University of P[lymouth]

The Perfect Lo[cation]... [for... Adventure?]

◆ one of the largest universities in the UK
◆ an excellent international reputation for teaching and research
◆ students from over 100 countries
◆ guaranteed approved accommodation for your first year

The University has seven dynamic Faculties in the beautiful South West:

The Faculties of Science, Technology and Human Sciences, the Business School and the Postgraduate Medical School are in the thriving city of Plymouth, close to beautiful beaches and countryside.

The Faculty of Arts & Education has campuses in the busy historic city of Exeter and the lively seaside town of Exmouth.

The Seale-Hayne Faculty - offering courses in agriculture, food, rural land use, hospitality and tourism - is based on a magnificent country estate near the market town of Newton Abbot.

As well as superb academic facilities, we offer an impressive range of leisure and cultural opportunities.

To find out more, please contact:
The International Office, University of Plymouth, Drake Circus, Plymouth, Devon, PL4 8AA, United Kingdom.
Tel: +44 (0)1752 233345   Fax: +44 (0)1752 232014
Email: intoff@plymouth.ac.uk
Web site: http://www.plymouth.ac.uk/

UNIVERSITY OF PLYMOUTH

A World Centre for the Study of Education

The Institute of Education, a graduate college of the University of London, is a world centre for the study of education. Our international renown attracts students from over 80 countries every year.

RESEARCH degree provision at the Institute, leading to an MPhil, PhD, EdD or DEdPsy degree, is second to none. We also provide an unrivalled range of courses leading to Master's degrees, Advanced Diploma and Associateship awards.

THE INSTITUTE is justifiably proud of its excellent library, which is the largest collection in Europe of books and periodicals concerned with educational studies. A range of computing facilities, including dedicated computing support for doctoral students, is available, and we also offer precessional and insessional support in English language to our international students.

The Institute is situated in the heart of the attractive Bloomsbury district of central London, close to its own hall of residence and to the major cultural attractions of the capital. A number of nearby underground stations provide for easy and swift travel in the London area.

FOR FURTHER INFORMATION ABOUT OUR PROGRAMMES OF STUDY, OR ABOUT ANY OTHER ASPECT OF OUR ACTIVITIES, PLEASE CONTACT:

THE REGISTRY, INSTITUTE OF EDUCATION
20 Bedford Way, London WC1H 0AL

Telephone:	020 7612 6101 (Master's and Diploma awards)
	020 7612 6670 (doctoral degrees)
Fax:	020 7612 6097
Email:	fpd.enquiries@ioe.ac.uk *or* doc.enquiries@ioe.ac.uk

INSTITUTE OF
EDUCATION
UNIVERSITY OF LONDON

Pursuing Excellence in Education

Contents

2000 @CAVE

Art & Design

Business

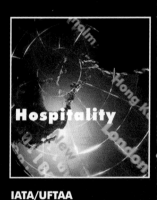

Hospitality

Art & Design Foundation

Graphic Design

Creative Advertising

Interior Design Architectural Foundation

Photographic Studies

Fashion Design

Fashion Marketing

Make up & Beauty

Acting, Directing & TV/Film Production

Chartered Institute of Marketing (CIM)

Higher National Diploma in Business (BTEC)

Business & Marketing Diploma

International Managment Marketing & Communications

International Trade - Import/Export

Investment & Portfolio Management

Integrated Secretarial Executive Secretarial

IATA/UFTAA Travel Agents Diploma

IATA/UFTAA International Travel Consultants Advanced Diploma

Fares & Ticketing

Tour Guide Operations

Travel and Hotel Operations Management

Hotel and Catering Management

Computer Reservations

http://www.cavendish.ac.uk

avendish College welcomes students from all parts of e world and therefore its courses are designed to meet e high demands of the global market place. The rectors of course development and planning at avendish aim to provide, within a study programme, ·st a basic working understanding of the subjects, then ·rther exploration and analysis, and ultimately the ·plication of acquired knowledge and skills to practical, ·eryday work situations.

NDISH

Computing

EFL

English as a Foreign Language

TEC HND in oftware Engineering

·ogramming

usiness Computing & ystem Design

/eb Site Design

·ultimedia Design

·omputer Graphics

·omputer Animation

·omputer-Aided Design

General English Examination Preparation Advanced English Intensive Study Skills

Preparation for IELTS

English for Business and Commerce

English for Tourism

General English Plus Extra Conversation

One to One Tuition

Cavendish College

35-37 Alfred Place London WC1E 7DP Tel: 0207 580 6043 Fax: 0207 255 1591
http://www.cavendish.ac.uk
e-mail: learn@cavendish.ac.uk

h t t p : / / w w w . c a v e n d i s h . a c . u k

Publishers

Jeremy Hunt, Mike Elms

Editor

Alice Kodell

Production Manager

Jo Flood

Graphic Design

Alex Faiers

Sub Editor

Josh Low

Editorial

Chris True, Yolande Taylor, Sarah Petheram,
Susie Stewart, Robby Elson

Advertising Sales

Schalk Cloete, Sarah John, Claire-Maria Harrison

The publishers and editors make strenuous efforts to ensure that the
information in this guide is correct at time of going to press but can accept no
responsibility for any errors or omissions. Colleges reserve the right to make
changes to their curriculum, course content, and prices at any time.

ISBN 1 898730 40 7
© Elms Hunt International Limited 2000

On Course Publications
121 King Street, London W6 9JG UK
Tel: 020 8600 5300 Fax: 020 8741 7716
Email: jeremy@oncourse.co.uk
Web: www.oncourse.co.uk

Using the Guide

using the guide using the guide using the guide using the guide

Welcome to the World Study Guide: Study in Britain Handbook 2000/2001. Our guides are designed to provide you with everything you need to make a success of studying abroad. Whether it is a short course in furniture design or a research degree in environmental engineering, then the following pages should have all the information you need.

Structure of the guide

As with all the On Course guides, the Study in Britain Handbook is set out for easy, accessible referencing. If you are not British, the early section from pages 12 to 64 will tell you what you need to know about the British education system. It also covers visa and immigration requirements, and aspects of British culture which may be unfamiliar. If you are British, you may want to skip this section.

The 'A to Z of subjects' follows starting on page 65, with chapters covering all the main subject areas you might want to study. These include information on degree programmes and short vocational courses. Whether it is an MA in English Literature or a four-week secretarial course, you will find a number of courses profiled here to give you an idea of what's available. It is not, however, a comprehensive list. There are so many thousands of courses at different places in Britain that it would be logistically impossible to write details about them all in a book of this size. However, the main subject areas offered by different higher education institutions are listed in the course directory at the back from pages 488 to 498. Use this to get a more complete picture.

The 'A to Z subject' chapters also contain tables showing how well higher education institutions fared in independent inspections of their teaching quality and research capability. Bear in mind that not all institutions have been assessed for all subjects and as a result many of the tables are incomplete: in 1992 and 1996 an official assessment was carried out into the quality of research at different universities. Although they are primarily of interest

to postgraduate research students, we have included the results in every chapter for your reference.

The teaching quality in university departments is tested every four years on a rolling programme. Some are about to be inspected for a second time, whereas some are still awaiting inspection for the first time. Therefore, there may be a number of universities providing excellent courses which haven't been inspected. You should therefore use the course directory (page 488) for a more comprehensive list of courses by institutions.

The tables are for higher education only. For vocational and further education, there are no independent assessments available, and the best thing to do is to visit a college before enrolling to check that it looks likely to suit your requirements.

The 'A to Z of subjects' section is followed by detailed profiles of a selection of universities and colleges in Britain. Use these to get a feel for universities you are considering applying to, and to find out key information such as whether it is a campus or town university, which subject areas are particularly strong, and whether the facilities meet your requirements. You can also find further information at www.oncourse.co.uk or the University and College Admissions Service (UCAS) website at www.ucas.ac.uk

If you want a prospectus for any of the universities or colleges listed in the guide to be sent to you free of charge, just fill in the Reader Information Service postcard at the front of the guide.

Throughout the guide, for reasons of consistency and brevity, certain conventions are observed. All internet addresses omit the 'http://' and start with 'www' followed by the address. All telephone numbers are written as if dialled from within the UK unless otherwise stated. If you are dialling internationally you need to add the international code +44 for the UK before the number written, leaving out the initial 0. At the time of going to press (April 2000), a series of changes will be made to UK dialling codes, in Coventry, Cardiff, Portsmouth, London and Northern Ireland. In addition, all local numbers in these regions will become eight-digit numbers. For new dialling codes see the table below.

The index and the contact details at the back of the book are full of useful names and addresses you might need.

Remember if you have any suggestions for the next issue of this guide, please do not hesitate to contact On Course on 020 8600 5300, fax 020 8741 7716, or email jeremy@oncourse.co.uk. The best letters get a free copy of next year's edition, or indeed any other On Course guide if you would prefer.

New dialling codes, as from April 22 2000

Region	Dialling code	eight-digit local number starting with	Example
London	**020**	7/8	**020 7** 1234567
			020 8 1234567
Cardiff	**029**	20	**029 20** 123456
Coventry	**024**	76	**024 76** 123456
Portsmouth	**023**	92	**023 92** 123456
Southampton	**023**	80	**023 80** 123456
N Ireland	**028**	Varies according to area	

Britain and the British

britain
britain
britain
britain

Britain, said the English author J B Priestly, "is just pretending to be small." And nothing could be more true. With an area of 240,000 sq km, 600 miles from south to north and under 300 miles at its widest point, Britain is holding a population of almost 57 million people with an average of 236 inhabitants per sq km, making the island one of the most jam-packed in the world.

You might already have several images of the typical Brit – perhaps a bowler-hatted businessman, the Queen or even the Spice Girls – but you'll probably be surprised by the diversity of lifestyles, characters and nationalities you find during your visit.

Whatever your impressions are of Britain and the British, the many different people, places and cultures will undoubtedly be an eye-opener. Although typically known for their politeness, reserve, eccentricity and strange sense of humour, it won't be long before you grow to understand the British people's ways and love their individuality, openness and kindness.

Even the name of the place can be puzzling. Should you tell people you're off to study in Great Britain, the United Kingdom (UK) or the British Isles? Well, it depends on what you mean. Great Britain comprises England, Wales and Scotland; the United Kingdom is Northern Ireland, England, Wales and Scotland, and the British Isles refers to Northern Ireland, the Republic of Ireland, Wales, Scotland and England. In this guide, we have generally used the UK, or Britain where we are not including Northern Ireland.

Recently, with the establishment of the Welsh assembly and the Scottish parliament there has been a lot of debate over regional identity. Some would say that the United Kingdom is not united at all. The UK is, in fact, four countries, each with its own flag, identity, traditions, and even ancient languages. Though there are disagreements over the new political roles of Scotland, Wales and Northern Ireland, they all have fixed political boundaries. However, the boundaries marking the North, the Midlands and the South are

John o'Groats
Inverness
Aberdeen
SCOTLAND
Dundee
St Andrews
Glasgow
Edinburgh
Newcastle
Belfast
Leeds
York
Manchester
Liverpool
Sheffield
Nottingham
Stafford
MIDLANDS
Norwich
Aberystwyth
Birmingham
Cambridge
Cheltenham
WALES
Oxford
Cardiff
Swansea
Bristol
London
Dover
Exeter
Brighton
Portsmouth
Plymouth
Land's End

Galway
Dublin
IRELAND
Limerick

ATLANTIC
OCEAN

IRISH SEA

NORTH
SEA

CELTIC SEA

ENGLISH CHANNEL

Le Havre
Brest
Paris
FRANCE

USEFUL INFORMATION

Capital	London
Population	56.7 m
Area	244,820 sq km
Official Language	English, Welsh, Scottish Gaelic
Currency	British pound (GBP)

South-East England

more arguable and inhabitants often have strong opinions about where they come from and whether they are a Northerner or a Southerner. See map of the UK on page 13.

Wherever you decide to study, whether it is St Andrews in Scotland, Cardiff in Wales, Manchester in England or Queen's in Belfast, you will be in easy reach of cities, countryside and coastline. And you'll only be a train ride away from the rest of Europe.

ENGLAND

As a newcomer, you might find England easier to understand if you divide the country up into broad areas, as the map on page 13 illustrates. If the rush and bustle of city life doesn't appeal to you, then you can escape the densely populated urban centres and retreat to one of the many unspoilt areas of English countryside or coastland. England boasts nine national parks, six forest parks, 200 country parks, over 600 miles of heritage coastline, as well as thousands of historic buildings and gardens.

South and South-East England

This is a large area encompassing the country's capital, London, the surrounding counties referred to as

the Home Counties, and some coastal towns and ports. The Home Counties offer peaceful green land-scapes whilst still within reach of the attractions of the capital. Fast train connec-tions serve all the commuters well. Many of the universities in this area are located in beautiful countryside, such as Buck-inghamshire College and the University of Surrey. Further east and en route to mainland Europe, Kent is traditionally known as the Garden of England, but other areas along the south coast could claim this title. There are several universities in the coastal towns and ports of the south of England in Brighton, Portsmouth, and Southampton. Here, picturesque villages merge with small towns. The South Downs Way will give you great views of the coast. And along the seafront, tourists can find the mixed attractions of chalky cliffs, amusement parks, shingle beaches and Victorian piers.

London

London is Europe's largest city and one of the most cosmopolitan places in the world. Its main geographical feature is the river Thames, which divides the city into northern and southern halves. Sometimes, especially during the summer months, it can feel like everyone on the planet has come to visit with 26 million tourists expected every year.

Many people are attracted to London as a place to study, particularly if they have visited the capital as tourists and seen its beautiful old buildings, elegant streets and spacious parks, and returned home long enough to forget its pollution and high prices.

South-West England

CHELTENHAM
GLOUCESTER
SWINDON
BRISTOL
BATH
WESTON-SUPER-MARE
EXETER
PLYMOUTH   TORQUAY
FALMOUTH

London offers a huge number of education opportunities. Forty per cent of all university students in Britain study in London, and there are hundreds of private language and specialist colleges.

If you are ever feeling homesick you are guaranteed to find a sample of your home country in London, be it food, cinema, newspapers, books or drama. But, on the downside, if you are looking to improve your English, you may find it hard to escape the international community. Meeting people from all over the world is certainly one of the benefits of studying in the capital but you may not speak to as many native English speakers as you would like, particularly if you are studying in a language school.

South West England

The region can be divided between Devon and Cornwall in the far west, and Dorset, Wiltshire and Somerset in the east. The south-westerly tip of England is bathed by the Gulf Stream, so it tends to be warmer than the rest of the country, and is a popular holiday destination. Although generally a peaceful part of the country, Cornwall and neighbouring Devon are prone to traffic jams of tourists in summer.

Devon and nearby Somerset are known for their traditional cream teas (tea served with cakes, scones, jam and clotted cream) and scrumpy, farm cider (a strong alcoholic drink made from the fermented juice of apples).

The scenery here is rich and varied, with upland moors, steep river valleys and a magnificent, rocky coastline with sandy coves. As well as the requisite pubs, college bars, and nightclubs, students in the south west have easy access to the many water sports on offer, such as sailing, surfing, wind-surfing and diving. With relatively high unemployment in the south west, many people depend entirely on the summer tourist trade to make a living. Consequently, the region has some of the cheapest accommodation in the UK. Cornwall is approximately five hours drive from London.

The Midlands

The Midlands is a term you will hear used to describe central England. This region was once the centre of England's manufacturing industry. Although industry now has less prominence across the region, Birmingham (the second largest city in Britain) is still a major manufacturing centre. Frequently hailed as the best place in Britain to buy a curry (it even has its own dish, the 'Balti'), it is home to some of the largest Asian communities in the country. Other large cities in the area like Leicester, Birmingham and Coventry have at least two, sometimes three universities. The rest of the Midlands has its fair share of tourist

15

The North and the Midlands

art galleries, and museums to suit all tastes. The cost of living is generally much cheaper than in the south.

Manchester

Manchester is often regarded as Britain's second city, with a population of 2.6 million. Due to host the Commonwealth Games in 2002, it is a commercial, educational and cultural capital of the North West of England. There is also a vast student population.

SCOTLAND

Scotland's landscape varies from the rolling hills of the Borders – the lowlands roughly to the southwest of Edinburgh – to the stark and uninhabitable crags of the Cairngorms. The countryside has an unrivalled variety of wildlife, with some species not found anywhere else in Britain. It's an often underrated country and few English realise what an extraordinary neighbour they have.

Scotland is also home to one of the world's leading cultural events – the annual Edinburgh International Festival. This is the largest arts festival in Britain and a must if you are interested in seeing fringe theatre, music, and poetry being performed to audiences from all over the world. If you are interested in science you will be pleased to hear Edinburgh also hosts the world's biggest single-city science festival. Scientists in Scotland are at the forefront of research into the human equivalent of BSE and Aids. Roots and heritage are heavily romanticised in Scotland, and Celtic culture is very much in evidence today. Gaelic, Celtic in origin, is spoken by over 60,000 people, most of whom reside in the Western Isles. Although this may seem like a fraction of the total population of Scotland, government

attractions, with historic villages and towns including Stratford-upon-Avon where William Shakespeare, the English dramatist and poet, was born and died.

North England

The North is a mix of mountainous scenery and farmland, and industrial towns and cities. The east and west sides of Northern England are divided by the Pennines – a range of hills and valleys that extends from Derbyshire towards the Scottish border. The Yorkshire Moors and the Yorkshire Dales offer plenty of hilly terrain for walkers. The region used to be heavily industrialised. Liverpool, Sheffield and Newcastle all have a history of industry whether it be a busy dock or steel or coal production. In the 1980's, these areas saw high unemployment, particularly in Liverpool. However, northern cities are now striving to be major centres of communication and commerce and most offer a host of theatres, concert halls, sports venues,

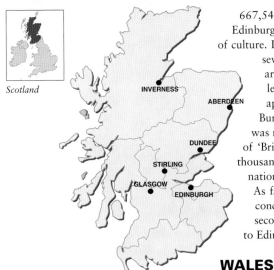

Scotland

667,540 people, and rivals Edinburgh and London as a city of culture. In Glasgow you will find several large theatres, great art galleries and major collections of fine and applied arts, such as the Burrell Collection. The city was recently awarded the title of 'Britain's friendliest city' by thousands of readers of an international traveller's magazine. As far as food and culture is concerned, it comes a close second to London and equal to Edinburgh in atmosphere.

support for Gaelic education and Gaelic organisations demonstrate that it is an important part of Scottish culture and heritage.

There are similarities and close links with England but there are also considerable differences. Scotland has its own currency, but all notes and coins are legal tender in the rest of the UK. The education system is different to England and is covered in detail in 'The British Education System' from page 22 .

Edinburgh

Scotland's capital, Edinburgh, is an ancient city built on crags and cliffs, with serpentine streets that rise and dip. During the late 18th and early 19th centuries, Edinburgh was the focus of an age of Scottish cultural brilliance which produced philosophers such as David Hume. Today its castles and palaces, its Great Kirk, its ancient streets and galleries are major attractions for tourists and for the students who attend its universities.

Glasgow

Scotland's largest city is home to over

WALES

The principality of Wales boasts cosmopolitan cities – Cardiff for example has some fantastic architecture, Victorian arcades and elegant public buildings – and some of the most stunning scenery in the British Isles. Rugged and imposing mountains, rolling hills, moorlands, forests and valleys are major attractions for visitors from all over the world. Snowdonia, the Brecon Beacons and the Pembrokeshire Coast have been protected by the creation of great national parks. Until recent decades, coal and steel production were the centre of the Welsh economy. The coal industry has now largely died out due to competition in prices from abroad and the switch to other methods of supplying electricity. And, while steelmaking remains significant, the largest area of expansion has been in the service industry and the development of technology.

England and Wales were united by the half-Welsh king, Henry VII, in 1485, so Wales shares many of England's political and cultural systems including its currency and legal system. Nevertheless, Wales has its own flag, and is soon

17

Northern Ireland

musical history. Both are celebrated at some of the most respected arts festivals in Britain. Eisteddfods – literally meaning 'a sitting' – are cultural gatherings at which artists compete in music and literature, and only Welsh is spoken. The Llangollen International Music Eisteddfod takes place annually and celebrates music, dance and song from all over the world. The Royal National Eisteddfod, celebrating arts, crafts, literature, dance and drama, is held in a different location in Wales every year, and is chaired by the Arch Druid (member of ancient order of priests) of the Gorsedd (the bardic institution of the Eisteddfod).

to have its own parliament in the form of the Welsh Assembly. The Welsh language is believed to be one of the oldest in Europe (the Celts crossed from Europe to Wales in about 600 BC). It is still widely spoken by those living around Lampeter and Aberstwyth on the mountainous west side of the country, and in pockets in the north and centre. Until 1942, the Welsh language was suppressed, but the Welsh have since become more and more determined to keep their language alive. There are Welsh television and radio stations and all Welsh schools teach pupils Welsh up to the age of 16. At Welsh universities where there is no separate Celtic or Welsh department, the language is offered as an optional modern language which all students can learn free of charge alongside their major studies. All Welsh college and university courses are taught in English.

Every town and village has its own special local traditions and events. Wales is home to 'Town of Books' Hay-on-Wye which comes alive every year when its literary festival attracts internationally renowned poets, writers and celebrities. The country's strong literary tradition is matched by its

Cardiff

Cardiff, the capital of Wales since 1955, is in South Glamorgan. Its rich maritime heritage comes from its 19th-century growth as a port to ship coal produced in the Welsh valleys. At its centre is its castle, originally built in the 11th century but largely rebuilt in neo-Gothic style in the 19th century. As well as being a thriving cultural centre with excellent museums, such as the Welsh Folk Museum and the Maritime Museum, Cardiff is also the headquarters of Welsh rugby. Cardiff hosted the 1999 Rugby World Cup at its new sports venue, which will be the focus of many international events. The city's cultural status is enhanced by the fact that it has the largest concentration of film and TV production companies outside of London – resulting in plenty of media-related industries. In addition, you will find plenty of cafes, restaurants, pubs and bars in which to relax within view of some dramatic countryside scenery.

Wales

NORTHERN IRELAND

The north-eastern corner of Ireland is part of the United Kingdom and its official name is Northern Ireland. Despite it's immense beauty Northern Ireland has been plagued with tragedy.

Although there is some optimism around the current peace process, the situation remains incomplete.

Ireland was an independent state until, in 1171, the English kings made the first of a series of encroachments into Irish territory. Subsequently, English monarchs of the late 15th and 16th centuries waged a campaign against Irish dissidents. Since then, the history of Northern Ireland has been rife with political upheaval, fluctuating between uneasy peace and violent rebellions. In 1801 Ireland was officially united, under the Act of Union, with England and Scotland as the United Kingdom of Great Britain and Ireland. In 1916, a nationalist rising was quelled and its leaders executed.

Sinn Fein, the Irish Nationalist Party, declared Ireland a republic, and, in 1922, the country was given dominion status. The six northern counties of the ancient province of Ulster were given the right to opt out. When Ireland became fully independent in 1949, the Protestant majority in the northern counties opted to stay as part of the United Kingdom, with a separate parliament (Stormont) and limited self-government. From the beginning, Northern Ireland's parliament had a unionist majority from which ministers were drawn for government. Nationalists, resented this domination and their effective marginalisation from political life. After a sophisticated civil rights movement developed in the region during the 1960s, a series of sectarian insurrections erupted. This has been the root cause of the 'Troubles', as the province's civil and political problems are known. The Good Friday Agreement, signed in 1998, was meant to mark an end to sectarian violence and signal the beginning of peace talks involving all parties. Its success remains to be seen. The next stage for lasting peace in Northern Ireland is for both unionists and republicans to decommission illegal weapons.

Northern Ireland's cultural heritage is rich and varied. It has several museums including the Ulster Museum in Belfast, the Ulster Folk and Transport museum in County Down and the Ulster-American Folk Park. The latter successfully documents the history of Irish emigration to the United States of America. In addition, there are numerous locally funded museums and heritage sites. You will find plenty of local arts festivals in Northern Ireland, including the respected Belfast festival. The Arts Council for Northern Ireland supports local drama companies, music groups, orchestras, theatres, writers and artists groups, of which there are plenty.

Belfast

The city of Belfast is home to a third of Northern Ireland's population, nearly half a million people. The city grew rapidly in the 19th century with the expansion of industries such as linen, rope-making and shipbuilding. Industry has played an enormous part in developing the region. The city has been at the heart of the troubles but has more recently transformed itself into a city of culture and tourism. There are numerous museums chronicling Irish heritage. Many Irish people emigrated to America and New Zealand in the 18th and 19th centuries and many of their ancestral farmsteads have been preserved. The family homes of four American presidents can be visited in and around Belfast. Queen's University is half a mile away from Belfast itself.

THE WEATHER

One of the only things that you can count on with British weather is its unreliability. Weather forecasters are notorious for their inaccurate predictions. As a result, the most discerning Brits carry an umbrella at all times. British people also love talking about the weather. Most conversations in the winter begin with a brief complaint about the cold, rain or snow and, in the summer, people often end up complaining that it's too hot. Although British summers tend to be cooler than those on the continent, winters are significantly milder.

Despite the changeable nature of British weather, there are general climate characteristics in the British Isles. The western and northern parts of Britain have mild and stormy winters and cool and windy summers – the mountains in these regions produce an increase in rainfall. The flat regions of England have a climate similar to that on the continent. The south of Britain tends to be warmer than the north, whilst the west is generally wetter than the east. Mountainous regions are usually cloudy and windy. And it is worth remembering that cities tend to be warmer than rural areas.

One of the most noticeable climactic features in Britain is long summer days and short winter ones – getting dark at 10pm in July and 4pm in December. At the winter solstice in December it is light for only about eight hours a day, whilst at the summer solstice in June, it is light for up to 18 hours a day.

The basic rule of thumb is that weather changes quickly and often, even in locations which are relatively close to each other such as Glasgow and Edinburgh.

Preparing for the cold

You can see from the international weather comparisons opposite, there are a lot of myths about the British weather and the most important thing is not to be put off studying there. London can be warmer than Mexico City in the summer, and if you are expecting lots of rain you will be surprised to see that it has a lower rainfall than Hong Kong, Tokyo or Washington. If you are living in student accommodaation, do not forget to budget for an increase in heating costs over the winter.

INTERNATIONAL WEATHER COMPARISONS

Place	Month	Average temp max c	min c	Extreme temp max c	min c	Month	Average temp max c	min c	Extreme temp max c	min c	Rainfall
London	Jun-Jul-Aug	21	13	33	6	Dec-Jan-Feb	7	3	15	-9	611mm
Belfast	Jun-Jul-Aug	18	10	28	3	Dec-Jan-Feb	4	2	14	-12	951mm
Birmingham	Jun-Jul-Aug	20	12	32	5	Dec-Jan-Feb	7	3	14	-8.9	622mm
Cardiff	Jun-Jul-Aug	20	12	32	6	Dec-Jan-Feb	7	2	15	-11	1061mm
Edinburgh	Jun-Jul-Aug	18	11	28	4	Dec-Jan-Feb	6	2	14	-8	638mm
Plymouth	Jun-Jul-Aug	19	12	29	4	Dec-Jan-Feb	8	4	14	-7.3	982mm
York	Jun-Jul-Aug	20.3	15	32.2	3.7	Dec-Jan-Feb	6.6	1	16.5	-13	588mm
Buenos Aires	Jun-Jul-Aug	15	6	28	-5	Dec-Jan-Feb	28	17	39	5	950mm
Rio de Janeiro	Jun-Jul-Aug	24	18	33	11	Dec-Jan-Feb	29	23	38	15	1086mm
Hong Kong	Jun-Jul-Aug	30	26	35	21	Dec-Jan-Feb	18	14	27	3	2208mm
Beijing	Jun-Jul-Aug	31	20	41	12	Dec-Jan-Feb	3	-8	15	-20	624mm
Bombay	Jun-Jul-Aug	30	25	35	22	Dec-Jan-Feb	29	20	35	12	1811mm
Tokyo	Jun-Jul-Aug	27	20	36	12	Dec-Jan-Feb	9	-1	36	-12	1565mm
Kuala Lumpur	Jun-Jul-Aug	32	23	36	20	Dec-Jan-Feb	40	22	36	19	2448mm
Mexico City	Jun-Jul-Aug	20	6	29	9	Dec-Jan-Feb	39	12	24	-2	749mm
Lisbon	Jun-Jul-Aug	27	16	40	12	Dec-Jan-Feb	18	8	22	-1	708mm
Singapore	Jun-Jul-Aug	31	24	34	21	Dec-Jan-Feb	31	23	34	20	2415mm
Madrid	Jun-Jul-Aug	29	16	38	7	Dec-Jan-Feb	10	2	19	-9	682mm
Washington	Jun-Jul-Aug	29	19	40	9	Dec-Jan-Feb	7	-2	26	-26	1064mm

The British Education System

education
education
education
education

The British education system is divided into three categories: primary (five to 11 years), secondary (11 to 18 years), and tertiary (higher education), and is the same for both England, Wales and Northern Ireland, Scotland has its own distinctive system (the main difference is in the qualifications, awarded, which is explained later in this chapter).

School is compulsory for children between five and 16 years and there are two sets of official exams. Only the first, at 16, is compulsory. Most 17 year-olds are in some kind of further education or work-related training. Britains are getting used to the idea of retraining with the growing realisation that jobs are not for life. Adult education has become more popular, if only by necessity.

Every university has a group of mature students – although some fear that their number may be decreasing given the recently introduced university fees. With both schools and universities subject to league tables and rankings, the whole education system has become much more open.

INDEPENDENT AND STATE SCHOOLS

Education is divided into state-funded and privately-funded (independent) sectors. Independent schools charge fees and are 'independent' of state control. There are independent schools of all kinds up and down the country, charging a range of fees and catering for all ages and religious beliefs. Confusingly, they have been known historically as public schools but are usually referred to as being private. Independent schools for children aged between seven and 11 are termed preparatory (or prep) schools, traditionally preparing children for their public school.

The majority of schools are state-funded and free. Some are selective and have such good reputations that competition for entrance is fierce, with parents even moving to a particular street in order to increase the chance of their child being accepted. The majority of state schools are co-educational (mixed sex) and some have a religious bias, usually either Church of England or Roman Catholic, although state-funded Muslim schools have recently opened. The independent sector has more single sex schools and its fair share of religious schools.

CURRICULUM AND QUALIFICATIONS

England, Wales and Northern Ireland

GCSE and A level

All state schools and some independent ones follow the national curriculum, which prescribes a number of subjects to be studied by children up to the age of 16, when pupils sit GCSEs (General Certificate of Secondary Education), in about 6 to 10 subjects. These are graded from A* to G. Those students who have five or more GCSEs at grades A* to C can then study two or more A (Advanced) levels for two years before taking the A level examinations. Most A level students will only take between two and four subjects, in order to gain a greater depth on knowledge in each of them. The subjects chosen at A level often reflect what a student would like to continue to study at university.

In between GCSEs and A levels, there is the possibility of taking A/S levels (Advanced Supplementary), which are the same standard as A levels but cover half the syllabus. They were introduced as an attempt to broaden A level students' curriculum.

GNVQ and NVQ

Some students take GNVQs (General National Vocational Qualification). These operate on different levels but all are more vocational than GCSEs and A levels. A foundation GNVQ is broadly equivalent to four GCSEs at grades D to G, and an intermediate GNVQ is broadly equivalent to four GCSEs at grades A* to C. Students studying Advanced GNVQs can apply to universities and, in 1996, 92 per cent of such applicants were offered a place.

Students no longer have to stick to rigid educational paths and can mix and match A levels with GNVQs, although in practice this is only happening gradually.

NVQs (National Vocational Qualifications) are work-related, practical qualifications relevant to a particular occupation. Standards are set by employers, trade unions and professional bodies. Each level is competence-based and there is no time restriction for acquiring the appropriate level. Students working for GNVQs and NVQs are continually assessed.

Diplomas

GNVQs are gradually replacing diplomas. Eventually GNVQ level 4 will replace the Higher National Diploma (HND). However, HND's are still available. First Diplomas are available in subjects related to work and are the equivalent to four GCSEs grades A* to C. The National Diploma is at a higher level and is also available in subjects related to work. Both are assessed by final examination and continual assessment. An HND is a higher education qualification which combines career preparation with opportunities for further study. Students may convert an HND into a degree course, often missing out the first year of the degree.

Awarding bodies

There are different awarding bodies for GNVQs and NVQs. These names are often used in a course title.

BTEC: Business and Technology Education Council. BTEC is now part of EDEXCEL but its name is still used to describe courses. It covers areas such as technology, business, health and social care, and leisure and tourism.

C&G: City and Guilds of London Institute. C&G covers technology in traditional industries such as engineering, construction, catering.

RSA: Royal Society of Arts. RSA offer similar courses to both BTEC and C&G but also specialise in office skills, English teaching and English as a foreign language.

Scotland

SCE and Highers and Advanced Highers

Although unique in the UK, the Scottish education system has similarities to countries such as the USA, Australia and Japan.

The Scottish Certificate of Education (Standard Grade) is taken at 16 (4th Year), and has three levels – Foundation, General and Credit – awarded by Scottish Qualifications Agency. At 18, pupils take Highers and/or Advanced Highers, of which there are five levels – Access, Intermediate 1 and Intermediate 2, Higher and Advanced Higher. Higher Grades (known as 'Highers') are the university or college entrance requirement and are taken by students aged 17 years. Students who wish to begin university or college at 18 years – the same age as in the rest of the UK – stay on to take the Certificate of Sixth Year Studies qualifications in relevant subjects, or retake Highers to get better grades.

Scottish Vocational Qualifications

Assessment is now done mainly by the Scottish Qualification Authority. The new qualification system introduced in 1999 applies to further education colleges as well as secondary schools. Awards include: Scottish Vocational Qualifications (SVQs) designed by industry for industry and involving assessment in the workplace; National Certificate of Higher National Certificate; Higher National Diploma; GSVQs for school and FE students aged 16 to 19 and adult returners, providing core skills, broad training and progression to higher education; 'Higher Still' which is open to all FE students beyond Standard Grade.

For detailed information on education in Scotland contact: the Scottish Qualification Agency Hanover House, 24 Douglas Street, Glasgow G2 7NQ Tel: 0141 248 7900. Helpline: 0141 242 2214. Website: www.sqa.org.uk

SPECIALIST AND VOCATIONAL COLLEGES

A number of schools and colleges exist in Britain that specialise in particular subjects. Whether it is Christie's Modern Art Studies or the London

National framework of qualifications

ACADEMIC	PART-VOCATIONAL	VOCATIONAL
Higher Degree		NVQ5
Degree	GNVQ4 / HND	NVQ4
A / AS Level	GNVQ Advanced / National Diploma	NVQ3
GCSE A-C	GNVQ Intermediate / First Diploma	NVQ2
GCSE D-G	GNVQ Foundation	NVQ1

Centre for Fashion Studies, there are plenty to choose from in a wide range of areas. Many, such as the Vidal Sassoon School of Hairdressing offer vocationally based skills. Some offer degree courses; some do not. Many colleges offer a one-year diploma or foundation courses which can be a good way to learn about your chosen subject, prepare for a higher education course and get used to the British way of life.

There is sometimes confusion over the certificates and qualifications awarded at private colleges. Some offer the nationally recognised qualifications listed on page 27, and others offer foundation courses that can be a good stepping stone to degree courses offered by them or other academic institutions. But colleges offering a diploma bearing their own name as the ultimate accrediting authority should be considered with caution. If they are genuinely well-known, and you should do some research to find out if this is the case, then the diploma will be useful to you when you finish. But you need to check very carefully that the qualification you will be awarded is worth more than the paper it is written on.

Language schools

Many students come to Britain solely to study English; others plan to study something else later, but want to brush up on their English first. English is the language of international communication, and is also the language of tourism, aviation, navigation and scientific research. It is also the largest language in the world in terms of the number of words.

Why study English in Britain? If English is not your first language, you need to choose whether you would like to learn English in Britain, Australia, Canada, the United States of America or a host of other English speaking countries. The main reasons why Britain is a popular choice for language schools is the familiarity with the British Education System and the appeal of the British way of life. One of the main benefits of studying in England is that you have easy access to mainland Europe. As an English language student studying in Britain you are likely to be one of many nationalities in your classes. Many international students find this a great advantage as English becomes the only means of communication between students.

Accreditation for language schools

There are various accreditation and membership schemes for English language schools, but the best known is run by The British Council. For this, schools have to meet fairly strict criteria. They undergo a thorough inspection of teaching facilities, teacher qualifications and management. For schools that have received British Council accreditation there are two further associations. The British Association of State English Language Teaching (BASELT) is an association of state sector English language teaching institutions. The Association of Recognised English Language Schools (ARELS) is for schools in the private sector. Courses in the state sector are often run in further education colleges. Class sizes may be larger than at private schools, but courses are often cheaper. Universities and higher education colleges also run English language programmes (also accredited by the British Council). Studying at the place you may wish to apply for a degree or postgraduate course will help you decide whether it is the right place for you.

COLLEGES OF FURTHER EDUCATION

(see the chapter 'Access, Foundation and Diploma' on page 67.)

Many non-degree courses can be taken at colleges of further education. 'Further education' is the title given to any non-degree level qualification taken after the minimum school leaving age in Britain, which is 16. Further education colleges tend to offer more vocational courses. Until recently they did not recruit international students and were not accustomed to arranging and validating student visas. This situation is changing quickly, as demand from international students increases.

ADULT EDUCATION COLLEGES

Adult education courses are often run at the same colleges as further education, but tends to imply part-time classes taking place in the evening or at lunchtimes or weekends. Subjects range from cake-baking to salsa and last anything from a day to a year. Students pay very reasonable fees for a set number of sessions. Classes tend to be informal and friendly because they are mostly made up of people who are keen to learn and experience something new. Taking an adult education course in a large city is often a way of meeting people and making new friends. Further education colleges often become adult education centres in the evenings and offer a range of courses. Many offer Access courses, which are a fast track into university for mature British students who left school with limited qualifications. Significantly, such centres are now starting to offer English language

classes, often at rock-bottom prices. Publications like *On Course* magazine will give you full information on these courses in London.

COLLEGES OF HIGHER EDUCATION

Higher education traditionally describes academic and professional courses ranging from diploma level to a first degree and beyond. Colleges of higher education offer A levels or Highers in vocational subjects, often combined with professional qualifications, and degrees validated by local universities. These may be full-time degrees, an HND or a Diploma of Higher Education (DipHE). Often, the dividing line between colleges of further and higher education is not clear. In many ways the name is irrelevant. Just check that the qualification you will be awarded at the end of your course is the one you need.

UNIVERSITY EDUCATION

GETTING ONTO YOUR CHOSEN DEGREE COURSE

A levels and Scottish Highers are the traditional route of entry into British universities for British students. International students need to get equivalent qualifications. International qualifications are recognised by universities, but it is always best to check with the institution you are applying to that your qualifications are appropriate.

Foundation courses

One year foundation courses are generally tailored for international students (apart from foundation years in art and nursing which are for everyone) and they

English Language Examinations

Examining Board	Examination
University of Cambridge Local Examination Syndicate (UCLES) Syndicate Buildings 1 Hills Road Cambridge CB1 2EU England Tel: 01223 553311	Preliminary English Test (PET) First Certificate in English (FCE) Certificate in Advanced English (CAE) *Some UK universities accept this level of English* Certificate of Proficiency in English (CPE) *Acceptable level of English for most UK universities.* International English Language Testing System (IELTS) *Most UK universities expect students to reach between 5.5 and 6.5.*
TOEFL Educational Testing Service P O Box 6151 Princeton, NJ 08541-6151 USA Tel: 001 609 921 9000 Website: www.toefl.org	Test of English as a Foreign Language (TOEFL). *Popular with US universities and colleges. Currently most UK universities accept a score between 550 and 600 for paper-based tests and 5.5 for computer-based tests. The paper-based TOEFL is being phased out.*
Northern Examinations and Assessment Board Devas Street Manchester M15 6EX Tel: 0161 953 1180	University Entrance Test in English for Speakers of Other Languages (UETESOL) *Acceptable at most UK universities.*
English Speaking Board (International) Ltd 26a Princes Street Southport PR8 1EQ Tel: 01704 501730 Website: www.esbuk.demon.uk	English Speaking Board, English as an Acquired Language (ESB, EAL) *Oral assessments on several levels from pre-foundation through intermediate to advanced.*
Oxford – ARELS University of Cambridge Local Examination Syndicate 1 Hills Road Cambridge CB1 2EI Tel: 01223 553 538	ARELS Oral Exams: Preliminary Certificate Diploma Higher Certificate Oxford Written Exams: Preliminary Level Higher Level
Trinity College Exams 89 Albert Embankment London SE1 7TP Tel: 020 7820 6100	Spoken English 12 levels *Oral assessment at all levels, beginners to advanced.*

are a way of gaining entrance to university degree courses. Although you may have completed your secondary education in your home country, your qualifications may not be recognised by admissions tutors, or you may need to bring your qualifications up to the standard required for degree level courses. Foundation courses are seen as an alternative route to British universities, or as a bridge between your own qualifications and entry onto a degree course. Foundation programmes can also help to broaden your knowledge, improve your English, develop practical skills and provide a solid basis for university education. Foundation programmes are tailor-made, according to what subject you intend to study at university. In addition to your chosen core of subjects, classes can be taken in study and communication skills along with English language tuition. In essence, you are given the choice of a set of core modules that relate to the subject that you eventually wish to study at university. Depending on where you study, most students take a core course of three or four major modules and a couple of minor ones that carry less weight in the final marks awarded.

Some foundation programmes are independent and may be accepted by a number of universities. Others are approved by certain universities and guarantee entry into those universities for successful students. Staff teaching independent foundation courses can offer advice on the choice of degrees and universities, and the course might offer greater flexibility if you are not sure what university programme you want to study. However, it is important to check that this is the right course for you. Independent foundation courses are not generally acceptable to study medicine or for entry to Oxford and

Cambridge. Other foundation courses are associated with a particular group of universities, whereby successful completion of the course results in guaranteed entry into any one of the universities associated with the foundation course. One example of this is the Northern Consortium, which comprises 12 universities in the north of England. The Northern Consortium has partner institutions in Jordan, Pakistan and Kenya and can be contacted on tel: 0161 200 4029 (fax: 0161 228 7040).

Art foundation courses are slightly different. British students wishing to study art degrees at university have to complete a foundation course after A levels or Scottish Highers. Again, check with your chosen institution whether this is necessary.

Qualifications for entry

Criteria for entry on to foundation programmes vary. Depending on where you apply to study, you will be expected to have completed your secondary education, be at least 17 years old, and have achieved an intermediate level in English language. Some courses offer language classes to be held simultaneously with your studies. Enquire about these at specific universities or specialist colleges.

Access courses

Access programmes are another well-established alternative route to university education. These are specifically designed for mature students and for those who have been disadvantaged in terms of their education, for whatever reason. There are over 30,000 Access students in Britain and over 1,000 recognised Access courses throughout England, Northern Ireland and Wales.

A great number of Access courses are now discipline-related and geared towards a certain vocation, for example, Access to Humanities or Access to Business. UCAS *(see below)* has developed a website for Access programmes. You can search for subjects or courses region by region at www.ucas.ac.uk/access.

DEGREES

Undergraduate degrees

In the England, Wales and Northern Ireland the normal undergraduate degree is, generally, three years, resulting in an honours degree. In Scotland, students attend three years to gain an Ordinary degree and four years to get an Honours. There is no standardisation of degrees in Britain and the approach to teaching may differ from one university to another. Most universities, however, employ a combination of teaching styles that includes tutorials, lectures and seminars. Lectures are given to a large group of students, usually in an auditorium or lecture theatre, and students are expected to listen and take notes on what is being said.

Seminars include one or more staff members with a smaller group of students. Students are asked to prepare presentations for the group to discuss. Tutorials often involve a much smaller group – usually one member of staff with four or five students.

At some universities your results in the first year exams do not count towards your final degree. The second and third year exam results combined with a mark awarded for your undergraduate dissertation will make up your final degree result. A *modular* structure is adopted in other universities. Here, courses are made up of units

called modules. A credit rating, derived from the number of hours of tuition and private study, is given to each module. These modules can be transferable to other universities that operate the same type of system. Many universities offer students the chance to combine two or more subjects in a combined or a joint honours degree.

A *combined degree* will involve different subjects which will not necessarily have equal weighting. A *joint honours degree* will have two subject areas with equal weighting. It may involve two closely related subjects such as economics and mathematics or more distant, but still connected, subjects such as computing and psychology.

The grades you are awarded for your Bachelor's degree may be made up of points you have collected under a modular system, or they will be

---

Degree titles

BA – Bachelor of Arts

BBA – Bachelor of Business Administration

BEd – Bachelor of Education

BSc – Bachelor of Science

BD – Bachelor of Divinity

BTh – Bachelor of Theology Licence in Theology

LLB – Bachelor of Law

BMus – Bachelor of Music

---

awarded on the basis of your final examinations (usually called 'finals'). When you receive them they will be in denominations that may sound unfamiliar but which have been in use for generations. The top grade is a First Class (Honours) degree. The Upper Second (Honours), or 'two-one', is awarded more frequently than a first, followed by a Lower Second (Honours), or 'two-two', (popularly known amongst students as a 'Desmond' – after Desmond Tutu). There is also the Third Class (Honours) degree and a Pass or Ordinary degree. This last degree is not with Honours and although it counts as a degree it is not well respected. Ordinary degrees tend to be even rarer than firsts.

Sandwich courses

These courses are made up of a combination of periods of study and time spent in industry, commerce or administration relating to your course. This usually means that the course extends to four years instead of the usual three. Work experience can be carried out in one block, lasting a year, or two blocks, each lasting about six months. This last type of course is usually referred to as a 'thin-sandwich' course. In both cases you will return to university in your final year to complete your studies. This is often seen as a good way for students to gain valuable experience during their degree, so that they graduate not only with academic qualifications, but also with relevant work experience.

As an international student, you will either have a restriction or prohibition on your right to work in this country. This will be stamped into your passport on your arrival.

Now rules introduced by the UK government make it much easier for international students to get permission to work on a sandwich course. You should talk to your college or university to get some details.

Degrees with Study Abroad programmes

These days it is common for universities to offer students the opportunity to study for anything from a term to a year abroad. This used to only really be possible with language courses, whereby students could study abroad to practice their language skills. In these cases, degrees usually last for four years with students returning to university for their final year.

Britain is a good place to use as a base for travel abroad because of its proximity to mainland Europe and the relatively cheap flights you can get from there to anywhere in the world. If you do decide to leave Britain for a year you will need to check what documents are necessary for departure and re-entry. You should also check the visa requirements of the country you intend to study in or visit. It is to seek the advice of your head of department or the international officer.

Postgraduate degrees

Often referred to as 'higher degrees' there are generally two types of postgraduate degrees in Britain. These are the taught courses and research degrees. The PhD stands for 'Doctor of Philosophy' but has nothing to do with philosophy as a discipline. It is the highest postgraduate research degree and can cover research in any area. The MPhil is similarly mistitled. It is a one- or two-year research degree in any subject often converted into a PhD.

Taught courses

One of the most attractive things about British universities for international students is the fact that you can study for a master's degree in one year instead of the usual two. The chance to get a postgraduate qualification in one year, with all the savings in terms of time and money, has made taught masters' courses the most popular postgraduate courses in Britain at the moment.

Taught masters' courses allow graduates to specialise in their subject under the instruction of professional academic staff – by way of lectures, seminars and tutorials – whilst further developing the vital skills of research and independent study. Taught courses are useful for students wishing to acquire detailed knowledge of a particular subject that can be applied directly to work-related situations.

The first half of the year usually consists of a series of lectures, seminars and tutorials or laboratory work, depending on the nature of your subject. This is followed by a period of major research, known as a dissertation. These projects, chosen by you, will usually be relevant to your experience and career interests. This mode of study can either be seen as an end in itself or as an opportunity for students to further their knowledge of a particular field, gaining practical instruction and experience that will relate to a chosen career or profession. It can also be seen as an introduction to the type of study you will encounter as a doctoral research student.

You will normally be expected to have an undergraduate degree in the same or similar subject, although some master's courses are designed as a type of conversion course into a specific field. This is usually the case for IT related master's courses.

Research degrees

These take a minimum of three years and you will be expected to carry out original research and produce a thesis. PhD students are also often involved in teaching within their department.

> # Remember!
> **Don't be afraid to ask for help! The British approach to education encourages questions and general inquisitiveness. Tutors will want to know if you are finding things difficult. Universities are supportive environments and members of staff will be keen to help if they think you are having problems. But you need to tell them!**

Research bodies can provide funding for these degrees and they will be looking for motivated, dedicated students with original ideas.

A great deal of preparation is required to undertake a research degree. As a doctoral student you will be allocated a supervisor who will oversee your research. You may get a lot of guidance and advice from your supervisor, or you may be given a greater degree of freedom. You may find that you need more advice at the beginning of your course and that you need to meet your supervisor less and less as time goes on. It depends on the nature of your study.

Distance learning/external programmes

These programmes are available at most higher and further education institutions and are ideal for students who are not able to physically attend the institution at which they are studying. As such they may appeal to international students seeking a British qualification whose financial, family, work or other commitments prevent them from dropping everything and studying in the UK for three or four years. Tuition fees are considerably less and you don't have the living expenses of settling in the UK. In addition, you can actually carry on earning money as you study, because the programmes are flexible to suit your needs.

Students generally never need to attend the college in person, and generally are not taught 'face-to-face' by a college tutor. Instead, as an external student, you will be in charge of your own timetable and method of study. The institution at which you are registered will provide you with course materials which vary according to the course you are studying.

There are a wide range of institutions that offer distance learning programmes – from the traditional higher education institutions, such as the University of London, to further education colleges and professional bodies, such as the Association of

Certified Accountants. The qualifications available range from GCSEs, A levels and Scottish Highers to diplomas and BA (Hons) degrees. To study for a diploma you will probably be required to attend an officially recognised institution at home that will be able to prepare you for exams on behalf of the university at which you are registered. Diplomas are available in subjects like law, computing, and economics, and will serve as qualifications in their own right – important for personal development, or as a way to increase career prospects. However, they can also be used as an entry qualification to a corresponding degree course. For example, the Diploma in Law offered by the University of London External Programme is designed as an entry route to LLB courses.

Whether you are studying for an undergraduate or postgraduate course, you will take lessons in a written form, specifically designed for distance learning programmes. Whilst you will

Pictures courtesy of Queen Mary and Westfield College, University of Bath, Bath Spa University College, and The University of Central England, Birmingham

the Distance Learning web page, where all the UK institutions offering distance- learning programmes are listed, along with all the application details you need. The website address is *www.distance-learning.co.uk*

FURTHER SOURCES OF INFORMATION

Many libraries and careers offices in Britain have prospectuses and, if you live outside Britain, the British Council is a good source of information. They also publish the *British Education* guides which are usually available free of charge or for a very reasonable price.

British Council officers will put you in touch with UCAS (Universities and Colleges Admissions Service) if you are applying for an undergraduate degree course. UCAS is the central body through which students apply for full-time undergraduate university places from Britain or abroad (see 'Applying to Study' on page 34).

If you are applying for a postgraduate course, contact the universities you wish to apply to directly, as postgraduate applications themselves are done directly with the university or college.

Most universities operate a website on which it displays its prospectus plus up-to-date information about its courses, admissions procedures and so on. You can also try the UCAS website (*www.ucas.co.uk*) or the On Course website (*www.hotcourses.com*). Note: the easiest way to get information about universities or colleges in this guide is to use the reader information service postcard at the front of this book. Just fill in which places you are interested in, send the card to us, and we will arrange for the information to be sent to you free of charge. You can also call or fax the On Course Hotline and we can arrange for a prospectus to be sent to you, tel: 020 8600 5300, fax: 020 8741 7716.

receive written materials and be expected to study alone, you may also have to attend local seminars and study groups at certain times of the year when academics from the home institution visit. Some courses may require students to attend summer schools and revision courses for a short period of time in the UK. Work is mostly assessed by examinations at the end of the course but you may also be given written assignments to complete as assessed coursework.

Entrance requirements for all courses are discussed in detail in prospectuses and will vary between institutions. However, for most undergraduate courses, you will be expected to be over 17 years old and have the equivalent of two subjects at GCSE level or SCE and two further subjects at A level or Scottish Highers. Mature students will be considered on an individual basis often having gained equivalent professional experience. If you are interested in a diploma, entrance requirements vary, although GCSE/SCE standard qualifications are usually satisfactory.

Applications should be made directly to the institution, and not through UCAS. For more details look at

Applying to Study

applying applying applying applying

Y ou must always fill in applications forms correctly, which means they must always be fully completed. For the majority of courses, including language courses, vocational courses and postgraduate courses, you need to apply directly to the institution. Each requires slightly different things, but you will not usually be required to come to Britain for an interview – a correctly filled-in application form plus deposit is generally enough. For full-time undergraduate courses, you must apply through UCAS, the Universities and Colleges Admissions Service.

SPECIALIST, VOCATIONAL AND LANGUAGE SCHOOLS

The application process will depend on the type of college in question. If you are applying to a specialist college to do a non-degree course, you simply need to write, call, fax or email the college and ask for an application form. They will also tell you the submission deadline for applications and anything else about the college you need to know. You may be asked to send a deposit to secure your place when you return the completed application form. Deposits are often non-refundable, but you should always ask if the amount can be deducted from your fee if you decide to take your place. For art courses you may well have to produce proof of your ability, such as a video or portfolio.

UNIVERSITY DEGREE PROGRAMMES

There are a number of things to consider when choosing whether you want to study for an undergraduate degree. The two major decisions are what you want to study, and where.

Choosing a course

Choosing the right course can seem a nightmare. These guidelines below may help.

- Get a good idea of the range of courses available. Read through course descriptions in university prospectuses and get an idea of entrance requirements. Refer to the UCAS *Big Guide* (available through UCAS on 01242 544610), which has information on virtually all UK undergraduate courses.

- Narrow your choice down to a list of your top subjects or combinations.

- Assess your criteria: what are your reasons for wanting to study the subject at the top of your list? Do you have the qualifications you need to be accepted? Is your English fluent enough to allow you to study in English? What would you like to do after you have finished your degree? Will the degree be accepted in the country where you want to work? How long are you prepared to study for?

- Estimate how much it will cost: consider the cost of travel to and from your country; the total fee for the duration of the course; the costs of books and equipment; term-time and vacation accommodation costs; living expenses; how you will finance your studies.

Choosing a university

There are a number of things to consider when choosing a university. The geographical location is one factor; you may want to be near London, or you may want to escape to the countryside.

Another key factor is choosing between a campus university or a university in the middle of a town. On campus universities, students tend to live, study, eat and socialise within the university grounds and the nearest town may be too far or inconvenient to get to. This may result in you getting to know your fellow students more quickly. Other universities can offer students the usual deal of a lively social life revolving around halls of residence, students' unions and bars, but with the town's theatres, museums, parks, cinemas, bars, pubs and concert venues to escape to if the student scene becomes repetitive and you feel like a change.

UNDERGRADUATE COURSES

UCAS processes applications for all full-time, Higher National Diploma (HND), Diploma of Higher Education (DipHE), and first degree courses at UK universities, with the exception of the Open University. UCAS handles more than 450,000 applications each year, including over 50,000 from international students.

Before you apply

Before applying you should check you have the necessary qualifications. These are normally shown in university or college prospectuses. See the *British Education System* chapter for information on university foundation programmes and comparative qualifications.

When to apply (UK/EU)

If you are applying from the UK/EU, whatever your nationality, your application form must arrive at UCAS between September 1 2000 and December 15 2000 except for the following important exceptions:

You must apply to UCAS by October 15 2000 for courses at Oxford University or Cambridge University, or for courses in medicine (courses codes A100, A101, A103, A104 or A106), dentistry (course codes A200, A203, A204, A205 or A206) or veterinary medicine/science (course codes D100 or D101).

For Art and Design "Route B" courses you must apply to UCAS between January 1 2001 and March 24 2001. We recommend that you apply by March 9 2001 if possible.

The universities and colleges guarantee to consider your application if UCAS receives your form by the appropriate deadline. If you send in your form after the deadline date but before June 30 2001, they may consider it at their discretion, but they do not have to.

When to apply (non UK/EU)

If you are a student of any nationality applying from outside the EU you can apply at any time between

September 1 2000 and June 30 2001, unless you are applying for Oxford or Cambridge, medicine, dentistry, veterinary medicine/science or Route B art and design courses (see above). You must read the next paragraphs carefully before you decide when to apply. Most applicants apply well before June 30 and, if you want to be sure that a place is available on your chosen course, you should not wait until then to apply. UCAS cannot guarantee that applications for places on popular courses at some universities and colleges will be considered if they receive the applications after December 15 2000. You should check with individual universities and colleges if you are not sure.

If you think that you may be assessed as a 'home' student (UK or EU) for fee purposes, you should apply by December 15 2000, exactly the same as if you are applying from an EU country.

If you apply early this will give you enough time to make immigration, travel and accommodation arrangements. These arrangements may take a lot of time, particularity during the summer when immigration departments are extremely busy.

If you are a student from a non-EU country wishing to apply to one choice only and you already have the necessary qualifications, you may apply at any time. However, before completing an application form you should contact UCAS or your chosen university or college for advice.

How to apply

To apply for full-time undergraduate courses you need to apply through UCAS and the process is the same for both UK and international students. The UCAS system is sometimes considered bureaucratic but it does have the following benefits:

- you can apply for up to six different universities or colleges on one application form. When you receive offers of a place, you can then choose which one to accept.

- all UCAS institutions are recognised by the government or they offer courses that are validated by government-recognised universities.

- UCAS makes sure that applicants receive fair treatment and detailed impartial advice.

- UCAS can also provide advice on the admissions system including how to provide the information that selectors are looking for.

You may apply for up to six universities/colleges by completing a single UCAS application form (but you should not complete more than one form). Six is the maximum number of choices for all courses except medicine and dentistry, for which you may only enter four choices (plus two other non-medicine, dentistry courses if you wish). You can apply to just one course, and add further choices at a later stage up to the maximum of six.

Enter the institutions you have chosen in the order they appear in the UCAS handbook, *not* in your order of preference. You only declare your preference after you have received back offers from the institutions you list.

A sterling cheque or banker's draft for the correct fee (£15) must be sent with your application. If you make a single application initially and wish to add other choices later you will be asked to pay an additional fee of £10 (for 2001 entry). UCAS will shortly be offering payment by credit card.

How to pay (UK applicants)

You can pay by personal cheque, postal order, credit card or debit card. If you pay by cheque, please make it payable to UCAS Applications Account and cross it 'account payee only'. You should write on the back the applicant's full name and the seven-digit number from the top right corner of the front page of the application form. If you want to pay by credit/debit card, please complete the coupon at the back of this booklet.

Some schools and college prefer to collect individual applicant fees themselves, and send UCAS one payment to cover all their applicants. Before you send in your form, please check if your school or college does this.

If you are using EAS (the Electronic Application System), please consult the on-screen help section for details of how to pay.

How to pay (non-UK applicants)

You can pay by credit/debit card (see above), or by sending one of the following:

a. evidence that you have arranged payment by an international money order.

b. evidence that your bank has arranged payment by a bank draft payable at a UK bank.

c. a sterling cheque payable at a UK bank.

d. evidence of direct payment such as Economy International Money mover to to the following bank

account: UCAS International Account at Lloyds Bank plc,

Montpellier Branch, sort code 30-95-72, account number 0188578.

On the back, you should write your name, address and seven-digit number from the top right corner of the front page of the application form.

Art and Design courses

Selection for courses in art and design is normally by interview or inspection of a portfolio of work. You should contact any institution to which you are considering applying before completing the application form. This will establish what arrangements can be made to submit a portfolio and whether an interview will be necessary. You can apply through 'Route A' (closing date December 15 for following September entry) or 'Route B' (closing date March 24 for entry in September of the same year).

Route A

Applicants may enter up to six choices on the UCAS application form but may, if they wish, reserve up to three choices for later application through Route B. The choices must be listed in the order in which they appear in the UCAS handbook. Copies of the application form will be sent simultaneously to each institution listed.

Route A timetable

December 15 is the closing date for all applications.

March 31	Last date for decisions by institutions.
July 1	Last date for replies by applicants.

Late applications received up to 30 June will be sent to the universities and colleges for consideration at their discretion. Applications received after the 30 June will be entered in clearing.

Route B

Applicants may enter up to three choices in the order in which they appear in the UCAS handbook. Applicants should indicate on a separate form, supplied with the UCAS application form, the order in which they wish to be interviewed or to have their portfolios considered by the institutions. The copy forms will be sent to the institutions in that order.

Route B timetable

March 24	Closing date for applications.
April 3	First round of interviews and portfolio inspection commences.
May 18	Second round of interviews and portfolio inspection commences.
June 12	Third round of interviews and portfolio inspections commences.

Late applications received between March 24 and June 12 will be referred to institutions in the next available round. Applications received after June 12 will be entered in clearing.

FILLING IN THE UCAS FORM

The UCAS form is four pages long and looks rather complicated, especially if English is not your first language. However each form is supplied with a booklet called 'How to Apply' which contains detailed instructions on how to complete the form. On the next few pages are a few hints and tips to explain how to fill it in.

• Fill in the form completely. Do not leave any unanswered questions or leave out any information.

• Fill in the form in black ink. The form has to be photocopied and red or blue ink does not photocopy well.

• Fill in the form neatly. Bear in mind that there are many thousands of forms passing through UCAS and the offices of each college and university – a messy, illegible or grammatically incomprehensible form will not do you any favours. Photocopy the blank form and practice filling in the copies before you fill in the real form.

• UCAS will not accept:
  – a photocopy or faxed copy of the completed form. You must send the original.
  – separated pages. You must keep the original form intact.
  – extra sheets. You must write everything you have to say in the boxes. However, you can write to the admissions offices of the colleges or universities you are applying to and give them any extra information.

• Photocopy your completed application form, and your cheque for £15, in case the original is lost.

• With the application form you will have received a small reply card. Write your name and address on the back and send it to UCAS with your completed application form. It will be posted to you when UCAS has received your application.

• Send the original form by registered or express post.

HINTS FOR FILLING IN THE UCAS FORM

Heading

Read the pamphlet UCAS sent to you with your application form, entitled *'Instructions for completion of the application form by international students'*.

You must attach payment or proof of payment for £5 (for one application) or £14 (for six applications) to this page. Write your name and address on the back of the reply card you received from UCAS and attach that to the form.

Post the form to UCAS.

The number in this box helps UCAS to process the form. Do not mark or damage the box in any way.

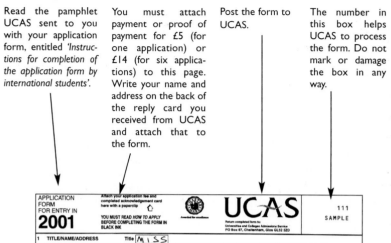

Section 1

Give the address where you want UCAS and the universities to send correspondence.

Write your forenames here. If you have a patronym, you should write it here.

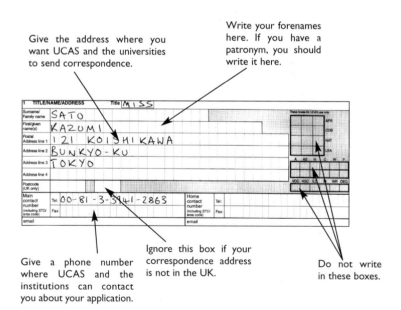

Give a phone number where UCAS and the institutions can contact you about your application.

Ignore this box if your correspondence address is not in the UK.

Do not write in these boxes.

Section 2

If you have a medical condition that needs special care, read the list below and enter the number of your disability. If you do not have an illness or disability, enter 0.

Enter one of these numbers in the box:
- **0** I do not have a disability
- **1** I have dyslexia
- **2** I am blind/partially sighted
- **3** I am deaf/hard of hearing
- **4** I have mobility difficulties/I use a wheelchair
- **5** I need personal care support
- **6** I have mental health difficulties
- **7** I have an unseen disability (eg. diabetes, epilepsy, asthma)
- **8** I have two or more of the above disabilities
- **9** I have a disability not listed above

If you are taking a BTEC/SCOTVEC or GNVQ/GSVQ qualification write your registration number in this box.

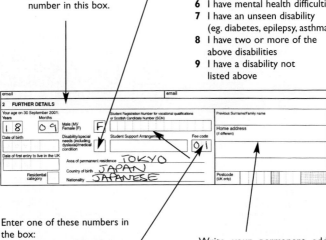

Enter one of these numbers in the box:
- **01** I am financing myself/ my parents are financing me
- **02** I am an EU resident applying for assessment of tuition fee contribution to a local education authority (LEA), Student Awards Agency for Scotland (SAAS) or Northern Ireland Education and Library Board.
- **06** I have an international student award from the UK government or the British Council
- **09** I'm financed by a non-UK government, university or industry
- **90** I'm financed by another sponsor, not listed above
- **99** I don't know yet. If I can't find a sponsor I may have to defer my application until 2000

Write your permanent address here if different from your correspondence address. Don't forget to let UCAS know if you change your address while your application is with UCAS.

Section 3 and 4

List the institutions and courses you want to apply for in this section, one college or one course per line *in the order they appear in the UCAS handbook.*

Only tick this column if you are going to live with friends or relatives while you are studying in the UK.

If you intend to defer any course for a year, write a 'D' in the box in this column.

If the institution has agreed to let you enter directly into other than year one of your course, write 2 or 3 etc. here. If you're going straight into the first year, do not enter anything.

3	APPLICATIONS IN *UCAS DIRECTORY* ORDER					If you wish to apply later for Art & Design Route B course please tick (✓)		
(a) Institution code name	(b) Institution code	(c) Course code	(d) Campus code	(e) Short form of the course title	(f) Further details requested in the *UCAS Directory*	(g) Point of entry	Home	Defer entry
GREEN	G7	0 0 1 6 0		BSc/EB				
GREEN	G7	0 0 1 6 1		BSc/EBES				
PLYM	P60	0 D 1 2		BSc/MrBec				
READ	GR1	2 0 1 6 0		BSc/EnvBio				

If you have previously applied to any institution(s) listed above enter the institution code(s) and your most recent UCAS application number (if known)

4	SECONDARY EDUCATION/FE/HE		From		To		PT,FT SW	UCAS SCHOOL OR COLLEGE CODE
			Month	Year	Month	Year		
	KOISHIKAWA HIGH SCHOOL		04	94	03	97	FT	

5	Tick (✓) if you have a National Record of Achievement or Progress File (UK applicants only)	pre-16	post-16

6 ADDITIONAL INFORMATION (not used for selection purposes)

A   Occupational Background _____

B   Ethnic Origin (UK applicants only)

C   UCAS may send you information from other organisations about products and services directly relevant to higher education applicants. Please tick the box if you *do not* want to receive it.

Page

Write the name and address of the last three educational institutions you attended (school, college, university) and the date(s) when you studied there.

International students can ignore sections 5 and 6.

This means:
PT = part-time
FT = full-time
SW = sandwich course.

Ignore this box if this is your first application to study in the UK.

Section 7A

7A QUALIFICATIONS COMPLETED (Examinations or assessments (including key/core skills) for which results are known, including those failed)

Examination/Assessment centre number(s) and name(s)

TOKYO METROPOLITAN HIGH SCHOOL ENTRANCE EXAM

Month	Year	Awarding body	Subject/unit/module/component	Level/qual	Result Grade Mark or Band	Month	Year	Awarding body	Subject/unit/module/component	Level/qual	Result Grade Mark or Band
02	94		MATHEMATICS		65						
02	94		JAPANESE		70						
02	94		ENGLISH		75						
02	94		SCIENCE		70						
02	94		HISTORY		68						

NATIONAL FIRST EXAMINATION FOR ENTRY TO STATE UNIVERSITY

Month	Year	Awarding body	Subject/unit/module/component	Level/qual	Result Grade Mark or Band						
02	97		MATHEMATICS		160						
02	97		JAPANESE		180						
02	97		ENGLISH		195						
02	97		BIOLOGY		87						
02	97		GENERAL SCIENCE		70						
02	97		WORLD HISTORY		95						
02	97		SOCIAL STUDIES		80						

7B QUALIFICATIONS NOT YET COMPLETED (Examinations or assessments (including key/core skills) to be completed, or results not yet published)

Examination/Assessment centre number(s), name(s) and address(es)

In the box above you have to write a list of all the examinations you have taken (whether you passed or failed). The column headings relate to UK examinations. If you have taken non-UK examinations, please write them along the horizontal rules, ignoring the vertical columns. You should also indicate the name of the examining body.

Section 7B

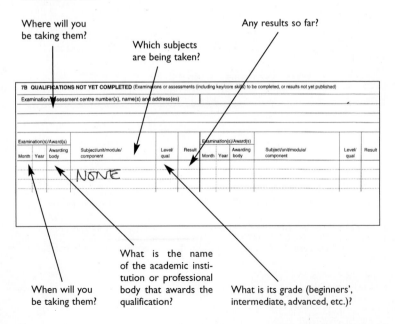

Where will you be taking them?

Which subjects are being taken?

Any results so far?

7B QUALIFICATIONS NOT YET COMPLETED (Examinations or assessments (including key/core skills) to be completed, or results not yet published)

Examination/Assessment centre number(s), name(s) and address(es)

Month	Year	Awarding body	Subject/unit/module/component	Level/qual	Result	Month	Year	Awarding body	Subject/unit/module/component	Level/qual	Result
			NONE								

When will you be taking them?

What is the name of the academic institution or professional body that awards the qualification?

What is its grade (beginners', intermediate, advanced, etc.)?

Sections 8, 9 and 10

Have you ever had a job or spent some time in work experience? Write down the details here.

If you put a number in the disability/special needs square in Box 2 (see page 48) you should explain here what your disability is and what special needs you have.

USE BLACK BALLPOINT OR BLACK TYPE

8 SPECIAL NEEDS or SUPPORT required as a consequence of any disability or medical condition stated in Section 2.

9 DETAILS OF PAID EMPLOYMENT TO DATE Names and addresses of recent employers	Nature of work	From		To		PT/
		Month	Year	Month	Year	FT
NONE						

10 PERSONAL STATEMENT (do NOT attach additional pages or stick on additional sheets)

Name of applicant

I've been fascinated by the sea since I was small. As part of my examination course, I'm studying the effects of pollution on marine life in Tokyo Bay. I've had to analyse water samples over a period of six months. Biology is my best subject at school. There's such a wide range of courses on offer in the UK for someone with my interests. I emailed each of the institutions I've chosen to ask for more information. I didn't know what Environmental Studies, for example, involved. I wanted to be sure that I chose something I was good at, as well as developing my particular interest in Marine Biology. My English exchange partner works for the Environment Agency in Huntingdon and I've learnt a lot from accompanying her on field trips on two recent visits to England. I'm hoping to do a longer period of job observation this summer before starting university. When I finish, I'd like to work in conservation, maybe in England. The English always seem so involved in conservation issues. That's one of the things that made me want to study here. I started working as a volunteer with the Tokyo Friends of the Earth Agency at the beginning of my final year in high school. I learnt a great deal from this experience - current issues concerning the environment, working with other people on group projects, the importance of efficient administration, and broad based IT skills. Apart from my academic studies I enjoy going to the cinema, books by Ruth Rendell, tennis, hiking and Tae Kwon Do.

11 CRIMINAL CONVICTIONS: Do you have any criminal convictions? See *How to Apply* YES ☐ NO ☐

12 DECLARATION: I confirm that the information given on this form is true, complete and accurate and no information requested or other material information has been omitted. I have read *How to Apply*, I undertake to be bound by the terms set out in it and I give my consent to the processing of my data by UCAS and educational institutions. I accept that, if I do not fully comply with these requirements, UCAS shall have the right to cancel my application and I shall have no claim against UCAS or any higher education institution or college in relation thereto.

	tick one
I have attached payment to the value of £15.00/£5.00	
or	
I have attached a complete credit/debit card payment coupon	

Applicant's Signature.................... Date ....

REMEMBER TO KEEP A PHOTOCOPY — SEE APPLICANT CHECKLIST ON BACK OF *HOW TO APPLY*   Page

Don't forget to sign and put the date.

Remember to attach your cheque or bank draft to the form before you put it in an envelope. Don't forget to post it.

Reference

You should get a teacher or some other responsible person to write a statement about you. This needs to corroborate what you have said in your personal statement, and give some indication of your academic performance. This should give a university confidence that you will work hard and complete the course successfully. The statement should also explain anything unusual in your history such as poor results, absence through illness etc. Do not copy the example below.

USE BLACK BALLPOINT OR BLACK TYPE

REFERENCE
Do NOT attach additional pages

UCAS
PO Box 67, Cheltenham, Glos GL52 3ZD
UCAS is a Registered Educational Charity
UCAS Ref No UC-0003A/01

4 4 4
SAMPLE

Name of referee		Type of school, college or training centre	
Post/Occupation/Relationship		Dates when the applicant is unavailable for interview due to examinations, etc.	
Name and address of school/college/organisation			
		Total number in post-16 education	Full time / Part time
Tel:	Fax:	Number normally proceeding to higher education each year	
email:			

Name of applicant (block capitals or type)

I have known Kazumi Sato for eight years, since she began at the Tokyo Girls High School. She has worked consistently hard, and achieved high results, especially in the sciences.

She is particularly interested in Marine Biology and is currently completing a final year project in the effects of pollution on fish in the Tokyo Bay. I have supervised this project in my capacity as Head of Biology and have been impressed by the thoroughness of her research. I am sure that Kazumi would perform well on any course with an individual research component.

Kazumi is equally talented in languages, as is shown by her proficiency in English. She has participated in various educational exchanges, and received a prize for her progress in English over the last academic year.

Kazumi is a bright and motivated pupil of the school. She is sociable, and popular with staff and students alike. I recommend her highly to the UK institutions she has chosen.

Section 7 checked as correct?	Yes		Referee's Signature:	
Correct fee and stamped acknowledgement card enclosed?	Yes		Date:	

Page 4 — **SEE REFEREE CHECKLIST ON BACK OF *HOW TO APPLY***

Referee should check section 7 if appropriate.

Your referee must sign his or her statement and write the date.

44

CHECKLIST
Information to include in the personal statement

- ☐ **Why have you chosen the course(s) listed in Section 3?**

- ☐ **What do you already know about the subject(s) you wish to study?**

- ☐ How did you acquire that knowledge?

- ☐ **Are you currently involved in any work or activity that relates to the subject(s) you wish to study?**

- ☐ What particular aspects of your current studies do you enjoy most?

- ☐ **Why do you want to study in the UK?**

- ☐ What do you plan to do with your higher education qualification?

- ☐ **What other interests, (e.g. cultural, sporting) do you have?**

- ☐ Are there any non-examined subjects which you are studying?

- ☐ **Have you been involved in any activities where you have been in a position of authority or have had to demonstrate communication skills?**

- ☐ Have you obtained, or applied to any industrial or professional sponsorship or placement? If so give details.

- ☐ **Are you planning to defer entry to the year 2001? If so, give your reasons for doing so.**

- ☐ Apart from any English language test results you have included in Section 7 what other evidence can you give of your ability to successfully complete a higher education course taught in English? For example, if all or part of your studies have been conducted in English it is important to mention it.

After you have applied

UCAS will send a copy of your application form to the institutions you have named. The institutions will each consider your application and tell UCAS whether they wish to make you an offer of a place.

If you have already achieved the entrance qualifications for the course, the offer will be unconditional. If you still have to take qualifying examinations, any offer you receive will be conditional on passing those examinations at specific grades. UCAS will pass this decision on to you, although the institutions may also write to you directly. You should not reply to any offers you receive until you are asked by UCAS which offers you wish to accept. You may hold no more than two choices: your first choice/firm acceptance and your second choice/ insurance acceptance. Your reply should be sent to UCAS who will then send it on to the institutions.

Accepting an offer

You must think very carefully about your replies to any offers, as you will be expected to keep to them and not change your mind later. When your examination results come out you must send a copy of your results slip to the university/college at which you are holding conditional offers.

If you have met the conditions of any offer you are holding, the institution will make the place unconditional. If firm acceptance of the first choice institution is confirmed, your insurance offer is automatically cancelled. If you didn't quite achieve the desired grades, you must still send a copy of your results to the universities. One of them may still send you an unconditional offer through UCAS.

UCAS will notify you of the final decision. If you receive a confirmed offer of a place you must return the slip UCAS sends with it immediately, direct to the institution, to confirm whether or not you are accepting the offer. If you do not get accepted because you have missed the required grades you can always join the Clearing process.

Clearing

UCAS operates a service known as 'Clearing' in August/September each year to help candidates who have been unsuccessful in finding a place at their preferred institution, or who have applied late. You would be eligible for Clearing if you fall into one of the following categories:

- Having applied to UCAS in the normal way you receive no offers from any of your choice institutions.

- You receive offers from some of your choices, but your subsequent examination results are not good enough for you to be accepted.

- If you have applied through UCAS for the first time after June 30 (or June 11 for Art and Design Route B courses) you will automatically be sent a Clearing Entry Form (CEF) by UCAS with the necessary details and information on how to proceed.

Finances

As an international student you will be responsible for paying fees to cover tuition, accommodation and expenses. When you arrive in the UK you will have to prove that you are here to study and that you can fund your studies. You must organise adequate sponsorship from individuals or organisations at home before you leave. Immigration restrictions prevent you from working solely to fund your studies whilst you are in the UK.

To be eligible for a mandatory award (local education authority grant), or a

Pictures courtesy of Queen Mary and Westfield College, University of Bath, Bath Spa University College, and The university of Central England, Birmingham

student loan, you have to have been 'ordinarily resident' in the UK for three years before the day you start your course. You may be entitled to an award or a student loan if you are on a full-time course and you are from a European Economic Area country or if you can show that your husband/wife or either of your parents has migrant worker status.

You may also qualify for an award or a loan if you are recognised by the British government as a refugee.

Applying for postgraduate courses

Unless you are applying for post-graduate studies in teaching or social work (see Education and Economics chapters) there is no central admissions body, like UCAS, that deals specifically with postgraduate applications. You will have to contact the relevant institutions directly. Some universities will have a separate department that deals with postgraduate admissions, others will expect you to apply to the relevant tutor directly.

Your first step should be getting hold of prospectuses for graduate studies from the institutions you wish to apply to. This will give you general information about the university and its departments. Using the information in this prospectus, you can then request individual departmental prospectuses.

Application procedures differ from one university to the next. Generally, however, you will be asked to complete a detailed application form in which you will be asked about academic qualifications, work experience, and your reasons for wanting to study the course. If you are applying for a research place, you may be asked to outline a proposal for your research. Even if you are applying for a taught course, there will be a small research component at the end of the year.

Finance

As an international student, you will be responsible for finding the funds to cover registration and tuition fees, living expenses, books and travel expenses. Although tuition fees and living expenses vary from university to university and region to region, there are approximately standard rates throughout the UK – arts courses are in the region of £6,000, science courses cost around £8,000, and clinical courses cost around £14,000. If you are an EU student, then you pay the same as British students, namely around £1,040 per year. Bear in mind that these fees only cover your tuition costs. You will also need to calculate how much you'll need for accommodation, food, travel, etc.

As an international student you may be able to apply for funding through your own government. Alternatively, you might find help from other sources: the British Council awards bursaries, and the Foreign and Commonwealth Office and Overseas Development Administration run scholarship and awards schemes.

What if I choose the wrong course?

When you study in the UK you often have the option of choosing from a range of different modules – short courses in some specialist aspect of the broad subject you are studying. Inevitably some students gradually realise that they are more interested in a subject that was not their original course. If this happens, then don't panic.

At almost every British university you will be allocated an academic tutor. If you are serious about changing, make an appointment to see your tutor, they will be able to advise you on how to proceed.

Arriving in Britain

If and when you decide you want to come to Britain to study, you will need to make a number of arrangements before leaving for the UK, otherwise you may be refused entry in to the country or have to leave your course for some other reason. You may have military service obligations for example or need permission to leave your country. The British High Commission, British Embassy, British Consulate (General), or the British Council may be able to help by providing supporting documents. Your government may impose restrictions on the transfer of currency to the UK.

VISAS AND IMMIGRATION

The basic division is between European Economic Area citizens (European Union plus Iceland and Norway), people from other countries who do not need a visa to enter Britain ('non-visa nationals') and people from countries who do need a visa before entering Britain ('visa nationals'). The Home Office divides the categories as follows:

European Economic Area

If you are a national of a European Union country or are from Norway or Iceland you are free to enter the UK to study, live and work and you do not need a visa. European Union citizens face fierce competition from British students and also have to contribute towards their course – depending on

European Economic Area

Austria, Belgium, Denmark, Finland, France, Germany, Greece, Holland, Iceland, Ireland, Italy, Liechtenstein, Luxembourg, Norway, Portugal, Spain, Sweden, United Kingdom

financial circumstances. Icelandic and Norwegian students have to pay full fees as international students, but do not need work visas and so can fund their course by working.

Non-visa Nationals

Non-visa nationals are from countries that don't require a visa to enter Britain. You can arrive with the necessary documentation and be issued the visa when you arrive. You need:

- Proof that you have been accepted onto a full-time course at a UK school, college or university (totalling 15 or more hours a week).

- A letter from your new school, college or university, on their official

Non-Visa Nationals

Andorra, Argentina, Australia, Botswana, Brazil, Canada, Costa Rica, Japan, Korea (South), Malaysia, Malta, Mexico, Monaco, Namibia, New Zealand, San Marino, Singapore, South Africa, South Korea, Swaziland, Switzerland, USA, Zimbabwe

headed paper, to state that you have paid your deposit and/or your tuition fees.

- Proof that you have the funds to pay for your study and living expenses. This could be in the form of traveller's cheques in sufficient quantity to cover your expenses, a bank draft drawn on a UK bank, letters or bank documents from sponsors, or a combination of all these things. You will have to show that you will not have 'recourse to public funds' – that you can support yourself financially without relying on the British welfare state or by working to fund your studies.

If you are staying for longer than six months, your finances will be inspected much more rigorously. It is advisable to submit your documentation to the British Embassy/High Commission in your own country and get entry clearance (a visa) prior to arrival. Your status can still be challenged but you have the right to lodge an appeal and remain in Britain while your case is heard. If you were intending to be issued with a visa on arrival you could be sent back at your own expense. There are plenty of scare stories around, but this is unlikely to happen in practice unless you have done something that arouses suspicion. This might include travelling back and forth from Britain a number of times over a short period, appearing to have little money, or enrolling at a school with a reputation as a 'visa factory'.

You can bring your partner/husband/ wife or children with you. However, they will require a separate 'student dependent visa', which they must obtain before they arrive (even though

Visa Nationals

Afghanistan, Albania, Algeria, Angola, Armenia, Azerbaijan, Bahrain, Bangladesh, Belarus, Belize, Benin, Bhutan, Bolivia, Bosnia-Herzegovina, Brazil, Burkina Faso (Upper Volta), Burma (Myanmar), Brunei, Bulgaria, Burundi, Cambodia (Kampuchea), Cameroon, Cape Verde, the Central African Republic, Chad, China, Colombia, the Congo, Cuba, Cyprus, the Democratic Republic of the Congo (Zaire), Djibouti, the Dominican Republic, Ecuador, Egypt, Equatorial Guinea, Eritrea, Ethiopia, Fiji, Gabon, the Gambia, Georgia, Ghana, Guinea, Guinea-Bissau, Guyana, Haiti, India, Indonesia, Iran, Iraq, the Ivory Coast, Jordan, Kampuchea (Cambodia), Kazakhstan, Kenya, Kirgizstan, Korea (North), Kuwait, Laos, the Lebanon, Liberia, Libya, Macedonia, Madagascar, Malawi, the Maldives, Mali, Mauritius, Moldavia (Moldova), Mongolia, Morocco, Mozambique, Myanmar (Burma), Nepal, Niger, Nigeria, Oman, Pakistan, Palestine, Papua New Guinea, Peru, Philippines, Qatar, Romania, Russia, Rwanda, São Tome e Príncipe, Saudi Arabia, Senegal, Serbia, Sierra Leone, Somalia, Sri Lanka, Sudan, Surinam, Syria, Tanzania, Taiwan, Thailand, Togo, Tunisia, Turkey, Turkmenistan, Uganda, the Ukraine, Upper Volta (Burkina Faso), Uzbekistan, Vietnam, The Yemen, Yugoslavia, Zambia

your own visa can be issued on arrival). To obtain this you will have to show that you can support them out of your own pocket. Remember that it can be very difficult to find accommodation for families and what there is tends to be expensive, so try and make arrangements before you arrive. Most universities can offer family accommodation, but space is limited. Be as organised in your arrangements as possible, as this will make you look more credible in the eyes of immigration officials.

You could also enter Britain as a tourist. In theory, non-visa nationals can then apply to have it changed to a student visa without leaving the country as an 'in-country application'. In practice this is not advisable as the immigration department is inherently suspicious of people who change the purpose of their stay while they are in Britain. You may succeed in getting your visa changed this way, but you will get a grilling in the process. Many people come to Britain on a tourist visa, and then look around for a school to enrol in. Be careful, because you could end up being deported if you are thought to have deliberately deceived the immigration department. The best thing to do is to apply for a 'prospective student visa' in your home country.

You will need to show that you have the finances to support your course and will be allowed to stay in the UK for a maximum of six months.

Visa nationals

Visa nationals need to get a student visa from their nearest British Embassy, Consulate or High Commission before arriving in Britain. In order to get this you will need to show the following:

- Proof that you have been accepted for a full-time course (15 or more hours a week) at a reputable UK college or university. If it is at a language school it is preferable for it to be an ARELS or British Council accredited school.

- A letter from your new school, college or university, on their official headed paper, to state that you have paid your deposit and/or tuition fees.

- Proof that you have the funds to pay for your study and living expenses. This could be in the form of traveller's cheques in sufficient quantity to cover your expenses, a bank draft drawn on a UK bank, letters or bank documents from sponsors, or a combination of all these things.

- Immigration officials prefer a bank draft as this is the most difficult to forge and can be checked with the issuing bank. You will have to show that you will not have 'recourse to public funds'. The longer your proposed stay, the more convincing your financial credentials will need to be.

You will need to get your visa, and bring it along with all the above documentation when you enter Britain, as immigration officials may

Pictures courtesy of Queen Mary and Westfield College, University of Bath, Bath Spa University College, and The university of Central England, Birmingham

wish to see on arrival. If you have been given entry clearance in your home country this is usually sufficient. However, your right of entry may be challenged if immigration officials believe that there has been a change of circumstances or you have not disclosed, or have hidden, some relevant information. In this situation, you have the right to remain in Britain while you lodge an appeal.

If you entered the UK as a tourist you will not be able to get your tourist visa changed to a student visa in Britain. You will have to leave the country, and re-apply for a student visa before re-entering.

IF YOU HAVE PROBLEMS

You should not fear problems at the immigration desk, but you should be prepared to be questioned quite closely. Immigration officials will be trying to establish whether you are a genuine student, and not coming to the UK for the purpose of work or permanent residence. They also want to be sure you will go home when you have finished your studies.

If, for any reason, the officials are dissatisfied with your answers and decide to hold you at the immigration stage, airport officials will provide you with an interpreter if necessary. It can be a scary experience and the best thing to do is ask officials to contact the college or university where you have a place, or anyone else who can help you by supporting your case. The best advice is to be honest and direct. Immigration officials become even more suspicious if they detect even the smallest half-truth or lie.

If you have entry clearance and choose to appeal you can then contact an immigration solicitor. It is important that you use a reputable firm. There is an organisation called UKCOSA, specifically set up to help students in such situations. They can recommend a reputable solicitors, or take on your case.

UKCOSA Council for International Education
9-17 St Albans Place
London
N1 ONX
Advice Line: (Mon-Fri 1pm to 4pm)
Tel: 020 7354 5210

Another organisation that may be of use is the Joint Council for the Welfare of Immigrants (JWCI), although they mainly deal with people coming to settle rather than study in the UK.

Joint Council for the Welfare of Immigrants (JCWI)
115 Old Street
London
EC1V 9JR
Advice Line: (open Mon, Tue, Thu 2pm to 5 pm).
Tel: 020 7251 8706

If you use a solicitor and have problems with the firm, you can contact the Law Society on 020 7242 1222. Or contact the Immigration Law Practitioners Association on 020 7251 8383. They can give you the names and addresses of immigration solicitors and advisers.

You can get further information on general immigration issues by writing to the Foreign Office at:

The Correspondence Unit
Migration and Visa Division
Foreign and Commonwealth Office
1 Palace Street
London
SW1E 5HE

Registration and visa obligations

Registering with the Police

If you are from a visa-national country that is not a member of the Commonwealth and you are going to be in Britain for more than six months you will be required to register with a local police station. If you are in London, you should visit the Alien Registration Office at 10 Lambs Conduit Street, High Holborn, London (Mon – Fri 9.30am – 4.45pm), tel: 020 7230 1208. Residents outside London should register at the local central police station. When you go to register, you must take your passport, travel documents, any appropriate home office documents, two passport-size photos and a £34 registration fee. If you later change address, course or any aspect of your registration details, you must return to the same office and alter you record.

Registration with your embassy

You should also register with your national embassy in London in case you lose your passport and other travel documents, or are involved in an incident of any kind. If you are living outside London, you will have to contact the embassy by telephone and request the appropriate registration forms. Otherwise, it is always possible to go there and register in person. It may be sensible to call up first in case you need to make an appointment. (Check with Yellow Pages or directory enquiries (Tel: 192) for the correct telephone number).

Extending your student visa

This is best done by post as the queues at immigration offices tend to be painstakingly long. You need to write to the Application Forms Unit at the Immigration and Nationality Directorate (address below), and send the original copies of relevant documents by registered or recorded delivery. You must provide original documents. Photocopies will lead to your application being instantly dismissed.

The documents you will need include proof of your school or college registration and if you are trying to get an extension of your student visa, proof of an 80 per cent or better attendance record to date. If you have attended fewer than 80 per cent of your lectures, seminars and other course requirements, you will have to show a medical certificate or similar evidence to justify your absence. This medical certificate also has to be presented in its original form and not as a photocopy.

If you are applying in person, you can go to any one of the Immigration and Nationality Directorate offices up and down the UK. Application forms may be obtained by writing to:

Immigration and Nationality
Directorate
Block C,
Whitgift Centre
Croydon
CR9 1AT
For immigration application forms
tel: 0870 241 0645
For general enquiries
tel: 0870 606 7766
For individual case enquiries
tel: 0870 608 1592

This is the nearest office for the London area, in Croydon, and not surprisingly it is also the busiest, with queues regularly forming from six in the morning. Bring breakfast and you may even need a packed lunch. For this reason, use one of the non-London offices if you can.

Other Offices:
Belfast
Immigration Office
Olive Tree House
Fountain Street
Belfast BT1 5EA
Tel: 0870 606 7766

Birmingham
Immigration office
(Cargo Terminal)
Birmingham Airport
Birmingham B26 3QN
Tel: 0121 606 7345

Glasgow
Immigration Office
Dumbarton Court
Argyll Avenue
Glasgow Airport
Paisley PA3 2TD
Tel: 0141 887 2255

Liverpool
Immigration Office
Graeme House
Derby Square
Liverpool L2 7SF
Tel: 0151 236 8974

You can also look on the Immigration and Nationality Department website: www.homeoffice.gov.uk/ind/hpg.htm

TRAVEL

Britain may be a relatively small country, but it can still be complicated to get around when you are not familiar with the system.

When you first arrive in Britain, you will have to get from the airport, port or railway station to your destination. If you are enrolling at a university, its international officer should have sent you a map and instructions on how to

travel. They may even have arranged to meet you at your point of entry. Heathrow, Gatwick, Stansted and Luton airports are all on the outskirts of London and you have to take a train, tube or bus to get into town. There are major international airports all over the British Isles, including Edinburgh, Glasgow, Derry, Prestwick, Birmingham, Cardiff, and Bournemouth. Many students flying to regional airports use Amsterdam rather than London's crowded Heathrow as a hub.

Travel from Heathrow

If you are travelling between Heathrow airport and London, you can either take the Heathrow Express service to Paddington station (£12 for a 15-minute, one-way journey), or the underground train. Heathrow is on the Piccadilly line and a one way ticket to or from central London will cost £3.40 for a one-hour journey. The underground is safe and cheap, although you will have to negotiate escalators with all your luggage. You can use the Airbus service, which leaves every 30 minutes, costs around £6. The A2 Airbus goes to Russell Square via Holland Park tube, Baker Street tube and Euston Station. If you want to experience one of London's many black taxi cabs and you have pounds and pounds at your disposal, the journey will cost you about £45 plus a 10 per cent tip. It may take longer than the tube if the traffic is bad, especially during rush hours.

Travel to and from Gatwick

You can travel easily to and from Gatwick airport via the Gatwick Express, from Victoria station. Trains leave every 15 minutes and cost £10.20 for a one way journey. Trains run until 11.40 pm. Coaches run regularly between Gatwick and Victoria and cost £5 for a one-way journey. The last coach leaves Gatwick at 10pm and the last to leave Victoria is at 11.30pm. They run regularly from early morning. The coach enquiry line is 0990 747 777.

Travel to and from Stansted

Stansted is further away from London than Heathrow and Gatwick airports. Perhaps because of this it is usually quiet and pleasant to use. Trains from Stansted to Liverpool Street, in central London, take about 40 minutes and cost £12 for one way.

Regional airports

If you are going to a college or university outside London, you may be able to fly directly there from your home country with or without stops en route to airports like Manchester. If you land at Aberdeen, Edinburgh or Glasgow, your best option for getting to your destination is to take a taxi

TAXI SAFETY TIPS

❑ If the taxi is not a black cab, always make sure the driver has an identification card

❑ Always tell someone where you are going and which company you booked through

❑ If you are female try not to travel alone late at night

from the taxi rank at the airport (costing between £8 and £15).

You may find there is a long queue of people also waiting for taxis. It is considered to be rude and unfair for people to 'jump' the queue or push in front of others, so be warned! There may be a bus that serves the airport from the station on a circular route, which will be cheaper than a taxi. Taxis are cheaper outside London, and probably the best option.

Living and Studying in Britain

LIVING IN BRITAIN

Accommodation

The key thing to find out from the institution you will be studying at is whether they can make accommodation arrangements or whether they expect you to do this yourself. The options are: university or college accommodation; flat or house share arrangements; or 'homestay' (living with a British family). Unless your university is arranging accommodation for you, it is advisable to view accommodation before committing to taking it or, more importantly, before paying a deposit.

College/university accommodation

Generally, you should have guaranteed accommodation at least during your first year. It is best to accept any offers of accommodation as early as possible. Few universities have enough room to accommodate all of their students, therefore they need to know as early as possible if rooms are going to be free.

Universities have invested in new accommodation in recent years to cater for increasing numbers of students. Most have accommodation that ranges from old-style single, double and triple study-bedrooms that have a shared kitchen and bathroom in a hall of residence, to new apartments in a 'student village', with single rooms for about eight students with a shared kitchen, bathroom and living room. Some universities have also purchased houses close to campus, which they have adapted for use by students. There are also some schemes in existence whereby private landlords allow their buildings to be managed by universities for students.

The more traditional halls of residence are usually supervised by university staff. Some halls provide two meals a day, and others provide facilities for students to cater for themselves. Although these self-catering halls are usually cheaper, you may prefer to pay extra to have your meals cooked for you. Meal times can be a good opportunity to meet people and make new friends. Most halls of residence usually have laundry facilities as well as cleaning staff who will change bedsheets and empty dustbins.

Halls of residence

Though some halls are stricter than others permission can usually be obtained to allow overnight guests to stay. Generally few people bother to seek this permission. Spare rooms can sometimes be booked in advance for visiting parents/friends.

Living in student halls of residence is a great way to meet new people and make lasting friendships. The stresses that can sometimes be associated with 'living out', such as bills and landlords, are avoided in halls where you have the benefit of being part of a large group, plus you have privacy if you need it. Living in halls of residence also means that you can take part in activities organised by people in the halls.

Bearing all this in mind, it is worth noting that the rules can be restricting. You may be incompatible with your fellow students and prefer a noisier/quieter environment. The predominating culture, be it partying or studying, does not suit everyone. However, as they are owned and run by universities, halls can provide a supportive environment.

Not all halls provide accommodation for the whole year, and will require you to clear your room during the holidays. Check with your international officer whether this is the case. Most universities will make exceptions for international students and allow you to stay in halls during vacations. Some may charge extra. In any case it will probably be possible for you to store luggage in secure storage space if you are going home for the holidays.

HOST
HOSTING *for*
OVERSEAS STUDENTS

Host is a voluntary organisation supported by the British Council and the British Foreign Commonwealth office, organising international students to stay with British residents to get to know the people, culture and ways of life. Contact 0207 494 2468 or www.hostuk.org

Houseshare and Flatshare

In most instances halls of residence are only on offer for one or two years of a three-year course: usually the first and/or third years. It is for this reason that flat and house sharing tends to be popular with long term students. Students enrolled on short courses tend not to want the hassle of arranging their own accommodation.

Flats and houses for rent are advertised in local papers and in accommodation offices in universities. In London the papers to look in are *Loot* and *The Evening Standard*. *Loot* also has a good website: www.loot.co.uk. Prices vary widely, depending on the location and standard of accommodation required. Generally, the best time to look for accommodation is before the end of the summer term – June/July. Bear in mind that if you find a flat or house at this time of year, you will need to pay for it over the summer. If you enjoy independence and cooking for yourself (and occasionally others!) then sharing a flat or house is probably best for you.

Homestays

This is a popular option for language school students. You live in the home of a host family, where you have your own study bedroom and a certain number of meals with the family. Arrangements are flexible according to the needs and wants of the student, although it is usually seen as a kind of cultural exchange. The host family may be interested in getting to know you in the same way that you may be interested in their culture and traditions. Complete immersion in British life is often the best way to practice language and understand the culture and customs of a British family.

You will be expected to respect and

abide by basic rules that the family may impose. However, you are paying, so services, such as baby-sitting, are entirely at your discretion and not part of the deal.

Homestays can work very well for students who value security and prefer a home environment. However, if the host family has young children you may not find it the best environment for studying. The real advantage is that you will speak English daily and improve your conversational skills. But you may be living some distance away from college and other students, and you might not enjoy the cooking!

Homestays can be arranged for the duration of your course, either privately or through the institution you are going to attend. Some international offices arrange a short one-off weekend homestay as a way of introducing you to British culture and home life. They can also be arranged through organisations such as local churches, temples, mosques or synagogues, and charitable organisations with overseas links. You may prefer to get in contact with people who you know through family or friends. They may be able to suggest where you can stay.

Bedsits

Short for 'bedroom/sitting room', a bedsit is a one-room apartment in a larger building. A single or double bed with a washing area, cooker and bathroom are usually common in all bedsits. They can be any size from reasonably spacious to extremely cramped. Although very cheap, bedsits can be lonely unless you are in a building with lots of other students. Noisy neighbours can also make it almost an impossible environment to write essays and read in, and landlords may not be as sympathetic or supportive as in halls of residence, particularly if you have any delays in

payment of rent. But, for independent students, bedsits can be a good way of assuring your peace and quiet and freedom!

Lodgings

This is a room in a family house – just like a homestay – but the relationship is purely commercial. You will have fairly little to do with the family and will be treated as a tenant rather than as a paying guest.

As a paying lodger, you are entitled to privacy, respect and a decent standard of living, although the family may have rules about bringing guests and friends into the house. Lodgings are usually advertised locally in shops and super-markets, or through students' accom-modation offices and religious and char-itable organisations.

FINANCES
Working in the UK

If you have a student visa, immigration laws will not permit you to work as a means of financing your studies. You can, however, work for up to 20 hours a week, on a part-time basis. You are allowed to work full time in the holidays. The UK government has recently simplified the rules to make it easier to work. One of the useful changes is that a spouse is now allowed to do full time work provided his or her partner is in full time study.

• You are not working to finance your studies.

You will also need to present your passport and a local police registration certificate so your temporary student resident status can be checked. Job centres are listed in the local telephone book under 'Employment Services and Job Centres'.

Working without a permit is illegal and means that you will not be protected by employment laws. Employers caught employing illegal workers are fined when found out, and illegal employees are deported instantly.

Bank accounts

As a student on a full-time course of two years or more, you are entitled to open a student bank account. These usually have interest-free overdrafts, and other attractive offers such as rail tickets, mobile phones, record tokens, and sometimes cash gifts.

As a student you will normally be offered a current or student account that entitles you to a cheque-book, and a cheque guarantee and cash point card – for use at cashpoint machines. You can also use it as a debit card (used like a credit card in shops, but the money is automatically deducted from your account in about three working days from purchase).

Cheques are commonly used as a method of payment in Britain, and a few important points should be remembered when filling them in:

- Do not leave any gaps.

- Sign your name in a way that is difficult to imitate (using Japanese characters if you are Japanese is more sensible that signing in English). Keep your cheque-book separate from your cheque guarantee card at all times.

You will be asked if you require an overdraft when you open an account. This is a good idea, as becoming over-drawn without an authorised overdraft can be very expensive as you might be charged interest. Most student overdrafts are interest-free, although some banks may charge extra fees for handling cheques.

Read all the relevant literature available before you choose where

to bank. Banks tend to range from the large, nationwide operations (eg Midland, Royal Bank of Scotland, Barclays, Lloyds TSB, National Westminster) to smaller regional banks (eg Clydesdale – in Scotland) and building societies (Nationwide, Cheltenham and Gloucester) that offer very competitive terms for students. It is worth joining a bank or building society near your college or university as staff are more likely to be used to dealing with students.

Student loans

Student loans are offered as part of the financial support package for higher education students. Although essential to students in the UK, they are unlikely to apply to international students. Student loans are arranged with the Student Loans Company Ltd, based in Glasgow, and offer more competitive rates than high street banks. To qualify you need to have been a resident in the UK for the three years immediately before the first day of your course, and attending a full-time course of higher education (15+ hours per week), or a Postgraduate Certificate in Education (PGCE).

Loans must be repaid in monthly instalments over five years, or seven if the student has taken out loans for more

than five academic years. Repayments include interest. Contact the Student Loans Administrator in the Student Finance Department at your university/college for details. Although loans are arranged through your university, you can ask questions about eligibility at: The Student Loans Company Ltd 100 Bothwell Street Glasgow G2 7JD Tel: 0800 405 010. Postgraduate research students are not eligible for loans, partly because graduates can more easily obtain loans from banks.

HEALTH AND WELFARE

Registering with doctors and dentists

If your course is longer than six months you are entitled to free treatment within the National Health Service (NHS). There may be a surgery attached to your college or university, and it is a good idea to register here. Staff are used to student patients, and the location is likely to be convenient. If not, you should apply to a local surgery and ask if you can register. You can find the nearest one in the Yellow Pages or by asking your local chemist. Take proof of your student status with you. Once you have registered you will be sent an NHS medical card with an individual identity code.

Do not lose this card, as you will also need it to register with a dentist. Students are entitled to free dental treatment on the NHS although this is not available from all dentists.

NHS prescriptions for medicines cost £5.80 per item. You will be exempt from this charge if you are under 19 years old and in full-time education, or if you are pregnant or have had a baby within the last year. There is no charge for prescriptions for contraceptive tablets or devices.

Prepayment certificates are available if you are likely to need medicines frequently, where you pay £30.80 (for four months) or £84.60 (for 12 months) in advance, which may mean a saving in the end. For example, it's worth it if you are an asthmatic who needs more than one kind of inhaler at all times, because each inhaler and each cylinder of medication incurs a separate prescription charge.

FOOD

If you are catering for yourself while you study, you will soon realise that Britain has an excellent range of shops selling food for all tastes. Nowadays you can usually buy a surprisingly wide range of foods even in smaller towns. London, in particular, has shops selling authentic ingredients from all over the world. There are Chinatowns in most of larger cities such as Manchester, Birmingham and Liverpool. Local shops tend to be more expensive than large supermarkets, but if you do not have access to a car, or if the public transport serving out-of-town supermarkets is poor, then these may be your lifeline. Food will cost you at least £25 per week, depending on your dietary requirements. Vegetarianism and veganism are common in Britain, and are well-catered for in towns and cities by a range of health-food specialists and well-stocked supermarkets. Even in small towns it is now possible to eat only organically-grown produce, or buy from free-range farms.

In most towns and cities you will find excellent restaurants from many different countries serving food such as European, Indian, Thai, Chinese and Greek and Turkish food. Fish and chips is probably the most famous British dish, although chicken tikka masala is the most widely eaten! You can find fish and chip shops all over England, from the smallest towns to the largest cities. 'Greasy spoon' café's, appropriately named after the cutlery you might find there, are the best places to try a traditional English breakfast. This typically consists of fried tomatoes, fried bread, sausages, bacon, fried eggs, fried mushrooms, fried potatoes, baked beans, black pudding, and a hot cup of tea. Not for the faint-hearted. And of course fastfood take-away burger and chicken bars, and pizza parlours can be found almost everywhere in the country. Look out for restaurant guides in local and regional newspapers and listings magazines.

ENTERTAINMENT

With very few exceptions, all universities in the UK have unions that are affiliated to the National Union of Students (NUS). When you register at university you will be issued with an NUS card and a student identity card. You can also apply to your school or university for an International Student Identity Card (ISIC). Both are proof of your student status and entitle you to concessions.Whilst a student living allowance rarely stretches to luxurious pursuits, a lot of good fun can be had for very little money. Cinemas in towns with colleges or universities often offer student discounts, and most universities have a film society showing films at unbeatable prices. Theatre is a very popular form of entertainment in Britain and as a student, you will be given discounts or cheap seats, especially for matinée (afternoon) performances. Your NUS card will get you discounts on most things from nightclubs and shopping, to bungee jumps and health centres.

You will probably be attracted to at least one society connected to your college or university. This may be the best way to take part in and organise events that relate to your specific interest, be it rock climbing or wine-tasting.

Cities such as London and Manchester are famous for their nightclubs. In reality the best clubs are dotted all over the country, and it is common for clubs to tour the country – spending a few months of every year at a particular venue. Clubbing can be expensive and sometimes drinks on sale there are almost double the price that they are in pubs. Dance music and clubs are commonly associated with the drug 'ecstasy'. Some clubs tend to be frequented by people buying and selling drugs, and therefore by police, so be warned! Drug related deaths and subsequent media attention have resulted in there being increased police interest in nightclubs.

You will find music of all types in every large city: orchestras and choirs, classical music, and rock, jazz and folk bands playing in clubs and pubs. Pubs are the best known social centres in Britain. They sell alcohol and soft drinks and sometimes have live music and stand-up comedy acts.

British people are often at their most relaxed in a pub drinking beer or lager in pint glasses. People often spend the whole evening playing darts or pool, taking part in quizzes, or karaoke, or simply chatting and listening to a band. Pubs are equally inviting during cold winters when you can often find a burning log fire, or during the summer when drinkers can bask in the sun on outdoor tables. Many colleges and almost all universities have at least one bar, usually in the students' union. The bar is often the focus of student life, a place where people gather between lectures or at the end of the day. Groups of friends often meet at a pub before going off somewhere else for the rest of the evening. English licensing laws forbid the sale of alcohol after 11pm.

SIGHTSEEING

The UK is relatively small, yet a great deal is crammed into its borders. It can offer the visitor outstandingly beautiful landscapes, historic buildings and vibrant cities, and because of its size it is easy to travel between places of particular interest. Don't be fooled, however, into thinking you can 'do' the major sights in a long weekend; there are so many places worthy of a visit it is important to allow enough time for each one.

You should take advantage of any opportunity to get off campus, and make sightseeing a regular feature of your stay. Whether you prefer the many attractions of London, the ancient mystery of Stonehenge, the tranquil beauty of the Lake District or the stunning coasts of Cornwall and west Wales, you will be sure to find something of interest.

Getting around

To get around London it is sensible to invest in a tourist map and a one-day four-zone travel card that will allow you to use most public transport in the London area.

Stations and trains

If you enjoy beautiful scenery and appreciate the English countryside, then you'll turn a blind eye to the frequent delays, inflated prices, and sub-standard buffet services on British trains.

Buying a ticket in a busy London station can be an effort. Try to find out the time of the train that you want to catch, and the name of your destination station before you buy your ticket.

Stations are often very noisy places, and customers are separated from ticket vendors by thick glass screens. You will need bionic ears and a clear loud voice to get what you want. Another way to buy them is to go on-line. www.trainline.com.

Trains that travel between cities ('Inter-City' trains) usually have a buffet carriage or trolley, depending on the length of the journey. You may also be lucky enough to find a telephone (extortionately more expensive than normal payphones). Services are relatively reliable. Trains that run along short local routes rarely have anything but a lavatory, however, and the services can be prone to delays and cancellations.

The following rules tend to operate on public transport:

- Don't get on a train without a ticket that is valid for your entire journey. There will be an inspector checking every ticket, possibly more than once, on every mainline train and usually on the tubes. Immediate fines apply (£10 on the London Underground), even if you profess ignorance.

- There is a no-smoking rule on most public transport – although Inter-City trains usually have one carriage reserved for smokers. The London Underground is strictly non-smoking.

Buses and coaches

In London you can catch a coach from Victoria Coach Station (near Victoria Railway Station) to most parts of Britain. Coach journeys take a lot longer than journeys to the same destination by train, seating is more cramped, and facilities are minimal – if they exist at all. However, the fares are a lot cheaper, and if you get a journey scheduled at night, you can try and sleep all the way. Most towns and cities have coach stops, and some coach services form transport links for small towns with no railway station. Buses usually operate local routes in rural areas and small towns, and district routes in cities. London has its famous red London buses, and most cities have a multi-coloured range of buses all owned by different companies. Fares vary according to where you start your journey and how far you travel. City bus routes are much more frequently served than rural routes, which often take in every village in an area.

Your ISIC or NUS card will enable you to buy coach tickets at a discount, and you can also apply for a Young Person's Railcard if you are under 26 years old or in full-time education. This will enable you to get a third off all rail tickets at a cost of £18 for one year.

STUDYING IN ENGLISH

If English is not your first language then you may find yourself struggling through the first few weeks of your chosen course. Whether you are studying mechanical engineering or dance and drama you will invariably find yourself having to study the English language very intensively. You will be expected to understand what is being said at normal speed in classes; take notes; understand classmates when they talk to you and each other as well as read and write reasonably quickly. However familiar you are with the English language, you may need time to adjust to taking in large amounts of information all day long.

If you are having serious difficulties there will always be people who are willing to help you in your period of adjustment, however long. If you are at university the international officer, in particular, will understand the difficulties you may be facing. If, as sometimes happens, one of your teachers or lecturers speaks too fast or with an accent you have trouble understanding, you should not be afraid to let them know. They should take your needs into consideration, and speak more clearly and slowly if necessary. Above all, don't be afraid to ask for help.

One way to overcome these problems is to arrive a few weeks before your course starts and enrol in a language course. Most colleges, universities and English language schools offer summer courses at all levels. Some also offer courses in 'study skills' that prepare you for things like essay writing, planning workloads, and so on. Learning in this environment before you start a university or college course may be useful as you will become familiar with learning in English, and hearing it in an academic environment. Don't panic if you find things difficult. Ask for written notes from your teachers to supplement your own notes if it helps. They should be more than happy to help.

Many colleges arrange special language and 'study skills' classes for their international students. These classes are usually free of charge so take advantage of the opportunity. The main thing to remember is that you will find that things should become easier as time passes. Most international students say they start to feel much more confident after a month to six weeks.

Regional accents

As in any country, Britain displays a wide range of regional accents. Whereas the spoken language is the same, pronunciation of words and expressions differ markedly from

Great Britain Main Railway

Principal routes
Other selected routes
Airport interchange
Railair coach link with Heathrow Airport
Ferry interchange

London Terminals

C	Charing cross
E	Euston
F	Fenchurch Street
K	Kings Cross
L	Liverpool Street
P	Paddington
S	St Pancras
V	Victoria
W	Waterloo

International direct services
LILLE, BRUSSELS, PARIS

National Rail Enquiries
0345 48 49 50

region to region. This diversity is no greater than in other countries such as the USA or Japan, but may be a surprise to an international student who is expecting to hear either the stereotypical 'cockney' or 'Queen's English' accents. Bear in mind that wherever you go you will probably need time to adjust to the way local people speak, and the phrases they use. In any case, if you are planning to study at university or college, you will soon realise that your fellow students are from all over the country. This is because most British students move away from their home town to study at university.

USEFUL INFORMATION

TRANSPORT
London Black Cabs (24-hour bookings)	020 7272 0272
Underground enquiries	020 7222 1234
National Rail	0345 48 49 50
Brittany Ferries	0990 360 360
P&O Ferries	0990 980 980
Gatwick Airport general enquiries	01293 535353
Heathrow Airport	020 8759 4321
Eurostar	0990 300 003

GENERAL
British Tourist Authority	020 8846 9000
Irish Tourist Board	020 7493 3201
Scottish Tourist Board	020 7930 8661
Welsh Tourist Board	020 7409 0969

HEALTH SERVICES
Aids Helpline	020 7242 1010
Emergency services	999
Drug, Alcohol Help Advice Line	020 8200 9575
Family Planning	020 7837 5432
Life (free pregnancy tests, counselling)	020 7637 1529
Rape Crises Centre (24 hours)	020 7837 1600
Samaritan's Helpline	020 7734 2800

TELEPHONE
Operator	100
Directory enquiries	192
International operator	155
International directory enquiries	153

The first thing you will need to decide is which subject you would like to study, and this section will give you an outline of what is on offer. It is designed to cover not just the traditional academic disciplines such as physics, law and economics but also more vocational areas such as graphic design, fashion and media studies. This is not a comprehensive list of subjects, but most of the main ones are included.

Each of the following chapters are divided into three parts. The first part of each chapter gives an introduction to the general subject area, explaining such things as the history of a subject, the various branches it has (the difference between civil engineering and chemical engineering, for example) and will describe how it is studied in Britain.

The second section of the chapter concentrates on specialist and vocational courses that tend to be offered at private institutions. These courses can last anything from one week to three years, but are generally one-year courses. Featured in this section are a number of independent colleges that specialise in courses for international students.

The third section of each chapter profiles some undergraduate and postgraduate degree courses on offer. This contains a selection of courses available at various institutions, including some of those which scored highly in the 1996 research assessment exercise, or in recent teaching quality assessments. For reasons of space many universities with Excellent ratings in the teaching quality assessments or 5 ratings in the research assessment exercises are not featured, and should be given equal consideration. Each profile finishes with a reference to the page number in the final chapter which contains further information and/or contact details of institutions.

Research ratings and teaching quality assessments

These chapters also include tables showing the results of independent assessments of standards at universities and colleges. These assessments are carried out on a subject-by-subject basis. One assessment is carried out for the quality of research in a particular subject. This is known as the research assessment exercise (RAE), and these were last carried out in 1996. For this the assessors look principally at the number of papers published nationally and internationally in a particular field. These tables are probably more relevant to postgraduate students. Scores range from 5* for departments recognised as having the highest standards of research to 1 for departments with weaker research capabilities. This, however, does not necessarily mean that teaching standards at such a university are any worse. On the contrary, it could be possible that lecturers at a university with less research capabilities have more time to devote to undergraduate students. The research assessment exercise is carried out every four years.

The second assessment is for the quality of teaching, known as the teaching quality assessment (TQA). These are probably more significant to undergraduate courses but also include taught master's programmes. The TQAs are performed by separate organisations in England, Scotland and Wales. Because it can take up to three years to assess a subject and the process is still in its early days, many are not yet complete. As the TQAs are performed separately for England, Scotland and Wales, there are some subjects that have been completed for Scotland and Wales but not for England. The Scottish TQAs also have an extra category, Highly Satisfactory, which can make it difficult to make comparisons.

Another complication is that recently the system of scoring has changed for TQAs in England. Departments used to be given an Excellent, Satisfactory or Unsatisfactory ratings, but now are given a score out of a maximum of 24. This score is based on curriculum design, teaching, student progression, student support and guidance, learning resources and quality control.

So you will find tables that are incomplete, use conflicting systems, apply to one part of Britain but not another and are generally totally confusing. But despite all this, we have decided that it is, nonetheless, important information, and that it is therefore better to include it with these caveats than not to include it at all. But be careful not to see these as the whole picture.

Sample table from the teaching quality assessments

TEACHING QUALITY ASSESSMENTS

Finance and Accounting
(England 1995/96)

Institution	Grade	Institution	Grade
Bath	Excellent	Brighton	Satisfactory
City, London	Excellent	Brunel	Satisfactory
Cranfield	Excellent	UCE, Birmingham	Satisfactory
De Montfort	Excellent	Doncaster College	Satisfactory
Imperial, London	Excellent	Durham	Satisfactory
Kingston	Excellent	Huddersfield	Satisfactory
Lancaster	Excellent	Hull	Satisfactory
London Business School	Excellent	Kent at Canterbury	Satisfactory
LSE, London	Excellent	Loughborough College	Satisfactory
Loughborough	Excellent	Nene College	Satisfactory
Manchester	Excellent	N.E. Worcestershire College (Revisit)	Satisfactory
Northumbria at Newcastle	Excellent	Plymouth	Satisfactory
Nottingham	Excellent	Portsmouth	Satisfactory
Nottingham Trent	Excellent	Queen Mary and Westfield, London	Satisfactory
Open University	Excellent	Reading	Satisfactory
Surrey	Excellent	Salford	Satisfactory
UMIST	Excellent	Sheffield Hallam	Satisfactory
Warwick	Excellent	Southampton	Satisfactory
UWE, Bristol	Excellent	Suffolk College	Satisfactory
Anglia Polytechnic	Satisfactory	Swindon College	Satisfactory
Birmingham	Satisfactory	Teesside	Satisfactory
Blackburn College	Satisfactory	Ulster	Satisfactory
Bradford	Satisfactory	Wolverhampton	Satisfactory
Bradford and Ilkley College	Satisfactory		

Source: HEFCE, SHEFC, HEFCW latest available ratings
For a more complete list of institutions offering these courses at undergraduate level refer to the Course Directory

Access, Diploma and Foundation Courses

So you're considering studying in the UK. You might even have identified a course that takes your fancy or chosen a place that suits your academic and social needs. Before turning up at your first-day lectures, however, there are often quite a few other requirements that you may have to meet. Although British universities do recognise many international qualifications, it may be the case that they don't accept those that you hold, or that your level of education or knowledge of the English language is not of the necessary standard to begin the course you want. Don't be disheartened if these are the problems that you face, as there are a number of alternative routes available that can provide a recognised step to higher education.

While A levels and Highers are the traditional route into higher education for British students, international students can take foundation, Access and diploma courses at universities and higher education institutions around the country, as well as at a range of further education colleges that often provide a relatively low-cost pathway to higher education. In recent years these have developed a range of resources to cater for the needs of international students.

Foundation courses usually last one year and aim to provide students with a solid basis for progressing onto higher education. In addition to covering core subjects, programmes develop practical, communication and IT skills, as well as offering students the chance to improve their English proficiency. Some foundation programmes are offered in association with higher education institutions, while others are independent but have qualifications that are widely accepted by universities and colleges. The advantage of associated courses is that they can guarantee a place on a degree course at that institution. The advantage of an independent foundation course, on the other hand, is that it can offer impartial advice on degrees and universities and greater flexibility if you are not sure what you want to study.

Access courses, recognised by universities as an alternative to A levels or Highers, are specifically designed for mature students and those who have been disadvantaged in terms of their education. For many people, Access courses can provide a second chance to pursue academic opportunities and in general they have no formal entry requirements. Courses cover a wide range of topics and include guidance and support for students with university applications.

Diploma courses can be taken in a variety of subjects and are available at higher and further education institutions as well as a number of independent schools and colleges. Diplomas are not specifically designed for entry to higher education, concentrating instead on a certain subject and the skills required to succeed in a relevant profession. Completion of a diploma course does not guarantee a place at a higher education institution but it could be the key qualification for entering a particular profession, such as modelmaking or alternative medicine, that does not have an equivalent degree programme.

Bromley College of Further and Higher Education
Cambridge Business Skills

This is a one-year full-time foundation course run by the Faculty of Business and Management, and is designed to prepare students for undergraduate study. It emphasises the skills required for successful study at degree level, like independent work and research. Covering modules such as business communication, marketing, the world of business, meeting and presentation skills, and finance, the course also includes teaching of English as a Foreign Language where appropriate. Teaching takes place at the college's Rookery Lane site. There are currently around 20 international students enrolled on the course. Contact details p478.

Chichester College of Arts Science and Technology
Academic Foundation Course

The academic foundation courses have been specifically designed for those students who are intending to follow undergraduate or postgraduate study in the UK. The college runs a number of English language courses that are designed to develop language, communication and IT skills, with qualifications available in Cambridge Proficiency, NVQ English and RSA CLAIT (Computer Literacy and Information Technology), amongst others. There is also an English language summer school that is popular with international students. A two-year Foundation Course in Medical, Dental and Veterinary Science provides an academic programme of A level subjects accepted by universities, complemented by periods of work experience. There is also a range of music courses available including a pre-professional music course, a BTEC National Diploma in Popular Music and a foundation in music lasting two years. A one-year

Access Diploma in Jazz Studies offers intensive formal training for those students who are interested in the fields of jazz and Afro-American music. Chichester is a historic cathedral city by the coast and is surrounded by beautiful countryside. It has good road and rail links to London and major air terminals, and France can be easily reached via the nearby Portsmouth ferry terminal. Chichester College was the Beacon Award Programme Winner of the 1999 British Council Award for International Student Support. Contact details p479.

City College Manchester
Foundation Economics and Social Studies

The course, run by City College, in conjunction with the University of Manchester, covers economics, politics, mathematics and information technology. Although a certain standard of English is expected of prospective students, language support is provided. The programme is designed to bridge the possible gaps in knowledge and skill, between the student's home-country qualifications, and those needed to enter a British university. Students who successfully pass the course with appropriate grades gain a place at one of the linked university faculties. These include: the University of Manchester, where students can study subjects ranging from anthropology and business studies, to economics and social policy; the University of Manchester Institute of Science and Technology (UMIST), where students can take management, and management and IT; and Manchester Metropolitan University, where students can study accounting and finance, economics, business, financial services, hotel management with tourism and international business. The college also offers Foundation Studies in Science and Engineering. Linked to the University of Manchester,

this course allows students to go on to study computer science, engineering, mathematics, chemistry, physics, biological sciences, materials science or earth sciences. Contact details p479.

David Game College

A private college situated in a modern building in London's Notting Hill Gate, David Game College has been running pre-university courses for international students since 1974. The University Foundation Programme offers guaranteed progression onto virtually all university degree courses, except medicine. To date, over 1,500 students have successfully completed this option, going on to degree courses at over 60 universities in the UK. The University Foundation Programme is a full-time course structured to provide flexibility. At its core are three compulsory modules in mathematics, information technology and communication skills. In addition, students select three further modules that are most relevant to their intended degree course. This choice is made from a wide range of subjects in the fields of art and design, business studies, science and mathematics, and social sciences. The programme runs from September to June or from January to August. Both intakes aim at university entry the following October. Contact details p479.

Dudley College

Dudley College is set in the West Midlands, the centre of England. It offers Access courses in a number of different subjects including computing, teacher training and business. The courses are designed to allow people with non-typical qualifications to enter higher education. More than 300 students successfully enter higher education and degree-level programmes each year from Dudley College. This transition is helped by the college's guidance service, which gives students assistance in making university choices.

Students at Dudley may benefit from the college's libraries and study centres. The library contains over 38,000 books, some 200 specialist periodicals, up-to-date reference books and useful services such as a photocopier and computer access. More than 200 study places offer both group and individual work areas while quiet room facilities are ideal for completing assignments or concentrating on exam revision. The college has places to eat and meet with friends – in addition to the main restaurant, a health food bar and the lively Rendezvous Piazza are very popular with students at all times of the day. Contact details p479.

St Austell College
International Foundation Programmes

St Austell College provides a number of one-year programmes for international students wishing to progress to study at university. Foundation courses on offer are: business management, subject to validation from the University of Plymouth; an introduction to law, maths, physics and computer science, in conjunction with the University of Exeter; and hospitality and catering, subject to validation from the University of Surrey. Further courses are planned in art and design, and tourism. Each course is structured with core modules covering English and communication, information technology, and study skills for higher education, which are designed to improve a student's English language skills and aid their application to university. There are also a number of defined modules in each programme that provide an introduction to the chosen area of study. Assessment is through assignments and examinations, and university staff monitor all results and grades. Progression onto a degree or HND course is often guaranteed if students reach the required standard and all programmes are worth 120 points on the university Credit Accumulation Transfer (CAT) scheme. St Austell, a small town in Cornwall, is close to many beaches and beautiful countryside. Plymouth is the nearest major town, an ancient port with extensive shopping facilities. The college is located next to the bus and train station with services throughout the area and there are also flights from London (Gatwick) to Newquay airport. Contact details p477.

The Arts Institute at Bournemouth
Diploma in Foundation Studies in Art and Design

The Arts Institute at Bournemouth was established around 1900 and it has developed to provide the education and training necessary for students to take up careers in the world of art, design and media. This is an intensive and demanding course during which time you will build up a portfolio of work in a particular area. The course is divided into two stages. In the first, students work on a variety of creative projects integrating subjects such as drawing, printmaking, photography and computer -aided design. The second stage allows students to explore their own creative skills in order to prepare themselves for a specialist area. Options available include graphic design, fashion and textiles, and fine art. The course takes place full time over one year or part time over two years. Practical studio work is combined with lectures and seminars. Educational visits to national centres, galleries and museums are an integral part of the course. Applicants will be required to submit a portfolio of recent work. Contact details p477.

Accountancy and Finance

Accountancy had never had the liveliest of images but, despite its reputation, it has leapt into the 21st century with great enthusiasm. The accountant's world is exciting and globally motivated. Offices are smart, busy and use the latest technology, and the ever-complicated nature of many people's income, company accounts and business dealings means that accountants themselves are in more demand than ever.

Many of the largest accountancy firms in the world, from Pricewater-houseCoopers to KPMG, are based in the UK, and accountancy or finance related occupations are popular careers to enter for young graduates, because they provide financial security, as well as intellectual stimulation.

As an accountant you may be involved in audit, tax, corporate finance, insolvency, financial consultancy or management accounting, and qualification is highly regarded and is seen in the UK as being solid business grounding.

To qualify as an accountant in Britain, you have to sit professional exams set by one of six institutions (these are taken after you have done your first degree, which does not necessarily have to be in accountancy).

Since a great deal of accountancy deals with processing financial information and giving detailed business advice to clients, those thinking of pursuing it as a career need to think logically and show a proficiency in all business areas.

You do not necessarily have to be highly numerate to be an accountant, but for certain business areas, such as auditing, it can certainly be beneficial.

Accounting and finance degrees in Britain concentrate on the disciplines that form the foundation of an accountant's skills, such as economics, statistics and law. Degree courses tend not to stray too far from these theoretical foundations, as accountancy or finance graduates wishing to start working professionally will have to take a further course before the professional examinations.

Teaching is by way of lectures, tutorials and workshops or seminars. The emphasis is usually on private study rather than class interaction and most courses will have some practical element, familiarising students with spreadsheets and basic computer skills at an early stage.

There are also courses available for those who wish to study finance as a whole, usually with reference to the constantly changing global economy. Students develop an understanding of the theory of finance and stock markets, and knowledge of financial instruments and treasury management. Finance can also be studied as a joint honours degree, linked with such subjects as accountancy, computer science, economics, or specialisms such as sports or hotel management.

Some courses contain an element of practical work experience, as well as theoretical study, so students form outside the European Union should be aware that they may be restricted by visa requirements.

SPECIALIST AND VOCATIONAL COURSES

City of London College

Established in 1979, and set in close proximity to the financial heart of the capital – The City of London – this private college specialises in adult training courses on a full- or part-time basis. Courses on offer can lead to masters level qualifications awarded by UK universities, or directly to the professional job market. The college is fully accredited by the British Accreditation Council. Students can study an integrated programme to combine various accountancy skills. The college can also assess candidates who are not attending its courses but who wish to be examined. Most courses last from two to three terms. City of London College is approved for and offers the Association of Accounting Technicians (AAT) course. The foundation courses cover subjects such as accounting for cash and credit transactions, and business skills including data processing, and health and safety. At the intermediate stage, there are two central assessments – financial accounting and cost accounting. Students prepare an accounting portfolio that comprises simulations or workplace records. Students are also trained and assessed on information technology skills. The technician stage course includes aspects of accounting and business specialised skills. Contact details p479.

London City College

The college has been in operation since 1982. It is part of the Royal Waterloo Centre, a six-storey building housing educational facilities situated next to the River Thames. The college offers courses ranging from Master of Business Administration (MBA) degrees to diplomas in Marketing, Travel and Tourism, Hotel and Catering, Art and Design, and Shipping and Transport. The college's MBA in Finance is awarded by Leicester University, but all lectures and examinations take place at the London City College. The aim of the programme is to introduce and develop an understanding of the concepts of finance and the role of financial management in a variety of organisations – industrial, commercial and public sector. The full-time, 12-month course includes areas such as strategic management, economics, accounting for managers, business policy, international finance and corporate finance. It costs £6,400. (See also Business and Travel chapters). Contact details p482.

DEGREE COURSES

University of Abertay Dundee
BA (Hons) Accounting

This degree is fully accredited by the Institute of Chartered Accountants of Scotland, England and Wales; the Chartered Institute of Public Finance and Accountancy; and the Chartered Association of Certified Accountants. The course is primarily designed for students who wish to pursue a career as a chartered accountant, and is tailored to meet the needs of the profession. Like other courses at the university business school, the course is fully modularised, and offers students the choice and flexibility to adapt their course according to individual interests and career aspirations. The course introduces students to, and develops their understanding of, the accounting principles of financial and management accounting, IT taxation and accounting theory and practice in chartered, certified and public accountancy. In their final year, students complete a project on a chosen accounting or finance topic. Notable features of the course include instruction in industry-standard accounting packages, a European language option and access to modern teaching, learning and library facilities. Contact details p477.

University of Abertay Dundee
Accountancy and Financial Services

The department, recently awarded an Excellent in the teaching quality assessments, offers two undergraduate degrees, the BA (Hons) Accounting and the BA (Hons) Financial Services. The accounting degree is fully accredited by the professional accountancy bodies and includes specialist options in accountancy, business finance, and management and information systems. The other is a specialist finance degree, ideally suited to students interested in pursuing a career in banking. Research interest covers four main areas: social and environmental accounting, financial reporting theory and practice, management accounting and auditing, and financial markets. Research degrees may also be a good starting point for doctoral study in the department. Contact details p477.

University of Glasgow
Accounting

There are several variants of the accountancy course at the University of Glasgow. The study tends to cover aspects of the business environment: financial and management accounting practice, business law, economics, taxation, information and computer systems, and business finance. The following BAcc Accountancy courses are available: BAcc Accountancy, BAcc with Languages, BAcc with Finance, BAcc with International Accounting, and BAcc Joint Honours in Accountancy and Economics. The BAcc provides exemption from the examinations of the UK Institutes of Chartered Accountants – all of which provide world-recognised professional qualifications. The course with international accounting is particularly relevant for international students who can benefit from the international research focus of the department. There are currently about 15 international

TEACHING QUALITY ASSESSMENTS

Finance and Accounting
(Scotland 1995/96)

Institution	Grade	Institution	Grade
Dundee	Excellent	Stirling	Highly Satisfactory
Edinburgh	Excellent	Abertay Dundee	Satisfactory
Aberdeen	Highly Satisfactory	Napier	Satisfactory
Glasgow	Highly Satisfactory	Paisley	Satisfactory
Glasgow Caledonian	Highly Satisfactory	Strathclyde	Satisfactory
Heriot-Watt	Highly Satisfactory		

Finance and Accounting
(Wales 1997/98)

Institution	Grade	Institution	Grade
Aberystwyth	Excellent	Glamorgan	Excellent
Cardiff	Excellent		

Source: HEFCE, SHEFC, HEFCW latest available ratings

For a more complete list of institutions offering these courses at undergraduate level refer to the Course Directory

students on accounting courses at the University of Glasgow. Contact details p480.

London Guildhall University

BA (Hons) Financial Services

This course focuses on the study of financial services in an integrated and international framework. It draws on a variety of academic disciplines to examine the development and significance of financial services in the modern world. There is a strong emphasis on theoretical knowledge and its practical application in the financial services industry. The degree is multidisciplinary in nature, making use of accounting, economics, investments theory, law and management. It allows considerable flexibility, with students being able to take up to two specialist pathways in areas such as banking, financial services management, insurance, investment and law. The system of options permits the study of a modern European language throughout the degree. Students can specialise in up to two of the following pathways: banking, financial services management, insurance, investment and law. Contact details p482.

The Manchester Metropolitan University

Accountancy and Finance

With over 2,300 full-time and 2,600 part-time students, the Faculty of Management and Business at Manchester Metropolitan is one of the largest in the UK. It is situated in the city centre in the Aytoun Building which recently received a Royal Institute of British Architects award. This new building contains a split-level library and computer facilities. Subjects available in the faculty range from international business management to public relations and marketing. The BA (Hons) Accounting and Finance course is a three-year, full-time course which aims to provide a critical awareness of the role and techniques of accounting and finance in both the public and private sectors. There is a high level of information technology involved

Top International Accountancy Firms

Source: *Accountancy* magazine, Institute of Chartered Accountants in England and Wales 1999/2000

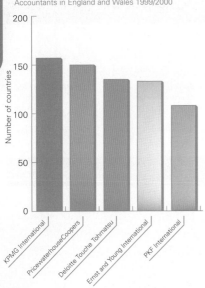

Interesting facts

- Asia, the Middle East, eastern Europe and Central America are the most sought-after countries for firms seeking further expansion

- The world Scrabble champion is an accountant

- Accountancy dates back to ancient Greek farmers, who wanted to keep financial control of their land

throughout the course, as well as specialist options in financial management, auditing, systems and taxation. Contact details p483.

University of North London
MA International Finance
This one-year taught course is designed for graduates from accounting, economics, business and related disciplines. Students examine both the developing world of international finance and the management of finance, through the examination of such issues as the current state of global finance and economics, and the impact of international finance on economic and political activity. Core modules on the course include global financial markets, finance and quantitative analysis, and investment research methods, whilst options include mergers and acquisitions and strategic management control. Teaching and learning methods involve group discussions, problem analysis and videos, as well as conventional lectures, seminars and a 12,000 to 15,000 word dissertation. Students may apply to develop their dissertation topic into an MPhil/PhD programme. Contact details p483.

South Bank University
MSc/PG Dip Accountancy and Finance
This is a specialised course for current or intending finance professionals seeking to obtain a masters qualification in accounting and finance, whilst simultaneously studying for the final professional stage examinations of the Association of Chartered Certified Accountants (ACCA). Qualified professional accountants may enter at the dissertation stage. Subject to demand each year, it may be possible to begin the course in either September or February. The syllabuses are based on ACCA syllabuses for papers 11 (taxplanning), 12 (management and strategy), 13 (financial reporting environment) and 14 (financial strategy). As stated, this enables students to study simultaneously for a masters degree and for the ACCA professional stage examinations. Contact details p486.

oncourse·co·uk
The ultimate guide to courses

ACCOUNTANCY

RESEARCH RANKINGS

Accountancy

Institution	Grade	Institution	Grade
Manchester	*5	Bristol	3a
Edinburgh	5	Central Lancashire	3a
Exeter	5	Queen's Belfast	3a
LSE	5	Thames Valley	3a
Strathclyde	5	Middlesex	3b
Brunel	4	Portsmouth	3b
Dundee	4	Hull	2
Essex	4	Liverpool	2
Glasgow	4	Newcastle	2
Stirling	4	Paisley	2
Aberystwyth	4	Southampton Institute	2
Aberdeen	3a		

source: RAE 1996

Agriculture and Land Management

Britain can claim to be an ideal place to study agriculture. It was one of the first countries in the world to move towards scientific methods of farming, and has managed to maintain its technological lead today. The massive increase in productivity as a result is now giving way to a greater concern for the way in which we farm the land and the consequences for the environment. This has to be weighed against the dietary demands of an ever-increasing world population and the livelihood of millions of farmers. This is just one of the dilemmas facing all future farmers and land managers.

Under the loose heading of agriculture and land management come a number of courses ranging from agricultural science, tree management, horticulture, forestry and greenkeeping to environmental or countryside management, mechanisation, horse care and floristry. Many of these will have certain core courses and then options for specialised study – you may have a particular interest in maintenance and repair of agricultural machinery or tropical agricultural development. It may also be possible to gain qualifications that are a legal requirement for operators in the industry (UK), for example NPTC Crop Sprayers.

You should be aware, however, that teaching will probably be based around the practices in the UK or other countries with similar methods, rather than worldwide. If you are particularly interested in use of the land in other countries, you will need to check courses offered very carefully to ensure they contain elements that will be most relevant to you.

Agriculture

The study of agriculture involves farming methods, crop and livestock production and, increasingly, the relationship between farming and the protection of our environment. Common elements include accounting for agricultural businesses, farm planning, animal production, and animal nutrition.

Arboriculture

This is the science and practice of cultivating trees and shrubs. It is similar to forestry but less concerned with timber production and concentrates more on conservation. Subjects studied include tree nursery work, plant science, mechanisation, establishing plantations, landscape design, countryside management and timber harvesting. Practical skill such as working in a sawmill and using chain saws may also be covered.

Horticulture

The production and use of plants both for eating and creating an attractive environment in which we can live. Course content may include plant growth, development, protection and selection; preparing sports areas, ecology, alternative ways of growing plants; propagation; and garden centre skills.

Countryside Skills and Conservation

This kind of course provides the skills and knowledge to carry out conservation and management work in the countryside. Core modules may include plant science, countryside awareness, ecology, climate and conservation law.

TEACHING QUALITY ASSESSMENTS

Agriculture, Forestry and Agricultural Sciences
(England and N Ireland 1997/98/99)

Institution	Grade	Institution	Grade
Oxford	24	Buckinghamshire College	20
Harper Adams	23	Sparsholt College	20
Nottingham	23	Leeds	20
Cranfield	22	UWE	20
Newcastle upon Tyne	22	Greenwich	20
Plymouth	22	Lincolnshire and Humberside	19
Wye College	22	Pershore and Hindlip College	19
Askham Bryan College	21	Writtle College	19
Queen's Belfast	21	Central Lancashire	18
Reading	21	De Montfort	16
Bournemouth	20		

Agriculture and Forest Science
(Wales 1996/97/98/99)

Institution	Grade	Institution	Grade
Bangor (Forest Sciences)	Excellent	Aberystwyth (Rural Studies)	Satisfactory
Bangor (Agriculture)	Satisfactory		

Source: HEFCE, SHEFC, HEFCW latest available ratings
For a more complete list of institutions offering these courses at undergraduate level refer to the Course Directory

DEGREE COURSES

Bishop Burton College

BSc (Hons) Countryside Management and Ornithology

Bishop Burton College is a national Beacon of Excellence and Accredited College as awarded by the government. Situated in East Yorkshire, it specialises in education and training for those interested in careers in the countryside and land-based industries. Being located close to many sites of international importance for birds, such as the Humber Estuary Special Protection Area, and having its own 340 hectare farm and woodland estate, the college is ideally positioned for studying ornithology. You will be involved in monitoring and research work based at the college. The BSc (Hons) in Countryside Management and Ornithology aims to prepare students for the role of countryside manager specialising in the area of ornithology. The countryside management element looks at subjects such as ecology, countryside conservation, rural resource management, business management and environmental policy. You will also follow a skills development programme and take part in career development workshop. On this course, you will undertake research into avian biology/ecology at Spurn Point Bird Observatory, where you will be resident for one week. Modules include: bird biology, bird ethology, bird population studies, avian habitat exploitation, birds and man, policy and legislation for bird conservation, and field research in ornithology. In addition you will be expected to study a dissertation topic in a research area of your interest. Contact details p477.

AGRICULTURE

University of Plymouth
Seale-Hayne Faculty

The Seale-Hayne Faculty specialises in rural development and land use, agriculture, food quality and product development, hospitality and tourism. Situated in South Devon, the faculty was founded in 1914. It is now a part of the University of Plymouth. In the 1997 teaching quality assessment Seale-Hayne was awarded 22 out of 24 for agriculture, food science and land and property management related courses. The faculty has a farm of 166 hectares whose enterprises include a dairy herd of around 120 cows, an indoor pig unit and a 225 strong flock of sheep. Although the farm is used for educational purposes, it also operates as a separate financially viable unit. Courses on offer include BSc degrees in agriculture, tourism, hospitality, animal production, crop science, food biology, food production and quality, rural estate management and rural resource management. Contact details p484.

Interesting facts

- About two thirds of the world's fresh water flows from the Amazon River. It can even be found on the sea's surface 40 miles away

- By 2015, 26 cities in the world are expected to have 10 million people or more. To feed a city of this size today at least 6,000 tonnes of food must be imported a day

- 77 per cent of the land in Britain is used for food production, agriculture, commercial horticulture and the leisure industry

The University of Reading
MSc Tropical Agricultural Development

This MSc has been taught since 1969. International students usually comprise about 70 to 80 per cent of those on the course. Most of these are already professionals within their own country, who return, following the course, to senior positions in organisations such as the Ministry of Agriculture and research institutes. The degree aims to teach a specialised knowledge of the science and practice of tropical crop production in the wider context of aspects of tropical agricultural development, including the physical, economic and social environments. Students are also exposed to the process of identifying and examining the effects of both crop and environmental parameters. In lectures and seminars students learn about the core modules – subjects such as agricultural production, tropical environments and rural economics – and more specialised modules – areas such as crop science, breeding, biotechnology, crop-water relations and irrigation. Students must also write a dissertation. Contact details p484.

Sources of Power in Developing Countries
Source: Food and Agriculture Organisation of The United Nations

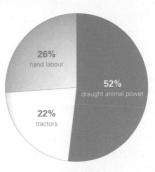

University of Wales, Bangor

The School of Agricultural and Forest Sciences

Agriculture and forestry have been taught at Bangor for over 100 years and this is reflected in the programmes available. BSc can be taken in subjects including Agriculture, Forestry, Agroforestry, Rural Resource Management, Environmental Science and Environmental Conservation. All courses are modular based, so that students can expand their knowledge of important subject areas, and develop some new interests. There are also opportunities to develop skills in other languages. Students may be able to study abroad through exchange programmes to countries such as Finland and Canada. Extensive use is made of the university's Hill and Upland Research Centre for both teaching and research. Study tours in agriculture, forestry and conservation are organised to many parts of the UK every year. In addition to the school's laboratories and computing facilities, a new science library was opened in 1999. For more information visit their website at www.safs.bangor.ac.uk/ Contact details p477.

Warwickshire College

City & Guilds National Certificate in Horticulture (Garden and Landscape Design)

Warwickshire College, situated in the heart of Shakespeare country, specialises in practical, vocational courses. The City & Guilds National Certificate in Horticulture is a one-year full-time course that takes place four days a week. The practical nature of the syllabus is intended to develop skills enabling students either to find work with landscape companies or to go on to further levels of study. Subjects that you will study include garden history and development, landscape design, computer aided design, plant selection and recognition, principles of horticulture, and machinery and equipment. There is also the possibility of studying towards Computer Literacy and Information Technology (CLAIT) qualifications. Assessment is on-going combined with formal exams. There are no formal entrance requirements but a good level of Maths and English are important and prospective students should be able to demonstrate a suitable level of practical ability. Contact details p487.

AGRICULTURE

RESEARCH RANKINGS

Agriculture and Land Management

Institution	Grade	Institution	Grade
Reading (Plant Sciences)	5*	Bangor	4
Edinburgh	5	Cranfield	3a
Newcastle upon Tyne	5	Exeter	3a
Nottingham	5	Wye College	3a
Queen's Belfast	5	Aberystwyth	3b
Aberdeen	4	Harper Adams	3b
Leeds	4	De Montfort	2
Natural Resources Institute	4	Portsmouth	2
Reading (Agriculture, Soil Science, Agricultural Economics and Management)	4	Wolverhampton	2
Stirling	4	Writtle College	2
		Plymouth	1

source: RAE 1996

Archaeology and Anthropology

archaeology
archaeology
archaeology
archaeology

Even though it has been 100,000 years since the evolution of man, there have been very few physical changes to the human form. Yet culturally, socially and economically, humankind has advanced beyond recognition, and it is this evolution that fascinates anthropologists and archaeologists alike. Archaeology and anthropology are both multidisciplinary and can be studied either together or as separate subjects.

Archaeology

Archaeology, in its simplest terms, is about digging up the past and studying human societies from their material remains. Discovering a coin from two thousand years ago, for example, goes some way in revealing the existence at that particular time of a market economy and some minting technology. With such "real" evidence, archaeology is an exciting area with frequent new developments and interpretations.

Both science and arts students should be well equipped to study archaeology. The first year of an archaeology course is often a general introduction to the subject and methods surrounding it. Modules may then include biological and social evolution of Homo sapiens; the Neolithic revolution and the advent of farming; technology and adaptation; and ethics. Over the following years, students have more of a choice and specialise in a dissertation or project. There is a practical side to archaeology and some departments, at Oxford, Durham and UCL (London), demand that students complete a minimum period of fieldwork. Archaeological digs help bring the theory to life and have a reputation for being fun and sociable.

Britain has many interesting archaeological sites. In Wales, for example, there are prehistoric hill forts, Roman gold mines and mediaeval castles.

Anthropology

Anthropology combines the study of man and his biology, his environment and his society from the past to the present day. The programmes at British universities focus on one of these strands or a combination of the three. The latter style of course gives students an unusually broad foundation including elements of the social sciences, sciences and humanities.

The content of anthropology courses can vary extensively. Like archaeology, a general introduction to the subject in the first year is typically followed by specialisation. Students often complete a project or dissertation on anything from the death customs of the Dinka of Sudan to the rituals of English witchcraft. The evidence for anthropology comes from the rather misleadingly titled 'field studies' which involves observing a community to gain an understanding of the lifestyles of inhabitants.

DEGREE COURSES

Bournemouth University

MSc/PGDip Forensic Archaeology

Forensic archaeology is the application of archaeological principles and methods within the constraints of the criminal

TEACHING QUALITY ASSESSMENTS

Anthropology
(England and N ireland 1994/95)

Institution	Grade	Institution	Grade
Brunel	Excellent	Oxford Brookes	Excellent
Cambridge	Excellent	Oxford	Excellent
Durham	Excellent	SOAS	Excellent
Kent at Canterbury	Excellent	Sussex	Excellent
LSE	Excellent	UCL	Excellent
Manchester	Excellent	Goldsmiths	Satisfactory

Source: HEFCE, SHEFC, HEFCW latest available ratings
For a more complete list of institutions offering these courses at undergraduate level refer to the Course Directory

justice system. The course integrates archaeological, legal and managerial aspects, and is designed for archaeologists who wish to work in crime investigation, police officers who may want to strengthen their investigative capacity, or graduates who would like to work in this area. It aims to provide the student with the specialised skills necessary to carry out scene-of-crime investigations, allowing them to gather evidence safely and accurately, so that it can be presented in a courtroom. The course lasts for one year, on a full-time basis, with some weekend units. In 1994 the course received the Queen's Award for course design and structure. Contact details p478.

University of Cambridge
Social Anthropology

Sir James Frazer, author of The Golden Bough, and one of the most influential anthropologists at the turn of the century, studied at Cambridge. Students of the social anthropology tripos (Part 1), explore the interaction of society, culture and biology from the time of the earliest known human remains, up to the late twentieth century. This integration of archaeology with social and biological anthropology is unusual in a first year undergraduate course. In the second year (part IIA of the tripos)

students specialise in social anthropology, but may also keep up one other interest, as there are exams in four subjects. Year three of the tripos (part IIB) is intended to allow students to explore their chosen discipline in greater depth, and either produce a dissertation, or combine a number of advanced topics. After specialisation in the second year, students may still able to carry on with other courses throughout the degree. For example, you may take a course in either history or archaeology. The application process is controlled by the colleges. In your first term there are approximately eight lectures and two seminars per week. There are 10 to 12 supervisions (tutorials involving one or two students and one supervisor) per term, each one leading to an essay. In addition to this programme of study, the department estimates that students should undertake two hours private study a day. Contact details p478.

University of East Anglia, Norwich
BA Anthropology, Archaeology and Art History

The Department of Art and Cultural History is characterised by its interdisciplinary approach to the fields of art history, archaeology and anthropology. This course concentrates on the theoretical, methodological and political issues that are relevant to all three disciplines. Students can choose from a wide range of specialist subjects in one of the three areas of study. Archaeological and anthropological material is evaluated throughout the course. This unusual combination of subjects is complemented by a component in museum studies – with numerous visits to museums around the country. The university's Sainsbury Centre houses a vast collection of world and European art, and a large reference library of non-Western art. There are opportunities for archaeological fieldwork with the Norfolk Archaeological Unit, and travel in Europe. Contact details p479.

University of Wales, Lampeter
BA (Hons) Anthropology

Anthropology has moved on considerably since the first few decades of the 20th century, when the great founders of the subject, such as Malinowski and Evans-Pritchard, established overseas fieldwork as the basis of our knowledge of other societies. Living, as these two scholars did, with the Trobriand islanders, or with the Nuer of Sudan, was a far more satisfactory way of trying to understand peoples than simply relying on the reports of missionaries and colonial administrators. Today, however, it is not just the apparently technologically-simple societies in Africa or the Pacific that interest anthropologists. Scholars from the Third World are now engaging in their own analysis of society from an insider's perspective, and there is an increasing amount of interest in the anthropology of Europe, America and other, more developed, regions of the globe. A social or cultural anthropologist trained in Britain might specialise in the religious rituals of an African 'tribe', in the language use of the Hebridean Islanders, contemporary English witchcraft or the workings of the European Commission, to give just a few examples. An undergraduate course in anthropology reflects this diversity as well as providing a grounding in the theories and perspectives which characterise British anthropology. Contact details p481.

Age and Gender of Archaeologists Working at Universities

Source: "The Top 10 of Everything: 2000"
Russell Ash, Dorling Kindersley 1999

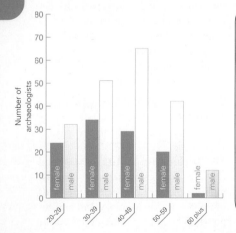

Interesting facts

• There are 4,425 people employed in archaeology in the UK. The whole profession could sit in London's Royal Albert Hall

• In late Bronze Age Britain, around 1800 BC, houses were solid, wooden, circular structures about 100 metre squared. Clusters of between two and 10 of these made up the first hamlets

RESEARCH RANKINGS

Anthropology

Institution	Grade	Institution	Grade
Cambridge	*5	Queen's Belfast	4
Brunel	5	St Andrews	4
Goldsmiths	5	Sussex	4
LSE	5	Hull	3a
Manchester	5	Kent at Canterbury	3a
SOAS	5	Oxford Brookes	3a
UCL	5	Roehampton Institute	3a
Durham	4	Swansea (Department of Sociology and Anthropology)	3a
Edinburgh	4		
Oxford	4	Swansea (Centre for Development Studies)	3a

Archaeology

Institution	Grade	Institution	Grade
Cambridge	*5	Glasgow	4
Oxford	*5	Liverpool	4
Sheffield	*5	Cardiff	4
Bradford	5	York	4
Durham	5	Exeter	3a
Leicester	5	Nottingham	3a
Queen's Belfast	5	Lampeter	3a
Reading	5	Bournemouth	3b
Southampton	5	Newcastle upon Tyne	3b
UCL	5	Trinity College, Carmarthen	3b
Birmingham	4	Newport	3b
Bristol	4	King Alfred's College	2
Edinburgh	4	Staffordshire	2

source: RAE 1996

ARCHAEOLOGY

School of Oriental and African Studies (SOAS)

BA History of Art and Archaeology and Social Anthropology

This is a combined degree course which covers a particular area or region such as Africa or the Middle East. Students consider aspects of the history of paintings, sculpture, architecture, costume, applied art and objects unique to the culture concerned. This combination deepens the students' understanding of the meaning and value of a 'work of art' for the culture that produced it and questions assumptions about western conceptions of art. SOAS was donated by Sir Perceval David in 1950, a huge collection of Chinese ceramics numbering approximately 1,700 pieces. Both departments were awarded Excellent in the 1996 research assessment exercise and anthropology was judged to be Excellent in the 1995 teaching quality assessments. Contact details p485.

Architecture and the Built Environment

architecture architecture architecture architecture

I t was the Greeks who came up with the term 'architect' and the Romans who invented concrete and the first ever leisure complexes. The long history of this discipline has seen Britons contributing to some of the world's finest architectural achievements. London's first square at Covent Garden was designed by Inigo Jones (1573 to 1652). Sir William Talman (1650 to 1719), a contemporary of Sir Christopher Wren, is most famous for Chatsworth House in Derbyshire, a beautiful country house that is definitely worth a visit. More recently, we have seen the meteoric rise of Sir Norman Foster (1935-) with many achievements to his name, and Mike Davies, creator of the controversial Millennium Dome in London.

Architecture

Studying architecture in Britain has several advantages. Firstly, teacher: student ratios tend to be more favourable than in the rest of Europe; teaching may well be less theoretical than in your home country; and you are able to specialise in architecture as a first degree, which is not possible in the USA. British architecture degrees eventually lead to professional membership of the Royal Institute of British Architects (RIBA). You need to pass RIBA Parts 1, 2 and 3 to qualify. The traditional route to qualification starts with a three-year undergraduate programme. Depending on the university, graduating with a degree in architecture may exempt you from the RIBA Part 1 exam. The degree is followed by a year in professional practice which in turn leads to a two-year graduate programme. Part 2 exams are then taken, followed by a second year of professional practice at the end of which you sit your Part 3s. For a work placement in a UK practice, international students should check their visa requirements.

Built environment

The complexity of the social, environmental and aesthetic issues involved in building and land usage is reflected in the variety of degrees on offer, the possible combinations of majors and the range of interdisciplinary modules that make up the course. Town and country planning, for example, is concerned with using social, economic and ecological knowledge to manage change and development in the built and natural environment. The subject covers such elements as the development process; planning skills, such as graphics, communication skills and statistical methods; urban politics; and transport planning. Some colleges and universities offer the chance to study part of the degree elsewhere in Europe. Other significant areas of study include quantity surveying, which is concerned with the organisation and financial management of building and civil engineering work, and construction management, which aims to produce professional managers capable of understanding the technology of buildings as well as the business aspects of running a construction company.

DEGREE COURSES

University of Bath
MA Architectural Design

This is a 12-month, full-time programme that starts in September each year. It is concerned with the architectural design of a selected European city – last year Rome, and currently Granada in Spain. Students study the historical and cultural dynamics of the chosen city and, working with students on the MA Architecture degree programme, they each focus on developing a specific building brief before designing a modern building. A written dissertation is an integral component of the degree. Two students graduated last session, and there are two students currently enrolled.Contact details p477.

The University of Edinburgh
MA (Hons) and BArch in Architectural Design

This is a vocational studio-based course that equips students with the knowledge and skills needed to enter the profes sion. Full-time study is complmented by periods of practical training in architects' offices. Six years of study is split between a four year MA (Hons) and two years BArch. Students not seeking a vocational qualification can leave after the MA. In the first two years, the course focuses on the theory and practice of architecture, the latter including a series of design exercises and projects. Architectural history is also covered and students may take an option from any subject offered by the major university faculties. The third and fourth years enable students to pursue their particular interests in architecture, two of which must be placements. The BArch develops individual design skills and seeks to pool creative and intellectual resources through group work. Urban design theory and building technology are accompanied by a city based project, and professional practice is developed during a further placement. See www.caad.ed.ac.uk/ for further information. Contact details p480.

Greenwich University
MA Urban Design

Over 20 per cent of students at the School of Land and Construction Management are international, and urban design students work on projects both from the UK and abroad. The current approach to urban design on the course is objective analysis wherever suitable and it concentrates mainly on morphology and context. Core subjects studied include urban design theory,

TEACHING QUALITY ASSESSMENTS

Architecture
(England and N Ireland 1994)

Institution	Grade	Institution	Grade
Bath	Excellent	Huddersfield	Satisfactory
Cambridge	Excellent	Kingston	Satisfactory
East London	Excellent	Leeds Metropolitan	Satisfactory
Greenwich	Excellent	Liverpool John Moores	Satisfactory
Newcastle upon Tyne	Excellent	Liverpool	Satisfactory
Nottingham	Excellent	Manchester Metropolitan	Satisfactory
Sheffield	Excellent	Manchester	Satisfactory
UCL	Excellent	Oxford Brookes	Satisfactory
York	Excellent	Plymouth	Satisfactory
Brighton	Satisfactory	Queen's Belfast	Satisfactory
De Montfort	Satisfactory	Westminster	Satisfactory

ARCHITECTURE

TEACHING QUALITY ASSESSMENTS

Architecture
(England and N Ireland 1997)

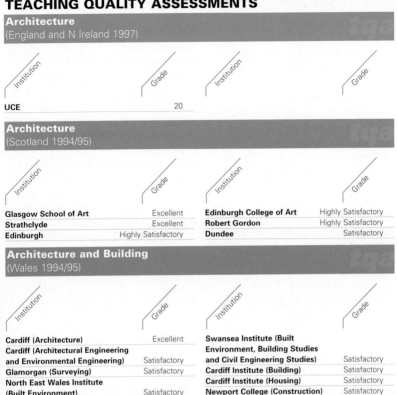

Institution	Grade
UCE	20

Architecture
(Scotland 1994/95)

Institution	Grade	Institution	Grade
Glasgow School of Art	Excellent	Edinburgh College of Art	Highly Satisfactory
Strathclyde	Excellent	Robert Gordon	Highly Satisfactory
Edinburgh	Highly Satisfactory	Dundee	Satisfactory

Architecture and Building
(Wales 1994/95)

Institution	Grade	Institution	Grade
Cardiff (Architecture)	Excellent	Swansea Institute (Built Environment, Building Studies and Civil Engineering Studies)	Satisfactory
Cardiff (Architectural Engineering and Environmental Engineering)	Satisfactory	Cardiff Institute (Building)	Satisfactory
Glamorgan (Surveying)	Satisfactory	Cardiff Institute (Housing)	Satisfactory
North East Wales Institute (Built Environment)	Satisfactory	Newport College (Construction)	Satisfactory

Source: HEFCE, SHEFC, HEFCW latest available ratings
For a more complete list of institutions offering these courses at undergraduate level refer to the Course Directory

urban design analysis, territorial projects, research methods, the urban block and urban design syntheses. Students also produce design projects and a dissertation. There are opportunities for multidisciplinary work. The school prides itself on its computing facilities and urban design students make use of techniques such as geographical information systems (GIS) and computer-aided design (CAD). In addition to urban design, the school has a unique combination of architecture and landscape architecture disciplines. In the 1994 teaching quality assessment it received an Excellent rating for architecture. Contact details p480.

The Manchester Metropolitan University
Architecture

The Manchester School of Architecture was formed in 1997 by the existing schools at The University of Manchester and The Manchester Metropolitan University, incorporating all their staff and facilities. The school has over 450 students with a high proportion from overseas. The BA (Hons) Architecture course is a three-year, full-time pro-gramme which is strongly design orientated and encourages both theoretical and practical approaches to the subject. A central part of the course is project work, through which students explore architecture at different levels of social and technical complexity. Study includes the technologies of construction and environment, settlement and social studies, history and theory, and processes and skills. There are also elective elements which allow the development of an individual approach to architecture. Contact details p483.

The University of North London
Architecture and Interior Design

The school runs undergraduate BA (Hons) degrees in architecture and in interior design. These have been combined to form an undergraduate scheme in which students take the majority of modules from their main area of study alongside some from the complementary area. An architecture student, for example, would therefore gain some knowledge of interior design through integrated project work. All courses in the school have a strong design focus and aim to build on each student's individual creativity. There is also an access to architecture and interior design course, which provides a foundation for students to prepare for a degree in a related field. This includes modules in ideas and issues, practical skills and model making, and drawing and visual communication alongside a design project. Contact details p483.

The University of Reading
The Reading MSc in Construction Management

This is a one-year, full-time course looking at projects from their inception and design, through to their construction and management. The course aims to give students a thorough grounding in all aspects of financing, procurement, design and management of construction projects from both the client and constructor's perspective. The course programme includes two 10-week terms

that are taught by leading researchers in the field of construction management. The core subjects covered include professional construction management, international construction, construction law, information technology, environmental engineering, financial engineering and organisational management. There is also a one-month spell spent on a unique 'on-site' project and a research-based dissertation produced at the end of the course. The Department of Construction Management and Engineering at The University of Reading received a 5* rating in the latest research assessment exercise (RAE). Contact details p484.

University of Salford
MSc Information Technology in Property and Construction

This postgraduate course focuses on the management of IT for people working in the field of property and

TEACHING QUALITY ASSESSMENTS

Town and Country Planning and Landscape
(England and N Ireland 1996/97/98)

Institution	Grade	Institution	Grade
Greenwich	24	Leeds Metropolitan	21
Kingston	24	Newcastle upon Tyne	21
Oxford Brookes	24	Northumbria at Newcastle	21
Liverpool	23	UCE	20
Nottingham	23	Manchester	20
Sheffield	23	Manchester Metropolitan	20
UWE	23	Westminster	20
Reading	22	Anglia Polytechnic	19
Salford	22	Coventry	19
Sheffield Hallam	22	Doncaster College	18
South Bank	22	Liverpool John Moores	18
Queen's Belfast	22	Southampton Institute	18
Cheltenham and Gloucester College	21	Edge Hill College	17
De Montfort	21	North East Surrey College	15

City and Regional Planning
(Wales 1996/97/98)

Institution	Grade	Institution	Grade
Cardiff	Excellent		

Source: HEFCE, SHEFC, HEFCW latest available ratings
For a more complete list of institutions offering these courses at undergraduate level refer to the Course Directory

construction. The programme consists of four modules: technologies and systems; databases, CAD and visualisation; advanced software technologies and techniques, and IT management and strategies. Students also complete a dissertation. Salford's Research Centre for the Built and Human Environment was graded 5* in the 1996 research assessment exercise. It has a postgraduate community involving some 70 PhD and MPhil students. The department is setting up a number of distant learning courses. Contact details p485.

The University of Sheffield
BA (Hons) Urban Studies and Planning

Sheffield was the first university in the UK to establish a separate Faculty of Architectural Studies which comprises

Interesting facts

- The Eiffel Tower can be laid down inside the Millennium Dome with 60 metres to spare. The Royal Albert Hall in London can also fit inside it 13 times over

- The Eiffel Tower can 'grow' or 'shrink' as much as six inches depending on the temperature

- The largest pyramid in the world is not in Egypt but in Cholula, Mexico. It is 177 ft tall and covers 25 acres. It was built sometime between 6 AD and 12 AD

the School of Architectural Studies and the Departments of Landscape and Town and Regional Planning. The BA (Hons) in Urban Studies and Planning looks at how people relate to their environment. The course covers a wide range of academic disciplines including sociology, economics and politics. The three-year course begins with a basic introduction to urban development and planning and its justification. Modules include such subjects as urban history, graphics and town planning and design. The following two years build on this foundation and allow you the chance to specialise in a particular area. For those wishing to become town planners, students can, after the course, complete a one-year diploma course which is accredited by the Royal Town Planning Institute. The department has received 23 out of 24 for teaching quality and a top rating of 5B for research. Contact details p485.

Tallest Habitable Buildings

Source: "*The Top 10 of Everything: 2000*" Russell Ash, Dorling Kindersley 1999

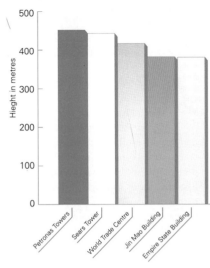

RESEARCH RANKINGS

Built Environment

Institution	Grade	Institution	Grade
North East Wales Institute	1	South Bank	1
Plymouth	1	Staffordshire	1
Southampton Institute	1	UCE	1

source: RAE 1996

Town and Country Planning

Institution	Grade	Institution	Grade
Westminster	3a	De Montfort	2
Manchester	3b	Dundee	2
Nottingham	3b	East London	2
Queen's Belfast	3b	Edinburgh College of Art	2
Sheffield Hallam	3b	Manchester Metropolitan	1
UWE	3b	Paisley	1
Anglia Polytechnic	2	UCE	1

source: RAE 1996

Art, Design and History of Art

Although Britain has always maintained a tradition for producing great artists, the last 30 or 40 years have seen British designers and artists establish themselves as the vanguard of modern, fine art and design. Artists like Damien Hirst, and his dissected animals preserved in formaldehyde, or 1998's Turner Prize winner Chris Ofili, who has a habit of incorporating elephant dung into his paintings, have ensured British art and artists a front-page position in the media, as well as a central position in public debate. The Sensation exhibition, for instance, provoked outrage in London, where demonstrators threw eggs at Marcus Harvey's painting of convicted child murderer Myra Hindley, as well as in New York, where mayor Rudolph Giuliani described it as "sick". If, as the cubist Georges Braque claimed, "Art is meant to disturb", then it looks as if British artists are doing something right, and this makes Britain perhaps the most vibrant, and exciting place for artists to work and study in the world.

Art schools have been very quick to adapt to the ever-expanding range of media within which artists can now work. As such, most courses offer the chance to experiment, or specialise, in areas such as typography, textile design, graphic design, interior design, photography, film-making, animation, jewellery and computer-aided design (commonly known as CAD).

It is possible to study art either at a university or at a specialist art and design college. Either type of institution typically offers both specialist courses as well as those covering a whole range of artistic media and skills. At many art colleges it is possible to study informally, for as long as you like, and in any medium you like, without necessarily having to work towards a qualification. Entrance onto degree courses, for British students, will typically depend on an interview at which a student's portfolio of work is shown and discussed. Admission procedures for international students are often different, however, and full details are given from page 34.

Courses usually last four years, the first year being a foundation year in which students study as wide a range of artistic disciplines as time allows. This provides students with the chance to make a practical decision about which areas they would most like to specialise in later on in their studies. Some students complete their foundation year at one school and then apply elsewhere. Similarly, if you have studied art in your own country, it is sometimes possible to be admitted directly into the second year of an art degree. Students should check at the international office of a university or college to see if this is possible.

Whilst all art courses will involve a certain amount of theory, in the form of either the history of art, or the philosophy of art, it is also possible to study this side of art separately. History of art courses are purely theoretical and can be studied singularly, or combined with subjects like archaeology or philosophy.

SPECIALIST AND VOCATIONAL COURSES

Blake College

This independent art college offers courses that are suited to both beginners and advanced students. Named after the 18th-century painter, William Blake, and set in a converted Victorian warehouse, the college has up-to-date facilities including a print room and fully-equipped dark room. The college provides scholarships for a small number of talented EU students on a limited budget. Students are multinational and classes are small. Classes are supplemented by visits to galleries, museums, and exhibitions as appropriate. There are national museums and art galleries, inter-nationally renowned design consultancies and arts organisations, such as the Design Council, in the immediate vicinity of the college. Blake College was the first independent college in the UK to receive full validation from BTEC for its foundation diploma in art and design. Courses generally last for one academic year although there is flexibility for students who join later in the year or wish to study for shorter periods. Courses are available in a variety of practical disciplines including life drawing, painting and drawing, sculpture, history of art and design, printmaking, graphics, fashion and interior design as well as photography, video and film. Contact details p477.

Cavendish College

Established in 1985, and set in the heart of central London, this private college specialises in full- and part-time courses in business, art and design, hospitality and computing. Offering modern and spacious facilities including a lecture theatre, specialist creative studios and five computer laboratories, the college has recently established its own cyber café where students can relax and use the Internet for recreational purposes in between their classes. Due to the vocational nature of a lot of the courses on offer, the college updates course content regularly to keep abreast of contemporary developments in particular fields. The college has a large international community with students coming from over 80 different countries around the world. The creative department offers a variety of courses at different levels that cater for both the beginner and advanced student. The Foundation Diploma includes all aspects of painting, drawing, graphic design and photography. In addition to the foundation course the creative department offers diplomas in graphic design, interior design, fashion design and fashion marketing. Diploma programmes run for the whole academic year and students can take additional subjects to further their skills and interests. Facilities include well-equipped art studios, workshops and photography dark rooms. Contact details p478.

TEACHING QUALITY ASSESSMENTS

Art and Design
(England and N Ireland 1998/99)

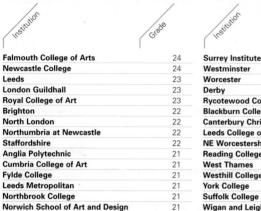

Institution	Grade
Falmouth College of Arts	24
Newcastle College	24
Leeds	23
London Guildhall	23
Royal College of Art	23
Brighton	22
North London	22
Northumbria at Newcastle	22
Staffordshire	22
Anglia Polytechnic	21
Cumbria College of Art	21
Fylde College	21
Leeds Metropolitan	21
Northbrook College	21
Norwich School of Art and Design	21
Ripon and York St John	21

Institution	Grade
Surrey Institute	21
Westminster	21
Worcester	21
Derby	20
Rycotewood College	20
Blackburn College	19
Canterbury Christ Church	19
Leeds College of Art	18
NE Worcestershire College	18
Reading College of Art and Design	18
West Thames	17
Westhill College	17
York College	17
Suffolk College	15
Wigan and Leigh College	13

Art, Design and Art History
(Wales 1995/96)

Institution	Grade
Cardiff Institute	Excellent
Swansea Institute	Excellent
Aberystwyth	Satisfactory
Cardiff Institute (Ceramics, Fine Art, Internal Architecture)	Satisfactory

Institution	Grade
Newport College	Satisfactory
North East Wales Institute	Satisfactory
Carmarthenshire College of Technology and Art	Satisfactory

Fine Art, Printmaking, Sculpture and Painting
(Scotland 1995/96/97)

Institution	Grade
Dundee	Highly Satisfactory
Edinburgh College of Art	Highly Satisfactory

Institution	Grade
Glasgow School of Art	Highly Satisfactory
Robert Gordon	Satisfactory

Graphic Design and Textile Design
(Scotland 1995)

Institution	Grade
Dundee	Excellent
Edinburgh College of Art	Highly Satisfactory
Glasgow School of Art	Highly Satisfactory

Institution	Grade
Robert Gordon	Highly Satisfactory
Scottish College of Textiles	Highly Satisfactory

Source: HEFCE, SHEFC, HEFCW latest available ratings
For a more complete list of institutions offering these courses at undergraduate level refer to the Course Directory

ART AND DESIGN

93

Christie's Modern Art Studies

The Modern Art Studies programme offered by Christie's Education was established in 1976. It offers a survey of the key ideas and developments of modern art from the origins of Impressionism to the present day. The three nine-week terms consist of slide lectures and gallery visits presented by art historians, critics and writers. The course also includes visits to museums, auction houses and galleries as well as weekend trips abroad. The course attracts students of all ages, nationalities and academic backgrounds. Some take part purely for pleasure, while others are looking for a recognised qualification to further their career. It is possible to take it as a year-long examination course, leading to the UCLES Christie's Education Diploma in Modern and Contemporary Art – cost £7,800 + VAT = £9,165. It is also possible to take short courses lasting one term only or concentrating on one particular subject. Subjects on offer include modern art in depth, issues in modern art, Courbet to the Fauves, Cubism to World War II and Abstract Expressionism to the present. Lecture courses cost £1,175 a term and £3,290 a year. Contact details p479.

City and Guilds of London Art School

This small, independent school was established in Kennington by the City and Guilds Institute in 1879 as an extension of the Lambeth School of Art. Originally it provided training, mainly in carving, modelling and architectural decoration. Over the years, it has expanded its activities and courses and now attracts students from abroad and throughout the UK. Architectural Stonecarving and Ornamental Wood-carving and Gilding continue the tradition and are incorporated into the Conservation Department, which also runs a full-time, three-year BA (Hons) in Conservation Studies. The Department of Fine Art offers three-year full-time BA (Hons) courses in Painting and Sculpture, as well as a one-year full-time MA in Fine Arts. The Department of Applied Arts runs three-year diploma courses in Architectural Glass, Decorative Arts and Illustration. The Foundation course (one-year, full-time) has a success rate of over 80 per cent of students gaining entrance to their first choice of subsequent specialist art course. All students are required to study life drawing. Housed in a terrace of 18th-century houses, the facilities include purpose-built fine art studios, stonecarving workshop, printroom, wood workshop, drawing studio and a specialist library to back up the humanities programme – an important component of the full-time courses. Contact details p479.

The Hampstead School of Art

Founded in 1965, the Hampstead School of Art is a registered charity dedicated to the field of art and design. The school is open to applicants of any age or academic background. Most of the classes teach both beginners and more experienced students. It is located in the King's College campus in Hampstead. Courses on offer range from part-time, pre-foundation and A level art to one-week summer courses in pottery and life drawing. The pre-foundation art course, for example, prepares students for entry to a BA Art and Design course. Lasting three terms (30 weeks), the course costs £3,200. Entry is by interview and candidates are expected to show evidence of previous work. Specialist subjects studied include mosaics, silk painting and colour theory. Previous students have been accepted by major art schools,

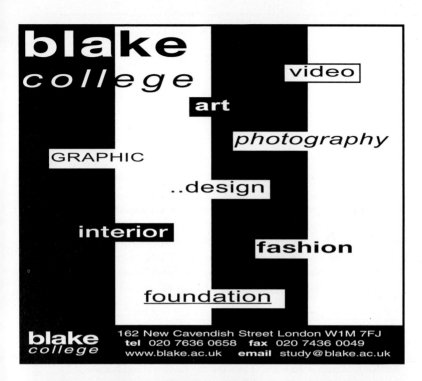

THE
THOMAS CHIPPENDALE
SCHOOL OF FURNITURE

Learn how to Design, Make & Restore Furniture

The Thomas Chippendale School of Furniture is an independent school dedicated to the design, making and conservation of furniture. The aim of the school is to develop craftsmen and women with expertise and professionalism, to create experts who have a sound practical knowledge. Our unique 30-week course is designed to ensure that students have the skills and knowledge to establish their own business or to secure positions in professional workshops or the arts and museums.

From fine classic pieces to bespoke commissions, students on our intensive course gain hands-on experience in a stimulating workshop environment, situated in the heart of the beautiful Scottish countryside, yet near the vibrant city of Edinburgh.Success in the world of furniture also requires strong business skills. The Thomas Chippendale School of Furniture will ensure you gain that vital commercial knowledge and understanding.

For information on our course commencing in October 2000,
please contact the Principal,
leaving your name, address and telephone number:

The Thomas Chippendale School of Furniture
Gifford, East Lothian EH41 4JA Scotland
Tel: (44) (0) 1620 810680
Fax: (44) (0) 1620 810701
www.chippendale.co.uk

For information on short courses in individual aspects of furniture making and restoration run by our American sister school please contact:

Ben Farrell in South Carolina, USA
Tel: (00 1) 803 892 4153

such as Central Saint Martins, Chelsea and the London College of Printing, and during the last year there was a 100 per cent acceptance rate. The school has a friendly, welcoming atmosphere and maintains a high level and quality of teaching in small class groups. Contact details p480.

Heatherley School of Fine Art

Heatherley's was established more than 150 years ago by a group of students unable to tolerate the academic restrictions imposed on them at the Government School of Design. It is now the oldest independent art school in London. Since then the college has moved to a 19th-century building in Chelsea, within walking distance from the King's Road and Chelsea Harbour. The building has purpose-built studios with north-east light. All members of staff, including the principal, are practising artists. Courses are for beginners and experienced artists and include a two-year diploma in portraiture, a one-year foundation/portfolio course, a one-year continuing studies course and part-time and short courses in subjects such as life drawing, oil painting, watercolour, printmaking and figurative sculpture. The diploma in portraiture, introduced in 1994, aims to prepare students for professional practice as portrait painters. It has external examiners chosen by the Royal Society of Portrait Painters. In addition, the school has recently introduced a two-year diploma in sculpture. The school's Open Studio, founded in 1845, is based on the French atelier system – a tutored class with a model allowing for any level of ability or attendance – and can be joined at any time in the academic year. Flexible tickets are available for 10 two-and-a-half hour lessons at a cost of £120. Contact details p481.

The Tate Gallery of British Art

The Tate Gallery of British Art, at Millbank, is one of London's most famous and popular galleries, housing a permanent collection of British art from the 16th century to the present day. Since 1984, it has hosted the Turner Prize, which provides an opportunity to view the work of contemporary British artists. As part of its interpretation and education programme, the gallery offers a variety of courses that relate to all aspects of its collection, major exhibitions, special displays and other art-historical themes. Course sessions may take place in the Clore Gallery auditorium or in the galleries in front of the works. Where courses are linked to an exhibition, a visit to the show is often included in the fee. Courses are designed to suit a range of different audiences from the art specialist to the absolute beginner. Course themes for 2000/2001 include: William Blake; Turner; 19th-century British art; the Pre-Raphaelites, British art in the Tate and National Gallery collections; 20th-century British art; and the Turner Prize and contemporary art. Contact details p486.

The Thomas Chippendale School of Furniture

Established in 1985, this private school specialises in the design, making and conservation of furniture. The school aims to develop craftsmen and women with practical, technical and theoretical expertise. The school is set in four acres of grounds in the rolling hills of the East Lothian countryside, only half-an-hour away from the historic city of Edinburgh. The school offers a full-time 30-week course, leading to a diploma, teaching the skills involved in antique restoration, and bespoke furniture design and manufacture. Students are

TEACHING QUALITY ASSESSMENTS

History of Art, Architecture and Design
(England and N Ireland 1996/97/98/99)

Institution	Grade	Institution	Grade
Birkbeck	24	Northumbria at Newcastle	21
SOAS	24	Open University	21
UCL	24	Staffordshire	21
Courtauld Institute	23	Warwick	21
Leeds	23	York	21
Nottingham	23	Bristol	20
Oxford Brookes	23	Falmouth College of Arts	20
Reading	23	Kingston	20
Birmingham	22	Sheffield Hallam	20
Cambridge	22	Southampton	20
East Anglia	22	Sussex	20
Essex	22	UCE	20
Kent at Canterbury	22	Central Lancashire	19
Leicester	22	Derby	19
Manchester Metropolitan	22	Goldsmiths	19
Middlesex	22	London Institute	19
Royal College of Art	22	Anglia Polytechnic	18
Brighton	21	Southampton Institute	18
De Montfort	21		
Manchester	21		

History of Art
(Scotland 1995/96)

Institution	Grade	Institution	Grade
Aberdeen	Highly Satisfactory	Glasgow	Highly Satisfactory
Edinburgh	Highly Satisfactory	St Andrews	Highly Satisfactory

Source: HEFCE, SHEFC, HEFCW latest available ratings
For a more complete list of institutions offering these courses at undergraduate level refer to the Course Directory

also taught to apply their theoretical and practical skills in a professional commercial environment. The course is spread out over three 10-week terms. Teaching is by way of lectures, demonstrations, and visits to view furniture in private houses, galleries and professional workshops. Specialist tutors are invited as guest lecturers in specific subject areas. Students are encouraged to work on their own designs, and can exhibit these works at the graduation evening at the end of the course. Modern facilities include spacious 6,500sq ft workshops with well spaced-out benches, purpose-built wood turning and sanding rooms, and 2,000 sq ft of exhibition and function space. Full fees are £9,450 per year. Thomas Chippendale also have a sister school in South Carolina, USA, which runs short courses on individual aspects of furniture making and restoration. Contact details p487.

DEGREE COURSES

Bath Spa University College
BA (Hons) Graphic Design and
Pre-degree Art and Design Course
This course offers students the opportu-

nity to specialise in photography, video animation, illustration or multimedia. Supporting studies are also possible in three-dimensional design and print media. Experimental learning is developed through studio and workshop activities, encouraging students to make use of craft and technological learning skills. The course strives to prepare students for the competitive world of design and equip them with skills that can be used in any international context. Students are also encouraged to develop cultural, social, historical and professional awareness in the hope that they become able to formulate independent judgement of their work. Famous designers and artists regularly give lectures. Due to the strong professional element to the course students are encouraged to take part in as many competitions as possible. International students can prepare for direct entry into the BA (Hons) Graphic Design with the Pre-degree Art and Design Course, which combines the foundation study of art and design with English language teaching. Contact details p477.

Bradford College
BA Art and Design

The BA Art and Design course enables students to identify their strengths by allowing them to choose from different media areas before specialising in two areas for their final year. Students study drawing and theoretical studies as a core programme. Two specialist areas may be chosen for their studio practice units from ceramics, painting /fine art, graphic design, print making, illustration, photography and textiles. Depending upon the choice of specialisms, students may apply to specialist degree titles in fine art, graphic/ media communication or textiles. There are currently 15 international students on the course. Contact details p478.

The Courtauld Institute of Art
BA (Hons) History of Art

The Courtauld Institute of Art is a relatively small organisation that provides training solely in the subject of history of art. Its size is an advantage in that class sizes are small with usually no more than eight students, and there is the opportunity for closer contact between students and staff members. The institute was awarded the highest possible grading in the 1996 Research Assessment Exercise, and received 23 in the recent Teaching Quality Assessments. The BA (Hons) in History of Art is a three-year course that concentrates solely on the history of Western art. In the first year, students cover a all periods of western art, and at least two periods must be studied in-depth during the second year. Students are encouraged to take a broad range of courses until the third year when there are opportunities to specialise. Courses are taught through visits to galleries, museums and monuments, as well as through the more traditional method of lectures, seminars and classes. All students attend a course to gain a reading knowledge in French, German or Italian; useful for studying art history as well as studying elsewhere in Europe. Contact details p479.

Coventry University
MA Automotive Design/
Automotive Design Research

These courses provide students with the skills and understanding to become creative automotive designers, or to pursue a research-based examination in the field of experimental learning. The courses contain elements of two- and three-dimensional design, and students can practice advanced CAD technology and traditional drawing, with clay modelling in industry-based projects. The research-based course involves

Most Expensive Painting Sold at Auction

Source: *"The Top 10 of Everything: 2000"*
Russell Ash, Dorling Kindersley 1999

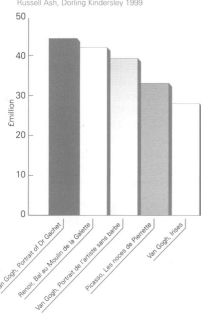

Interesting facts

- The world's largest art gallery is the Winter Palace and Hermitage in St Petersburg, Russia. Visitors would have to walk 15 miles to see the 322 galleries which house nearly three million works of art

- In 1998, Sotheby's in the UK sold a tin containing the faeces of Italian artist Piero Mazzoni for £17,250

- During a career that lasted just 10 years, Vincent Van Gogh painted 800 works of art and sold just one

elements of design management, research preparation, and CAD and design contextual study. Graduates from these courses are currently employed at styling studios at Volvo, Jaguar, Ford, Rover, and other car manufacturers, freelance design, and teaching or design management. International students will have the opportunity to work in a studio environment and have contact with practising designers and industry methods. There are currently four international students on the course. Contact details p479.

Falmouth College of Arts
Art, Design and History of Art

In 1999 Falmouth College of Arts received 24 out of 24 in teaching quality assessments for its art and design provision, one of only two institutions in the UK to receive such a rating. The college's foundation art and design programme aims to help students assess their potential as an artist or designer by working with a wide range of materials and techniques and then allowing them to specialise. In fine art the principal areas of studio practice are painting, sculpture and printmaking. History of modern art is available at BA and postgraduate level. BA (Hons) programmes in design include opportunities in graphic design, illustration, photography, interior and landscape design, studio ceramics, textiles and 3D design. Students receive a thorough grounding in both practical skills and theoretical issues. The PG Dip in Creative Advertising aims to mirror as closely as possible professional life in an agency creative department. Recent graphic design graduates have found employment in a number of leading London consultancies, including Newell and Sorrell, BBC Presentation Graphics

ART AND DESIGN

and MPL. The college's illustration programme has well-developed contacts with the design industry in London, New York and Amsterdam where there is a substantial market for such work. Contact details p480.

Goldsmiths, University of London
BA (Hons) Fine Art

The programme is taught within the Visual Arts Department, which was one of only two university art departments in the UK to receive the top rating of 5* in the 1996 research assessment exercise. Through the exploration of contemporary practice and theory, the degree aims to enable students to discover and develop their abilities, in order that they may practise independently as a creative individual. Students are expected to be highly motivated and hard-working and are encouraged to develop self-discipline, self-confidence and self-evaluation. The fine art degree combines three years of studio and workshop practice with lectures and seminars in contemporary art theory. Contact details p480.

The London Institute, Camberwell College of Arts
MA Conservation

This course is concerned with the conservation of paper-based artifacts and includes the broad range of materials found in libraries archives, and prints and drawings collection. The full-time, two-year programme progresses through two stages. In stage one (one year), the emphasis is on building the skills base, which includes: collections care and preservation; conservation procedure and treatments; the materials and conservation science underpinning conservation practice; and an historical studies programme that focuses on the importance of history in relation to

conservation issues. The emphasis in stage two is on individual conservation and research projects, and the development of an ability to deal with more complex and demanding conservation problems. During the summer period, students also take part in a professional placement. Graduates with relevant professional experience in paper conservation may be considered for direct entry into the third term for year one. International students often wish to learn about British conservation methods and how these may be used in conjunction with their own, traditional methods. Contact details p482.

Southampton Institute
BA (Hons) Fine Arts Valuation

This degree course is a unique blend of specialist study areas in fine and decorative arts and chattels (moveable items of personal property such as furniture and paintings) together with legal, financial and management studies. During the course students cover such areas as architectural appreciation of buildings, interiors and gardens, the historical influence of the Renaissance, the Orient and Islam, object analysis, valuation and business studies, business practice and auction law, European furniture, ceramics and fine art. Students also complete a dissertation on a chosen topic. Students have regular access to the institute's study collection which includes furniture, ceramics, glass, metalwork and paintings, as well as access to computer-based information through the Internet, Art Quest and Thesaurus. In addition, there is a programme of visiting lecturers and

oncourse·co·uk

The ultimate guide to courses

visits to auction houses and collections, and a European trip in the second year. Contact details p486.

Staffordshire University
BA (Hons) Design

This three-year, modular degree scheme offers students the chance to specialise in one of 11 design areas including ceramics, glass, media production, photography and product design. It is possible to combine this first choice with another design subject as a minor study. The university has a gallery in New York for staff and student exhibitions and most staff are active as artists, designers or researchers. This connection with the world of art and design practice is reinforced by visiting lecturers. Workshops cater for hot and cold glass working, monochrome and colour printing, screen printing on textiles and paper, audio/video production and editing, studio photography and the use of wood, metal, plastics and ceramics. As would be expected from the university's location in Stoke-on-Trent (which has a long history of ceramics), there are more students studying ceramics here than anywhere else in the country. Contact details p486.

University of Sunderland
BTEC Diploma Foundation Studies in Art and Design

This foundation course leads directly into the university's undergraduate degree programme in art and design. It is a nationally recognised pre-undergraduate qualification. The purpose of the course is to provide a bridge from secondary-level art education to the academic standards of higher education. All students who complete the course will be offered a place on the undergraduate degree programme. Students are taught to develop practical studio skills, and to consider the theories and history behind issues relating to art. Students are given practical assistance in portfolio development throughout the course. There are various study visits to museums, galleries and craft centres around the country. All teaching staff are professional artists and designers who teach through lectures, seminars and group workshops. Students are assessed through a combination of examinations, essays and presentations. Contact details p486.

The Surrey Institute of Art and Design
MA Design Management

This course, which falls under the aegis of The Surrey Institute's faculty of Design, allows students to design their own project. The options range from research into design practice, including corporate communications, brand development and product design, to the examination of how design management fits into business or education. Alternatively students may investigate the relationship between design practice and adjacent disciplines such as marketing or advertising. The degree can be completed in one year. Contact details p486.

The Surrey Institute of Art and Design
BA (Hons) Graphic Design

Students learn a number of graphic specialisms including typography, illustration and computer animation. Beyond the fundamentals of graphic design there are options which allow students to take an individual direction. This includes a largely electronic route encompassing computer animation and multimedia. This course is part of The Surrey Institute's Faculty of Fashion and Communication, and is based at the Epsom campus. Contact details p486.

RESEARCH RANKINGS

Institution	Grade	Institution	Grade
Brunel	5*	Central School of Speech and Drama	3b
Goldsmiths	5*	Dartington College	3b
UCL	5*	De Montfort (Design)	3b
Dundee	5	Derby	3b
Open University	5	Glasgow School of Art	3b
Oxford	5	Hertfordshire	3b
Wimbledon School of Art	5	Keele	3b
Bournemouth	4	Kent Institute	3b
Brighton	4	Leeds Metropolitan	3b
Coventry (Design)	4	Lincolnshire and Humberside	3b
Middlesex (Electronic Arts)	4	Liverpool John Moores	3b
Reading (Fine Art)	4	Napier	3b
Reading (Typography and Graphic Communication)	4	Newcastle	3b
		Newport College	3b
Royal College of Art	4	Norwich School of Art and Design	3b
Sheffield Hallam	4	Oxford Brookes	3b
Southampton	4	Portsmouth	3b
Ulster	4	Staffordshire (Design)	3b
Westminster	4	UCE	3b
Bath Spa	3a	Anglia Polytechnic	2
Bretton Hall	3a	Central Lancashire	2
Buckinghamshire College	3a	Guildhall, London	2
Cardiff Institute	3a	Huddersfield	2
Cheltenham and Gloucester College	3a	Liverpool Hope College	2
Coventry (Fine Art)	3a	Loughborough College	2
De Montfort (Fine Art)	3a	North East Wales Institute	2
East London	3a	North Riding College	2
Edinburgh College of Art	3a	Roehampton Institute	2
Falmouth College	3a	Salford College	2
Kingston	3a	Scottish College of Textiles	2
Lancaster	3a	Southampton Institute (Design Innovation)	2
London Institute	3a	University College Chichester	2
Loughborough	3a	Wolverhampton	2
Manchester Metropolitan	3a	Bolton Institute	1
Middlesex (Fine Art)	3a	Canterbury Christ Church	1
Middlesex (Design Disciplines)	3a	Chester College	1
Northumbria at Newcastle	3a	Edge Hill College	1
Nottingham Trent	3a	Glasgow Caledonian	1
Plymouth	3a	La Sainte Union College	1
Robert Gordon	3a	Newman College	1
Southampton Institute (Fine Art Practice)	3a	Ripon and York St John	1
Staffordshire (Fine Art)	3a	Surrey Institute	1
Sunderland	3a	Swansea Institute	1
UWE	3a	Teesside	1
Aberystwyth	3b	Westhill College	1

source: RAE 1996

University of Wales Institute, Cardiff

International Foundation in Art and Design

This course allows students to train as professional artists in whatever field they choose in addition to building up a portfolio of work, in preparation for application to higher education courses in art and design. Having built up a substantial portfolio, students can then progress to an honours degree programme. Students begin the course with an intensive look at drawing, colour, and a range of basic two- and three-dimensional processes, including printmaking, ceramics and jewellery. Students can specialise in a number of subjects in the second term, from fine art and graphic design to textiles and theatre design. There is a major end-of-year exhibition, which students will prepare for in the final term. Contact details p478.

Wimbledon School of Art
Foundation Course in Art and Design
The foundation course in art and design is a one-year, full-time course which offers an introduction to the specialist areas within art and design. The course enables students to choose which areas of art and design are of the greatest interest and progress on to suitable degree courses. The course starts with a diagnostic phase which allows students to try out different areas. Students then apply for specialist options and can choose between fashion and textiles, fine art, graphic design and illustration, lens media, theatre design and three-dimensional design. Contact details p487.

oncourse·co·uk
The ultimate guide to courses

RESEARCH RANKINGS

History of Art, Architecture and Design

Institution	Grade	Institution	Grade
Cambridge	5*	Glasgow	3a
Courtauld Institute	5*	Loughborough College	3a
Sussex	5*	Manchester Metropolitan	3a
Essex	5	Middlesex	3a
Leeds	5	Nottingham	3a
Open University	5	Plymouth	3a
SOAS	5	Aberdeen	3b
UCL	5	Bristol	3b
Birkbeck	4	De Montfort	3b
East Anglia	4	Goldsmiths	3b
Edinburgh	4	Hertfordshire	3b
Kent at Canterbury	4	Leicester	3b
Manchester	4	Northumbria at Newcastle	3b
Newcastle	4	Southampton	3b
Oxford Brookes	4	Surrey Institute	3b
Reading	4	Cardiff Institute	2
Royal College of Art	4	Central Lancashire	2
Southampton Institute	4	Glasgow School of Art	2
St Andrews	4	Kent Institute	2
Warwick	4	London Institute	2
Birmingham	3a	UCE	2
Brighton	3a	Wimbledon School of Art	2
Derby	3a	Kingston	1
Falmouth College of Arts	3a		

source: RAE 1996

Business, Management and Marketing

According to UCAS, business courses in the UK have recently experienced a higher increase in applications than any other subject. Business-related subjects are becoming increasingly popular as both students and employers come to recognise their value. In Britain, business "heroes" like Richard Branson, and Archie Norman, the former chairman of supermarket chain Asda, regularly receive praise and media attention. Success stories like these are inspirational and encourage many to gain an understanding of both the operations of individual businesses and the trends that affect them.

There are a number of subjects that come under the heading of 'business and management' and if you are interested solely in business, you may be forced to narrow down your interests. In general, business courses aim to prepare managers for the decisions they are likely to make in the real business world. This can include areas like strategic planning, finance, coping with change, marketing and general management. Law and economics also affect the way businesses work and are often incorporated into the course. Courses may focus on a single subject area, such as marketing, and offer minor modules in other subjects. Alternatively, there are joint courses that balance areas equally, for example business and accountancy.

Undergraduate courses in business studies typically last between three and four years. The key concepts learnt in the first year underlie the theory and practice studied in following years. Many courses also emphasise the importance of practical experience and include visiting speakers, role plays and work experience. Some business studies courses, referred to as sandwich courses, include a six-month or one-year placement in the business world.

At postgraduate level, there is an increasing level of specialisation, with the possibility of studying technology management or personnel management, for example. The MBA (Master of Business Administration), developed in the USA, is now very popular in the UK. To follow an MBA you need a minimum of three years work experience, a good first degree in any subject and often a satisfactory Graduate Management Admissions Test (GMAT) score (630 to 650 is about average for good schools). Due to their popularity, gaining entrance to courses at some of the internationally renowned institutes is difficult and expensive. However, if you do succeed, you will obtain a highly-respected qualification, hopefully making you more employable.

Short courses in a number of business-related areas can also be taken on a part or full-time basis at private colleges. These may provide a good starting point for students considering going into higher education or for those wanting some initial training.

SPECIALIST AND VOCATIONAL COURSE

Babel Technical College

This small college was established in 1984 and is based in David Game House in Notting Hill, London. Specialising in computing, the college offers several courses aimed at improving business and office skills. The City and Guilds diploma and advanced diploma in modern office skills, for example, teaches students such areas as word-processing, spreadsheets, touch-typing and databases. It is also possible to study English for business communications. Fees are £2,920 for the diploma and £4,530 for the advanced diploma courses. Diplomas are Level 2 and advanced diplomas Level 3 vocational qualifications. The college also offers private tuition and short and part-time courses. Contact details p477.

The Bell Language Schools

Bell, a registered charity, was founded by Frank Bell in 1955 to promote international understanding through quality language teaching. The Bell Educational Trust has six language centres in England and four in Europe, and has 18 associate schools in Europe and Asia. The University Access Course in Business Studies, run at Saffron Walden is a 25-week-long course designed for international students whose academic qualifications are insufficient for university entrance or who wish to develop their language and study skills. Completion guarantees entry to a business studies degree course at Anglia Polytechnic University in Cambridge. The English for Business (18 plus), Capital and Premier Professional English (24 plus) courses are designed for people needing to communicate in English in their work environment. Language development, communication skills and cultural awareness provide the basis for these programmes, by focusing on specific commercial or business contexts and improving fluency and confidence. The combination of the Intensive English Plus programme with one of the business-based courses would help the student who wishes to study for a business degree or diploma in English. The new Bell Executive Centre in Bath, offers language development and business skills training programmes which are intensive, small-group classes combining group work with personal one-to-one tuition. The executive centre is a dedicated centre with office-to-office facilities and support, excellent study resources and multi-media centre with Internet access. Contact details p477.

Bromley College of Further and Higher Education

HND in Business Studies

The HND in Business Studies is run by the college's Faculty of Business and Management, and offered through the associate college agreement with the University of Greenwich. The course lasts two years, each year consisting of two semesters. The first year includes modules in communications, law, accounts, marketing and personnel. In the second year students follow compulsory modules such as operation management and strategy as well as selecting choices from a range of units. Options include small business management, managing human resources, and financial services. Students have the opportunity to pursue a specialist route within the diploma, such as finance or personnel. Assessment is by a combination of coursework and assignments, including case studies, projects, group problem solving, computer exercises and the compilation of a portfolio of work. Contact details p478.

BUSINESS

Cavendish College

Established in 1985, and set in the heart of central London, this private college specialises in full- and part-time courses in business, art and design, and computing. Offering modern and spacious facilities including a lecture theatre, specialist creative studios and five computer laboratories, the college has recently established its own cyber café where students can relax and use the Internet for recreational purposes in between their classes. Due to the vocational nature of a lot of its courses, the college updates its course content regularly to keep abreast of contemporary developments in particular fields. The college has a large international community with students coming from over 80 different countries around the world. The business studies department offers a wide range of courses that aim to prepare students for work in the international business world. Intensive diplomas can be obtained in either six or nine months in subjects including marketing, PR, and advertising, and communications. Other courses include diplomas in international management, import/export, investment analysis, creative advertising and executive secretarial studies. The college offers specialised computer training in all its business courses, and students are encouraged to use the college's extensive computing facilities at every opportunity. Contact details p478.

City Business College

The City Business College is a private college situated near the City of London within easy walking distance of Barbican Underground station. It provides a full range of accredited courses in business, management, accounting, marketing, tourism and computing which prepare students for examinations set by professional bodies such as the Association of Business Executives (ABE), the Institute of Commercial Management (ICM), the Institute for the Management of Information Systems (IMIS) and the Chartered Institute of Marketing (CIM), leading to internationally recognised certificates, diplomas and advanced diplomas. All courses are offered on a full-time basis and postgraduate qualifications are also available – with the Diploma in Management Studies (DMS) and Masters of Business Administration (MBA). Students are taught in small, friendly classes by fully qualified teachers who are experienced in guiding international students towards successful completion of their studies. The college administration is always available to assist students with visa requirements and any other problems they may encounter. An accommodation service is provided and there is a variety of sports and leisure activities within easy reach of the college, as are the famous attractions of London. Contact details p479.

EF International Language School

EF does a range of Business English courses. Details p480.

Hove College

Founded in 1977, Hove College is a specialist private college situated less than one mile from Brighton, which is on the South coast of England. To gain acceptance onto a course here, although it is preferable that prospective students have gained previous relevant educational qualifications, the level of motivation of the individual is the single most important factor. The Business Department offers several courses; for example the European Business and Personnel Diploma covers information technology, business administration, shorthand and European languages for business. The course lasts 24 weeks and

109

costs £3,883. The Executive Media Assistant Diploma includes modules on information technology, shorthand, European languages for business, business travel planning, public relations and advertising. The course lasts 24 weeks and costs £3,883. These two courses have three start dates throughout the year. There are shorter courses available within the department. A full range of accommodation is available at the college; prices vary from £55 to £70 a week for a flat or house share, to £70 to £80 a week for a one-bedroom apartment. Contact details p481.

Kensington College of Business

Kensington College of Business was established in 1982 as a specialist training centre for management qualifications. Originally situated in Kensington, the college has expanded rapidly and now operates from two large centres in central and west London, in addition to conducting courses nationwide in areas including Birmingham and the Channel Isles. The college currently has over 1,000 students from all over the world studying on a full-time, part-time and distance learning basis. The college offers two main types of qualification: professional qualifications such as examinations of The Association of Business Executives (ABE), The Institute of Secretaries and Administrators (ICSA), The Chartered Institute of Marketing (CIM) and The Chartered Institute of Business Administration (IBA); and BA, BSc, LLB and MBA degrees awarded by Glamorgan, London and Thames Valley universities. The facilities of the college are complemented by the administrative staff who are always willing to assist students with any academic, career or

TEACHING QUALITY ASSESSMENTS

Business, Management and Marketing
(England and N Ireland 1994)

Institution	Grade	Institution	Grade
Bath	Excellent	Brighton	Satisfactory
City	Excellent	Brunel	Satisfactory
Cranfield	Excellent	Doncaster College	Satisfactory
De Montfort	Excellent	Durham	Satisfactory
Imperial	Excellent	Huddersfield	Satisfactory
Kingston	Excellent	Hull	Satisfactory
Lancaster	Excellent	Kent at Canterbury	Satisfactory
London Business School	Excellent	Loughborough College	Satisfactory
Loughborough	Excellent	North East Worcestershire College	
LSE	Excellent	(Revisit)	Satisfactory
Manchester	Excellent	Plymouth	Satisfactory
Northumbria at Newcastle	Excellent	Portsmouth	Satisfactory
Nottingham Trent	Excellent	Queen Mary and Westfield	Satisfactory
Nottingham	Excellent	Reading	Satisfactory
Open University	Excellent	Salford	Satisfactory
Surrey	Excellent	Sheffield Hallam	Satisfactory
UMIST	Excellent	Southampton	Satisfactory
UWE	Excellent	Suffolk College	Satisfactory
Warwick	Excellent	Swindon College	Satisfactory
Anglia Polytechnic	Satisfactory	Teesside	Satisfactory
Birmingham	Satisfactory	UCE	Satisfactory
Blackburn College	Satisfactory	Ulster	Satisfactory
Bradford and Ilkley College	Satisfactory	University College Northampton	Satisfactory
Bradford	Satisfactory	Wolverhampton	Satisfactory

Source: HEFCE, SHEFC, HEFCW latest available ratings
For a more complete list of institutions offering these courses at undergraduate level refer to the Course Directory

City of London College

Courses commence: September, January, April & July of each year

Accountancy
(AAT – Found., Inter., Tech.)
(ACCA – Technician Level A, B, C)

Business Studies
(DBA, ABE Diploma Level I, II, Adv. Diploma)
(CIM – Cert., Adv. Cert., PGDiploma)

Computer Studies
(C&GLI – 424 Preliminary Cert. in App. Prog'g)
(IMIS – Diploma, Higher Dip., Graduate Dip.)

Travel & Tourism
(Diploma in Travel & Tourism Management)
(IATA / UFTAA Standard & Advanced Diploma)

Hotel Management
(Diploma, Advanced Diploma, Higher Diploma)

Secretarial
(Diploma Certificate in Legal Secretaries)

Masters in Business Administration
(Degree awarded by Washington International University – USA)

ACCESS COURSES

One year Graduate Diploma in Information Systems (IMIS)
(Entry to Masters Degree in the Management of Information Systems – MSc)

One year Postgraduate Diploma in Management Studies
(Entry to Masters Degree in Hospitality Management)

One year Higher Diploma in Hotel Management
(Entry to final year BA (Hons) Hospitality Management)

STUDENTS' COMMENTS:

"Attending first lecture at the College reassured me that I had made the right decision in joining the City of London College."
Mr G. Patrick – AAT student

"I was nervous about coming to London, but the staff at City of London College could not have made it any easier for me to settle down."
Ms S. L. Ng – CIM student

"The experience in joining the Diploma in Travel & Tourism course at City of London College has been invaluable. The lecturers have been a great help."
Ms M. Chiba – T&T student

"I am glad that I chose City of London College to gain IMIS qualifications. I have enjoyed not only the learning but the international social life at the College."
Ms M. Daet – IMIS student

 Accredited and recognised as efficient by the British Accreditation Council

personal problems. The college has an accommodation list to help students find accommodation within easy reach of the college. Contact details p481.

London College of International Business Studies

London College of International Business Studies (LCIBS) specialises in training international students and offers management courses in international business, marketing communications and tourism. Their training aims to develop students' practical business knowledge and to improve their professional English. The programmes are flexible, allowing students to choose subjects suited to their careers and if necessary, a timetable to suit individual circumstances. All courses include study skills and professional English communications and involve lectures, video presentations and practical case study assignments. Research projects and work experience are also included on the long diploma programmes. All tutors have commercial experience in their fields and class sizes are kept small to ensure maximum possible personal attention. The student body is diverse with many areas of the globe represented. Students include school leavers, graduates and working professionals; the average age is 25. LCIBS diplomas are awarded to successful candidates who can go on to jobs with international companies or further their studies at university. Tourism students can obtain OAG and IATA certificates. The college also offers executive/PA training and these students also sit Pitman qualification exams. According to the college, over 90 per cent of their job-seeking graduates find employment within six months of graduation. Contact details p482.

London City College

London City College has been in operation since 1982. It is part of the Royal Waterloo Centre, a six-storey building housing educational facilities situated in London, next to the River Thames and South Bank complex. The college offers courses ranging from Master of Business Administration (MBA) degrees in Marketing or Finance to courses in general English language, Shipping and Transport, Marketing, Travel and Tourism, Hotel and Catering, and Art and Design. London City College has been accredited and 'recognised as efficient' by the British Accreditation Council (BAC). The college's MBA degree is awarded by Leicester University, but all lectures and examinations are taken at London City College. The 12-month course includes the study of strategic management, economics, accounting for managers, and organisation analysis and control. Students can take options in areas such as international marketing, marketing management and public sector management. The course costs £6,400 for the year. Specialist MBA programmes are also available in Maritime Management, Marketing, and Finance. The one-year, full-time course in Shipping Management covers both specialist shipping subjects and general management subjects. Core modules include shipping finance, maritime law and strategic management, and options are available in such areas as dry cargo chartering, international marketing and marine insurance. Assessment is 50 per cent examination and 50 per cent continuous assessment. Contact details p482.

London Institute of Technology and Research

London Institute of Technology and Research (LITR) was initially set up in 1987 as a training and research consultancy and is a non-profit making educational institution, situated in the commercial heart of London, near

of assistantships available. The LITR accommodation office maintains lists and can help students to find suitable local housing. Contact details p482.

Lucie Clayton College

Founded in 1928, originally as a finishing school, the secretarial college was established in 1968. Lucie Clayton College is housed in a large residence near Kensington Gardens in London and has a buttery (café), drawing room and student accommodation on site. The secretarial college offers one-, two- and three-term executive business courses. All include the core secretarial skills of shorthand, typing, word processing, audio typing and computing. The one-term course combines academic study with business skills. Popular with university graduates and gap year students, the aim is to acquire high and accurate skills in a short time. Business support subjects studied include commercial English, finance for the office and administration. The three-term course is suitable for students interested in PA work. Covering advanced computer packages, advertising, public relations, marketing and law, it also includes a three-week work experience programme at prestigious companies in London. The college also offers short courses of two and four weeks in touch-typing, word processing and IT. Contact details p483.

Oxford Media and Business School

The Oxford Media and Business School is situated in the centre of this ancient university city. The school offers a range of intensive, modular business programmes ranging in length from three months to one year, with the option of going on to study for an MBA at a British university. In addition to business theory, courses place a great deal of emphasis on practical

Borough underground. The faculty is led by its executive president who has taught and researched in England, the USA, Africa, the Middle East and Asia. LITR is accredited with applicant status by the British Accreditation Council (BAC) and is a full member of the European Commission for Business Education (ECBE) and the Association of Collegiate Business Schools and Programmes, USA. Courses available at the institute include an MBA programme which can be studied either on campus or by distance learning. It is offered on a full- or part-time basis, which means that students have the option of combining study with employment and can finish the course at their own pace. Fees are £3,450 a year and the course lasts one to two years. For students in financial difficulties, there are a limited number

management ability. This includes training in key skills such as the use of the latest computer office systems and the preparation and delivery of an effective business presentation using audio-visual aids. Students are sent on a two-week company placement during courses of six months or more, as well as going on selected company visits to learn from the real-life workplace. The school also runs a nine-month executive assistant diploma course incorporating a full range of executive secretarial training, along with an option in a second or third language for multilingual career roles. All students receive professional help with both career planning and job interview techniques. A full-time student accommodation manager offers help with accommodation in Oxford, and most international students stay in college-owned flats and houses. Help with English language is available for international students who require it. Contact details p484.

Purley Secretarial and Language College

This private college, established in 1928 and set in a large house in the centre of Purley, specialises in language and business training. The college selects local host families for students who need accommodation, which gives them an extra opportunity to improve their language skills. The college holds business and secretarial courses. Students are prepared for external examinations including OCR (RSA) and Pitman qualifications. Those who wish to extend their knowledge may take English lessons alongside their studies. Courses are available in business, computing and personal assistant skills, and last from six to 36 weeks. Subjects include word processing, audio transcription, shorthand, business administration and communication skills. Short courses are available in

keyboarding and word processing. See EFL chapter for details of other courses. Contact details p484.

Queen's Business and Secretarial College (Cambridge and London)

Queen's was founded in 1924 and has two schools, one in Cambridge, one in London. It caters for school leavers, graduates, mature students and international students, running courses of varying lengths which cover business and computing skills and business English. There are three courses with a business focus and these require students to have a high level of English language skills. The Marketing and Business Skills Diploma (£2,695 London, £2,450 Cambridge a term) lasts three terms and is for students at A level or degree standard. The course includes general office software and procedures and runs courses on marketing, public relations and advertising. The Executive and Personal Assistant's Diploma runs for two or three terms depending on a student's ability. Those at GCSE level opt for the three-term course (£2,590/£2,070 a term) while A level or mature students may complete the course in two terms (£2,590/£2,150 a term). Both courses include general office administration and computer software as well as shorthand, desktop publishing, finance, and career development. Students on both diplomas complete two weeks' work experience. A one-term course in intensive business skills or intensive business technology is completed in 12 weeks (£2590/£2285 a term). It is designed to complement a diploma or a degree course and is suitable for mature students or those at A level standard. The technology course emphasises information technology and business finance, while on the business skills course students learn shorthand.

Short courses are available offering a range of computer training. Contact details p484.

The Spectrum Group

Spectrum works with 20 government colleges and universities in London and throughout Britain. All offer modern study facilities for international students, with small classes, and a varied sports and social programme. Accommodation ranges from hostel to homestay. These institutions offer a range of first, intermediate and advanced diploma courses as well as higher national diploma (HND) and degree courses in business studies, business administration, accounting, finance, information technology, law, management, marketing, retail and secretarial studies. These last for one, two or three years and lead to internationally-recognised qualifications. Fees start from £2,700 per year for a diploma course; £4,950 per year for an HND or a degree; and £4,800 for an international University foundation year programme. Some colleges also offer short specialist courses lasting a few weeks in aspects of international business and related areas. Contact details p486.

West London College

West London College moved to its modern premises in the heart of London's West End, only a few minutes from Bond Street station, in 1997 (it had occupied its previous site since the 1930s). The college is a BAC accredited business school which attracts over 1,000 students each year, from over 100 countries, to study business, hotel management, travel and tourism, computer science and English. The Department of Business offers a completely flexible entry system whereby students of all levels can join a study programme which culminates in an MBA. Applicants with GCSEs can start with a Basic Business Certificate, whereas A level holders can join at Diploma in Business Administration level. Graduates or holders of relevant professional qualifications are given direct entry to an 18-month Masters in Business Administration programme, which is run in association with Heriot-Watt University. Contact details p487.

Top Full-time Student Enrolment on First Degree Business and Administration Courses by Year

Source: UCAS

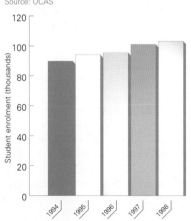

Interesting facts

- Nearly half a million people start a business in the UK each year

- Out of 14,110 directors surveyed in the UK, only 5,284 had any kind of qualification (1,778 had a university degree and 204 had an MBA)

- According to *Forbes* magazine, Bill Gates is the richest man in the world. His fortune is estimated at £60 billion

BUSINESS

DEGREE COURSES

University of Abertay Dundee
MBA

This full-time one-year course is aimed at prospective or existing managers who wish to further their career interests through a postgraduate degree. Students are encouraged to develop analytical and practical skills throughout the course that eventually help them to formulate and implement strategic change and innovation in a corporate environment. The course also provides students with a detailed understanding of the public and private sector organisations that make up the business environment, whilst developing their knowledge of international and ethical issues. A modular system allows students to take a group of core modules and one optional module per semester. Students are also able to take an additional language option. Courses include a class in research methods, which helps students prepare for their dissertations to be completed in the final stages of the course. Contact details p477.

Bournemouth University
BA (Hons) Advertising and Marketing Communication

This course covers the management of marketing communication with a particular focus on advertising. Many of the teaching staff have professional experience in marketing companies and large advertising agencies. Students spend six weeks in industrial placement within marketing, media and advertising companies such as Saatchi & Saatchi Advertising, Coca-Cola, and Gillette. Modules within the course include consumer behaviour, advertising and society, marketing planning, and persuasion and influence. In the most recent teaching quality assessment the School of Media Arts and Communication received a rating of 22.

Students are expected to conduct presentations, and to complete a dissertation. Graduates have gone on to find employment with companies such as Zenith, and advertising agencies such as SCRS and TBWA Simon Palmer. Contact details p478.

Bradford College
MA Marketing Practice

The MA covers marketing management, marketing communications, international marketing, and strategy marketing. It places marketing within an international context. The course aims to give students the skills to: analyse and understand marketing processes and practice; develop marketing skills and knowledge; improve potential effectiveness; and enhance career practice. The course is designed to accommodate candidates holding a good relevant degree or having appropriate work experience and professional qualifications. The course is a vocationally-oriented programme relevant for careers in a variety of public and private sector organisations. Contact details p478.

Brunel University
BSc (Hons) in Management Studies

The School of Business and Management, which is based on the Uxbridge and Osterley campuses of the university, offers single- and joint-honours programmes as well as several MSc courses, MPhil and PhD programmes, and the Brunel MBA. The BSc (Hons) in Management Studies aims to provide a business and management education to answer the demands of highly-qualified managers. An important feature of the management course at Brunel is that it allows students the scope to specialise in particular areas or maintain a more general approach. Courses can be taken in functions such as marketing, personnel and industrial relations. During a

management degree, options can be taken in foreign languages and there is the chance to spend some time abroad. In the final year of the course all students undertake a 15,000-word project that contributes to the degree classification. Contact details p478.

Cardiff University
MBA

The Cardiff Business School is one of the largest in Britain and received a 5 rating in the latest research assessment exercise. The MBA is a one-year course that leads to an international qualification. The course aims to provide training in the skills and knowledge relevant to a career in industry, commerce or the public sector. Students study core courses in: organisation and personnel; strategy and the environment; and information and control. Students then choose two elective courses of study from a set of options. The course is completed with a dissertation on a career-related project. The Cardiff MBA programme has an international perspective with pastoral care offered to all international students. Contact details p478.

University of Essex
BSc Business Management (with English)

Essex has offered degrees in accounting, finance and management for several years, but this new course is specifically aimed at international students, wishing to combine a reinforcement of language proficiency with a study of business management. Some students can proceed directly to the three-year study of management, finance, IT, accounting, marketing and related topics. The first two years of this are composed of compulsory courses in areas such as economic theory and policy, operations management, and financial reporting and analysis. The final year allows students to take options in areas such as strategic marketing, cultural aspects of management and managerial decision making. Many international high school leavers require a foundation year in English and study skills, which leads to a separate award of the Certificate of English for Academic Purposes. Contact details p480.

European School of Economics
International MBA

The International MBA takes 12 months for full-time participants and between 18 and 20 months for part-time students. The course is divided into five periods of study including core modules, elective modules and placement and project research work. Students specialise in the fourth term in one of the following areas: international marketing; finance and investment; art and heritage management; or fashion management. On the course, students are exposed to several methodologies of study including individual work, small discussion groups, conferences, seminars and traditional lectures. A number of international students follow the course and the school has links with many international companies. Contact details p480.

Greenwich School of Management
BSc (Hons) in Business Management and Information Technology

The Greenwich School of Management was founded in 1974 and is an affiliated college of The University of Hull. The undergraduate programmes at the school are accelerated courses that take two years to complete. Start dates are flexible and students can commence courses in February, June or October. The degree in business management and IT is split into three parts, each consisting of two semesters. In part one students study modules ranging from statistics and computing, C programming and systems analysis and design, to business organisation and policy, management and an introduction to accounting. Part two includes Visual Basic programming, telecommunications, database systems, organisational behaviour and marketing, whilst part three covers project management, corporate strategy, information systems and human resources management. Assessment is by examination at the end of each module, as well as course and project work. The school's library has a large study area, a range of books, periodicals and journals, as well as CD-ROM and Internet access. Contact details p480.

Greenwich University
International MBA
This course aims to provide a broad understanding of business which it combines with practical application. Core subject areas studied include marketing, leadership and team-building skills, operations management, international financial management, information technology in business, change management, strategic management, capital markets and creative problem solving. Much of the work involves problems currently being investigated by collaborating companies and, at the end of the programme, students conduct a consultancy exercise with one of these companies to demonstrate the skills they have learnt. Students also spend two weeks in Lille, France, studying with French students (the subject is taught in English) to provide additional cultural diversity. There are currently 15 international students on the course. Contact details p480.

Gyosei International College
BA Business Studies
This course is geared towards interna-

tional, non-British students and has a mix of international and British lecturers. 180 international students currently study the course which leads to both BA and licentiate qualifications. Core modules on the business course include computer studies, business concepts, quantitative methods, English for business and economics. The course lasts between three and four years, and includes a compulsory dissertation. Students benefit from links with Japanese and UK businesses, with trips, placements and project work. Each course takes place over a ten week term and includes an examination. Resits are possible where necessary. Contact details p480.

Heriot-Watt University
BA/MA/MSc Business and Finance
The undergraduate and postgraduate business and finance degrees at Heriot-Watt aim to provide students with the business, financial, and managerial skills to enable them to progress onto managerial roles within the manufacturing or services industries. Undergraduate business and finance degrees at the university share a common first year with other degrees offered at the School of Management. The modular structure of the course provides students with a flexibility and breadth of subject matter. Modules in accountancy, finance, management, economics and statistics are studied throughout the duration of the course. There is also a range of elective modules for students to choose from, according to their interests and career aspirations. With their combined theoretical and practical approach, these degree courses are intended to be relevant to today's world of business and commerce and allow students to attain relevant transferable skills. Contact details p481.

121

University of Hull
MBA General Management

There are 45 international students taking this course at present, which covers all aspects of management, including global marketing and international business, management of information technology and creative problem solving. Candidates should ideally hold a first degree from a recognised university, a postgraduate diploma or a suitable professional qualification. Applications, however, are welcomed from successful business people who do not hold the usual academic qualifications. Those individuals whose mother tongue is not English must provide evidence of their proficiency in the language. This course can also be followed on a part-time, distance-learning basis, which normally takes two years to complete. In this case, applicants should have a minimum of at least three year's work experience. Contact details p481.

King Alfred's College
BA (Hons) Business Administration

This course is designed as a one-year, full-time, top-up programme which builds on past experience gained on a course leading to an HND or its equivalent. In comparison to other BA degree courses it is a way of quickly achieving honours degree status. Students study a range of traditional business disciplines, including a range of modules such as platform for change, information systems for business, financial management, decision and control, and strategic management. Students are encouraged to confront and appraise their preconceptions and to carry out independently managed work programmes. Contact details p481.

Leeds Metropolitan University
Business and Management

The Leeds Metropolitan University (LMU) business and management courses are offered at higher national diploma, bachelor and postgraduate level. LMU's students are based in Leeds Business School, one of the largest business schools in Europe, which has links with business schools in many countries including Malaysia, India, China, Hong Kong and the USA. The school's academics come from a variety of professional backgrounds, for example management, economics, accounting, human resources, marketing and public relations. MBA students have the choice of starting their course in February or September. The course focuses on practical management skills and includes a work placement in a local company. Contact details p482.

London Guildhall University
BA (Hons) Business Studies

As an integrated sandwich course, this degree combines an academic grounding with a practical business training. After spending two years at the university, full-time students undertake an assessed one-year training period in industry or commerce. The university assists in arranging placements, and members of staff visit students to guide their progress during the placement. Students work full-time and are paid a salary. At the beginning of the fourth semester, students begin to specialise in an optional subject such as banking, corporate finance, human resources management, insurance, marketing, transport and distribution, or securities and commodities. Other courses available within the department include: BA (Hons) Business Administration and BA (Hons) European Business Studies, which includes a compulsory placement year abroad in a French, German or Spanish speaking environment. Contact details p482.

Loughborough University
Business
Loughborough University Business School received an Excellent rating in the 1994 teaching quality assessment. The school offers six undergraduate degree programmes, including BSc (Hons) programmes in accounting and financial management, banking and finance, and international business. The BSc International Business course, for example, lasts four years and prepares students for a career in management, including those careers which require fluency in a second language. French, German or Spanish are studied for the duration of the course and the international emphasis involves an examination of the cultural, political and economic structures in other countries which have a bearing on business operations. The third year is spent in a professional placement either in the UK or abroad. Contact details p482.

London School of Economics and Political Science, University of London (LSE)
BSc Management
This degree provides an opportunity for critical and theoretical study, and aims to give students a broad preparation for management drawing on the range of social science disciplines taught at LSE. BSc Management is a three-year course. In the first year, which provides a foundation for specialism in the second and third years, students take compulsory courses in economics, quantitative methods and industrial enterprise in comparative perspective. They also take one optional course. In the second and third years, students continue to take some compulsory courses in management, accountancy and finance and economics, but also options in areas covering the international context, public and voluntary sector management, and human and organisational aspects of management. The school is a member of the Community of European Management Schools (CEMS) which offers students the opportunity to gain an additional qualification (the CEMS Master). To do this, students undertake a period of study and work in another member country. They must also demonstrate fluency in three languages. Contact details p482.

University of Luton
MBA International Business
The course focuses on strategic areas of marketing and finance, as well as the way international trading relations develop. Assessment of the programme involves a variety of methods, including formal examinations and coursework components. The most significant element in the overall assessment of the programme is the dissertation, which involves an in-depth study of a problem or issue of interest to business or management. It will often be based upon a particular organisation or business sector. A student may undertake a dissertation some distance from Luton, providing a number of conditions are met concerning access and ongoing contact. Students wishing to pursue a dissertation with an international dimension are welcome. Applicants will need to have experience in a managerial or administrative role. Contact details p483.

Middlesex University
BA Marketing
This course is designed for students who wish to follow a professional career in marketing. The modules that make up the programme are designed to develop

skills that will help you in today's competitive marketing environment. They include quantitative methods for business, organisational behaviour, strategic marketing, advertising and sales promotion. You may choose the three-year course or the four-year programme with its placement year. The Business School at the university is the only business school that offers successful students the Chartered Institute of Marketing Advanced Certificate in Marketing. Contact details p483.

Napier University
Master of Business Administration

The MBA can be divided into three distinct parts. Stage one involves financial analysis, data analysis, human resource management, marketing management, operations management and managerial economics. Stage two brings students on to the study of corporate strategy, finance, marketing management, human resource management, operations management and research methods. A group project must also be completed. Stage three concerns themes and issues in strategic management plus two electives from: marketing communications strategy; international business; public sector management; innovation and new venture creation; world-class operations; strategic financial management; growth venture management; and human resource management. Electives offered are dependent on minimum numbers. The programme also includes a final dissertation that will normally be concerned with an investigation of management and strategic issues which are of significance and interest to the participant's organisation. Contact details p483.

University of North London
MA/PgDip International Public Administration

This course is an intensive, applied policy and public management-oriented programme intended for graduates who are working, or intending to pursue careers, in public administration. The overall aim of the course is to equip public service practitioners with the skills and understanding to become administrators and managers who can be innovative and implement change in their home environment. It is also intended for students from outside of the UK; the course runs in six cities across the world, so overseas internships are organised as part of the programme. The work placement could be within a London-based public service organisation. Scholarships are available. At present there are 100 international students on the course. Contact details p483.

Oxford Brookes University
MSc International Management

In 1998/9, there were 46 international students on this course designed mainly for recent graduates wishing to pursue a career in international organisations. The philosophy of the course is based upon the belief that managers at all levels in organisations need an awareness and understanding of the integrative nature of global business. The course, now in its fourth year, provides students with an opportunity not only to gain knowledge of the theory and concepts of international business and management, but also to gain interpersonal skills through group and team issues. There are three core modules: one explores the global environment, including ecological issues; a second includes an investigation of setting up companies overseas; and the third introduces the skills essential for career development in a hands-on manner. Running alongside the core modules is a research methodology course which helps prepare students for their final 20,000 word project. Teaching takes place in groups of approximately 25. Contact details p484.

LONDON
CITY COLLEGE

London City College (LCC) is an international college recognised by the **British Accreditation Council** (BAC) offering the following prestigious qualifications, in association with **Leicester University**.

- **MASTER OF BUSINESS ADMINISTRATION (MBA)**
- **MBA (MARKETING)**
- **MBA (MARITIME MANAGEMENT)**
- **MBA (FINANCE)**
- **GRADUATE DIPLOMA IN MANAGEMENT**

OTHER COURSES OFFERED: MARKETING • SHIPPING AND TRANSPORT • IMPORT AND EXPORT • HOTEL AND CATERING • TRAVEL AND TOURISM • BUSINESS ADMINISTRATION • INTERNATIONAL BUSINESS • ADVERTISING AND PUBLIC RELATIONS • ACCESS COURSES • ENGLISH LANGUAGE COURSES • PSYCHOTHERAPY AND COUNSELLING.

Courses start in September, October, January and June. For a prospectus contact:

Admissions Director, London City College
51/55 Waterloo Road, London SE1 8TX.
Tel: 020 7928 0901/0938/0029
Fax: 020 7401 2231
E-mail: lcclist@aol.com

University of Portsmouth
BA (Hons) in Business Administration

Between 20 and 30 international students are currently studying for a BA (Hons) in Business Administration at the university's business school. The course includes areas such as accounting, statistics, business information systems, economics, law and quantitative methods. The business school has expanding local, national and international links that can often benefit students. Modules can be taken in travel and tourism or international business and marketing. There is an optional project in the final year of this course. Contact details p484.

University of Salford
Master of Business
Administration (MBA)

The Salford MBA is divided into three areas. Foundation subjects include economics, finance/accounting, information technology and marketing. The core courses are strategy, management

decision making and international business. There are electives in human resource management and development, multinational finance, manufacturing and automation, intelligent knowledge-based systems and engineering. The course has an international emphasis with aspects of business activity such as international business, international marketing and international accounting. The course was launched in 1984. The Graduate School of Managements now runs nine separate, yet integrated, degree courses which have attracted students from over 80 countries. There are currently more than 25 international students on the MBA. Contact details p485.

South Bank University
MSc International Business

This course focuses on the complex and changing character of international business in the modern world. The aim of the course is to develop students' knowledge, analytical awareness and critical understanding of international business. However, it is anticipated that students will also gain skills that will enhance their effectiveness in employment. An important element of the course is that it will enable students to gain an understanding of major global trends and strategic decision-making within international companies. The major issues created by the growth of international business for developed and developing countries are explored at regional and global levels. Thus students learn to analyse trade policy, industrial policy, regional policy, taxation policy and exchange rate policy. Contact details p486.

Southampton Institute
BA (Hons) International Business

The Business School at Southampton Institute has recently been formed following the merger of the Business Management and Business Finance Faculties. It has a number of undergraduate and postgraduate courses supported by a team of 100 full-time academics and about 80 part-time staff. There are currently around 3,200 full-time students. On the BA degree in International Business, students study areas such as economics, quantitative methods, language, information systems, marketing, European business, financial decision making, strategic management, global marketing strategy, international human resource management and international accounting and finance. Students also study a foreign language and spend one semester of their second year studying abroad at a higher education establishment in Spain, Germany, France, Italy, Finland, USA or Canada. Contact details p486.

University of St Andrews
Department of Management

The Department of Management offers degrees that can be combined with a variety of arts and science subjects giving greater flexibility. The courses aim to develop critically-thinking individuals with a strong multidisciplinary, multicultural approach to management. The first level programme of study covers economic, political, social and technological aspects of organisations within the business world. Students choose optional modules from a selection that includes employee relations, teamworking theory and practice, alliances and networks, health economics and managerial economics. Contact details p485.

University of Stirling
MSc Marketing

The programme is a 12-month course comprising taught units and a dissertation. The taught units are delivered using lectures, case studies, and small group and individual projects. Subjects covered include contemporary issues in marketing, research techniques and applications, and professional skills in marketing. Options can be taken in areas such as international marketing, logistics and channel management, and retail buying and merchandising. Currently there are 45 international students on the programme. Graduates of the course have gone on to work in internationally-based companies operating in product management, market research, media planning, and account management and the public services. Contact details p486.

University of Sunderland
BA Business Administration

This is a broad-based degree programme that offers students the opportunity to study a wide range of business disciplines. The first and second years cover all the essential components required for a career in business, whilst the final year offers the chance for students to specialise in areas such as marketing, human resource management, finance and legal studies. Business is one of the most transferable subjects one can study at university. The principles of business are the same all over the world, and this programme is offered with an international perspective. Students gather both knowledge and transferable personal and business skills throughout the course, through a mixture of lectures, seminars, tutorials and practical work. In years one and two, students run their own business, and in the final year undertake a project with a company where they research an active business problem and make appropriate recommendations. There are currently 50 international students on this course. Contact details p486.

University of Teesside
School of Business and Management

The school offers a wide range of modular courses at both undergraduate and postgraduate level. Courses include undergraduate degrees in marketing, business studies, international business studies, accounting and finance, human resource management and leisure management. Postgraduate courses available include MSc Management Studies and MA Human Resource Management. All courses are underpinned by the development of relevant theoretical knowledge while the opportunity to undertake projects with businesses gives courses a practical emphasis. Through an international exchange programme the school offers the opportunity to experience a different culture and way of learning. International students particularly enjoy the opportunity to participate in a wide range of learning activities. The school has recently benefited from a complete refurbishment and boasts up-to-date facilities for study including three high-specification IT laboratories running

the latest hardware and software. Contact details p486.

University of the West of England
BA (Hons) Business Administration, Bristol Business School

The three-year, full-time undergraduate degree provides students with a comprehensive business education, in which they have the opportunity to analyse and evaluate business organisations and understand the way in which they operate. Students study the key business functional areas of accounting, finance, employee relations, marketing and operational management. The programme has a dedicated international administrator and many of the modules have an international bias. The Bristol Business School has links to many EU institutions, through the Socrates scheme, giving a multicultural mix of students. Contact details p487.

University of Wales Institute, Cardiff
MBA

This is an internationally-recognised qualification for senior management. Students are prepared for leadership in the international marketplace. This MBA programme concentrates on four core business management modules, with two optional modules in areas such as international marketing or finance management. A module on self-development runs throughout the course, and involves a residential weekend to help students develop an understanding of their own learning needs. There is also a specialist dissertation that enables students to concentrate on a particular area of interest. The course is designed for students to work closely with their tutors in small groups. There is considerable choice and guidance on specialist option modules, dissertation topics, and commercial or industrial placements for research. Assessment is by examinations, coursework and dissertation at the end of the year. There are currently 28 international students on this course. Contact details p478.

University of Wales, Bangor
School of Accounting, Banking and Economics

The School of Accounting, Banking and Economics offers courses in business and financial studies at both undergraduate and postgraduate level. The multidisciplinary nature of the school ensures that students have the opportunity to study a broad range of business subjects, with lecturers who are active researchers within their field, including accounting, banking, finance, economics, management and marketing. All single honours students follow the same core modules in their first year, which enables them to experience many business subjects before making a final commitment to their main degree specialism. The school aims to place emphasis on friendly and informal relationships between staff and students. Courses at the school can be studied at undergraduate level. There is the possibility of progression to an MA, MPhil or PhD on completion of this course. International students currently make up about 30 per cent of the school's numbers. For more information visit the school's website at www.bangor.ac.uk/ab/sabe.htm/ Contact details p477.

BUSINESS

128

Classics and Ancient History

classics
classics
classics
classics

Students following classics and ancient history courses study the classical civilisations of Greece and Rome. Some also learn the ancient languages of Greek and Latin. This discipline was, until relatively recently, a necessity for the educated person. George Bernard Shaw once wrote that knowledge of Greek "stamped a man at once as an educated gentleman". Although the subjects that make up classics and ancient history are no longer a compulsory part of British school curriculums, they remain valuable and respected humanities, and thrive in British universities.

The Greco-Roman past ran from before the year zero (BC) to the fall of the Roman Empire in 476 AD. The Romans invaded Britain twice with Julius Caesar in 55 BC and then again in 43 AD. This period's cultural and linguistic influences still touch life today. Roman numerals, ruins and roads, for example, can be detected throughout Europe and classical authors, such as Aristotle and Homer, are still familiar names in academia. Latin served for 1,000 years as the principle means of writing in the British Isles and is the language of St Bede, the Domesday Book and the Magna Carta. The terminology of Latin and Greek still features in science and mathematics today. The Greek and Roman empires were so far reaching geographically that classical culture continues to provide a common heritage shared by people from Ireland to the Balkans.

The classics can be divided into the two cultures, Greek and Roman, and there are four main areas of study: literature, history, philosophy and language. These components are combined at universities and provide a host of courses: BA (Hons) in Classics, Latin, Classical Studies and Ancient History to name just a few. What's more, these subjects lend themselves to joint honours degrees and are often studied with philosophy, th ology, modern history or archaeology. Single honours classics degree courses are typically based on Latin and/or Greek literature and language. Modules such as Greek language, Latin poetry of love, Greek tragedy, and Greek and Latin textual criticism are often offered. On the other hand, courses entitled classical civilisations or ancient history study the whole Greco-Roman achievement. This can include study of the thought, religion and culture of these civilisations. Most ancient history or classics courses culminate in a dissertation where students are able to focus on an area that particularly interests them.

Prospective students for any classics or ancient history course should be able to demonstrate a broad interest in the field. Most university departments allow some flexibility so that a student following a single honours Latin course could opt for some ancient history modules. Similarly students studying ancient history may want, or be required, to take up Greek and Latin. Most British universities will teach beginners in these languages if they can show an aptitude for learning languages.

DEGREE COURSES

University of Birmingham
BA (Hons) in Classical Literature and Civilisation

The Classics Department at the University of Birmingham focuses on development through challenging courses centred on the literature and the culture (rather than the history) of antiquity. Immediately on arrival students are introduced to teamwork and the practical use of the Internet as a first step in developing effective skills. Single honours students take a four-week study tour, visiting Greece and Italy, with financial support from the university. They must study Latin or Greek in their first two years, normally from beginners' level and they also usually study another subject outside Classics (as one-sixth of their work). Joint honours students benefit from the literary and cultural core with provision for advanced option courses in such subjects as mythology, philosophy and film. They are not required to study Latin and Greek. The BA (Hons) in Classical Literature and Civilisation may be combined with English, music, history of art, Italian, philosophy and many other subjects. Contact details p477.

University of Newcastle upon Tyne
MA Museum Studies

The curriculum covers study of the museum past, present and future. As part of the course students examine subjects such as museum and collections management, personnel, finance, museums education, services, and marketing and museum communication. It is possible to specialise in a particular area such as art, education, natural sciences, archaeology, social history, interpretation or management. These are taught through hands-on work with collections, an extended placement in a museum or gallery and individual research for presentation as a dissertation. International students might be attracted to the course for a number of reasons. The course includes both theory and

The 10 Longest Standing Roman Emperors from 31 BC to 200 AD
Source: www.ghgcorp.com

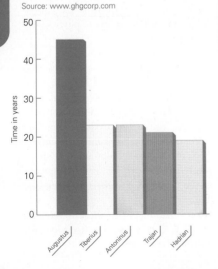

Interesting facts

- The ancient Olympic Games began in the year 776 BC, when Koroibos, a cook from the nearby city of Elis, won the stadium race, a foot race 600 feet long

- Aristotle wrote accounts of the constitutions of 158 Greek states

- The Colosseum in Rome, home to the fights of the Gladiators, could hold up to 50,000 spectators

- A crooked nose was a sign of leadership among the ancient Romans

practice and is taught by practising museum curators as well as by academic staff. It can be completed in one year. One recent graduate returned to America to work for the National Parks Service at the Golden Gate Park in San Francisco, whilst another has recently become Head of Education with the Irish Heritage Service. Contact details p483.

University of Wales, Lampeter

Classical Studies

Greek and Latin are at the heart of British and European culture. In Part one of the course, the modules are: myth and literature, life and livelihood in ancient Athens, aspects of love, Augustus and the Roman world, beginner's Latin or beginner's Greek. Modules are usually taught in small classes to give opportunity for discussion. In the final year there is a research project of the student's choice. In Part two, the choice of modules includes: the epic, satire, tragedy, Greek and Roman architecture, Greek anthropology, historians of imperial Rome, Alexander the Great, the later Roman empire, Roman Egypt, Justinian and the sixth century, ancient technology, ancient civilisations of Asia Minor and Sparta. There is a summer workshop in Greek and Latin, attended by people from all over the world. Contact details p481.

TEACHING QUALITY ASSESSMENTS

Classics and Ancient History
(Wales 1997/98)

Institution	Grade	Institution	Grade
Lampeter	Excellent	Swansea	Excellent

Source: HEFCE, SHEFC, HEFCW latest available ratings
For a more complete list of institutions offering these courses at undergraduate level refer to the Course Directory

RESEARCH RANKINGS

Classics, Ancient History, Byzantine and Modern Greek Studies

Institution	Grade	Institution	Grade
Cambridge	5*	Leeds	4
Institute of Classical Studies	5*	Liverpool	4
King's College	5*	Manchester	4
Oxford	5*	Newcastle upon Tyne	4
UCL	5*	Swansea	4
Birmingham (Byzantine, Ottoman and Modern Greek Studies)	5	Warwick	4
		Keele	3a
Bristol	5	Nottingham	3a
Exeter	5	Open University	3a
Reading	5	Queen's Belfast	3a
Royal Holloway	5	Birmingham (Classics and Ancient History)	3b
St Andrews	5	Kent at Canterbury	3b
Durham	4	Lampeter	3b
Edinburgh	4	St Mary's College	2
Glasgow	4		

source: RAE 1996

CLASSICS

Drama and Dance

drama and dance
drama and dance
drama and dance
drama and dance

From The National Theatre on London's South Bank, to the popular musicals of the West End, British drama and dance is known and respected all over the world. With great British exports such as Shakespeare, Charlie Chaplin and Dame Margot Fonteyn, it would hard to find a better place to study drama and dance than in the UK. Rich in culture, rich in history and often daring and experimental, the British theatre has become a melting pot of new ideas and old traditions. On one hand, there are the ballerinas at the Royal Opera House performing classics such as Tchaikovsky's Swan Lake, and on the other there is the dance troop "Stomp" storming through the world with rhythmical routines involving dustbin lids.

For aspiring actors, there are two types of places to study drama in Britain: at university, where you will get a broader academic qualification, or at a school, where you will be trained in a more practical environment for work as a professional actor.

Certain British drama schools are considered to be of undisputed excellence, with long traditions in the performing arts. The Royal Academy of Dramatic Art (RADA), the Central School of Speech and Drama, the Guildhall School of Music and Drama, to name but a few. There are hundreds of drama schools throughout the UK, catering for students at all levels. The Conference of Drama Schools, available on the Internet, and the National Council of Drama Training (NCDT) provide a list of approved courses. Entrance to drama school is by audition, based on your talent and potential. Drama schools aim to train their students in performance and to equip them with the skills they need to work professionally in acting. The practical aspects of working in the entertainment industry, such as dealing with agents and film administration, are also covered. In performance studies, students are taught about several styles of theatre, including Greek, Shakespearean, Restoration and 20th century.

A drama or theatre studies degree, with its more academic approach, will also include such areas as the history of theatre, playwrights and the history of directing. The main thing to remember is that courses vary considerably from university to university. If you are interested in oriental theatre, for example, the Middlesex University course has elements like Kabuki and Peking Opera.

Study in dance can also take place either at universities or, more commonly, at specialist schools. At universities, courses sometimes combine music, drama and dance or include a dance module in a drama course, as with Royal Holloway's drama degree. Alternatively, some universities, for example the University of Surrey, and the more specialist dance schools focus exclusively on dance. Gaining a qualification in dance may lead to a professional career with a dance company, or it may take you into such areas as dance therapy, community dance, or even into acting.

TEACHING QUALITY ASSESSMENTS

Dance, Drama and Cinematics
(England and N Ireland 1997/98)

Institution	Grade	Institution	Grade
Hull	24	Liverpool Community College	21
Kent at Canterbury	24	East Anglia	21
Lancaster	24	Liverpool John Moores	21
Reading	24	Manchester	21
Warwick	24	Queen Mary and Westfield	21
Bristol	23	Roehampton Institute	21
Brunel	23	Salford	21
Central School of Speech and Drama	23	Southampton Institute	21
Dartington College	23	University College Chichester	21
Loughborough	23	North Riding College	20
Manchester Metropolitan	23	Rose Bruford College	20
Northern School of Contemporary Dance	23	St Mary's College	20
Royal Holloway	23	Surrey	20
Bournemouth	22	East London	19
Bretton Hall	22	King Alfred's College	19
Canterbury Christ Church	22	Liverpool Hope College	19
De Montfort	22	St Martin's College	19
Exeter	22	Sheffield Hallam	19
Goldsmiths	22	Wolverhampton	19
Leeds Metropolitan	22	Derby	18
Middlesex	22	Suffolk College	18
Newcastle College	22	Chester College	17
North London	22	Huddersfield	17
Northumbria at Newcastle	22	City College Manchester	16
Ulster	22	Hertfordshire	15
Birmingham	21	Edge Hill College	14

Drama
(Scotland 1998)

Institution	Grade	Institution	Grade
Glasgow	Highly Satisfactory	Royal Scottish Academy of Music and Drama	Highly Satisfactory
Queen Margaret University College	Highly Satisfactory		

Drama
(Wales 1994/95)

Institution	Grade	Institution	Grade
Welsh College of Music and Drama	Satisfactory		

DRAMA COURSES

Goldsmiths, University of London
BA (Hons) Drama and Theatre Arts

The drama and theatre arts degree offers the opportunity to explore the theory and practice of performance, as it is produced in a range of media. Students on the programme are led through a range of material including: basic technical skills; the physical investigation of, and reflection upon, modes of performance; close analysis of performance and written text; study of the intercultural history of the theatre; an understanding of how performance affects audiences; and an ability to define what performance actually is. In addition to this broad knowledge, students are given a chance to specialise in both study and production of a piece of physical theatre. This could be in areas such as community theatre, radio drama or theatre administration. The department has working relationships with theatre companies, media organisations, and professional specialists and practitioners and seeks to keep its students in contact with the latest work in the theatre as it happens in London. Contact details p480.

University of Hull
Drama

The Department of Drama at the University of Hull has good practical facilities. The department offers a wide range of academic and practical options, enabling joint honours students to choose modules from American studies, theology, music and a variety of languages. The selection process varies according to the type of degree. Singles honours students are invited for a whole or half-day interview; selected candidates will then participate in a practical seminar/interview. Joint honours candidates are expected to attend an open day. The usual workload in the first semester consists of eight to 10 contact hours a week, a concentrated practical week, open-ended intense practical work for two to six weeks, two essays and a two-hour exam. Course assessment is based on a modular system of credits. Credits are gained through a variety of means such as assignments, exams, a dissertation and a practical portfolio. The department has an extensive list of famous alumni including TV presenter Juliet Morris, actor Malcolm Sinclair and author/director Bob Carlton. Contact details p481.

University of Kent at Canterbury
Drama

Single honours drama offers an intensive approach to all aspects of the subject, both academic and practical, on a roughly 50:50 basis. It is unique in being a four-year course with the final year devoted entirely to a practical group project in an area of the student's choice. Drama achieved full marks (24/24) in the recent teaching quality assessment exercise, with positive feedback from current students. The joint honours in drama, whilst not neglecting the practical side, focuses primarily on an academic approach. The BA (Hons) in Visual and Performed Arts provides an opportunity to combine the study of drama with that of art history. The drama department at the University of Kent at Canterbury is able to count comedian Alan Davies and actor Ramon Tikaram amongst their recent graduates. Contact details p481.

King Alfred's College
MA Theatre for Development

This one-year, full-time postgraduate degree integrates community drama and theatre practices with development studies. It offers frameworks of communication through which specific groups and communities can further their self-development. Curriculum modules include research methodology, issues in development, integrated workshops in theatre for development, and a major practical project. This project is run by students in the field either in the UK or overseas. Students write a 15,000 word dissertation under supervision on a topic of their choice. The course will be of interest to students who aspire to careers in community theatre, non-government organisations or community development. Contact details p481.

Top Five Highest-Grossing Films of All Time

Source: "*The Top 10 of Everything: 2000*" Russell Ash, Dorling Kindersley 1999

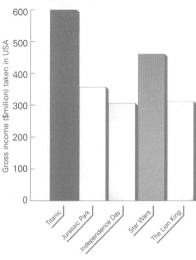

Interesting facts

- The Academy Awards were first held in 1929 with fewer that 250 people attending

- The longest-running musical in the UK is *Cats* by Andrew Lloyd Webber, which has been showing since 1981

- The Shakespeare play to have been produced the most in the UK is *Twelfth Night*

Rose Bruford College

BA (Hons) Theatre Design

The course covers theatre design (set and costume), theatre studies (play analysis), costume history, theatre styles and genres, theatre history, skills classes (model making, technical drawing, life and costume drawing), and involves a placement in a professional theatre company giving students contacts and experience in the world of theatre. In addition, the college's numerous shows offer students the chance of practical experience. Each student has his, or her, own individual studio space. Contact details p484.

DANCE COURSES

The Royal Academy of Dancing

The Routemaster Programme

The Royal Academy of Dancing, which incorporates the Benesh Institute, offers a comprehensive package of education and training programmes. These diplomas and degrees include a Diploma in Classical Ballet Teaching; a BA (Hons) in Classical Ballet Teaching; a BA (Hons) in the Art and Teaching of Ballet; BPhil (Hons) in Ballet and Contextual Studies; Diploma in Classical Ballet Teaching for Professional Dancers; Diploma in Benesh Movement Notation; and a BA (Hons) in Benesh Movement Notation. The academy headquarters is conveniently located in a courtyard setting by the River Thames in Battersea. There are local shops, restaurants and the famous Kings Road nearby. Contact details p485.

The Royal Ballet School, London

Pupils at this famous performing arts school, are predominantly from the UK, though about 30 per cent are international. The RBS is composed of two campuses, the Lower School is for 11 to 16 year olds and the Upper School, based in Barons Court, is for students aged 16 and over. Famous past members of the RBS include Darcey Bussell and Dame Margot Fonteyn. In the Upper School students can study subjects such as classical ballet, contemporary dance and teaching. The RBS also runs summer schools. Candidates should possess a good standard of English at comprehension level as classes are all conducted in English. Accommodation is arranged for students at the Upper School. Entry to the school is based on talent and potential. All candidates are auditioned providing they meet the minimum standard requirement. The school states that no applicant should be deterred by a lack of financial means. Contact details p485.

University of Surrey Roehampton

The University of Surrey Roehampton, situated in southwest London, has courses suitable for those students who wish to enter the performing arts, including those people who do not wish to commit themselves to a specific area of study. Approximately 15 to 20 international students (mainly from Japan, USA, Norway and South Korea) attend these courses and are guaranteed on-campus accommodation if they wish. The undergraduate degrees on offer include a BA in Dance Studies (single or combined honours) and a BA

in Drama and Theatre Studies, Dance, Music and MA/Graduate Diplomas in Ballet Studies, Dance Movement Therapy, Drama Therapy and Music Therapy. Fees for international students attending these programmes vary accordingly to the programme chosen, and all programmes offer a valuable balance between theory and practice. An English language level of TOEFL 550, IELTS 6.0 or equivalent is required, and for students who have still to reach this level the institute can offer a range of foundation programmes including the popular English for academic purposes programme. This enables students to improve their English language skills whilst spending some time on the academic programme they wish to follow. Contact details p486.

oncourse·co·uk
The ultimate guide to courses

RESEARCH RANKINGS

Dance and Performing arts

Institution	Grade	Institution	Grade
Royal Holloway	5*	De Montfort	3b
Warwick	5	East Anglia	3b
Birmingham	4	Manchester Metropolitan	3b
Bristol	4	Ulster	3b
Exeter	4	Worcester College	3b
Glasgow	4	Bournemouth	2
Goldsmiths	4	Bretton Hall	2
Hull	4	Central School of Speech and Drama	2
Kent at Canterbury	4	Dartington College	2
Lancaster	4	Huddersfield	2
Manchester	4	Liverpool John Moores	2
Reading	4	London Institute	2
Roehampton Institute (Dance)	4	Middlesex	2
Surrey	4	Queen Margaret University College	2
Aberystwyth	3a	Salford College	2
City	3a	St Martin's College	2
Loughborough	3a	Chester College	1
Nottingham Trent	3a	Ripon and York St John	1
Roehampton Institute (Drama and Music)	3a	Coventry	1
University College Chichester	3a	North Riding College	1
Brunel	3b	Northumbria at Newcastle	1

source: RAE 1996

Economics, Sociology and Development

Economics and sociology are two of the pillars of social science. Studying either subject will bring you into contact with principles and theories from Marx to Keynes via Weber. In both subjects, theories are studied alongside what happens in practice within society or the economy.

Economics

The basis of economics is that human wants are insatiable whilst resources are scarce. Economists are fascinated with the mechanisms, such as price, that solve this problem and distribute resources. This fundamental problem takes them into the realms of inflation, taxation, interest rates and unemployment. Economics degrees can pave the way into finance, accountancy, industry or the public sector.

Britain was home to the most famous economist of them all, John Maynard Keynes, and steeped in such tradition, is a good place to study the subject. It has some of the world's centres of economic study including Oxford University and The London School of Economics and Political Science.

To start on an undergraduate economics course, it is not always essential to have previous economics qualifications. However, entrance requirements will often stipulate a level of mathematical knowledge and that the student has an interest in numeracy and computing.

Sociology and Social Work

Early sociologists, such as Max Weber, introduced scientific methodology to the study of both society and the individuals within it. This involves gathering, analysing and presenting data, statistics and information; formulating theories and modules; and checking such theories against more statistics and information. Sociology is often linked with cultural studies, courses examining aspects such as ethnicity, gender, the family and the media.

Sociology has an interdisciplinary nature and can be combined with economics, history, anthropology or psychology. Courses can lead to either BA or BSc degrees.

Social work is both academic and vocational (in contrast to sociology, which is primarily academic). It is about working in the community and supporting people within the UK social services system. International students should be aware that situations and government policies in the UK might differ from those in their home country. A Diploma in Social Work is recognised for entry into the UK profession, although courses can be taken that provide more advanced qualifications.

Development Studies

Development studies, a relatively new degree subject offered by about ten universities, involves tracing developing countries. Courses look at the experiences, institutions, social processes and strategies of developing countries, and their relationships with one another and with developed countries.

Few institutions offer straight, single honours degree in development studies. It is typically combined with international relations, peace studies, geography, economics or sociology.

TEACHING QUALITY ASSESSMENTS

Economics
(Scotland 1993)

Institution	Grade	Institution	Grade
Aberdeen	Excellent	Glasgow	Satisfactory
Dundee Institute of Technology	Excellent	Heriot-Watt	Satisfactory
St Andrews	Excellent	Napier	Satisfactory
Stirling	Excellent	Paisley	Satisfactory
Dundee	Satisfactory	Strathclyde	Satisfactory
Edinburgh	Satisfactory		

Economics
(Wales 1997/97)

Institution	Grade	Institution	Grade
Aberystwyth	Excellent	Bangor (Economics and Financial and Management Studies)	Satisfactory
Cardiff	Satisfactory		
Swansea	Satisfactory		

Social Policy and Administration
(England and N ireland 1994/95)

Institution	Grade	Institution	Grade
Bath	Excellent	Open University	Excellent
Brunel	Excellent	Sheffield	Excellent
Edge Hill College	Excellent	Ulster	Excellent
Hull	Excellent	York	Excellent
Kent at Canterbury	Excellent	Birmingham	Satisfactory
Lancaster	Excellent	De Montfort	Satisfactory
London Guildhall	Excellent	East London	Satisfactory
LSE	Excellent	Leeds Metropolitan	Satisfactory
Manchester	Excellent	Luton	Satisfactory
Newcastle upon Tyne	Excellent	North London	Satisfactory

Social Policy and Administration
(Scotland 1997/98)

Institution	Grade	Institution	Grade
Edinburgh	Excellent	Glasgow	Excellent

Source: HEFCE, SHEFC, HEFCW latest available ratings
For a more complete list of institutions offering these courses at undergraduate level refer to the Course Directory

DEGREE COURSES

University of Bath
BSc (Hons) Economics and International Development

This course aims to train students who wish to follow careers related to international development, in government, the private sector, international organisations or non-governmental organisations. Students will acquire an interdisciplinary understanding of the recent development of the world economy, and an ability to use appropriate techniques to analyse specific problems. The course content includes economic theory, politics, development economics, international relations, international trade and finance, quantitative methods and languages. A particular attraction of the course is the opportunity to do a relevant 12-month placement in the third year, which will allow for an appreciation and application of economics to the practice of international development. Most placements will be with organisations either in the UK or overseas, which offer an opportunity of work experience in a developing country context. Contact details p477.

The University of Birmingham
BA (Hons) in Sociology

The sociology programme at the University of Birmingham has three distinctive features. Firstly, the version of sociology that they teach reflects their location within the Department of Cultural Studies. The department was ranked first in a survey of British universities in The Guardian, October 1999. Throughout the degree they engage with the growing importance of cultural form and practices in contemporary life. Secondly, the department's presence in the city of Birmingham influences their teaching. The changes underway in Birmingham exemplify many of the key issues of the degree: economic restructuring, urban regeneration, multiculturalism, and the influence of global forces on localities. Birmingham is thus an ideal city in which to study sociology. Thirdly the department places emphasis on the cultivation of research skills. Students' degrees culminate in a dissertation on a topic of their choice. All the staff in the department are active researchers and through their teaching impart both the substance of their work and the skills that independent research requires. Contact details p477.

University of Bristol
BSc Economics and Accounting

First- and second-year students on this course study core subjects in microeconomics and macroeconomics and take units in quantitative methods (mathematics, statistics and econometrics). Options are available in the final year and students may also take language modules.

The economics department places emphasis on the practical application of statistics and offers extensive experience in the use of computers. Economics and accounting is deemed a "relevant" degree by professional accounting bodies exempting students from the foundation stage of major UK professional accountancy bodies. There are number of combined degrees available including a BSc in Economics and Accounting with Law. Research in the department covers such areas as privatisation and regulation, the structure of financial markets and managerial information systems. The department has its own website: www.ecn.bris.ac.uk Contact details p478.

Brunel University
Economics and Business Finance

Brunel's courses are largely based on the semester pattern and students progress

ECONOMICS

Top 5 Countries with the Most Workers

Source: "*The Top 10 of Everything: 2000*" Russell Ash, Dorling Kindersley 1999

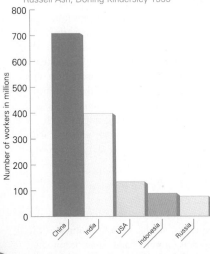

ECONOMICS

through three levels of study each lasting for two semesters. The various economics and finance courses at Brunel cater for many student interests and aptitudes. Economics and business finance is the most popular programme and caters for those aiming to enter the financial service sector. The integrated sandwich degree course combines taught principles with experience and practice. Each side of this type of course helps support the other and, given that work placements are often paid, it can be of significant financial benefit.

Teaching in this department combines lectures, workshops, seminar groups, written tests and assignments. Students receive instructions in presentation skills and are given the opportunity to develop these skills through seminars. There are currently 50 international students in this department. Contact details p478.

City College Manchester
Economic and Social Studies Foundation

In conjunction with the three universities in Manchester, this one-year foundation course is aimed at international students wishing to progress onto a first degree in economic and social science subjects. The programme includes subjects such as economics, government and politics, mathematics, information technology and English support. Students who successfully complete the course are offered a place on a degree course at one of the linked universities. Degree courses available for those who pass include sociology, econometrics, accounting and finance and anthropology. Assessment is by coursework, class tests and end of unit tests. Facilities at the college include a learning resource centre with an IT centre and a well-stocked library.

There is also a Fast Track foundation course of 30 hours a week. The course starts in January each year and is available to students who cannot begin the one-year course in September. As with the one-year foundation course, it aims to fill the gap in knowledge and skills between the student's home country and the entry requirements for university in the UK.

TEACHING QUALITY ASSESSMENTS

Sociology
(England and N Ireland 1996)

Institution	Grade	Institution	Grade
Birmingham	24	Portsmouth	20
Open University	24	Roehampton Institute	20
Sussex	24	Salford	20
Greenwich	23	St Mary's College	20
York	23	Trinity and All Saints	20
Bath Spa	22	University College Northampton	20
Brunel	22	Wolverhampton	20
College of St Mark and St John	22	Bath	19
Essex	22	City	19
Keele	22	East London	19
Liverpool Hope College	22	Leicester	19
Reading	22	Nottingham Trent	19
Thames Valley	22	South Bank	19
Bristol	21	Southampton Institute	19
Exeter	21	Teesside	19
Goldsmiths	21	Central Lancashire	18
Kent at Canterbury	21	Derby	18
Kingston	21	La Sainte Union College	18
Lancaster	21	Liverpool John Moores	18
Liverpool	21	Luton	18
Manchester	21	UCE	18
Manchester Metropolitan	21	Bradford	17
Oxford Brookes	21	Ripon and York St John	17
Sunderland	21	De Montfort	17
Surrey	21	London Guildhall	17
Worcester College	21	Staffordshire	17
Anglia Polytechnic	20	Ulster	17
Cheltenham and Gloucester College	20	Buckinghamshire College	16
LSE	20	East Anglia	16
Northumbria at Newcastle	20	Lincolnshire and Humberside	16
Plymouth	20		

Sociology and Social Policy
(Wales 1994/95)

Institution	Grade	Institution	Grade
Bangor	Satisfactory	Swansea	Satisfactory
Cardiff	Satisfactory		

Social Work
(Scotland 1995/96)

Institution	Grade	Institution	Grade
Edinburgh	Excellent	Paisley	Highly satisfactory
Dundee	Highly satisfactory	Robert Gordon	Highly satisfactory
Glasgow	Highly satisfactory	Stirling	Highly satisfactory
Glasgow Caledonian	Highly satisfactory	Strathclyde	Highly satisfactory
Northern College of Education	Highly satisfactory	Moray House Institute	Satisfactory

Source: HEFCE, SHEFC, HEFCW latest available ratings
For a more complete list of institutions offering these courses at undergraduate level refer to the Course Directory

TEACHING QUALITY ASSESSMENTS

Applied Social Work
(England 1994/95)

Institution	Grade	Institution	Grade
Anglia Polytechnic	Excellent	De Montfort	Satisfactory
Bradford and Ilkley College	Excellent	Derby	Satisfactory
Bristol	Excellent	East London	Satisfactory
Durham	Excellent	Exeter	Satisfactory
East Anglia	Excellent	Hertfordshire	Satisfactory
Huddersfield	Excellent	Leicester	Satisfactory
Hull	Excellent	Liverpool John Moores	Satisfactory
Keele	Excellent	Manchester Metropolitan	Satisfactory
Lancaster	Excellent	Middlesex	Satisfactory
LSE	Excellent	Northumbria at Newcastle	Satisfactory
Oxford	Excellent	Nottingham	Satisfactory
Queen's Belfast	Excellent	Open University	Satisfactory
Sheffield	Excellent	Portsmouth	Satisfactory
Southampton	Excellent	Reading	Satisfactory
West London Institute	Excellent	South Bank	Satisfactory
York	Excellent	Stockport College	Satisfactory
Bath	Satisfactory	Sussex	Satisfactory
Buckinghamshire College	Satisfactory	Ulster	Satisfactory
Central Lancashire	Satisfactory	University College Northampton	Satisfactory
Croydon College (revisit)	Satisfactory	Warwick	Satisfactory

Applied Social Work
(Wales 1993/94)

Institution	Grade	Institution	Grade
Bangor	Satisfactory	Swansea	Satisfactory
Cardiff	Satisfactory	Newport	Satisfactory
Cardiff Institute	Satisfactory	North East Wales Institute	Satisfactory

Sociology
(Scotland 1996)

Institution	Grade	Institution	Grade
Aberdeen	Excellent	Glasgow Caledonian	Highly Satisfactory
Edinburgh	Excellent	Paisley	Highly Satisfactory
Glasgow	Excellent	Strathclyde	Highly Satisfactory
Stirling	Excellent		

Source: HEFCE, SHEFC, HEFCW latest available ratings
For a more complete list of institutions offering these courses at undergraduate level refer to the Course Directory

A foundation certificate is awarded by the University of Manchester and City College Manchester. Fees are £4,250. Contact details p479.

University of East Anglia, Norwich
BA/BSc (Hons) Development Studies
This interdisciplinary programme provides students with a critical

ECONOMICS

understanding of development, as well as skills that are valued in development advocacy and practice. The outlook is primarily an international one, with emphasis on developing countries. It encompasses social, economic and environmental sciences within one department. The department received an Excellent rating in the 1994 teaching quality assessments, and the research conducted at the department was awarded the highest rating of any development studies centre in the UK in 1996. The BA degree programme covers economics, sociology and social policy. The BSc degree programme covers subjects such as natural resources and the environment. Regular speakers from government, and non-governmental organisations contribute to the learning programmes at the department. The Rt Hon Clare Short MP, Minister for the Department for International Development was a recent visitor to the school. There are currently 26 international students studying the course. Contact details p479.

Gyosei International College
BA Culture Studies

After three or four years study at Gyosei International College, students can obtain an honours degree in Culture Studies. Students pass examinations in 27 courses in total at three levels over three years. There is also a dissertation requirement. Students take core courses in the main business subjects. These include marketing, production, personnel, economics and accounting. This is then supplemented by specialisms such as psychology, sociology, history, politics and education. Each course takes place over a ten week term and includes an examination. There are many supports in place to help students such as opportunities to resit examinations. 90 international students currently study the course which leads to both BA and licentiate qualifications. Contact details p480.

Kingston University
BA Hons Economics/Financial Economics/Business Economics

The School of Economics at Kingston offers three related courses, but students may also combine other subjects such as languages, social sciences or history. Economics students undertake a rigorous academic treatment of economic theory and its application. Theory is used to analyse areas such as policy making and implementation on issues such as unemployment, inflation, the single European currency and the risks of futures trading. The degree course offers a broad base for a variety of financial careers but also allows specialisation for final-year students. Staff emphasise computer literacy and presentation and communication skills. Graduates leave to start careers in manufacturing, accountancy, financial institutions and retail management positions. There are currently 23 international students on the course. Contact details p481.

ECONOMICS

University of Leeds
Development Studies

By concentrating on the past and present relationships between the now developed countries and the poorer countries of the South, the BA (Hons) in Development Studies at Leeds aims to provide a sound basis for the analysis of current issues in international development. Internal and international determinants of poverty in the developing world are studied and prospects for change investigated. Development studies is structured on a major-minor basis, with minor subjects chosen from economics, geography, politics, sociology or theology to provide complementary disciplinary specialisation. Teaching is by a combination of lectures, seminars and tutorials. All core units are supported by weekly tutorials. Modules in the first year include the Making of the South; and Contemporary Development Issues. There are opportunities for study abroad in the second year at the University of Zimbabwe or the Middle East Technical University, Ankara, Turkey. For more information, students can visit their website at www.leeds.ac.uk/devstud/ Contact details p481.

London School of Economics and Political Science, University of London (LSE)
Economics

The London School of Economics can count five Nobel Prize winners in economics amongst its number. The list includes Sir John Hicks who developed modern microeconomic theory in the 1930s; Ronald Coase who established the theory of the firm, or why production operates effectively within the structure of a company; and Hayek, who is credited with being the brains behind the Thatcher/Reagan

RESEARCH RANKINGS

Social Policy and Administration

Institution	Grade	Institution	Grade
LSE	5*	Royal Holloway	3a
Bath	5	Sussex	3a
Bristol	5	Brighton	3b
Kent at Canterbury	5	Buckinghamshire College	3b
York	5	Edge Hill College	3b
Birmingham	4	Glamorgan	3b
Brunel	4	Leeds Metropolitan	3b
Edinburgh	4	Lincolnshire and Humberside	3b
Glasgow	4	Liverpool John Moores	3b
Hull	4	Northumbria at Newcastle	3b
Keele	4	Portsmouth	3b
Manchester	4	Queen's Belfast	3b
Middlesex	4	Sheffield Hallam	3b
Open University	4	Thames Valley	3b
Sheffield	4	Cheltenham and Gloucester College	2
South Bank	4	Glasgow Caledonian	2
Ulster	4	London Guildhall	2
Bangor	4	Luton	2
Goldsmiths	3a	North London	2
Leicester	3a	Sunderland	2
Newcastle upon Tyne	3a	St Martin's College	1
Oxford	3a	Newport	1

source: RAE 1996

RESEARCH RANKINGS

Economics and Econometrics

Institution	Grade	Institution	Grade
LSE	5*	Reading	4
Oxford	5*	St Andrews	4
UCL	5*	Stirling	4
Birkbeck	5	Strathclyde	4
Bristol	5	Surrey	4
Cambridge	5	Sussex	4
Essex	5	Swansea	4
Exeter	5	Bath	3a
Newcastle upon Tyne	5	City	3a
Nottingham	5	East London	3a
Southampton	5	Heriot-Watt	3a
Warwick	5	Hull	3a
York	5	Leicester	3a
Aberdeen	4	Manchester Metropolitan	3a
Birmingham	4	Portsmouth	3a
Dundee	4	Queen's Belfast	3a
East Anglia	4	Salford	3a
Edinburgh	4	SOAS	3a
Glasgow	4	Aberystwyth	3b
Keele	4	De Montfort	3b
Kent at Canterbury	4	London Guildhall	3b
Liverpool	4	Northumbria at Newcastle	2
Loughborough	4	Nottingham Trent	2
Manchester	4	Staffordshire	2
Queen Mary Westfield	4	Abertay Dundee	1

source: RAE 1996

RESEARCH RANKINGS

Social Work

Institution	Grade	Institution	Grade
Stirling	5*	Liverpool	3a
East Anglia	5	Queen's of Belfast	3a
Lancaster	5	Southampton	3a
Warwick	5	Brunel	3b
York	5	Exeter	3b
Bristol	4	Kent at Canterbury	3b
Edinburgh	4	Luton	3b
Huddersfield	4	Middlesex	3b
Keele	4	Ulster	3b
Leicester	4	Anglia Polytechnic	2
Swansea	4	De Montfort	2
Bath	3a	Goldsmiths	2
Birmingham	3a	Liverpool John Moores	2
Bradford	3a	Manchester Metropolitan	2
Dundee	3a	North East Wales Institute	2
Hull	3a	Staffordshire	2

source: RAE 1996

RESEARCH RANKINGS

Sociology

Institution	Grade	Institution	Grade
Essex	5*	Exeter	3a
Lancaster	5*	Greenwich	3a
Edinburgh	5	Kent at Canterbury	3a
Goldsmiths	5	Plymouth	3a
Loughborough	5	Portsmouth (Cultural Theory and Historical)	3a
Manchester	5	Royal Holloway	3a
Oxford	5	Strathclyde	3a
Surrey	5	Teesside	3a
Warwick	5	Derby	3b
Brunel	4	Keele	3b
Cambridge	4	Liverpool	3b
Cardiff	4	Manchester Metropolitan	3b
City	4	Nottingham	3b
Glasgow	4	Nottingham Trent	3b
Leeds	4	Oxford Brookes	3b
Leicester	4	Portsmouth (Sigma)	3b
LSE	4	Reading	3b
North London	4	Roehampton Institute	3b
Open University	4	Ulster	3b
Queen's Belfast	4	UWE	3b
Salford	4	Anglia Polytechnic	2
Staffordshire	4	Bath Spa	2
Sussex	4	Central Lancashire	2
York	4	Liverpool Hope College	2
Aberdeen	3a	London Guildhall	2
Bath	3a	Northumbria at Newcastle	2
Bradford	3a	St Mary's College	2
Bristol	3a	Worcester College	2
Durham	3a	Coventry	1
East London	3a	Trinity and All Saints	1

source: RAE 1996

era of free market principles. LSE's reputation as one of the world's leading centres of social and economic thinking continues today with some of its members of staff currently advising the government on employment and welfare policy. For undergraduates, LSE offers BScs in economics, economics with economic history, econometrics, mathematical economics, geography with economics, environmental policy with economics, government and economics, philosophy and economics, and mathematics and economics. A number of MScs are offered including economics, econometrics and mathematical economics, global market economics, and public finance policy. The school's reputation attracts students from all over the world, and has internationally renowned research programmes in employment and labour market policy, econometrics, macroeconomics, microeconomics and financial markets. Research takes place in small, active groups and students have reasonable access to the academics. Contact details p482.

University College London (UCL)
Economics

UCL offers both undergraduate and postgraduate degrees in economics and is one of only three Economics Departments to be awarded the 5* rating for its research in the subject. For undergraduates there is a specialist BSc

ECONOMICS

degree in Economics and a range of joint honours programmes, including Economics and History, Economics and Geography, Economics and Statistics, and Philosophy and Economics (BA). The Economics BSc includes an option for students who do not have maths A level. In addition, the Mathematics Department offers a degree in Mathematics with Economics (BSc or MSci). UCL offers MSc programmes in Economics, Environmental and Resource Economics. The one-year MSc in Economics provides a good background for entry into doctoral research in the department. Contact details p487.

University of Manchester
BA (Hons) Economics

This is the largest degree in the university with 800 UK students and 215 international students from 40 different countries. It is a broad-based, flexible degree organised by the Faculty of Economics and Social Studies. Students can specialise in one or two of the following subjects: accounting, business studies, economics, econometrics, economic history, finance, government, sociology, social anthropology or social policy. Modules are available in law and modern languages and many have an international content – international accounting, multinational corporate finance, economics of the European Union and ethical issues in world politics, for example. The main features of the degree are its flexibility, the range of options on offer and the principle that students make strategic decisions about their areas of specialisation as they progress through the three years. Contact details p483.

University of Oxford
Economics and Statistics

Oxford has long been noted for the study of economics. Its Politics, Philosophy and Economics (PPE) honours degree, has many famous alumni including some former Prime Ministers. Today, PPE is the most popular undergraduate degree course at Oxford. Students have to study all three subjects in their first year, and can then specialise in the last two years. If you are a keen economist, you can do up to three quarters of your finals degree in economics. Oxford now offers a degree in economics and management, and there are also two four-year specialist degrees available that combine economics and management with engineering or metallurgy. At postgraduate level Oxford offers an Economics MPhil. This course lasts for two years and goes into far greater depth than some of its counterparts. It is a theoretical course and requires a good level of mathematical proficiency. Many students use the MPhil as a way to further research; the thesis needed to complete the MPhil can be extended to form the basis of an MLitt or a DPhil. The well-established pool of expert knowledge at Oxford is one of the clear benefits of conducting research there. Some notable areas of current expertise are industrial economics, labour economics and developing economies. Contact details p484.

Queen Mary and Westfield College, University of London
BSc in Business Economics

The BSc in Business Economics concentrates on those aspects of economics most relevant to business and finance, and incorporates subjects such as accounting and law. The first year contains basic courses in micro- and macroeconomics, as well as quantitative analysis. Following this, the course concentrates more on microeconomics and quantitative techniques and, in the third and final year, includes the study of finance theory, futures and options. A number of options are also available to students, particularly in the final year. Choices could include foreign languages, further economics courses, law, the workings of stock exchanges, and business studies, or could come from a wide range of courses offered in other departments. Contact details p484.

Royal Holloway, University of London
Department of Social and Political Science

The Department of Social and Political Science at Royal Holloway offers a stimulating environment in which to study topics across the social sciences. Students may select from single and joint honours degrees in sociology, social policy and politics, in addition to programmes offered by other departments, such as management and economics. The flexible system ensures a high level of choice and the opportunity to specialise in subjects that are of particular interest. Many students go on to further study. The programmes may be attractive to international students since the kind of skills and knowledge gained in the course of study can be applied around the world. The demand among public and private sector employers for trained social scientists has never been greater. Contact details p485.

University of York
Economics and Finance

This popular undergraduate degree course combines financial analysis with the tools and techniques of the economist. After an introductory first year, the second and third years include modules in accountancy, financial management, capital markets, banking economics, monetary theory, economics for business decisions and business finance. The appeal of this course lies in its practical nature. For students wishing to work in a business environment it provides a solid grounding in economics allied to an understanding of the applications of economics in the business world. As one of the largest economics departments in the UK, the department at York contains a wide range of expertise and is able to offer its students a high degree of flexible module choice. Graduates from this course have gone onto work in a number of different professions. Whilst many go on to work in management in industry and the financial sector, others have excelled in public administration, social welfare, teaching and media professions. Contact details p487.

Education

education
education
education
education

"Education is the passport to the future," wrote Malcolm X, and undeniably it has a huge influence on where we go and what we become. You are probably testimony to this yourself by reading this guide and considering study in Britain. If you study education and become a teacher, you are given the opportunity to put back into the system and gain enormous emotional rewards.

The common perception of the British education system is of public schools with teachers in mortarboards and gowns. The reality, in fact, is completely different with about 85 per cent of secondary school children attend comprehensive schools, which, as the title implies, cater for all.

To qualify as a primary or secondary school teacher in Britain and gain Qualified Teacher Status (QTS), students can chose between two main routes. There is the specialist teaching degree, the Bachelor of Education (BEd), or the one-year Postgraduate Certificate in Education (PGCE) which is taken after having completed an undergraduate degree in another subject.

The majority of British primary teachers (nearly 70 per cent) do an undergraduate teaching degree – normally three- or four-year BEd. These courses train students to teach all subjects, although normally with an area of specialisation, and include a certain amount of time in the classroom with supervision from a mentor. Some BEd courses are available for potential secondary school teachers – in physical education or design and technology for example. Another alternative is to take a BA or BSc degree with greater specialisation in one subject that includes QTS. At Canterbury Christ Church College, for example, you can take a BA in History with QTS.

Nine times out of 10, secondary school teachers have done a postgraduate teaching course. The PGCE is the standard, one-year, full-time postgraduate teaching course. Courses vary in their structures but most consist of three main areas: practical experience of teaching in a school; study of a main subject area, which is normally the subject in which a graduate has their first degree; and the theory and role of the teacher. It is also possible to take a PGCE in primary education.

As the approach to teaching varies between countries, it is important for international students to consider where they eventually wish to teach. Qualifications gained in the UK may not be recognised outside the European Union or may require a conversion course. Similarly qualifications from outside of Europe may not be sufficient to start a British QTS course. A further route into British teaching is via the Overseas Trained Teacher Scheme, which leads to QTS and can take between one term and three years. It provides teachers who have a degree in education or postgraduate qualification and one year's teaching experience with a way into the British system by combining teaching experience with training in a school.

TEACHING QUALITY ASSESSMENTS

Education
(Scotland 1994/95)

Institution	Grade	Institution	Grade
Moray House Institute	Highly Satisfactory	**Stirling**	Highly Satisfactory
Paisley	Highly Satisfactory	**Strathclyde**	Highly Satisfactory
St Andrew's College	Highly Satisfactory	**Northern College**	Satisfactory

Education
(Wales 1997/98)

Institution	Grade	Institution	Grade
Cardiff	Excellent		

Source: HEFCE, SHEFC, HEFCW latest available ratings
For a more complete list of institutions offering these courses at undergraduate level refer to the Course Directory

DEGREE COURSES

Institute of Education, University of London
MA in the Teaching of English to Speakers of Other Languages

This postgraduate course is aimed at students seeking a practical orientation to high-level professional education. In 1998/9, there were 76 international students on the course. The course has a more theoretical approach to applied linguistic orientation than some institutions offer. Students cover the fundamental issues in language and teaching including the sociolinguistic and psycholinguistic contexts of language teaching. There is also a range of study options available including discourse analysis and language acquisition. Contact details p481.

Institute of Education, University of London
BEd (Hons) for Serving Teachers

This first-degree level course is aimed at trained and qualified teachers from the UK and overseas. It is divided into two parts. Part I aims to develop a broad, mature and accurate understanding of educational issues; part II offers an opportunity to specialise in areas of educational studies or in curriculum areas. Modules are chosen with regard to candidates' previous experience and they include areas such as child development, contemporary schooling, psychology of education or the learning and teaching of English. The course includes a programme of visits to enable international students to gain first-hand experience of some aspects of the British school system. In 1998/9, there were 11 international students on the course. Contact details p481.

University of Northumbria at Newcastle
MA Education

This is a one-year course that has a number of different pathways. Topics include: approaches to practitioner enquiry, research design and collaborative enquiry, leadership in education, managing the curriculum, and professional learning in education. The course permits qualified and experienced teachers from overseas to add specialist knowledge to their existing expertise in fields such as education management or special needs education. Entry is in February and September. There are currently 24 international students on this course. Contact details p483.

University of Oxford
Postgraduate Certificate of Education

This is awarded after a one-year full-time course of teacher training for graduates. The emphasis of the course lies upon professional preparation in partnership with associated schools in local education authorities. The work is designed for intending secondary school teachers wishing to specialise in a subject. A range of subsidiary courses is offered and all course members take part in a cross-curricular programme of activities. Members of the course are required to become members of a college. Full advice on this matter is given to all successful applications for admission. The Department of Education also offers part-time continuing profession development for teachers leading to diplomas and opportunities for research work leading to the degrees of MSc, MLitt and DPhil. Contact details p484.

University of Stirling
Education

Stirling offers a concurrent degree programme, which means that students learn to teach while studying another subject at degree level. For example, it is possible to study for a BSc or BA in English, French, German, history, mathematics, religious studies, amongst others, and at the same time gain a Diploma in Education. The concurrent course takes three and a half or four and a half years, depending on whether you wish to graduate with a general or honours degree. Once qualified, you may work as a teacher in a school, just as you would if you had completed a PGCE at other universities. The course involves a similar level of practical work as the PGCE, although Stirling offers its own Microteaching course. This involves bringing small groups of young children into the university to give students 'hands-on' experience of teaching. Contact details p486.

Number of Teachers in Primary and Secondary Schools Across the UK
Source:www.statistics.gov.uk

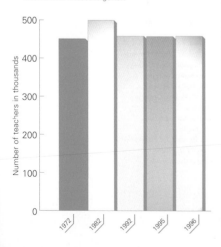

Interesting facts

- In 1885 there was an educational qualification in English elections, as graduates were allowed to cast two votes
- School canteen guidelines, due to come into force from 2001, specify that chips or other fried potatoes should not be served more than three times a week, and baked beans not more than once a week
- 60 per cent of people remember a good teacher, compared to 75 per cent who remember a bad teacher

RESEARCH RANKINGS

Education

Institution	Grade
Institute of Education	5*
King's College	5*
Bath	5
Birmingham	5
Bristol	5
East Anglia	5
Lancaster	5
Leeds	5
Newcastle upon Tyne	5
Oxford	5
Open University (Educational technology)	5
Sheffield	5
Stirling	5
Aberdeen	4
Cambridge	4
Cardiff	4
Durham	4
Edinburgh	4
Exeter	4
Goldsmiths	4
Manchester	4
Nottingham	4
Open University (Education)	4
Southampton	4
Surrey	4
Sussex	4
Warwick	4
York	4
Queen's Belfast	4
Ulster	4
Canterbury Christ Church	3a
Dundee	3a
Glasgow	3a
Greenwich	3a
Heriot-Watt	3a
Homerton College	3a
Hull	3a
Keele	3a
Leicester	3a
Liverpool	3a
Liverpool John Moores	3a
Moray House Institute	3a
Northumbria at Newcastle	3a
Reading	3a
Sheffield Hallam	3a
Bangor	3a
Swansea	3a
Aberystwyth	3b
Anglia Polytechnic	3b
Aston	3b
Brighton	3b
Brunel	3b
City	3b

Institution	Grade
East London	3b
Hertfordshire	3b
Leeds Metropolitan	3b
Loughborough	3b
Manchester Metropolitan	3b
Middlesex	3b
North London	3b
Nottingham Trent	3b
Oxford Brookes	3b
Plymouth	3b
Strathclyde	3b
University College Northampton	3b
UWE	3b
Worcester College	3b
Bath Spa	2
Bretton Hall	2
Central Lancashire	2
Central School of Speech and Drama	2
Cheltenham and Gloucester College	2
College of St Mark and St John	2
De Montfort	2
Edge Hill College	2
Huddersfield	2
King Alfred's College	2
Kingston	2
Lincolnshire and Humberside	2
North East Wales Institute	2
Portsmouth	2
Roehampton Institute	2
St Martin's College	2
South Bank	2
St Andrew's College	2
Sunderland	2
Thames Valley	2
UCE	2
University College Chichester	2
Westhill College	2
Westminster College	2
Chester College	1
Derby	1
La Sainte Union College	1
Liverpool Hope College	1
Newman College	1
Northern College	1
North Riding College	1
Paisley	1
Swansea Institute	1
Teesside	1
Trinity and All Saints	1
Cardiff Institute	1
Wolverhampton	1

source: RAE 1996

Engineering

engineering
engineering
engineering
engineering

Engineers are the silent stars behind our everyday lives. Every time we catch a tube or train, every time we drive across a bridge or plug in our electronic game consoles, engineers are in some way responsible.

Traditionally, Britain's strengths in engineering have been in inventiveness and innovation rather than in manufacturing. In recent years, however, there has been a great deal of investment in production facilities. The UK now leads the way in aerospace and automotive research, for example, with many of the world's Formula One teams being based in Britain.

Engineering degrees in the UK last between three and five years, and lead to a Bachelor of Engineering (BEng) or a Master of Engineering (MEng) qualification. Students are sometimes expected to spend one year on an industrial placement. Following graduation, a further period of employment allows students to become a chartered (CEng) or incorporated (IEng) engineer.

All engineers need technical and managerial skills, and the knowledge to understand the design, construction, operation and maintenance of products. Apart from these general principles, however, engineers specialise in a chosen field. There are a large number of specialisms under the general heading of engineering, but those most commonly studied include chemical, civil, computer, mechanical and electrical engineering. If you are planning to do an engineering course, you need to consider the type of engineering you are most interested in. If you are unsure, then university courses that include an introductory or foundation year might offer the answer. These allow you to cover a broad range of topics and get to know the different parts of the subject before choosing the area in which you wish to specialise.

Group work and imaginative problem solving are important features of all engineering courses. Design and research projects also play a part in the development of students' knowledge. With regard to specific courses, each engineering degree normally begins with an introduction to the basic principles of engineering. Subjects relevant to the particular specialism are then studied in more depth from the second year onwards. Chemical engineers, for example, cover areas such as chemical technology, unit operations, plant engineering, and physical chemistry. Civil engineers, on the other hand, tackle subjects like geology, soil mechanics, water resources and fluid mechanics.

Teaching methods usually consist of a combination of studio, laboratory and project work, lectures and tutorials. Some courses may involve an element of field work. Teaching assignments generally look to provide an industrial and practical relevance to the development of knowledge-based material and group presentation work is usually involved. Assessment is by a combination of written examinations, essays, laboratory practicals, design projects and presentations.

DEGREE COURSES

University of Abertay Dundee
BEng (Hons) Civil Engineering

This course is recognised by the Engineering Council as providing the initial academic qualification for membership, at chartered engineer level, of the Institutions of Civil and Structural Engineers. In the first three years of the course, students take a range of civil engineering subjects. In their final year, students specialise from a range of subjects, including environmental engineering, structural engineering, rock mass engineering, highways engineering, and construction organisation and management. Students also undertake a major project on an individual basis within an area of personal interest. For two periods in the degree programme, students undertake relevant paid industrial training. This is viewed as a very important part of the course because it allows students to gain relevant work experience as well as a deeper understanding of the issues that influence the practical application of engineering principles. This work experience can also count towards the professional experience required before obtaining chartered engineer status. Contact details p477.

Bradford College
BEng Software Engineering

Software engineering is the establishment and use of sound engineering principles for the design, development, implementation and maintenance of software products. This is an innovative degree aimed at providing candidates with first order technical skills in the field of software development. The course content includes computer platforms, systems analysis, software constructions and tools, computing solutions, networking data analysis and database design, programming,

software engineering implementation /techniques, communications technology, quality management, data structure and algorithms, and software engineering development /programming. Successful candidates can expect extensive career opportunities in informatics. There are currently 20 international students on the course. Contact details p478.

University of Bradford
BEng Mechanical Engineering

On this course, students acquire the skills needed to conceive, design and produce the moving parts, components and machinery used in every aspect of modern life. Modules in the mechanics of machine solids and fluids are backed

ENGINEERING

154

up by the development of mathematical and computing skills. Considerable time is spent on practical work in the laboratory. There is also an introduction to business and communication skills. In the final year, there is a choice of modules, including computer-aided engineering, robotics, energy engineering and business studies. A project must also be completed. The department received a rating of 4 in the 1996 research assessment exercise. Other related courses available include: mechanical and automotive engineering, manufacturing systems with mechanical engineering, mechanical engineering with management, and manufacturing systems with management. Contact details p478.

University of Bristol
MEng in Computer Science

Bristol computer science students complete a substantial piece of project work as well as studying within four main areas: hardware, software, applications and cross disciplines. The course has recently been revised to match students' needs as well as to meet the skills required by future employers. Staff aim to develop students' practical and theoretical capabilities and there are opportunities to work on industrial projects. The first two years of study contain core subjects in software engineering and computer architecture. Third- and fourth-year students choose such courses as artificial intelligence, computer graphics, databases and systems architecture. Contact details p478.

Brunel University
BEng (Hons) in Electronic and Electrical Engineering

The Faculty of Technology, in which the Department of Electrical Engineering is based, is located on the university's main campus at Uxbridge.

The department aims to encourage students to give their best and maintain the highest academic standards. Boards of study have been established to help achieve this and every member of the academic staff is also a personal tutor. Undergraduate courses are based on a semester structure that preserves the four-year integrated thin sandwich degree but allows students to opt for a four-year thick sandwich course or a three-year non-sandwich course if they prefer. The first four semesters are devoted to fundamental subjects and in the final year, semesters five and six, a selected number of subjects are studied in depth. The overall intention of the course is to produce well-rounded engineers who are capable of pursuing interesting careers in research, design, management, finance and marketing. Contact details p478.

Cardiff University
Engineering

Cardiff School of Engineering offers a number of engineering courses including: civil; electrical and electronic; architectural; environmental and mechanical engineering, which all lead to a BEng or MEng. Teaching quality in the department has been rated as Excellent and all the degrees are recognised by the relevant professional institutions. The school is located in the modern complex known as the Queen's Buildings, close to other academic departments, the students' union and the city centre. It houses well-equipped teaching and research laboratories, a large library, the latest computer technology and quiet study areas. The school has strong links with industry and aims to produce work of a world-class standard. There are currently 80 international students on engineering courses that last between three and five years. Contact details p478.

TEACHING QUALITY ASSESSMENTS

General Engineering
(England 1996/97)

Institution	Grade	Institution	Grade
Open University	24	Wolverhampton	20
Cambridge	23	De Montfort	19
Imperial	23	Queen Mary and Westfield	19
Oxford	23	South Tyneside College	19
Southampton	23	Southampton Institute	19
Brunel	22	UCE	19
Durham	22	Bournemouth	18
Lancaster	22	Coventry	18
Sheffield Hallam	21	Doncaster	18
Warwick	21	Lincolnshire and Humberside	18
Bradford	20	University College Northampton	18
Central Lancashire	20	Buckinghamshire College	17
Cranfield	20	Greenwich	17
Exeter	20	Leeds Metropolitan	17
Hertfordshire	20	South Bank	17
Leicester	20	Bradford and Ilkley College	16
Liverpool	20	Ryecotewood College	15
Ulster	20		

Chemical Engineering
(England and N Ireland 1995/96)

Institution	Grade	Institution	Grade
Cambridge	23	Bath	20
Imperial	22	Bradford	20
Loughborough	22	UCL	20
UMIST	22	Aston	19
Birmingham	21	Leeds	19
Newcastle upon Tyne	21	South Bank	18
Nottingham	21	Surrey	18
Queen's Belfast	21	Teesside	17
Sheffield	21		

Chemical Engineering
(Scotland 1997/98)

Institution	Grade	Institution	Grade
Strathclyde	20	Heriot-Watt	19
Edinburgh	19		

Chemical Engineering
(Wales 1997/98)

Institution	Grade	Institution	Grade
Swansea	Excellent		

Source: HEFCE, SHEFC, HEFCW latest available ratings
For a more complete list of institutions offering these courses at undergraduate level refer to the Course Directory

ENGINEERING

Coventry University
BSc International Disaster Engineering and Management

This course is aimed at developing skills and experience in complementary areas of study in disaster management, in particular sustainable human development, health, management processes and disaster relief. It provides a blend of academic and skills based study, enabling students to develop technological and disaster management expertise. The programme is designed to enable students to study engineering, management and international studies together with field skills training, which is viewed as an essential feature of the course. The syllabus also provides opportunities for students to practice some of the skills in a field environment. The course has a strong international theme with many international case studies. It is ideal for international students who wish to assist in capacity building and development initiatives in developing countries. Contact details p479.

The University of Edinburgh
BEng or MEng (Hons) in Engineering

In the broad Scottish tradition, students may apply to either a specific department (Mechanical, Civil, Electrical and Electronic or Mechanical Engineering) or as a general engineering undergraduate. Lectures in the first year enable them to confirm their choice of department and then choose from 26 more advanced and specialised honours courses. The University of Edinburgh also offers joint honours programmes that combine engineering disciplines with construction management (civil), computer science, software engineering and physics (electronics), or management techniques (mechanical). As might be expected in the capital city of Scotland that draws tourists from all over the world, the engineering community at Edinburgh includes a diverse mix of nationalities. In the Division of Engineering, staff are from Europe, Asia, Australia and North America. There are around 150 international students currently studying engineering at the University of Edinburgh. Contact details p480.

University of Essex
Electronic Systems Engineering

This department is very specialised and focuses on the growth areas of electronics – electronic systems telecommunications and computer engineering. UK applicants are invited to an interview. Courses are designed around a nominal workload of 40 to 45 hours per week, with 17 direct contact hours (lectures, seminars, etc). At entry level, all undergraduates in the department study the same things. Students only go on to specialise in the last two years of the course and are free to change course within the department. Assessment combines tests and continuous assessments (throughout the year) and formal examinations (at the end of each year). Students have access to the university library and there are computer facilities for undergraduates within the department. The provision of computers has been worked out so that any student should have access to one whenever they need it. There are about 50 workstations for undergraduates and 30 PCs for course teaching. Famous alumni include Peter Cochrane – a senior spokes person for British Telecom. Contact details p480.

University of Kent at Canterbury
BEng/MEng in Electronic Engineering

Engineering can be taken at different levels at the University of Kent at Canterbury. Specialisations are offered in electronic engineering, communications engineering, electronic

TEACHING QUALITY ASSESSMENTS

Civil Engineering
(England and N Ireland 1996/97/98)

Institution	Grade	Institution	Grade
Plymouth	23	Bradford	20
Bath	22	Liverpool John Moores	20
Bristol	22	Newcastle upon Tyne	20
Kingston	22	Nottingham Trent	20
Liverpool	22	Portsmouth	20
Loughborough	22	South Bank	20
Nottingham	22	Westminster	20
Queen's Belfast	22	Wolverhampton	20
Southampton Institute	22	City	19
Surrey	22	Coventry	19
UMIST	22	Derby	19
Birmingham	21	Leeds	19
Brighton	21	Salford	19
East London	21	Teesside	19
Greenwich	21	UCL	19
Imperial	21	Ulster	19
Leeds Metropolitan	21	University College Northampton	19
Oxford Brookes	21	Hertfordshire	18
Sheffield	21	Manchester	18
Southampton	21	Sheffield Hallam	18
Anglia Polytechnic	20	Stockport College	15
Aston	20	Wigan and Leigh College	15
Bolton Institute	20		

Source: HEFCE, SHEFC, HEFCW latest available ratings
For a more complete list of institutions offering these courses at undergraduate level refer to the Course Directory

engineering with medical electronics, and computer systems engineering. Foundation courses are available for students who do not possess the qualifications for direct entry to the department. All courses are accredited by the Institution of Electrical Engineering. A new programme in multimedia technology and design is being proposed for introduction in September 2000. In both the research assessment exercise and teaching quality assessment the department was rated as Excellent. Contact details p481.

Kingston University
MEng/BEng/BSc/HND Aerospace Engineering
Kingston runs one of only two courses in the UK that combines air and spacecraft engineering. The course (at all levels) has a strong emphasis on engineering, design and business issues and is specifically for students intending

to work in the aerospace industry. The curriculum covers aerodynamics and propulsion, aerospace structures and materials, astronautics and space systems, flight dynamics, and business management. Assessment is based on group reports, design drawings, laboratory reports, oral presentations and exams. Students on the course have been able to visit aerospace facilities such as the Mig aircraft factory in Russia and the Star City cosmonaut training facility. Contact details p481.

Loughborough University
Electronic and Electrical Engineering
The Department of Electronic and Electrical Engineering is one of the largest departments at Loughborough, with 40 full-time staff and a similar number of support staff. The broad areas of research within the department are communications and signal

processing, electronic component technology, electrical power and control systems. All of these cover a range of interests which includes lasers, robotics and underwater communications. In 1997, the department was rated amongst the highest in the country in the teaching quality assessment, receiving 22 out of 24. Programmes available include a three-year BEng and a four-year MEng degrees in Electronic and Electrical Engineering, Electronic and Computer Systems Engineering and Electro-Mechanical Power Engineering. Contact details p482.

University of Newcastle upon Tyne
MSc Environmental Engineering

The University of Newcastle has 40 years of experience in the field of civil engineering. The department scored well in both teaching and research, gaining a score of 20 out of 24 in the 1996/7 teaching quality assessment and a 5* in the 1996 research assessment exercise. Based on current developments, the postgraduate MSc in Environmental Engineering covers a variety of subjects including water pollution assessment, waste water engineering, water supply, environmental impact assessment, air pollution modelling, and chemical and biological assessment of aquatic systems. Students also undertake individual research for presentation as a dissertation. Graduates from the course go on to work in industry, government agencies, academic organisations and research institutions, and Newcastle alumni include senior industrial and academic figures, the Ministers of Environment for Portugal and Singapore and the Minister of Water Resources for Sierra Leone. Contact details p483.

University of Plymouth
BSc/BEng/MEng Civil Engineering

In the School of Civil Engineering students can study a range of subjects which include civil engineering, civil and coastal engineering, building surveying and the environment, quantity surveying and the environment and civil engineering, design and computing. Amongst the school's research projects it has developed unique instrumentation systems for wave measurements and for testing the dynamic response of structures. The main structures laboratory contains a 2,000KN universal loading rig which provides facilities to test wall elements up to 5m high and up to 3m (3m in plan), under both vertical and horizontal loads. The school offers unique modules in diving and underwater technology allowing selected students to obtain a commercial diving qualification. Contact details p484.

ENGINEERING

Queen's University of Belfast
BEng (Hons) Electrical and
Electronic Engineering

This course is accredited by the Institute of Electrical Engineers and the content is chosen to prepare students for a career in any branch of electrical or electronic engineering. Subject speciali-sation includes power systems, intelligent control signal processing, computing, telecommunications and microelectronics. The department was awarded a 5 in the research assessment exercise and the maximum 24 points for teaching quality. State-of-the-art technology is available in the Northern Ireland Technology Centre. Contact details p484.

TEACHING QUALITY ASSESSMENTS

Civil Engineering
(Scotland 1993)

Institution	Grade	Institution	Grade
Aberdeen	Highly Satisfactory	Heriot-Watt	Highly Satisfactory
Dundee	Highly Satisfactory	Napier	Highly Satisfactory
Dundee Institute	Highly Satisfactory	Paisley	Highly Satisfactory
Edinburgh	Highly Satisfactory	Strathclyde	Highly Satisfactory
Glasgow	Highly Satisfactory	Glasgow Caledonian	Satisfactory

Civil Engineering
(Wales 1996/97/98)

Institution	Grade	Institution	Grade
Cardiff	Excellent	Glamorgan	Satisfactory
Swansea	Excellent		

Mechanical Engineering
(Scotland 1995)

Institution	Grade	Institution	Grade
Strathclyde	Excellent	Paisley	Highly Satisfactory
Aberdeen	Highly Satisfactory	Robert Gordon	Highly Satisfactory
Abertay Dundee	Highly Satisfactory	Edinburgh	Satisfactory
Glasgow	Highly Satisfactory	Glasgow Caledonian	Satisfactory
Heriot-Watt	Highly Satisfactory	Napier	Satisfactory

Mechanical Engineering
(Wales 1993/94)

Institution	Grade	Institution	Grade
Cardiff	Excellent	North East Wales Institute	Satisfactory
Cardiff Institute	Satisfactory	Newport	Satisfactory
Carmarthenshire College	Satisfactory	Swansea	Satisfactory
Glamorgan	Satisfactory	Swansea Institute	Satisfactory

Source: HEFCE, SHEFC, HEFCW latest available ratings
For a more complete list of institutions offering these courses at undergraduate level refer to the Course Directory

ENGINEERING

University of Sheffield
Electronic and Electrical Engineering

This department is one of only three in the country to score 5* in the 1996 research assessment exercise. It was also graded with 24 marks out of 24 in a teaching quality assessment. The department is home to the ESPRC's national centre for III-V semi-conductor materials and devices and has extensive outdoor test facilities at nearby Buxton. There are currently 112 staff with 425 students, of which 128 are from overseas. The department offers six undergraduate degrees in electrical engineering, electronic engineering, or electronic engineering with a choice of four specialisms, namely communications, computing, solid-state devices and systems, all of which can be taken as a three-year BEng or a four-year MEng. The final decision on whether to take a three- or four-year course and the choice of specialism need not be made until the end of the first year. At postgraduate level there is an MSc in Data Communications which is taught jointly with the Department of Computer Science. Contact details p485.

Southampton Institute
BSc (Hons) Media Technology

The course aims to provide the broadcast, cinema and entertainment industries with a potential source of technical support engineers.

There are two strong themes to the course: the operation of media production equipment coupled with electronic engineering at systems level. This is a vocational degree in so far as it has been specifically designed to meet the future needs of the media and entertainment industries. During the three-year course students cover a range of areas which include computing, mathematics, electrical principles and integrated electronics, magnetic recording, audio and video systems, microprocessor-based multimedia and telecommunications. Industrial practitioners teach on the course and the technical content is updated in the face

TEACHING QUALITY ASSESSMENTS

Mechanical, Aeronautical and Manufacturing Engineering
(England 1996/97/98)

Institution	Grade	Institution	Grade
Kingston	24	Anglia Polytechnic	19
Nottingham	24	City	19
Cambridge	23	Southampton Institute	19
Loughborough	23	Sunderland	19
Bristol	22	UCE	19
Cranfield	22	Writtle College	19
Hertfordshire	22	Bournemouth	18
Imperial	22	Coventry	18
Queen's Belfast	21	East London	18
Sheffield Hallam	21	Lincolnshire and Humberside	18
Southampton	21	Loughborough College	18
Birmingham	20	Farnborough	17
Brunel	20	Leeds Metropolitan	17
Liverpool	20	Sandwell College	17
Manchester	20	South Bank	17
Newcastle	20	Wigan and Leigh College	15
UMIST	20		

Source: HEFCE, SHEFC, HEFCW latest available ratings
For a more complete list of institutions offering these courses at undergraduate level refer to the Course Directory

TEACHING QUALITY ASSESSMENTS

Electrical and Electronic Engineering
(England 1996/97/98)

Institution	Grade	Institution	Grade
Birmingham	24	Hertfordshire	20
Bristol	24	KCL	20
Essex	24	Luton	20
Huddersfield	24	Manchester	20
Hull	24	Nottingham Trent	20
Imperial	24	Portsmouth	20
Queen's Belfast	24	Staffordshire	20
Sheffield	24	Ulster	20
Southampton	24	Anglia Polytechnic	19
York	24	Bournemouth	19
Cambridge	23	De Montfort	19
Leeds	23	Derby	19
Surrey	23	East Anglia	19
Coventry Technical College	22	Middlesex	19
Loughborough	22	Oxford Brookes	19
North London	22	South Bank	19
Northumbria at Newcastle	22	Southampton Institute	19
Nottingham	22	Sunderland	19
UMIST	22	UCE	19
UCL	22	Blackburn College	18
Aston	21	Coventry	18
Bradford	21	Doncaster	18
Brunel	21	Lincolnshire and Humberside	18
City	21	Liverpool John Moores	18
Kent at Canterbury	21	Loughborough College	18
Kingston	21	University College Northampton	18
Liverpool	21	Plymouth	18
Manchester Metropolitan	21	Sheffield Hallam	18
Newcastle upon Tyne	21	North West London	17
Queen Mary and Westfield	21	Greenwich	17
Reading	21	Leeds Metropolitan	17
Sussex	21	Sandwell College	17
Teesside	21	Liverpool Community College	16
UWE	21	Salford	16
Westminster	21	Central Lancashire	15
Bath	20	East London	15
Bolton Institute	20	Stockport College	15
Brighton	20	Wigan and Leigh College	15

Source: HEFCE, SHEFC, HEFCW latest available ratings
For a more complete list of institutions offering these courses at undergraduate level refer to the Course Directory

of rapidly changing technology. Specialist facilities include two television studios, a film studio, five radio studios, several machine edit suites and a multitrack hard-disk recording studio. Contact details p486.

University of Southampton
Department of Electrical Engineering

The courses offered by the Department of Electrical Engineering are broad-based and can include electronics, computing, information processing, mechanics and control theory. An emphasis on breadth, fundamentals and applications is in line with the department's opinion that a good command of engineering principles is essential. Subjects are compulsory for the first and second year but in the subsequent years students get considerable choice. The main focus of the third year is a challenging individual

The Five Longest Suspension Bridges

Source: "*The Top 10 of Everything: 2000*" Russell Ash, Dorling Kindersley 1999

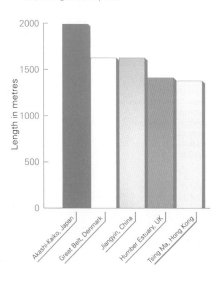

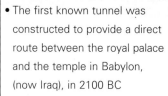

Interesting facts

- The first known tunnel was constructed to provide a direct route between the royal palace and the temple in Babylon, (now Iraq), in 2100 BC

- The first paved roads, using blocks of stone, are thought to have been laid when the Great Pyramids at Giza, Egypt, were constructed around 2500 BC

- The biggest railway station in the world is Grand Central Terminal, New York City, USA. The station covers 48 acres on two levels, with 41 tracks on the upper level and 26 on the lower

RESEARCH RANKINGS

Civil Engineering

Institution	Grade	Institution	Grade
Imperial	5*	UCL (Photogrammetry and Surveying)	4
Newcastle upon Tyne (Civil Engineering)	5*	Abertay Dundee	3a
Swansea	5*	Birmingham	3a
Bradford	5	Leeds	3a
Bristol	5	Napier	3a
Cardiff	5	Paisley	3a
City	5	Queen Mary and Westfield	3a
Dundee	5	Salford	3a
Nottingham	5	Strathclyde	3a
UCL (Civil Engineering)	5	Surrey	3a
Edinburgh	4	UMIST	3a
Glasgow (Civil Engineering)	4	Brighton	3b
Glasgow (Naval Architecture and Ocean Engineering)	4	Portsmouth	3b
Heriot-Watt	4	Plymouth	2
Liverpool	4	South Bank	2
Loughborough	4	Teesside	2
Manchester	4	Westminster	2
Newcastle upon Tyne (Surveying)	4	Bolton Institute	1
Queen's Belfast	4	East London	1
Sheffield	4	Kingston	1
Southampton	4	Oxford Brookes	1
		Southampton Institute	1

source: RAE 1996

ENGINEERING

RESEARCH RANKINGS

Chemical Engineering

Institution	Grade	Institution	Grade
Imperial	5*	Queen's Belfast	3a
Bath	5	Surrey	3a
Birmingham	5	Swansea	3a
Cambridge	5	Heriot-Watt	3b
UMIST	5	Leeds (Chemical Engineering)	3b
UCL	5	Nottingham	3b
Leeds (Fuel and Energy)	4	Glasgow Caledonian	2
Loughborough	4	South Bank	2
Bradford	3a	Strathclyde	2
Edinburgh	3a	Teesside	1
Newcastle upon Tyne	3a		

source: RAE 1996

project. The department can has a 100 per cent employment record for its graduates. Contact details p486.

University of Sunderland
BEng Automotive Design and Manufacture

A three-year undergraduate programme, or four-year sandwich course that incorporates one year working in industry. The degree programme was developed in collaboration with leading companies in the automotive design industry. These companies provide materials and equipment for the course in addition to guest lecturers from time to time. Academic studies are supplemented by hands-on practical projects throughout the course. These projects lead up to a large final-year project that is usually related to a topical area. Through the course students become equipped with the knowledge and transferable skills that will enable them to seek careers in professional automotive design or manufacturing. Teaching methods include a combination of lectures, seminars and tutorials. Students are assessed by written exams, multiple-choice and computer-based tests, and research dissertation projects. Contact details p486.

University of Sussex
MEng/BEng in Engineering

The School of Engineering and Information Technology acts as a closely integrated, non-departmental centre for both teaching and research activities. The four-year MEng degree programmes are enhanced versions of the three-year BEng courses, with additional project work and business management studies in the third and fourth years. It is possible to change from a BEng to a MEng at the end of the first year. Both courses embrace a wide range of engineering disciplines from computer, electronic, mechanical and control engineering to robotics, opto-electronics, product design and manufacturing systems. Both the BEng and MEng programmes are available in specialist and interdisciplinary fields.

Students who do not have the normal entrance requirements are able to enrol on four-year BEng degree programmes where the first year is a foundation course. Contact details p486.

oncourse·co·uk

The ultimate guide to courses

ENGINEERING

University of the West of England

MEng/BEng (Hons) in Electrical and Electronic Engineering

The engineering award can last from three to five years at UWE depending on whether the programme is a masters or a bachelor degree, and whether it includes a sandwich year or not. There are currently 16 international students on the programme of study. Graduates in electrical and electronic engineering are likely to pursue careers as electrical and electronic system designers to solve engineering problems for communications and power generation/distribution companies. Throughout the programme emphasis is placed on practical and project work often based around a number of advanced laboratories. The award is recognised as satisfying the educational requirements for membership of the Institution of Electrical Engineers. The programme has a vocational nature and provides students with good access to industry. There is the opportunity to study a foreign language. Contact details p487.

RESEARCH RANKINGS

Electrical and Electronic Engineering

Institution	Grade	Institution	Grade
Edinburgh	5*	Northumbria at Newcastle	3a
Sheffield (Electrical and Electronic Engineering)	5*	Nottingham	3a
		Reading (Electronics - Cybernetics)	3a
Southampton	5*	Bradford	3b
Surrey	5*	City	3b
UCL	5*	Hull	3b
Bristol	5	Manchester Metropolitan	3b
Glasgow	5	Napier	3b
Imperial	5	Nottingham Trent	3b
Queen Mary and Westfield	5	Plymouth	3b
Queen's Belfast	5	Portsmouth	3b
Sheffield (Automatic Control and Systems Engineering)	5	Westminster	3b
		Bolton Institute	2
Strathclyde	5	Bournemouth	2
UMIST (Instrumentation and Analytical Science)	5	De Montfort	2
		Glamorgan	2
Aston	4	Huddersfield	2
Bath	4	Liverpool John Moores	2
Birmingham	4	Middlesex	2
Cardiff	4	Reading (Electronics - Engineering)	2
Essex	4	Sheffield Hallam	2
Heriot-Watt	4	South Bank	2
Kent at Canterbury	4	Brighton	1
KCL	4	Central Lancashire	1
Liverpool	4	Coventry	1
Loughborough	4	Derby	1
Newcastle upon Tyne	4	East London	1
Swansea	4	Glasgow Caledonian	1
UMIST (Electrical Engineering)	4	North London	1
York	4	Paisley	1
Brunel	3a	Staffordshire	1
Bangor	3a	Teesside	1
Leeds	3a	University College Northampton	1
Manchester	3a	UWE	1

source: RAE 1996

ENGINEERING

English Language

Chinese may be spoken more widely as a first language, but the dominance of English as the world's favourite second language looks set to increase. It is the international language of science, medicine, aviation, tourism and navigation. Learning from books and cassettes can be a good starting point but nothing can compare with going to a country and soaking up the language. Learning about the culture and the people will also give you an insight into some of the quirks of a language. Choosing to study in the UK may be because you want to come here and sample the way of life, history, entertainment, even the pubs. You may not want to come for the weather but remember that although Cambridge cannot compete with California on a sunshine level, its architecture is great and it doesn't get earthquakes.

There are thousands of language schools throughout the UK and choosing one may seem difficult when they all seem to offer the same thing. Your budget will probably be a major factor in the decision process and the school's location may also be important. The quality of teaching, however, can make or break your progress with the language. The British Council, a government-sponsored body, was established by Royal Charter in 1934 and one of its roles is the monitoring of English language teaching in Great Britain through the British Council Accreditation Scheme. Schools that apply for accreditation are rigorously inspected every three years. Two inspectors spend several days within each school examining the general and academic management, the teaching premises, the student accommodation, teaching equipment, books, and welfare and social provisions. The British Council monitors the teachers, who should all hold a recognised teaching qualification.

There are two further associations linked to this scheme, for schools that have received British Council accreditation. The British Association of State English Language Teaching (BASELT) is an association of state sector English language teaching institutions, whereas the Association of Recognised English Language Schools (ARELS) is for schools from the private sector.

Many universities provide English classes either as summer schools or for students who are enrolling on an undergraduate or a graduate course and feel that their English is in need of some first aid. This may include English for academic purposes; writing a 5,000-word essay will involve different English to emailing the person you were chatted up by the night before in the college bar.

SPECIALIST AND VOCATIONAL COURSES

The Bell Language Schools

Bell, a registered charity, was founded by Frank Bell in 1955 to promote international understanding through quality language teaching. The Bell Educational Trust has six language centres in England and four in Europe, and has 18 associate schools in Europe and Asia. The UK centres – Bath, Cambridge, London, Oxford, Norwich and Saffron Walden – offer English language courses that focus on the vocational, professional and personal development needs of language learners. The Intensive English Plus programme improves English language knowledge, builds confidence, develops communication skills and applies English language skills to specific contexts. The Core programme focuses on language development through grammar activities, vocabulary building, pronunciation activities and skills development. The Plus programme activates the English learned through options of language clinics, English in vocational contexts, English for study purposes or English for personal interests such as literary, cultural, social and media studies. Bell has three exam preparation courses for IELTS, TOEFL and Cambridge, and prepares students – through the Intensive English Plus course – for other English language exams for business and vocational purposes. Bell's reputation is based on its quality of teaching and personal attention, study and multimedia centres, and student care. On-site sports and recreational facilities are available at most of the centres. Contact details p477.

Bromley College of Further and Higher Education

English as a Foreign Language

The Faculty for Community and

ENGLISH LANGUAGE

Continuing Education offer a full range of courses for students wishing to study English as a Foreign Language. All levels are catered for, including Cambridge KET, PET, First Certificate, Advanced and Proficiency. It is also possible to study for NVQs in English at both levels one and two. The college's language centre provides a number of modern multimedia resources, including interactive tape recorders and CD-ROM computers, allowing students the opportunity to study at their own speed. There are currently around 50 international students enrolled on the various courses. Contact details p478.

Christie's Modern Art Studies

The Modern Art Studies programme offered by Christie's Education was established in 1976 and offers a survey of the key ideas and developments of modern art from the origins of Impressionism to the present day. One of the course options on offer is in modern art and languages, designed for students of art whose first language is not English. This full-time course includes the core lectures – Courbet to the Fauves, Cubism to World War II and Abstract Expressionism to the present – alongside sessions of English language studies for special purposes and classes with an art history specialist who teaches students in their own language. Only a small number of students are accepted each year and acceptance is by interview. Successful students are awarded the UCLES Christie's Education Diploma in Modern Art and Language Studies. Contact details p479.

City Business College

Based in London's financial centre, City Business College is a private college situated within walking distance of the Barbican. The college runs its own accommodation service and sport and leisure activities are available nearby. Due to the large number of international students it attracts the college is used to providing information, advice and assistance on obtaining visas. The college aims to support students as they make choices about their qualifications and careers. The college offers full- and part-time English language courses at all levels from elementary to proficiency stages. Students learn in small classes with highly qualified and trained teachers. Courses include elementary English, Cambridge First Certificate and advanced English. Contact details p479.

David Game College

This independent college is part of the David Game Group, a large education organisation incorporating colleges throughout the UK and abroad, including Pakistan and Turkey. The college is fully accredited by the British Accreditation Council. David Game students can study English as a foreign language at the Kensington Academy of English, a division of the college. Courses are available at all levels, beginners to advanced. There are general courses and others leading to recognised examinations such as IELTS, TOEFL and the Cambridge range. Some students progress to the college's pre-university courses and receive full university entrance counselling. The University Foundation Programme is a one-year, full-time course designed as an alternative to traditional A levels, for international students wishing to apply to British universities. Tailor-made courses prepare students for study at degree level in a chosen subject alongside English language and study-skills classes. The course structure consists of six modules, spread over the three phases of the course. Three of these modules are major, relating to the students' future degree subject, and the other three minor modules broaden and balance the

workload. Minor modules available for all students include mathematics, IT and communication skills. Major modules include art, economics, law, science and social studies. Contact details p479.

EF International Language Schools

EF International Language Schools are truly international with students from countries as far apart as Thailand, Russia, Portugal and Chile. Together, these students form an exciting international community. There are EF language schools in London, Bournemouth, Brighton, Hastings and Cambridge. All these schools offer a range of English courses. Students can follow general English courses, summer courses or highly intensive one-to-one business courses. EF also offers courses to prepare students for internationally recognised exams including TOEFL, IELTS, Cambridge Proficiency, Cambridge Advanced and First Certificate.Classes at EF are carefully graded and run at all levels from beginner to higher advanced. All students are tested on their first day at school to ensure that they are assigned to the correct level of study. EF activity co-ordinators help students to organise their free time and have fun with their fellow classmates. They organise theatre visits, student parties, sports events and barbecues. At weekends, EF students have the chance to explore more of the UK with trips to cities such as Oxford, Edinburgh and Bath. Family accommodation and home-cooked meals are all included in the price of the course, although campus accommodation can be arranged if preferred. Contact details p480.

Gyosei International College
Diploma in British Studies

The aim of the programme is to give students an insight into British culture and to help them become fluent in both written and spoken English. In the first year the main emphasis is on improving English, whilst in the second year students are free to choose from the whole college curriculum including other European languages.

The Diploma in British Studies is a unique combination of language and culture courses which enable students to learn about Britain and its people as well as improving students' English. There are many opportunities to visit local places of historical interest, schools and businesses, as well as a study tour to another region of Britain. Contact details p480

King Street College

King Street College (KSC) was founded over 10 years ago with the aim of providing good quality, affordable English courses. It is based at two centres in west London, both opposite underground stations and only 15 minutes from the centre of London. The centres offer the same English language courses, which range from

general English to business English to small group IELTS courses. The general English plus conversation class, for example, combines a 15-hour week general English course with an hour a day of conversation practice in a small group. There is also an intensive course that lasts six hours a day. Students can enrol on courses lasting anything from one week to one year. Course start every Monday. Preparation classes for Cambridge exams (FCE, CAE, CPE and Cambridge Business Certificate) are always available. The school has a year-round social programme and welfare support for its students. Both centres are equipped with self-study rooms, coffee bars, email access and small libraries. The college has its own student hostel and accommodation can be arranged with local families. Contact details p481.

London College of English

The London College of English is a private college which is recognised by the Association of British Language Schools and provides English tuition for international students in small groups. It is situated near the City of London within walking distance of the Barbican underground station. Courses are available on a full-time basis at all levels from elementary to proficiency. They are designed to prepare students for the examinations in English set by Cambridge University which are recognised across the world. All teachers are fully–qualified, native English speakers who are experienced and aim to provide students with maximum benefit and enjoyment from their time at the college. The college administration is always available to assist students with visa requirements and any other problems that they may encounter. A full accommodation service is provided and there is a variety of sports and leisure activities within easy reach of the college, as are the famous attractions of London. Contact details p482.

London English Language Academy

London English Language Academy was established in 1997 and since its opening has trained over 2,000 students. The courses on offer are specific and aimed at improving students' oral and technical command of the English language. The main courses on offer are English at beginners or advanced level, and students can take a number of Cambridge exams including the Preliminary English Test (PET), First Certificate in English (FCE), Certificate in Advanced English (CAE) and the Certificate of Proficiency in English (CPE). It is also possible to study for the International English Language Testing System (IELTS), a certificate often required by universities for entrance to degree courses. The London English Language Academy also offers computer courses suitable for beginners and those wishing to improve existing skills. Courses available include computer keyboard skills, Windows, Excel, Access and Sage. The school also organises accommodation nearby and takes students on day trips to sightseeing attractions. Contact details p482.

London Institute of Technology and English

London Institute of Technology and English (LITE) has two centres: LITE Camden Town and LITE West End which are both examination-approved City and Guilds centres. LITE offers a wide range of English courses from elementary to proficiency to cater for their multinational classes. LITE aims to offer high-quality tuition. The teachers aim to be friendly and patient. The centres both offer courses in accountancy and travel and tourism as well. Contact details p482.

TEACHING QUALITY ASSESSMENTS

English
(England and N Ireland 1994/95/96)

Institution	Grade	Institution	Grade
Anglia Polytechnic	Excellent	Canterbury Christ Church	Satisfactory
Bath Spa	Excellent	Central Lancashire	Satisfactory
Birkbeck	Excellent	College of St Mark and St John	Satisfactory
Birmingham	Excellent	De Montfort	Satisfactory
Bristol	Excellent	East Anglia	Satisfactory
Cambridge	Excellent	Essex	Satisfactory
Chester College	Excellent	Greenwich	Satisfactory
Durham	Excellent	Huddersfield	Satisfactory
East London	Excellent	Hull	Satisfactory
Exeter (revisit)	Excellent	Keele	Satisfactory
Kingston	Excellent	Kent at Canterbury	Satisfactory
Lancaster	Excellent	King Alfred's College	Satisfactory
Leeds	Excellent	KCL	Satisfactory
Leicester	Excellent	Luton	Satisfactory
Liverpool	Excellent	Manchester Metropolitan	Satisfactory
Newcastle	Excellent	Manchester	Satisfactory
North London	Excellent	North Riding College	Satisfactory
Northumbria at Newcastle	Excellent	Nottingham Trent	Satisfactory
Nottingham	Excellent	Portsmouth	Satisfactory
Oxford	Excellent	Reading	Satisfactory
Oxford Brookes	Excellent	Royal Holloway	Satisfactory
Queen Mary and Westfield	Excellent	St Mary's College	Satisfactory
Queen's Belfast	Excellent	Staffordshire	Satisfactory
Sheffield	Excellent	Sunderland	Satisfactory
Sheffield Hallam	Excellent	Teesside (revisit)	Satisfactory
Southampton	Excellent	Trinity and All Saints	Satisfactory
Sussex	Excellent	UCE	Satisfactory
UCL	Excellent	University College Chichester (revisit)	Satisfactory
UWE	Excellent	Westminster	Satisfactory
Warwick	Excellent	Wolverhampton	Satisfactory
York	Excellent	Worcester College	Satisfactory
Aston	Satisfactory		

Source: HEFCE, SHEFC, HEFCW latest available ratings
For a more complete list of institutions offering these courses at undergraduate level refer to the Course Directory

Oxford House College

Oxford House College is located in central London on Oxford Street. The college is accredited by the British Council and is a member of ARELS. English courses are available for all levels, from beginners to advanced. There are courses in general English and also in more specialist areas such as business and executive English, English plus travel and computing, and conversation and pronunciation. Students can study for IELTS, in July and August, and academic English and Cambridge exams. There is a maximum of 16 students in each class, with an average of 12. General English, for example, is available as a full-time programme (15 hours a week), an intensive programme (30 hours a week) or part-time (six hours a week). Listening and speaking are the areas the college concentrates on most, but students get practice in reading, writing, grammar and vocabulary. Course costs vary according to the length and intensity of the programme – for example, a full-time, two-week course costs from £92 to £136 and a full-time, 36-week course costs from £1,284 to £1,817. Business English courses start every Monday or Tuesday and cover such areas as company structure, public relations, banking and negotiating. Lasting eight weeks the course costs £516. It is possible to take a BEC or LCCI exam at the appropriate level. Contact details p484.

Purley Secretarial and Language College

This private college, set in a large house in the centre of Purley, specialises in language and secretarial training. The college selects host families for students who need help finding accommodation; this is of particular assistance to international students as it provides an extra opportunity to improve their language skills. On arrival at the college, students are assessed on their language ability and placed in an appropriate class – Beginners, Elementary, Intermediate, First Certificate, Advanced or Proficiency. Emphasis is placed on communication, so listening, reading, speaking and writing skills are developed, alongside classes in English literature, history and culture. Learning resources include up-to-date audiovisual material. Students are prepared for external examinations held throughout the year, including IELTS, TOEFL, Institute of Linguists, and Cambridge UCLES exams. In addition to general part- and full-time English classes, the college offers intensive English for Special Purposes that last from one to four weeks, for example in trade, tourism and marketing. Students are encouraged to take part in sporting and social activities arranged by the college. See secretarial chapter for details of other courses. Contact details p484.

Queen's Business and Secretarial College

Queen's offers a range of courses which are detailed in the Business, Management and Marketing and IT and Computing chapters. There are two courses which meet the specific needs of international students: the English and Secretarial course for overseas students and Business English with Computer Skills (£2,590 London, £2,285 Cambridge a term). The former is a three-term course, designed for students with intermediate English language skills. Students focus on business English in the first part of the course as well as word processing and business administration. They complete a two-week work placement in January. In February students sit two exams: Pitmans text processing and LCCI English for Business level 1. The second half of the course continues with business English and advanced word processing

TEACHING QUALITY ASSESSMENTS

English and Associated Studies
(Wales 1994/95)

Institution	Grade	Institution	Grade
Aberystwyth	Excellent	Cardiff (Literature)	Satisfactory
Cardiff (Language)	Excellent	Lampeter (English and	
Glamorgan (Creative Writing,		Victorian Studies)	Satisfactory
Theatre, Media Drama)	Excellent	Swansea	Satisfactory
Bangor (Literature)	Satisfactory		

Source: HEFCE, SHEFC, HEFCW latest available ratings
For a more complete list of institutions offering these courses at undergraduate level refer to the Course Directory

and introduces shorthand and further computer applications. Students complete a further two weeks on a work experience placement and take LCCI English for Business level 2 and RSA Text Processing and Word Processing in June. Business English with computer skills is designed for students of upper intermediate level. Students study business English and take courses in keyboarding and word processing and learn a number of computer applications. The course is for 12 weeks (one term). Contact details p484.

Sels College London

Sels College is situated in the heart of London, close to the Royal Opera House in Covent Garden, accredited by the British Council. Students can study general English in small groups of between five and nine, as well as business or academic English. One-to-one tuition is also offered and can be combined with group tuition. Students can take various examinations including the Cambridge FCE, CAE or CPE and IELTS. All of the college's teachers are university graduates trained to teach English to international learners. Students have an average age of 23 and come from all over Europe and the Far East, with a few from Latin America. In order to maintain its friendly atmosphere, and personal tuition, Sels College does not accept group bookings from any single country, with no more than two students from the same source accepted at any one time. Accommodation can be arranged with families, hotels or hostels in central London. Professor AC Gimson, of London University, described the college as "a school with a heart," and the college aims to ensure the students derive maximum benefit and enjoyment from their stay. Contact details p485.

The Spectrum Group

Spectrum works with 20 government colleges and universities in London and throughout Britain. All offer modern study facilities for international students, with small classes, and a varied sports and social programme. Accommodation ranges from hostel to homestay. Most colleges in the group belong to the British Association for State English Language Teaching (BASELT), which guarantees the quality of their English language courses. General English courses are offered at elementary, intermediate and advanced levels, leading to TOEFL, IELTS and Cambridge exams. Fees start from £390 for four weeks, from £625 for three months and from £1,680 for one year. Courses last from a few weeks to a year or more, and several colleges run summer schools in July and August. Courses in English Plus (English language with a vocational subject) are increasingly popular, usually lasting for one year. Choices include business, art and design, computing, tourism, beauty therapy, hospitality, fashion, photography and music technology. Several institutions also run courses for international teachers of English – TEFL, TESOL and CEELT. Contact details p486.

St Patrick's International College

St Patrick's International College is based in a large five-storey building in a quiet street in the heart of London's West End. Open all year, facilities include a library, language laboratory, Internet room and multimedia computer rooms. English language courses at all levels start every Monday throughout the year. The minimum stay is one week and students can study for as long as they need. The college is accredited by the British Council and is a member of the Association of Recognised English Language Services (ARELS). St Patrick's

is also a recognised examination centre for the London Chamber of Commerce and Industry and Trinity College, London. Computer training departments at both sites offer courses at all levels using the latest software. Also on offer are courses in web design and MCP/MCSE training. All students can use the facilities at the nearby International Students' House, including a café, restaurant, cinema, gymnasium, pool, travel service, bar and cyber café. There is also a comprehensive social, cultural and sports programme throughout the year. Contact details p485.

The Old Vicarage

This private residential college for girls is set in a large Regency house on the outskirts of Marden village, Kent. Placing emphasis on the individual development of each student, the school helps them to acquire a range of skills and abilities. The Old Vicarage provides a relaxed but stimulating environment for students while they continue with their education and develop practical skills. International students have found that studying English language classes with a practical subject provides the chance to use spoken English and widen their vocabulary. Short flexible courses in English language are available, in addition to courses that lead to examinations in English as a foreign language. Courses are arranged throughout the year. Fees are £2,610 per 10 week term or £7,830 per year. Short courses are £326 to £435 per week depending on teaching hours and subject. Short courses for students under 18 years are £270 per week, inclusive of board and accommodation, tuition and tax. Contact details p484.

oncourse·co·uk
The ultimate guide to courses

DEGREE COURSES

Anglia Polytechnic University
BA (Combined Hons) English Language and Business

This degree enables students to develop English for business whilst studying modules in business issues. These modules are both theoretical and practical and range from the analysis of corporate culture to professional business presentations. Students do not have to make their choice of modules before starting the course which gives them a chance to find out about the courses before committing themselves. Coursework assignments often place students in realistic business situations and the work undertaken may involve writing business reports, preparing consultancy papers and making presentations. There are currently 45 international students on the course. Contact details p477.

Bath Spa University College
Comparative International Studies (CIS)

The one-year CIS programme allows entry into a number of undergraduate degrees for international students whose English language skills are below the usual entry requirements. The programme combines the study of academic subjects in year one of the university college's modular scheme with subject-related English language support and cultural and social activities. International students take classes alongside their British counterparts whilst receiving additional help with seminar presentations, essay writing and language skills. Up to three subjects are studied together with British students in year one of the modular degree programme. Successful completion of the CIS programme qualifies students for entry into the second year of a

degree programme at Bath Spa. The programme can also be used as a bridging qualification into other higher education institutions in the UK. This programme is a particularly popular route into the BSc (Hons) Business Studies, Creative Arts or Social Sciences programmes on offer at the university college. Contact details p477.

City College Manchester
English for Speakers of Other Languages

The college offers full-, part-time and evening courses for those wishing to obtain qualifications in English as a foreign language. Qualifications include IELTS, University Entrance Test, and Pitman basic and elementary. Students can study for up to 22 hours a week and are free to use the college's facilities, including a multi-gym, a leisure centre, music studios and an IT suite. Through one-to-one tutorials, students work with tutors to identify their needs and design an individual learning programme. Courses are based at the Abraham Moss Centre in the north of Manchester, and the Fielden Centre in the south. English language provision at the college is accredited by the British Council and is a part of the BASELT organisation. Tuition fees for a one-year, full-time course are £2,900. Contact details p479.

Executive Centre, International House
Specialised Professional English

International House is one of the most well-known names in the UK for English language learning and teacher training. The London branch is based on Piccadilly in the centre of London. The Executive Centre has been operating an independent programme of courses since 1983. The specialised English courses offer professionals the chance to study the language and language skills relevant to their own area of expertise. English for lawyers, journalists and executive secretaries is offered as well as tailor-made courses for doctors and for the tourism industry. Effective communication is the main emphasis of the course and techniques such as role-play and simulation are used to give participants plenty of opportunity to practice and develop their language skills. Facilities include a resource centre with video and computers, a listening library, and a range of material suitable for self-study. Delegates on the course are offered accommodation in hotels and private homes. There is also an airport transfer service on arrival and departure between the airport and the accommodation. Contact details p480.

University of Essex
BA Teaching English as a Foreign Language

This degree course is designed for those interested in a career in teaching English as a foreign language (TEFL). The three-year degree also incorporates the award of a TEFL certificate. It provides an introduction to aspects such as the structure of contemporary English and an understanding of the way in which language learning takes place in classrooms, as well as evaluating current materials and methods used in TEFL. It is also possible to take options in linguistics. The course is taught within the Department of Language and Linguistics which was founded 30 years ago and comprises some 50 members of teaching and research staff. There are currently 13 international students on the course. Contact details p480.

Lancaster University
MA in Language Teaching

This degree is designed for people professionally concerned with language teaching. Most students on the course

Countries With The Most English Language Speakers

Source: "*The Top 10 of Everything: 2000*"
Russell Ash, Dorling Kindersley 1999

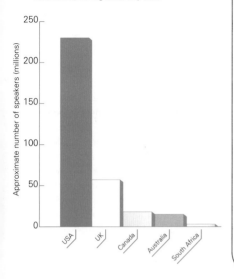

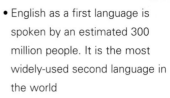
are EFL or ESOL teachers and come from or have taught all over the world. As a result, students and staff can benefit from sharing ideas and developing skills on a truly international basis. There are two schemes available within the programme. One, the TESOL scheme, places more emphasis on professional development, while the other, the Applied Linguistics scheme, is more broadly based, and has more of a research orientation. Both schemes, however, share common elements. They are both taught course, taking place over three terms. Students chose six modules from such choices as: Language Issues in Adult Literacy; Gender and Language; Language Test Construction and Design; Managing Innovation: The Project Approach; and Language, Ideology and Power. Each module is assessed by a 5,000-word essay, the mark for which counts towards your degree. You can also choose one or two courses to audit – this means you take part on the course

but do not have to do the essay at the end. You write the dissertation in June and July under the guidance of a supervisor who has a particular interest in your field. To help students, there are several workshops and support courses, a departmental library and a computer laboratory (postgraduate only). Contact details p481.

Middlesex University
International Foundation Course

This course has been designed to provide English language and specialist subject tuition. Two-thirds of the course is spent studying English language, and the remainder is spent studying your chosen specialist subject. After completing the course, students then go on to study a degree course at the university. There is a wide range of subjects to study alongside English language. These include art and design (preparation for portfolio), business studies, computer graphics, politics, music, technology/engineering, law, hospitality, marketing and fashion. Students study at one of the university's partner colleges, and alongside their subjects, are prepared for education at a British university. This one-year course begins with a free-of-charge, residential orientation week. Students on the foundation programme have access to all the facilities of the university, including learning resources and recreational facilities. Contact details p483.

Oxford Brookes University
International Foundation Diploma

This course is run by the International Centre for English Language Studies (ICELS) at Oxford Brookes. The course is a mixture of compulsory and optional modules. The three compulsory modules are English language, study skills and an individual research project involving the subject the student is intending to study. Five further modules are taken at foundation and under-graduate levels from a range of options that includes business, tourism, law, media, social sciences and computing. The centre is based in a new building on the main campus close to the library, computer centre, languages centre, sports centre and refectories. 87 international students from over 40 countries attended ICELS courses in 1997/8. Contact details p484.

College of Ripon and York
International Short Course Centre

The centre offers courses in English language at both intermediate and advanced level throughout the year. Students can study for periods of one to three months on intensive English programmes, staying with specially selected host families in York. Students can also study for the Certificate in BA Foundation Studies which is a one-year programme validated by the University of Leeds to give students the English language, study skills and subject knowledge to progress onto

an undergraduate degree. Contact details p484.

University of St Andrews
English Language Teaching Department

The English Language Teaching Department at St Andrews provides undergraduate and postgraduate access courses for international students before they study for their degrees. These aim to enable international students to study successfully at degree level. Each course has three main components: academic English; lecture courses; and general English. Students are able to live in the university halls of residence whilst they participate on the course. Passing the undergraduate English language course gives students automatic entry to the university. The department is staffed by qualified language professionals, most of whom have experienced teaching in other countries. Great emphasis is placed on student support, by way of individual tutorials, counsellors from the same country and schemes to help international students integrate into British life. Courses have been running for over ten years and there is a 100 per cent success rate in placing students who choose not to stay at St Andrews. Contact details p485.

University of Surrey Roehampton
English for Academic Purposes

This is a bridging/foundation course aimed at students preparing for undergraduate and postgraduate study. Students are trained in English reading, writing, listening and speaking skills. Study skills should be improved through the teaching of critical and analytical methods. The course also aims to give international students an understanding of British culture and society. In the second semester students sit in on lectures and seminars of the

undergraduate or postgraduate course they are intending to join the following year. This gives students a chance to familiarise themselves with the format of the course as well as giving staff a chance to get to know the students.

Students have pastoral support which includes personal tutorials. Previous students have gone on to degrees at Roehampton Institute and to other universities in the UK. Contact details p486.

RESEARCH RANKINGS

English Language and Literature

Institution	Grade
Cambridge (Anglo-Saxon, Norse and Celtic)	5*
Cambridge	5*
Oxford	5*
UCL	5*
Birmingham	5
Cardiff	5
Leeds	5
Queen Mary and Westfield	5
Sussex	5
York	5
Birkbeck	4
Bristol	4
Durham	4
East Anglia	4
Edinburgh	4
Essex	4
KCL	4
Lancaster	4
Leicester	4
Liverpool	4
Manchester	4
Nottingham	4
Reading	4
Royal Holloway	4
Sheffield	4
Southampton	4
St Andrews	4
Warwick	4
Aberdeen	3a
Aberystwyth	3a
Bangor	3a
Dundee	3a
Glasgow	3a
Goldsmiths	3a
Hull	3a
Keele	3a
Kent at Canterbury	3a
Loughborough	3a
Newcastle	3a
Nottingham Trent	3a
Queen's Belfast	3a
Roehampton Institute	3a
Sheffield Hallam	3a
Stirling	3a
Strathclyde	3a
Swansea	3a

Institution	Grade
Ulster	3a
Anglia Polytechnic	3b
Cheltenham and Gloucester College	3b
De Montfort	3b
Exeter	3b
Hertfordshire	3b
Lampeter	3b
Liverpool John Moores	3b
Manchester Metropolitan	3b
Middlesex	3b
Open University	3b
St Mary's College	3b
UWE	3b
Bath Spa	2
Bolton Institute	2
Brunel	2
Edge Hill College	2
Huddersfield	2
Kingston	2
Liverpool Hope College	2
North London	2
Oxford Brookes	2
Plymouth	2
Ripon and York St John	2
St Martin's College	2
Staffordshire	2
Sunderland	2
Trinity College, Carmarthen	2
UCE	2
University College Chichester	2
University College Northampton	2
Westminster	2
Westminster College	2
Worcester College	2
Bretton Hall	1
Chester College	1
College of St Mark and St John	1
Derby	1
King Alfred's College	1
La Sainte Union College	1
Luton	1
Northumbria at Newcastle	1
Norwich School of Art and Design	1
Teesside	1
Trinity and All Saints	1

source: RAE 1996

English Literature

The French philosopher Descartes said: "The reading of good books is like a conversation with the finest persons of past centuries." As such, a degree in English literature can be seen as an extended discussion with the likes of Shakespeare, John Milton and Charles Dickens, an exciting prospect in anyone's book.

English is, surprisingly, quite a modern subject. Although the British literary tradition goes back hundreds of years, until the 20th century British education was preoccupied with Greek and Latin texts. These days, as the English language has spread in influence throughout the globe – it is the second most widely spoken language in the world – and Britain itself has absorbed countless cultural influences into a multicultural society, so English literature has come to represent these changes. Although degree courses still require students to study what are known as the 'canonical' texts, including Shakespeare, Chaucer, Pope and Milton, they increasingly include authors as culturally and geographically diverse as Milan Kundera, Arthur Miller and J M Coetzee, winner of the 1999 Booker Prize.

Most universities, colleges and private schools offer English, and many will also offer English as a Foreign Language (EFL). The courses are radically different, however, and students should be careful not to confuse the two. A course in English literature will invariably involve a lot of reading, but it is also likely to involve the discussion of subjects and ideas as far reaching as politics, philosophy, art, history and science. The ability to write clearly and concisely is a must, as is the ability to develop and articulate arguments.

At undergraduate level, a degree in English usually lasts three years. The content of each course can vary considerably between universities, as can the diversity of choice offered to students. Some courses concentrate primarily on more traditional texts, allow scope for more unusual, and more diverse study including, in some cases, television and film. The first year of a course will usually include the canonical texts and provide an introduction to critical theories as well as important cultural sources such as Darwin, the Bible, Marx and Freud. The following two years will then allow students a certain amount of freedom to structure their own course of study. Teaching is generally carried out through a combination of lectures, seminars and tutorials, where students may be expected to do presentations or read out their essays, as well as engage in discussion and debate.

At postgraduate level it is possible to do research, a taught MA or even a postgraduate diploma course in almost any area imaginable. Choices could include critical theory, modern English language or Shakespeare studies, or the possibility to branch out further afield into subjects like American literature and culture.

TEACHING QUALITY ASSESSMENTS

Institution	Grade	Institution	Grade
Anglia Polytechnic	Excellent	Canterbury Christ Church	Satisfactory
Bath Spa	Excellent	Central Lancashire	Satisfactory
Birkbeck	Excellent	College of St Mark and St John	Satisfactory
Birmingham	Excellent	De Montfort	Satisfactory
Bristol	Excellent	East Anglia	Satisfactory
Cambridge	Excellent	Essex	Satisfactory
Chester College	Excellent	Greenwich	Satisfactory
Durham	Excellent	Huddersfield	Satisfactory
East London	Excellent	Hull	Satisfactory
Exeter (revisit)	Excellent	Keele	Satisfactory
Kingston	Excellent	Kent at Canterbury	Satisfactory
Lancaster	Excellent	King Alfred's College	Satisfactory
Leeds	Excellent	KCL	Satisfactory
Leicester	Excellent	Luton	Satisfactory
Liverpool	Excellent	Manchester Metropolitan	Satisfactory
Newcastle	Excellent	Manchester	Satisfactory
North London	Excellent	North Riding College	Satisfactory
Northumbria at Newcastle	Excellent	Nottingham Trent	Satisfactory
Nottingham	Excellent	Portsmouth	Satisfactory
Oxford	Excellent	Reading	Satisfactory
Oxford Brookes	Excellent	Royal Holloway	Satisfactory
Queen Mary and Westfield	Excellent	St Mary's College	Satisfactory
Queen's Belfast	Excellent	Staffordshire	Satisfactory
Sheffield	Excellent	Sunderland	Satisfactory
Sheffield Hallam	Excellent	Teesside (revisit)	Satisfactory
Southampton	Excellent	Trinity and All Saints	Satisfactory
Sussex	Excellent	UCE	Satisfactory
UCL	Excellent	University College Chichester (revisit)	Satisfactory
UWE	Excellent	Westminster	Satisfactory
Warwick	Excellent	Wolverhampton	Satisfactory
York	Excellent	Worcester College	Satisfactory
Aston	Satisfactory		

Source: HEFCE, SHEFC, HEFCW latest available ratings
For a more complete list of institutions offering these courses at undergraduate level refer to the Course Directory

DEGREE COURSES

Bath Spa University College
MA Creative Writing

This programme, located in the Faculty of Humanities, is concerned with imaginative writing, which includes poetry, fiction, play-writing and scriptwriting. Whilst the course challenges the dimensions between genres and experiments with language and form, it also also addresses traditional literary practices. Students are encouraged to pursue a particular direction with their writing, and their creative writing skills are developed to further their careers as journalists, writers, novelists or poets. The course is structured in a modular form, and includes writing workshops, two compulsory context modules such as postmodernism, writing and the Irish famine, suspense fiction and a two-stage writing project. Assessment is on the basis of a folder of creative writing, and each of the context modules are assessed by 3,000 word essays. There are no written examinations. The course attracts a variety of students from a many different backgrounds. Guest writers are invited to give seminars and readings throughout the course. Visiting writers have included Fay Weldon. Contact details p477.

ENGLISH LITERATURE

University of Birmingham
English

The English programme at Birmingham allows students to follow a syllabus reflecting their own interests, selecting courses in both literature and language, or specialising in literary or linguistic study. English can be studied as a single honours degree or as a joint honours degree in combination with subjects including African studies, American studies, drama and dance. After a common first year, in their second year and third years students choose from around 100 modules covering a range of writers, genres and types of literature from the middle ages to present, as well as advanced work in English language. Choices include a module devoted to Shakespeare, which draws upon the resources of the unique Shakespeare Institute in Stratford-upon-Avon and involving visits to performances by the Royal Shakespeare Company. Compared with school or college, students have fewer contact hours with staff, and are encouraged to work independently outside lectures, seminars and tutorials. Assessment is by essays, oral presentations and written

ENGLISH LITERATURE

TEACHING QUALITY ASSESSMENTS

English and Associated Studies
(Wales 1994/95)

Institution	Grade	Institution	Grade
Aberystwyth	Excellent	Cardiff (Literature)	Satisfactory
Cardiff (Language)	Excellent	Lampeter (English and	
Glamorgan (Creative Writing,		Victorian Studies)	Satisfactory
Theatre, Media Drama)	Excellent	Swansea	Satisfactory
Bangor (Literature)	Satisfactory		

English
(Scotland 1996/97/98)

Institution	Grade	Institution	Grade
Dundee	Excellent	St Andrews	Highly Satisfactory
Glasgow	Excellent	Edinburgh	Highly Satisfactory
Stirling	Excellent	Strathclyde	Highly Satisfactory
Aberdeen	Highly Satisfactory		

Source: HEFCE, SHEFC, HEFCW latest available ratings
For a more complete list of institutions offering these courses at undergraduate level refer to the Course Directory

The World's Highest Book Sales

Source: "The Top 10 of Everything: 2000"
Russell Ash, Dorling Kindersley 1999

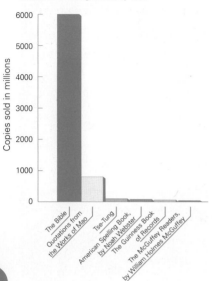

Copies sold in millions

6000
5000
4000
3000
2000
1000
0

The Bible
Quotations from the Works of Mao
Tse-Tung
American Spelling Book, by Noah Webster
The Guinness Book of Records
The McGuffey Readers, by William Holmes McGuffey

Interesting facts

- The best selling fiction writer of all time is the British crime writer Agatha Christie. Her 78 novels have been translated into 44 different languages and have sold approximately two billion copies
- The most expensive manuscript ever sold at auction is a notebook formerly owned by Leonardo da Vinci. Called *The Codex Hammer*, it was brought by Bill Gates for £19.23 million in 1994
- The most prolific novelist ever to have lived is the Brazilian writer José Carlos Ryoki de Alpoim Inoue. In the 10 years leading up to 1996, he published a total of 1,046 novels

ENGLISH LITERATURE

examinations, together with a final year dissertation. English graduates develop skills in critical thinking and articulate expression, and many go on to work in publishing, journalism and teaching. Contact details p477.

University of Cambridge
BA (Hons) in Anglo-Saxon, Norse and Celtic

The Anglo-Saxon, Norse and Celtic (ASNC Tripos) course at the University of Cambridge is the only one of its kind in the country. It offers students the chance to study the history, language and literature of Anglo-Saxon England, the Celtic lands of Ireland, Scotland, Wales and Brittany, and Viking Scandinavia, including Iceland and Russia. The course is, however, flexible enough to allow students to focus on areas that particularly interest them. The first year

involves studying three subjects chosen from a range of 10. These include four historical papers, five language and literature papers (Insular Latin, Old English, Old Norse, Medieval Welsh and Medieval Irish), and a paper on paleography. The same courses are studied through the second year, along with the chance to choose another three from a range comprising the 10 first-year courses, a special subject and a dissertation. It is also possible to select up to two papers from four other, related triposes. The third year allows students to take four subjects from a choice of 15, providing the chance to specialise more closely in particular subject areas. Further details can be found at the department's website: www.asnc.cam.ac.uk Contact details p478.

University College London, University of London

BA (Hons) English

UCL has a solid history in taking English as an academic subject seriously before any other university in the UK and has constantly achieved top ratings for both teaching and research. In addition to the single honours English Literature course it is possible to combine English study with German or History of Art. The first year of the

RESEARCH RANKINGS

English Language and Literature

Institution	Grade	Institution	Grade
Cambridge (Anglo-Saxon, Norse and Celtic)	5*	Ulster	3a
Cambridge	5*	Anglia Polytechnic	3b
Oxford	5*	Cheltenham and Gloucester College	3b
UCL	5*	De Montfort	3b
Birmingham	5	Exeter	3b
Cardiff	5	Hertfordshire	3b
Leeds	5	Lampeter	3b
Queen Mary and Westfield	5	Liverpool John Moores	3b
Sussex	5	Manchester Metropolitan	3b
York	5	Middlesex	3b
Birkbeck	4	Open University	3b
Bristol	4	St Mary's College	3b
Durham	4	UWE	3b
East Anglia	4	Bath Spa	2
Edinburgh	4	Bolton Institute	2
Essex	4	Brunel	2
KCL	4	Edge Hill College	2
Lancaster	4	Huddersfield	2
Leicester	4	Kingston	2
Liverpool	4	Liverpool Hope College	2
Manchester	4	North London	2
Nottingham	4	Oxford Brookes	2
Reading	4	Plymouth	2
Royal Holloway	4	Ripon and York St John	2
Sheffield	4	St Martin's College	2
Southampton	4	Staffordshire	2
St Andrews	4	Sunderland	2
Warwick	4	Trinity College, Carmarthen	2
Aberdeen	3a	UCE	2
Aberystwyth	3a	University College Chichester	2
Bangor	3a	University College Northampton	2
Dundee	3a	Westminster	2
Glasgow	3a	Westminster College	2
Goldsmiths	3a	Worcester College	2
Hull	3a	Bretton Hall	1
Keele	3a	Chester College	1
Kent at Canterbury	3a	College of St Mark and St John	1
Loughborough	3a	Derby	1
Newcastle	3a	King Alfred's College	1
Nottingham Trent	3a	La Sainte Union College	1
Queen's Belfast	3a	Luton	1
Roehampton Institute	3a	Northumbria at Newcastle	1
Sheffield Hallam	3a	Norwich School of Art and Design	1
Stirling	3a	Teesside	1
Strathclyde	3a	Trinity and All Saints	1
Swansea	3a		

source: RAE 1996

ENGLISH LITERATURE

single honours English course consists of a foundation course covering critical method and narrative texts from the Anglo-Saxon period to the present, with excursions into background texts, such as Homer and Freud and the Bible. In the second and third years, students take two 'core courses' in Chaucer and Shakespeare, plus six more courses chosen from language and literature options. There are one-to-one tutorials once a fortnight. The degree is graded according to assessment throughout the whole course, and by long essays and exams in the second and third years. There are only 80 places to read English at UCL including the joint honours programmes and as a result admission grades to the department are high – A level grades are AAB, with the A in English. Contact details p487.

Falmouth College of Arts
English with Media Studies

This programme encourages students to use literature, philosophy, sociology and media studies to bring an informed and critical analysis to their own reading and writing. It aims to provide undergraduates with the theoretical tools to analyse such texts as Victorian fiction and poetry, American Realism, television soap operas or even a website, for their role in the construction of meaning and identity. A distinctive regional emphasis introduces students to authors such as A L Rowse, Quiller Couch, Caroline Fox and Daphne du Maurier, and to ecclesiastical miracle plays in translation from the original Cornish. Small learning teams, seminars, assignments and independent research projects are designed to equip students with interpersonal and communication skills and the confidence needed for independent study. Undergraduates are guided and supported by tutorial staff with their own research interests and professional experience. The programme aims to provide graduates with a wide range of career opportunities, particularly in publishing, journalism, editing and other disciplines demanding critical and written skills. Contact details p480.

University of Leeds
English

The single honours English degree programme at the University of Leeds gives students the opportunity to study a broad range of English literature and language from the medieval period to the present day. The flexible nature of the course means that after students have taken prescribed core modules in each year, introducing important issues, approaches, and skills in English language and literature, they are then free to choose options from the variety on offer. Options can change from year to year and reflect the research interests of members of staff. These allow students to specialise in topics raised in the core topics or to branch out into new areas, and they help to give each degree an individual character. The School of English teaches across a wide range of English studies, from Old English to contemporary literary theory, including English language, Commonwealth and American literature, and modern theatre. The school was rated as Excellent in the most recent teaching quality assessments and received a 5 in the research assessment exercise. A number of scholarships are offered to prospective international undergraduate students. Contact details p481.

oncourse·co·uk
The ultimate guide to courses

University of Oxford
English Language and Literature

Oxford is renowned for postgraduate English whilst the undergraduate english language and literature course is always over-subscribed, with about 300 international students accepted each year. Oxford has well known academic professors such as Terry Eagleton, as well as the world-famous Bodleian Library. In addition to the BA in English Language and Literature, English is now offered as part of a joint degree with Modern History, Classics or Modern Languages. The course is non-modular, and you will be introduced to, and will write essays on, the whole range of English writing to which you may add a few options including classical literature, linguistics, American literature and major poets. Assessment involves one exam at the end of the first year (Honour Moderations), and then a final examination at the end of the third year. This system gives students the opportunity to deeply explore the subject in depth and develop their skills without exam stress in the second year, although it means the final exam period is more than usually pressured. As with all Oxford undergraduate programmes, students have a tutor to supervise progress and provide support in one-to-one sessions. Contact details p484.

University of Sussex
English Subject Group

English at Sussex has been highly rated in the government's research assessment exercises. It was also awarded a grade of Excellent in the most recent assessment of teaching quality. English has always aimed to be especially innovative at Sussex. It has a special study pattern for its degrees, giving students the opportunity to explore a range of topics alongside literature. The choice of courses available is wide, and students are able to put together a programme that suits their own individual interests. Most of the teaching is in seminar groups of about 12 students, and a number of courses are supported by lectures. In the spring and summer terms of year two, students are eligible to spend the spring semester at Rutgers University, New Jersey, as part of an exchange programme. English graduates from Sussex have been employed in a wide range of fields including writing, theatre, journalism, television, publishing, teaching and the civil service. Contact details p486.

University of York
BA (Hons) English

Literature is a particularly diverse and exciting subject, encompassing most of human life. The English Department at York seeks to reflect that diversity in a course of historical and geo-gra-phical breadth in which students are introduced to a variety of critical approaches while being encouraged to develop and express their own ideas. Options on the course range from Anglo-Saxon literature to modern Irish poetry. Staff interests also include several international literatures. The flexibility of the course can be seen not only from the variety of literary options, but also from the opportunities students have to substitute standard courses for subjects such as creative writing or play productions. A new programme starting in 2000 focuses on English Writing for Performance (Drama, Film and Television). Assessment methods are inventive and include long essays, oral assessment and seven-day open papers, to take account of the variety of strengths the department expects its students to acquire. Contact details p487.

Fashion and Beauty

The UK fashion industry has undergone something of a revival in the last five years or so. The 1990s have seen the emergence of British designers such as Alexander McQueen, Vivienne Westwood and John Galliano, not to mention Stella McCartney. In 1997, just 18 months after graduating from Central Saint Martins College of Art and Design in London, she replaced Karl Lagerfeld as head of the Parisian design house Chloé. Britain it would seem, and London in particular, is an ideal place to study for careers in both fashion and beauty.

The two subjects are usually treated separately and there are very few schools in the UK (the London College of Fashion – London Institute, is one exception), where it is possible to study both under one roof. Both subjects require a good deal of practical work, and there are an almost countless number of courses, and types of qualification available. Many private and specialist schools offer courses, and frequently their own diplomas, but it is also possible to take university and college courses at an undergraduate, or postgraduate level.

Fashion

The term 'fashion' covers a spectrum of activities. From high-street design to the catwalk; from fashion buying and marketing to textile design; and from photography to journalism, there are a number of ways into the industry, and a number of different courses available. Design-based courses will typically try to broaden a student's experience of fashion, whilst simultaneously developing their artistic skills and individual style. Other courses may deal primarily in the business side of the industry, be it in marketing, promotion or journalism.

Beauty and Make-up

There is a vast, and often confusing, range of make-up and beauty courses available in the UK. Before starting any course, you should gather as much information about what it involves, and what it qualifies you for, before committing yourself and your cash. It is also important to be aware of the many different areas within the general terms of 'beauty and make-up'.

Beauty therapy may involve massage, manicure, waxing and facials and respected qualifications include the International Hair and Beauty Certificate (IHBC), City & Guilds or NVQs. In addition, well known accreditation bodies, such as the Comité Internationale d'Esthetique et Cosmetologie (CIDESCO), and its counterpart, the British Confederation of International Beauty Therapy and Cosmetology (CIBTAC), test and inspect establishments before allowing them to display their names.

Those interested in make-up may have to decide between a fashion-based course and a special effects-based course. A fashion styling for hair and make-up course will teach students to prepare models for promotional, catwalk or photographic work. A course in theatrical make-up, on the other hand, may teach the various techniques for creating fake wounds, or period looks for the stage or screen.

SPECIALIST AND VOCATIONAL COURSES

Blake College

This independent art college offers courses that are suited to both beginners and advanced students. Set in a converted Victorian warehouse, the college offers up-to-date facilities. It provides a small number of scholarships for talented EU students on a limited budget. Fashion illustration students are initially familiarised with figure drawing. Different media are used including crayons, large and small brushes or a combination of these to produce theme boards and alternative drawing techniques. Students develop their own personal style in research and drawing, and complete projects based on historical and contemporary sources. Courses in pattern cutting and garment construction allow students to

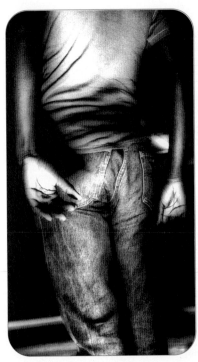

make their own clothes. Teaching covers the skills required for producing sleeves, pockets, trousers, pleating, and gathering in addition to sewing with electric machines and producing toiles. Students begin with simple projects such as making an A-line dress, and graduate onto producing a collection for the yearly student fashion show. Textiles students are taught to produce designs for fabrics and other materials for fashion or interiors, using a multitude of effects and techniques. Eventually students create and explore their own techniques and themes of research. The course covers a number of application techniques including screen printing, dyeing and silk painting. There are also courses in graphic and interior design. Contact details p477.

Birmingham College of Food and Tourism

NVQ Level 2 and 3 Hairdressing and Beauty Therapy

Students can focus their studies on either hairdressing or beauty therapy (two-year courses) or combine the subjects (three-year course). The content of the programme is 80 per cent practical and 20 per cent theory and students learn about such aspects as skin care, electrotherapy, non-surgical face-lift, nail and eye treatments, cutting, blow-drying, colouring and perming. Training is undertaken in a practical working environment in the college's two hair salons and beauty therapy suites which are all open to the public. New HND programmes include business with salon management.

The majority of the programmes start in September each year. However it is also possible to enrol in February. Course fees are £3,300 a year and this includes English language tuition. Contact details p477.

London Centre for Fashion Studies

London Centre for Fashion Studies (LCFS), working with Middlesex University, aims to be a leader in professional design, merchandising and technical training for the fashion industry. The director of studies at LCFS, Martin Shoben, has been a trainer and educator for the past 25 years. He is the author of books on pattern cutting, design and grading. The centre provides both full-time and part-time courses. The one-year Professional Diploma in Fashion Design and Technology, for example, caters for all levels from beginners to professionals wishing to learn new techniques. Studies cover women's day wear, evening wear, wedding wear, sports wear, children's wear, men's casual and formal wear and lingerie. Students learn about all stages of production from design and portfolio presentation to sewing and production methods. The course also includes industrial placements in clothing companies. It costs £1,800 for 12 weeks and £5,400 for 36 weeks. Another option at the centre is the two-year BA (Hons) in Fashion Product Management, which involves the study of three major areas: fashion product management, fashion business skills, fashion design and garment technology. This course costs £10,500 a year. Contact details p482.

London Esthetique

Located in the centre of London, close to Oxford Street, London Esthetique offers an educational programme covering full-, part-time and evening classes. The school adheres to the philosophy that educators must both teach and 'do' and therefore their team of instructors are also active participants in the beauty industry. London Esthetique's education director,

Beryl Barnard, is particularly involved with the school. She has 20 years of experience in the beauty industry, of which she is a well-respected member, working in France and the USA, as well as in the UK. Students at London Esthetique come from all over the world and an interpreter may be supplied if necessary. The courses on offer are diploma-based, either NVQ Level 2 and 3 or IHBC. Class sizes are kept small and the school continues to provide students with career advice and support after they have left. Educators at the school include the prestigious make-up artist, Ruby Hammer. Contact details p482.

Oxford International College of Beauty

Oxford International College of Beauty was founded in 1980 by Erika Oswin. It is set in a seventeenth-century building in the historical town of Witney, near Oxford. Witney is a typical Cotswold town, complete with ancient buildings, yet it boasts a number of modern facilities including a large sports and leisure centre, cinema, nightclub and modern shopping arcades. Beauty therapy can be a fascinating and challenging career. The college aims to provide students with comprehensive and professional training in all aspects of beauty and holistic treatments of the body. Courses include electrolysis, aromatherapy, reflexology and beauty therapy. Classes are kept small, with a maximum of 10 students enabling a more personal and intensive training. Oxford International College of Beauty is registered with ITEC (International Therapy Examining Council), and CIBTAC (Confederation of International Beauty Therapy and Cosmetology), both of which are recognised worldwide. Opportunities for graduates are considerable. Some may seek employment in salons, hotels or health spas, whilst the more adventurous may opt for cruise liners or airlines. Accommodation is available at the college, with local host families or in guesthouses. Contact details p484.

Oxford Media and Business School

The Oxford Media and Business School is situated in the centre of this ancient university city. The school offers a range of specialist fashion publishing, advertising and graphic design management programmes through its specialist media school. Nine-month courses available include a Fashion Publishing Diploma for those seeking a career with a fashion magazine, the fashion department of a newspaper, or even within fashion promotion. The syllabus includes coverage of the structure of the fashion industry, editorial, magazine production, and the business of publishing. The course also involves a practical publishing project/case study and visits to fashion shows, fashion houses and fashion magazines. All students receive professional help with career planning and interview techniques from the college's in-house recruitment service, Careers Direct. A full-time student accommodation manager offers help with accommodation in Oxford and most international students stay in college-owned flats and houses. Help with English language is available for international students who require it. Contact details p484.

The Old Vicarage

This private residential college for girls is set in a large Regency house on the outskirts of Marden village, Kent. Placing emphasis on the individual development of each girl, the school helps students to acquire a range of skills and abilities from dressmaking and entertaining to sugarcraft and childcare. The Old Vicarage provides a relaxed but stimulating environment for girls while they continue with their education and develop practical skills for use in later life. The school aims to produce 'talented, relaxed and well-adjusted adults'. Short courses are available in beauty culture, fashion and grooming, and clothes co-ordination throughout the year. The Art Department at the school also offers tuition in design and needlework, fashion and dressmaking. Students who successfully complete the course are awarded the school diploma. Fees are £2,610 per 10-week term or £7,830 per year. Short courses are £326 to £435 per week depending on teaching hours and subject. Contact details p484.

DEGREE COURSES

London Guildhall University
BA (Hons) Silversmithing, Jewellery and Allied Crafts

The opportunity to enter the world of jewellery design is provided by the BA (Hons) at London Guildhall University. The three-year, full-time degree is designed to be as flexible as possible to allow students the freedom to explore and develop their own creative and design skills. The course will appeal to students who have a particular interest in entering silversmithing and jewellery as managers, designers, and creative artists in fashion and accessories. The three levels of the course cover topics such as basic materials and processes, history of art and design, introduction to mixed media, new product development (silversmithing), and application of colour processes in design. Options from other departments in the university may also be taken, for example photography, computer-aided design and print making. The course includes an industrial placement period and has wide-ranging industry contacts; students can go to companies involved in fashion jewellery, silversmithing, glass, blacksmithing, theatre props, sculpture and millinery. A review in 1998 by the Quality Assurance Agency for Higher Education awarded the department a high score of 23 out of 24. Contact details p482.

University of Northumbria at Newcastle

Design

The Postgraduate Diploma/MA in Design at the University of Northumbria at Newcastle can include specialisms in fashion, design for industry and 3D design. The course has a good international reputation. It recently won an award from a leading German fashion magazine for having the best fashion design course in the world. Contact details p483.

Westminster University

BA (Hons) Fashion Merchandising Management

This four-year course has been developed in close consultation with representatives of the fashion industry and is taught jointly by the School of Communication, Design and Media and the Harrow Business School. Graduates will have the skills necessary for entry into the fashion business industry, as well as a broad understanding of the international industry. Students spend a year on a work placement and can participate in exchanges with the Fashion Institute of Technology in New York. Contact details p487.

oncourse·co·uk
The ultimate guide to courses

The World's Richest Supermodels

Source: *Eurobusiness* magazine, as reported in British Vogue

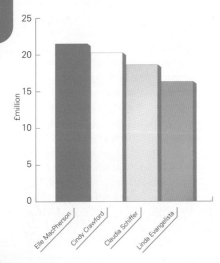

Interesting facts

- Top Shop's three-level store at Oxford Circus in London is the world's largest high street fashion store, covering an area of 7,897 square metres

- Selling more than 10 million bottles every year, Chanel No 5 is the world's biggest-selling designer perfume on the market

- 43-year-old Cindy Jackson has spent £66,000 on cosmetic surgery. Her 27 operations have included three full facelifts, thigh liposuction, breast reduction and semi-permanent make-up

FASHION AND BEAUTY

195

LONDON ESTHETIQUE
THE LONDON ACADEMY OF BEAUTY & MAKE-UP

Full and part-time available, day and evening classes

BEAUTY THERAPY COURSES

Internationally recognised for its comprehensive
training in all aspects of beauty therapy and make-up.
Post graduate classes are available in aromatherapy.
Excellent career opportunities through our close
connections within the industry on cruise ships,
spas and prestigious UK stores

MAKE-UP COURSES

Situated in the heart of London's fashion industry
we offer training by top international make-up artist's to
those who wish to make a career in the world of high fashion
make-up. Ranging from basic to creative level including
photographic, TV and film. Also available
"The One Day Ruby Hammer Masterclass"
(Post-graduate)

Leading to international diplomas in:
IHBC (International Health and Beauty Council)
NVQ Levels 2&3 (National Vocational Qualification)

Further Education Funding Available
Call or write for information pack:
London Esthetique, 75–77 Margaret Street, London W1N 7HB
Tel: 020 7636 1893 Fax: 020 7323 1805
Affiliated to Southgate College of Further Education
www.lond-est.com

Environmental Studies

environmental environmental environmental environmental

Many different subjects and courses come under the general heading of environmental studies. Some degrees can take a very broad approach, a BSc in Earth Studies for instance, and others can be more specific, such as a BSc in Coastal Studies. Earth scientists seek to understand the make up of the planet, the evolution of different forms of life and the origins of the atmosphere. It is an area of discovery, investigating changing patterns of land and sea, and changing climates. Studying geography can also involve many aspects of earth science, but it tends to be broader in scope and can include anything from geology to demographics.

Geography

Geography courses can involve the study of both natural and social sciences, from meteorology, urban design and planning, to demographics, social change and world cultures. Many degree courses provide students with a general grounding in a range of topics before giving them the chance to specialise in a particular area. It is also possible to focus on the practical application of geographical knowledge. A BSc or MSc in Geographical Information Systems, for example, involves using data collected from aircraft and satellites for purposes such as navigation, weather forecasting and disaster management.

Geology

Geology is the study of the earth, including its composition, structure, processes and history. Such things are not only constantly changing, but also affect how we use the land around us. Courses often reflect this by including a large practical element, including structural analysis and surface mapping for example, as well as a good deal of field work. Geological training is an essential foundation for many specialist careers. Those interested in working in the energy industry might consider taking a course in industrial or petroleum geology. In fact, it is possible to specialise in almost any geological area; some, for instance, focus on the study of fossils, and even link those studies with a course in archaeology.

Environmental science

Environmental science courses study the relationship between humans and their environment. With the increased concern over global warming, it is an area of both growing interest and importance. Course typically examine the impact that human activity has on the earth and, vice versa, the way the humans are affected by their environment, for instance, by volcanoes and earthquakes.

Ocean studies

There are not a vast number of courses in ocean studies or oceanography available in the UK. The courses that do run usually offer a good degree of specialisation. Some, for instance, are biased towards studying the physical and biological aspects of the ocean whilst others tend towards a technological focus and consider the operations that are carried on, and under, the sea. Other courses emphasise the legal and economic side of shipping.

TEACHING QUALITY ASSESSMENTS

Geography
(England and N Ireland 1994/95/96)

Institution	Grade	Institution	Grade
Birmingham	Excellent	Sheffield	Excellent
Bristol	Excellent	Southampton	Excellent
Cambridge	Excellent	UCL	Excellent
Canterbury Christ Church	Excellent	Birkbeck	Satisfactory
Cheltenham and Gloucester College	Excellent	Central Lancashire	Satisfactory
Coventry	Excellent	Hull	Satisfactory
Durham	Excellent	Kent at Canterbury	Satisfactory
East Anglia	Excellent	King Alfred's College	Satisfactory
Exeter	Excellent	Kingston	Satisfactory
KCL	Excellent	Leicester	Satisfactory
Lancaster	Excellent	Liverpool	Satisfactory
Leeds	Excellent	LSE	Satisfactory
Liverpool Institute	Excellent	Loughborough	Satisfactory
Manchester	Excellent	Manchester Metropolitan	Satisfactory
Nottingham	Excellent	Newcastle	Satisfactory
Open University	Excellent	Northumbria at Newcastle	Satisfactory
Oxford Brookes	Excellent	Salford	Satisfactory
Oxford	Excellent	SOAS	Satisfactory
Plymouth	Excellent	Sunderland (revisit)	Satisfactory
Portsmouth	Excellent	Ulster	Satisfactory
Queen Mary and Westfield	Excellent	Worcester College	Satisfactory
Reading	Excellent		

Geography
(Scotland 1993/94)

Institution	Grade	Institution	Grade
Aberdeen	Excellent	Strathclyde	Excellent
Glasgow	Excellent	Edinburgh	Highly Satisfactory
St Andrews	Excellent	Dundee	Satisfactory

Geology
(England 1994/95/96)

Institution	Grade	Institution	Grade
Birmingham	Excellent	Oxford	Excellent
Cambridge	Excellent	Plymouth	Excellent
Derby	Excellent	Queen's Belfast	Excellent
Durham	Excellent	Reading	Excellent
Imperial	Excellent	Royal Holloway	Excellent
Kingston	Excellent	Southampton	Excellent
Leeds	Excellent	UCL	Excellent
Liverpool	Excellent	Bristol	Satisfactory
Manchester	Excellent	Exeter	Satisfactory
Newcastle	Excellent	Leicester	Satisfactory
Open University	Excellent	Oxford Brookes	Satisfactory

ENVIRONMENTAL STUDIES

DEGREE COURSES

Coventry University
MSc Environmental Monitoring and Assessment

Students wishing to complete this course must first complete a post-graduate diploma, and if they wish to continue may go on to complete the MSc. Students are taught the processes of industrial environment, and maintaining good industrial practice in terms of water and air quality, and safe disposal of waste. Students develop their skills in assessing and solving environmental problems. They first study a core course consisting of environmental chemistry and management in terms of monitoring and analysing industrial environment. The final year of the MSc course involves studying environment regulation and management, with specialisation in waste management, air, water and noise pollution, and contaminated land. Graduates of this course have gone on to work in environmental agencies, consultancy and environmental quality control in industry and commerce. Contact details p479.

Kingston University
BSc/HND Geographical Information Systems

Geographical information systems is a rapidly growing branch of information technology which combines the skills of the geographer with IT and complementary disciplines. The course at Kingston is designed to link technical skills with the understanding of geographical problems and issues concerning the handling, manipulation and analysis of spatial information. Students undertake plenty of 'hands-on' practical work to reinforce theory and tackle real-world issues relating to spatial problem solving and decision making. The course includes options on remote sensing, surveying and programming. Students learn through computer-based practicals, workshops and seminars. There are currently 11 international students on the course. Contact details p481.

University of Leeds
Geology and Geophysics

Undergraduate degrees are available in geological sciences, geophysical sciences and environmental geology. All courses are taught by the School of Earth Sciences which received an Excellent rating in the 1995 teaching quality assessments. The geological sciences course involves the study of the whole range of earth sciences. The environmental geology course is concerned with the processes occurring at, or near, the earth's surface. This includes natural hazards and ground-water pollution. In the final year of both courses undergraduates follow a mixture of compulsory and optional modules chosen from around twenty subject

areas. The geophysical sciences course is a multidisciplinary degree programme. Over three years students take modules chosen from the departments of Earth Sciences, Mathematics and Physics. As the programme progresses, there is an increasing emphasis on specially tailored geophysics modules. The university also offers students the chance to participate in their North America programme. This is available for all three degree courses and lasts for four years, instead of three. The additional year is spent at a North American university, chosen from Penn State University, the University of Santa Barbara, the University of California or Queen's University, Ontario. The extra year studying means that students graduate with either an MGeol or MGeophys. Contact details p481.

Liverpool Hope University College

MA Contemporary Urban Renaissance

This course offers postgraduate students the opportunity to develop their understanding of current approaches to the study of urban issues. Set in the context of urban regeneration, the course provides a contemporary discourse on the future of post-industrial cities. Students investigate concepts and theories in urban geography and apply these to processes that have shaped cities in recent decades. A balance of academic and skills-based courses is offered. In addition to taught core modules such as practice and procedures, and concepts and theories in urban renaissance, students can also gain practical experience during work placements in development agencies, planning consultancies or local authorities. Optional modules include urban ecology and tourism, heritage and urban renewal. Students undertake research in a topic of their own choice. Contact details p482.

London School of Economics and Political Science, University of London (LSE)

Geography and Environment

Undergraduate programmes are offered in geography, geography and economics, and geography and population studies. All these courses reflect the economic, social and environmental problems which have resulted from location and spatial interaction, and provide students with an understanding of the social, political and economic forces which shape development and social change in our interdependent global economy. At postgraduate level, LSE's geography and environment courses concentrate on the socio-economic aspects of the subject, placing great emphasis on multi-disciplinary teaching and research and focusing strongly on policy-relevant work. Research primarily takes place in three cluster groups which focus on economic performance and regulation; the social institutions of economic transformation; and environmental policy, planning and regulation. Staff in each of these areas have responsibility for teaching specialist masters courses, which means that students benefit from an up-to-date understanding of the issues involved. Staff interests range from environmental regulation to the use of geographical information systems (GIS). Contact details p482.

The University of Reading

MSc/Diploma Applied Meteorology

The course aims to prepare students with a scientific background for work in all branches of applied meteorology, including agricultural meteorology. Core subjects include courses in atmospheric physics, global ecology and measurements and instrumentation, and these are followed by advanced options in subjects such as hydrometeorology,

TEACHING QUALITY ASSESSMENTS

Geology
(Scotland 1993/94)

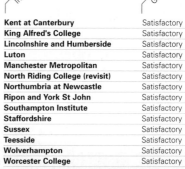

Institution	Grade	Institution	Grade
Edinburgh	Excellent	Aberdeen	Highly Satisfactory
Glasgow	Excellent	St Andrews	Highly Satisfactory

Environmental Studies
(England and N ireland 1994/95/96/97)

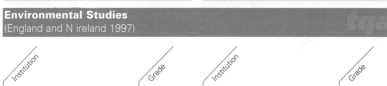

Institution	Grade	Institution	Grade
Bath	Excellent	Kent at Canterbury	Satisfactory
East Anglia	Excellent	King Alfred's College	Satisfactory
Greenwich	Excellent	Lincolnshire and Humberside	Satisfactory
Hertfordshire	Excellent	Luton	Satisfactory
Lancaster	Excellent	Manchester Metropolitan	Satisfactory
Liverpool	Excellent	North Riding College (revisit)	Satisfactory
Liverpool Institute	Excellent	Northumbria at Newcastle	Satisfactory
Plymouth	Excellent	Ripon and York St John	Satisfactory
Reading	Excellent	Southampton Institute	Satisfactory
Southampton	Excellent	Staffordshire	Satisfactory
Ulster	Excellent	Sussex	Satisfactory
Anglia Polytechnic	Satisfactory	Teesside	Satisfactory
Central Lancashire	Satisfactory	Wolverhampton	Satisfactory
De Montfort	Satisfactory	Worcester College	Satisfactory

Environmental Studies
(England and N ireland 1997)

Institution	Grade	Institution	Grade
Nottingham	23		

Environmental Studies
(Scotland 1994)

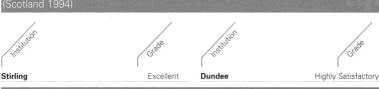

Institution	Grade	Institution	Grade
Stirling	Excellent	Dundee	Highly Satisfactory

Environmental Studies
(Wales 1994/95)

Institution	Grade	Institution	Grade
Cardiff (Environmental Engineering)	Excellent	Trinity College, Carmarthen (Rural Environment and Health and the Environment)	Satisfactory
Bangor (Environmental Sciences)	Satisfactory		
North East Wales Institute (Environmental Sciences)	Satisfactory		

ENVIRONMENTAL STUDIES

climate change and statistical climatology. The third term is spent on a topic of the student's choice. Students also have the opportunity to work on a team project, investigating an issue such as the 1997 El Niño phenomenon, and to attend a short course on weather forecasting at the UK Meteorological Office College. The department has links with the Met Office and the European Centre for Medium Range Weather Forecasts. A highlight of the course is the weekly current weather discussion, where the week's weather is compared with forecasts. Contact details p484.

Royal Holloway, University of London
BA/BSc Geography

The Department of Geography was awarded a 5 rating in the last research assessment exercise. Teaching focuses on both human and physical geography. Fieldwork trips in the UK and overseas add a strong practical element. Topics presently studied by students range from urban regeneration to environmental sustainability and, by the final year, a substantial amount of study time is spent completing ones own research and dissertation. The large size of the Geography Department means that there is a large choice of course units. Students with a strong interest in earth science may study in the Geology Department (which shares the same building) for a joint honours degree. Trained geographers are in increasing demand as governments and organisations around the world seek to better manage and protect resources and the environment. Contact details p485.

TEACHING QUALITY ASSESSMENTS

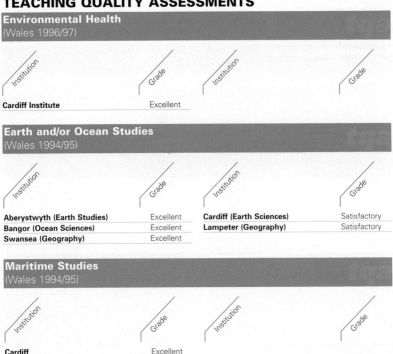

Environmental Health
(Wales 1996/97)

Institution	Grade	Institution	Grade
Cardiff Institute	Excellent		

Earth and/or Ocean Studies
(Wales 1994/95)

Institution	Grade	Institution	Grade
Aberystwyth (Earth Studies)	Excellent	Cardiff (Earth Sciences)	Satisfactory
Bangor (Ocean Sciences)	Excellent	Lampeter (Geography)	Satisfactory
Swansea (Geography)	Excellent		

Maritime Studies
(Wales 1994/95)

Institution	Grade	Institution	Grade
Cardiff	Excellent		

Source: HEFCE, SHEFC, HEFCW latest available ratings
For a more complete list of institutions offering these courses at undergraduate level refer to the Course Directory

ENVIRONMENTAL STUDIES

The Five Largest Cities in Europe by Population

Source: *"The Top 10 of Everything: 2000"*
Russell Ash, Dorling Kindersley 1999

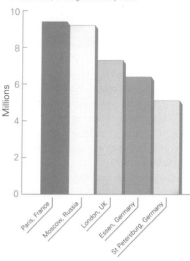

Interesting facts

- The city of La Paz, in Bolivia, is so high above sea level, at 12,000 ft, that there is barely enough oxygen to support combustion

- The average thickness of Antarctica's ice sheet is 7,200 feet. It holds 90 per cent of all the ice in the world and 70 per cent of all the fresh water

- Historians estimate that an earthquake in the eastern Mediterranean in 1201, killed over one million people

University of Southampton
Oceanography

The University of Southampton's School of Ocean and Earth Sciences is part of the Southampton Oceanography Centre. The school offers courses in marine sciences, marine environmental chemistry, and oceanography combined with marine biology, geology, physical geography, mathematics or physics. In both the oceanography courses and marine environmental chemistry, oceanography comprises at least 50 per cent of the courses' content. The marine sciences degree is designed to provide the student with a broad marine education, without having to specialise in any particular area. The course is also available combined with French, and both combined and single honours students spend a year studying at an oceanography department in France. The university has recently introduced a new, four-year, programme for undergraduates. The MOcean in Oceanography allows the opportunity for students to study outside of the school, and to specialise within marine sciences in the third and fourth years. All degrees emphasise practical skills and encourage students to gain experience in other marine institutes. Contact details p486.

ENVIRONMENTAL STUDIES

health and medicine
health and medicine
health and medicine
health and medicine

Health and Medicine

Britain has an illustrious tradition of medical innovation and excellence. As far back as the middle of the 19th century, Joseph Lister, who studied at University College London (UCL), introduced antiseptic techniques into surgery. More recently James Whyte Black, a graduate of the University of St Andrews, shared the Nobel Prize for Physiology and Medicine for developing the first beta-blocker drug, used to relieve angina. What is more, Britain's renowned National Health Service not only provides world-class health services free of charge, but it is the largest employer in Europe. This makes Britain an ideal place to study medicine, or pursue a career in healthcare.

The heading Health and Medicine covers quite a number of different career areas and subjects, from dentistry, nursing or optometry, to pharmacology, physiotherapy and training to become a doctor. It is also possible to study subjects such as anatomy, immunology or physiology at BSc, MSc or MPhil level, with many science faculties treating them as separate subjects in their own right.

Medicine and Dentistry

Britain's teaching hospitals count amongst the best in the world. Unfortunately, their excellent reputation for teaching and research attracts applications to British medical schools in huge numbers, both from Britain and abroad. On average, there are around three applicants for every available place in a British medical school. Some often receive in excess of 20 applicants per place. Naturally then, competition for places is very fierce and it is not unusual for applicants with three A grades at A level to be turned down. Furthermore, the government restricts the number of undergraduate places offered to international students, and some medical schools will restrict the offer of international student places to those whose own countries lack adequate training facilities.

There are about 30 schools of medicine in the UK, 14 of which also offer dentistry, which is similarly oversubscribed. The chance of being accepted onto a course may be improved by applying to some of the less-famous schools with less-rigid admissions policies. The University of Bristol, for example, has been known to admit students with unusual medical backgrounds, including a practising acupuncturist seeking to broaden his medical knowledge. Medical and dental schools will also be impressed by applicants with a high standard of spoken and written English and the ability to demonstrate previous interest and experience in their chosen field, possibly by way of voluntary work in a hospital, for instance.

Both dental and medical courses last five years. Traditionally, the first two years are 'pre-clinical', introducing students to the theoretical aspects of anatomy, physiology and dental science, for instance, followed by three 'clinical' years mixing study with practical experience on a ward. Some schools,

TEACHING QUALITY ASSESSMENTS

Anatomy and Physiology
(England and N Ireland 1998/99)

Institution	Grade	Institution	Grade
Newcastle	24	Sunderland	23
Loughborough	24	Luton	22
Liverpool	23	Northampton	22
Manchester	23		

Anatomy and Physiology
(Wales 1997/98)

Institution	Grade	Institution	Grade
Cardiff	Excellent		

Dentistry
(England and N Ireland 1998/99)

Institution	Grade	Institution	Grade
Belfast	24	UCL, Eastman Dental Institute	23
Leeds	23	Birmingham	22
Newcastle	23	Liverpool	21

Dentistry
(Scotland 1996)

Institution	Grade	Institution	Grade
Dundee	Highly Satisfactory	Glasgow	Highly Satisfactory

Dentistry
(Wales 1997/98)

Institution	Grade	Institution	Grade
Cardiff	Excellent	College of Medicine	Excellent

Dietetics and Nutrition
(Scotland 1997/98)

Institution	Grade	Institution	Grade
Queen Margaret College	Excellent	Glasgow Caledonian	Highly Satisfactory
Robert Gordon	Excellent		

HEALTH AND MEDICINE

however, are adopting a more integrated approach. Courses are intensive, and the disadvantage of combining academic study with practical experience is that students often only get evenings and weekends to study. In the last two years of a course students also lose their long summer vacations and have to work 48 weeks of the year.

Dental training ends at graduation when students are immediately qualified for practice. There are opportunities to specialise in areas such as orthodontics or restorative dentistry, for instance, and though a career in general practice is a popular choice, there are also opportunities in the armed forces, hospitals or academic dentistry. To specialise in oral surgery, however, you will first have to qualify as a doctor.

Medical training does not end at graduation. To be registered as a medical practitioner with the General Medical Council (GMC), graduates must first spend a year as a house officer. This is a kind of apprenticeship, served in a hospital under the supervision of a fully-licensed practitioner, and although hours are not legally supposed to exceed 56 hours a week, many house officers often work in considerable excess of this.

Upon registration, doctors can begin specialist training in any number of areas, be it as a General Practitioner (GP), or in surgery, pathology or anaesthesia. There are also opportunities in postgraduate research as well as in independent research organisations such as the Institute of Cancer Research. Research institutions will accept most international medical qualifications, but some research grants are only available to graduates of British medical schools.

Related areas

Doctors and dentists may be the most high profile members of the health services, but they are by no means the only ones. There are also nurses, pharmacists, opticians or optometrists, radiographers, dieticians, physiotherapists, podiatrists and occupational and speech therapists, to name but a few. It is possible to study and practice all of the above at British universities and medical schools. There are two routes open to those wishing to qualify as nurses, via a diploma of higher education in nursing (DipHE) or a pre-registration nursing degree. The minimum entrance requirements are five GCSEs. Both the diploma and degree programmes integrate theory and supervised practice in hospital and community settings. The courses usually last three years (sometimes four), and are typically split into two periods of 18 months. The first involves studying the Common Foundation Programme, and the second allows for specialist experience in areas such as mental health or learning disabilities. Accelerated diploma programmes, lasting 24 months, are sometimes available for those who already hold a health-related degree. Courses are run by some universities, and a number of smaller, specialist colleges. For a complete list, and further information on nursing in the UK, contact the National Board for Nursing, Midwifery and Health Visiting, between 10am and 3pm, at the appropriate number below. England: 020 7388 3131. Northern Ireland: 01232 238152. Wales: 01222 261 400. Scotland: 0131 225 2096.

Pharmacists dispense drugs for the treatment of illness and disease, and must possess an expert knowledge of the physical sciences. A Master of Pharmacy (MPharm) usually lasts four years and, along with a year of supervised employment following graduation, allows graduates to register as a member of a professional body, such as the Royal Pharmaceutical Society, and dispense drugs.

Students of optometry learn to examine the eye, to diagnose defects and diseases and treat them with therapy or lenses. A BSc degree usually lasts three years and will include studying the anatomy and physiology of the eye, visual optics and clinical practice. Students can go on to register with the General Optical Council by completing a postgraduate year of training under the supervision of a qualified optometrist, and passing the professional examinations.

Radiography has two principal branches. The first is primarily diagnostic and involves using x-rays and other electromagnetic radiation to produce images of the body's internal structures, and is an important process in the diagnosis of abnormalities and diseases. The second is therapeutic and uses ionising radiation to treat things like malignant diseases. BSc degree courses last between three and four years, include a clinical placement, and generally cover areas such as radiation science and technology, human biology, anatomy and physiology.

Nutrition is the scientific study of the foods we eat, what they contain, what happens to them in the body and what effect they have on our health. Dietetics is the application of nutrition with the aim of promoting better health, preventing nutrition-related problems and treating diseases through diet. BSc degrees usually combine both aspects and last between three and four years depending on whether a placement is part of the course. Graduates can go on to work in hospitals, but nutritional expertise can also be put to good use within the food industry.

You need high grades to study physiotherapy in the UK, at least BBC at A level, including physics at GCSE level or higher. The three- to four-year BSc degree is accepted all over the world, although physiotherapists qualified in the UK sometimes find it difficult to practice in certain states of the USA, despite the fact that many Americans come to the UK to train. Courses generally include options such as care of the spine, sports medicine or care of the elderly, and clinical placements are integrated into the study programme.

DEGREE COURSES

University of Bradford
BSc (Hons) Biomedical Sciences

The course covers the investigation and diagnosis of disease, health screening, the development of new drug therapy and the analysis of the effects of pollution upon the mammal. Although it has a broad basis, it includes significant specialist options. Cellular pathology examines cell function and the inter-relationships between cells. Medical biochemistry studies the body's biochemical responses to various injurious factors. Medical microbiology covers the natural history of microbial disease and the changing patterns in the epidemiology of infectious disease. Pharmacology

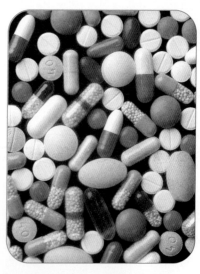

TEACHING QUALITY ASSESSMENTS

Medicine
(England and N Ireland 1998/99)

Institution	Grade	Institution	Grade
Liverpool	24	Birmingham	20
Newcastle	24	Sheffield	19
Leicester	23	Leeds	18
Queen's Belfast	22	Derby	16
UCL	21		

Medicine
(Scotland 1996/97)

Institution	Grade	Institution	Grade
Aberdeen	Excellent	Edinburgh	Highly Satisfactory
Dundee	Excellent	St Andrews	Highly Satisfactory
Glasgow	Excellent		

Medicine
(Wales 1997/98)

Institution	Grade	Institution	Grade
Cardiff	Excellent	College of Medicine	Excellent

Nursing
(England and N Ireland 1998/98)

Institution	Grade	Institution	Grade
Buckinghamshire College	23	Liverpool John Moores	21
Luton	23	Sheffield	21
Bournemouth	22	Sheffield Hallam	21
Brighton	22	St Martin's College	21
Canterbury Christ Church	22	Wolverhampton	21
Edge Hill College	22	City	20
Northampton	22	Leeds	20
Homerton College	21	Suffolk College	20
Keele	21	Thames Valley	20
KCL	21	Derby	19
Leeds Metropolitan	21		

Source: HEFCE, SHEFC, HEFCW latest available ratings
For a more complete list of institutions offering these courses at undergraduate level refer to the Course Directory

investigates how drugs and toxic substances interact with cells and tissues. Students are also expected to complete a substantial research project. Before entering the final year, there is an option to gain practical experience in a relevant working environment, for example in the pharmaceutical industry or in a medical research laboratory. In the 1996 research assessment exercise the department was awarded a rating of 4. Contact details p478.

University of Cambridge
Medicine

Cambridge's medical course consists of the three-year preclinical Medical Sciences Tripos, leading to a BA degree, and a two-and-a-half-year period of clinical study in a teaching hospital working toward the final Bachelor of Medicine and Bachelor of Surgery (MB BChir). Cambridge offers an MB/PhD programme, which includes three years of research combined with clinical training. The Cambridge Clinical School also offers a GP Parallel Track Course for students who want to go into general practice. You need AAA at A level to be admitted. The Clinical School gained high ratings in pharmacology and pharmacy, anatomy and physiology, hospital- and community-based clinical subjects, and clinical laboratory sciences in the 1996 research assessment exercise. Contact details p478.

City University
BSc Optometry

Of the six courses in this subject in the UK, this is the only one that is taught in London. Optometry is the study of visual defects and the ways in which these can be corrected or relieved. The course covers anatomy, physiology, pathology, optics, visual optics, computing and mathematics, clinical methods, binocular vision, contact lenses, visual perception, pharmacology, microbiology, professional and legal studies, perception and the environment. The qualification is recognised worldwide, which is why it is attractive to international students; there are 25 studying this course at the moment. Alumni are engaged in practice and research in over 50 countries. As well as academic qualifications, good communication and interpersonal skills are necessary. Contact details p479.

TEACHING QUALITY ASSESSMENTS

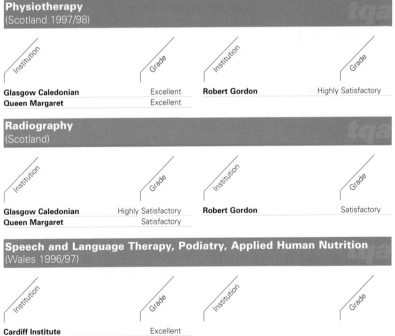

Physiotherapy
(Scotland 1997/98)

Institution	Grade	Institution	Grade
Glasgow Caledonian	Excellent	**Robert Gordon**	Highly Satisfactory
Queen Margaret	Excellent		

Radiography
(Scotland)

Institution	Grade	Institution	Grade
Glasgow Caledonian	Highly Satisfactory	**Robert Gordon**	Satisfactory
Queen Margaret	Satisfactory		

Speech and Language Therapy, Podiatry, Applied Human Nutrition
(Wales 1996/97)

Institution	Grade	Institution	Grade
Cardiff Institute	Excellent		

Source: HEFCE, SHEFC, HEFCW latest available ratings
For a more complete list of institutions offering these courses at undergraduate level refer to the Course Directory

Largest Human Organs by Weight

Source: "*The Top 10 of Everything: 2000*" Russell Ash, Dorling Kindersley 1999

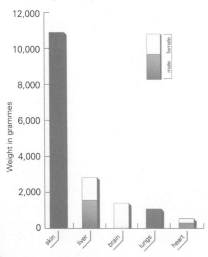

Guy's, King's and St Thomas's Hospitals Medical and Dental School
Medicine and Dentistry

King's College London and UMDS (the United Medical and Dental Schools of Guy's and St Thomas's Hospitals) merged in August 1998, bringing together three of London's most famous hospital campuses. The academic tradition of medicine at King's College London was established in the 19th century by pioneering doctors such as Lord Lister and continues today with scientists such as Sir James Black, who won the Nobel Prize for his development of certain life-saving drugs. St Thomas's Hospital was founded in the 12th century and for six hundred years was the only hospital in south London. Guy's Hospital was built close to St Thomas's and its first patients were admitted in 1786. Previous links were re-established when, in the early 1980's, Guy's and St Thomas's were incorporated to become UMDS. Medical and dental students are taught in their first two years at a newly-developed centre at the Guy's campus at London Bridge. Teaching in years three to five principally takes place at St Thomas's, King's College Hospital at Denmark Hill, Guy's and in the community. Some students of medicine and dentistry can choose to take a one-year intercalculated BSc programme. It is also possible for students to undertake a period of work abroad. Contact details p480.

The School of Pharmacy
MSc in Clinical Pharmacy: International Policy and Practice

Areas covered in the course include pathology and therapeutics, drug delivery, rational prescribing and pharmacovigilance, drug evaluation and service development. The international perspective deals with issues of healthcare policy, drug regulation and rational drug use. Supervised clinical placements are offered in a range of specialities, such as cardiology and respiratory medicine. The degree is the only one of its kind in the UK and is specially designed for the international pharmacist. Its purpose is to develop the ability of qualified pharmacists to provide clinical pharmacy services relevant to their own countries. There is a wide range of clinical specialisms available and the course has, in recent years, attracted senior employees of major pharmaceutical companies and professional leaders, as well as community and hospital pharmacists. The course is based in the University of London and two of London's 12 teaching hospitals, amongst one of the world's most enduring scientific communities. Contact details p485.

University of Teesside
Health

This school offers a range of under-graduate and postgraduate programmes

RESEARCH RANKINGS

Anatomy

Institution	Grade	Institution	Grade
Birmingham	5*	Dundee	4
Royal Free Hospital	5*	Glasgow	3a
UCL	5*	Nottingham	3b
Cambridge	5	Edinburgh	2
Liverpool	5	Queen's of Belfast	2
Oxford	5		

source: RAE 1996

Clinical Laboratory Sciences

Institution	Grade	Institution	Grade
Institute of Cancer Research (Biological Clinical Laboratory Sciences)	5*	UCL	4
Oxford (Dunn School of Pathology)	5*	Wales, College of Medicine	4
Royal Postgraduate Medical School	5*	Aberdeen	3a
Birmingham	5	Leeds	3a
Cambridge	5	Leicester	3a
Institute of Cancer Research (Medical Physics)	5	Liverpool	3a
London School of Hygiene and Tropical Medicine	5	Newcastle	3a
Oxford (Clinical Laboratory Sciences)	5	Nottingham	3a
Bristol	4	Manchester	3b
Dundee	4	Queen's Belfast	3b
Edinburgh	4	UMDS Guy's and St Thomas's Hospitals	3b
Glasgow	4	KCL	2
Imperial	4	Queen Mary and Westfield	2
Royal Free Hospital	4	Roehampton Institute	2
Southampton	4	Sheffield	2
		St George's Hospital	2
		Bournemouth	1

source: RAE 1996

Clinical Dentistry

Institution	Grade	Institution	Grade
UMDS Guy's and St Thomas's Hospitals	5*	Liverpool	3a
Manchester	5	Newcastle	3a
UCL, Eastman Dental Institute	5	Sheffield	3a
Bristol	4	Wales, College of Medicine	3a
KCL	4	Birmingham	3b
Leeds	4	Glasgow	3b
Queen Mary and Westfield	4	Queen's of Belfast	2
Dundee	3a		

source: RAE 1996

for people wishing to enter the health and allied professions. These include degrees in physiotherapy, health sciences, and occupational therapy. There are postgraduate qualifications on offer in a number of subjects, including medical ultrasound, rehabilitation sciences and a doctorate in clinical psychology. There

211

RESEARCH RANKINGS

Community Based Clinical Subjects

Institution	Grade	Institution	Grade
Cambridge	5*	Leicester	3a
KCL (Institute of Psychiatry)	5*	Liverpool	3a
Oxford	5*	Queen's Belfast	3a
London School of Hygiene and		Birmingham	3b
Tropical Medicine	5	Dundee	3b
Royal Free Hospital	5	Exeter	3b
UCL	5	Glasgow	3b
Wales, College of Medicine	5	KCL	3b
Brunel	4	Leeds	3b
Edinburgh	4	Newcastle	3b
Manchester	4	Nottingham	3b
Queen Mary and Westfield	4	Southampton	3b
UMDS Guy's and St Thomas's Hospitals	4	St George's Hospital	3b
York	4	Hull	2
Aberdeen	3a	Keele	2
Bristol	3a	Sheffield	2
Charing Cross and Westminster	3a	De Montfort	1
Imperial	3a	Westminster	1

source: RAE 1996

Hospital–Based Clinical Subjects

Institution	Grade	Institution	Grade
Imperial (National Heart and Lung Institute)	5*	UMDS Guy's and St Thomas's Hospitals	4
Oxford	5*	Wales, College of Medicine	4
UCL (Institute of Opthalmology)	5*	Aberdeen	3a
Cambridge	5	Bristol	3a
Edinburgh	5	Charing Cross and Westminster	3a
Exeter	5	Leeds	3a
Royal Postgraduate Medical School	5	Leicester	3a
UCL (Institute of Child Health)	5	Manchester	3a
UCL (Institute of Neurology)	5	Newcastle	3a
Birmingham	4	Nottingham	3a
Glasgow	4	Queen Mary and Westfield	3a
Imperial	4	St George's Hospital	3a
KCL	4	Dundee	3b
Royal Free Hospital	4	Keele	3b
Sheffield	4	Liverpool	3b
Southampton	4	Queen's Belfast	3b
UCL	4	Hull	2

source: RAE 1996

are also courses for students wishing to pursue nursing and social work. The School of Health maintains close links with employers and professional bodies, and teaching programmes are continually updated to reflect trends in professional practice and delivery. Most courses include relevant clinical placements. The

school also offers the opportunity for graduate students to continue their studies through a range of taught postgraduate modules or research. There are international students from Norway, USA, Mauritius, Trinidad, Sierra Leone and Singapore on the school's course. Contact details p486.

HEALTH AND MEDICINE

RESEARCH RANKINGS

Nursing

Institution	Grade
KCL	5
Manchester	4
Surrey	4
Institute of Cancer Research	3a
Leeds	3a
Liverpool	3a
RCN Institute	3a
Edinburgh	3b
Glasgow Caledonian	3b
Hull	3b
Liverpool John Moores	3b
Nottingham	3b
Sheffield	3b
Ulster	3b
Birmingham	2
Brighton	2
Central Lancashire	2
Glasgow	2

Institution	Grade
Hertfordshire	2
Oxford Brookes	2
Portsmouth	2
Robert Gordon	2
Swansea	2
Thames Valley	2
Anglia Polytechnic	1
Buckinghamshire College	1
City	1
Coventry	1
De Montfort	1
Manchester Metropolitan	1
Middlesex	1
North East Wales Institute	1
St Martin's College	1
Southampton	1
UCE	1
Wales, College of Medicine	1

source: RAE 1996

University of Wales Institute, Cardiff

BSc Biomedical Sciences

This course is designed for students who wish to work as biomedical scientists in hospitals, research organisations or industry. The four-year course involves a one-year clinical placement between the second and third years. The course is arranged within a modular framework. The main areas of biochemistry, cell and molecular biology and physiology lead to specialised courses in medical laboratory sciences, pharmacology and biotechnology. Students are assessed continually through examinations, assignments and projects. The department has a long tradition of educating international students, particularly from South East Asia and the Arabian Gulf. An Erasmus funded programme has established links with various institutions in France, Denmark, Finland, Ireland and Greece. Contact details p478.

Interesting facts

- In 1991, Katherine O'Hanlan of Stanford University Medical Centre, USA, removed a multicystic mass of the right ovary that weighed 137.6 kilograms. The patient made a full recovery

- Daniel Canal of Miami, USA, has undergone three, multi-organ transplants and received a total of 12 new organs in the process

- In 1957, on the island of Papua New Guinea, an outbreak of Creutzfeldt-Jakob disease (CJD) killed hundreds of women and children. The epidemic spread because they were eating their dead relatives

HEALTH AND MEDICINE

RESEARCH RANKINGS

Other Studies and Professions Allied to Medicine

Institution	Grade
Southampton (Nutrition)	5*
Strathclyde	5*
Ulster (Biomedical Sciences)	5*
Cardiff	5
Loughborough	5
Surrey (Toxicology)	5
Aston	4
Bradford (Biomedical Sciences)	4
Bradford (Optometry)	4
Glasgow	4
Greenwich	4
KCL (Gerontology)	4
KCL (Nutrition)	4
Napier	4
Portsmouth	4
Sheffield Hallam (Biomedical Sciences)	4
Surrey (Nutrition)	4
UMIST	4
City (Clinical Communication Studies)	3a
City (Optometry and Visual Science)	3a
East Anglia (Health Policy and Practice)	3a
Glasgow Caledonian (Vision Sciences)	3a
Liverpool John Moores	3a
North London	3a
Queen Margaret College (Nutrition)	3a
Queen Margaret College (Speech and Language Disorders)	3a
Central Lancashire	3b
Glasgow Caledonian (Biomedical Sciences)	3b
KCL (Physiotherapy)	3b
Queen Margaret College (Social Sciences in Health)	3b
Robert Gordon	3b
Salford College	3b
UCL	3b
Ulster (Rehabilitation Sciences)	3b
UWE	3b

source: RAE 1996

Institution	Grade
Bath Spa	2
Brighton	2
Canterbury Christ Church	2
Cardiff Institute	2
Chester College	2
College of St Mark and St John	2
Coventry	2
Derby	2
Glasgow Caledonian University (Other Professions Allied to Medicine)	2
Goldsmiths	2
Hertfordshire	2
Huddersfield	2
Kingston	2
Leeds	2
Leeds Metropolitan	2
Manchester Metropolitan	2
Northumbria at Newcastle	2
Queen Margaret College (Physiotherapy)	2
Sheffield Hallam (Health Care Practice and Evaluation)	2
Southampton (Occupational Therapy and Physiotherapy)	2
St Martin's College	2
Teesside	2
University College Northampton	2
Wolverhampton	2
Anglia Polytechnic	1
Brunel	1
City (Radiography)	1
East Anglia (Occupational Therapy and Physiotherapy)	1
East London	1
Oxford Brookes	1
Ripon and York St John	1
UCE	1
Westhill College	1

Pharmacology

Institution	Grade
Leicester	5*
Royal Free Hospital	5*
UCL	5*
Bristol	5
Cambridge	5
Liverpool	5
Oxford	5
Dundee	4

source: RAE 1996

Institution	Grade
Edinburgh	4
Nottingham	4
Queen Mary and Westfield	4
Birmingham	3a
Leeds	3a
Hertfordshire	2
East London	1

History and Politics

History and politics are two closely linked subjects that are central to our everyday lives. They are determining forces in how we live as individuals and as a society, and they are essential to our national identity. Studying the past not only involves a fascination with how we have evolved but also generates the vain hope that we might learn lessons from our history and avoid repeating the same costly mistakes. While historians pick over the bones of episodes past, politicians look to the future hoping that they can plan a better place to meet the needs of a changing world.

Britain has played a major part in global civilisation and it has a rich historical and political heritage. One only has to think of major British landmarks, such as the Houses of Parliament or Nelson's Column, or leading figures such as Queen Victoria or Margaret Thatcher to illustrate Britain's varied past and the extent of its influences. Studying in Britain can give international students an indication of the culture and surroundings that underpin the country's history, and it can provide a good experience of the politics of one of the world's oldest democracies.

History can be studied as a single subject or it can be combined with a number of different disciplines such as languages or archaeology. It is also possible to study courses such as economic and social history as degrees in their own right. Most history degrees give students a general overview of the subject in the first year with modules covering broad periods and themes in history or concentrating on study skills or historiography – the study of theories and approaches to history. In the second and third years, most courses will allow students to pick and choose more specialist topics from the range offered by their department.

Politics degrees, like history degrees, can often be combined with a number of subjects and can vary in nature from institution to institution. Most courses will include an overview of the subject in the first year with courses on how politics and political thought have developed, how power is distributed and how government interacts with society. In the second and third years, students can usually choose options covering differing political theories and philosophies, or the politics of countries around the world. Degrees can also be taken in international relations, which examine the underlying mechanisms of affinity and exploitation that draws nations together, or not, as the case may be.

To study history or politics, students need to have the ability to think critically, and the necessary skills to analyse evidence and present cogent arguments. Teaching on history and politics courses is usually through lectures and seminars and assessment by exams at the end of the academic year. Many courses will also offer the opportunity of a dissertation in the final year contributing to the overall degree mark. History and politics graduates are generally recognised as being flexible, adaptable and able to fit into a variety of positions in modern life.

SPECIALIST AND VOCATIONAL COURSES

University of Bradford
Peace Studies

Established in 1973, this is now the world's largest university centre for peace studies. This course is concerned with the analysis of issues of international, social and interpersonal violence. The areas covered include conflict resolution, defence and security, development, international relations, politics and society. The foundations of the courses are drawn from politics, sociology and international relations, social psych-ology, history, philosophy and eco-nomics. In the final year, students must complete a dissertation. All courses are taught using a combination of lectures, seminars and tutorials. Options include modules such as: the United Nations, peacekeeping and intervention, development and democracy in Latin America, nationalism and ethnicity in post-Cold War politics, and the Middle East: areas in conflict. The department's inter-national standing has been recognised by Rotary International which has selected it as one of only seven departments worldwide to receive its postgraduate scholarships. Contact details p478.

DEGREE COURSES

Institute of Education, University of London
MA in Education and International Development

Students on this degree course study two foundation modules in education development and international develop-ment. They also take a range of optional modules on such subjects as education planning, curriculum and teacher education in developing countries, and women and health.

Lasting one year full time and two to four years part time, the course can be structured to suit the student's own needs. It is aimed at professionals and educators working in ministries of education, non-government organisations, donor agencies and schools abroad. In 1998/9 there were 23 international students on the course. Contact details p481.

University of Wales, Lampeter
BA (Hons) History

The University of Wales, Lampeter, is well placed for field trips to medieval and pre-modern towns, churches, castles and monasteries. Students are encouraged to attend seminars at the University of Wales conference centre, Gregynog Hall, in the countryside of mid-Wales. Here, students and staff can relax socially with colleagues from other universities within Wales. The History Society, run by students, also organises a programme of speakers, visits and social events, all with the idea of fostering the pleasures of studying history. From the outset of the course, students are introduced to the nature and problems of historical enquiry. This training aims to develop skills in research, assimilation, comprehension and analysis as well as in writing critically, sensitively and relevantly, and in making and communicating clear and coherent judgements. All such skills are transferable to the employment market and recent Lampeter graduates have gone on to a variety of jobs in teaching, archive administration, the Civil Service, accountancy, law, banking, management and social work. Contact details p481.

oncourse · co · uk
The ultimate guide to courses

TEACHING QUALITY ASSESSMENTS

History
(England and N Ireland 1993/94)

Institution	Grade	Institution	Grade
Birmingham	Excellent	Derby	Satisfactory
Cambridge	Excellent	East Anglia	Satisfactory
Canterbury Christ Church	Excellent	Essex	Satisfactory
Durham	Excellent	Goldsmiths	Satisfactory
Hull	Excellent	Keele	Satisfactory
KCL	Excellent	King Alfred's College	Satisfactory
Lancaster	Excellent	La Sainte Union College	Satisfactory
Leicester	Excellent	Leeds	Satisfactory
Liverpool	Excellent	Manchester	Satisfactory
LSE	Excellent	Newcastle	Satisfactory
Oxford	Excellent	North London	Satisfactory
Queen's Belfast	Excellent	Northumbria at Newcastle	Satisfactory
Royal Holloway	Excellent	St Martins College	Satisfactory
Sheffield	Excellent	Sheffield Hallam	Satisfactory
UCL	Excellent	Southampton	Satisfactory
Warburg Institute	Excellent	Staffordshire	Satisfactory
Warwick	Excellent	Sussex	Satisfactory
York	Excellent	Trinity and All Saints	Satisfactory
Anglia Polytechnic	Satisfactory	University College Chichester	Satisfactory
Bath Spa	Satisfactory	UWE	Satisfactory
Bristol	Satisfactory	Wolverhampton	Satisfactory

History
(Scotland 1995/96)

Institution	Grade	Institution	Grade
Edinburgh	Excellent	Glasgow	Highly Satisfactory
St Andrews	Excellent	Stirling	Highly Satisfactory
Aberdeen	Highly Satisfactory	Strathclyde	Highly Satisfactory
Dundee	Highly Satisfactory		

History
(Wales 1993/94)

Institution	Grade	Institution	Grade
Swansea	Excellent	Cardiff	Satisfactory
Aberystwyth	Satisfactory	Glamorgan	Satisfactory
Bangor	Satisfactory	Lampeter	Satisfactory

Politics
(Wales 1995/96)

Institution	Grade	Institution	Grade
Aberystwyth	Excellent	Swansea	Satisfactory
Cardiff	Satisfactory		

Source: HEFCE, SHEFC, HEFCW latest available ratings
For a more complete list of institutions offering these courses at undergraduate level refer to the Course Directory

TEACHING QUALITY ASSESSMENTS

Politics
(Scotland 1996)

Institution	Grade	Institution	Grade
Strathclyde	Excellent	Edinburgh	Highly Satisfactory
Aberdeen	Highly Satisfactory	Glasgow	Highly Satisfactory
Dundee	Highly Satisfactory	Stirling	Highly Satisfactory

Source: HEFCE, SHEFC, HEFCW latest available ratings
For a more complete list of institutions offering these courses at undergraduate level refer to the Course Directory

London Centre of International Relations (University of Kent)

MA International Relations / MA International Conflict Analysis / MA International Relations and European Studies and MPhil/PhD

The University of Kent's London Centre of International Relations was established in 1990 and now comprises half the total number of graduate students in the department of politics and international relations. Forming a significant part of Kent's Graduate School of Politics and International Relations, teaching on the MA programmes stresses the cutting edge of theoretical and philosophical debates in the study of global politics, while being at the same time engaged with specialised areas covering the research interests of staff based at the London centre and the department as a whole. All three MA programmes share core courses in international relations theory and methodology, while diversifying into separate areas through mandatory and elective modules. The MA in International Relations familiarises students with contending approaches to the subject and its history, while providing them with more contemporary challenges from ethics, critical theory, post-structuralism and feminism. The MA in International Conflict Analysis covers the various explanations and understanding of international conflict from classical thought on war to more contemporary approaches to the study of political violence and peace. Topics covered include: conflict and social change; the politics of identity; the ethics of war and peace; women and war; international and inter-communal conflict resolution; and peace building in post-conflict societies. The MA in International Relations and European Studies seeks to integrate the centre's expertise in both international relations and European studies. While it contains core courses in theories and methodologies of international relations, this programme emphasises a detailed interpretation of European international politics, with particular focus on topics such as: European governance; the institutions and politics of the European Union; and the international politics of East-West relations. Elective modules on offer to all students at the LCIR may include: human rights; international political economy; environmental politics; security studies; and critical approaches to war and peace. The three MA programmes are available on a full - and part-time basis. Contact details p482.

University of Sheffield
Politics

The department received a 5 rating in the 1996 research assessment exercise. Research and teaching covers a wide area including political parties, international political economy,

European public policy, political theory, British politics and political methodology. The department houses the Mohan Memorial library which has a collection of books with a particular strength in the fields of international politics and third world politics. The 655 full-time students can choose from a variety of single and dual honours courses adding the following subject areas to politics: economics, geography, Japanese studies, sociology, modern history, philosophy, or languages such as French, German, Hispanic or Russian. There are eight MA courses in British politics, democracy and democratisation, European political economy, international political economy, public policy, political economy, politics and intern-ational studies as well as an MSc in research methodology. Contact details p485.

School of Oriental and African Studies (SOAS), University of London
BA History and Politics

This combined degree offers students the opportunity to explore a range of political and cultural traditions within a unique comparative historical framework. In addition to developing knowledge of the core intellectual and theoretical concepts of the disciplines, students are offered a range of specialist options in international and regional topics such as gender history of the modern Middle East and Africa, or Chinese politics of the 20th century, to name just two. The regional aspect of this course (you choose a region or area) enables students to really focus on one culture, illuminating issues such as imperialism, colonisation and de-colonisation. Contact details p485.

Interesting facts

- Henry VIII, reigning from 1509 to 1547, was the fattest King of England with a 52 inch waist, Charles I, 1625 to 1649, was the smallest standing at 4'9" while George III, 1760-1820, went slowly insane, which all makes the present Royal Family seem quite normal

- On November 5 1605, Guy Fawkes was arrested for trying to blow up the British Parliament, the King, and his Lords. The occasion was known as the Gunpowder Plot and the date has been celebrated annually ever since with fireworks, bonfires and the burning of a 'guy'

The Youngest British Prime Ministers

Source: "*The Top 10 of Everything: 2000*" Russell Ash, Dorling Kindersley 1999

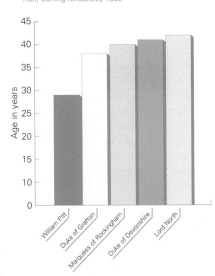

RESEARCH RANKINGS

Politics and International Studies

Institution	Grade	Institution	Grade
Essex	5*	Leeds	3a
KCL	5*	Liverpool	3a
LSE	5*	Open University	3a
Oxford	5*	Oxford Brookes	3a
Aberystwyth	5	Nottingham	3a
Glasgow	5	Plymouth	3a
Institute of Commonwealth Studies	5	Reading	3a
Sheffield	5	SOAS	3a
Strathclyde	5	St Andrews	3a
Sussex, Science Policy Research Unit	5	Stirling	3a
Aberdeen	4	Warwick	3a
Birkbeck	4	Westminster	3a
Bradford	4	Coventry	3b
Bristol	4	Durham	3b
Edinburgh	4	East Anglia	3b
Exeter	4	Guildhall	3b
Hull	4	Huddersfield	3b
Keele	4	Leeds Metropolitan	3b
Leicester	4	Manchester (Policy Research in Engineering, Science and Technology)	3b
Manchester (Government)	4	Manchester Metropolitan	3b
Newcastle upon Tyne	4	Middlesex	3b
Queen Mary and Westfield	4	Northumbria at Newcastle	3b
Queen's Belfast	4	Nottingham Trent	3b
Southampton	4	Robert Gordon	3b
SSEES	4	Staffordshire	3b
Sussex (International Relations and Politics)	4	Ulster	3b
Swansea	4	Glasgow Caledonian	2
York	4	Greenwich	2
Birmingham	3a	Liverpool John Moores	2
Brunel	3a	Teesside	2
De Montfort	3a	Wolverhampton	2
Dundee	3a	Southampton Institute	1
Kent at Canterbury	3a		
Lancaster	3a		

source: RAE 1996

University of Sussex
MA International Relations

This taught postgraduate programme is designed for students who wish to extend their knowledge of international relations as well as those who require an introduction to the subject. The course begins with a group of core subjects which are theoretical and historical in nature, thereby offering students a challenging approach to study. In the second term, in addition to an introduction to relevant research practices, students can choose two options from a wide range of course modules, from foreign policy analysis, international conflict analysis, to the globalisation of business, or war, state and society. The course is progressive in nature, and is moved primarily by contemporary social analysis and critical theory, rather than by classical international theory or traditional history associated with most international studies programmes. The wide range of course options allow students to pursue their own research interests closely. Contact details p486.

HISTORY AND POLITICS

RESEARCH RANKINGS

Institution	Grade
Cambridge	5*
KCL	5*
LSE (Economic History)	5*
Oxford	5*
SOAS	5*
UCL	5*
Warwick	5*
Birkbeck	5
Birmingham, School of History	5
Bristol	5
Durham	5
East Anglia	5
Edinburgh (Economic and Social History)	5
Hull (Economic and Social History)	5
Hull (History)	5
Imperial	5
Institute of Commonwealth Studies	5
Leeds	5
Leicester (Economic and Social History and English Local History)	5
LSE (International History)	5
Manchester	5
Open University	5
Royal Holloway	5
Sheffield	5
St Andrews	5
Strathclyde	5
Sussex	5
Ulster	5
Aberystwyth	4
Birmingham (Economic and Social History)	4
Cardiff	4
Edinburgh (History)	4
Essex	4
Exeter (History)	4
Glasgow (Economic and Social History)	4
Goldsmiths	4
London Guildhall	4
Institute of Historical Research	4
Keele	4
Kent at Canterbury	4
Lancaster	4
Leicester (History)	4
Liverpool (History)	4
Newcastle upon Tyne	4
Nottingham	4
Oxford Brookes	4
Queen Mary and Westfield	4
Queen's Belfast (Economic and Social History)	4
Queen's of Belfast (Modern History)	4
Reading	4
Sheffield Hallam	4
Southampton	4
SSEES	4
Stirling	4
Warburg Institute	4
York	4
Aberdeen	3a
Bangor	3a
Bath Spa	3a
Canterbury Christ Church	3a
Central Lancashire	3a
Dundee	3a
Exeter (Economic and Social History)	3a
Glasgow (History)	3a
Huddersfield	3a
Liverpool (Economic and Social History)	3a
North London	3a
Northumbria at Newcastle	3a
Roehampton Institute	3a
St Mary's College	3a
Swansea	3a
Teesside	3a
UWE	3a
Wolverhampton	3a
Anglia Polytechnic	3b
De Montfort	3b
Edge Hill College	3b
King Alfred's College	3b
Kingston	3b
Lampeter	3b
Liverpool John Moores	3b
Manchester Metropolitan	3b
Middlesex	3b
North Riding College	3b
Portsmouth	3b
Staffordshire	3b
Sunderland	3b
Trinity and All Saints	3b
University College Chichester	3b
Westminster	3b
Bolton Institute	2
Cheltenham and Gloucester College	2
Chester College	2
Glamorgan	2
Glasgow Caledonian	2
Hertfordshire	2
La Sainte Union College	2
Liverpool Hope College	2
Luton	2
University College Northampton	2
Nottingham Trent	2
Ripon and York St John	2
St Martin's College	2
Thames Valley	2
Worcester College	2
Derby	1
Westhill College	1

source: RAE 1996

HISTORY AND POLITICS

221

Hotel Management, Catering and Food Studies

The hospitality industry has changed considerably since Cesar Ritz, the celebrated hotelier, first opened his hotel doors in London and Paris at the beginning of the 20th century. Nowadays, catering and hospitality are an integral part of the service sector and are widely recognised as economic growth areas. In the UK alone there are over 260,000 hotels, restaurants, cafés, pubs and clubs, and an estimated 100,000 catering outlets, employing 10 per cent of the country's workforce. These range from a small number of very large hotel and catering groups, such as Radisson or Forte operating on a worldwide scale, to the numerous smaller establishments which can be found in every town, city or village.

Apart from being geographically diverse, the hospitality and food and drink industries also offer a wide range of jobs. So, before choosing a course, it may be worth taking time to think exactly just what sort of career you would like to pursue. Some studies place greater emphasis on the business and management side of hotel and catering, and students on these courses are prepared for such roles as catering supervisor, publican, or hotel manager. Other courses will concentrate on the actual cooking and serving of food and drink, and there are plenty of courses and training schemes for those who want to be chefs or wine waiters. Whilst Britain is not traditionally renowned for its cuisine, the situation has been changing over the last few years with people eating out more and becoming more adventurous in their choice of dishes.

Whereas hotel management and catering is more focused upon providing customers with an enjoyable stay or a tasty dinner, food studies is concerned with what makes up the food we eat, how it affects us and what happens to it during processing, storage and distribution. This can encompass a number of subjects from product development, manufacturing and retail, to food policies and nutrition. These are generally more science-based disciplines so, if you want to develop a diet that will produce a supermodel's waif-like figure or tackle the thorny problem of genetically modified food you will probably need to have the relevant scientific background.

There are three main routes into the hospitality or food industries: attending a college or university, joining a training programme or going straight into employment. At college and university level, the teaching usually involves a mixture of lectures and seminars with practical sessions in the laboratory for food sciences, or in the kitchen for cookery and catering. Most courses will also involve some sort of work placement in a hotel, restaurant or the food and drinks industry. Practical experience is an important learning aid providing students with a useful introduction to their chosen field and it is invaluable for helping to put that first foot on the rung of the career ladder.

SPECIALIST AND VOCATIONAL COURSES

Butlers Wharf Chef School

Providing training for aspiring and experienced chefs and restaurant personnel, the Butlers Wharf Chef School is located on the southeast side of Tower Bridge in the Cardamom Building on Shad Thames. The school opened in late 1995 and has provided training for over 1,500 individuals. Training at the school focuses on its 60-seat restaurant, 'The Apprentice', where trainees are supervised by leading chefs and restaurateurs. A wide range of full-, part-time and specialist courses operate from introductory to advanced levels. All courses are validated by nationally recognised bodies or Butlers Wharf certification. Programmes include a professional chefs diploma, a profes sional restaurant diploma and a hospitality diploma. Courses start throughout the year. The school also offers regular one-day and evening, food and cookery courses for amateurs. Training programmes are designed around the individual and supported by regular theory sessions, specialist lectures and guest chef and restaurant master classes. Facilities include a training kitchen, a fully-operational restaurant, a demonstration theatre and study facilities. Staff and students at the school regularly compete in national and international competitions and have won a number of awards including the Gold Award in Le Parade de Chefs in 1999. Contact details p478.

Le Cordon Bleu, London

Le Cordon Bleu was founded in Paris in 1895. Today, there are 12 centres throughout the world. Founded in 1933, the London school was set up by a graduate of the Paris school. Internationally famous for cuisine and

Butlers Wharf Chef School
Incorporating the apprentice restaurant

Situated 2 minutes from Tower Bridge, this award winning School offers a wide range of full time, day release and specialist courses for aspiring and experienced chefs and restaurant personnel. In addition to courses for keen amateurs.

Training is intensive, focused on the acquisition of modern skills, techniques and experience. Leading Chefs, Restaurateurs, food & wine experts work closely with the School with course start dates all year round

- Hospitality Diploma/Advanced Diploma – 1/2 years full time •
- Professional Chefs Diploma – 1 year full time •
- Professional Restaurant Diploma – 1 year full time • Catering Certificate – 12 Weeks full time •
- Chef Certificate – 6 weeks full time • Chef Diploma – 16 weeks full time •
- Advanced Chef Diploma – 24 weeks full time •
- Restaurant Certificate – 6 weeks full time • Restaurant Diploma – 16 weeks full time •
- Advanced Restaurant Diploma – 24 weeks full time • Day release chef & restaurant training – one day per week •
- One day & evening Wine courses •
- One day and evening cookery courses for keen amateurs •
- Chef Masterclasses – monthly • Guest Chef demonstration dinners – monthly •

For details, contact: 020 7357 8842
Butlers Wharf Chef School, The Cardamom Building, 31, Shad Thames. London. SE1 2YR
Fax: 020 7403 2638
Email: enquiries@chef-school.co.uk   Website: www.chef-school.co.uk

TEACHING QUALITY ASSESSMENTS

Dietetics and Nutrition
(Scotland 1998)

Institution	Grade	Institution	Grade
Queen Margaret College	Excellent	**Glasgow Caledonian**	Highly Satisfactory
Robert Gordon	Excellent		

Food and Hospitality Management
(Wales 1996/97)

Institution	Grade
Llandrillo College	Satisfactory

Food Science
(England and N Ireland 1997/99)

Institution	Grade	Institution	Grade
Harper Adams	23	**Lincolnshire and Humberside**	20
Nottingham	23	**Oxford Brookes**	20
Plymouth	22	**Bournemouth**	19
Reading	22	**Manchester Metropolitan**	19
Queen's Belfast	21	**North London**	19
Surrey	21	**South Bank**	18
Huddersfield	20	**Teesside**	17
Leeds	20		

Food Science
(Wales 1996/97)

Institution	Grade
Cardiff Institute	Satisfactory

Hospitality Studies
(Scotland 1995)

Institution	Grade	Institution	Grade
Dundee	Highly Satisfactory	**Strathclyde**	Highly Satisfactory
Napier	Highly Satisfactory	**Glasgow Caledonian**	Satisfactory
Queen Margaret College	Highly Satisfactory	**Robert Gordon**	Satisfactory

Source: HEFCE, SHEFC, HEFCW latest available ratings
For a more complete list of institutions offering these courses at undergraduate level refer to the Course Directory

patisserie, it attracts students from all over the world. The London school alone has a large international community with students from over 50 different countries. All aspects of fine cuisine are taught by a team of Master Chefs, who instruct groups of 10 students, ensuring a large degree of individual attention. In addition to the teaching staff, guest chefs visit the school and give demonstrations and lectures to students. Modern facilities include close circuit television to enable students to witness, close up, the chef's hands at work. The Patisserie School is based on the same premises, and offers courses to cater for beginners and advanced students.Courses range from the comprehensive Classic Cycle course, to a range of short day or evening classes. Skills taught range from basic techniques to highly skilled cake decoration or patisserie classes. Contact details p481.

Leith's School of Food and Wine
Cookery and Wine Appreciation

Leith's School of Food and Wine was set up in 1975 with the aim of providing both professional training for career cooks and short courses for amateurs. The school teaches classical techniques and methods, but with a fresh, modern approach, in a professional but informal atmosphere. Leith's School of Food and Wine is an independent company owned by Christopher Bland and Caroline Waldegrave. The company is made up of Leith's School of Food and Wine and Leith's List - an agency for cooks. The course for those with professional ambitions is the Diploma in Food and Wine. Students attend daily demonstrations and practical classes each about two and a half hours long. Diploma students study menu planning, budgeting and wine appreciation. There

Interesting facts

- Chicken tikka masala is now the most popular dish in Britain replacing the long-term favourite, fish and chips. Following a close third is the traditional roast beef and Yorkshire pudding

- The UK has 650 McDonald's restaurants, which is the fifth largest number in the world, behind the USA (12,094), Japan (2,004), Canada (992) and Germany (743)

are opportunities to do work experience in London restaurants, visit Smithfield, Billingsgate and Covent Garden Markets, and hear lectures from gastronomic celebrities, head chefs and famous food writers. There are also visits from chefs specialising in international cuisine. The Diploma can be achieved in three terms (starting in October) or two terms starting in January (if students possess enough basic knowledge of cookery). Other food and wine courses offered by the school include holiday, evening and part-time courses for the enthusiastic amateur. Contact details p482.

London Hotel School

London Hotel School is located in the centre of London's West End. The school offers two types of qualifications: the American Hotel and Motel Association Diploma in Hotel Management and the London Hotel School Diploma. Both of these count as credits credit for the BA (Hons) degree in Hospitality Management at Middlesex University and Oxford Brookes University. The American Hotel

and Motel Diploma is modular, consisting of 12 units, meaning students can start when they want and study one or two courses each month until they have the 12 course credits needed for their qualification. General modules on offer include facilities management, hospitality computing, food and beverage management, sales and marketing, hospitality accounting and international tourism. It is also possible to take this diploma with a focus on finance, human resources, tourism or sales and marketing. If students complete the course with good marks and attendance, they can take the London Hotel School Diploma. This involves a one-year, full-time work experience placement in a London hotel (work permits are arranged). The school and the employing hotel both supervise students' training in one or two departments. London Hotel School also runs an open learning programme on which students can study at home using course books, self tests and telephone support. Contact details p482.

The Queen's University of Belfast

BSc (Hons) Food Science/Food Technology

The BSc in Food Science or Food Technology covers three or four years depending on the student's qualifications on entry to the university. Both subjects are multidisciplinary in approach and require a sound knowledge of the basic sciences but vary in their emphasis on chemistry, micro biology, mathematics, engineering and management when applied to the food industry. In the first year all students share a common syllabus, in which basic modules in chemistry and microbiology are complemented by applied modules in biochemistry, food composition and statistics, mathematics and information technology. At the end of this year students may change course before the next stages of study when the degrees in food science and food technology become more specific to their relevant fields. Before entering the final year, students taking either degree will normally be required to undertake at least ten week's approved vacation work in a food factory and/or food laboratory and may, if they wish, take a year out of university to gain appropriate industrial experience. Since the degree in food science was first introduced in 1971, 55 per cent of graduates have entered the food industry, 13 per cent into government or other advisory bodies, 12 per cent into postgraduate research and 15 per cent into teaching. Contact details p484.

Tante Marie School of Cookery

Founded in 1954, the Tante Marie School of Cookery is one of the largest and one of the oldest independent

The Top Five Tea Drinking Countries

Source: "*The Top 10 of Everything: 2000*" Russell Ash, Dorling Kindersley 1999

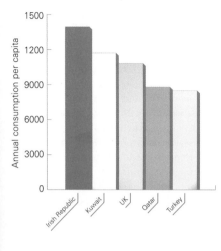

Annual consumption per capita

1500
1200
9000
6000
3000
0

Irish Republic   Kuwait   UK   Qatar   Turkey

cookery schools in Britain. It is the only cookery school to be accredited by the British Accreditation Council and qualifies for a 23 per cent vocational training tax relief on all course fees, available to international students intending to stay in the UK for six months or more. Set in a large Victorian house and surrounded by its own gardens, where vines and culinary herbs for the kitchen are grown, the school's facilities include five comprehensively-equipped teaching kitchens for groups of no more than 12 students, a lecture room and an impressive demonstration theatre. Courses available include the 36-week Tante Marie Diploma Course for complete beginners who are planning a career in catering and hospitality. The 24-week Tante Marie Intensive Diploma Course is ideal for mature students who already have some prior cookery experience. The 12-week Tante Marie Certificate Course is very popular with students who plan to travel and wish to make sure that they have employable catering skills. Tante

Marie welcomes and encourages international students who wish to improve their knowledge of the English language in a warm and friendly environment. Homestays can also be arranged. Contact details p486.

The Old Vicarage

This private residential college for girls is set in a large Regency house on the outskirts of Marden village, Kent. Placing emphasis on the individual development of each girl, the school helps students to acquire a range of skills and abilities from dressmaking and entertaining to sugarcraft and childcare. The Old Vicarage provides a relaxed but stimulating environment for girls while they continue with their education and develop practical skills for use in later life. The school aims to produce 'talented, relaxed and well-adjusted adults'. The cookery programme at the school introduces students to simple techniques and progresses onto more advanced traditions such as cordon bleu. The course incorporates home economics and household skills with sugarcraft and cake decoration. All students who successfully complete the course are awarded the school diploma. Fees are £2,610 a 10-week term or £7,830 a year. Short courses are £326 to £435 per week depending on teaching hours and subject. Contact details p484.

West London College

West London College moved to its modern premises in the heart of London's West End, only a few minutes from Bond Street station, in 1997 (it had occupied its previous site since the 1930s). The college is a BAC accredited business school which attracts over 1,000 students each year from over 100 countries to study business, hotel management, travel and tourism, computer science and English. The college offers two main courses: the Confederation of Tourism, Hotel and Catering Management (CTHCM) Diploma in Hotel Management and the (CTHCM) Advanced Diploma in Hotel Management. Both last for one year and are designed for those aspiring to management roles. Students on the Advanced Diploma course are given practical training at Thames Valley University and many conclude their training with three months practical experience at a London Hotel. Contact details p487.

DEGREE COURSES

Heriot-Watt University
BSc (Hons) in Food Science, Technology and Management

First introduced in 1999, this inter-disciplinary degree draws on the expertise of the Departments of Biological Sciences and Mechanical and Chemical Engineering and The School of Management. The course aims to provide the skills in science, engineering and management necessary for a managerial career in the food and drinks industry, or any other related industry. The BSc in Food Science, Technology and Management essentially combines the biochemistry and micro-biology of foods with a broad base of management skills. The structure of this course necessarily differs from other courses in the Department of Biological Sciences. Although it retains the first year in common with other biology degrees, modules in management and marketing are introduced in the second year and continue through to the final year. Food process technology is introduced in the third year as well as the biological fundamentals essential to the modern food technologist. All students are expected to pursue a summer placement in industry during the vacation between third and fourth years and this can often lead to subsequent employment. Contact details p481.

RESEARCH RANKINGS

Food Science and Technology

Institution	Grade	Institution	Grade
Leeds	5*	Lincolnshire and Humberside	2
Nottingham	5*	Robert Gordon	2
Heriot-Watt	4	South Bank	2
Queen's Belfast	4	Bournemouth	1
Reading	4	Huddersfield	1
Surrey	4	Leeds Metropolitan	1
Natural Resources Institute	3b	Manchester Metropolitan	1
Cardiff Institute	2		

source: RAE 1996

Information Technology and Computing

We now live in an age where computers shape so much of our of everyday lives, from cash machines to air traffic control, that we take their benefits for granted. Not only do they play an important part in how we work, with few businesses able to operate efficiently without them, but they are also playing an increasingly important role in our leisure pursuits. The advent of email and the Internet has meant that we can now chat with friends, do our shopping or book a holiday, all at the touch of a button. Despite much of the technological impetus coming from the US, with the huge influence of Microsoft and Intel, Britain has a long tradition of research and development in computers, having devised the first working prototypes in the 1940s and 1950s.

Computer science is essentially the study of information and computation. Its multidisciplinary nature means that it has ties with a number of other subjects including psychology, maths and engineering. Most degree courses will introduce the fundamentals of computing in the first year. Typical modules will include the mathematical foundations of computing, basic programming and the practical aspects of computer systems and their applications. The following years allow students to specialise in fields such as computer architecture, system modelling or artificial intelligence. Teaching is usually through lectures and seminars and most courses involve laboratory work with hands-on computer experience. Many courses will involve a placement in industry, either during the summer vacation, or through a sandwich year as part of the course.

As the importance of computers in all aspects of our lives continues to grow, so too does the range of courses available. Apart from degrees, there are many postgraduate and research opportunities, and courses which can be used as a conversion from another subject. Many institutions also offer HND courses which have a more practical emphasis towards the fundamentals of computing, focusing, perhaps on software engineering or systems programming. For those who want a practical introduction to the basics such as word processing, spreadsheets or databases there are also a large number of shorter courses found at private or specialist colleges and adult education centres.

Almost everyone has some regular contact with IT, yet there are still relatively few people who have an in-depth knowledge of how computers and information systems work. This has meant that over recent years the IT sector has been growing much faster than the supply of skilled workers it requires. Computing can lead to a number of different jobs, from designing and building large and complex computer systems, to writing programming languages or designing web pages. Whatever the job, computer scientists need to be equipped with a broad knowledge and adaptable skills that allow them to adjust to the needs of a rapidly changing industry.

SPECIALIST AND VOCATIONAL COURSES

Babel Technical College

This small college was established in 1984 and is based in David Game House in Notting Hill, London. The college provides practical, vocational and academic courses in computing and information technology at a level suitable for the office and at more advanced computing and programming levels. All the courses are certified by external institutions such as City and Guilds, Pitman and Cambridge University. City and Guilds diplomas and advanced diplomas are offered in computer applications, business and office technology, dataprocessing and information systems and in programming, with a large range of modules including 3D Studio, web page design, desk top publishing (DTP), computer-aided design (CAD), networking, Java, Visual Basic and C++ programming. Diploma courses are for two terms and advanced diploma courses for three terms; full-time, part-time or evening. Prices range from £330 to £1,730 a term depending on the level and number of modules studied. Students are taught in small groups, averaging seven, using lectures and supervised hands-on experience in the college's five computer laboratories. It is also possible to do GCSE and A level computing courses in association with the David Game Tutorial College. Contact details p477.

Cavendish College

Established in 1985 in the heart of central London, this private college specialises in academic and vocational courses. Both full- and part-time course can be taken in business studies, hospitality and tourism, secretarial training, creative studies, computer studies, media studies and English language. The college offers modern facilities and has recently established its own cyber café where students can relax and use the Internet for recreational purposes. Courses are continually updated to reflect the market and therefore meet changing student demand. The college has a diverse international student population from over 80 different countries around the world. The Computer Studies Department offers courses that aim to prepare students for work in a rapidly changing environment. Diploma courses are offered in computer animation, computer graphics, multimedia design, website design, computer visualisation, business computing and systems analysis, programming, and business computing. Facilities include five well-equipped computer suites offering the latest software packages and students are encouraged to make full use of these facilities in their own time. Contact details p478.

David Game College

This independent college is part of the David Game Group, a large education organisation incorporating private colleges throughout the UK and abroad, including Pakistan and Turkey. The college is fully accredited by the British Accreditation Council, and is housed in purpose-designed premises incorporating fully-equipped laboratories, computer rooms, a library and student services. The college offers a wide range of pre-university courses, and also vocational full- and part-time courses in IT and modern office skills. The small student tutorial groups are supported by four computer laboratories, continually updated with new hard- and software. Students are prepared for City and Guilds and other recognised examinations, in IT and computer applications. Other courses at GCSE, A

INFORMATION TECHNOLOGY

233

TEACHING QUALITY ASSESSMENTS

Computer Science
(England and N Ireland 1994/95)

Institution	Grade	Institution	Grade
Cambridge	Excellent	Kingston	Satisfactory
Exeter	Excellent	Lancaster	Satisfactory
Imperial	Excellent	Leeds	Satisfactory
Kent at Canterbury	Excellent	Luton	Satisfactory
Manchester	Excellent	Newcastle upon Tyne	Satisfactory
Oxford	Excellent	Northumbria at Newcastle	Satisfactory
Southampton	Excellent	Nottingham	Satisfactory
Teesside	Excellent	Nottingham Trent	Satisfactory
Warwick	Excellent	Open University	Satisfactory
York	Excellent	Oxford Brookes	Satisfactory
Blackburn College	Satisfactory	Plymouth	Satisfactory
Bournemouth	Satisfactory	Queen Mary and Westfield	Satisfactory
Brighton	Satisfactory	Queen's Belfast	Satisfactory
Buckinghamshire College	Satisfactory	Reading	Satisfactory
Canterbury Christ Church	Satisfactory	Royal Holloway	Satisfactory
Chester College	Satisfactory	Sheffield	Satisfactory
City	Satisfactory	Sheffield Hallam	Satisfactory
De Montfort	Satisfactory	Suffolk College	Satisfactory
Derby (revisit)	Satisfactory	Sunderland	Satisfactory
Durham	Satisfactory	Thames Valley (revisit)	Satisfactory
Essex	Satisfactory	Ulster	Satisfactory
Farnborough	Satisfactory	UMIST	Satisfactory
Hertfordshire	Satisfactory	UCL	Satisfactory
Huddersfield	Satisfactory	University College Salford	Satisfactory
Keele	Satisfactory		

Computer Studies
(Scotland 1994)

Institution	Grade	Institution	Grade
Edinburgh	Excellent	Dundee	Satisfactory
Glasgow	Excellent	Glasgow Caledonian	Satisfactory
Heriot-Watt	Highly Satisfactory	Napier	Satisfactory
St Andrews	Highly Satisfactory	Paisley	Satisfactory
Strathclyde	Highly Satisfactory	Robert Gordon	Satisfactory
Aberdeen	Satisfactory	Stirling	Satisfactory
Abertay Dundee	Satisfactory		

Computer Science and Computer Studies
(Wales 1993/94)

Institution	Grade	Institution	Grade
Swansea	Excellent	Glamorgan	Satisfactory
Aberystwyth	Satisfactory	Newport	Satisfactory
Cardiff	Satisfactory	North East Wales Institute	Satisfactory
Cardiff Institute	Satisfactory	Swansea Institute	Satisfactory

Source: HEFCE, SHEFC, HEFCW latest available ratings
For a more complete list of institutions offering these courses at undergraduate level refer to the Course Directory

INFORMATION TECHNOLOGY

level and foundation level can lead to university entrance, for which a full counselling service is provided. Shorter vocational courses in all forms of modern secretarial skills and office practice are also available. Contact details p479.

London Institute of Technology and English

London Institute of Technology and English (LITE) has two centres, LITE Camden Town and LITE West End, which are both City and Guilds examination-approved centres. A wide range of courses are on offer such as MS Office 2000, Web Design and Java among others. Classes are taught using the latest equipment in small groups. Instructors aim to be friendly, patient and professional. Courses in travel and tourism, and accountancy are also offered at both centres and students may take relevant examinations. Contact details p482.

Oxford House College

Oxford House College is located in central London on Oxford Street. Full-time courses lasting three, six and nine months, are available in office applications, desktop publishing, graphics, website design, programming, networking and PC hardware. Students can also study for City & Guilds OCR and Microsoft qualifications, and all full-time students have free Internet access and the use of the latest hardware and software. The college is accredited by the British Council for English language training and is a member of ARELS, and it is possible to combine English and computer courses. They offer tailor-made English courses for executives that can help prepare for a vital meeting or presentation. Learning is in small groups and/or with private teachers. Contact details p484.

Purley Secretarial and Language College

This private college established in 1928 and set in a large house in the centre of Purley, specialises in language and business training. The college selects local host families for students who need accommodation, which gives them an extra opportunity to improve their language skills. The college holds business and secretarial courses. Students are prepared for external examinations including OCR (RSA) and Pitman qualifications. Those who wish to extend their knowledge may take English lessons alongside their studies. Courses are available in business, computing and personal assistant skills, and last from 6 to 36 weeks. Subjects include word processing, audiotranscription, short-hand, business administration and communication skills. Short courses are available in keyboarding and word processing. Contact details p484.

Queen's Business and Secretarial College

Queen's was founded in 1924, and has two schools, one in London and one in Cambridge. It runs courses in business and computing skills and business English. There are also a number of short courses for those wishing to learn a wide range of software packages. One- to six-week full-time courses run all year round for students who want to gain good information technology skills as quickly as possible. Students may select modules to suit their requirements. Courses include keyboarding, word processing, spread sheets, databases and presentation packages. Fees vary, but a four-week full-time course in London costs £630 (students can save 23 per cent as tax relief), a one-week desk top publishing course costs £160 and a two-week keyboarding course

£320. Cambridge fees are slightly less. Contact details p484.

St Patrick's International College

St Patrick's International College is based in a large five-storey building in a quiet street in the heart of London's West End. Open all year, facilities include a library, language laboratory, Internet room and multimedia computer rooms. English language courses at all levels start every Monday throughout the year. The minimum stay is one week and students can study for as long as they need. The college is accredited by the British Council and is a member of the Association of Recognised English Language Services (ARELS). St Patrick's is also a recognised examination centre for the London Chamber of Commerce and Industry and Trinity College, London. Computer training departments at both sites offer courses at all levels using the latest software. Also on offer are courses in web design and MCP/MCSE training. All students can use the facilities at the nearby International Students' House, including a café, restaurant, cinema, gymnasium, pool, travel service, bar and cyber café. There is also a comprehensive social, cultural and sports programme throughout the year. Contact details p485.

Westminster College of Computing

Westminster College of Computing, located London's West End, is an institute providing modern training in various aspects of information technology and e-commerce. The college's computer laboratory includes the latest Pentium Multimedia PCs on Novell 4.11, Windows 95 and Windows NT 4.0. All students have access to the Internet and free email facilities. Maximum class sizes at the college are,

in most cases, between eight and 10. The college offers full-time diploma courses in programming, networking and database management that cost around £2,000 a year. There are short-term and part-time courses available. The subjects taught by the college include: object orientated programming, web technology, RDBMS, system analysis and design, computer system and network management. Westminster College of Computing is an examination centre for Oxford and Cambridge RSA, and City & Guilds. Students are also prepared for Microsoft, Oracle and Sun certifications in relevant technologies. The college has a software development and research wing with special interests in e-commerce and active web database technologies. Students are encouraged to take part in ongoing projects. Contact details p487.

DEGREE COURSES

University of Essex

MSc Computer and Information Networks

This nine-month course aims to provide authoritative and up-to-date information on the principles of computer networks and the services they support. Core subjects are network computing, network concepts, network engineering and networked information. Specialist options include ATM and IP net-working, internet communication and telecommunication networks. This relatively new course is taught in the Department of Electronic Systems Engineering, which has a history of co-operation with the nearby national research laboratories of British Telecommunications. In the teaching quality assessment of 1997, the department received the highest possible score of 24 out of 24. Current research grants total £3.7 million. At present

INFORMATION TECHNOLOGY

237

there are 15 international students on the course. Contact details p480.

Goldsmiths, University of London

BA Computing, Operational Research and Statistics for Business

This new degree has been designed for students who wish to acquire computing, mathematical and statistical skills which will be useful in the worlds of business, finance and industry. It aims to produce numerate graduates who: have a knowledge of how mathematical and statistical techniques can be applied to the management of resources; are able to apply statistical techniques to analyse business problems; are versed in the theory and practice of modern computing; and are educated in the theory, techniques and good practice of information technology in business systems. The three-year course is made up of a combination of core subjects, including operational research, linear models and mathematical modelling, and options such as graph theory, optimisation, artificial intelligence or numerical analysis. It is also possible to do a four-year course in which the third year is spent on supervised work experience involving some agreed aspects of mathematics, statistics or computer science. Contact details p480.

University of Greenwich

Msc in Computing and Information Systems

There is a need in the computing industry for people with high level creative skills together with the ability to communicate effectively. Many graduates in disciplines other than computing are well-equipped to fill this need, but lack a basic training in computing. However, with the advent of powerful computing tools, which were specially designed for non-specialist use, there is an increasing opportunity for industry to make use of these graduates in a computing environment. The MSc in Computing and Information Systems provides graduates with an awareness of high-level, modern computing tools and of the environment in which they are used. The course aims to provide non-computing graduates with sufficient understanding to allow them to contribute to the design of information systems and to make informed decisions concerning their use. The course covers such topics as database design, Internet programming, operating systems and distributed information systems. This is a conversion course and in order to gain admission, an applicant must have a good first degree in any discipline. It is not necessary for the student to have studied computing. Contact details p480.

Greenwich School of Management

BSc (Hons) in Business Management and Information Technology

The Greenwich School of Management was founded in 1974 and is an affiliated college of The University of Hull. The undergraduate programmes at the school are accelerated courses that take two years to complete. Start dates are flexible and students can commence courses in February, June or October. The degree in business management and IT is split into three parts, each consisting of two semesters. In part one students study modules ranging from statistics and computing, C programming and systems analysis and design, to business organisation and policy, management and an introduction to accounting. Part two includes Visual Basic programming, telecommunications, database systems, organisational behaviour and market-

ing, whilst part three covers project management, corporate strategy, information systems and human resources management. Assessment is by examination at the end of each module, as well as course and project work. The school's library has a large study area, a range of books, periodicals and journals, as well as CD-ROM and Internet access. Contact details p480.

Liverpool Hope University College

Information Technology

Courses are available here at undergraduate and postgraduate level. The MSc in Information Technology is designed as a conversion course to allow graduates of other subjects to develop IT expertise. Students choose to follow a course of study either in sound and multi-media or environmental information technology. Taught course modules include database analysis and design, applications of the worldwide web, recording studio techniques and systems analysis. Students also undertake research in a topic of their own choice. Both the undergraduate and postgraduate courses are modular and allow a significant element of choice. Whilst students on the post graduate course can gain work experience as they study, undergraduate students can study English Language Studies alongside their degree course. The undergraduate course teaches students to develop computer applications in their chosen areas of interest, which may include visual communications, software design, education and training, and hardware and communications. IT graduates are highly sought in all areas of employment. Contact details p482.

Loughborough University

Computer Science

In 1969, Loughborough University became one of the first universities in Great Britain to introduce a single honours degree in computing. The Computer Science Department was the first in the country to introduce the UNIX operating system in its teaching. There are four undergraduate degree programmes available which all involve theory and practice. A new four-year programme offers a Master of Computer Science degree (MComp) which includes the study of areas such as computer architectures, digital computer systems, programming languages, algorithm analysis, and legal and professional issues in computing. Students at Loughborough can also

Westminster College of Computing

5, Sherwood Street, Piccadilly Circus, London, United Kingdom, W1V 7RA
Tel: (+44) 020 7287 6299 Fax (+44) 020 7287 6297 e-mail: training@wcc.co.uk

One and Two Year full-time Diploma & Advanced Courses
3,6, & 9 Months full-time courses

System Analysis and Programming
Relational Database Management Systems
Network and Systems Management
e-commerce and Active Web Technologies
Application software and Conversion Courses

Part-time (Day, Evening & Weekend) Courses for Beginners

Introduction to Personal Computers
Microsoft Office – Word, Excel, Powerpoint, Access
Introduction to Internet, Keyboard Skills

Part-time (Day, Evening & Weekend) Courses for Advanced Users

SQL, SQL Server, Oracle, Access Client/Server, Data Warehousing
Web Design, Internet Connectivity, TCP/IP, Microsoft Frontpage Java
Script, VB Script, Active Web databases, Active Server Pages (ASP),
e-commerce, Active-X, Intranets, Visual Basic, Visual Basic
for Databases and Client/Server, VB for Internet, Java, Visual J++,
J Builder, C++, Visual C++, PC assembly & support, System
Engineering, PC Networking, Windows NT/2000, Novell Netware,
Exchange Server, IIS, Unix, AIX, Sun Solaris, Open Systems and Linux
Preparation for MCSE, MCP, Oracle(OCP) & SUN (Java) Certifications

**Please visit our web-site www.wcc.co.uk to enroll now.
Our modern facilities include free internet access and e-mail
facilities for full time students. Overseas students enjoy a very
good stay with us with our excellent student welfare programs.
Nearest tube – Piccadilly Circus**

Westminster College of Computing is a registered examination centre for Oxford and Cambridge
RSA and City and Guild Examinations in IT and affiliated with Institute of Para Legal Studies.

combine computer studies with management or languages. Contact details p482.

University of Manchester
BSc Computer Science

In 1948 the Department of Computer Science developed the world's first stored program computer and computer science research has continued here for the last fifty years. Thirty years ago this led to the establishment of the UK's first undergraduate computer science programme. In 1994 the department was inspected as a part of the teaching quality assessment, for which computer studies were graded as Excellent. Teaching in the department is modular. This means that the BSc Hons in Computing Science gives students the opportunity to select the range and depth of subjects they wish to study. Possible course units include object-oriented programming, software engineering, distributed operated systems, computer networks, computer graphics, management information systems, A1 programming, neural networks, mobile robotics and VLSI systems design. Contact details p483.

Napier University
MSc/PgDip Information Technology

The course allows students to pursue various specialisms including: information systems; computer-aided engineering; engineering design; mechatronics; multimedia technology; and software engineering. It is divided into a taught component of 31 weeks, leading to a postgraduate diploma qualification, and a project of 15 weeks which leads to the masters qualification. The project may be based in industry or in the university. Progress to the second component is subject to satisfactory performance in the postgraduate diploma. The course aims to provide students with a sound theoretical and practical knowledge in the application of IT to both industry and research. The emphasis throughout is placed on practical 'hands-on' experience, making use of the school's extensive computer, networking and industrial applications. Contact details p483.

University of Newcastle upon Tyne
MSc Computing Science

Newcastle has one of the largest departments of computing science in the UK. The research programme incorporates both individual research work and group projects. Students learn about the practical aspects of computers and software development including developing programming skills in C++. It is possible to take options in subjects such as computer networks and applications of artificial intelligence. During the final three months of the MSc, work is devoted to a project which provides an opportunity for collaborative work with industry. Graduates in the past have gone on to find employment as software engineers and consultants, or have taken research degrees which have led to lectureships and professorships in the UK and the USA. Contact details p483.

The Nottingham Trent University
MA/PGD Online Journalism

A focused, largely practical course providing training in the production of online information and news. It will interest high-calibre graduates and professionals with the imagination and enthusiasm for writing and broad-casting in new media forms. The Centre for Broadcasting and Journalism operates from the former home of BBC East Midlands, in the heart of the city of Nottingham. It offers the opportunity to study for a specialist qualification in an environment equipped to broad-casting standards. The faculty also offers two other unique, specialist courses. The MA/PGD in Television Journalism, the UK's first MA focused on education and training for television news. The MA/PGD in Investigative Journalism is the only substantive course in investigative journalism in Europe and is designed to equip the student with the knowledge and skills for working as a researcher in features, documentaries or current affairs. The preliminary Foundation in Journalism course is integral with all three MAs, and includes introductions to media law, government and politics, journalism skills and information technology. Contact details p484.

Oxford Brookes University
BSc Computing

The course at Oxford Brookes is modular so that students can select the areas that are of particular interest to them or are relevant to their career intentions. This means it is possible to take a broad computer course or to specialise in an area such as software engineering, knowledge based systems or information systems. It is also possible to combine computing with another subject area such as publishing, history, statistics, ecology or law. For students holding good diplomas in computing from local colleges, the university offers entry with credit which shortens the course. So far over 300 international students who entered with credit have successfully completed the course. Contact details p484.

University of Portsmouth
BSc (Hons) Business Information Technology

This four-year undergraduate course studies the application of information technology in a business environment. The emphasis is on competitiveness and business decision-making. It is a flexible course that allows students to change degree path. The third year is spent in industry where students are able to put their knowledge to the test. The areas of study include accounting, economics, law, marketing, systems analysis, multimedia and programming. Contact details p484.

Queen Mary and Westfield College, University of London
MSc in Internet Computing

Introduced in 1999, the MSc in Internet Computing is a new, postgraduate course, designed to equip students with the skills to succeed in the Internet computing industry. It is intended for both graduates of related disciplines, as well as industrialists who already have some experience of working in information technology, and who wish to obtain a formal qualification. Combining network and software technologies, modules range from the basic principles of digital networks through to research level techniques, technologies and services. Students have the chance to specialise in different areas and, in particular, to focus on either network-level or applications-level issues. Contact details p484.

The Queen's University of Belfast
BSc (Hons) or BEng (Hons) Computer Science

The core components of the course are computer programming, computer architecture, data structures and algorithms, data processing and database systems, software engineering, computation theory, parallel programming, networks and communications, multimedia systems, formal methods, systems software, artificial intelligence, image processing and neural networks. Queen's supplies a number of graduates to the rapidly expanding software industry in the region. International students have the option of spending a year gaining experience in industry in a paid full-time post, something which nearly all take up. The department gained a 4 in the research assessment exercise. Contact details p484.

Staffordshire University
Computing Degree Scheme

Staffordshire has one of the largest higher education Computing Schools in the UK (approximately 100 academics, 2,000 full-time students) housed in a new £10 million computer centre. Within a wide portfolio of programmes, the School of Computing offers the 'Computing Degree Scheme'. This is an undergraduate award in which students share a common first year studying computer science before specialising in one of ten different areas, leading to awards of a BSc (Hons), a BEng (Hons) or MEng. Course titles range from the general, such as Computing Science, Software Engineering and Information Systems through to specialist titles like Internet Technology, Computer Graphics Imaging and Visualisation, Computing with Applicable Mathematics, Multimedia Computing and Intelligent Systems. The degrees include one-year, paid work placements and are recognised by the British Computer Society and the Engineering Council for exemption from all examinations for membership. Contact details p486.

Purposes For Using The Internet: British Adults That Are Regular Users
Source: The CommerceNet/Nielsen Media Internet and Ecommerce Survey, October 1999

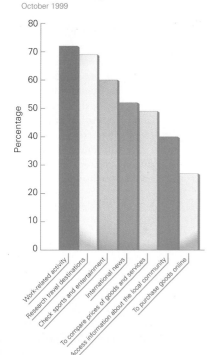

Interesting facts

- In May 1997, Sir Paul McCartney received the most questions ever on an Internet site, around three million, when promoting his album *Flaming Pie*

- The most frequently-used search word on the Yahoo engine is 'sex' with an average of 1.55 million searches a month. In second place is 'chat' with 414,320 searches

- The British Department of Trade and Industry appointed Lara Croft, heroine of the Tomb Raider series of computer games, the UK's Ambassador for Scientific Excellence in November 1998

South Bank University
Computing Courses

The department offers many courses, but, in general, there is a strong emphasis on computer engineering. Students may specialise in fields such as human-computer interaction, systems analysis and design, computer systems management, and multi-media. The proximity of the university to the city means that there is a good insight into the demands that the business world makes on information technology. Conventional lectures and tutorials make up only a small part of courses and much of the students' time is taken up working in the school's computer laboratories. An MSc conversion course is available for non-computing graduates. The university lays particular emphasis on Java programming and maintains close links with the software houses leading this field. Contact details p486.

University of Teesside
Computing and Mathematics

Undergraduate courses range from computer science, information technology and informatics to innovative programmes in leading-edge areas such as multimedia, visualisation and creative visualisation. New courses have been developed in virtual reality, computer animation and interactive entertainment systems. Postgraduate courses include MScs in Information Technology, Multimedia Applications and Computer-Aided Graphical Applications. The computing and IT courses at Teesside received an Excellent rating in the most recent teaching quality assessments. Many courses involve a year's paid work experience, and this along with the emphasis on practical skills means that the university has a good employment record in this area. Contact details p486.

Thames Valley University
IT and Computing

IT and computing covers a wide area at Thames Valley University (TVU), from basic computing, information and knowledge management and information systems, to multimedia computing and digital arts. This range caters both for people wishing to enter the IT profession and those who wish to develop their creative side while using computers. Information systems' graduates can expect to find a range of attractive career opportunities, both directly in information technology and infor-mation management, and in any organisation using technology. The pathway is designed to give the student a good understanding of relevant people-issues, as well as a sound knowledge of which computer-based solutions are appropriate to meet business objectives. Digital arts, with its combination of art and design, the latest technology and the option to study a related subject in parallel, aims to provide a solid foundation for anyone looking to develop a digital-media career. Students receive a thorough grounding in the concepts and creative skills involved in digital media, including 2D graphics, text, animation, video and sound. This enables students to develop their own creative voice using digital arts techniques and gain practical skills in relevant software packages. Contact details p486.

University of Wales, Bangor
BSc in Computer Science

The BSc in Computer Science in the School of Electronic Engineering and Computer Systems is probably the newest programme of its kind in the UK. It was launched in 1999, yet draws on 10 years' experience in running a family of computer systems pro-grammes. Given this experience, the emphasis of the computer science scheme is on the definition, design and implementation of software systems using modern programming languages and design methodologies. Students undertake projects in both the second and third year which provide opportu- nities to apply new ideas in a significant piece of work. The central software systems theme is complement- ed with carefully selected theoretical material, project management skills, Internet technology and a full range of subjects you would expect to find in a

RESEARCH RANKINGS

Computer Science

Institution	Grade	Institution	Grade
Cambridge	5*	Hull	3a
Glasgow	5*	KCL	3a
Imperial	5*	Leicester	3a
Oxford	5*	Liverpool	3a
Warwick	5*	Manchester Metropolitan	3a
York	5*	Open University	3a
Bath	5	Stirling	3a
Bristol	5	Strathclyde	3a
Dundee	5	Sunderland	3a
Edinburgh	5	Ulster	3a
Lancaster	5	UWE	3a
Manchester	5	De Montfort	3b
Newcastle upon Tyne	5	Keele	3b
Southampton	5	Nottingham Trent	3b
Sussex	5	Paisley	3b
UCL	5	Plymouth	3b
Aberdeen	4	Robert Gordon	3b
Aberystwyth	4	South Bank	3b
Aston	4	Brunel	2
Birmingham	4	Cardiff Institute	2
Cardiff	4	Goldsmiths	2
Durham	4	Huddersfield	2
East Anglia	4	Kingston	2
Essex	4	Leeds Metropolitan	2
Exeter	4	Liverpool John Moores	2
Heriot-Watt	4	Middlesex	2
Hertfordshire	4	Napier	2
Kent at Canterbury	4	North London	2
Leeds	4	Northumbria at Newcastle	2
Loughborough	4	Oxford Brookes	2
Nottingham	4	Sheffield Hallam	2
Queen Mary and Westfield	4	Teesside	2
Queen's Belfast	4	Westminster	2
Reading	4	Wolverhampton	2
Royal Holloway	4	Abertay Dundee	1
Sheffield	4	Bournemouth	1
St Andrews	4	Chester College	1
Swansea	4	Coventry	1
UMIST (Computation)	4	Derby	1
UMIST (Language Engineering)	4	London Guildhall	1
Birkbeck	3a	Luton	1
Bradford	3a	Portsmouth	1
Brighton	3a	Staffordshire	1
City	3a	Swansea Institute	1
Glamorgan	3a		

source: RAE 1996

INFORMATION TECHNOLOGY

modern computer science programme. Bangor has links with the computer industry and a strong research base in software engineering, databases, intelligent systems and object-orientated programming. The links with industry ensure that courses reflect recent developments. Staff are practising professionals who act as consultants to industry. Sponsorship and scholarship opportunities are available on a competitive basis. For more information visit the website: www.sees.bangor.ac.uk/ Contact details p477.

University of York

The Department of Computer Science at York scored both a 5* in the research assessment exercise of 1996 and an Excellent rating in the 1994 teaching quality assessment. It aims to provide its students with good computing facilities and in 1997 moved into a new, specially-designed building. The BEng/BSc programme covers all the main topics of computer science including theory, practice, hardware (electronics) and software (programs) which are inte-grated into the design of systems. The early part of the course provides a foundation in the subject while years two and three allow for some specialisation. Much emphasis is placed on practical and project work throughout the course. The final-year project offers the opportunity for individual work. Project supervision is carried out by staff who are themselves involved in research and development. Particular interests are in the areas of software engineering, real-time systems, human-computer interaction and machine learning. Contact details p487.

INFORMATION TECHNOLOGY

Law

law
law
law
law

Most of us will feel the long arm of the law at some time in our lives. This is not because there are a lot of naughty people around, but for the simple reason that the law is our lives. It is concerned with nearly every human activity and it provides the guidelines upon which our society is based. Many countries' legal systems are often a reflection of the political, cultural, economic and religious forces that have shaped its history, which happens to be the case with England and Scotland. The laws in Scotland and many other European countries are based on statute, or written law, which was derived from the system first codified by Roman legal theorists in the 6th century. England, the former countries of the Commonwealth and the US, on the other hand, use a common law that is based on precedent, which means, in theory, that the law could change from week to week.

We've all seen the courtroom scenes on film and TV where the high-flying barrister wins a famous victory, convincing the jury of their client's innocence. In reality a legal career can be very different and cover a wide range of, sometimes, mundane topics. The areas covered on law courses vary between institutions but most will include the seven foundation subjects currently required by the UK legal authorities to become a practising lawyer. These are constitutional and administrative law, criminal law, law of tort, law of contract, land law, law of trusts and European Community law.

Apart from these subjects, students can specialise in any range of topics, from patent law or French law to taxation law or medical ethics and the law.

Most students taking a law course will hope either to become barristers, qualified to practice in higher courts, or solicitors, advising clients and preparing cases for barristers. Professionally qualified lawyers, however, play many roles in society; they are employed not only in private practice but also in the legal departments of the civil service, local government, industrial and commercial firms, banks and international organisations. A law degree also involves many skills highly valued by employers and it is often the case that many students prefer to go into administration, management or accountancy.

To study law you do not need to have taken any particular subject at school or college. All you need is to have shown academic ability and possess a range of skills that include an ability to think clearly, logically and critically, an aptitude for analysing complex problems and distinguishing fact from fiction, and a capacity for communicating clearly, both orally and in writing. Teaching methods are through lectures, seminars and tutorials but most courses include discussion groups, mock trials and case studies. For many students a law degree will involve a certain amount of independent study in the library or legal research. Assessment is generally by examination at the end of each academic year.

DEGREE COURSES

University of Aberdeen
Law

Law has been taught at Aberdeen since 1495, when the university was founded by Bishop William Elphinstone. Nowadays the Law Faculty is located in King's College in Old Aberdeen and comprises the modern Taylor Building and the recently extended and refurbished law library. The LLB is a three-year course while the LLB (Hons) involving more specialist and in-depth study takes four years. Both degrees offer a wide and varied choice of courses and a flexibility that enables students to construct their own programme. Law can be combined with French, German, Spanish, accounting, economics or management studies. Options can also be taken in French, German, Spanish or Belgian law which require students to study for a year abroad in a European law school. In addition it is possible to study subjects offered in other departments and count them towards a law degree. Up to one third of a student's curriculum could comprise non-law courses. The faculty maintains close links with the legal profession in Aberdeen and in the most recent research assessment exercise it was the only law school in Scotland (and only one of eleven in the UK) to receive the top rating of 5. Contact details p477.

University of Bristol
Law, Law and French, Law and German (LLB), Chemistry and Law (BSc)

The teaching of law began at Bristol many years before the faculty was established in 1933. More recently, it was rated Excellent in the teaching quality assessment. The faculty offers both undergraduate and postgraduate degree programmes. Undergraduates on the LLB programme have a chance to transfer to European legal studies and have a year of study in Europe. In addition to the usual compulsory units in legal principles and philosophy, a wide range of options are available in specialist legal and socio-legal fields. Students can choose a degree programme combining the study of law with either French, German or chemistry. Contact details p478.

Cardiff University
LLB in Law

Cardiff Law School received a 5 rating in the latest research assessment exercise. All degrees are fully recognised by the Law Society of England and Wales, and the Bar Council. With an academic staff of 70 (including 14 professors) and over 1,100 undergraduates, the Law School has degrees ranging from the traditional LLB Law degree to LLB degrees in Law and Politics or Law and Sociology. Students at Cardiff have the opportunity to complete their professional training at the Centre for Professional Legal Studies, part of the Cardiff Law School. Cardiff Law School offers a number of pastoral care facilities exclusively dedicated to international students, including: a legal study skills course; legal English language classes; and a pastoral care officer. With 25 per cent of students coming from overseas, there is also an emphasis on transferable legal studies for international students. Contact details p478.

University of Kent at Canterbury
The Law School

Creative thought and response to the rapidly changing legal world is promoted in the Law School at the University of Kent. In recent years they have added modules in the rapidly developing areas of intellectual property, banking, environmental and medical law

TEACHING QUALITY ASSESSMENTS

Legal Studies
(Scotland 1995/96)

Institution	Grade	Institution	Grade
Abertay Dundee	Satisfactory	Napier	Satisfactory
Glasgow Caledonian	Satisfactory	Robert Gordon	Satisfactory

Law
(England and N Ireland 1993/94)

Institution	Grade	Institution	Grade
Bristol	Excellent	UWE	Excellent
Cambridge	Excellent	Birmingham	Satisfactory
Durham	Excellent	Bournemouth	Satisfactory
East Anglia	Excellent	De Montfort	Satisfactory
Essex	Excellent	Derby (revisit)	Satisfactory
KCL	Excellent	Exeter	Satisfactory
Leicester	Excellent	Hertfordshire	Satisfactory
Liverpool	Excellent	Hull	Satisfactory
LSE	Excellent	Leeds	Satisfactory
Manchester	Excellent	Middlesex	Satisfactory
Northumbria at Newcastle	Excellent	North London	Satisfactory
Nottingham	Excellent	Queen Mary and Westfield	Satisfactory
Oxford	Excellent	Southampton Institute	Satisfactory
Oxford Brookes	Excellent	Sussex	Satisfactory
Queen's Belfast	Excellent	Ulster	Satisfactory
Sheffield	Excellent	University College Northampton	Satisfactory
SOAS	Excellent	Westminster	Satisfactory
UCL	Excellent	Wolverhampton	Satisfactory
Warwick	Excellent		

Law
(Scotland 1995/96)

Institution	Grade	Institution	Grade
Aberdeen	Highly Satisfactory	Glasgow	Highly Satisfactory
Dundee	Highly Satisfactory	Strathclyde	Highly Satisfactory
Edinburgh	Highly Satisfactory		

Law
(Wales 1993/94)

Institution	Grade	Institution	Grade
Aberystwyth	Satisfactory	Swansea	Satisfactory
Cardiff	Satisfactory	Swansea Institute	Satisfactory
Glamorgan	Satisfactory		

Source: HEFCE, SHEFC, HEFCW latest available ratings
For a more complete list of institutions offering these courses at undergraduate level refer to the Course Directory

LAW

amongst others. Core modules have small seminar group teaching on a weekly basis alongside two hours of lectures a week. The Law School aims to be at the forefront of legal education in two other ways. Firstly, the Kent Law Clinic allows students contact with real clients, under guidance, which teaches skills that traditional approaches do not touch on. Secondly, the Law School has also invested heavily in electronic legal resources (if you have access to the Internet you may wish to look at their website www.ukc.ac.uk/law/ and clicking on the LAWLINKS button). The school has three-year single and joint honours LLB programmes and four-year courses with languages. They also have postgraduate taught courses in international commercial law, European law, environment law, medical law and criminal justice. Research degrees can be undertaken in a number subject areas. Contact details p481.

London School of Economics and Political Science, University of London (LSE)
LLB Bachelor of Law

LSE encourages students to develop a broad outlook on legal issues and gain an understanding of the functions of law in society, the legal system and the formal rules of law. The LLB consists of three parts, the intermediate, part I and part II examinations, taken over three years. In the first year, students take the subjects necessary for the intermediate examination, introducing such subjects as public law, obligations (tort and contracts), law of property, the legal system and criminal law. In the second and third years, students take optional subjects such as law of evidence, intellectual property law or law of business associations. The third year includes a compulsory course in jurisprudence. LSE also offers an LLB in French law and a joint honours law course with anthropology. Contact details p482.

University of Luton
LLB (Hons) Law

The LLB course is aimed not only at those interested in a career in law, but also at those who wish to develop transferable skills. The degree is recognised by the Law Society and the Council for Legal Education as giving exemption from the Common Professional Examination, provided the appropriate class of honours is obtained. Alternatively, law can be combined with another subject as a major, minor or joint programme within the university's modular degree scheme. This leads to a BA (Hons) with the advantage of gaining an understanding of law alongside another discipline, such as marketing. There are eight full-time modules a year, assessed by a combination of coursework and examination. Option modules are taken in the second and third years. Contact details p483.

University of Manchester
LLB (Hons) and LLM Law

The Faculty of Law was established as part of The University of Manchester in 1872 and is one of the oldest in the country. Over the years it had some celebrated graduates including Christabel Pankhurst, the founder of the Suffragette Movement, and Sir Gordon Borrie, former Director General of Fair Trading. Many of the staff have come from, taught or studied overseas. On the LLB (Hons) Law degree programme, students study a number of basic subjects that the faculty regards as essential to any understanding of law. In the second and third years of the course students choose optional modules from a list that includes international law of trade, EC social and labour law, business taxation and medicine and ethics. This degree provides exemption from the Common Professional Examination. At postgraduate level the faculty offers four courses: International Business Law, European Law, European Law and Policy, Law and Economics and a Diploma in Legal Studies. Contact details p483.

Napier University
LLM/PgDip International Law

This taught programme aims to provide in-depth, specialised coverage of key areas of contemporary international law. Four subjects from the following must be chosen: sources and methods of international law 1 and 2; the role of the United Nations in contemporary international society 1 and 2; international human rights 1 and 2; international regulation of environmental resources 1 and 2; and international regulation of trade 1 and 2. A dissertation on an approved topic of approximately 15,000 to 20,000 words is required for submission one year after admission to the programme to gain the

LLM qualification. A candidate who fails to submit a dissertation but satisfies the assessment requirements of the eight modules will be awarded a Postgraduate Diploma in International Law. By looking at issues in a theoretical and practical context the programme is aimed at both those who wish to pursue their academic research and those who are confronted with problems in international law within their professional environment. Contact details p483.

The Nottingham Trent University
MBA in Legal Practice

The Nottingham Law School MBA provides a synthesis of current management principles and techniques, and applies them to the particular demands of legal practice. In order to meet the needs of the busy professional, the first year of the MBA (the PGD year), is built around four, intensive study weekends, spread to allow preparatory work and follow-up assignments to be undertaken at the most convenient time for course participants. The second year (the MBA year) then builds on the PGD year to provide a greater depth of understanding of economics and the management of groups of professionals, knowledge and change. Participants who have benefited from the MBA include lawyers, senior administrative staff from virtually all types and sizes of law offices and legal departments, in the UK and overseas. The Nottingham Law School also offers an LLM in Advanced Litigation, which is the only course of its kind. Contact details p484.

University of Oxford
Law

As at Cambridge, successful graduates in law gain a BA (Hons). Unlike most other universities, undergraduates are expected to rely on primary sources for their work rather than being taught through lectures. There is a high premium placed on students' facility in English as undergraduates are expected to write one essay a week for each of the taught subjects. Oxford now offers a four year law with law studies in Europe course which includes a year at university in the European Unions. At postgraduate level there are various options: the BCL (Bachelor of Civil Law) and the MJur (Master of Jurisprudence) are both taught courses, the MSt (Master of Studies) is one year's training in legal research, assessed through a research paper which can then be followed by an MLitt or a DPhil. Contact details p484.

University of Sheffield
Law

The Department of Law is one of the three largest English university law schools outside Oxbridge and London. The 1996 research assessment exercise awarded the department a score of 5 and the teaching quality assessments rated the department as Excellent in 1993. The department has six research clusters: the Centre for Criminological and Legal Research, the Centre for Comparative International and European Law, the Centre for Socio-legal Studies, the Institute for the Study of the Legal Profession, the Institute for Commercial Law Studies and the Sheffield Institute for Biotechnical Law and Ethics. There are currently 65 staff and 970 full-time students of which 216 are international. At undergraduate level students can choose from degrees in law, law and criminology and law with French, German or Spanish. Level one offers an introduction to the subject and students can subsequently choose a path suited to their own area of interest from a choice of some 40 options. Postgraduates can study an MA in Law, Law with International Criminology, Biotechnology Law and Ethics or

Interesting facts

- The longest prison sentence ever given was to Chamoy Thipyaso and seven of her associates who were found guilty of swindling in public. They were jailed for 141,708 years by a Bangkok criminal court, Thailand, on July 27 1989

- Duelling is legal in Paraguay as long as both parties are registered blood donors

- In England in 1571, a man could be punished with a fine for not wearing a wool cap

Socio-legal Studies. The department also offers an LLM and a diploma in legal practice. Contact details p485.

University of Southampton
LLB (Hons) Law

The Faculty of Law has been established for 50 years at the University of Southampton and enjoys strong connections with the legal profession. The faculty has 30 full-time members of staff and achieved a 5 rating in the last research assessment exercise. Students shape their LLB course by choosing from options during all three years. There is the chance to specialise in a particular field such as commercial or international law. Each subject is assessed at the end of the academic year by a variety of methods including examinations and course work. The university also offers an LLB course in European legal studies which includes spending a year in a European country. Law can also be studied as an additional option subject in the Faculties of Arts or Social Sciences. Contact details p486.

LAW

Staffordshire University
LLM Law

For students who have taken an undergraduate law degree or equivalent, this one-year, taught LLM is a modular award enabling students to accumulate credits through individual subject modules and a dissertation. It allows students to choose one of 12 named routes so that they can tailor the course to follow their own individual interests. Options include international law, international business law, employment law and intellectual property law. Staffordshire University's Law School is located in a £3 million, purpose-built facility, which incorporates a law library, two mock courtrooms and legal practice suites. The law school is the first in the country to offer Malaysian law options. It has a specially designated international students' tutor to look after the welfare of international students. Contact details p486.

University of Sussex
LLM International Commercial Law

Expansion of legal studies at Sussex has enabled the university to extend the range of research, and introduce new taught postgraduate programmes. The course is designed to be relevant to the process of international commerce. It allows students to pursue topics in domestic and international law that are economic and comparative in nature. The course consists initially of a core element comprising modules on domestic and international sale of goods, and payment and finance. Students can then pursue a range of modules that are commercial, comparative or economic in nature. There is a vast choice of modules, which include French law of obligations, investment laws of developing countries, Japanese trade law and EC market law. Students are assessed by unseen examinations at the end of the year, extended essays and a dissertation. Contact details p486.

Thames Valley University
LLB (Hons) Law

Whether you wish to become a barrister or solicitor, or simply gain a deeper understanding of the law, a legal training will always stand you in good stead. Thames Valley University's (TVU) LLB degree is fully validated by the Law Society and aims to provide a solid foundation for a legal career. To become a solicitor or barrister you must first obtain a qualifying law degree – you will need to have studied law as one of your subjects throughout the three years of your degree, and taken it as the dominant subject in your second and third years. The LLB pathway is recommended to those who intend to practice. At TVU you can also study law with a number of options. Whether you specialise or follow the combination route, your studies will cover civil and criminal law (process and in context), the criminal trial and applied civil process, contracts, tort, criminal and land law, remedies and legal skills, foundations of EU law and public law,

Average Prison Population of England and Wales

Source: "The UK in Figures 1999" Government Statistical Service

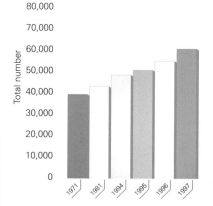

and the foundations of equity and trusts. Contact details p486.

University of the West of England
LLB (Hons) Law, Faculty of Law

This long-established programme provides an understanding of legal concepts, their practical application and the role of law in society. Students have access to video-equipped courtrooms. Graduates of the programme are exempt from the first stage of academic training in relation to both the Bar's and the Law Society's requirements. The faculty has links to many international institutions and bursaries are available. Each year

visits are arranged by the department to institutions in Brussels, Luxembourg and Strasbourg. Contact details p487.

Warwick University
BA in Law and Business Studies

This joint degree covers the many areas of overlapping interest between the business and legal professions, such as the structure of companies, business organisation, competition law and the regulation of markets, finance, financial markets and taxation. There are currently 18 international students on the course out of 75 students in total. Students study in both the Law School and the Warwick Business School. Contact details p487.

RESEARCH RANKINGS

Law

Institution	Grade	Institution	Grade
Cambridge	5*	Hull	3a
Oxford	5*	Lancaster	3a
Aberdeen	5	Liverpool	3a
Birkbeck	5	Newcastle upon Tyne	3a
Cardiff	5	Queen's Belfast	3a
Essex	5	Reading	3a
KCL	5	Sheffield Hallam	3a
LSE	5	SOAS	3a
Manchester	5	Sussex	3a
Nottingham	5	City	3b
Sheffield	5	Coventry	3b
Southampton	5	De Montfort	3b
UCL	5	Nottingham Trent	3b
Birmingham	4	Southampton Institute	3b
Bristol	4	Swansea	3b
Brunel	4	Ulster	3b
Dundee	4	UWE	3b
Durham	4	Anglia Polytechnic	2
Edinburgh	4	East London	2
Glasgow	4	London Guildhall	2
Institute of Advanced Legal Studies	4	Huddersfield	2
Keele	4	Manchester Metropolitan	2
Kent at Canterbury	4	Staffordshire	2
Leeds	4	Westminster	2
Leicester	4	Bournemouth	1
Queen Mary and Westfield	4	Derby	1
Strathclyde	4	Glamorgan	1
Warwick	4	Luton	1
Aberystwyth	3a	Northumbria at Newcastle	1
Central Lancashire	3a	Teesside	1
East Anglia	3a	Thames Valley	1
Exeter	3a	Wolverhampton	1

source: RAE 1996

Library and Information Studies

For many people, the word librarian conjures up an image of a stern old lady who keeps everyone in her library in a state of absolute silence. The reality of a job in this sphere is very different.

For hundreds of years, librarians have been evolving ways of indexing, abstracting and retrieving information. By creating a controlled vocabulary they organise resources so that others can use them effectively and efficiently. The growth of the Internet means there is now an ever greater need to make the mass of available information work for, rather than against, us – in June 1996 there were 230,000 websites on the Internet, now there are too many to count. Information specialists are no longer the preserve of libraries and are much in demand in a number of areas including banking, education, the media, computing and, in fact, anywhere information systems are used.

There is a great deal of innovation in the UK library environment, with projects such as the Electronic Libraries Programme and the New Library People's Network, and other countries have often adopted British models for librarianship and information services. The first BSc in Information Science was introduced in 1967 at the University of Newcastle. Degrees in this field have since evolved enormously, in line with the widening job description and latest developments in computer technology. As a result, students come from a variety of academic backgrounds, ranging from chemistry to English. The ability to speak a language other than English is a great advantage and is becoming increasingly necessary. A high degree of computer literacy is essential.

Library and information degrees come under a variety of headings, including: library and information studies; information management; and information systems. Students can apply for either a BA or BSc degree. On a BA course, first-year core modules might include: IT and systems; communication methods; and research methodology. The second and third years then allow students to specialise in areas such as: business information studies; information and library services; or multimedia publishing. A BSc degree, on the other hand, may have a more scientific, management or computing focus and can often be combined with a computing course.

The majority of library and information courses, however, are studied at postgraduate level. MSc and MA taught courses normally last for one year and it is possible to do research to PhD level.

Most degree courses are accredited by the two main professional bodies for librarians and information managers: The Library Association (LA); and the Institute of Information Scientists (IIS). For full lists of these courses contact: The Library Association, 7 Ridgmount Street, London WC1E 7AE. Tel: 020 7636 7543, Fax: 020 7436 7218, website: www.la-hq.org.uk/ or The Institute of Information Scientists, 44-45 Museum Street, London WC1A 1LY. Tel: 020 7831 8003, Fax: 020 7430 1270, website: www.iis.org.uk.

DEGREE COURSES

Leeds Metropolitan University
Librarianship

Leeds Metropolitan University (LMU) offers a range of courses which focus on the skills of information specialists working in a variety of professions and sectors. Courses at bachelor degree and masters degree level include information management, information studies, library studies and business information technology. The masters' courses last one year and some are conversion courses, designed for students with a first degree in a different subject area. All the courses have a practical base and are taught by staff from diverse professional backgrounds. Students are based in the School of Information Management on LMU's Beckett Park Campus, set in 100 acres of parkland. Contact details p482.

Loughborough University
Information Science

Loughborough is unusual among UK institutions offering library studies in that it has undergraduate courses in this field. BAs in Library and Information Management, Information Management and Business Studies, Publishing with English, Information Management and Computing, can be studied for three or four years. The four-year course entails a year working and earning money in industry, as well as gaining an extra qualification – the Diploma in Professional Studies. The department also offers postgraduate courses and was

TEACHING QUALITY ASSESSMENTS

Information and Library Studies
(Wales 1994/95)

Institution	Grade	Institution	Grade
Aberystwyth	Excellent		

Source: HEFCE, SHEFC, HEFCW latest available ratings
For a more complete list of institutions offering these courses at undergraduate level refer to the Course Directory

RESEARCH RANKINGS

Library and Information Management

Institution	Grade	Institution	Grade
City	5*	Manchester Metropolitan	3b
Sheffield	5*	Queen Margaret College	3b
Loughborough	5	UWE, Bristol	3b
Salford	4	Bath	2
Strathclyde	4	Central Lancashire	2
Northumbria at Newcastle	3a	Leeds Metropolitan	2
Queen's Belfast	3a	Liverpool John Moores	2
Robert Gordon	3a	UCL, London	2
Aberystwyth	3b	Bath College	1
Brighton	3b	La Sainte Union College	1
UCE, Birmingham	3b	Thames Valley	1
De Montfort	3b		

source: RAE 1996

The Five Largest Library Collections in the World

Source: Public Lending Right

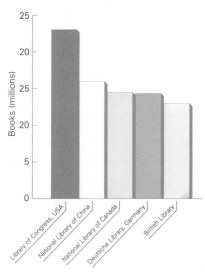

awarded 5 in the 1996 research assessment exercise. Contact details p482.

University of Sheffield
Information Studies

Sheffield's Department of Information Studies offers BAs in accounting and financial management and information management and in business studies and information management, MAs in librarianship and in library and information management, MScs in information management and in information systems, a Diploma/MSc in health information management and a certificate in networked learner support. The department was awarded 5* in the 1996 research assessment exercise. Contact details p485.

University of Wales Aberystwyth
Information and Library Studies

Programmes available in the Department of Information and Library Studies include undergraduate degrees in information and library studies, information management, and information management, accounting and finance. The department also offers a UDIP/MScEcon in Archive Administration, distance learning courses, and runs an International Graduate Summer School. Contact details p477.

University of Strathclyde
MSc/PG Dip in Information and Library Studies

Designed for those aiming for a career in information and library work, both PG Dip and MSc students follow a nine-month taught course. MSc students go on to study for a further three months during which time they are expected to produce a dissertation. PG Dip students who meet the required standard may transfer to the MSc course. The nine months are split into two semesters. The first semester incorporates core classes whilst the second semester involves a five-week placement and a choice of elective classes. Contact details p486.

oncourse . co . uk
The ultimate guide to courses

LIBRARY STUDIES

Mathematics and Statistics

Mathematics has been studied in its own right for centuries because of its elegance and the interest that it generates. The curiosity that inspires the mathematician has often lead to unexpected connections – the work of logicians and algebraists of the last 100 years, culminating in the building of the first computer, is one good example.

Broadly speaking mathematics can be divided into two main areas; pure and applied. Pure mathematics is the cerebral subject – maths for maths sake, you might say. Applied mathematics is the exploration of a problem in the real world – such as locating the eyes of a car driver using an in-car camera and then monitoring the blink rate as an indicator of the driver's drowsiness – and can lead into physics, statistics and operational research.

Isaac Newton is the grandfather of mathematics in the UK and his influence still seems to pervade the higher education sector, attracting many international students. It has been suggested that the Newtonian heritage and a tradition of pragmatism have contributed both to the quality of mathematics research at UK institutions and to the British emphasis on applied mathematics. While academics on the continent have racked their brains over the vagaries of pure mathematics, the UK has continued to maintain a tradition of excellence in the application of the subject. This generalisation should not be taken too far, however, as pure mathematics also thrives in British universities, and countries such as France and Germany have proved their skills in applied mathematics with the quality of their engineering.

The areas covered in a mathematics degree will vary from institution to institution, as will the permutations of subjects that can be combined with mathematics. Some departments offer separate courses in individual branches of mathematics such as pure mathematics, business mathematics and computing mathematics. This is also true of statistics with divisions including applied statistics, business statistics and medical and health statistics. As a result of their close relationship sometimes statistics is studied as part of a mathematics degree and sometimes vice versa.

Most degrees last for three years and are normally divided into modules. In the first year of both mathematics and statistics degrees you are likely to cover the basic principles of the subjects. For mathematics these include: calculus; algebra; and computing skills; for statistics: probability; foundations in statistics; and computational methods.

Specialisation normally takes place in the second and third years of the course. Examples of such modules for mathematics may include: mechanics; abstract algebra; and linear systems; for statistics: distribution theory; theoretical artificial intelligence; and techniques of operational research. In the final year it is often possible for students to undertake a project on a topic of their choice, under the super-vision of an academic tutor, in lieu of one of these modules.

DEGREE COURSES

University of Cambridge
Applied Mathematics and Physics Theoretical

The Mathematical Tripos has been in place since 1780 making it one of the oldest existing mathematics examinations in the world. Mathematical study is divided between two departments: the Department of Applied Mathematics and Theoretical Physics (DAMTP) and the Department of Pure Mathematics and Mathematical Statistics (DPMMS). Cambridge has the most mathematics undergraduates of any comparable department in the UK and almost all accepted applicants have straight As at A level. The degree (Parts One and Two of the Tripos) lasts three years and is entirely devoted to mathematics. The best candidates from Cambridge and high–calibre students from elsewhere also apply to continue their studies by taking Part Three of the Tripos – a taught master's course. The Statistical Laboratory carries out research into engineering, financial services, and technological problems. Contact details p478.

Heriot-Watt University
BSc/MSc/Diploma Actuarial Mathematics and Statistics

Actuarial work can be described as the application of mathematics and statistics to the analysis of financial problems in areas such as life insurance, pensions, general insurance and investment. Heriot-Watt had the first department for actuarial mathematics and statistics in the UK and is one of the few universities to offer the subject at postgraduate level. Postgraduate taught courses are available in actuarial science or financial mathematics and research areas include risk theory, permanent health insurance, wave energy statistics and statistical education. At undergraduate level it is possible to study BSc degrees in Statistics and Actuarial Mathematics or Statistics. Graduates have gone on to careers in insurance houses and finance houses. At present there are 48 international students on the undergraduate courses and 12 on the postgraduate courses. Contact details p481.

University of St Andrews
Mathematics and Computational Sciences

The University of St Andrews offers courses and options from the entire spectrum of mathematical science and provides a structure that is sufficiently

Interesting facts

- Archaeologists have found evidence of games of chance on prehistoric digs, showing that gaming and gambling have been a major pastime for different peoples since the dawn of civilisation

- The Babylonian number system used base 60 rather than the base 10 of our present system. They divided the day into 24 hours, each hour into 60 minutes, each minute into 60 seconds. This form of measuring time has survived for 4000 years

- The longest-standing maths puzzle was Fermat's Last Theorum. It was finally proved by Andrew Wiles (UK) in 1995, having baffled the world's greatest mathematicians for over 350 years

MATHEMATICS

RESEARCH RANKINGS

Statistics and Operational Research

Institution	Grade
Cambridge	5*
Bath	5
Bristol	5
Imperial	5
Lancaster	5
Queen Mary and Westfield	5
Southampton (Operational Research)	5
Warwick	5
Birmingham	4
Brunel	4
Edinburgh	4
Glasgow	4
Kent	4
LSE	4
Newcastle	4
Nottingham	4
Open University	4
Oxford	4
St Andrews	4
Salford	4
Sheffield	4
Southampton (Statistics)	4
Strathclyde	4
Surrey	4
UCL	4
Aberdeen	3a
Durham	3a
Essex	3a

Institution	Grade
Heriot-Watt	3a
Leeds	3a
Liverpool	3a
Manchester	3a
UMIST	3a
Reading	3a
Swansea	3a
Abertay Dundee	3b
Birkbeck	3b
City	3b
De Montfort	3b
East Anglia	3b
Exeter	3b
Goldsmiths	3b
Greenwich	3b
Keele	3b
Napier	3b
North London	3b
Nottingham Trent	3b
Sussex	3b
Bournemouth	2
Coventry	2
Dundee	2
Northumbria at Newcastle	2
Plymouth	2
UWE	2
Oxford Brookes	1

source: RAE 1996

TEACHING QUALITY ASSESSMENTS

Mathematics, Statistics and Operational Research
(England and N Ireland 1998/99)

Institution	Grade	Institution	Grade
Bristol	23	Hertfordshire	21
East Anglia	23	KCL	21
Sheffield Hallam	23	Liverpool John Moores	21
Sussex	23	Nottingham Trent	21
Brighton	22	Queen Mary and Westfield	21
Canterbury Christ Church	22	Sheffield	21
Exeter	22	Bolton Institute	20
Hull	22	De Montfort	20
Keele	22	Essex	20
Leeds	22	Wolverhampton	20
Manchester	22	Central Lancashire	19
York	22	Greenwich	19

Mathematics
(Wales 1995/96)

Institution	Grade	Institution	Grade
Aberystwyth	Satisfactory	Glamorgan	Satisfactory
Bangor	Satisfactory	Swansea	Satisfactory
Cardiff	Satisfactory		

Mathematics and Statistics
(Scotland 1994)

Institution	Grade	Institution	Grade
Edinburgh	Excellent	Heriot-Watt	Highly Satisfactory
St Andrews	Excellent	Napier	Highly Satisfactory
Aberdeen	Highly Satisfactory	Paisley	Highly Satisfactory
Abertay Dundee	Highly Satisfactory	Robert Gordon	Highly Satisfactory
Dundee	Highly Satisfactory	Stirling	Highly Satisfactory
Glasgow	Highly Satisfactory	Strathclyde	Highly Satisfactory
Glasgow Caledonian	Highly Satisfactory		

Source: HEFCE, SHEFC, HEFCW latest available ratings
For a more complete list of institutions offering these courses at undergraduate level refer to the Course Directory

MATHEMATICS

flexible to permit students to specialise or acquire a broad expertise. Mathematics and/or statistics can be studied from within either the arts or science faculty. The department has been highly rated in research and received Excellent in teaching quality assessments. It aims to provide students with good facilities and small tutorial group support. Courses in mathematics and statistics can be taken as part of a number of joint degrees and may, for example, be combined with computing. The Computer Science School is compact; the small tutorial groups, laboratory sessions, informal contact and discussion allow students and staff to get to know each other. All computers have fast link networks to the worldwide web and internet. 24-hour access to laboratory facilities is provided from the second year onwards. Degree courses in computer science at the University of St Andrews have full accreditation with the British Computer Society and the Engineering Council for the first part of the Chartered Engineer qualification. Contact details p485.

University of Teesside
Computing and Mathematics

Undergraduate courses range from computer science, information technology and informatics to innovative programmes in leading-edge areas such as multimedia, visualisation and creative visualisation. New courses are being developed in virtual reality, computer animation and interactive entertainment systems. Postgraduate courses include MSc's in Information Technology, Multimedia Applications and Computer-Aided Graphical Applications. The computing and IT courses at Teesside have been awarded Excellent ratings in the most recent teaching quality assessments. Many courses involve a year's paid work experience, and this along with the emphasis on practical skills means that the university has a good employment record in this area. Contact details p486.

RESEARCH RANKINGS

Applied Mathematics

Institution	Grade	Institution	Grade
Cambridge	5*	Reading	3a
Oxford	5*	Royal Holloway	3a
Aberystwyth	5	Surrey	3a
Bath	5	York	3a
Bristol	5	City	3b
Durham	5	Coventry	3b
Exeter	5	Glasgow Caledonian	3b
Heriot-Watt	5	Hull	3b
Imperial	5	Northumbria at Newcastle	3b
King's	5	Nottingham Trent	3b
Leeds	5	Oxford Brookes	3b
Nottingham	5	Portsmouth	3b
Queen Mary and Westfield	5	Abertay Dundee	2
St Andrews	5	Bangor	2
UCL	5	Bradford	2
Birmingham	4	Chester College	2
Brunel	4	De Montfort	2
Dundee	4	Derby	2
East Anglia	4	Glamorgan	2
Edinburgh	4	La Sainte Union	2
Glasgow	4	London Guildhall	2
Keele	4	Manchester Metropolitan	2
Liverpool	4	Napier	2
Loughborough	4	Paisley	2
Manchester	4	Plymouth	2
UMIST	4	Staffordshire	2
Newcastle	4	Teesside	2
Sheffield	4	UWE	2
Southampton	4	Central Lancashire	1
Strathclyde	4	Goldsmiths	1
Sussex	4	Middlesex	1
Kent	3a	Robert Gordon	1
Leicester	3a		

source: RAE 1996

Fields Medal-Winning Countries*

Source: Bellevue Community College
*The Fields Medal is the mathematical equivalent of the Nobel Prize.

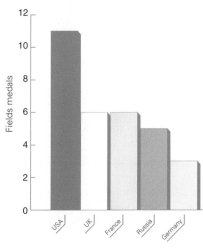

Warwick University

BSc in Mathematics, Operational Research Statistics and Economics (MORSE)

MORSE, in the Faculty of Social Science, teaches a balance of mathematical theory and practical work to produce high quality graduates who are mathematically equipped for the practical problems of finance, business and industry. It is an interdisciplinary programme across four top-rated Warwick departments. MORSE has an annual intake of 70 of which there are currently 22 international students. There is a four-year variant of the programme which provides specialised study of actuarial and financial mathematics – an expertise in growing demand across the world. Contact details p487.

RESEARCH RANKINGS

Pure Mathematics

Institution	Grade	Institution	Grade
Imperial	5*	Royal Holloway	4
Oxford	5*	St Andrews	4
Warwick	5*	Swansea	4
Bath	5	York	4
Cambridge	5	Aberdeen	3a
Cardiff	5	Bangor	3a
Durham	5	Central Lancashire	3a
East Anglia	5	Essex	3a
Edinburgh	5	Exeter	3a
KCL	5	Goldsmiths	3a
Leeds	5	LSE	3a
Liverpool	5	Newcastle	3a
Manchester	5	North London	3a
Queen Mary and Westfield	5	Queen's Belfast	3a
Sussex	5	Reading	3a
UMIST	5	Sheffield	3a
UCL	5	Southampton	3a
Birmingham	4	Aberystwyth	3b
Bristol	4	East London	3b
Glasgow	4	Leicester	3b
Hull	4	Open University	3b
Lancaster	4	Stirling	3b
Nottingham	4		

source: RAE 1996

MATHEMATICS

Media and Communication Studies

The 20th century has witnessed a boom in media and communications not seen since the invention of moveable type in the 1450s. Newspapers, magazines, television, radio, cinema and advertising, and all have a massive, daily impact on our social and cultural lives. The recent introduction of digital television, and the rising popularity of the Internet suggests that mass media will, for the foreseeable future, continue to dominate our lives. Britain's most popular tabloid, *The Sun*, has a higher daily circulation than any other English language paper in the world, and only Japan and the United States have more Internet users.

Courses in media and communications can either be wholly practical, wholly theoretical, or a mixture of the two. They can be highly specialist, providing specific skills in media technology for instance, or take a broader approach to the subject involving anything from semiotics (the study of signs and symbols) to censorship and the cultural and political influence of media proprietors. The type of course you study is very important. No degree, no matter how vocational, can ever guarantee a successful career, and the media industry is more competitive than most. Where you study can also be important. Some universities and colleges are more reputable than others within the industry. For instance, employers looking for journalists often prefer to recruit from courses associated to the National Council for the Training of Journalists (NCTJ).

For students aiming to work in a specific area of the media, it might be preferable to take a related training course. Increasingly, these are available through universities, but the majority can be found at colleges and specialist institutions. Journalism, for instance, is available on short courses or at NVQ and postgraduate level. There are also courses available in everything from scriptwriting, directing and animation, to lighting and sound engineering. Such courses are likely to concentrate primarily on practical and technical skills.

Students wishing to gain a theoretical understanding of the media may be more interested in less vocational degrees in media studies, or communication studies. A media studies degree might cover the historical development of mass media, politics and propaganda, photojournalism or media ethics. A degree in communication studies typically revolves around the problems and issues associated with both interpersonal and mass communication. For instance, students may study the role of language in interviews, or children's response to television programmes. Although both degrees involve the discussion and application of theoretical models, they also feature practical work. Some courses will allow students to develop their practical interests in areas such as photography, writing or television, and others can include a short work placement at a communications-related business, such as an advertising company or public relations agency.

SPECIALIST AND VOCATIONAL COURSES

Blake College

Set in a converted Victorian warehouse, this independent art college offers part- and full-time courses with up-to-date facilities. The video, film and photography department offers many courses including video production, film studies, practical photography, photography workshop, and multimedia studies. There is strong emphasis on practical work on these courses. Video production students experience scripting, directing, editing and camera operation. Students are taught the stages of video production, from planning in pre-production, through to the shoot, and editing in post-production. Technical workshops are supplemented with tutorials and classes. Project briefs include non-sync narrative, music video, documentary or drama and an individual project where the crew consists of fellow students. The department has a fully equipped AVID suite for editing, digital cameras and full ancillary equipment. Film is studied as an art form during the film studies course. Classes include the structure of the industry, film form and narrative, history, and critical approaches to Hollywood, British and alternative styles of cinema. Students carry out an in-depth study of a particular genre. Practical photography courses teach camera functions, processing and darkroom skills as well as printing techniques and presentation. Colour digital photography is also introduced using photoshop. Photography workshops allow students to explore photographic techniques, equipment and materials. Presentations, museum and gallery visits, and practical work are a major part of the course. History and science is a theory course and rounds off the full-time students' experience. Contact details p477.

Oxford Media and Business School

The Oxford Media and Business School is situated in the centre of this ancient university city. The school offers a range of specialist advertising, graphic design management and fashion publishing programmes through its specialist media school. Nine-month courses available include an Advertising Account Executive Diploma, for those seeking a career in advertising or as a brand manager in the marketing department of a large firm. There is also a Design Assistant Diploma, incorporating a greater emphasis on practical business IT skills, for those aiming to work as a PA or marketing assistant. Both courses look at the role of marketing, the principles of advertising and the use of PR, as well as giving students training in the latest professional graphics software such as QuarkXPress and Photoshop. In addition, there is also a nine-month Fashion Publishing Diploma, and a specialist three-month Art Director Certificate aimed at design graduates seeking practical print production and work training to help them secure their first design job. All students receive professional help with both career planning and interview techniques. A full-time student accommodation manager offers help with accommodation in Oxford, and most international students stay in college-owned flats and houses. Help with English language is available for international students who require it. Contact details p484.

DEGREE COURSES

Anglia Polytechnic University

BSc (Hons) Multimedia Systems

This degree offers creative students of any discipline the opportunity to design and develop multimedia systems using

TEACHING QUALITY ASSESSMENTS

Communication and Media Studies
(England and N Ireland 1997/98/99)

Institution	Grade	Institution	Grade
University College Chichester	24	South Bank	20
East Anglia	23	Staffordshire	20
Reading	23	City	19
Warwick	23	College of St Mark and St John	19
Westminster	23	Cumbria College of Art and Design	19
Bournemouth	22	Greenwich	19
Central Lancashire	22	Leeds Metropolitan	19
Goldsmiths	22	Sheffield Hallam	19
Leeds (revisit)	22	Wolverhampton	19
Liverpool John Moores	22	Warrington Institute	19
LSE	22	Anglia Polytechnic	18
Luton	22	Buckinghamshire College	18
Sunderland	22	Coventry	18
UWE	22	Falmouth College	18
Leicester	21	Huddersfield	18
Nottingham Trent	21	King Alfred's College	18
Oxford Brookes	21	Southampton Institute	18
Ravensbourne College	21	Thames Valley	18
Sussex	21	Derby	17
UCE	21	Farnborough College	17
Ulster	21	London Guildhall	17
University College Northampton	21	Lincolnshire and Humberside	17
Bolton Institute (revisit)	20	North London	17
Brunel	20	Surrey Institute	17
Canterbury Christ Church	20	Trinity and All Saints	17
Cheltenham and Gloucester	20	East London	16
De Montfort	20	St Helens College	15
Edge Hill College	20	Suffolk College	15
Kent at Canterbury	20	Wirral Metropolitan	15
London Institute	20	Sandwell College	13
Ripon and York St John	20		

Mass Communication
(Scotland 1996)

Institution	Grade	Institution	Grade
Glasgow Caledonian	Highly Satisfactory	Stirling	Highly Satisfactory
Napier	Highly Satisfactory	Queen Margaret College	Satisfactory

English and Associated Studies
(Wales 1994/95)

Institution	Grade	Institution	Grade
Aberystwyth (Theatre, Film and Television Studies)	Satisfactory	Cardiff (Mass Communication)	Satisfactory
Cardiff (Journalism)	Satisfactory	Trinity College, Carmarthen (Theatre, Music and Media Studies)	Satisfactory

Source: HEFCE, SHEFC, HEFCW latest available ratings
For a more complete list of institutions offering these courses at undergraduate level refer to the Course Directory

MEDIA

computers. Consideration is given to the wider impact such systems have on our lives, so the course includes design technology alongside psychology and business applications. During the first two years of the course students cover a broad range of activities including software evaluation, developing an internet site, making videos, photography, sound mixing and building multimedia kiosks. In the final year they can specialise in either marketing and commercial media or multimedia in education. The proximity of ULTRALAB at the Chelmsford site provides opportunities to form links with an international company that develops educational CD-ROM and Web learning materials. Contact details p477.

European School of Economics

BA (Hons) Communication and Media, Specialisation in Advertising and Company Imaging

Students follow a core programme of modules and select options from their specialisation such as advertising management or consumer and buyer behaviour. All students study two foreign languages and carry out 10 months of work placements in at least two countries. 70 per cent of undergraduates on the course are international students. Contact details p480.

Falmouth College of Art

PgDip Professional Writing

This programme is designed to enable people from a variety of backgrounds to learn the skills of professional writing, combined with the study of narrative and literary theories. It provides the opportunity to become acquainted with different genres such as corporate writing, writing for performance, journalistic writing and literary writing. The aim is to produce a combination of writer, editor and media specialist, for

Interesting facts

- England was the first country to have a regular, high-definition television broadcasting service. The BBC began televising experiments in 1932 and began a full service in 1936

- China holds the record for the country with the most TV sets, where a staggering 227.5 million households have a television

- The most expensive advert ever made was only shown once. A commercial for Apple Computers Inc, it cost nearly £1 million to produce and air, and was directed by Ridley Scott of *Alien* fame

example someone who can co-ordinate the transformation of complex technical information into an entertaining screenplay, a web page or a reader-friendly manual. This course is intended to meet the need for people to produce specialist trade and in-house magazines, or to take on roles in the area of public relations. Contact details p480.

King Alfred's College

BA (Hons) Media and Film Studies

This is an academic degree concerned with theories and approaches to media and film. Attention is paid to the historical and cultural conditions within which media and cinema are produced and students analyse a wide range of both contemporary and past film and media texts. Although primarily theoretical, students on single honours and major pathways have the opportunity to take optional modules in video production and screenwriting. All students acquire a variety of transferable

BUSINESS COURSES

with an INTERNATIONAL FOCUS
Start: January, April or September

L CIBS – London's leading business career training college for international students. Specialise in:

- **International Business Management**

- **Marketing Communications and**

  Public Relations

- **International Tourism Management**

All courses are during the day and may be studied either full-time or part-time. Training in Professional English communications and Business Computing is included on all diploma courses.

Top Five English Language Daily Newspapers

Source: "The Top 10 of Everything: 2000" Russell Ash, Dorling Kindersley 1999

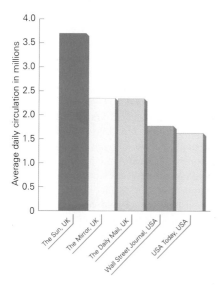

creative writing, creative computing and cultural studies in the contemporary world, aim to complement and extend the theoretical and practical base of the core courses. In the second and third years, students are introduced to specific media areas with core courses on understanding television and advanced digital video production. In the third year, a range of options and core modules are offered to extend the skills acquired in the first two years. Euryn Ogwen Williams, S4C's Digital Development Consultant, has said that the degree scheme is "most refreshing in an area of academic study that has failed to catch up with the reality of the new media." Students also benefit from the university's purpose-built Media Centre which houses a video conferencing suite, a television studio, digital editing suites, a production gallery, a subtitling raining suite and digital and still cameras. Contact details p481.

skills including computer literacy. Some students go on to work in media-related industries, others use the skills they have acquired in areas such as retail management, public service, administration and teaching. Contact details p481.

University of Wales, Lampeter
BA (Hons) Media Studies

The degree scheme in media studies was launched in September 1999. It has a strong interdisciplinary approach, combining both theoretical and practical modules. In the first year students study a broad range of historical and theoretical perspectives whilst key issues such as realism, representation, gender and narrative are investigated via analysis of specific texts from soap opera, news, documentary, advertising and drama. An introduction to digital video production introduces students to technical and practical elements, whilst

The Nottingham Trent University
BA (Hons) Design for Television

This unique course involves a wide range of creative, communicative and intellectual skills by which the visual style of any television programme, video, film or series is determined. The course places strong emphasis on developing those qualities which are essential to a successful and fulfiling career in this field, including imagination, creativity, practical and interpersonal skills, as well as team-working and communicative qualities. The course is practically based and taught through a series of real situation design projects. A close working relationship with the television industry has been established from the outset, and a significant part of the course is delivered by professional practitioners. This is the first graduate-level training

MEDIA

within the UK which is dedicated to providing the specialists who will one day maintain the worldwide reputation of British television production design. Contact details p484.

College of Ripon and York
BA (Hons) Theatre, Film and Television

This programme takes an integrated approach to the study and practice of theatre, film and television. 60 per cent of the degree comprises production activity in well-equipped, purpose-designed studios and workshop areas. The course is vocational with many graduates gaining employment in television, theatre and independent production companies. The degree also considers the aesthetic, cultural, industrial and technological aspects necessary for students in this field. The course has close links with local theatre andtelevision companies and includes a work placement. Contact details p484.

University of Stirling
MPhil in Publishing Studies

The MPhil in Publishing Studies aims to reflect the international nature of modern publishing and covers the whole publication process from planning through production and marketing. To keep up to date with the changing nature of publishing, the details of the course content change every year. Generally, however, students cover the theory and practice of publications, editorial and production, marketing, publishing law, intellectual property, business and finance, design and typography, desktop and electronic publications, Internet and online publishing, image and text manipulation, sales, distribution and new media developments. The course aims to provide students with the intellectual and practical skills required to succeed in such a highly competitive industry, and is popular with both postgraduates entering publishing for the first time, and with established professionals

MEDIA

RESEARCH RANKINGS

Communication, Cultural and Media Studies

Institution	Grade	Institution	Grade
East Anglia	5	London Institute	3b
East London	5	Luton	3b
Stirling	5	Middlesex	3b
Sussex	5	North London	3b
Warwick	5	Queen Margaret College	3b
Westminster	5	Thames Valley	3b
Birmingham	4	De Montfort	2
Goldsmiths	4	Leeds Metropolitan	2
UWE	4	Southampton Institute	2
Cardiff	3a	Staffordshire	2
Leicester	3a	Sunderland	2
Nottingham Trent	3a	Bournemouth	1
Sheffield Hallam	3a	City	1
Ulster	3a	London Guildhall	1
Coventry	3b	King Alfred's College	1
Glasgow Caledonian	3b	Surrey Institute	1
Leeds	3b	Wolverhampton	1
Liverpool John Moores	3b		

source: RAE 1996

aiming to enhance their skills. It also attracts international students who value its approach to publishing as a global enterprise. Contact details p486.

The Surrey Institute of Art and Design
BA (Hons) Film and Video
This course, which is part of the Arts and Media faculty is based at the Surrey Institute's Farnham campus, and currently has about 20 international students enrolled on it. It aims to develop creativity and practical abilities by providing a broad grounding in production, sound, art direction, post-production, lighting and camera. The degree is accredited by BKSTS and BECTU, and is particularly popular due to the current renaissance of the British film industry. Contact details p486.

University of Surrey Roehampton
BA Film and Television Studies
This degree blends practical work with theory. In their first year, students take modules designed to introduce them to the subject. These include the study of developments in the moving image, television institutions and audiences, reading film narrative and video production. In years two and three students can specialise in such areas as documentary film and television, writing for the screen, media presentation, film as art, dance as television and screen acting. The institute has a fully-equipped, professionally-staffed television studio on campus. In addition, it is close to the British Film Institute (BFI), Institute of Contemporary Art (ICA) and the Museum of the Moving Image (MOMI). This programme used to be a part of the institute's drama course which counts Vivien Leigh amongst its graduates. Contact details p486.

Warwick University
MA in Creative Industries
This is a new postgraduate programme, launched in 1999. It is a taught programme studying the convergence of broadcasting corporations, the music industry, publishing and film. It looks at the emergence of a new cultural economy driven by creative entrepreneurs and is the first course in the UK to focus specifically on this phenomenon. It has developed from the MA in European Cultural Policy and Administration which combines cultural study with finance, marketing and applied arts management. Contact details p487.

MEDIA

oncourse.co.uk
The ultimate guide to courses

Modern Languages and Area Studies

How many times have you been in a different country and found yourself unable to say what you want, or indeed anything that makes the slightest bit of sense. A language barrier can often be very frustrating to overcome, whether you are simply ordering a cup of coffee, or are involved in a more complex discussion about politics. Nowadays it is not acceptable to try and get your message across with a combination of hand signals and talking loudly, as the world we live in is becoming a smaller place. Not only is our knowledge of once far-flung places increasing, but the technological advances of the 20th century are making communication far easier. This all means that the ability to communicate in another language is a highly valued skill that is much sought after by any business or industry.

Studying a language other than English in the UK may initially seem like an odd idea. However, there are several reasons why it could be a good option. The quality of teaching, the research opportunities and the range of facilities in a British university sometimes exceed those available in the countries where the language is spoken. Most universities will have good links with other institutions around the world, especially those in Europe. Also, there is a vast range of languages to choose from, many of which can often be combined with other academic disciplines.

Modern language degrees, and the range of subjects they can be combined with, can vary between institutions.

Some institutions take a more traditional approach with emphasis on literature and history, while others have a more contemporary outlook concentrating on business skills and modern culture. All courses, however, will include a main element of written and spoken language study, which can include laboratory work and conversation with native speaking assistants. Aside from this, most courses will offer options covering an array of topics including the literature, culture, history, politics, linguistics, philosophy or society of the countries speaking the language in question. Area studies, such as African or Celtic studies, will cover many of these topics as they are highly multi-disciplinary in nature and focus on nearly every aspect of a particular country, region or culture. Most also include an option to study a language.

Almost all modern language and area study degrees last four years and typically include a year spent in a country of the language studied. This usually takes place in the third year and can involve studying at a university, working as a language assistant or, in some cases, full-time employment can be arranged. Some institutions have a fairly rigid structure for what the year abroad should include while others will leave students pretty much to their own devices. Most students will usually have studied the language at A level or equivalent but most institutions will accept beginners and run special courses in the first two years of the degree programme.

DEGREE COURSES

University of Bath
MA Diploma in Interpreting and Translation

This is a one-year, full-time course. Languages offered include Chinese, English, French, German, Italian, Japanese, Russian and Spanish. The course is taught over two semesters with examinations in the summer. Students may follow one of two possible paths: either two foreign languages working into English, or one language working both from and into English. The course contains core subjects such as documentary translation, consecutive interpreting, simultaneous interpreting and elective subjects such as inter-cultural communication training. Candidates who wish to proceed to the MA must present a 15,000-word dissertation after successful completion of the above course of study. Former students have reached positions of responsibility in many international organisations, for example the head of English interpreting at the European Parliament and the head of translation at the European Monetary Institute. Contact details p477.

University of Hull
Hispanic Studies

This department achieved 24 (out of 24) in the teaching quality assessments. The department aims for its undergraduates to achieve near native fluency in Spanish. Even those without A level Spanish, who study the language as part of a joint honours degree, are encouraged to reach a very high standard of linguistic skill by the end of the course. Language learning is integrated into the study of broader aspects of Hispanic culture including Spanish cinema, Latin American history, or business Spanish. Second-year students also have the opportunity to study Portuguese. The department has a flexible approach to students with non-standard entry qualifications and to those who want to change courses once they have been accepted. Linguists at Hull benefit from the facilities of the university library, the language institute, and the computer centre. Assessment varies between modules, but may take the form of coursework, a single long essay or an exam. Second-year students have the chance to gain the *Certificado de Español Comercial* from the Madrid Chamber of Commerce and finalists with outstanding spoken Spanish gain a distinction in spoken Spanish as part of their degree. Contact details p481.

University of Hull
MA South-East Asian Studies

This multidisciplinary, 12-month programme offers seminar or course options, organised into two streams: development problems and policy and politics, and international relations. Each of these streams provides a working knowledge of research methods for those who plan to proceed to the doctoral programme or to undertake field research for non-governmental organisations or other public or private agencies. For those international students who wish to take a preparatory year before the MA, there is a 12-month Foundation Diploma in South-East Asian studies available. In co-operation with the Institute of Pacific Asia Studies, South-East Asian Studies offers weekly seminars on topics of current interest, often with distinguished scholars or diplomats as participants. Contact details p481.

Liverpool Hope University College
BA European Studies

European Studies equips students with an understanding of the development, structure and challenges of modern day Europe. A wide range of options can be studied including political, social, environmental, legal and cultural

TEACHING QUALITY ASSESSMENTS

American Studies
(England and N Ireland 1996/97/98)

Institution	Grade	Institution	Grade
Central Lancashire	24	Derby	21
East Anglia	24	Kent at Canterbury	21
Keele	24	Liverpool John Moores	21
Hull	23	Reading	21
Leicester	23	Wolverhampton	21
Birmingham	22	Liverpool Hope College	19
Middlesex	22	King Alfred's College	18
Nottingham	22	University College Northampton	18
Ulster	22	Ripon and York St John	17
Brunel	21	Thames Valley	15
Canterbury Christ Church	21		

Dutch
(England and N Ireland 1996)

Institution	Grade	Institution	Grade
UCL	22	Hull	20

East and South Asian Studies
(England and N. Ireland 1996/97/98)

Institution	Grade	Institution	Grade
Cambridge	23	Oxford	22
Leeds	23	Sheffield	22
SOAS	23	Durham	21
Westminster	23	King Alfred's College	20
Hull	22		

European Languages
(Scotland 1998)

Institution	Grade	Institution	Grade
Aberdeen	22	Heriot-Watt	21
Glasgow	22	Stirling	20
St Andrews	22	Napier	19
Strathclyde	22	Paisley	19
Edinburgh	21	Robert Gordon	19

Source: HEFCE, SHEFC, HEFCW latest available ratings
For a more complete list of institutions offering these courses at undergraduate level refer to the Course Directory

MODERN LANGUAGES

modules. Students start the course with six core modules, including the history of Europe since 1945 and an introduction to the European Union. There is an optional period of study abroad for one semester at one of the college's partner universities in France, Germany, Finland, Holland or Spain. Students are

TEACHING QUALITY ASSESSMENTS

French
(England and N Ireland 1995/96)

Institution	Grade	Institution	Grade
Portsmouth	23	Warwick	21
Westminster	23	Bristol	20
Aston	22	Keele	20
Durham	22	Lancaster	20
Exeter	22	Queen's Belfast	20
Leeds	22	Ulster	20
Liverpool	22	Birkbeck	19
Oxford Brookes	22	Leicester	19
Sussex	22	Manchester	19
Hull	21	Wolverhampton	19
KCL	21	Birmingham	18
Reading	21	British Institute in Paris	18
Royal Holloway	21	Edge Hill College	17
Sheffield	21	Sunderland	17
UCL	21	Nottingham	16

English and Associated Studies
(Wales 1994/95)

Institution	Grade	Institution	Grade
Aberystwyth (American Studies)	Satisfactory	Swansea (American Studies)	Satisfactory

French Studies
(Scotland 1997)

Institution	Grade	Institution	Grade
Aberdeen	Excellent	Edinburgh	Highly Satisfactory
Glasgow	Excellent	Stirling	Highly Satisfactory

German
(England and N Ireland 1995/96)

Institution	Grade	Institution	Grade
Exeter	24	KCL	20
UCL	23	Reading	20
Warwick	23	Sheffield	20
Aston	22	Westminster	20
Durham	22	Birmingham	19
Leeds	22	Keele	19
Nottingham	22	Lancaster	19
Bristol	21	Liverpool	19
Hull	21	Oxford Brookes	19
Leicester	21	Royal Holloway	19
Manchester	21	Ulster	19
Portsmouth	21	Sunderland	17
Birkbeck	20	Wolverhampton	17

Source: HEFCE, SHEFC, HEFCW latest available ratings
For a more complete list of institutions offering these courses at undergraduate level refer to the Course Directory

MODERN LANGUAGES

required to undertake an individual project, where appropriate, researched during study abroad. There is also the opportunity to learn a second European language (French, German or Spanish). Non-native speakers of English may be able to take English language studies. Graduates of this course have gone on to work in exports, banking, the civil service, publishing, local government and research consultancies. Contact details p482.

University College London
French

French can be studied at UCL as a single honours degree or combined with a number of subjects including German, Italian, Russian, an Asian or African language, philosophy, history of art or Scandinavian studies. The Department

of French has structured its four-year degree so that after studying core courses in French literature, language and culture in the first year, students have a degree of flexibility in the subjects they study later on. Second-year courses usually involve a choice of lecture and seminar courses that cover topics in critical theory, French society, or literature from the medieval to the modern period. There is also the choice of film studies and literature from other French-speaking countries. The third year is spent abroad, either as a teaching assistant, as a full-time student at a university or at the British Institute in Paris, or occasionally in employment that has been arranged independently. The fourth year is devoted entirely to seminar work in which students can build on the

TEACHING QUALITY ASSESSMENTS

Iberian Languages and Studies
(England and N Ireland 1996)

Institution	Grade	Institution	Grade
Hull	24	Manchester	20
KCL (Portuguese)	23	Wolverhampton	20
Birmingham	22	Birkbeck	19
Bristol	22	UCL	19
KCL (Spanish)	22	Portsmouth	18
Leeds	22	Sunderland	18
Liverpool	21	Ulster	18
Queen's Belfast	21	Westminster	18
Sheffield	21	Nottingham	17
Exeter	20	Durham	16
Lancaster	20		

Italian
(England 1995/96)

Institution	Grade	Institution	Grade
Birmingham	22	Leicester	20
Exeter	22	Portsmouth	20
Hull	22	Reading	20
Bristol	21	UCL	20
Royal Holloway	21	Leeds	19
Warwick	21	Manchester	19
Durham	20	Westminster	19
Lancaster (with Iberian Studies)	20		

Source: HEFCE, SHEFC, HEFCW latest available ratings
For a more complete list of institutions offering these courses at undergraduate level refer to the Course Directory

TEACHING QUALITY ASSESSMENTS

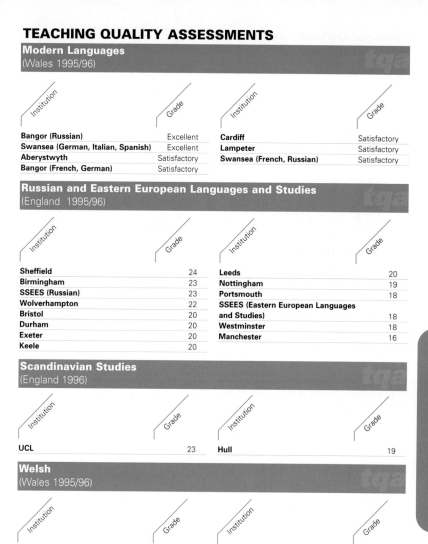

Modern Languages
(Wales 1995/96)

Institution	Grade
Bangor (Russian)	Excellent
Swansea (German, Italian, Spanish)	Excellent
Aberystwyth	Satisfactory
Bangor (French, German)	Satisfactory

Institution	Grade
Cardiff	Satisfactory
Lampeter	Satisfactory
Swansea (French, Russian)	Satisfactory

Russian and Eastern European Languages and Studies
(England 1995/96)

Institution	Grade
Sheffield	24
Birmingham	23
SSEES (Russian)	23
Wolverhampton	22
Bristol	20
Durham	20
Exeter	20
Keele	20

Institution	Grade
Leeds	20
Nottingham	19
Portsmouth	18
SSEES (Eastern European Languages and Studies)	18
Westminster	18
Manchester	16

Scandinavian Studies
(England 1996)

Institution	Grade
UCL	23

Institution	Grade
Hull	19

Welsh
(Wales 1995/96)

Institution	Grade
Aberystwyth	Excellent
Bangor	Excellent
Cardiff	Satisfactory

Institution	Grade
Lampeter	Satisfactory
Swansea	Satisfactory

Source: HEFCE, SHEFC, HEFCW latest available ratings
For a more complete list of institutions offering these courses at undergraduate level refer to the Course Directory

knowledge and critical skills that they have acquired in previous years. Each of the final-year options explores the research interests of lecturers in the department. Contact details p487.

University of Nottingham
Slavonic Studies

The Department of Slavonic Studies, established in 1916, teaches two areas of Slavonic culture: Russian studies and Southern Slavonic studies (the latter covering the countries of the former Yugoslavia). The degree courses on offer are all modular and last four years with the third year spent abroad. Russian or Serbo-Croat can be studied for a single honours degree, a joint honours degree, or as part of a degree

Lanuages Officially Spoken in the Most Countries

Source: "The Top 10 of Everything: 2000" Russell Ash, Dorling Kindersley 1999

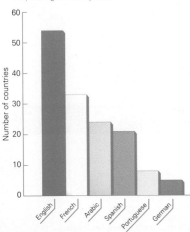

MODERN LANGUAGES

combining two or three subjects. Slovene modules can also be taken in conjunction with any degree. Certain modules are compulsory, and each degree course has its own framework, but students have some freedom to decide the content of their own degrees. Modules are offered in language, literature, drama, philology, and cultural history, and students are encouraged to take modules from other departments in related or new subjects. The courses aim to help students develop linguistic competence and a specialist knowledge of Russia and/or Slavonic studies. They also provide an opportunity for students to develop their communicative, study and IT skills both in English and in the target languages. In the last national assessment of research, the department was one of the only two in the country to receive the top rating of 5*. Contact details p484.

University of Portsmouth
BA (Hons) European Studies

As part of this three-year programme in the Faculty of Humanities and Social Sciences, students specialise in one foreign language. Spanish, Italian, German, Russian and Portuguese can all be studied from beginners' level. The faculty has strong links with European schools and colleges that will help those doing European studies. Students learn about features of Europe such as institutions, public policy and culture. 20 international students are on the European Studies course this academic year. Contact details p484.

The Queen's University of Belfast
MA Irish Studies

The Institute of Irish Studies was established to encourage interest and co-ordinate research in those fields of study which have a particular Irish interest. The masters degree run by the institute involves interdisciplinary study in areas including history, politics, literature and drama, geography, archaeology, social anthropology and Irish language. The institute received 5 in the latest research assessment exercise, and has Nobel Laureate and former Queen's graduate Seamus Heaney as an Honorary Fellow. Contact details p484.

TEACHING QUALITY ASSESSMENTS

Linguistics
(England and N Ireland 1996)

Institution	Grade	Institution	Grade
Lancaster	23	College of St Mark and St John	21
Central Lancashire	22	Wolverhampton	21
Durham	22	Hertfordshire	20
Newcastle upon Tyne	22	SOAS	20
Roehampton Institute	22	Westminster	20
Sheffield	22	Birkbeck	19
Sussex	22	Reading	19
Thames Valley	22	Ripon and York St John	19
UCL	22	East London	18
Essex	21	Leeds	17
Luton	21	Exeter	16
Manchester	21		

Middle Eastern and African Studies
(England and N Ireland 1997/98)

Institution	Grade	Institution	Grade
Birmingham	23	Westminster	22
Cambridge	23	Leeds	21
Durham	22	Exeter	20
Oxford	22	Manchester	20
SOAS	22	Salford	20

Modern Languages
(England and N Ireland 1995/96/97)

Institution	Grade	Institution	Grade
Northumbria at Newcastle	23	La Sainte Union College (revisit)	19
Queen Mary and Westfield	23	Leeds Metropolitan	19
Cambridge	22	Liverpool Institute	19
Newcastle upon Tyne	22	Liverpool John Moores	19
Oxford Brookes	22	London Guildhall	19
South Bank	22	Middlesex	19
York	22	Roehampton Institute	19
Anglia Polytechnic	21	Sheffield Hallam	19
Central Lancashire	21	Queen's Belfast	19
Coventry	21	Bournemouth (revisit)	18
Kingston	21	Bradford	18
Manchester Metropolitan	21	Derby	18
Oxford	21	East London	18
Staffordshire	21	Southampton	18
UWE	21	Surrey	18
Brighton	20	Thames Valley	18
Luton	20	UMIST	18
North London	20	De Montfort	17
Salford	20	Goldsmiths	17
Bath	19	Nottingham Trent	17
Bolton Institute	19	Sussex	17
Chester College	19	Trinity and All Saints	17
De Montfort (Bedford)	19	Hertfordshire	16
East Anglia	19	Huddersfield	15
Kent at Canterbury	19		

MODERN LANGUAGES

279

University of Salford
MA/PgDip in Translating and Interpreting

This course is designed to meet the international demand for highly-trained translators/interpreters and linguists, as well as meeting the needs of students who are planning a career in international and government departments, regional organisations and the freelance sector. Students come from all over the world and there are currently 10 international students on the course. The school normally expects all students to undertake a short work placement in an interpreting environment. Graduates of the course often work in these companies, as well as becoming freelance translators or interpreters. Students take modules in lexicography/terminology, principles of translation and information technology in consecutive and simultaneous interpreting and can specialise in either translation or interpreting. Students learn through a mixture of laboratory exercises, seminars and lectures. Contact details p485.

School of Oriental and African Studies (SOAS)
BA African Language and Development Studies

This is a combined four-year degree course. Students can visit the chosen region and learn the language in a safe and structured way. Students taking Swahili and development studies, for example, spend the first two terms of their third year studying in Tanzania. African languages that are normally available are Amharic, Hausa, Swahili, Somali, Yoruba, Arabic and Zulu, and no previous knowledge is expected. The degree emphasises the role that language plays in giving access to a particular culture, as well as the importance that the developing world exerts on the global scene in terms of cultural enrichment, expressed through texts, orality and music. Contact details p485.

University of Southampton
BA (Hons) British Studies

British studies is a new course established by the University of Southampton to respond to the needs of international students who wish to learn about British culture, society and the English language. The course looks at the distinctive features of British culture, society and its institutions through history, language, the social sciences, art, music, fashion and written culture. Core modules are taken in society, politics, culture and ideology in the British Isles. Students also choose from courses as diverse as archaeology, art, cultural studies, economics and media studies. The course lasts three or four years depending on a student's academic qualifications and proficiency in English. Contact details p486.

Westminster University
BA (Hons) Modern Languages/Modern Languages with English Literary and Cultural Studies, with English Language or Linguistics

Westminster has a large modern language department which scores well in teaching quality assessments. Students on this four-year course can choose between the following languages: French, Spanish, Italian, Russian, Chinese, German, Arabic and English language. You can also choose a combination of two languages, or study one with linguistics, or with English literature and cultural studies. Students are encouraged to spend the third year at a partner university abroad in order to perfect their language skills. English studies or English language and linguistics are also available as separate degrees. Contact details p487.

Music

music
music
music
music

"Music creates order out of chaos", said the British musician Sin Yehudi Menuhin. There was a time when music, as taught at universities, was thought of as the audible manifestation of mathematics: a science, allied to geometry and astrology. Today, although music has retained some of its mathematical associations, especially with regard to technicalities such as acoustics and temperament, there is more of a tendency towards viewing it as a creative art, and a form of self-expression.

There has been a startling array of musical genres originating in the UK. These include those started by Elgar, Purcell, The Beatles or the Spice Girls, Elton John, George Michael or even Oasis. For many years, the UK has been the place for musical innovation, with the British invasion in the 60s, and the birth of Britpop in the 90s. The UK is also home to some of the finest orchestras in the world, such as the London Symphony Orchestra and the Scottish National Opera. Top musicians from all over the world have come to London to study at the Royal College of Music, and every year London is host to one of the most prestigious events in the music calendar, the Proms.

A degree in music can be studied in a number of ways leading to a BA, BMus or BEng, say in music technology. Many universities also provide combined studies degrees with arts, humanities and social science subjects. Although music studies are traditionally associated with the classical, popular music has recently been introduced into various university faculties. Other specialist degrees include: commercial music; composition; contemporary music; electronic music; ethnomusicology; jazz; music technology; and performance studies.

The majority of academic music courses aim to give students both an understanding of European traditions, from medieval times to the present day, and enable them to develop individual interests in historical, creative or practical fields. Courses introduce students to different kinds of study – historical, critical, analytical, technical, compositional and performance-related. The proportion of theory and performance in different courses can vary enormously. Conservatories such as the Royal College of Music and the Royal Northern College of Music are likely to concentrate on performance whereas universities may pursue a more theoretical approach to the subject.

International students should remember that methods of teaching music in the UK might be different from other countries. Musical training in the UK is geared towards interpretation and this is in contrast, say with the Eastern approach that is often more technical. It is advisable to consult all prospectuses to find out exactly what each course entails and to talk to someone in the department before you apply.

Entrance requirements vary considerably, but performance-based courses will demand a standard of instrumental skill from applicants.

DEGREE COURSES

The University of Birmingham
BMus Music

The Department of Music at the University of Birmingham, together with the University Music Society and the Barber Institute, promotes a range of musical activities, including concerts by visiting artists, occasional professional operas and a festival of early music. Those who come to Birmingham to study music are provided with tuition in music as an academic discipline, in composition, and in performance, both as an individual and in ensembles. Facilities include a suite of practice rooms, electroacoustic music studios, early instruments and computing facilities. Degree programmes aim to give a general grounding in music, whilst at the same time offering students the chance to develop special interests and fulfil individual potential. The first year comprises courses in music history, composition, harmony and counterpoint, and tuition as a performer in two studies. In the second and final years the work becomes increasingly specialised, and students can choose from various different options including studies of certain genres or composers, and technical disciplines such as editing and analysis. Contact details p477

University of East Anglia, Norwich
BA Music, BA Music with English Language Foundation

The first year of the BA Music with English Language Foundation combines the study of music with English language subjects. The following three years are spent primarily on studying music with the opportunity to continue with English to a lesser degree. Both courses revolve around the core elements of developing practical skills with the history and theory of music. Specialist modules include performance, conducting, musicology and composition. Assessment varies according to the nature of the module. Performers are assessed through recitals; composers are assessed on a portfolio of pieces; and conductors are assessed through the performance of choral and orchestral works. Continuous assessment is common in all courses. The School of Music, based at the Music Centre, has a multipurpose concert room, rehearsal spaces, electroacoustic studios and an open-air amphitheatre. The department also maintains a close relationship with musical organisations in the region, such as the Aldeburgh Festival and Norwich Cathedral. Contact details p479.

King's College London, University of London
Music

King's College London places equal emphasis on performance and general musicianship, free composition, musical analysis and the history of music.

TEACHING QUALITY ASSESSMENTS

Music
(England 1994/95)

Institution	Grade	Institution	Grade
Anglia Polytechnic	Excellent	Sussex	Excellent
Birmingham	Excellent	Trinity College	Excellent
Cambridge	Excellent	UCE	Excellent
City	Excellent	Ulster	Excellent
Goldsmiths	Excellent	York	Excellent
Huddersfield	Excellent	Bretton Hall	Satisfactory
Keele	Excellent	Bristol	Satisfactory
KCL	Excellent	Canterbury Christ Church	Satisfactory
Lancaster	Excellent	Durham	Satisfactory
Leeds	Excellent	East Anglia	Satisfactory
Manchester	Excellent	Exeter	Satisfactory
Nottingham	Excellent	Hertfordshire	Satisfactory
Open University	Excellent	Hull	Satisfactory
Queen's Belfast	Excellent	Kingston	Satisfactory
Royal Academy of Music	Excellent	Liverpool	Satisfactory
Royal College of Music	Excellent	Liverpool Institute	Satisfactory
Royal Northern College	Excellent	Middlesex	Satisfactory
Salford College	Excellent	Newcastle upon Tyne	Satisfactory
Sheffield College	Excellent	Oxford	Satisfactory
SOAS	Excellent	Reading	Satisfactory
Southampton	Excellent	Royal Holloway	Satisfactory
Surrey	Excellent		

Music
(Scotland 1994)

Institution	Grade	Institution	Grade
Royal Scottish Academy of Music and Drama	Excellent	Glasgow	Highly Satisfactory
Edinburgh	Highly Satisfactory	Napier	Satisfactory

Music
(Wales 1994/95)

Institution	Grade	Institution	Grade
Bangor	Excellent	Trinity College, Carmarthen (Theatre, Music and Media Studies)	Satisfactory
Cardiff	Satisfactory		
Welsh College of Music and Drama	Satisfactory		

Source: HEFCE, SHEFC, HEFCW latest available ratings
For a more complete list of institutions offering these courses at undergraduate level refer to the Course Directory

Comprehensiveness is the underlying theme of the BMus degree programme, the academic rigour of the analytical, historical and theoretical teaching being balanced by the strong practical elements of the course. Individual tuition is organised by the Royal Academy of Music and participation in performances of chamber music and choral works is obligatory. Furthermore, it is possible to play in the orchestra as well. There is scope for extra curricular

Top Five Countries at The Eurovision Song Contest, 1975–1998

Source: www.kolumbus.fi/jarpen/points.htm

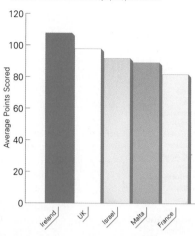

musical activities thanks to the department's computer studio, music processing and recording facilities. Budding composers at King's have the opportunity to hear their works performed in workshops by distinguished professional ensembles. The music department has its own library and computer facilities for undergraduates. Famous names associated with the department include Harrison Birtwistle (a professor at King's), Michael Nyman and John Eliot Gardiner. Contact details p481.

Rose Bruford College
BA Music Technology/BA Sound and Image Design

The BA Music Technology course teaches music composition utilising computer software as a form of music technology. It covers sound recording, sequencing synthesis, digital audio, language of music, composition and pop promos. The BA in Sound and Image Design covers many of the same areas, but also includes digital visual media manipulation. London's appeal as possibly the music technology capital of the world, is a major draw for this course. Contact details p484.

Royal College of Music
BMus Music

Famous alumni at the RCM include Benjamin Britten, Dame Joan Sutherland and Anne Dudley – the Oscar-winning composer of the music for *The Full Monty*. The degree here involves practical training with a strong emphasis on performance and opportunities to perform in public. More than 250 concerts are given each year. Application involves an audition at which set works are played and a range of general music skills are tested. First-year undergraduates can expect a weekly workload of a principal study, aural lessons, stylistic and historical studies and academic seminars (a total of 20 hours a week). A pre-degree course for talented musicians and a BSc in Physics with Studies in Musical Performance, offered in conjunction with the neighbouring Imperial College of Science, Technology and Medicine, are also available. A significant number of graduates find employment with major international orchestras, opera companies, choirs and chamber ensembles. There are many opportunities for RCM students to gain experience both within the UK and abroad. The facilities available at the RCM include the Museum of Instruments, the Department of Portraits and Performance History, a library and computer facilities. The RCM also has its own studios for recording and composition. Contact details p485.

School of Oriental and African Studies (SOAS)
Music Studies

Students interested in something other than classical Western training may consider the music courses on offer at SOAS. In keeping with the SOAS specialism, undergraduate degrees are based on ethnomusicology and the selected musical traditions of Asia and Africa. Music can be studied either as a single subject – music studies, or in conjunction with another subject to create a broader cultural study. The courses include performance in non-Western forms of music and professionals are available for tuition on specific instruments such as the sitar or the koto. In the second and third year, students choose to focus on the music of two areas: South East Asia, South Asia, the Near and Middle East, East Asia or Africa. The centre also offers a taught masters degree (MMus in Ethnomusicology) and research degrees. Contact details p485.

RESEARCH RANKINGS

Music

Institution	Grade	Institution	Grade
KCL	5*	Lancaster	4
Liverpool	5*	Reading	4
Manchester	5*	Surrey	4
Oxford	5*	Sussex	4
Royal Holloway	5*	Bangor	3a
SOAS	5*	Bretton Hall	3a
Birmingham	5	Canterbury Christ Church	3a
Cambridge	5	Glasgow	3a
City	5	Newcastle upon Tyne	3a
Durham	5	Salford College	3a
Goldsmiths	5	Thames Valley	3a
Leeds	5	Anglia Polytechnic	3b
Nottingham	5	Bath College	3b
Open University	5	Dartington College	3b
Queen's Belfast	5	East Anglia	3b
Royal Academy of Music	5	Hertfordshire	3b
Royal College of Music	5	Kingston	3b
Royal Northern College of Music	5	Oxford Brookes	3b
Sheffield	5	UCE	3b
Southampton	5	Ulster	3b
York	5	Brunel	2
Bristol	4	Coventry	2
Cardiff	4	King Alfred's College	2
De Montfort	4	Liverpool Hope College	2
Edinburgh	4	Nottingham Trent	2
Exeter	4	University College Chichester	2
Huddersfield	4	College of St Mark and St John	1
Hull	4	Edge Hill College	1
Keele	4		

source: RAE 1996

MUSIC

Philosophy, Theology and Religious Studies

Have you ever asked yourself the question "What came first, the chicken or the egg?" Well, if you have, maybe philosophy is the subject for you.

For over 3,000 years, from Plato and Aristotle to Hume and Kant, philosophers have tried to find answers to questions about humankind and the world we live in. Literally meaning 'love of wisdom', philosophy thrives on discussions about human existence, the mind, free will and determinism. Studying philosophy is a matter of teaching students to use their own minds - to reason and argue rather than simply asserting things dogmatically.

Ever since the Middle Ages, thinkers from the British Isles have been at the forefront of Western philosophy. Writing in Church Latin, figures such as Roger Bacon and Duns Scotus were admired across Latin Christendom. Later, John Locke and David Hume became giants of the Enlightenment. Even Karl Marx and Friedrich Engels spent much of their working lives in Britain.

The study of philosophy at university is normally centred around five main areas: logic; epistemology (the theory of knowledge); metaphysics (the study of the nature of reality); moral philosophy; and social and political philosophy. These introductory subjects are likely to be studied in the first year, with the opportunity to specialise in the second and third years. Later options could include political philosophy, symbolic logic, aesthetics or philosophy of religion.

Theology and Religion

Theology can be traced back as one of the core subjects taught in Britain's oldest universities. Today, subjects such as religious studies have replaced theology in many universities, reflecting perhaps, Britain's present multicultural society.

Theology comes from two Greek words, *theos*, meaning God, and *logos*, meaning word, or reason, and describes the study of divine things. In its narrow sense theology means the doctrine of God and His works, but on a broader scale it points to the sum of Christian doctrine. Religious studies, by contrast, looks at various faiths and their impact on culture and history. Both subjects deal with issues in anthropology, sociology, language, history, art and philosophy.

It is important to remember that university courses are both secular and academic, and that you don't have to be religious to study religion, although many students are.

Most theology and religious studies degrees last for three years. In the first year, religious studies students are likely to study introductory modules, such as religion in contemporary Britain and may go on to study modules such as: religion and working classes in 19th century England. Studying theology will normally involve looking in depth at the texts of both the Old and New Testaments, as well as Church history, and possibly biblical languages such as Greek and Hebrew. There may also be the opportunity to study other related subjects such as archaeology, psychology and philosophy.

DEGREE COURSES

University of Stirling
Religious Studies

Stirling is one of the few universities in the country to offer degree programmes in religious studies rather than in theology. The difference is essentially that a religious studies degree puts the theme of religion at the centre of the subject, and studies the faiths of the world and approaches to religion. A comparative religious studies degree such as those offered at Stirling, the University of Wales, Bangor and Lancaster University is more akin to a social science such as anthropology. At Stirling the approach to religion is thematic and options cover such themes as the social anthropology of religion, the psychology of religion, and women and religion. However, part of the teaching does focus on specific faiths such as Theravada Buddhism, Mahayana Buddhism, Christianity and Islam. Students study a minimum of two out of three core courses in their first year and a half at Stirling. These three core courses cover such areas as religion, myth and meaning, religion ethics and society and religion in the modern world. Following that, you can choose any course from a range of options. During your first semester you can expect a workload of around six hours of lectures and one to two hours of private study per week. Many of the courses are assessed through an even balance of exams and continuous assessment. Contact details p486.

Lancaster University
BA(Hons) Philosophy

The BA (Hons) degree course in philosophy at Lancaster University offers an introduction to some of the perennial and central problems of philosophy, and some of its vocabulary and techniques, at a level that assumes no previous knowledge of the subject. Topics include: knowledge, truth and scepticism; theories of mind, soul and person; freedom and responsibility; the nature of reasoning; and facts and values. Eight courses are taken in the second and third years with options such as ethics; Plato and Aristotle; and aesthetics and the arts. There are two hours of lectures a week and a one-hour seminar. Coursework amounts to two-thirds of the degree, and one-third is based on an exam. Up to four courses may be assessed by dissertation instead of exams. In addition there are opportunities for students to spend a few months of their degree course in a European country. Contact details p481.

University of Glasgow
Course Titles: BD Divinity, MA Religious Studies

The Faculty of Divinity at the University of Glasgow offers an MA in Religious Studies and a BD degree in Divinity. All students take first-level courses in Religious Studies, Philosophy, the Bible, theology, Church history and one appropriate area in the Arts, Social Sciences or Science Faculties. Students are then advised about their second-level modules. If, at the end of the first two years, the standard of achievement in course and exam work has been high enough, students may be admitted to study for an Honours degree, which allows for some specialisation. Teaching is carried out through regular lectures and seminars. Performance is assessed through coursework leading up to the end-of-course degree exams. Around one third of the students in the Faculty of Divinity have well-defined vocational aims, principally the ministry and teaching religious education. Contact details p480.

TEACHING QUALITY ASSESSMENTS

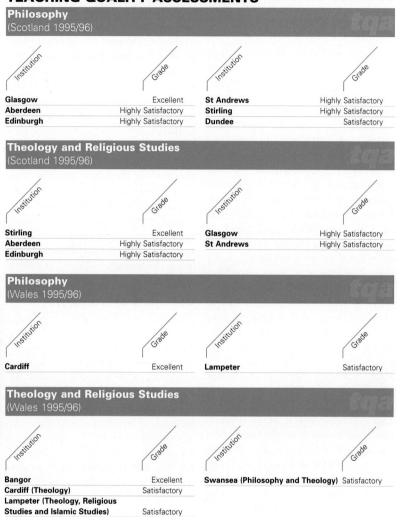

Philosophy
(Scotland 1995/96)

Institution	Grade
Glasgow	Excellent
Aberdeen	Highly Satisfactory
Edinburgh	Highly Satisfactory

Institution	Grade
St Andrews	Highly Satisfactory
Stirling	Highly Satisfactory
Dundee	Satisfactory

Theology and Religious Studies
(Scotland 1995/96)

Institution	Grade
Stirling	Excellent
Aberdeen	Highly Satisfactory
Edinburgh	Highly Satisfactory

Institution	Grade
Glasgow	Highly Satisfactory
St Andrews	Highly Satisfactory

Philosophy
(Wales 1995/96)

Institution	Grade
Cardiff	Excellent

Institution	Grade
Lampeter	Satisfactory

Theology and Religious Studies
(Wales 1995/96)

Institution	Grade
Bangor	Excellent
Cardiff (Theology)	Satisfactory
Lampeter (Theology, Religious Studies and Islamic Studies)	Satisfactory

Institution	Grade
Swansea (Philosophy and Theology)	Satisfactory

Source: HEFCE, SHEFC, HEFCW latest available ratings
For a more complete list of institutions offering these courses at undergraduate level refer to the Course Directory

University of Oxford
Philosophy

With 1,000 students engaged in philosophical studies and about 50 philosophers employed as full-time teaching staff, Oxford has the largest provision for philosophy study of any university in the United Kingdom. There is no single subject philosophy course for undergraduates at Oxford. There are a number of joint honour degrees which combine philosophy with maths, physics, theology, modern languages, physiology and psychology. However, the two best known courses involving philosophy are *literae humaniores* (or greats) and politics, philosophy and economics, commonly shortened to PPE. At postgraduate level the most popular degree is the

The Four Largest Religions in the World

Source: www.adherents.com

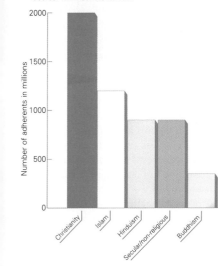

Number of adherents in millions

Christianity, Islam, Hinduism, Secular/non-religious, Buddhism

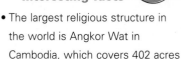

Interesting facts

- The largest religious structure in the world is Angkor Wat in Cambodia, which covers 402 acres

- Pope John Paul II has created more saints than any other pope. By January 1999 he had canonised 283 people and beatified 805

- Thales, the first philosopher proposed that water was the primary substance from which all things were derived

Bachelor of Philosophy (BPhil) although DPhil, MLitt and MSt qualifications are also available. Contact details p484.

University of Sheffield
Biblical Studies

The Department of Biblical Studies at the University of Sheffield was established in 1948 in the wake of the introduction of compulsory secondary school education. Many schools in Britain are denominational and the government was worried that there would be a shortage of Biblical scholars to teach RE (religious education). The degree course and the department are therefore unique in Britain in that they are centred around the Bible and its role in the contemporary world. The strength of this department is its research record particularly in classical Hebrew. Undergraduates are taught by scholars who are themselves undertaking research. The department attracts students from Christian communities all over the world and may be suitable for those who, though not necessarily religious themselves, are interested in the impact of Christianity in shaping the modern world. Contact details p485.

PHILOSOPHY

Science and Technology

science science science science science

Science seems to be a word regularly used in conversation, and yet most of us, in all honesty, would be hard pressed to give a precise definition of the word. Before you go rushing off to grab the nearest dictionary here is the *Chambers* version of what 'science' actually is. Science is "the systematic study of the nature and behaviour of the material and physical universe, based on observation, experiment, and measurement, and the formulation of laws to describe these facts in general terms". Seems simple enough, doesn't it? Yet within the term science there are many, many branches and specialisms. Science can be broadly split into three main categories: biology, chemistry and physics. These categories can then be split further into subjects such as biochemistry, environmental science, psychology, anatomy, biotechnology, botany, microbiology, pharmacology and zoology. The good news is that all these subjects, and more, can be studied at university.

Science, and scientific research in particular, has had a long and proud history in Britain. Sir Isaac Newton, Charles Darwin, Stephen Hawking and Richard Dawkins are just a few British scientists who have pioneered new and exciting theories, and helped changed the face of history. Whether at undergraduate or postgraduate level, there can be few places in the world that offer as much opportunity to study scientific disciplines to the extent or depth offered in Britain. Cambridge University alone has won 68 Nobel prizes for science-related subjects, and

with a history going right back to Newton can rightly claim a central role in defining physics.

Science degrees normally last three to four years and a great number of institutions are now offering sandwich placements, so that students can go off for a year and work in industry to gain the relevant practical experience needed for their course. This, in turn, improves the employability of any student entering the workplace after university.

First-year students studying any science subject normally have to take core modules before moving on to more specialised areas. For example, students studying physics are likely to cover the basic principles of physics and mathematics, such as mechanics, nuclear physics, dynamics and quantum physics, before going on to more specialist subjects such as chaos theory and optics. Biology students, on the other hand, concentrate initially on the core elements of biology, namely cell biology, genetics, ecology and the form and function of living organisms, before moving onto different specialisms.

All science subjects at university involve an amount of practical work, with some time spent in laboratories and in the field conducting experiments. Students should be aware, if they are choosing to study biology or a biology-related subject, that some departments across the country practise vivisection. Courses are concerned with the properties of living cells and tissues of animal and man, and as there are no alternatives to this, animals are used.

SPECIALIST AND VOCATIONAL COURSES

Faculty of Astrological Studies

The Faculty of Astrological Studies was founded in London in 1948 and over the years has provided training for more than 9,000 students from over 90 countries. The faculty aims to produce professional astrologers with a high degree of integrity who will be able to contribute to the advancement of knowledge, and who will maintain standards that command public respect. It is a non-profit making organisation, run by a democratically elected council. The faculty offers several courses of tuition which can either be attended at classes given in London or through its original method, the correspondence course, which enables students throughout the world to receive astrological education. After a year of preliminary training, the student is eligible to take the faculty's certificate exam. This is followed by a diploma course, lasting approximately three years, and culminating in the award of the Diploma of the Faculty of Astrological Studies. There are many ways in which astrology can be applied to everyday life, including the analysis of political events, financial trends, and medicine. Contact details p480.

DEGREE COURSES

Anglia Polytechnic University

BSc (Combined Hons) Forensic Science

This undergraduate course encompasses the study of forensic chemistry, forensic pathology, forensic toxicology and human genetics. It is sufficiently grounded within analytical chemistry to provide appropriate experience and knowledge necessary to work in the field, whilst providing scope for students to acquire a solid foundation in other disciplines

SCIENCE AND TECHNOLOGY

291

central to the study of forensic science. Anglia Polytechnic University is one of only eight institutions that offer forensic science as an undergraduate programme. The combined honours feature of this course allows it to be studied not only in combination with other sciences, but also with law and criminology. This gives international students the opportunity to make a comparative study of forensic science in the UK in a legal and social context. Students have access to up-to-date facilities and purpose-built laboratories, with extensive IT provision. Contact details p477.

City College Manchester
Science and Engineering Foundation

In conjunction with the University of Manchester, this one-year, full-time programme is aimed at international students wishing to progress onto a first-degree programme in science or engineering. The programme consists of compulsory units in mathematics, IT and an investigative project, plus a range of options in physics, chemistry and biology. In addition, an intensive course in English is integral to the programme, leading to an internationally recognised English test (for example IELTS). Successful completion of the

TEACHING QUALITY ASSESSMENTS

Chemistry
(England and N Ireland 1993/94)

Institution	Grade	Institution	Grade
Bristol	Excellent	Huddersfield	Satisfactory
Cambridge	Excellent	Keele	Satisfactory
Durham	Excellent	KCL	Satisfactory
Hull	Excellent	Kingston	Satisfactory
Imperial	Excellent	Leeds Metropolitan	Satisfactory
Leeds	Excellent	Liverpool	Satisfactory
Leicester	Excellent	Liverpool John Moores	Satisfactory
Manchester	Excellent	Manchester Metropolitan	Satisfactory
Nottingham	Excellent	North London	Satisfactory
Nottingham Trent	Excellent	Portsmouth	Satisfactory
Open University	Excellent	Reading	Satisfactory
Oxford	Excellent	Salford	Satisfactory
Southampton	Excellent	Staffordshire	Satisfactory
Aston	Satisfactory	Sunderland	Satisfactory
Bath	Satisfactory	Sussex	Satisfactory
Birmingham	Satisfactory	Teesside	Satisfactory
De Montfort	Satisfactory	UMIST	Satisfactory
East Anglia	Satisfactory	UCL	Satisfactory
Essex	Satisfactory	Warwick	Satisfactory
Exeter	Satisfactory	York	Satisfactory
Greenwich	Satisfactory		

Chemistry
(England and N Ireland 1997/98)

Institution	Grade	Institution	Grade
Canterbury Christ Church	21		

Source: HEFCE, SHEFC, HEFCW latest available ratings
For a more complete list of institutions offering these courses at undergraduate level refer to the Course Directory

programme at the appropriate level will gain students access to one of the following degrees at the University of Manchester: engineering (aerospace, civil, electrical, electronic and mechanical); chemistry; computer science; earth sciences; materials science; mathematics; physics; and biological sciences. A foundation certificate is awarded by the University of Manchester and City College Manchester. Course fees are £4,500. Contact details p479.

TEACHING QUALITY ASSESSMENTS

Chemistry
(Scotland 1993/94)

Institution	Grade	Institution	Grade
Edinburgh	Excellent	Aberdeen	Highly Satisfactory
Glasgow	Excellent	Abertay Dundee	Highly Satisfactory
Glasgow Caledonian	Excellent	Heriot-Watt	Highly Satisfactory
Robert Gordon	Excellent	Napier	Highly Satisfactory
St Andrews	Excellent	Paisley	Highly Satisfactory
Strathclyde	Excellent	Dundee	Satisfactory

Chemistry
(Wales 1993/94)

Institution	Grade	Institution	Grade
Bangor	Excellent	Swansea	Satisfactory
Cardiff	Excellent	North East Wales Institute	Satisfactory
Glamorgan	Satisfactory		

Materials Technology
(England 1996/97/98)

Institution	Grade	Institution	Grade
Imperial	24	Nottingham	21
Bolton Institute	23	Birmingham	20
Cambridge	23	Brunel	20
Oxford	23	Leeds	20
Southampton	23	Liverpool Community College	20
Cranfield	22	London Guildhall	20
Manchester Metropolitan	22	Newcastle upon Tyne	20
Sheffield Hallam	22	Nottingham Trent	20
Sheffield	22	Queen Mary and Westfield	20
Surrey	22	UMIST	20
London Institute	22	De Montfort	19
University College Northampton	22	North London	19
Bath	21	Plymouth	19
Exeter	21	Southampton Institute	19
Liverpool	21	Sandwell College	17
Loughborough	21	Staffordshire	17
Manchester	21	Bradford and Ilkley College	16

Source: HEFCE, SHEFC, HEFCW latest available ratings
For a more complete list of institutions offering these courses at undergraduate level refer to the Course Directory

TEACHING QUALITY ASSESSMENTS

Molecular Biosciences
(England 1998/99)

Institution	Grade	Institution	Grade
Kent at Canterbury	24	Luton	22
Nottingham Trent	24	Queen Mary and Westfield	22
Salford	24	UCL	22
Sunderland	24	De Montfort	21
UWE	24	Lancaster	21
Aston	23	Northumbria at Newcastle	21
Birmingham	23	Queen's Belfast	21
Manchester	23	Surrey	21
Southampton	23	Westminster	21
Warwick	23	Greenwich	20
East Anglia	22	East London	19
Imperial	22	Liverpool	19

Organismal Biosciences
(England and N Ireland 1998/99)

Institution	Grade	Institution	Grade
Kent at Canterbury	24	Luton	22
Nottingham Trent	24	Newcastle upon Tyne	22
Oxford	24	Queen Mary and Westfield	22
Salford	24	Sussex	22
Sunderland	24	Bath Spa	21
UCL	24	Canterbury Christ Church	21
UWE	24	Lancaster	21
Aston	23	Liverpool Hope College	21
Edge Hill College	23	Suffolk College	21
Manchester	23	Surrey	21
Roehampton Institute	23	Queen's Belfast	21
Southampton	23	Westminster	21
Warwick	23	Greenwich	20
Bolton Institute	22	East London	19
Bristol	22	Liverpool	19
East Anglia	22		

Physics and Astronomy
(England and N Ireland 1998/99)

Institution	Grade	Institution	Grade
Bath	24	Surrey	23
Durham	24	Exeter	22
Manchester	24	KCL	22
Birmingham	23	Sheffield	22
Bristol	23	Staffordshire	22
Cambridge	23	Canterbury Christ Church	21
Hull	23	UMIST	21
Leicester	23	Queen Mary and Westfield	21
Loughborough	23	Portsmouth	20
Northumbria at Newcastle	23	Central Lancashire	19
Royal Holloway	23		

Source: HEFCE, SHEFC, HEFCW latest available ratings
For a more complete list of institutions offering these courses at undergraduate level refer to the Course Directory

University of Dundee
BSc Biochemistry

The Biochemistry Department at Dundee has 200 scientists and support staff, including 30 academic staff members. A typical honours programme in biochemistry begins in the first year with modules in the biosphere, mechanisms of life and chemical principles. Modules in cellular and molecular biology, comparative physiology and diversity of life, plus three modules chosen from genetics, organismal biology, metabolism and energy, drugs and drug targets, biological chemistry or chemistry, are taken in the second year. Four modules providing an advanced treatment of molecular and cellular aspects of biochemistry are taken in the third year. The fourth year extends the depth of treatment in selected areas of biochemistry. Practical work is a very important element of the course. In the fourth year this takes the form of a two-term research project within one of the research groups. Students benefit from the extensive programme of invited seminar speakers. Applications with exceptionally good qualifications may be allowed to enter directly into the second year of the course. Contact details p479.

The University of Edinburgh
Quantitative Genetics and Genome Analysis

The course in Quantitative Genetics and Genome Analysis lasts one year. It is designed to provide students with the required knowledge to apply quantitative genetic theory to practical problems in the biomedical and agricultural industries. Students also undertake research on problems related to quantitative genetics, population and genome analysis. Teaching takes the form of lectures, tutorials, seminars and laboratory practicals. Research is an important element of the course; a major project during the summer months being supplemented by mini projects during each term. The first term is devoted to the genetics of populations, then term two focuses on quantitative trait analysis and genomics. The final term's choice of modules covering human genetics, principles of livestock improvement and in-depth literature review is followed by a four-month research project. See www.gradlife.ed.ac.uk/msc-qg.htm for further details. Contact details p480.

University of Glasgow
BSc (Hons) Physics

The BSc (Hons) in Physics is a course run as part of the Department of Physics and Astronomy in the Faculty of Science. The course covers all the main topics of modern physics and astronomy such as relativity, quantum physics, electromagnetism and modern optics. There are options available on many topics in the third and fourth year.

Countries With The Most Computers

Source: "The Top 10 of Everything: 2000" Russell Ash, Dorling Kindersley 1999

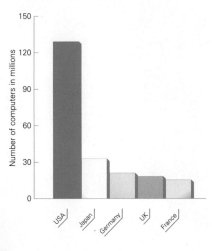

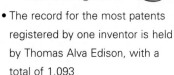
Physics may be studied either as a single honours or along with another subject: physics with geology; chemical physics; astronomy and physics; mathematics and physics; physics and electronic engineering; physics and music; or philosophy. Physics and astronomy have been taught at the university since its earliest times and have been rated as Excellent. Contact details p480.

Heriot-Watt University

BSc/MSc/Diploma Brewing and Distilling

Heriot-Watt is the only UK university to offer these courses. Organised with the co-operation of senior representatives of the industry, they are taught in the International Centre for Brewing and Distilling. Students learn about the scientific principles of malting, brewing and distilling and, in both the undergraduate and postgraduate courses, there are modules in biology and chemical engineering as well as brewing and distilling science. On the postgraduate courses, students holding a first degree which has covered sufficient biological and chemical areas are offered alternative subjects such as business studies. A specialist area of study at Heriot-Watt is fermentation technology of beer, wine and spirits. Students also go on regular visits to breweries and distilleries. Graduates have gone on to careers in research and development or management in the industry (one of the largest and most stable in the UK). At present, international students comprise 50 per cent of postgraduate classes. Contact details p481.

University of Luton

International Foundation Course (Science, Technology and Design)

This course combines the study of English language with one of the following subjects: science, technology, computing or design. The aim is to develop the individual's communication skills in English to the level required

SCIENCE AND TECHNOLOGY

TEACHING QUALITY ASSESSMENTS

Physics
(Scotland 1994/95)

Institution	Grade	Institution	Grade
Edinburgh	Excellent	Glasgow Caledonian	Highly Satisfactory
Glasgow	Excellent	Heriot-Watt	Highly Satisfactory
St Andrews	Excellent	Robert Gordon	Highly Satisfactory
Strathclyde	Excellent	Napier	Satisfactory
Dundee	Highly Satisfactory	Paisley	Satisfactory

Physics
(Wales 1995/96)

Institution	Grade	Institution	Grade
Swansea	Excellent	Cardiff (Physics and Astronomy)	Satisfactory
Aberystwyth	Satisfactory		

Psychology
(England and N Ireland 1998/99)

Institution	Grade	Institution	Grade
Central Lancashire	24	Manchester	22
Lancaster	24	Manchester Metropolitan	22
Loughborough	24	Northumbria at Newcastle	22
Nottingham	24	Nottingham Trent	22
Queen's Belfast	24	Roehampton Institute	22
Sheffield Hallam	24	Surrey	22
Durham	23	City	21
East London	23	King Alfred's College	21
Hertfordshire	23	Suffolk	21
Oxford Brookes	23	Warwick	21
Portsmouth	23	Canterbury Christ Church	20
Plymouth	23	Chester College	20
Staffordshire	23	Derby	20
Essex	22	Huddersfield	20
Goldsmiths	22	University College Worcester	20
Greenwich	22	Liverpool John Moores	19
Liverpool	22	Southampton Institute	19

Psychology
(Scotland 1995/96)

Institution	Grade	Institution	Grade
Dundee	Excellent	Abertay Dundee	Highly Satisfactory
Glasgow	Excellent	Edinburgh	Highly Satisfactory
St Andrews	Excellent	Glasgow Caledonian	Highly Satisfactory
Stirling	Excellent	Paisley	Highly Satisfactory
Aberdeen	Highly Satisfactory	Strathclyde	Highly Satisfactory

Source: HEFCE, SHEFC, HEFCW latest available ratings
For a more complete list of institutions offering these courses at undergraduate level refer to the Course Directory

SCIENCE AND TECHNOLOGY

for entry to a degree or HND at the University of Luton, while providing the necessary background knowledge and technical skills for the subject of choice. In order to apply for this course, there are certain criteria which must be met. The student's first language must not be English, a qualification which is suitable for entry to a higher education programme in the UK is needed, and entry is for those of 18 years of age and over. To complete each part of the course, four core modules must be passed. These include English language for academic purposes, contemporary English language 'A', contemporary English language 'B' and information technology. Contact details p483.

University of Plymouth
Maritime Studies

For more than 130 years the waters of the world, their use and resources have been the subject of teaching and research at the Institute of Marine Studies. It has developed into one of the largest teaching and research departments in the UK, with over forty academic staff, a similar number of research staff and over 700 students. These students come from all over the world, reflecting the global nature of the marine industry which operates in every continent and often across frontiers. The institute is currently involved in collaborative ventures abroad and has links with international agencies and institutions. 100 students are studying on taught postgraduate programmes, and BSc (Hons) programmes on offer include Fisheries Science, Hydrography, Marine Navigation, Marine Technology, Maritime Business, Ocean Science and Underwater Science. Students gain a broad understanding of marine studies in their first year before entering a more

focused programme in the later stages of their course. For further details see the institute's website at: www.science.plym.ac.uk. Contact details p484.

Queen Mary and Westfield College, University of London
Science and Engineering Foundation Programme

The foundation programme for science and engineering forms the first year of a four-year degree programme for students who have non-standard entry qualifications. The course provides a broad foundation to a number of BEng and BSc courses, from aeronautical engineering, astronomy or civil engineering to chemistry, computer science and environmental science. All relevant degree courses are fully accredited by the appropriate professional science and engineering institutions and students who successfully complete the foundation programme are guaranteed a place at Queen Mary and Westfield College. For the benefit of international students, the foundation programme contains two course units of English language, taught by teachers with years of experience in teaching English for academic purposes at university level. Contact details p484.

Royal Holloway, University of London
BSc Biology

This degree programme covers a broad range of topics, drawing upon the diverse research specialisms within the school. Students can choose from courses in botany, zoology, cell biology, genetics, ecology and biochemistry. By the final year students are expected to undertake their own detailed research project, providing the kind of training which enables many of the graduates to go on to study for a PhD or follow a career in research. The School of Biological Sciences recruits students from many countries and prides itself on its aim to understand the differences in the education systems around the world and provide a good environment to study in which all students can be accommodated. Students benefit from the support of tutors and personal advisors whilst also being encouraged to work independently and develop their own ideas. Contact details p485.

University of St Andrews
Psychology

The School of Psychology at St Andrews was rated as Excellent in the most recent teaching quality assessments. The school's teaching can also capitalise on its 5* research rating that puts it in the top four UK psychology departments in this respect. The current research grant income of the school is in excess of £2 million and it pursues research in most areas of psychology. The School of Psychology has its own library and there is, in addition, a large collection of books and journals in the main library. Psychology is studied up to honours level in both the Faculty of Science and the Faculty of Arts. In the first two years, all students take the same modules in psychology before specialising in the last two. At this level,

students usually attend a reading party and have the benefit of meeting distinguished visiting psychologists. Contact details p485.

University of Surrey Roehampton
BSc Psychology

During the first year of this undergraduate programme students study areas such as social psychology, child development and cognitive processes. In years two and three they can specialise in areas such as communication and social interaction, cognition and emotion, counselling, human socioecology and intervention. The programme takes on board contemporary developments in psychology such as neuropsychology and criminal psychology. It is both theoretical and practical and is taught through a combination of lectures, practical laboratory sessions, seminar groups, workshops and individual project supervision. Recent graduates have gone into fields such as counselling, education and psychology. The programme is recognised by the British Psychological Society as a pathway onto graduate courses such as the MSc in Counselling Psychology at the institute. Contact details p486.

SCIENCE AND TECHNOLOGY

Travel, Tourism and Leisure

From the days of Marco Polo to the discovery of the New World by Christopher Columbus in 1492, travel has been a thing of excitement, anticipation and discovery. These days, with a significant increase in people's freetime and disposable income over the last fifty years, the leisure and tourism industry has become big business. In the UK alone, the travel and tourism industry is set to become one of the biggest sources of foreign income. It is the country's fourth largest sector in employment terms and according to the English Tourist Board, is now worth more than £33 billion a year.

Travel and tourism courses in the UK are geared towards producing graduates for a specific industry, so they are often more vocational than other subjects offered at colleges and universities. Tourism courses at university level tend to last three or four years and lead to BA degrees. Some concentrate on the management side of the industry and may be related to hotel and catering courses. Others focus more on analysing the sociological aspects of the tourist industry. Then there are also courses that combine both these practical and theoretical sides. A general BA in tourism could include the study of such subjects as tourism and mass communication; entertainment and event management; travel and tourism law; and marketing. Some courses also offer students the opportunity to spend a year within the industry, whether it be working for an airline, a hotel or a tour operator.

Travel subjects are usually studied at colleges and private schools rather than at universities, as they tend to have a more vocational bias. Courses are available that teach students the skills needed to work in various areas of the travel business, such as air fares and ticketing, cabin crew and travel agencies. These can be found in conjunction with language courses in English and business English. It is often worth checking whether courses are accredited by associations such as the Association of British Travel Agents (ABTA), the International Air Transport Association (IATA) or by internationally recognised companies such as British Airways (BA) or GALILEO, which supplies the airline reservation system most widely-used by travel agents.

There are several subject areas closely related to travel and tourism, not least of which is transport. This is generally a three or four-year BSc (Hons) degree and covers a range of areas, including: transport law; logistics and distribution; transport research methods; passenger transport; and freight transport. Other closely related subjects include languages, sport and leisure, entertainment industry management, hospitality management, business studies, marketing and PR, geography, sociology, and landscape or environment management – aspects of which are often included in a tourism course. It may also be possible to do more unusual courses such as international travel law and rural or countryside tourism.

SPECIALIST AND VOCATIONAL COURSES

Bromley College of Further and Higher Education
HND in Leisure Management

The HND in Leisure Management is run by the college's Faculty of Business and Management, and offered through the associate college agreement with the University of Greenwich. The course lasts two years, each year consisting of two semesters. The first year concentrates on the management of business resources. It includes modules in business organisations, an introduction to leisure, leisure management, marketing, sports coaching and sociological issues in sport. Year two concentrates on business policy and decision making and covers work-based learning, event management, sports development and outdoor recreation. Students are required to complete a professional project at the end of year two. Assessment is by a combination of coursework and assignments, including case studies, projects, group problem solving, computer exercises and the compilation of a portfolio of work. Contact details p478.

City of London College

Established in 1979, and set in close proximity to the financial heart of the capital – the City of London – this private college specialises in adult training courses on a full- or part-time basis. Courses on offer can lead to masters level qualifications in UK universities, or directly into the professional job market. The college is fully accredited by the British Accreditation Council. The Diploma in Travel and Tourism Management provides adequate training for the start of a career in the travel industry, or for those who wish to expand their professional knowledge. The course also provides students with knowledge of a wide range of business management issues, and information technology, that relates to the travel and tourism industry. The course is operated on a modular system and students take up to four modules each term. To qualify for IATA approved travel agency operations, students must achieve a total of 40 points. Course modules include IATA level 1 and 2 airline fares and ticketing, world travel geography, business communication, marketing, and computerised reservation systems. The diploma course lasts for three terms, and begins in September, January, and April of each year. Contact details p479.

Hove College

The specialist travel division is an accredited training centre for British Airways, LCCI, City & Guilds, ABTA and Galileo. The travel industry offers employment opportunities to all age ranges and therefore there is no lower or upper age limit for applicants to these courses. The International Travel Diploma covers a range of topics, among them travel geography, cabin crew training, customer service skills and overseas courier training. The course lasts 24 weeks and costs £3,883. Galileo computerised reservations training includes modules on timetables and availability, fare quotes, currency conversions and hotel reservations. The course costs £258 and takes up to 60 hours. Hove College is within walking distance of Brighton town centre, a historic and lively coastal town. There is a range of accommodation available at the college, from house shares to one-bed-roomed flats. (See also Business chapter). Contact details p481.

Jetset Training

Jetset, established in 1963, is now one of the world's largest travel organisations

TEACHING QUALITY ASSESSMENTS

Hospitality Studies
(Scotland 1994/95)

Institution	Grade	Institution	Grade
Dundee	Highly Satisfactory	Strathclyde	Highly Satisfactory
Napier	Highly Satisfactory	Glasgow Caledonian	Satisfactory
Queen Margaret University College	Highly Satisfactory	Robert Gordon	Satisfactory

Hotel, Tourism and Leisure
(Wales 1996/97)

Institution	Grade	Institution	Grade
Cardiff Institute	Satisfactory		

Sports Science
(Wales 1996/97)

Institution	Grade	Institution	Grade
Cardiff Institute	Satisfactory		

Food and Hospitality Management
(Wales 1996/97)

Institution	Grade	Institution	Grade
Llandrillo College	Satisfactory		

Source: HEFCE, SHEFC, HEFCW latest available ratings
For a more complete list of institutions offering these courses at undergraduate level refer to the Course Directory

with a network of offices and companies in 26 countries and an annual turnover of £650m. The organisation's training centre, situated in London's West End, offers courses accredited by the International Air Transport Association (IATA) and can award up to 30 IATA points. Classes are kept to a maximum of nine students ensuring each pupil has individual attention. Jetset has links with over 1,000 independent travel agencies plus many larger companies. These companies contact the Jetset Training Centre advertising their vacancies. In addition to the IATA air travel courses, Jetset run courses in Galileo, travel geography, independent travel planning, travel selling skills and inclusive travel planning. No formal qualifications are required for most of the courses but students should be competent in written and spoken English. Certificates are awarded on the completion of courses. Contact details p481.

TRAVEL

Oxford House College

Oxford House College is located in central London on Oxford Street. The college is accredited by the British Council and is a member of ARELS. Currently the college offers travel courses in: British Airways (BA) Fares and Ticketing Levels I and II and First Class Galileo Computer Reservation Systems. The fares and ticketing courses are taught by approved BA trainers and are available full-time or part-time or via distance learning. Level I, for example, covers such areas as itinerary planning, encoding and decoding, computer reservation systems and flight arrangements. Level II is a higher-level qualification covering such topics as checking availability, ticketing and displaying seat configuration. Both courses last three weeks and cost £310 (plus £20.85 exam fees). The Galileo course is computer-based and students learn how to use this central booking system which allows travel agents direct access to the booking of airline tickets, hotel rooms and car hire. It is taught on flexitime over sixty hours, which means that students can choose the hours they study, and costs £220 (plus £20.85 exam fees). (See also Business and EFL chapters). Contact details p484.

The Spectrum Group

Spectrum works with 20 government colleges and universities in London and throughout Britain. All offer modern study facilities for international students, with small classes, and a varied sports and social programme. Accommodation ranges from hostel to homestay. These colleges offer a range of first, intermediate and advanced diploma courses as well as higher national diploma (HND) and degree courses in travel and tourism, leisure, sports studies and tourism/leisure management. These last for one, two or three years and lead to internationally-recognised qualifications. Fees start from £2,700 per year for a diploma course and from £4,950 per year for an HND or a degree. There are also many short intensive courses available leading to specific examinations such as ABTAC 1 and 2, IATA Fares and Ticketing, Galileo Computerised Reservation Systems. Contact details p486.

West London College

West London College moved to its modern premises in the heart of London's West End, only a few minutes from Bond Street station, in 1997 (it had occupied its previous site since the 1930s). The college is a BAC accredited business school which attracts over 1,000 students each year from over 100 countries to study business, hotel management, travel and tourism, computer science and English (see Business and Hotel and Catering chapters). The travel and tourism department offers a range of part-time courses including: British Airways Fares and Ticketing, which can be taken during the evenings or at weekends throughout the year; one-year, full-time programmes in travel agency management and tour operation which start in January, June and September; six-week intensive summer programmes in British Airways Fares and Ticketing; and Galileo Computer Reservation Systems starting in June, July and August. The college offers an advice service for young people who are interested in working in the travel industry and has a welfare department which can offer hostel-type accommodation if required. International students are welcome and the college can provide assistance with visa extensions if necessary. Contact details p487.

DEGREE COURSES

Bournemouth University

Masters in Tourism Programme

The establishment of the International Centre for Tourism and Hospitality Research within the university's School of Service Industries has expanded the range and depth of expertise in this area. The school itself has been awarded 'Centre of Excellence' status by the World Tourism Organisation making Bournemouth one of only 15 universities worldwide to receive this distinction. The centre was founded by leading international academics in the tourism field, each with their own substantial research and publication track record. The centre has developed a range of specialised tourism courses with the aim of producing graduates with strongly-focused skills and expertise. The courses are suited to anyone wishing to pursue a career in tourism and include specific degrees in: tourism and hospitality management; tourism management and planning; tourism management and marketing; tourism and environmental management; tourism and hospitality education; and tourism management. Contact details p478.

European School of Economics

BA Hons International Business, Specialisation in Sports and Leisure Management

Students on this course follow the core modules in international business, including business administration, information technology, microeconomics and private law. In addition, there are specialised modules which include sports philosophy, sports law and sports history. As with all courses at the school, students carry out ten months of work placements over the four-year course. Similarly, two languages are studied and time is spent in one of these countries. Contact details p480.

Greenwich School of Management

BSc (Hons) in Business Management: Travel and Tourism Pathway

The Greenwich School of Management was founded in 1974 and is an affiliated college of The University of Hull. The undergraduate programmes at the school are accelerated courses that take two years to complete. Start dates are flexible and students can commence courses in February, June or October. The degree is split into three parts, each consisting of two semesters. In part one, students study modules ranging from business law, statistics and computing, to management, business organisation and policy, and introductions to accounting and the macroeconomic environment of business. Part two includes the economics of travel and tourism, retail travel and tour operations, information technology and organisational behaviour, as well as modules in marketing and management accounting. Part three covers international marketing for travel and tourism, total quality management, financial management, human resources management, information systems management and corporate strategy. Assessment is continuous and based 30 per cent on coursework and 70 per cent on examination. The school's library has a large study area, a range of books, periodicals and journals, as well as CD-ROM and Internet access. Contact Details p480.

Leeds Metropolitan University

Tourism and Hospitality Management

Leeds Metropolitan University's School of Tourism and Hospitality Management is one of the largest schools of its type. Its industrial placement scheme and its courses aim to help students think strategically and gain an understanding of how companies and organisations grow and develop. The school welcomes international students, and students in the past have come from countries such as Norway, South Africa, Malaysia and Cyprus. Students can choose to take an international degree which includes language options and an overseas placement. Contact details p482.

Manchester Metropolitan University
MSc Tourism Management

The MSc is an advanced course that seeks to equip students with the knowledge, skills and techniques to follow an international management career within a global industry. Tourism is predicted to be the world's largest industry in the new millennium and is growing in importance in many areas of the world, so, naturally, both the subject and the course have an international focus. The year-long course is split into three semesters. During the first semester students take courses in tourism studies, current issues in tourism, research methods, and a group management consultancy project. The second semester includes the study of service operations management, strategic marketing, information management, finance, employment issues and interdisciplinary studies. The final semester is principally dedicated to individual dissertations. Contact details p483.

University of Northumbria at Newcastle
MSc Sport Management

The programme focuses on the management of sports organisations and facilities. Sport is treated as a progressive industry requiring high-level management skills. Course leaders have a number of international contacts and students have gone on to work for the International Olympic Committee, the Commonwealth games, Adidas, and Newcastle United Football Club. Units

TRAVEL

The Worlds Busiest Airports, 1998

Source: www.airports.org

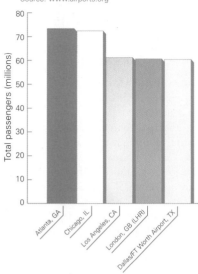

of study include: comparative sport management, research design, sport development, sport event/project management, sport facility management, sports marketing, managing sport performance and European sport management. Students can opt to complete the course with a European focus and may study for part of their course with a European university. Contact details p483.

Oxford Brookes University

School of Hotel and Restaurant Management

The MSc in International Hotel and Tourism Management offers aspiring managers the opportunity to obtain professional expertise as well as academic qualifications. For those with an unrelated first degree, there is the opportunity to take an introduction to work internship programme prior to the masters which enables you to experience work in the hotel and tourism industry and to gain academic credit for your learning. The MBA (Hospitality) is an open learning programme which allows participants to study without taking extensive periods of time off work and away from home. The programme can be tailored to meet the specific needs of individual managers and the knowledge and skills gained will enhance career prospects within the hospitality industry. Contact details p484.

College of Ripon and York

BA (Hons) Leisure & Tourism Management

This course is designed for future managers in the tourism and leisure industries. Emphasis is placed on the acquisition of both theoretical knowledge of business and practical skills in managing people and resources. The curriculum covers management disciplines such as marketing, economics, financial accounting, organisational behaviour and information systems, exploring them in relation to organisations within the leisure and tourism industries. The course includes an eight-week industrial placement and a major research assignment. Contact details p484.

TRAVEL

Thames Valley University
BA (Hons) Tourism Management/BA (Hons) Hospitality Management

The Faculty of Tourism, Hospitality and Leisure at Thames Valley University (TVU) is located in west London and has been teaching students for over 50 years. The interrelated programmes in hospitality, leisure and tourism management offer relevant learning associated with their specialist industry and aim to provide an insight into available careers. The school has links with industry and students gain practical experience as a part of their course. The university offers a number of other hospitality and catering programmes ranging from two-year diplomas/HNDs, to masters' level study. These pathways have been designed to provide essential training for a career in one of the world's largest industries and offers students the opportunity and flexibility to develop knowledge and acquire skills that are in strong demand. A combination of academic learning and practical, industry-focused study, with a stimulating mix of visits, industry speakers, sponsored work projects, core studies and multimedia applications, including industrial trips and a 12-month placement, all aim to help open up widespread opportunities in the sector. Contact details p486.

Westminster University
BA (Hons) Tourism and Planning

This course is very flexible within three core themes: tourism industry and impacts, tourism planning and management, and tourism business and management. Students then have a choice of optional modules allowing them to specialise in an area of particular interest such as tourism, languages, business and management or development and planning. In addition to the subjects covered in the degree programme, students are encouraged to develop written and oral presentation skills and IT skills. Final-year students can work in a tourism-related industry in their last year. Contact details p487.

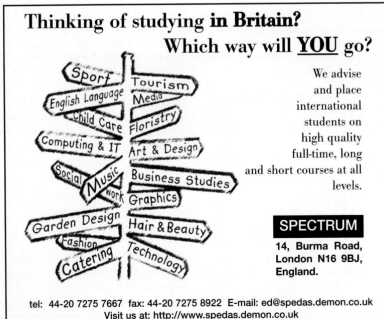

Veterinary Medicine

If you have a love for animals and a fascination for medicine, then veterinary medicine may be the degree for you. However, this combination alone will not secure you a place at one of the six veterinary schools and faculties in the UK, where entrance is fiercely competitive. In general, there are about three applicants to every place on veterinary medicine courses, which means that universities can afford to keep their entrance requirements high – two As and a B at A level is the usual minimum requirement. A level chemistry is compulsory whilst the other two subjects can be offered in biology, physics or mathematics. Some, but not all universities will accept one non-science subject. As well as being one of the hardest degrees to enter, veterinary medicine is probably the most expensive – about £13,500 a year – which is even more costly than medicine.

It is essential for students to have good English and all-round communications skills as they will be dealing not only with animals but also with their owners as well. Anyone seriously considering studying veterinary medicine should gain practical experience of working with animals. A good place to start is by shadowing a qualified vet in vacations or at weekends. It is also advisable that candidates spend time working in a variety of environments such as a dairy farm or in kennels or stables. All this shows motivation and commitment at interview.

Like medicine or dentistry, a Bachelor of Veterinary Science (BVSc) degree is intensive – working a minimum of 9am to 5pm every day – and very long – five years at most universities. In addition, students are required to do vacation work with licensed veterinary surgeons amounting to a total of 38 weeks unpaid work over the course of the degree. Courses also have a similar structure to those of medicine and dentistry. In the first two or three (depending on how the university divides it) pre-clinical years, students get a general grounding in the subject, studying topics such as cells, anatomy, pathology, genetics and animal husbandry. Students might then have the option of taking a break from their veterinary course to study for an intercalated BSc degree in a specialist area of research such as neuroscience, virology or pathological sciences. The last two or three clinical years mix continued study with clinical practice.

What distinguishes the study of veterinary medicine in the UK from many other countries in the world is that undergraduates do not specialise early on in the course. Students have to be equally knowledgeable about every type of animal - from the largest to the smallest. The advantage of this approach is that UK graduates are generally more employable than those from other countries. On graduating, students gain membership of the Royal College of Veterinary Surgeons (RCVS), which accredits all veterinary science degrees in the UK. This also entitles graduates to practice in Commonwealth countries or anywhere in the EU.

DEGREE COURSES

University of Bristol
Clinical

The Department of Veterinary Science at Bristol consists of four divisions: animal health husbandry, companion animals, food animal science, and molecular and cell biology. The university also has a veterinary pathology unit, part of the university's Department of Pathology and Immunology. The undergraduate course lasts five years and leads to a Bachelor of Veterinary Science (BVSc) qualification. Undergraduates spend one day a week at the Clinical Veterinary School at Langford and the rest of their time in the School of Veterinary Science, the School of Medical Sciences and the School of Biological Sciences. The department also has a variety of active research programmes. One advantage of studying veterinary science at Bristol is that there is a zoo on the outskirts of the city. Contact details p478.

University of Cambridge
Veterinary Medicine

The Department of Clinical Veterinary Medicine offers a six-year undergraduate course. The first three years cover preclinical sciences and lead to a BA degree. The second part of the course focuses on clinical instruction and leads to the further qualification – VetMB. The preclinical subjects are taught as part of the medical and veterinary science tripos and overlap to a great extent with the study of medicine at preclinical level. As part of their clinical training, students must complete 12 weeks farm practice and a minimum of 26 weeks "seeing practice" with a qualified veterinary surgeon in the UK. Final year students get the opportunity to work in the Queen's Veterinary School Hospital – the only university veterinary hospital approved by the RCVS – and also benefit from the proximity of the Cambridge University Farm. Contact details p478.

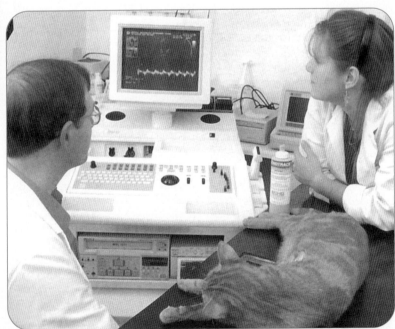

Picture courtesy of University of Bristol

Countries with the Most Threatened Species

Source: "*The Top 10 of Everything: 2000*" Russell Ash, Dorling Kindersley 1999

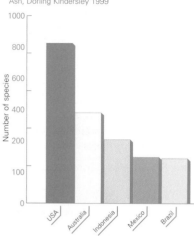

TEACHING QUALITY ASSESSMENTS

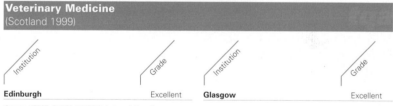

Institution	Grade	Institution	Grade
Veterinary Medicine (Scotland 1999)			
Edinburgh	Excellent	**Glasgow**	Excellent

Source: HEFCE, SHEFC, HEFCW latest available ratings
For a more complete list of institutions offering these courses at undergraduate level refer to the Course Directory

RESEARCH RANKINGS

Institution	Grade	Institution	Grade
Veterinary Science			
Bristol	4	**Glasgow**	4
Cambridge	4	**Liverpool**	4
Edinburgh	4	**Royal Veterinary College**	4

source: RAE 1996

University of Edinburgh
Veterinary Medicine

Edinburgh is considered by some to be the home of veterinary medicine. The faculty is made up of four departments which are located on two sites in Edinburgh and at the Veterinary Field Station just outside the city. As well as the five-year undergraduate vet course, there is a thriving postgraduate veterinary community at Edinburgh. The city has a zoo where vet students go to learn about exotics. Contact details p480.

University of Glasgow
Veterinary Medicine

The BVMS offered at Glasgow is unique in the UK, in that the entire course is taught on one campus. After the preclinical part of the course, there is increasing emphasis on paraclinical and clinical training. In the final year, there are no formal lectures and students take part in the work of the veterinary hospital. They also gain experience at the People's Dispensary for Sick Animals and spend two weeks at the University Veterinary Practice in Lanark. The Glasgow faculty has an international research reputation and attracts more funding than any other veterinary school in the country. Contact details p480.

The University of Liverpool
Faculty of Veterinary Science

The University of Liverpool awarded the first UK veterinary degree in 1950. Its Faculty of Veterinary Science incorporates three departments: veterinary preclinical sciences, veterinary pathology and veterinary clinical science and animal husbandry and offers a BVSc over five years. Some time is spent at the Veterinary Teaching Hospital in Leahurst, including a period 'living-in', and students are also required to participate in the night duty rota for the Small Animal Hospital in Liverpool. In addition to work with practising vets, vacation work includes work in stables, kennels and on farms during the first part of the course and in an abattoir during the fourth year. The university suggests that students should consider taking a gap year to gain necessary experience before applying for the course. Contact details p482.

The Royal Veterinary College
Veterinary Medicine

The Veterinary College, the predecessor of the current college, was founded in 1791 and established the veterinary profession in this country. The college is based on two campuses in Camden and in Hertfordshire and is organised into four academic departments: Veterinary Basic Sciences, Pathology and Infectious Diseases, Farm Animals, and Equine Medicine and Surgery. The first two years of the course are based at Camden in easy reach of London zoo and the Beaumont Animals' Hospital. Clinical training is carried out at the 230 hectare Hawkshead campus, and at the college farm, Bolton's Park. There are currently 50 international students from 18 different countries studying for the BVetMed course at the RVC. In addition, the college offers a number of MSc courses and a veterinary nursing course. Contact details p485.

The University of
Sussex
at Brighton

International and Study Abroad Office
Arts B, University of Sussex, Falmer
Brighton, BN1 9QN
Tel: **(+44 1273) 678422**
Fax: **(+44 1273) 678640**
Email: **International.off@sussex.ac.uk**
http://www.sussex.ac.uk

UNIVERSITY OF
SUSSEX
AT BRIGHTON

Universities and Colleges

This section contains details of a selection of universities and colleges in Britain, followed by a list of contact addresses for all UCAS institutions and a number of specialist and private colleges in the UK. Much of the information has been supplied by the institutions themselves, and, although it will be of interest to UK-based students, its primary focus is for students coming from overseas. Most universities now have international offices to deal with the special needs of international students. For this reason the contact details given here are generally those of the international office. If you are a British student interested in undergraduate courses, you should address your enquiry to the main admissions office. Postgraduate applicants can try either the admissions office or contact the university or college department directly. A good place to get contact details for these is via the university or college website. Where the university or college has a two-page profile, the information has been set out for easy reference which is explained on the following page.

Because much of the information is supplied by the universities or colleges, it is always worth sending for a prospectus before making your final decision and, if possible, making a visit to check whether the university or college has the atmosphere you are looking for. This is a good way to get an idea of available accommodation as well.

If you are unable to visit, you could try asking a friend in the UK to go on your behalf. And, if this is impossible, it is well worth arriving a few days or a week before your course starts, as most universities offer orientation weeks for international students that can help you to get settled in. It also means that you have a chance to sort out any problems that might arise before your course begins (if you want to change your accommodation for example).

Above all, we would like to hear about your experiences – so please write and let us know. Good, bad or indifferent – we will try to include your experiences in future guides so that they can be of benefit to other students. The best letters will be sent a copy of the next edition, or any other On Course guide if you prefer.

All universities now have international offices to deal with the particular needs of students coming from overseas. For this reason, the contact details given here (phone numbers, fax numbers, email addresses, etc) are generally those of the international office. For further details on international dialling codes, see Using the Guide on page 10.

Student numbers include both undergraduates and postgraduates followed by a breakdown into postgraduate numbers, if the institution offers such courses, and international student numbers, generally including those from European Union countries.

All website addresses listed omit the prefix http://.

Entrance requirements are included as an approximate guide only and grades required will vary according to the subject applied for. Universities assess applications individually and may welcome inquiries from students with more unusual qualifications and backgrounds.

EFL requirements refer to the various qualifications available in English as a Foreign Language. Only the minimum grade is given, you might need a higher standard of English for particular subjects such as English literature, law or medicine, so check with the university.

Write to: Kate Cohoon, International Office, Beyer Building, The University of Manchester, Oxford Road, Manchester M13 9PL

Tel: 0161 275 2059

Fax: 0161 275 2058

Email: international.unit@man.ac.uk

Website: www.man.ac.uk

Students: 23,496 in 1998/99 (5,471 postgraduate, 2,570 international, from over 130 countries), 48:52 male:female.

Accommodation: single sex, married, vacation – sometimes extra charge. Storage facilities. University residences from £43 to £57 a week self-catered, from £75 a week catered.

Entrance requirements: vary according to subject, generally three high grades at A level.

EFL: Cambridge Certificate of Proficiency in English Grade C. GCSE English Language Grade C, IELTS average 7.0 (not less than 6.0 in any one component), TOEFL 550.

Foundation: none on campus. Two available at City College, Manchester for entry to science and engineering programmes or economics and social studies.

Fees: classroom courses £6,800 a year, laboratory courses £9,000 a year, clinical courses £16,500 a year.

The accommodation section refers to types of residence available from the university or college, including whether it is possible to stay in married or family flats or rooms or in single sex accommodation. Single sex is usually taken to mean female only, and this may include instances whereby male and female students occupy different floors in a hall of residence. This section states whether students can stay in rooms during vacations and whether there is an additional charge on the normal rates. It also states if there are storage facilities for students' luggage. Prices for university/ college/institute residences generally include heating, water, electricity and cleaning costs. Prices for rooms in town generally exclude all additional costs.

All prices given for accommodation and fees are those supplied by the institutions at time of publication and you should be aware that these could change.

Foundation courses are available at many universities and are intended to bring students up to the required entrance level for a degree course. This section includes specific subjects available alongside study skills and English language classes. If completed successfully, some courses guarantee students a place on a degree programme at the university. For further information see The British Education System chapter on page 22 and contact the international office.

UNIVERSITY *of* ABERTAY DUNDEE

The University of Abertay Dundee

Write to: Judith Salters, University of Abertay Dundee, Bell Street, Dundee DD1 1HG

Tel: 01382 308 921

Fax: 01382 308 081

Email: j.salters@abertay.ac.uk

Website: www.abertay_dundee.ac.uk

Students: 3,528 in 1998/9 (613 postgraduates, 154 international, from 47 countries), 50:50 male:female.

Accommodation: single-sex, vacation extra charge in summer, storage facilities. University residences from £36 to £54 a week self-catered. Room in town from £30 to £50 a week.

Entrance requirements: generally two A levels or international equivalent (one A level for HND courses).

EFL: IELTS 5.5, paper-based TOEFL 550

Foundation: specialised one-year courses with English language, and pre-MBA courses.

Fees: undergraduate classroom courses £5,950 to £6,250 a year, postgraduate courses £6,250 to £7,175.

Dundee is Scotland's fourth largest city and lies on the north shore of the River Tay. Surrounded by some of the most beautiful scenery in Scotland, the rolling countryside of Perthshire and Angus Glens, Dundee and its neighbouring areas are rich in historical and cultural heritage. Glamis Castle, just a few miles north of Dundee, was the original setting for Shakespeare's Macbeth. Despite its proximity to the countryside, Dundee itself is at the centre of Scotland's road and rail network, allowing easy access to other parts of Scotland and the UK. The numerous pubs, theatres, clubs, cinemas, galleries, ballet and opera venues found here enrich the cultural life of the city.

The university is based on a city centre campus, with all of its buildings less than a quarter of a mile away from each other. All postgraduate management courses are taught at Dudhope Castle – only 10 minutes away from the main building. The main teaching site houses Old College, Graham, Baxter and Kydd buildings, where the majority of teaching departments are housed, in addition to the new purpose-built library centre which provides excellent facilities.

Academic strengths

The university's academic strengths include accountancy, management, computing, engineering and social

University Library, opened in 1998

sciences. The university operates a modular system for its degrees, allowing students the flexibility and choice to design courses to suit their individual interests. All courses are credit-rated and compatible with other institutions in Scotland and Europe. Teaching at the university aims to develop students' skills and teach them to apply these skills later in their professional careers.

Facilities include over 1,500 Pentium PCs with industry standard software, a video conferencing studio allowing students to participate in live lectures and seminars with other universities in the UK, and a newly refurbished university library featuring language laboratories and IT training clusters.

The following courses have been particularly popular with international students in the past: accounting, business studies and marketing, civil engineering, software engineering and mechatronics.

Student life

The students' union organises a range of social events and outings for students. This begins with 'freshers' fortnight' – two weeks of entertainment, induction courses, society fayres and other activities all designed to welcome incoming students. For international students this includes an orientation day, reception and welcome programme. There are many societies that operate through the union that cater for the recreational, cultural and/or religious interests of students. These include anything from the hockey club to the mountaineering society. Students can start their own societies if they wish. The International Student Association organises many social events and outings for the university's international students. Entertainment facilities on campus include a newly refurbished bar and disco, video games, and pool and table tennis rooms. Students interested in keeping fit can use the multi-purpose gym, complete with a fully qualified instructor. In addition, the association sells a sport and recreation card that allows students to use all the city council's sports facilities for free or at a heavily subsidised price. The surrounding areas are amongst the most popular in Scotland for skiers, water sports enthusiasts and golfers.

All students can use the university chaplaincy, regardless of their religious beliefs – meditation and prayer space is available. Anglican, Roman Catholic and Church of Scotland chaplains are available to give guidance and advice for those who request it. Students of other faiths can be put in touch with religious groups in the city through the chaplaincy.

"I recently graduated from the University of Abertay Dundee after completing a four-year BSc (Hons) in Quantity Surveying. My story may sound like an everyday tale of student achievement but I am no ordinary graduate! I am 43 years old and had, before my degree, been head of a family plumbing and heating business employing 12 people. It is not everyday that someone gives up a job as managing director to become a student but I had always wanted to become a quantity surveyor – it was just a question of taking the plunge. My motto fits in well with the Abertay Dundee ethos. Ernest Shackleton put it perfectly 'And for the future, my passion to be successful and to give my best to whatever I turn my hand to is undiminished. Never for me the lowered banner, never the last endeavour'."

William Alexander Burgess, Scotland

ANGLIA POLYTECHNIC UNIVERSITY

Anglia Polytechnic University

Write to: International Office, East Road, Cambridge CB1 1PT

Tel: 01245 493131

Fax: 01245 348772

Email: international@anglia.ac.uk

Website: www.anglia.ac.uk

Students: 13,000 in 1999 (2,000 postgraduate, 1,300 international, from over 90 countries), 66:33 male:female.

Accommodation: single-sex, vacation. University residences from £50 a week self-catered, £80 a week catered. Room in town from £50 to £60 a week.

Entrance requirements: generally one or two A level passes, or international equivalent.

EFL: for undergraduates, Cambridge First Certificate, IELTS 5.5, TOEFL 550.
For postgraduates, Certificate of Proficiency, IELTS 6.5, TOEFL 650.

Foundation: International Degree Access Course entrance: IELTS 4.5, TOEFL 450.

Fees: undergraduate and postgraduate courses £6,350 a year, access course £5,500 a year, classroom courses (master's) £5,950 a year, laboratory courses (master's) £6,350 a year, MBA £7,200 a year.

Spread across two campuses, Anglia Polytechnic University's teaching traditions extend back over 100 years. The Cambridge campus is located in the heart of the historic city with hidden courtyards and grand architecture. The old city has been an important market and centre of learning for hundreds of years. It is surrounded by fenlands to the north, and the rolling chalklands of the Icknield Way to the south. Footpaths, cycleways and bridle-paths litter the landscape, making the beauty of the countryside accessible to students.

Chelmsford campus has a range of student facilities. Queen Elizabeth II opened the student village in 1995. The campus offers disabled facilities, computer facilities, and a med-

The Learning Research Centre

ical centre including a dispensary. Chelmsford itself is a quiet market town, and has been the County Town of Essex for over 700 years. Extensive parks, and countryside sit alongside a thriving modern shopping centre and high-technology industry.

Academic strengths

A recent survey into the quality of teaching in British universities published by The Guardian placed APU in the top 50 institutions. There are several courses here that have been popular with international students. Most notable are the International MBA courses – which start in September and February, and can be completed in one calendar year – English language, computer science, music and optometry. Many courses are recognised by professional bodies, such as the ICSA, ACCA, RCIS and the Law Society.

The university offers a modular system, and with over 12,000 modules on offer, students can enjoy flexibility and diversity in their studies. Both campuses boast a range of up-to-date facilities and learning resources. These include art studios, a practice area for music students, a purpose-built computer facility, a drop-in information centre, and a specialist learning technology centre – concerned with software development, research and teaching of information technology. The modern language centre has multimedia language laboratories, with language and machine translation software, and television and satellite facilities.

Student life

All students can join a wide range of societies according to their cultural, religious, political or recreational interests. Students at the Cambridge site often socialise with students from Cambridge University, and get involved in jointly run societies. Every July in Cambridge, a series of festivals of classical music, art, theatre and film, are enjoyed by students and visitors alike. And, for sporty types, there are a range of facilities on offer, including tennis courts, a multi-gym, a sportsfield for outdoor sports and a swimming pool close by. On the Chelmsford campus, the gym is free, and students can enjoy most sports from hand gliding to wind surfing to golf to cricket, usually with a big discount.

The university also offers support services to all international students, such as pre-arrival information and advice, an orientation programme for new students, English language modules as part of studies, and a specially assigned tutor for international students.

"It was important for me to go to a business school which would provide me with the necessary education, that could not only focus on the 'job side' but also on the 'entrepreneurial side'. International exposure to business practices, issues, strategies, effective decision-making and a broad range of subjects was what I wanted to learn. Anglia Business School places an emphasis on small groups and small class sizes. The MBA at APU helped me not only to widen my horizons but also to look at issues differently and approach them strategically. I can say that my exposure at Anglia Business School in Cambridge has contributed immensely to my business thinking."

Dave Dilkush, India

Prifysgol Cymru · University of Wales
BANGOR

University of Wales, Bangor

Write to: Angharad Thomas
(from Europe and North America)
or Iwan Roberts (from other
countries), International Office,
University of Wales, Bangor,
Gwynedd, Wales LL57 2DG

Tel: 01248 382028

Fax: 01248 383268

Email: angharad.thomas@bangor.
ac.uk (for Angharad Thomas) or
international@bangor.ac.uk
(for Iwan Roberts).

Website: www.bangor.ac.uk

Students: 8,272 in 1998/99,
(838 postgraduates, 1,820
international students, from 90
countries), 46:54 male:female.

Accommodation: family,
vacation and single-sex available.
University accommodation from
£62 to £69 a week catered,
self-catered from £42 a week or £52 a
week with en suite bathroom.
Room in town from £35 a week.

Entrance requirements: A levels,
European or International
Baccalaureate and other qualifications
all considered.

EFL: IELTS 6 minimum with a TWE
written score of 4, TOEFL 560
minimum, Cambridge Proficiency
Higher pass.

Foundation: one, two and three
month pre-sessional courses between
June and September. Cambridge
examinations can be taken in June for
those needing a qualification for entry.

Fees: 1999-2000 classroom courses
£6,450, laboratory courses £8,530 and
MBAs £8,000.

The University of Wales, Bangor opened
in October 1884, housed in an old
coaching inn with 58 students (29 of
them women) and 10 teaching staff.
Nine years later it became one of the
three original constituent colleges of
the University of Wales. In 1911, the
university moved to a new site on a
hillside overlooking Bangor – the present
main university buildings.

Today the university offers over 250
degree courses. It has over 8,000
students, 17 academic departments and
over 300 teaching staff. The university
has a long tradition of welcoming
international students who make up
nearly a quarter of the student
population.

The cathedral city of Bangor is situated
on the coast and near the beautiful
Snowdonia mountains. Bangor cathedral
dates back to the sixth century and is
surrounded by many other historic
monuments and buildings. Two

The University of Wales campus

cultures, English and Celtic, have influenced the city. It can claim low crime rates, a healthy living environment due to low pollution levels and a relatively low cost of living. Bangor is central in Britain and a good starting point for exploring the country.

Academic strengths

The University of Wales, Bangor is in The Telegraph's 'first division' of UK universities and over half the departments have been awarded the top rating of Excellent in teaching quality assessment.

Students at the university can take advantage of a main arts and humanities library, a science library and six other subject-specific libraries. Computer resources include laboratories with access to the Internet, computer training and a helpdesk. A multimedia language centre provides facilities for learning and improving several different languages. Other services include an ocean-going research ship, botanical gardens, a natural history museum and two university farms.

Student life

The students' union has many activities and clubs to everyone's taste, including sports clubs and special interest groups. The union is a good meeting place in the daytime and evening, with cafes and "Time" nightclub. A newly opened sports centre on the Ffriddoedd campus has squash and badminton courts, weights room, a gym and cardiovascular room, and a large sports hall. Outside there is an all-weather pitch next to numerous football, hockey and rugby pitches. Students interested in music benefit from a varied programme of concerts including regular visits by the BBC National Orchestra for Wales and overseas orchestras including the university's own professional chamber ensemble. There are chaplaincies and religious organisations for most faiths.

International students are met by a university representative on arrival at bus or train stations and taken to their accommodation. An orientation day during welcome week consists of a half day of presentations and information, and a half day introduction and tour of the surrounding area. Pre-sessional courses are run during the summer in preparation for the start of the academic year in September. A dedicated international welfare adviser is on hand to provide support, advice, guidance and information on all aspects of international students' life in Bangor.

"I chose to study here because Bangor's ranking is high compared to other universities in the UK offering banking and finance. Bangor's scenic and coastal setting also appealed to me. I'm very pleased with my course, I can choose from lots of modules, so I follow my particular interests. The course has excellent web pages to support the learning, and I refer to them regularly. The university is smaller than some other city universities, so class sizes are smaller and you get more personal attention. I think Bangor pays close attention to its students. I've joined trips for international students to different parts of the UK and I've taken part in the HOST programme and I've made friends with students from many different countries all over the world. Because it's quiet, it's easier to study, but there are always plenty of things to do. There are a wide range of clubs and societies, so I've joined the photographic society."

Iroda Azizova, Uzbekistan

BATH SPA
UNIVERSITY
COLLEGE

Bath Spa University College

Write to: Doris Bechstein, The International Office, Bath Spa University College, Newton Park, Bath BA2 9BN

Tel: 01225 875 577

Fax: 01225 875 501

Email: international-office@ bathspa.ac.uk

Website: www.bathspa.ac.uk

Students: 3,000 in 1998/99 (600 postgraduate, 200 international, from 35 countries), 30:70 male:female.

Accommodation: single-sex, vacation, storage facilities – extra charge. University residences from £39 to £60 a week self-catered. Room in town from £50 a week.

Entrance requirements: three A levels or international equivalent.

EFL: From IELTS 6.0. Foundation IELTS 4.0 to 5.0.

Foundation: one-year courses with intensive English, Art and Design and Comparative International Studies (CIS) covers a range of undergraduate subjects.

Fees: undergraduate £6,890 a year, postgraduate £6,890 to £7,490 a year, Foundation Course £6,400 a year, Predegree Art and Design Course £6,200 a year, CIS programme £7,400 a year for 2000/2001.

Bath, in the west of England, is a city full of great historical and cultural interest. Being a major tourist destination, there are plenty of things to do and see in Bath. Amongst the many museums, theatres, galleries, bars and pubs are the world famous Roman Baths, after which the city is named, the Museum of Costume, the American Museum, the Theatre Royal, the Museum of East Asian Art and the Victoria Art Gallery. These attractions are all nestled in the city, from where surrounding parks, gardens and open spaces are always visible. Classical Georgian terraces in local honey-coloured limestone line the streets and the distinction of being England's only World Heritage City makes Bath a unique place to study. Nearby, students can enjoy the attractions of Bristol – only 30 minutes away. The Cotswolds to the north and the Mendips and Glastonbury to the

Bath Spa University College

UNIVERSITIES AND COLLEGES

322

south are ideal for visits to the English countryside.

Bath Spa University College is based on two campuses in Sion Hill in the north side of Bath, where all the university college's art and design courses are run, and Newton Park four miles west of central Bath, where all the other departments are located. Newton Park campus is a Georgian Manor House surrounded by landscaped gardens, parkland, a nature reserve and lake, woods and farmland. Famous alumni include Anita Roddick, founder of the world-famous Body Shop.

Academic strengths

Teaching quality assessments have resulted in the Departments of Art and Design, Sociology, English and Environmental Science being awarded Excellent ratings. The Higher Education Quality Councils who audit standards of universities noted that Bath Spa University College is "a close knit institution with a well developed sense of community and common purpose."

The university college is divided into four faculties of Applied Sciences, Art and Music, Education and Human Sciences and Humanities. Each department offers a diverse range of subjects at both undergraduate and taught postgraduate level. Courses popular with international students include art and design, business studies, music, health studies and teacher training programmes.

Both campuses have well-stocked libraries complete with CD-ROM, multimedia packs, and suites of networked computers. The university college provides a range of computer work-stations for general use in designated rooms and within some suject areas such as design and technology, education, geography and music.

Student life

The university college has a thriving students' union. Facilities include a bar for each campus, venues for live music, a laundrette and a general store selling stationary, art materials and books amongst other things. The union have persuaded the local bus company to run a direct service from Newton Park campus into town. There are societies to cater for the religious, political, national or cultural tastes of students including parachuting, chess, and the international society. The football society first team won their championship in the district Saturday league, as well as the 'Evening Chronicle' cup. The union also organises entertainment events that have made the university college a major venue of the south west. Events include comedy nights, discos and theme party nights and live music events. International students are welcomed with an airport pick-up, orientation day, induction week, and receive English language support.

"I am in my final year of a single honours Degree in Business Studies. I was recommended to study at Bath Spa by my brother, who also studied here. So far, I have learnt a great deal about business in Western culture. However, I need to prepare for my studies a lot more than British students. Bath is located in beautiful surroundings and I am sure this must be better for my wife and daughter, Risako, who was born during my studies here in Bath. It is impossible to live close to both nature and culture in Tokyo. This is my last year in Bath. I look forward to enjoying the last remaining days here with my family."

Takashi Asanuma, Japan

UNIVERSITY OF BATH

University of Bath

Write to: University of Bath, Bath BA2 7AY

Tel: 01225 826 832

Fax: 01225 826 366

Email: international-office @bath.ac.uk

Website: www.bath.ac.uk

Students: 7,000 in 1998 (2,000 postgraduate, 700 international students, from over 70 countries), 57:43 male:female.

Accommodation: single-sex, some married, vacation. University residences from £42 to £70 a week. Room in town from about £50 a week.

Entrance requirements: generally high: BBC or above at A level. Accept International or European Baccalaureate.

EFL: IELTS 6.0, TOEFL 580.

Fees: classroom courses £6,750 a year, laboratory courses £8,900 a year.

Situated on the outskirts of the city of Bath, the university received its royal charter in 1966. Thirty years later, following a national research assessment exercise in 1996, its Excellent results placed it among the top six universities in the UK. Bath's graduate employment rate is one of the highest in the country. The compact campus is well equipped with shops, cafeterias, lecture theatres, a bank, laboratories, student residences, a learning centre and library, and a lively students' union.

The city's history stretches back to Roman times, and it has since grown into one of the most architecturally and culturally renowned destinations in the world. As well as having several major tourist attractions such as the elegant Pump Rooms and the baths, Bath also has much to offer students in terms of shopping and nightlife. The countryside of the Cotswolds, the Wye Valley and the ancient Forest of Dean are nearby, and the attractions of Bristol are within easy reach. Bath is only an hour and a half away from London by train.

The university library

Academic strengths

The university offers undergraduate, taught postgraduate and research opportunities and comprises a School of Management and the Faculties of Science, Engineering and Design; Humanities, and Social Science. The Department of Mechanical Engineering holds a top 5* rating for research, combined with an Excellent rating for teaching and learning. Many international students apply to study engineering, business and management, social policy, administration and architecture. The university also specialises in education, modern languages, computer science, statistics, European studies, biology, chemistry, interpreting and translation, physics, mathematical sciences, pharmacy and pharmacology, social sciences, and sports science. The university's master's degree courses are also very popular.

Most courses at Bath contain a practical work experience element, placing a strong emphasis on education for the "real" world. The university year at Bath is split into two 15-week semesters, starting in February and September. All programmes are based on modules and Bath operates the transferable credit system. Study facilities include over 1,600 networked computers, most of which are connected to the campus-wide ethernet.

Student life

Bath is the only UK university to have hosted an Olympic Festival, and its 200-acre campus boasts sports facilities of a very high standard. These include playing fields, an indoor sports centre, two swimming pools (50m and 25m), four indoor and eight outdoor tennis courts and two floodlit all-weather astro-turf pitches. The students' union is very active, with over 100 clubs and societies. It also runs a newspaper, a magazine, a campus TV channel and a radio station.

The International Office at Bath, together with the chaplaincy, the medical centre, student counsellors and resident tutors, provide an information and support network for overseas students. The international office can offer advice on most things, including where to buy food from your native country. It also contacts overseas students before they leave home, and runs buses to collect them from the airport. They are guaranteed accommodation on campus or in the city of Bath for the duration of their course. They can also take classes in English and study skills at the English language centre.

"I first came to Bath in 1989 as a visiting scientist. It was one of several visits I've made during my career to universities overseas. In 1985 I went to Tsukuba International University near Tokyo, which is famous for horticulture – my field. I did a diploma course in vegetable seed, and learned Japanese. I was born and educated in Faisalabad in the Punjab, then in 1978 I went into government service. Before I went to Japan I'd got my MSc in horticulture from the Agricultural University of the Northwest Frontier Province. I came back to Bath in 1994 to do my PhD. I've been studying the cryopreservation of embryonic tissue – this subject is important to my country, but there are few people studying it. But I'll be going back soon, to my job in Pakistan. You see, I just heard, I got my PhD today."

Dr M H Bhatti, Pakistan

University of Bournemouth

Write to: Bournemouth University, Mr Chris Curran, International Office, Poole House, PG134, Talbot Campus, Fern Barrow, Poole BH12 5BB

Tel: 01202 595 651

Fax: 01202 595 287

Email: inta@bournemouth.ac.uk

Website: www.bournemouth.ac.uk

Students: 11,654 in 1997/8 (396 postgraduate, 316 international, from 63 countries), 47:53 male:female.

Accommodation: single sex, married/ family, vacation, storage facilities. University residences from £52 to £63 a week self-catered. Room in town from £65 a week.

Entrance requirements: generally two to three A levels or international equivalent.

EFL: IELTS 6.5, TOEFL 550.

Foundation: one-year courses in applied psychology and design, archaeology, electronics combined programme, environmental protection, heritage conservation, and product design.

Fees: classroom undergraduate and postgraduate courses £6,900 a year.

Nestled in the south coast of England, Bournemouth is sometimes referred to as the 'English Riveria' – with seven miles of golden beach stretching across the sea-front, and its reputation as the 'party capital' of the south coast, Bournemouth has all the cultural attractions of a larger town yet is small enough to retain an atmosphere of friendliness and safety.

Although around 200 years ago the area was little more than heathland, today you can see the results of years of nurturing and cultivation which has turned Bournemouth into a virtual 'garden city by the sea' – a UN organisation recently recognised it as one of the World Champion Floral Cities. Historically, Bournemouth has been the favoured place of residence for many a writer, poet, and artist: Mary Shelley, the creator of Frankenstein, is buried in Bournemouth, together with the heart of her husband, the poet Percy Bysshe Shelley. Robert Louis Stevensen lived and wrote Dr Jekyll and Mr Hyde

Students on Bournemouth University campus

here around 100 years ago. J.R. Tolkein, creator of the Hobbit, was also a long-time resident of one of the seaside hotels in Bournemouth.

There are plenty of theatre and concert venues catering for all tastes. Close by, Poole Harbour – Europe's largest natural harbour – is the region's centre for watersports, and the water-front is littered with pubs, cafés and restaurants. The historic town of Christchurch is nearby, with its 900 year old priory, whilst the rolling hills of the Purbecks and vast expanse of the New Forest are also within easy reach.

Academic strengths

Bournemouth University is divided into seven schools of study that reflect an emphasis on work-oriented education as an important part of career success: business; conservation science; design, engineering and computing; finance and law; institute of health and community studies; media arts and communication; and service industries. The School of Media Arts and Communication scored a high 22 out of 24 in the latest teaching quality assessment, and the university was awarded the Queen's Anniversary Prize for Higher and Further Education, for its innovative programmes of study.

Facilities include purpose-built libraries, laboratories and open learning centres. All students have access to Apple Macs, PCs and printing facilities in the university's computing centres 24 hours a day, 7 days a week. Bournemouth University is home to a number of specialist centres including the National Centre for Computer Animation, the Centre for Culinary Research and the International Centre for Tourism and Hospitality Research.

Student life

Bournemouth University students' union manages all the university bars and arranges a series of events throughout the year, such as live music, stand-up comedy and club nights which attract big-name DJs. More traditional events such as student balls and discos are also arranged on a frequent basis. Students can join any number of societies that operate from the union including chess, caving, film, Asian and Chinese, and Star Trek appreciation. The union operates an advice centre that can offer help on immigration, employment, financial, housing and personal or academic issues.

International students are welcomed on a first-come, first-served basis with an activities-packed orientation week. English language support is also available. Services also extend to a large team of chaplains who embrace all religions.

"I found that in my job as a senior town planner in Fiji, I wanted to know more about certain areas and decided that a master's degree would help me acquire this knowledge. Tourism is Fiji's main industry and I found that this high-quality course at Bournemouth is of huge relevance to me. The lecturers are great and they respect your individuality and different viewpoints. My fellow students are from all over the world, including Canada, Brazil and Egypt, and I have made many friends. I have no regrets about coming here, and the course is, arguably, the best in the world. Coming to Bournemouth to obtain my master's degree has been the best thing I've ever done in my life. I have learnt more form this one year of study than in my entire time at work in Fiji."

Viane Amato, Fiji

Bradford College

Write to: Howard Clough, Head of International Centre, The International Centre, Bradford College, Great Horton Road, Bradford, West Yorkshire BD7 1AY

Tel: 01274 753348

Fax: 01274 736175

Email: international@bilk.ac.uk

Website: www.bilk.ac.uk

Students: 35,000 in 1998/1999 (100 postgraduate, 500 international, from 56 countries).

Accommodation: married/family accommodation available. College residences from £39 to £52 a week self-catered. Room with family from £60 to £75 a week. Room in town from £38 to £95 a week.

Entrance requirements: refer to appropriate course for details.

Foundation: available in all disciplines.

Fees: English, foundation, vocational and technician courses £3,780 a year, higher technician and undergraduate courses £6,405 a year. Postgraduate courses on application.

Located in the geographical centre of the UK, Bradford is very much a university city that offers students a variety of cultural, historical and recreational experiences. The large student community is catered for by Bradford's many restaurants and bars, and the city is home to the National Museum of Photography, Film and Television, housing Britain's first IMAX cinema screen. Historically, Bradford was the centre of Britain's woollen industry. Now, engineering, electronics, finance, banking and commerce dominate, although the woollen industry is not completely forgotten.

All undergraduate and postgraduate courses are accredited by the University of Bradford, and other higher education

Bradford College

qualifications are awarded by Edexcel (BTEC).

Academic strengths

The college has 11 academic departments: Art and Design; Administrative Studies; Business Studies; Engineering and Construction; Management; Hospitality and Leisure; Information Technology (IT); Science; Teacher Education; Applied Social Science; and Applied Human Studies. Degrees and higher education qualifications have been developed, through consultation with both industrial and commercial sectors, to prepare students for their careers. All undergraduate courses are modular allowing students a large degree of flexibility and choice. The college runs an integrated computer network across the campus, both as a teaching facility and as a shared communication tool. IT courses are available at every level and, as a policy, the college has adopted industry-standard equipment and software. The library houses over 200,000 books, 1,200 journal titles and an extensive range of electronic information services, including Internet, email and CD-Rom databases. English language courses are available at all levels.

Student life

With both the college, and the University of Bradford, the city has a large student population and offers a lively nightlife, from bars and restaurants to theatres and sporting venues. Yorkshire's famous countryside is within easy reach and there are a number of opportunities for outdoor pursuits such as climbing, orienteering, fishing, sailing, flying, and pot-holing, as well as more sedate sports like golf. Most indoor sports are available at the college which houses a 25 metre swimming pool, squash courts, a gymnasium, sauna and solarium.

Students can also take advantage of the many societies operating through the student union, which cater for most cultural, political, sporting, intellectual and social tastes.

The college's international centre is the first point of contact that international students will have with the college. The centre aims to provide students with all appropriate course material and help guide them through the application process. It also ensures that students are given maximum credit for their previous work experience or education and offers information on visas and immigration. Specialist assistance is given to students experiencing difficulties with financial, medical or academic matters, or any other welfare issues. A 'meet and greet' service is available from both Manchester and Leeds/Bradford airports.

"After I finished my BA (Hons) Art and Design course at Bradford and Ilkley College I returned to Beijing before coming back to the college to further my studies. I am currently studying for an MA in Print Making. I enjoy living in Bradford, and have received a great deal of encouragement and assistance from the staff. There are many international students here, and I have made friends with students from most parts of the world. All areas of interest are catered for in the college, and there are excellent facilities in all areas of study which provide good opportunities for students. I've greatly enjoyed my time here and would recommend it to anyone."

Buri Gude Zhang, China

UNIVERSITY OF
BRADFORD

University of Bradford

Write to: International Office
University of Bradford,
Bradford, BD7 1DP

Tel: 01274 233023

Fax: 01274 235950

Email: international-office@
bradford.ac.uk

Website: www.brad.ac.uk

Students: 7,366 in 1999 (714
postgraduate, 660 international
students from nearly 100 countries),
54:46 male:female.

Accommodation: single sex,
vacation. University residences from
£38 a week self-catered. Room in
town from £28 to 35 a week.

Entrance requirements: generally
three Cs at A level but higher for
business and health-related courses

(optometry, pharmacy, physiotherapy).

EFL: IELTS 6.0, TOEFL 550.

Fees: classroom courses £6,550 a
year, laboratory courses £8,550 a year.

Bradford is a city university with its
main campus just five minutes' walk
from the centre of one of the 10 largest
cities in England. The National Museum
of Photography, Film and Television,
with its five-storey high IMAX cinema
screen is even closer, as is the magnificent
Alhambra Theatre. Bradford offers a
range of cultural, sporting and historic
attractions and is an excellent base for
trips to the magnificent scenery of the
Yorkshire Dales. The historic village of
Haworth, home of the Brontë family,
lies within the city boundary. Leeds/
Bradford International Airport is only
15 kilometres away. Sports facilities on

Students at the University of Bradford

campus include state-of-the-art fitness rooms, swimming pool and sports hall for badminton, basketball and five-a-side football.

Academic strengths

The university has particular strengths in engineering (chemical, civil, structural and environmental, computing, electrical and electronic, mechanical and manufacturing – including automotive) in health-related sciences (optometry, pharmacy, physiotherapy and radiography) and in business and management where its Management Centre was one of the first to be established in the UK.

In addition the university offers a range of innovative courses including Archaeological Sciences, Peace Studies (which is one of only seven departments worldwide to be selected by Rotary International for its scholarship scheme), Electronic Imaging and Media Communications, Cybernetics, Medical Engineering and Interdisciplinary Human Studies. Most courses, except those in health-related sciences, are happy to consider students who have taken courses in their own country which enable them to move directly into year two of Bradford degree courses.

The employment record of Bradford graduates is notable and reflects the practical and professional emphasis of the courses offered.

Student life

The university has 2,000 study bedrooms either on campus or within five minutes' walk. These almost all have telephone and computer network links which enable students to access computer facilities and to make and receive international calls from their rooms. Single international students on taught courses are guaranteed accommodation in university residences for their first year at Bradford and it is often possible to extend this to other years if students wish. However, accommodation in Bradford close to the university is cheap and easily available, and many students prefer to rent a house for between four or five people.

The students' union runs a wide range of social activities and has many international student societies. With 7,000 students living in and around the university there is always something to do for everyone, whatever their interest. On arrival all students are tested on their English language ability and the university offers a range of English and study skills programmes free of charge to international students.

"I wanted a broader background in communications but I had to be sure that Bradford was a top-quality university before I could get support from Mexico! The computer and microprocessor laboratories are very good, and so are the lectures. I find it very helpful that they give out notes so you can concentrate on listening rather than writing everything down. And they really prepare seminar and tutorial classes well, so you have the opportunity to practice what you are learning. Bradford is not a particularly beautiful city but I have been very surprised by the people. The people here are very warm and friendly. I had a problem soon after I arrived in Britain and I needed an operation in hospital. The staff in the University Health Service and the hospital were so helpful. In fact, everyone was helpful in making sure that I was able to keep up with my work."

Roberto Ramirez-Iniguez, Mexico

University of Bristol

Write to: Admissions Office, Senate House, Bristol BS8 1TH

Tel: 0117 928 7678

Fax: 0117 925 1424

Email: admissions@bristol.ac.uk

Website: www.bris.ac.uk

Students: 11,122 in 1998 (2,025 full-time postgraduate, about 1,000 international students, from over 100 countries), 51:49 male:female.

Accommodation: single-sex, some married, vacation. University residences from £45 a week self-catering from £55 a week catering. Room in town from £50 to £55 a week.

Entrance requirements: generally high – medicine; dentistry; veterinary science – As; many subjects – As and Bs. European and International Baccalaureate also accepted.

EFL: IELTS 6.5, TOEFL 620

Fees: classroom courses £7,306 a year, laboratory courses £9,609 a year, clinical medicine £17,805 a year.

Bristol University students

If you like city life, you'll love being at Bristol. Its several sites are spread across a lively, modern city, on two rivers. Bristol has been an important commercial port since medieval times. It was from Bristol that John Cabot set sail in 1497 on his voyage west to the coasts of Newfoundland and North America. Bristol's most famous sights are its three suspension bridges, one across the Avon Gorge and two across the Severn estuary, which link England with Wales and provide a fast route to the ancient Forest of Dean. Just to the east is the historic town of Bath, with its Roman ruins, ancient abbey, Georgian architecture, and varied museums. London is just ninety minutes away by train.

Academic strengths

Bristol's respected medical school was founded in 1833 while the university was founded in 1876. Today there are 36 applicants for every medical school place, and similar pressure for dentistry and veterinary science – the veterinary college in its rural setting away from the university's main city sites, is strong on farm animals and equine science.

Engineering and computer science are also major strengths; the faculties received Excellent ratings in teaching and research and both welcome students from all over the world every year. British Formula 1 racing cars have benefited from Bristol's forward-looking approach to aerospace engineering. Bristol is one of the world leaders in geography; it developed much of the technical equipment, such as night-eyes and other remote-sensing equipment used on geological surveys. Because Bristol is a focus for independent film and TV companies, its media courses receive a high number of applications for places.

International students often study law, economics and accountancy, or apply to the arts and social sciences departments, for which the university is also noted. The main library at the university has in excess of one million volumes and subscribes to over 6,000 periodicals. This library forms the focus of the library system and is supported by a further twelve branch libraries throughout the university. Networked computer rooms are located throughout the university precinct and all of the halls of residence. Each room is able to offer personal access to the Internet.

Student life

Bristol has entertainment of every kind, from the Old Vic, a leading provincial theatre, with its own theatre school, to a rock concert venue, and many clubs. The city has good shopping facilities and Clifton's sloping streets are full of antiques stores. There is yachting and water sports at the riverside docks.

The university has a large students' union with facilities including two theatres and a busy entertainments programme. Some of the union's members get involved in social work in the city – helping the homeless and other underprivileged groups. Bristol is a relatively safe city to walk around.

Single international students are guaranteed accommodation for the duration of their course in university residences, some in the city centre and others just on the edge of the city, up on the Downs, with fine views across the Avon Gorge. The international office is very experienced in welcoming and helping international students. There are events for new arrivals, English classes throughout the year, and a credit transfer system for students on year abroad schemes. Postgraduate research students often stick around, returning to do more research, or find work in the area.

"When I was 20, I was studying for a physics degree at Sogang, one of Seoul's top five universities. I was doing well, so my future was assured. Then I started an English course at the British Council, and I was gripped by the idea of studying in 'the land of physics', where Newton discovered gravity. The Times Higher Education Supplement listed Bristol among the top universities for physics, so I applied to enter the second year of a BSc. In the first year all I did was work. I was really isolated, but I had to keep up. I couldn't understand all the lectures. My maths bailed me out and some second-year English students in my residence helped me out. I passed, thank goodness, and this year I'm running for election to the students' union. I'm also applying to convert my course to a four-year MSc. Then I might go on to do a PhD in Cryogenics. Bristol holds the record for achieving the lowest-ever temperature."

Jisu Kim, Korea

Contact: Paul Higham, International Office, Bromley College of Further and Higher Education, Rookery Lane, Bromley BR2 8HE

Tel: 020 8295 7031

Fax: 020 8295 7051

Email: phigham@bromley.ac.uk

Website: www.bromley.ac.uk

Students: 6,000 in 1998/99 (2,500 full-time, 3,500 part-time, 200 international, from around 30 countries).

Accommodation: no college accommodation. Homestays £80 a week (including meals), vacation.

Entrance requirements: vary according to course of study.

Foundation: one-year Access courses in business, law, engineering and science, successful students guaranteed entry onto degree programmes at the University of Greenwich.

Fees: foundation courses £3,900 a year, HND courses £5,900 a year, undergraduate courses £5,900 a year.

Bromley College of Further and Higher Education is based on three sites in Bromley and Penge and is an Associate College of the University of Greenwich. Bromley is the largest of the London Boroughs with a population of around 300,000. It is mainly residential in character, with large areas of woodland and parks. Just under 20 minutes away from London by train, the college's students are never far away from the shops and nightlife of the capital, and Bromley town centre itself has over 450 shops and stores, as well as restaurants,

Bromley College

cafés, bars, a leisure centre, library and cinema. The college's main site is at Rookery Lane, just south of Bromley's town centre, and offers modern laboratories and workshops, a language centre, a library and a number of computer suites, allowing students free email and Internet access. The student union houses a refectory, bistro and student lounge, and the site's extensive grounds offer opportunities for both relaxation and exercise. The majority of the college's management training and social work courses are held in the college's second site in the Old Town Hall. Situated in the centre of Bromley, the grade 2 listed building houses a conference hall, seminar rooms, a library, IT suite and bar for both students and staff. The college's third site is the newly-refurbished Hawthorn centre, providing a range of training in areas such as IT, administration and childcare.

Academic strengths

A range of subjects are available at all levels from beginner upwards. Qualifications include GNVQs, NVQs, BTECs, AS levels, A levels, GCSEs, Higher National Diplomas and degrees. The college has approval to offer a number of University of Greenwich awards and students on approved courses are entitled to make use of the university's library and careers service. They also receive preferential consideration for progression, or transfer, to other university pathways. The library at Rookery Lane contains a range of books, newspapers, journals, videos, audio tapes, computer software and CD-ROMs. The library's learning resource centre provides specialist support for maths, English and IT. Along with the learning resource centre at the Old Town Hall, and the IT facilities available at all sites, students may benefit from modern multimedia resources and the latest computer hardware and software, including a TV-editing suite.

Student life

Many international students, aiming to improve their English skills, make their first visit to the college by attending its summer school. This provides a good opportunity for prospective students to assess the college and its facilities, as well as to enquire, first-hand, about their intended course of study and accommodation. The college's Student Services Department provides advice, information and counselling to those who require it. International students benefit from a free airport pick-up, an induction week upon arrival and English language support.

"I decided to come to the UK because the public security and welfare are good and it's easy to travel to other EU countries. I also wanted to study at a state college where there are many English people. I am studying English and business administration, including IT. There are many computers, a large library and good English teachers. I like the school environment, the student services and the fact that the college is so near to London. The college found my accommodation for me and I live in a house and cook for myself. I enjoy meeting and talking to students from other countries as it helps me gain knowledge about different cultures. The countryside is nice in the UK, though sometimes it can be a bit cold. I find most English people to be friendly."

Chia-Lung Chen, Taiwan

Brunel University

Write to: Caroline Browne, International Office, Brunel University, Uxbridge, Middlesex UB8 3PH

Tel: 01895 203076

Fax: 01895 203084

Email: international-office@brunel.ac.uk

Website: www.brunel.ac.uk/admin/registry/international

Students: 12,320 in 1998/99 (2,909 postgraduate, 714 international, from 90 countries), 55:45 male:female

Accommodation: single sex, married, vacation, storage facilities. University residence from £38 to £52 a week self-catered and from £56 to £60 a week catered. Room in town from £50 to £60 a week.

Entrance requirements: 20 points at A level. 26 to 36 in International Baccalaureate with grade 5 in specified subjects.

EFL: TOEFL 570 to 585, IELTS 6.5 to 7 or Cambridge level C.

Foundation: programmes available.

Fees: classroom courses £6,725 a year, laboratory courses £8,925 a year.

Brunel University was first established in 1966 and today has over 12,000 students. The university is located on the western outskirts of London near Heathrow, Windsor and central London. The four campuses are based at Uxbridge, Twickenham, Osterley and Runnymede. All the campuses have on-site halls of residences, social facilities, libraries, computer centres and welfare services. Brunel has traditionally

Brunel University campus

UNIVERSITIES AND COLLEGES

taught sciences and engineering, but in recent years there has been a substantial increase in the number of social sciences and arts courses. The university strongly promotes work experience and offers a number of four-year degrees with a "thin" or "thick" sandwich option.

Academic strengths

Brunel University is divided into five faculties: Arts; Professional Education; Science; Social Sciences; and Technology. In teaching quality assessments, the following departments were graded highly: American studies (21/24); anthropology (Excellent); drama, dance and cinematics (23/24); electrical and electronic engineering (21/24); general engineering (22/24); social policy and administration (Excellent); and sociology (22/24). Research in design received a 5* rating and anthropology a 5 rating in the 1996 research assessment exercise. Nine subject received 4 ratings.

Each campus library provides areas for private study, media rooms, video units and computer access. Media facilities include video editing suites and digital image and sound processing. Specialist teaching resources include sports amenities, engineering and science laboratories, design studios and dance studios. A new art complex and art gallery have recently been added to the university's facilities.

Student life

Brunel's students' union plays an active part at each campus with an office at each. The union provides a number of services including live entertainment, a free fortnightly magazine and a radio station. The union also supports around 90 different clubs and societies including those representing different ethnic groups. Sports facilities include three sports halls, squash courts, a weight room, fitness suite, tennis courts, playing fields, a running track and a boathouse.

A university counselling service is available to students on all four campuses and the medical centre also looks after student welfare. There is a union representative for international students. They co-ordinate a "meet and greet" service from Heathrow and an orientation programme for new students. Meeting houses are available for all faiths and weekly worship is arranged for Christians and Muslims.

A total of £210,813 from government access funds is available and in 1998/99 this was used to help 939 students. A small number of scholarships are also offered worth £2,000 for each year of full-time study.

"Having completed my undergraduate studies in the Department of Electrical Engineering and Electronics I am now studying for a postgraduate degree in microelectronics system design. My original choice of programme was based on Brunel's outstanding reputation in engineering. I decided to continue my studies for the following reasons. Firstly, I have found a sponsor for my degree through the department's industrial connections. This will hopefully give me the opportunity to gain an insight into the working of an international, broad-line manufacturer and supplier of integrated circuits. The second main attraction was the department itself. It has a good range of facilities which together with the enthusiastic and approachable lecturing staff constitutes an excellent working environment. Brunel University is a friendly, compact campus with everything close at hand, which makes it a great choice for students."

Christiana Krikis, Greece

UNIVERSITY OF CAMBRIDGE

University of Cambridge

Write to: Mrs Anne Newbould, Kellet Lodge, Tennis Court Road, Cambridge CB2 1QJ

Tel: 01223 333 308

Fax: 01223 366 383

Email: ucam-undergraduate-admissions@lists.cam.ac.uk

Website: www.cam.ac.uk

Students: 15,821 in 1997/8 (4,661 postgraduate; 2,339 international), 55:45 male:female.

Accommodation: varies according to each college. Single sex, (three all female colleges) married, vacation. University residences from £33 a week. Room in town from £50 a week.

Entrance requirements: 3 As at A level or equivalent (selection after rigorous assessment).

EFL: IELTS 7 with no individual element below 6, TOEFL 600, minimum score of 5 in TWE.

Foundation: none available

Fees: arts and maths £6,606, science, music, architecture, geography £8,652, clinical £16,014 a year. Undergraduates pay a college fee of £3,670, postgraduates a fee of £1,676.

The University of Cambridge was established in 1209 and colleges were set up in 1284. Today there are 31 colleges. Three admit women only and two are for graduates only. Their histories are very different and their internal procedures also vary. Each college is in some ways like a mini-university with its own statutes and regulations.

Undergraduate applications are made to an individual Cambridge college; there is also an open application route by which applications are allocated to a college by computer. There are some important things to remember: the closing date for applicatons to Cambridge is 15 October; forms must be received in Cambridge by this date and the UCAS form should be at UCAS by this date. You may not apply to Oxford and Cambridge in the same year.

Cambridge is a small market town, and its centre is dominated by students on bicycles and, in the summer months, scores of meandering tourists. The colleges that make up the town provide ample historical interest. However if you want to get away from 'quads' and gothic architecture, the countryside is never far away. Trips down the river

King's College Chapel

Cam (from where the town gets its name) take you into rural England.

Academic strengths

Cambridge University is famous for its high quality research and teaching whatever the subject. It consistently scores highly in research and teaching quality assessments. Some of the many subjects deemed Excellent in recent teaching quality assessments were anthropology, architecture, English, chemistry, geography, law, and computer science. Almost all the departments assessed for research gained a 5* in 1996. Students live and study at a college and mix with students from different subjects. Lectures are organised centrally, but the individual or two-to-one teaching that the university is famous for takes place in colleges. Each college has its own library, there are faculty or department libraries and the university library which is a copyright library. There are central computer resources, but again, each college has its own computer room usually with 24 hour access. The university attracts a number of distinguished speakers ensuring that students are part of an academic community that is wider than their own subject area.

Student life

Students have access to clubs and societies both in the colleges and in the university as a whole. The scope is vast. The university has the oldest student theatre run by the Amateur Dramatics Club (ADC), where many a now famous actor or comedian started life (including the likes of Michael Palin, Emma Thompson, Thandi Newton and Tilda Swinton). Sports such as rowing and rugby achieve international fame with 'varsity' matches (competition between Oxford and Cambridge). The usual student activities are there in greater abundance. Many colleges have a small theatre or have facilities for film screenings. Musicians can choose between orchestras, and the main university choir (there are several) is directed by Stephen Cleobury, director of music at King's College. The university is full of traditions. Some colleges are more traditional than others and demand gowns be worn at every dinner. Other students never even own a gown! Some colleges are as old as the university, others are still expanding and have the added attraction of modern accommodation. International students are supported through their college and each has a college representative to voice their concerns.

"I'm studying Natural Sciences – Physics at New Hall (one of the three all-female colleges). I made an open application to the university, which means that you do not specify a college. I was a little apprehensive about an all-female college at first, but New Hall is really friendly and has an informal atmosphere. I'm really glad that I'm here. I am in the third year of my course and have made some very good friends both British and from overseas. Last year I was the college international officer and helped organise social events for new international students. I also sent new students information about the college and university with advice about what to bring and what to expect. I didn't have too many difficulties with my English, but when I did have trouble (mainly with abbreviated words) other students were happy to help. I'm now the university student representative on the physics teaching committee and have recently taken up rowing. I'm very busy!"

Yvonne Deng, Germany

Cardiff University

Write to: Dr. Tim Westlake, Director of the International Office, Cardiff University, PO Box 921, Cardiff CF10 3XQ

Tel: 02920 874432

Fax: 02920 874622

Email: internat@cf.ac.uk

Website: www.cf.ac.uk

Students: 15,343 in 1999/00 (3,329 postgraduates, 2,577 international, from over 100 countries), 52:48 male:female.

Accommodation: single sex, married, some vacation, storage facilities over Christmas and Easter. University residences from £56 a week self-catered; room in town from £35 to £40 a week.

Entrance requirements: generally high, BBB in A levels or equivalent for most subjects. European and International Baccalaureates accepted.

EFL: IELTS 6.5, TOEFL 570

Fees: science courses £8,850 a year, arts courses £6,750 a year, MBA £9,900 a year (1998/9).

Cardiff is the capital of Wales, and the city's new Millennium Stadium recently played host to the Rugby Union World Cup. It is also home to a number of academic institutions, of which Cardiff University is the oldest. Situated adjacent to the city centre, it forms part of a central square that is home to the National Museum of Wales, the Welsh Office and the Welsh College of Music and Drama. The main building is Portland stone, which gives a grand and

Cardiff University's Main Building

UNIVERSITIES AND COLLEGES

imposing feel akin to some of the larger Cambridge colleges. You will be greeted by posters in the lobby showing how well Cardiff does in the research and teaching quality assessments.

As a city, Cardiff is relatively safe and has a reputation as being friendly. Most significantly for students, it has a much lower cost of living than London. If you like magnificent countryside, the Brecon Beacons and Gower Peninsula are nearby. There are also a number of beaches within easy access including Barry Island, Porthcawl and Penarth. As the capital city of Wales it offers a full range of social, cultural and sporting activities, and with a number of academic institutions based in the city there is a very active student scene.

Academic strengths

Cardiff is very proud of its record in both research and teaching. 21 departments got an Excellent rating for teaching, and 80 per cent of subject areas got a 4 or 5 for research. Business courses are very popular areas for international students and the Cardiff Business School has a wide range of undergraduate and postgraduate programmes. Architecture, computer science, engineering, journalism, film and broadcasting and pharmacy are also popular. On the postgraduate side, international students tend to go for the MBA, the MA in Journalism

Studies or one of the range of MSc Economics programmes. There are 11 libraries throughout the university as well as a number of 24-hour access computer rooms.

Student life

Cardiff students' union is one of the biggest in the UK and has a wide range of activities. Facilities include seven different food outlets, several bars, a shop, a games room, bank, nightclub and the Great Hall which has hosted bands such as Jamiroquai, Radiohead and Oasis in recent years. There are also a number of international societies which are well attended by British as well as international students. In addition there are Anglican and Roman Catholic chaplaincies on campus. All students are given a free email address. The university has three sports centres which include fitness rooms, tennis and squash courts a martial arts studio and a floodlit all-weather pitch. There is a hardship fund to support students in financial difficulties.

There is an induction week for international students prior to enrolment. This includes free coach collection from Heathrow and Cardiff airports, an information fair and a welcome reception. Free term time English language support is provided for full-time students assessed as in need by their departments.

"I chose Cardiff because I wanted to do law, and I liked the modular structure of their degree programme. This means that I do exams twice a year, spreading the burden rather than concentrating it all at the end of the year. Cardiff is also a great student city with plenty going on, especially if you like to go to parties once in a while. But it is not as overwhelming as London where there is so much happening I think I would find it hard to study. The Welsh countryside is also really beautiful in the summer. Having said that the weather was a shock when I first came – it just seemed to get colder and colder, not like the hot and humid tropical climate I am used to!"

Erleen Mokhtar, Malaysia

City College Manchester

Write to: Idoia Garcia, International Admissions Officer, City College Manchester, Fielden Centre, 141 Barlow Moor Road, West Didsbury, Manchester M20 2PQ

Tel: 0161 957 1609

Fax: 0161 957 8613

Email: igarcia@ccm.ac.uk

Website: www.manchester-city-coll.ac.uk

Students: 10,000 in 1997/8 (350 international, from 40 countries), 40:60 male:female.

Accommodation: single sex, married/family, vacation, storage facilities. Homestay from £70 a week including bills and meals. Room in town from £40 a week.

Entrance requirements: vary according to course, generally high school certificate or international equivalent.

EFL: HND programmes IELTS 5.0, FE courses IELTS 4.5, foundation courses IELTS 4.0-5.0.

Foundation: programmes in economics, finance, business studies, IT, art and design, science and engineering.

Fees: ESOL £2,900 a year, FE courses £3,900 a year, HE courses £5,100 a year.

The city of Manchester, with its 2.5 million inhabitants and student population of over 50,000, is a cosmopolitan blend of tradition and innovation. Two of the most famous football clubs in the world, Manchester United and Manchester City are based here.

Manchester has an unrivalled reputation for music and entertainment, too. Some well-known bands that started out in Manchester include M-People, The Smiths, the Bee Gees, Simply Red and Oasis. Students have easy access to the many bars, clubs, theatres, pubs and shopping facilities in the city. The renowned Hallé Orchestra is also based here. The areas surrounding Manchester include the rolling hills of the Pennines, the Peak District National Park and the Cheshire Plains.

Manchester City College is based at five centres across Manchester and is

Students at City College

one of the ten largest further education colleges in England. The college aims for an individual approach to each student and offers education and training in a range of subjects in a full-time, part-time, day release, evening or weekend capacity.

Academic strengths

The college offers a range of course subjects with flexibility in the mode of, and approach to study. Students can study subjects as diverse as performing arts, computing and IT management and child-care. All students of the college have full access to the facilities on offer.

English language provision is available from beginners to advanced level. International students have previously taken courses at the college to gain a place at a British university. Foundation programmes available are linked to a range of university degree programmes. Professional training courses are available for those who wish to work in industry and commerce – the vocational qualifications on offer at the college are acceptable and transferable throughout Europe. Courses in business management, IT and business administration have been popular with international students in the past.

Modern academic facilities include specialist photographic studios, a fully furnished IT suite, a recording studio, a business administration suite, theatre, drama and dance studios, fashion and textile studios and watch and technology workshops.

Student life

The students' union plays an active role in the full and varied social life enjoyed at the college. In addition to the large refectories and common rooms, sporting facilities include several multi-gyms and a leisure centre complete with a swimming pool. The college has a large performing arts department which has its own record label. Live concerts and plays are a regular feature of college life. The union organises a range of societies that cater to the recreational interests of students. The international society organises a programme of social activities throughout the year. Manchester has the largest concentrated student areas in Europe with its three universities and two large colleges, creating a thriving student scene. The college has links with universities in Manchester.

The college offers international students an accommodation service, free airport pick-up, English language support, counselling and guidance services, and a travel agent. There are strong links with the international society and, therefore, local denominations and religious groups.

"I came to City College Manchester as a student, and now I am the International Officer! I wanted to improve my English after finishing university in Spain. I heard about the college from one of my friends. I really enjoyed my time at the college. The teaching was excellent, the staff were very friendly, and eager to help. The college has good facilities, too. What I enjoyed the most was the diversity of the students and the mixture of people from different cultural backgrounds. The English I learnt enabled me to enrol on an MA course and find a job. Manchester is a vibrant city – the ideal place for a young person to live."

Idoia Garcia, Spain

COVENTRY
UNIVERSITY

coventry
coventry
coventry

Coventry University

Write to: Ann O'Sullivan, International Office, Coventry University, Priory Street, Coventry, CU1 5FB

Tel: 024 7683 8674

Fax: 024 7663 2710

Email: daya.evans@coventry.ac.uk

Website: www.coventry.ac.uk

Students: 16,000 in 1997/8 (5,000 postgraduate, 1,000 international from 90 countries), 50:50 male:female.

Accommodation: single-sex, vacation storage facilities – extra charge. University residences from £35 a week self-catered. Room in town from £30 to £40 a week.

Entrance requirements: generally two A levels or international equivalent.

EFL: IELTS 6, TOEFL 550.

Foundation: art and design, business computing, engineering, environment and sciences for entry to degree programmes.

Fees: for undergraduate courses £6,300 a year, Art and Design Foundation £4,300 a year; for postgraduate classroom courses £6,300 a year, laboratory-based courses, MBA and MA Marketing £7,300 a year.

Coventry University is based on a 25-acre purpose-built campus in the centre of the city. There is also a 20-acre site on the outskirts of the city centre, which is home to the university's Technology Park. The city of Coventry itself has a rich and varied past. In medieval times, Coventry was a wool and cloth manufacturing centre, and by the 14th century it had become the fourth largest town in England. During the Victorian industrial age, Coventry enjoyed a productive and inventive era and was the birthplace of the modern bicycle. The first part of the 20th century saw Coventry as Britain's motor and aircraft manufacturing centre. Today, modern and historical characteristics combine to make Coventry a lively cosmopolitan centre. The striking 20th

Coventry University

century cathedral is linked by an arch to the medieval shell of the original design. The Cathedral Quarter's cobbled streets are lined with pubs, restaurants and cafes.

Academic Strengths

All undergraduate courses at Coventry are in modular form. Students normally take up to eight single modules per year. The university also offers joint programmes to enable students to broaden their study to one or more subjects that are unrelated to their degree.

The library stocks nearly 350,000 books and over 2,600 current periodicals. There are over 1,150 study spaces, CD-ROM, multimedia, and Internet resources for students too.

Students can access computer services during the evenings and weekends. In addition to a range of word processing packages, students can also use graphics software. Tutorials are available for students who are not familiar with computers, and a team of advisers is available 12 hours a day for computer-related queries.

In the latest teaching quality assessment the departments of health and social sciences, geography and mechanical engineering were awarded Excellent ratings, and the following courses have been popular with international students in the past: business studies, engineering, transport design, autmotive engineering design, and international relations and European studies.

Student life

The students' union is at the centre of all student activity. As well as offering a range of welfare, personal development and representational services, the union also organises a busy entertainment programme. Students enjoy the bars, restaurants, clubs and societies run by the union.

International students are welcomed during the first week of term, when a programme of events is arranged, in addition to free airport pick-up and English language classes throughout term time. The International Office arranges a series of visits to local places of interest, and encourages students to participate in a variety of social and cultural events. There are two full-time international student advisers who are there to offer support and advice on various welfare matters including registering with the doctor, opening a bank account; extending one's visa and other matters relating to immigration.

Within the university there is a Muslim prayer room, and a Christian chaplaincy. The Chaplains can put students in contact with representatives of other faiths in the city.

"I came to England in 1992 to do an HND in mechanical engineering in Cheltenham, then I worked for Minolta in Malaysia. But with an HND I could enter directly into the second year of a degree course, so I applied to the government for a loan. If I get a first, I don't have to pay the loan back! I applied to Coventry because it's a new university. It used to be a polytechnic, so the courses are much more practical than theoretical and they're geared to work experience. Facilities are good here – the computer centre is open 24 hours – and the lecturers are really dedicated. Many are specialists in their field. Some of them talk very quickly, though, and it's difficult to understand. I like being at university in the town centre – here the cinema is right next door to the library."

Amir Sharrifuddin, Malaysia

edinburgh
edinburgh
edinburgh

The University of Edinburgh

Write to: Dr Tom Barron, The International Office, The University of Edinburgh, 57 George Square, Edinburgh EH8 9JU

Tel: 0131 650 4296

Fax: 0131 668 4565

Email: international@ed.ac.uk

Website: www.ed.ac.uk

Students: 20,185 students in 1998/99 (4065 postgraduates, 3114 international students, from 106 countries), male:female 47:53

Accommodation: married/family accommodation. University residence full board from £79 to £84 a week, self-catered from £50 to £64. Room in town £50 a week.

Entrance requirements: AAB to BBC in arts, divinity, law, music, medicine, social sciences and veterinary medicine. BCC to DD in education. ABB to CCD in science and engineering. International Baccalaureate 34 to 37 points for most programmes in arts, law, medicine, social sciences and veterinary medicine. 30 points in divinity, music, science and engineering.

EFL: TOEFL 550 to 580. 213 to 237 (computer). IELTS 6.0 to 6.5.

Foundation: contact international office.

Fees: classroom courses £6,970 a year, laboratory courses £9,160 a year, clinical courses £16,650 a year, MBA £10,000 a year.

Founded in 1583, the University of Edinburgh is one of the oldest and largest universities in the UK. Its various buildings – which range from 17th century to very modern – are integrated within the heart of Scotland's capital, Edinburgh. The city, which has half a million inhabitants and runs from the hills down to the sea, is compact enough to provide easy access to cultural, social, shopping and sporting facilities.

The university is firmly rooted in a Scottish educational tradition which places emphasis on breadth as well as depth of study. Notable alumni include: philosopher David Hume; biologist, Charles Darwin; novelists, Walter Scott and Robert Louis Stevenson; former Tanzanian president, Julius Nyerere; and senior British ministers, Gordon Brown and Robin Cook.

Academic strengths

The 2,500 staff at the University of Edinburgh are based in nine faculties. 94 per cent of staff submitted research in the most recent research assessment exercise and 90 per cent was rated 4, 5 or 5*. 34 subjects were assessed for the quality of teaching and 32 were within the top two levels, gaining the grade Excellent or Highly Satisfactory

The University of Edinburgh campus

(or the equivalent grades under the latest methodology). Ten subject areas: accountancy; biological sciences; chemistry; computer science; economic and social history; electrical engineering; geology and geophysics; pure mathematics; physics and astronomy and sociology have been rated both Excellent for teaching and 5 for research. Edinburgh was recently ranked sixth in a league of European universities published in Der Spiegel and eighth in The Times 'Good University Guide 1999'.

Student life

With over 150 different student societies, the university's student association is one of the largest in the UK. In addition to providing support services and a student voice in the university's decision-making process, the association hosts social events throughout the year. The Edinburgh University Sports' Union runs 50 sport clubs. Facilities include a well-equipped sports centre, grass and all-weather playing fields and a field centre in the Scottish highlands.

The university guarantees an offer of accommodation to all new first year students. Approximately 5,700 students are housed in university-owned accommodation, all first-year rooms have central heating, 99 per cent are single and 20 per cent have a private bathroom.

The university chaplain and his colleagues provide assistance to all students and staff, irrespective of religious allegiance. The university community includes individuals from a wide range of ethnic, national and religious bacgrounds, so there are many opportunities to meet socially or worship with members of the same faith or denomination.

International students are met in Edinburgh by Osprey, which is a support network for international students of the city's four universities. The international office co-ordinates an international day before the beginning of term and provides pastoral support throughout the year. A host programme, which links local families with new international students, is also active at the beginning of the year and at Christmas. Throughout the year, the international office continues to support students with facilities such as the international student centre and international women's club. The university administers a hardship fund to which international students may apply. Self-funded international students are also protected from economic instability by a mechanism allowing them to defer tuition payments if their currency depreciates by more than 20 per cent during the course of their studies.

"Before I came to Scotland, I knew that Edinburgh enjoyed a worldwide reputation for artificial intelligence. I had always wanted to study information technology, particularly its commercial applications, so I applied here. It was not hard for me to settle into life in Edinburgh. Most people here are very friendly and my husband (boyfriend when I came - we actually got married in Edinburgh) had been studying at Edinburgh for six months before I arrived. Academic work in artificial intelligence is extremely hard and intensive. I have occasionally had to work overnight to meet project deadlines, but I have a great sense of achievement now that I am approaching the completion of my studies. The past year has been so busy that I haven't even had time to look carefully around Edinburgh. I must catch up! I hope to study for a PhD here."

Yang (Stella) Xiao, China

European School of Economics

Write to: Steve Berridge, European School of Economics, 8/9 Grosvenor Place, London SW1X 7SH

Tel: 020 7245 6148

Fax: 020 7245 6164

Email: info@eselondon.ac.uk

Website: www.eselondon.ac.uk

Students: 1,289 in 1998/99 (86 postgraduate, 341 international, from 15 countries), 42:58 male:female ratio.

Accommodation: single-sex, vacation, storage. University residence from £87 a week half-board. Room in town from £70 to £85 a week.

Entrance requirements: 2 Bs at A level or a high school diploma valid for university entrance in the country of origin.

EFL: TOEFL 540 or IELTS 5/6.

MBAs: TOEFL 560 or IELTS 6/7.

Fees: £5,000 a year (EU students), £6,500 a year (non-EU students), plus £350 application and registration fee.

Foundation: Six month pre-BA course available, starting in October, January and May. Three month pre-MBA course available.

The European School of Economics (ESE) is a private university of economics, finance and management, with centres in London, New York and Shanghai. It is also the largest business school in Italy, with ten campuses spread throughout the country. The oldest campus is in the historical centre of Rome and the second oldest is close to the sea near Pisa. Other major cities in Italy with

European School of Economics

UNIVERSITIES AND COLLEGES

campuses include Milan, Bologna and Naples. The programmes offered at the European School of Economics are orientated towards the fastest growing segments of international business, management, politics, communication and sport, attracting individuals from a wide variety of cultural backgrounds. At present 38 nationalities are represented in the student body.

ESE states that its mission is to "prepare a new generation of entrepreneurs and public sector managers of international stature". The school aims to provide a "from school to career" education and bridge the gap between academic work and the business world.

Academic strengths

The European School of Economics runs a number of courses that have an international dimension including international business and international political studies. The courses are designed on a modular system and students that complete the four-year course are awarded a British BA with honours.

The first two years of study may be spent in either London or one of the school's Italian centres. The third year is then spent abroad, usually in two countries. In the final year students return to the country in which they began their studies. Here they may choose various options to deepen their knowledge in a particular field. All students must complete a dissertation. During the four years students undertake three practical training periods in international companies that last for up to ten months and help to give them a flavour of the real business world. Classes at ESE are kept small and the study of two European languages is a compulsory element of all courses.

The school has a multicultural international academic staff. An annual cycle of lectures is organised enlisting the participation of academics from European and American universities as well as professionals from multinationals. Facilities at the school include computer laboratories, electronic library facilities, self-access language laboratories, and television and music suites.

Student life

All the school's campuses have residential accommodation available and an office which assists students to find rented single or shared accommodation in the local area. Sports facilities are organised for students outside of the school. With campuses based in city centres, students can always take advantage of local entertainment.

"When I was choosing a university, I wanted one that would give me a well-respected degree and hands-on experience of the international business world. One of the biggest strengths of the European School of Economics is that it encourages personal responsibility in its students. When I went to carry out my first work placement for the Italian Trade Commission at the Atlanta Olympics in 1996, I was thrown into a new environment and immediately asked to put into practice the skills I had learnt over my first year. It was daunting at first but I was able to adapt to the environment and had a great time. More placements throughout my degree in large companies in France and the USA allowed me to develop my business skills further, and increased my confidence in dealing with individuals."

Marco D'Amico, Italy

University of Essex

University of Essex

Write to: Professor John Oliver, University of Essex, Wivenhoe Park, Colchester CO4 3SQ

Tel: 01206 873666

Fax: 01206 873423

Email: admit@essex.ac.uk

Website: www.essex.ac.uk/

Students: 5,700 in 1998/9 (1,592 postgraduate, 1,135 international, from 109 countries), 52:48 male:female.

Accommodation: single sex, married, vacation, storage facilities. University residences from £40 a week; £57 a week with en suite facilities self-catered. Room in town from £45 a week.

Entrance requirements: three good A levels or equivalent.

EFL: IELTS 6, TOEFL 540.

Foundation: nine-month bridging year with English language training if required, success guarantees entry to appropriate degree course at Essex. Teaching is within university and students have access to all its facilities.

Fees: classroom courses £6,600 a year, laboratory courses £8,820 a year, bridging course £6,660 for year.

The university received its royal charter in 1965. As it was conceived as a university town rather than a single building, the single-site campus incorporates teaching buildings, student accommodation, various shops, banks, a gallery, a theatre (the Lakeside Theatre), bars, cafes and sports facilities all on the one site. These are set in over 200 acres of parkland, much of which was landscaped in the 18th century. Famous alumni from Essex University include Virginia Bottomley MP, Dr Oscar Arias (the former president of Costa Rica and a Nobel prizewinner), and Dr Rodolfo Neri Vela (Mexico's first and only astronaut).

The university is two miles from the centre of Colchester, which is Britain's oldest recorded town and first capital. Today it has over 13,500 listed buildings. Amongst its cultural facilities are museums, galleries, an arts centre, a theatre and a multi-screen cinema. Colchester is less than an hour away from London. It also has transport links

University of Essex campus

with Stanstead Airport and the ferry port at Harwich.

Academic strengths

Essex undergraduate degrees aim to offer flexibility and choice. First year students can combine the core modules of their subject with options in other subjects such as linguistics, philosophy or computing. This allows the possibility of changing to another degree at the end of the year. There are 15 academic departments which are grouped into four areas of study – the Schools of Humanities and Comparative Studies, Social Sciences, Law, and Science and Engineering.

In the teaching quality assessments the University of Essex achieved an Excellent rating for law (1993) and scores of 21 for linguistics (1996), 22 for sociology (1995), 22 for art history (1998), 22 for psychology (1999) and 24 for electrical and electronic engineering (1997), out of a possible total of 24. Research areas at the university were assessed during the 1996 research assessment exercise and the following departments received a rating of 5 or 5*: law, economics and econometrics, politics and international studies, sociology and history of art, architecture and design.

Most departments have several one-year master's degrees as well as supervising PhD students. The university annually awards 50 scholarships to new postgraduate research students.

Amongst the university's facilities are nine computing laboratories which offer IT-based teaching and learning facilities. Three of the labs offer 24-hour access, whilst the others are generally available between 7am and midnight.

Student life

The university has a students' union offering services ranging from academic support to entertainment with over 100 clubs and societies. The entertainments manager co-ordinates a programme of events throughout the year. The sports clubs, which number around 40, offer students an opportunity to participate in a number of sports including gliding, Tai-chi, sub-aqua or orienteering. There is a multi-faith centre which is used by Anglican, Roman Catholic, Muslim, Buddhist, Hindu and Sikh students.

Essex has specific support services for international students. At the start of the year there are airport pick-ups, pre-session English classes and an orientation programme, while year-round facilities include advice and counselling, free in-session language classes for students and their dependants, an on-campus health centre, a travel shop and help with finding part-time jobs.

"I first heard about Essex at an education fair. I was looking for a foundation course and decided on the pre-degree bridging year at Essex. I particularly wanted to go on to study accounting and Essex has a department devoted to the study of accounting and financial management. In preparation for my degree I'm taking courses in mathematics and statistics, politics and economics and British institutions and culture. I have a lot of friends from other different countries and, despite my worries, it was easy to make friends when I first arrived. Some people say that English people are rather cold, but this is not true. I have found them to be warm and friendly."

Irene Ju-Yung Lai, China

Falmouth College of Arts

Write to: International Liaison Office, Woodlane, Falmouth, Cornwall TR11 4RH

Tel: 01326 211 077

Fax: 01326 212 261

Email: international@falmouth.ac.uk

Website: www.falmouth.ac.uk

Students: 1,500 in 1998 (10 per cent postgraduate, 10 per cent international), 50:50 male:female.

Accommodation: college residences from £57 a week. Room in town from £45 to £65 a week.

Entrance requirements: normally A level pass and three GCSE passes for foundation course and two or three grade C passes at A level for BA (Hons) courses, but emphasis placed on prior learning and experience.

EFL: evidence of ability to speak and understand English. Minimum requirements: IELTS 6.0, TOEFL 600.

Fees: foundation year £4,800 a year, BA (Hons) £5,800 to £6,300 a year, PGDip/MA £6,000 to £6,500 a year. MPhil/Phd research £6,000 to £6,500 a year.

Falmouth is a coastal seaside town in the picturesque south west of England. Falmouth College of Arts was established in 1902 and is a specialist college, with just over 1,500 students. Originally founded as an art school, the college now covers various areas of media and cultural studies, as well as art and design. The college's Woodlane campus is set in eight acres in its own subtropical garden, between the town of Falmouth, the harbour and the beaches. All students work in purpose-designed studios, workshops and other teaching facilities. Nearby annexe studios support those on the Woodlane site. The college's second campus at Tremough comprises an 18th century house and estate a few kilometres away. Set in 42 acres, the estate includes sports fields, tennis courts, gardens and parkland. Primarily for media and cultural studies students, development plans include the creation of a digital media centre.

Academic strengths

The one-year Art and Design Foundation course gives students hands-on experience in a wide range of subjects before entering a degree subject.

Students at Falmouth College of Arts

In a teaching quality assessment in 1999, Falmouth College of Arts was awarded 24 out of 24 for art and design provision. In recent years, Falmouth has also developed its media studies courses. The one-year full-time Post-graduate Diploma in Broadcast Journalism, recognised by the National Council for the training of Broadcast Journalists, has proved particularly popular. Several "now great-names" in broadcast media studied and gained experience at Falmouth, among them Hugh Pym, ITN's political correspondent.

The college library holds about 20,000 volumes, multimedia and computer resources, language materials, career reference information, newspapers and magazines. All the college's computer suites provide access to the Internet, with every student given an email address. Specialist computer studios provide digital video editing, three-dimensional animation, digital cameras, laptops, colour scanning and printing. Information Technology induction sessions and user support services are also provided. English language tuition is provided by a full-time tutor.

The college operates an international credit accumulation scheme. Apply to the college by the end of January for the foundation year, the end of February for the Postgraduate Diploma in Broadcast Journalism or Creative Advertising, and by June for other courses. Late applications will still be considered.

Student life

Falmouth students live in a pleasant town with few crime problems, just a few minutes walk from the college and the beach. A purpose-built student residence is located in Falmouth's town centre and provides accommodation for 156 students. Priority is given to international students and first-year students, whilst other students can choose from the excess of good accommodation in privately rented houses. The students' union organises regular entertainment and establishes links with local groups and societies, arranging student rates for many events and activities. A sports co-ordinator organises activities including riding, hand-gliding and rock-climbing. Being near the sea allows students to take part in many watersports such as surfing and sailing.

"I wanted to study journalism when I left school, but there are no journalism courses in Norway. At an exhibition I came across Falmouth's journalism courses. I wanted to find out what the college was like so I contacted some Norwegian students there through email. The college heard about this and they thought it was positive, so when I applied they made me an unconditional offer. The emphasis in the BA Honours course is more on analysis than practical work, but in this second year we're doing 12 weeks of online journalism and the Internet, which is really useful. The course is very wide-ranging, covering news stories in English, radio and TV, photography... so it's a lot of work, but it's the best of both worlds. I've been awarded a bursary and I'm looking forward to studying in Guatemala for six weeks after Christmas. I live in a house with other students and I've made a lot of friends – the people here are very friendly. What I like to do is get out and explore the coast and the Cornish countryside when I can."

Charlotte Bergloff, Norway

UNIVERSITY
of
GLASGOW

glasgow
glasgow
glasgow

University of Glasgow

Write to: Student Recruitment and Admissions, The University of Glasgow, Glasgow G12 8QQ

Tel: 0141 330 4241

Fax: 0141 330 4045

Email: sras@gla.ac.uk

Website: www.gla.uc.uk

Students: 19,918 in 1998 (2,635 postgraduates, 1,027 international, from over 20 countries), 49:51 male:female.

Accommodation: single and vacation. University rooms from about £45 to £55 a week self-catering,

Main University Campus

£67 catered. Room in town from £45 a week.

Entrance requirements: good grades at A level or equivalent (As for medicine, veterinary medicine, dentistry, law, accountancy).

EFL: Cambridge Certificates, IELTS 6.0, TOEFL 580.

Fees: classroom courses £6,930 a year, laboratory courses £8,800 a year. Medicine £13,640 a year. Postgraduate: various, check with admissions office.

The towers and pinnacles of George Gilbert Scott's neoGothic university buildings command wonderful views across a city that vibrates with activity. Glasgow is Scotland's largest city. It stands on the west coast, facing Edinburgh and is the gateway to the lochs, hills and Highlands, but with its medieval buildings, art galleries and museums, and Art Nouveau architecture, the city is itself a tourist attraction – it was recently nominated as Britain's third favourite tourist venue.

Glasgow and its oldest university have evolved together for, on completion of the city's great medieval cathedral in the mid-1400s, the Pope gave permission for a university to be founded there; the first lectures were held in the new nave. In 1870, the university moved to its present site, high on Gilmorehill, but today, the Faculty of Veterinary Medicine is out to the north; courses in agricultural science, food production, and leisure management are on the Scottish Agricultural College campus at

Auch-incruive, near Ayr; and Crichton College, home of a new MA (Liberal Arts) degree, is in nearby Dumfries. Glasgow has its own Marine Biology Research Station on the Firth of Clyde and a nuclear reactor at East Kilbride.

Academic Strengths

Glasgow University has many educational firsts to its name. In the 19th century, the medieval town was engulfed by industrial development, and in response, the university established the first Chair of Civil Engineering and the first Chair of Naval Architecture. Today, engineering, from aeronautical and aerospace to software, is one of its major academic strengths, and the courses in naval architecture with marine or ocean engineering are respected internationally. The Faculty of Medicine recently achieved a first among UK universities by directing the emphasis of its clinical training from science to patient care. In addition to engineering and medicine, accounting, finance and management studies attract students from all over the world. The university won high teaching quality assessment ratings for these subjects plus chemistry, computing, geography, geology, physics, astronomy, philosophy and sociology. The university library holds some two million works, available in forms ranging from vellum to satellite TV (and fast access to the libraries of seven other Scottish universities nearby). Glasgow also has a proportionally large postgraduate intake. In 1998/9, 30 per cent of postgraduate students came from overseas. The university has post-graduate accommodation and 60 to 70 flats for married students in town.

Student life

Glasgow has a new concert hall, several large theatres and a number of art galleries. The university has two students' unions competing for members, a debating society that has won the World Student DebatingChampionships five times, and exten-sive sports facilities. All students are guaranteed university accommodation – usually on the main campus – for at least a year.

The Student Recruitment and Admissions Service organises an orientation programme for international students that includes talks and tours of the university, city and surrounding countryside, as well as an opportunity to make friends. An international student adviser is available to provide students from overseas with confidential and practical help with aspects of living and studying in Glasgow.

"Studying in Britain is a tradition in my family. Since the second World War, my father and my uncles have all studied for a BSc in Mechanical Engineering in London or Scotland. I studied at Singapore Polytechnic for two years, so I could enter directly into the third year. Coming here is good for my English and I wanted to live with different people and stand on my own feet. People in Singapore think of England as a rich country and I was rather shocked, at first, to see poor people in the street. The hardest thing was learning how to get on with Europeans. They have a different way of thinking, and it took me three months to understand why they do some things. But learning to share other people's views is really good – it makes for success in work as well as in personal relationships."

Kelvin Hui, Singapore

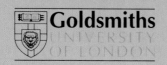

Goldsmiths University of London

Write to: Jill Thorn, International Office, Goldsmiths College, University of London, New Cross, London, SE14 6NW.

Tel: 020 7919 7700

Fax: 020 7919 7704

Email: international-office@gold.ac.uk

Website: www.goldsmiths.ac.uk

Accommodation: university residences from £54 to £69 a week self-catering.

Students: 5,280 students in 1998/9 (1,500 postgraduates, 393 international, from 15 countries), 34:66 male:female.

Entrance requirements: vary according to course applied for, generally two subjects at A level standard or equivalent.

EFL: IELTS 6.5, TOEFL 580 including 4.5 TWE minimum.

Foundation: extension degrees in visual arts, music, art history and fine art, mathematics, and textiles allows study for Goldsmiths BA (Hons) degrees. Certificate in English Language for the Arts and Social Sciences is sufficient for application for undergraduate degrees at Goldsmiths. Postgraduate Diploma in English Language sufficient for postgraduate study at Goldsmiths.

Fees: classroom courses £7,040 a year, laboratory courses £8,960 a year.

Goldsmiths, established in 1891, is a member of the University of London, and is set in historical southeast London. Nearby in Greenwich, the home of Greenwich Mean Time, you can stand above the Meridian line with one foot in the Western Hemisphere and the other in the Eastern. Although Goldsmiths' students are close to the attractions of central London, they are also in reach of the open spaces of Blackheath, Dulwich Park and the historic Thames waterfront.

The college is small enough to retain a friendly atmosphere and welcoming approach whilst being large enough to provide the facilities needed for students. The many different cultures, age ranges, and backgrounds of students reflect the many different courses on offer at the college.

Goldsmith University Campus

Academic strengths

Goldsmiths focuses on the study of creative, cultural and social processes. Whilst offering a combination of subjects, from mathematical sciences to educational studies to the performing arts, the college places great emphasis on combining theory and practice in academic studies, cultivating skills that can be transferred in the careers and lives of their students.

The most recent government teaching quality assessment awarded Goldsmiths college with Excellent ratings in the following subjects; Music, Sociology, Media and Communications, Drama, and Psychology. The 1996 research assessment exercise awarded the Art and Design Department a 5* rating – the highest mark possible.

Students at Goldsmiths can enjoy a wide range of study resources during their degree course. Some are offered by individual academic departments, although most can be found in the college's new Rutherford Information Services building. This houses the main college library, the computer services and language resource centre. There are also specialist purpose-equipped teaching rooms for language and computer-based teaching. Up-to-date facilities for sound processing and computer-based graphics are also available – scanners, MIDI interfaces, specialist equipment for slide input and generation, and video processing.

Time Out magazine, London's weekly entertainment listings bible, recently described Goldsmiths' library as "the best undergraduate library in London for contemporary social, cultural and media studies with an unusually comprehensive collection of periodical holdings". Students also have access to the University of London library, at Senate House, which has over a million volumes covering arts and humanities subjects.

Student life

Goldsmiths has an active students' union with a large number and wide variety of societies, including over 100 sports clubs, bars, a café and a subsidised shop. The union is renowned for its live concerts. International students have a special orientation programme at the start of term, English language support during term time, and a Sabbatical Officer to offer support, guidance and advice.

Within 10 miles of Goldsmiths, students can enjoy a host of modern facilities, such as over 15 sports centres, five football grounds, as well as five major museums, and art galleries.

The student chaplaincy welcomes members of all faiths, and offers meeting spaces for prayer or religious discussion.

"As an international student at Goldsmiths College, I have learnt lots of things which are becoming the foundation of my life in Japan. Because the education system is so different it was really difficult to settle myself into the course. However, all the tutors and technicians put me on the right path. They were really supportive and helped me like a friend. They treated me just like any other student. I enjoyed being on this course, as I am particularly enthusiastic about textiles."

Keiko Furubayashi, Japan

greenwich
greenwich
greenwich

Greenwich School of Management

Write to: Stephen Fettes, Greenwich School of Management, Meridian House, Royal Hill, Greenwich, London SE10 8RD

Tel: 020 8516 7800

Fax: 020 8516 7801

Email: enquiry@greenwich-college.ac.uk

Website: www.greenwich-college.ac.uk

Students: 600 in 1998/9 (300 postgraduate, 250 international, from 62 countries), 60:40 male:female.

Accommodation: single-sex, married/family, vacation, storage. Room in town from £60 a week.

Entrance requirements: school leaving certificate. For postgraduate courses, any degree.

EFL: competence in written and spoken English.

Foundation: access to BSc (Hons) courses.

Fees: from £3,000 a year. Postgraduate courses from £6,000 a year.

Greenwich School of Management is located in an historic area of London, close to both Greenwich Park and the River Thames. Greenwich has many entertainment and leisure facilities that are popular with both students and tourists from around the world. The area has recently received acclaim for the construction of London's Millennium Dome. The West End, London's major centre for the arts and entertainments, and the City, the capital's commercial heartland, are both a bus ride away. Greenwich is conveniently situated for travel both within the UK and abroad. Gatwick and Heathrow can be reached relatively

Greenwich School of Management

UNIVERSITIES AND COLLEGES

358

easily and Greenwich is the right side of London for crossing the channel.

Students from over 60 countries worldwide attend the school each year which helps create an international atmosphere. The largest single nationality of students attending the school is British, which allows opportunities for those from non-English speaking countries to improve their language skills.

Academic strengths

Greenwich School of Management runs a range of MBAs, postgraduate diplomas and undergraduate qualifications. Courses are available on a full- and part-time basis and last for between one and four years.

With the introduction of the BSc (Hons) in Business Management and Information Technology, the school has recently updated its IT resources. This includes the purchase of 12 new computers and the upgrading of existing equipment with new hard disks, increased RAM and, in some cases, new processors. All machines use Microsoft Visual C++ version 6.00.

The library at Greenwich School of Management has multiple Internet access. A total of eight computers have access to the Internet over the ISDN link, allowing information to be downloaded quicker and less time to be spent at machines. There are experienced staff on site to train any students that have not used the Internet before.

Student life

Greenwich School of Management is affiliated to the University of Hull and it is on occasions such as the degree conferment ceremony that students are strongly reminded of this connection. The programme produced for the occasion lists graduates of both institutions alphabetically, and full-time students from the Hull campus mix with students from the school. Students on the MBA and BSc programmes are welcome to use any of the University of Hull's facilities, including the university's career service.

International students at Greenwich School of Management may take advantage of the school's airport pick-up service which transports them directly to Greenwich. For those with basic English, pre-sessional courses can be arranged which allow students to settle in and make some friends before term begins. The school has a multi-faith feel and most religions can be practiced in the locality. Accommo-dation is relatively comfortable and reasonably priced given that it is near London.

"Before studying at the school I took an undergraduate degree in business at the University of Virginia and was working in an American company's marketing department. Whilst at Greenwich I followed an MBA, specialising in marketing, which taught some of the theory behind the work that I had been doing in practice. The Greenwich School of Management was small enough to be friendly and personal. I met people from all over the world and a lot of friendly 'locals' as well. There were good library, computing and television facilities and I loved the fact that I was so close to central London. The one thing I didn't like about England was that the portions of food were much smaller than I was used to! Apart from that though, my time at Greenwich was brilliant, it developed my personal skills and I now hope it will advance my career. Coming to Greenwich was one of the best decisions of my life."

Charlotte Hall, USA

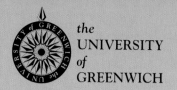
the
UNIVERSITY
of
GREENWICH

greenwich
greenwich
greenwich

The University of Greenwich

Write to: Enquiry Unit, Bank House, Wellington Street, Woolwich, London SE18 6PF

Tel: 020 8331 8590

Fax: 020 8331 8145

Email: courseinfo@gre.ac.uk

Website: www.gre.ac.uk

Students: 17,306 in 1999 (9,918 postgraduates, 848 international, from over 90 countries), 48:52 male:female.

Accommodation: single sex, vacation. University residences from £44 to £77 a week self-catering, £73 a week with breakfast and evening meal. Room in town from £45 a week.

Entrance requirements: generally two A levels plus three GCSEs Grade C, or equivalent. International Baccalaureate 24 points, a variety of local Diplomas and Higher Diplomas are accepted.

EFL: IELTS 6.0, TOEFL 550.

Fees: (in 1999) undergraduate/ postgraduate full-time £6,950 a year; MBA £9,450; MSc Financial Suite and MA Arts and Heritage courses £6,250.

Greenwich first opened its doors as Woolwich polytechnic, the second oldest polytechnic in the UK. Founded in 1891, five main campuses within the south east of London and Kent offer easy access to central London (about 30 to 45 minutes by train), the surrounding countryside and coast.

The new Greenwich Maritime University Campus houses the schools of PCET, Computing and Mathematical Sciences, and Law. This comprises of Sir Christopher Wren's Queen Anne Court and the restored dreadnought library originally built in 1764.

Woolwich University Campus is home to the schools of Chemical and Life Sciences, and Business and Humanities. It is a classic city campus with buildings spread around the town. Dartford University Campus, an elegant period house at Dartford in

The Maritime Greenwich World Heritage Site, including the University of Greenwich

Kent, is home to the schools of Land and Construction Management, and Architecture and Landscape. Medway University campus houses the schools of Earth and Environmental Sciences, Engineering and the Natural Recourses Institute. It is based in listed buildings near the historic cathedral city of Rochester. Avery Hill University campus hosts the schools of Education, Health and Social Sciences, on a parkland campus with an Italianate 19th-Century mansion that has a glass-domed conservatory.

Academic strengths

Greenwich is building a reputation for quality in teaching and research. Classed as the leading new university for research and consultancy income according to information released by the Higher Education Statistics Agency, it is one of the top two new universitites for research excellence in the latest quality assessment exercises. The schools of Architecture and Landscape, and Land and Construction Management were awarded maximum scores for 'excellence in teaching'. Environmental sciences and social sciences also achieved an Excellent rating. The university's curriculum includes courses on environmental control and conservation, heritage and tourism management, international business and marketing, MBA, business systems modelling, internet technology, architecture, and sports science, and combined degrees are also available. The academic year is split into two semesters of 15 weeks starting in September and February.

Student life

Greenwich has good sports facilities, ranging from football and mixed hockey to scuba diving and sailing. South east London has premier league football clubs within the vicinity, water sports on the nearby rivers, and the Crystal Palace sports stadium. Trips to Greenwich park and central London are the highlight of many weekends and evenings, with restaurants, cinemas, museums and markets all within easy reach. Kent students have easy access to historic cathedral towns, the channel tunnel and ports.

International students have the support of a specialist student service counsellor, English language skills and study skills tuition, accommodation and careers advice, and an international chaplaincy.

"After 12 years in the Chilean Navy, it was time for a change. I joined the Andean Mining and Chemicals Company as a sales representative and decided to further my career by studying for an MBA. I love travel so it had to be in London and the proximity to Europe made it an easy choice. I am very happy at Greenwich, the teaching levels are extremely good and I have developed some excellent relationships with my tutors who offered help and support. Each term brought new challenges, but teamwork has been the key to success. The subjects covered have given me a broader perspective and an opportunity to learn from people of vastly different backgrounds, ages and nationalities. I have been offered a promotion to Senior Manager of Operations on my return because of my MBA, and as I prepare to leave the UK, I must say that this course has been absolutely worthwhile."

Alejandro Natho, Chile

Gyosei International College

Write to: Mr William Unwin, Gyosei International College in the UK, London Road, Reading, Berkshire RG1 5AQ.

Tel: 0118 920 9335/9418.

Fax: 0118 931 0137.

Email: cityacadmin@gyosei.ac.uk or will@dial.pipex.com

Website: www.gyosei.ac.uk

Students: 300 in 1998/9 (10 post-graduates, 300 international students from 5 countries). 40:60 male:female.

Accommodation: vacation and storage. University rooms from £77 a week catered. Room in town from £150 a week.

Entrance requirements: One A level or the equivalent, and the motivation to study Japanese language and culture.

EFL: IELTS 5.0 or 4.5 with one month intensive course in September.

Foundation: available.

Fees: £6,450 a year (with Gyosei bursary).

The Gyosei Foundation dates back to 1881 when the first Gyosei High School was founded in the centre of Tokyo. In 1989, the first undergraduates began their studies at Gyosei International College at a campus in Reading. The town is the county town of Berkshire with thriving arts, commerce and industry, and a population of 200,000. It is a strategic travel link for all parts of the UK, benefiting from fast motorway and rail links to the capital (30 minutes by train).

Gyosei International College, now numbering 300 students, gears its education to non-native English speakers whose English is a second or third

Gyosei International College

language. The college has a bicultural and international perspective in all its work. The faculty of 50 staff are mainly Japanese and British academics with international teaching experience. Close links are maintained with universities and businesses in Japan, the UK and the USA.

Academic strengths

Gyosei International College is accredited by the British Accreditation Council, institutionally validated by the City University, and is an associate institution of Reading University. Four of the undergraduate courses are validated by a UK university. Students take between three and four years to complete their degrees. The degree is arranged in levels one to three (corresponding to years one to three) and students must pass nine courses per year and complete a dissertation to qualify for the degree. The degrees are bilingual, half the subjects may be studied and examined in Japanese, so that Japanese students are not linguistically disadvantaged

The degrees provide intensive knowledge of Japanese culture and business. Visits to businesses, placements and community projects are mixed, some in the UK and some in Japan. This aims to equip students to work either internationally or in Japan.

The Gyosei campus has academic facilities that include a library (with all the main English and Japanese textbooks), a resource centre with study materials for each course, a computer centre, a language laboratory and a careers support service. Students can also take advantage of City and Reading Universities' libraries and computer facilities.

Student life

Japanese and western students mix socially as well as on the courses. The college has a students' union with 22 clubs and societies. The students' union building, as well as housing these activities, has a restaurant, a cafeteria and a bar. The London Road campus also has senior and junior common rooms.

There are student newsletters, journals and other publications, regularly published. The students' union also organises a Matsuri festival on campus, which attracts a large crowd. When students arrive at Gyosei, there is an orientation week to give them a chance to settle in. Bursaries and scholarships are available.

"The City BA degree course is unique. Students can obtain a BA from the City University while studying at Gyosei International College in Reading. The staff are international and teach courses in subjects such as statistics, accounting and marketing. It is interesting to attend courses given by lecturers who are not only native English speakers. When I first came to the college I did have difficulty in understanding the English of non-native speaking lecturers. However, because I persevered I now find that it is relatively easy to understand. Assessment is mainly by essay. When I came to the college straight from senior high school in Japan, I had a very hard time as I was not used to writing essays. Essays are also the principal means of assessment in exams, and students have to answer three questions out of ten. Nevertheless, there is nothing more satisfying, when they are over, than sharing your thoughts about them (and a beer) with your friends."

Shiro Tamura

Heriot-Watt University
Edinburgh

Write to: Lorna Halliday, International Recruitment Office, Riccarton, Edinburgh EH14 4AS

Tel: 0131 451 3877

Fax: 0131 451 3630

Email: International@hw.ac.uk

Website: www.hw.ac.uk

Students: 5,025 in 1998/9 (1,207 postgraduate, 950 international, from 79 countries), 70:30 male:female.

Accommodation: single sex, vacation, storage facilities. University residences from £70 a week catered, £42 to £52 a week self-catered. Room in town from £42 to £46 a week.

Entrance requirements: generally BBC to DDD at A level.

EFL: IELTS 6.5, TOEFL 213.

Foundation: contact International Office for details.

Fees: classroom courses £6,500 a year, laboratory courses £8,500 a year, MBA £9,025.

Heriot-Watt University was established by Royal Charter in 1966. It traces its origins some 150 years earlier to the Edinburgh School of Arts. Today, Heriot-Watt is an integrated campus university. The 380-acre parkland campus is at Riccarton in the greenbelt of western Edinburgh. The university relocated here in the early 1990s and its buildings are entirely purpose-built. These are located in a natural setting of trees, lawns and a small loch.

Edinburgh is situated on the edge of a large loch, surrounded by volcanic hills. Its architecture ranges from Europe's largest area of Georgian buildings in the city's New Town to the 16th-century tenements and ancient castle high on the volcanic crag of Castle Rock. The city has 16,000 buildings that are listed as architecturally or historically important. Socially, there are over 700 pubs, plenty of restaurants and the population almost doubles in August during its International Festival. This is one of the

Statue of James Watt

largest arts festivals in the world, showing a range of theatre, comedy and dance from student productions to avant-garde professional companies. It has an airport and there are good rail and road links to London (four hours away by train).

Academic strengths

Courses at Heriot-Watt university are heavily weighted towards the engineering disciplines and natural sciences. In the 1996 research assessment exercise, the university had more top-graded engineering departments than any other Scottish university. Its mineral and mining engineering research received a rating of 5*, whilst applied maths and built environment research received scores of 5. There are also specialist courses available in Petroleum Engineering, International Banking and Finance, Actuarial Maths and Brewing and Distilling.

In the last 10 years, £60 million has been invested into the Riccarton campus and its facilities. Computing is integrated into most courses and students are encouraged to study using interactive learning techniques.

Student life

The student welfare services take care of accommodation needs and all new undergraduates are guaranteed a place in halls. They also run a counselling service and give advice on issues such as money, housing and immigration. International students can benefit from the airport pick-ups, two international student welcome weekends and weekend visits to scenic areas in Scotland. For students in serious financial difficulties, it is possible to apply to the university's hardship fund, which distributes money in the form of a grant. Overseas students can also apply for an Overseas Scholarship Award, available to new undergraduate and postgraduate students on taught courses. There is an interdenominational chaplaincy, which involves leaders from local churches. A special prayer room is provided for Muslim students.

The students' union is at the centre of the Riccarton campus. It has a representative for international students and there are international societies which organise events such as food days. Local culture also features, principally in the Scottish country dancing group and the Christmas ceilidh. There are also extensive facilities for sports and exercise at the university, including six football pitches and rugby pitches, a climbing wall, an international tournament centre for squash, and indoor badminton and hockey.

"After my government granted me a scholarship to go to the UK, I started looking for a place to study. Few universities offered international degrees that did not include a foreign language, so I chose Heriot-Watt. As a mature student I thought I would have problems adjusting to university life, as most students are quite young. But, to my surprise, I seem to be getting along well. In fact, I find the students in Heriot-Watt well-behaved. The lecturers and tutors are very supportive. I met other students from my country and we have all expressed our admiration for the place. Its history is written all over the place, even in the names of the buildings. It's amazing! I do look forward to my years of study at Heriot-Watt."

Gaositwe Pusumane, Botswana

THE UNIVERSITY OF HULL

The University of Hull

Write to: Admissions Office, Cottingham Road, Hull HU6 7RX

Tel: 01482 466 100

Fax: 01482 442 290

Email: admissions@admin.hull.ac.uk

Web: www.hull.ac.uk

Students: 11,425 in 1998 (2,561 postgraduate, about 8,864 international, from over 102 countries), 49:51 male:female.

Accommodation: single sex, married, vacation. University residences £30 to £50 a week self-catering. Room in town from £30 to £60 a week.

Entrance requirements: generally Bs and Cs at A level or equivalent qualification.

EFL: IELTS 6.0, TOEFL 5.5 or equivalent.

Foundation: international programme to improve qualifications to entrance requirement standards, includes English language.

Fees: foundation year £5,100 a year, classroom courses £6,200 a year, laboratory courses and postgraduate courses £8,200 a year.

The University of Hull began its life in 1928 and became England's 14th university in 1954. Today there are students from over 102 countries and members of staff from 38 countries on the campus, leading to the feel of an international university. Teaching and research at the university has had an international impact. For example, Hull's Department of Chemistry has developed liquid crystals which are now used worldwide for display systems. The university also prides itself on its expertise in environmental management and business skills; Hull's academics have pioneered roles in cancer and osteo-porosis research. Other developments from the university have included advances in work surface engineering, which is important to the UK manufacturing industry.

Students at The University of Hull

Academic strengths

The university was ranked in the top third of UK universities by *The Times*. Several of the university's departments have been awarded Excellent ratings in teaching quality assessments including areas such as European languages, Southeast Asian studies, history and engineering.

Areas which tend to be popular with international students include business studies, law, engineering and management. The university has various research centres such as the Centre for European Studies in which research is carried out into institutions and politics of the European Union. For those interested in environmental issues, there is an Institute for Environmental Science and Management which provides a focus for interdisciplinary research. The university develops and uses information technology for teaching and learning. For example, the CTI Centre for Modern Languages provides information on computer assisted language learning. There is also a dedicated centre for research in the field of virtual environments.

Student life

Hull is situated in the northeast of England. There are many places to go for entertainment such as pubs, clubs, theatres and shopping. The city centre is only ten minutes by bus from the university. It has good sea and air links to the rest of Europe and easy access to other part of England. Historic cities such as York and Lincoln are within easy reach. The town is safe and combines both the hustle and bustle of a city with a peaceful study environment. The university guarantees accommodation for unaccompanied international students for the duration of their course. The university owns and manages a range of accommodation. Nearly two thirds of students live in university flats, halls of residence and student houses – many of them close to the campus. Study bedrooms in halls of residence have direct access to campus computer networks and the Internet. The students' union has over 120 societies, including a range of sporting activities and a fully-equipped sports and fitness centre. The international office has a dedicated team of staff from five different countries who collectively speak more than seven different languages. The university also has an overseas students adviser, religious chaplaincies, careers advisers and counsellors.

"Study overseas was always my dream and it became a reality when I was offered the Sir Roy Marshall Scholarship to pursue my BEng Electronic Engineering degree at the University of Hull. The university has a beautiful campus, excellent facilities and close, friendly staff and student relationships. I enjoy my course on which I am given plenty of opportunities to learn and improve my , presentations and design troubleshooting skills. This has prepared and equipped me technically for a bright and challenging career in industry. The standard of teaching is high. The department has achieved the maximum score, 24, for the 1998 teaching quality assessment. My stay in Hull has provided me with valuable exposure and a better understanding of the local Yorkshire culture, which has enriched my life. Soon after completion of my degree, I intend to further my postgraduate studies in engineering before starting my career as an electronic engineer."

Don Ri Yuen, Malaysia

INSTITUTE OF EDUCATION
UNIVERSITY OF LONDON

london
london
london

Institute of Education University of London

Write to: The Registry,
Institute of Education,
University of London, 20 Bedford
Way, London WC1H 0AL

Tel: 020 7612 6000

Fax: 020 7612 6097

Email: ma.enquiries@ioe.ac.uk or
doc.enquiries@ioe.ac.uk

Website: www.ioe.ac.uk

Students: 4,421 in 1997/8 (all post-graduate, 400 international, from over 80 countries), 32:68 male:female.

Accommodation: single-sex, married, vacation. University residences from £86 a week catered. Room in town from £60 to £90 a week.

Entrance requirements: normally an approved first degree at second class honours level, some courses require professional experience.

EFL: foundation courses IELTS 5.0, TOEFL 500.

Foundation: 12 week pre-sessional course in English for academic purposes, eight-month English course leading to graduate certificate.

Fees: £7,053 a year.

Founded in 1902 as the 'London Day Training College', the Institute of Education is now a graduate college of the federal University of London. Today it has an international reputation as a centre of educational enquiry. Part of the institute's mission is to train high quality teachers and every year nearly 1,000 graduates undertake one of the institute's Postgraduate Certificate in Education courses offered in partnership with schools and colleges in the London area.

The institute is located in the Bloomsbury area of central London – a district renowned for its tree-lined squares and 17th and 18th century buildings. The main building of the institute was designed by the British architect Sir Denys Lasdun, creator of the Royal National Theatre and Genoa Opera House. A small number of academic and research units are based in Georgian houses in the vicinity.

The Institute of Education

The University of London's union, administrative buildings and library are all close by. So too are the shopping facilities of Oxford Street, Regent Street and Covent Garden and theatres, cinemas, galleries and museums, including the British Museum.

Academic strengths

In recent years the institute has widened the range of award-bearing courses offered from initial teacher training to further professional development and research degree programmes. In the 1996 research assessment exercise, the Institute of Education was one of only two institutions to receive the highest research ranking of 5*. Courses of interest to international students include teaching of English to speakers of other languages (TESOL), comparative education, child development, school effectiveness and policy studies. There is also a variety of short courses available for educational practitioners of all levels.

The institute is planning a Future Learning Centre which will provide the focus for collaborative experimentation in and evaluation of new ways of teaching and learning using developments in information and communication technology. As a forum for debate the institute has in the past hosted lectures on educational issues, delivered by the leaders of the main UK political parties, and a series of debates involving the Chief Inspector of Schools, Members of Parliament and editors of national newspapers.

Student life

The students' union is one of the main social centres of the institute. It is a self-contained unit, consisting of a large common room, with catering and bar facilities, meeting rooms, a shop and the union's offices. It has a number of societies including the African society, the multicultural society, the Hellenic society, the Hong Kong society, the Japanese society and the Latin American society. An annual feature of institute life is the Multicultural Extravaganza, featuring dance and drama from a number of countries with students wearing their national dress.

Some activities are aimed at international students. At the beginning of each academic session there is a free orientation course. For those requiring language tuition, spoken English classes are offered in the autumn and spring terms and writing workshops for research students are held regularly. A 12-week pre-sessional course in English is also available.

Accommodation for students is available in the institute's own hall of residence, the nearby John Adams Hall. Students are also entitled to live in any of the University of London's inter collegiate halls and use the university's medical and dental facilities.

"Immediately after taking a degree in psychology in Brazil, I moved to London in 1983 to undertake the MSc in Educational Psychology at the institute. Being exposed to a huge range of theoretical sources and to a very different culture was an enormously empowering experience. On returning home, I became a researcher and subsequently a lecturer at the Faculty of Education at the Federal University of Pelotas. I missed the institute and was therefore delighted to return as a doctoral student a decade later. My second stay was as rich and as interesting as my first, with the quality of supervision offered being particularly excellent."

Magda Flora Damiani, Brazil

Write to: Undergraduate or Postgraduate Admissions Office, The Registry, University of Kent at Canterbury, Canterbury, Kent CT2 7NZ

Tel: 01227 764000

Fax: 01227 827077

Email: admissions@ukc.ac.uk

Website: www.ukc.ac.uk

Students: 7,185 full-time students in 1998/9 (955 postgraduates, 2,312 international students, from 119 countries).

Accommodation: single, vacation and storage facilities. University residence from £47 a week self-catered and £60 a week catered. Room in town from £45 to £50 a week.

Entrance requirements: 18 to 26 points at A level, 68 to 78 points at European Bacccalaureate, 27 to 35 points at International Baccalaureate or other international qualifications on an equivalent basis.

EFL: TOEFL 580 points, for postgraduate courses 600 points. IELTS written 6.5.

Foundation: Not in lieu of A levels but as a bridging programme. Successful completion guarantees entry.

Fees: classroom courses £6,860 a year, laboratory courses £8,950 a year, law courses £7,300 a year, MBA £9,000 a year and Postgraduate Diploma in Management Studies and Business Studies £8,500 a year.

The University of Kent at Canterbury received its royal charter in 1965 and was one of seven new campuses founded in England in the sixties. The university is built in 300 acres of parkland, on a campus that overlooks the city of Canterbury.

Campus life centres around four colleges each named after distinguished British figures – Darwin, Eliot, Keynes and Rutherford. All students and academic staff belong to a college whether they live on campus or not. They are more than just halls of residence. In addition to living, social and catering facilities, they also house lecture theatres, seminar rooms, computer terminal rooms and each contain at least two of the academic departments. The aim of the college system, arranged around short corridors and staircases, is that students have access to a ready-made community from the moment that they arrive. A master heads each college and, along with the

University of Kent

porters and other staff, ensures that the college runs smoothly.

The campus is within walking distance of the town centre, that boasts a cathedral, medieval and Roman buildings and remains. Central London is just ninety minutes away by road or rail and the airports there are within easy reach. The Channel ports and tunnel are only 30 minutes away.

Academic strengths

The University of Kent at Canterbury offers over 300 degree programmes in 40 different subjects. The 19 departments are divided into three faculties: Humanities; Social Science; and Science, Technology and Medical Studies. Degrees can be single honours, joint honours involving two disciplines or multi-disciplinary honours. Many programmes offer the opportunity to study computing or learn a language, to take a year abroad, or in some cases, a year in industry.

The university's computing, library and language learning facilities are constantly being developed and expanded. The computing laboratory offers computing services to all areas of the campus including networks within the library, laboratories, colleges and a third of student residences.

Student life

The campus provides many opportunities for recreation. The sports centre has good facilities and offers coaching in many sports, both indoor and outdoor. The university has its own theatre that is a focus for professional, amateur and student drama; the region's only film theatre; its own orchestra; small music groups; jazz club; and choir. The students' union organises the central campus shop, and provides catering outlets in its purpose-built union building. The latter also houses "The Venue" nightclub.

The university has a multi-cultural flavour with international students from over 100 nationalities representing 25 per cent of the full-time student body. Baptist, Catholic, Methodist, Pentecostal, United Reformed Church, Society of Friends, Orthodox, Jewish and Muslim faiths are all represented at the university. International students benefit from airport pick-ups, an international students' orientation programme, freshers' week, a host family weekend and a free study centre with English language support. There are a limited number of scholarships for international students, a small hardship fund and some external scholarships.

"My three years at Kent were filled with all sorts of experiences – all of which contributed to my growth and learning progress. I learnt that attending university is not merely to do with a 'paper chase' – a great deal more lies beneath the surface. It had to do with adapting, coping, overcoming... or more simply put, surviving! Life at Kent was a degree programme in itself: where we were exposed to, and learned about, the many idiosyncrasies of the multitude of races and cultures that made up the population of UKC. It taught us tolerance, compassion, camaraderie - ingredients which prepare us to face the challenges of the 'big bad world'. This was especially useful to me doing the English studies degree which involved the study of a culture, language and way of life foreign to my own. My present job in Malaysia requires me to travel a fair deal; I am hoping that it will take me 'home' to Kent in the not-too-distant future."

Intan Darlinn Mahammad, Malaysia

King Alfred's Winchester

Write to: International Admissions, King Alfred's College, Sparkford Road, Winchester, Hants SO22 4NR

Tel: 01962 827235

Fax: 01962 827406

Email: international@wkac.ac.uk

Website: www.wkac.ac.uk

Students: 4,614 1998/9 (464 postgraduate, 140 international, from over 30 countries), 25:75 male:female.

Accommodation: single rooms or flats for married couples. College residences from £59 a week self-catered, £79 a week catered. Room in town from £55 to £75 a week.

Entrance requirements: 14 points at A level.

EFL: IELTS 6.0, TOEFL 560.

Foundation: Pre-sessional English language programmes.

Fees: £5,300 to £7,210 a year, postgraduate courses £5,350 to £7,210 a year.

King Alfred's College was founded by the Church of England in 1840 for the training of schoolmasters. Although teacher training still continues at the college today, the range of courses on offer has expanded to include subjects ranging from humanities and performing arts to business and psychology. King Alfred's runs its courses in association with the University of Southampton, which functions as the awarding body for its degrees. However, the college aims to award degrees and eventually to become the University of Winchester.

King Alfred's is a small, compact college and all accommodation is on campus or within a few hundred metres of the main buildings. Its size helps to encourage a sense of community amongst the students. Situated on a wooded hillside overlooking Winchester, students have easy access to the cathedral city. For centuries Winchester was the 'capital' of Wessex, and many monuments and historic buildings still remain. Today it is central to Hampshire's arts scene and it has theatres, a gallery,

King Alfred's College graduation ceremony

a museum and the Guildhall, which holds concerts, recitals and college balls. There are also pubs, shops and sports facilities including a swimming pool in the city. Southampton, a major shopping centre on the south coast is 15 minutes' away by rail or road and the New Forest, Stonehenge and the South Downs can be found in the surrounding countryside.

Academic strengths

Both undergraduate and postgraduate programmes are available at the college. Subject areas of interest to international students include business management and communications, dance, drama, English, sports studies, tourism and heritage management and psychology.

King Alfred's has good facilities to support students' studies. The college library covers three floors and houses a collection of almost 200,000 books and other resources and receives over 600 journals. There are study places for more than 450 readers, some of which are equipped with computers linked to the college network. Further PCs offering a range of software, access to the Internet and individual email are located in the college's IT Centres. Staff are on hand to provide assistance if needed and all students are provided with basic IT training. Photographic, video and audio equipment may be loaned. There is a fully-equipped television studio and post-production support is provided by non-linear video edit suites and video copying facilities.

Student life

King Alfred's caters for international students in a number of different ways. All international students are guaranteed accommodation on campus and receive a pre-arrival handbook. For international students there is an orientation programme at the start of their studies and free English language support for the duration of the study programme. All international students are allocated a personal tutor, and an international student welfare adviser is available to help with non-academic issues. Limited bursary support is also available on a competitive basis.

King Alfred's students' union provides welfare and academic advice to students. It also plays a role in providing leisure and recreation. Sport is organised by the athletic union and facilities include tennis courts, playing fields and a dance studio. Societies of the union include performing arts, film, radio, archaeology and an international student society.

"Although media, film and drama are closely related, they are still very different areas of study; the skills for which complement and contrast to create a varied and interesting course. We are encouraged to support our lectures with personal learning, and the college has many facilities which are beneficial for media and film students; video and audio equipment, research material and TV and editing suites are readily available. My chosen degree at King Alfred's has given me a far clearer vision of the direction I want my future career to take, and the skills and confidence to achieve these goals."

Jane Slingsby, United Kingdom

KINGSTON
UNIVERSITY

kingston
kingston
kingston

Kingston University

Write to: Student Enquiry and Applicant Services, Kingston University, Cooper House, 40-46 Surbiton Road, Kingston-upon-Thames KT1 2HX

Tel: 020 8547 7053

Fax: 020 8547 7080

Email: int.recruit@kingston.ac.uk

Website: www.kingston.ac.uk

Students: 16,270 in 1999 (3,366 postgraduate, 541 international, from 72 countries), 54:46 male:female.

Accommodation: single, some en suite, vacation. University residences from £50 to £60 a week self-catering. Room in town from £40 to £65 a week.

Entrance requirements: generally Cs at A level or equivalent (BBC for law and architecture, BCC for business studies). 24 to 30 in International Baccalaureate.

EFL: Cambridge Proficiency grade C, IELTS 6.5, TOEFL 550 plus written test grade 5 (computer-based test 213). Summer pre-sessional English courses available.

Foundation: one year course includes English language and chosen specialist subjects. Requires IELTS 4.

Fees: art and design foundation £4,200 a year, classroom courses £6,500 a year, studio-based design courses and some computing and science courses £7,500 a year, laboratory courses £8,000 a year.

The historic town of Kingston-upon-Thames is a busy retail centre with many shops, restaurants and clubs. The university is close to the town centre, which is now protected as a Conservation Area. Hampton Court Palace and the open spaces of Richmond Park are nearby. The university's four campuses are served by a free bus, and the university is only 20 minutes by train from central London and 30 minutes from Heathrow Airport. Kingston was voted the best place to live in the UK in the Guinness Survey 1999.

Academic strengths

Several courses have received maximum scores in recent teaching quality assessments including mechanical, aerospace and production engineering in the Faculty of Technology and surveying, and landscape architecture in the Faculty of Design. In 1999 The Financial Times placed Kingston fourth out of 97 institutions in the UK for teaching standards. Many of the staff have considerable industrial experience and most of Kingston's courses are strongly career-related. More traditional

Kingston Bridge

subjects rated Excellent in the most recent research assessment exercise include English literature and geology.

The Faculty of Business' undergraduate courses include business studies, business with French/German/Spanish, accountancy and finance, business information technology, LLB and law with business. The faculty received an Excellent rating in teaching quality assessments and offers a number of career-related postgraduate courses.

The Faculty of Human Sciences offers courses in business and financial economics as well as its full range of modular courses.

In the Faculty of Healthcare Sciences students of radiography, physiotherapy, nursing and midwifery are taught alongside medical students at St George's Hospital Medical School.

The Faculty of Art and Design covers fields such as architecture, landscape architecture, surveying, urban estate management, fashion, graphic design, fine art and music. International students often start on courses tailored to their individual needs which lead to degree study at the appropriate entry level.

Undergraduate courses range from two-year HNDs, to three-year degrees, four-year sandwich degrees (where the third year is spent in full-time employment) and four-year degrees in science and engineering which incorporate a foundation year.

Student life

Although Kingston takes large numbers of students, each campus aims to have a smaller 'community' feel - with its own library, bar, shop and student restaurant. There is a fully-equipped gymnasium and fitness centre, and the university has its own sports ground nearby. A large health centre on the main campus caters for students' medical needs.

International students follow a orientation programme on arrival to help them prepare for study at the university and adjust to life in the UK. All first-year students are guaranteed accommodation in modern self-catering halls of residence, after which they may move into the university's headed-tenancy housing in and around the town. International students are encouraged to join free English language and study skills classes. Each student is allocated a personal tutor and some courses offer a peer-assisted learning programme where older students take care of new arrivals. An international student adviser is also available to provide guidance and support. The students' union offers a varied sports and social programme.

"This is my final year in BEng (Hons) Electronic Engineering with Computing. I am so pleased that I chose Kingston. There is a really good campus atmosphere and the accommodation is excellent. Kingston is a lively town with plenty to do, but it is cleaner and safer than inner London. Heathrow Airport and central London are both nearby, which is very convenient. Adapting to British study methods was challenging, but the support services offered were brilliant. I felt very welcome and settled in quickly. I particularly benefited from PAL – a system of peer-assisted learning where new undergraduates are helped by second year students. The technical and research resources which are essential for my course are superb; excellent library facilities and no waiting for computer access as there are so many of them available. I am working hard, but really enjoying it and hope eventually to progress to a masters course." **Adeoti Olaiya, Nigeria**

University of Wales, Lampeter

Write to: Recruitment, Marketing and Admissions Department, University of Wales, Lampeter, Ceredigion SA48 7ED

Tel: 01570 423 530/422 351

Fax: 01570 423 530/423 423

Email: RECRUIT@admin.lamp.ac.uk

Website: www.lamp.ac.uk/recruitment

Students: 1,500 in 1998/9 (200 international, from 15 countries), 50:50 male:female.

Accommodation: single-sex, vacation–extra charge, storage facilities. University residences from £40 a week. Room in town from £25 to £45 a week.

Entrance requirements: 14 to 18 points at A level or international equivalent.

EFL: IELTS 6.5, TOEFL 600 to 800.

Foundation: access courses

University of Wales, Lampeter

available, applications considered on individual merit.

Fees: £1,025 a year (EU students); £5,000 a year (non-EU students). Postgraduate courses: £2,675 a year, full time, £1,350 a year, part time (EU students); £6,000 a year, full time, £2,000 a year, part time (non-EU students).

This compact campus is situated within reach of both mountains and the coast, in an area which has one of the lowest crime rates in the UK. The university was founded in 1822, and is situated in the market town of Lampeter, in western Wales. After the ancient universities of Oxford, Cambridge and Scotland, the University of Wales, Lampeter is the oldest university institution in Britain. For over 100 years it was an independent degree–awarding college, known as St David's College; in the 1960s it formed links with the University of Wales. Lampeter is surrounded by countryside, in an area of myth and legend – a cave near to Ystrad Ffin is said to have been the home of Tum Sion Cati, the Welsh Robin Hood. Although many people speak Welsh, all are bilingual, and the road signs are in Welsh and English. The nearest mainline train stations are at Carmarthen and Aberystwyth, and bus services run between these stations and Lampeter.

The nearest international airports are at Cardiff and Birmingham.

Academic strengths

Tuition is one to one, and each student has a personal tutor in their department.

The theology and religious studies course is particularly popular with international students, with research in this area receiving a rating of 4 in the 1996 research assessment exercise. The main university library contains 180,000 books, pamphlets and bound volumes. In addition, there is a research library, known as the 'Founders' Library', which contains books published before 1850. The collection was originally donated by three people, among them Thomas Burgess (Bishop of St David's and subsequently Bishop of Salisbury), who was the founder of St David's College (the precursor to the University of Wales, Lampeter). There is a media centre where video–conferencing on WelshNet and the Internet can take place. The Media Centre and the Department of Geography host new courses in media studies, creative studies and cultural studies.

Student life

Around 60 per cent of students live on campus, mostly in the first and last year of study; accommodation on site is guaranteed for all single first-year undergraduates. Accommodation varies from individually converted houses to purpose-built halls of residence with en suite facilities. Students can choose from over 70 different clubs and societies, or create their own if their particular interest is not covered. There are Rag events to participate in, for charity, and a Student Community Action Group, which works to bridge the gap between 'town' and 'gown' (the university) in the area. The students union bar has recently been extended, and a brand new nightclub venue added. The sports centre on campus includes a multi-gym, and courts for badminton, squash and tennis. There is a health practice adjacent to the campus, for all medical needs. Those students with children can take advantage of the child-care facility on offer, called 'Gwdihws' (pronounced 'goodyhoos', a Welsh word meaning 'Owls'). For those with financial difficulties, the access hardship fund is available on application after registration. There are specific meeting spaces on the campus for those of various religious persuasions, including the Anglican, Greek Orthodox and Roman Catholic faiths. International students benefit from a 'Welcome' week at the beginning of the academic year and English language courses are available.

"Coming from a big and hectic city like Copenhagen to a little quiet town like Lampeter is a big cultural change, at least so it seems at first. When I arrived in Lampeter, everything appeared different; but after just a few weeks, I realised that many things were similar to what I already knew from Denmark. Friends who already studied in Great Britain inspired me to apply here. The procedure was not as complicated as I had expected, actually it was easier to apply through UCAS than it was to apply through KOT in Denmark! There was a genuine interest in me as a student and as a person at Lampeter. It was explained what the University expected from me, and what I, as a foreigner, should be prepared for, to 'survive' the cultural change. The biggest difference was the change of language. After a short period of confusion, English becomes an unconscious part of your daily life. To study in a language which is not your first language is a challenge but also a big opportunity."

Thomas Dahl Jensen, Denmark

LEEDS METROPOLITAN UNIVERSITY

Leeds Metropolitan University

Write to: International Office, Leeds Metropolitan, Calverley Street, Leeds LS1 3HE

Tel: 0113 283 6737

Fax: 0113 283 3129

Email: international@lmu.ac.uk

Website: www.lmu.ac.uk

Students: about 25,000 in 1998/9 (approximately 1,000 from overseas).

Accommodation: university residences from £40 to £60 a week self-catering.

Entrance requirements: all types of qualifications and work experience are considered. IELTS 6.0, TOEFL 550

Foundation: one-year International Foundation Programme, guaranteed entry to many degree programmes on successful completion.

Entry requirements: include

IELTS 4.0/TOEFL 450

Fees: in 1999/2000, classroom courses £6,095 a year, laboratory courses £6,630 a year, MBA £7,700 a year.

Leeds is a popular university city, with plenty of entertainments and interesting historic attractions. It is located mid-way between London and Edinburgh. By train, London is just over two hours away and there are flights from the Leeds/Bradford Airport to many international destinations. As sports fans will know, Leeds is home to Headingley Cricket Ground and Leeds United. Leeds Metropolitan University itself has a long sporting tradition and the sports facilities on campus can be used at very little cost.

Academic strengths

Training people for trades and professions was the task of the 19th

Leeds Metropolitan University

century colleges from which the university has evolved. This tradition lives on today in courses which are designed to equip people for their future careers. Diploma, first-degree and postgraduate courses, as well as research degrees, are offered in the following subject areas; accounting and finance, applied science, architecture and landscape, art and design, built environment, business and management (including MBA), computing, cultural studies, economics, education, engineering, health education, hospitality management, information management, languages (including English as a Foreign Language), law, leisure and sport, professions allied to medicine, social sciences, technology and tourism management. There is also a wide choice of English language courses available throughout the year, short and long, to suit different levels of ability. The MBA and several other master's courses can be completed in one year and some offer a choice of entry in either February or September. There is also a foundation programme which provides successful students with guaranteed entry to a choice of undergraduate courses.

Student life

The shopping facilities in Leeds are excellent and the cost of living is lower than in many other parts of the UK. Leeds is a multicultural city with places of worship for most religions. Leeds Metropolitan University has two campuses. The City Campus is just a five-minute walk from the city centre. The Beckett Park Campus, set in beautiful parkland, is a short bus-ride away. Most student accommodation in Leeds is within easy reach of the two campuses. The options available include modern self-catering flats and an international residence.

Before your course begins, you are invited to a special introduction programme, where you can meet other new students and find out more about Leeds Metropolitan University. And if you need advice or just someone to talk to, the international student development officer is there to help.

During your spare time, you may wish to get involved in one of the student societies which are run by the students' union. These include the Malaysian Society, the Chinese Student's Society and clubs to suit many leisure interests such as walking and football.

"I gained a first-class degree in my BSc (Hons) in Applied Computing at Leeds Metropolitan. After completing a Higher Diploma in Malaysia I chose to top-up my qualification to a degree in one year. This is an option available within several subject areas at the university, including business, hospitality management, electronic engineering and computing. My course was very flexible and allowed me to pursue my own interests by choosing different subjects which suited me. I also selected my own dissertation title which was concerned with educational computing. The lecturers at the university were very supportive and the standard is very high. I'm thrilled to gain a first."

Arokia Mekala Soosay Manickam, Malaysia

Liverpool Hope University College

Write to: CELS, Liverpool Hope University College, Hope Park, Liverpool L16 9JD

Tel: 0151 291 3138

Fax: 0151 291 3836

Email: ashtonb1@hope.ac.uk

Web: www.livhope.ac.uk

Students: 5,000 in 1999 (697 postgraduate, 3 per cent from overseas, from over 20 countries), 30:70 male:female.

Accommodation: single sex, vacation. University residences from £47 to £65 a week. Room in town from £45 a week.

Entrance requirements: generally C grades in two A levels or equivalent.

EFL: Cambridge Advanced or Proficiency. IELTS 6.0, TOEFL 560.

Fees: English Language Studies £3,500 a year, all undergraduate and postgraduate courses £4,000 a year for tuition, and £6,200 a year including accommodation.

Foundation: none available

The key word at Liverpool Hope is change. Over the past two years the entire college, from its physical structure to the contents of its curriculum and the administrative team, has been given a complete overhaul. Buildings are being expanded and modernised, and better facilities for physically impaired students have been installed. Even the common room, which used to belong to the teaching staff, has been given to the students. Hope now possesses a nursery which serves its high proportion of mature students. It also owns a cyber-cafe, 'Hope on the Waterfront', at Liverpool's Albert Dock, which acts as its shop window.

Academic strengths

The college was founded in the 19th century as a group of three teacher training colleges for women (two Catholic and one Anglican) and in 1975 it diversified into BA and BSc courses. It is a University College, whose degrees are accredited by the University of

Students at Liverpool Hope

Liverpool. Today it retains its commitment to education and its BEd courses form a fundamental part of its curriculum – about half of Hope's students are studying for the BEd or the MEd (its strongest postgraduate course). It is currently developing into a liberal arts-style college with a strong social science/arts base, offering theology, women's studies and sports as some of its options. It offers mainly combined degrees for which students can choose from a stimulating range of topics: American and European studies, art and design, languages, geography and history, information technology, music, drama, biology and mathematics. Its full-time master's courses include information technology, ecology and environmental studies and urban regeneration and management.

Hope aims to have an approach to education which is best described as holistic. Students constantly reiterate this fact, and seem genuinely to be enjoying their experiences there. The college is especially concerned to provide education to those who are otherwise unable to benefit from it, so the entrance requirements are entirely flexible in order to widen access.

The Centre for English Language Studies (CELS) offers full-time English language tuition for international students who wish to improve their language competence before or during their degrees.

The academic year is divided into two semesters, starting in September and February. Courses are based on modules and there is a credit transfer scheme. There is a new, purpose-built library and learning resource facilities with excellent IT facilities.

Student life

Hope is a small college of about 5,000 students. It occupies a single campus in a residential suburb of Liverpool, about 15 minutes' drive from the city centre. It is a vibrant and lively place. The students' union has recently benefited from sizeable financial investment. There is an emphasis on sport at Hope, which has champion-level rugby, netball and soccer teams. There is a new floodlit outdoor pitch for hockey and other team games. The college also has an outdoor education centre at Plas Caerdeon in North Wales, which is used as much for social as for course-related activities.

"Studying and living in the UK was my dream and finally it came true. I attended English classes at Liverpool Hope with about ten students from different countries such as Korea, the Middle East, the Czech Republic, Poland, France, Germany and more. We often discussed our culture differences in class, which I think worked towards the benefit of my course in Sociology and European Studies. This course has just started and I am quite excited about it because it is much more interesting than I expected. I'm also looking forward to taking optional modules in other European languages, and doing community-based work experience. I am staying in accommodation off campus, sharing a big house with 11 other students from the all over the UK. I usually go out at the weekend and my favourite place at the moment is a new jazz cafe in the Albert Dock. I am really enjoying studying and living here and am glad that I can spend three more years at this friendly college."

Mariko Yamada, Japan

LONDON GUILDHALL
UNIVERSITY

London Guildhall University

Write to: Course Enquiry Unit, London Guildhall University, 133 Whitechapel High Street, London E1 7QA

Tel: 020 7320 1616

Fax: 020 7320 1163

Email: enqs@lgu.ac.uk

Website: www.lgu.ac.uk

Students: 14,639 in 1998/99 (1,719 postgraduate, 1,039 international, from 94 countries outside the EU), 46:54 male:female.

Accommodation: single-sex, vacation, storage facilities. University residences from £51 to £72 a week self-catered, from £74 a week catered; room in town from £55 to £80 a week.

Entrance requirements: generally two A level passes plus two other subjects at GCSE, or three A level passes plus one other subject at GCSE. 24 points in International Baccalaureate, 60 per cent in European Baccalaureate.

EFL: IELTS 6.0, TOEFL 550.

Foundation: University's English Language Centre offers foundation course for international students (one-year), exam preparation classes for Cambridge Advanced, Cambridge Proficiency and LCCI Business English exams, Foundation Certificate in English as a Foreign Language (one, two and three terms) and Cambridge First Certificate course (one, two and three terms).

Fees: HND and BA/BSc courses £6,430 a year. Supplements on some studio and laboratory-based courses.

In 1998 London Guildhall University celebrated its 150th anniversary. Its roots go back to 1848 when the Bishop of London, Bishop Blomfield, called upon the clergy to set up evening classes to improve the moral, intellectual and spiritual condition of young men in the metropolis. In 1861 the classes were reconstituted as the City of London College with the introduction of commercial and technical subjects. Today, over a century later, London Guildhall University is the only higher education institution located within the 'square mile' of the City of London. Its six teaching centres spread into Aldgate in East London and include historical sites such as the Jewry Street site built on the remains of the wall which the Romans built to protect Londinium. The university's Business School, in the

Jewry Street, London Guildhall University

City's financial district, is one of the largest in Europe. Alumni of the university include Vic Reeves, comedian, Mark Thatcher, son of Margeret Thatcher, and Wee Choo Keong, MP of Central Kuala Lumpur. The present patron is HRH Prince Philip.

Academic strengths

Several of the university's schools were originally private specialist colleges which means there is a diverse range of subjects on offer including courses in fine art, international relations, business and commerce, textile furnishing and interiors, musical instrument technology, business information technology, languages, law and silversmithing. In teaching quality assessments the university received 23 out of 24 for art and design, 20 out of 24 for materials technology in 1998 and an Excellent rating for social policy and administration in 1994.

Amongst the university's resources is its integrated learning resources centre which combines on one site computing, library and media services. It also has a seminar room, group study rooms, and an exhibition space. Other facilities are spread throughout the university's various sites. There are three libraries in total and the specialist Fawcett Library – a research library on the history of women and the women's movement.

Student life

On arrival international students can attend an orientation course to help them settle into student life in Britain.

This is a three-day residential programme and includes an introduction to the different university departments, tours of the campus and social events for both staff and students. During the course of their study they have the support of both the university and students' union international welfare officers. International students also have automatic membership of International House – a centre and club in London's West End offering facilities such as bars, restaurants, study rooms, a disco and a travel club. They are also guaranteed accommodation in halls of residence. Students requiring language tuition can take English language courses at the university. There is a university chaplaincy which is open to students of all faiths and spiritual traditions. An Anglican chaplain is based at the university and is joined by a visiting Roman Catholic chaplain and a Free Church chaplain. There are separate Muslim prayer rooms. For students with financial difficulties there is some limited help available.

"I have always been very interested in antique furniture and being a very hands-on person I wanted to do a degree where I could use these interests/skills. My careers tutor told me about the restoration and conservation degree at London Guildhall University; this sounded ideal as I could learn more about antiques and work with the materials used to restore and conserve them. Being in London too was very exciting as I could visit the many museums that are full of the artefacts I adore! The skills the course has taught me are fantastic. I could never have experienced this in a German University. I did my placement at a small furniture museum in East London where I worked on an eighteenth-century chair and some French picture frames. I have learnt so much doing this course. I would recommend it to anyone interested in learning the skills that breathe new life into antiques for future generation to enjoy."

Charlotte Hagemann, Germany

Loughborough University

Loughborough University

Write to: International Office, Student Recruitment and Admissions, Loughborough University, Loughborough, Leicestershire LE11 3TU

Tel: 01509 222 233

Fax: 01509 223 905

Email: international-office@lboro.ac.uk

Website: www.lboro.ac.uk

Students: 11,513 in 1998/9 (2,621 postgraduate, 818 international, from over 100 countries), 67:33 male:female.

Accommodation: single sex, married/family, vacation, storage facilities. University residences from £35 to £45 a week self-catered, £60 to £75 catered. Room in town from £32 to £49 a week.

Entrance requirements: for undergraduates combination of GCSE and A level passes, either in five subjects, with two at A level, or in four subjects with three at A level or international equivalent.

EFL: for undergraduates Certificate of Proficiency in English grade C, Certificate in Advanced English grade B. GCSE English grade C, IELTS 6.5, TOEFL 550; for postgraduates GCSE English, IELTS 6.5, TOEFL 550.

Foundation: one-year, full-time or two years, part-time for science and engineering or art and design.

Fees: classroom courses £6,465 a year, laboratory courses £8,461 a year.

Loughborough University dates from 1909, when a small technical institute was established in Loughborough town in the east Midlands. The college soon earned a national reputation for sporting achievement and joined the athletics union in 1929. By 1952 it had grown into four colleges specialising in technology, engineering, teacher training and art and design. The colleges of technology were granted university status in 1966

The town of Loughborough is about half an hour by car from Nottingham and Leicester and about an hour and a half from London by train. East Midlands airport is also close by. Once noted for lace-making and bell founding,

Loughborough University

Loughborough is now a market town with some light industry. The heart of the English countryside is close by; Charnwood Forest is close to the town and the neighbouring Peak District is popular for climbing, hang gliding and hiking.

Academic strengths

The university is divided into the faculties of engineering, science, and social sciences and humanities. In teaching quality assessments the university scored 22 or 23 out of 24 in several areas including electronic and electrical engineering (1997), mechanical, aeronautical and manufacturing engineering (1997) and drama, dance and cinematics (1997). In the 1996 research assessment exercise, Loughborough was awarded a 5 for research into professions allied to medicine, built environment, sociology, European studies, library and information management, and sports subjects.

The university's work with industry and commerce won Loughborough the Queen's Anniversary Prize in 1994, in recognition of teamwork with British Aerospace and Rolls-Royce. Sandwich degree students at the university can also often arrange their professional training outside of the UK. Academic facilities at the university include the Pilkington Library, containing books, journals and CD-ROMs, and the university's computing suites, to which students have access 24 hours a day.

Student life

Facilities on the campus include indoor and outdoor sports facilities, an arts centre, a free medical centre and a students' union building incorporating four banks, a dentist, an optician and several shops. English language is a concern for many students and the English language unit organises pre-sessional courses before the start of each academic year. Alongside English language tuition these include study skills and an orientation programme to help students settle into the town. Free coaches run from Heathrow Airport to the campus before each academic year starts. Facilities for worship include a Muslim prayer room and a chaplaincy, which can put students in touch with groups of other faiths. A number of scholarships and bursaries are available for students from specific countries and for those who perform well in such areas as music, sports, science and engineering.

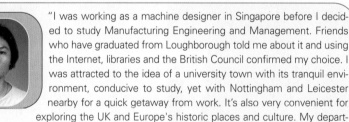

"I was working as a machine designer in Singapore before I decided to study Manufacturing Engineering and Management. Friends who have graduated from Loughborough told me about it and using the Internet, libraries and the British Council confirmed my choice. I was attracted to the idea of a university town with its tranquil environment, conducive to study, yet with Nottingham and Leicester nearby for a quick getaway from work. It's also very convenient for exploring the UK and Europe's historic places and culture. My department places a lot of emphasis on group work. The lecturing style aims to encourage self-learning and research amongst students, whilst lecturers provide a very rewarding and supportive environment. Living in halls has given me valuable exposure to British culture and there is a good mix of international students. Different cultures, traditions, recipes and food are often exchanged during meals. As well as getting a good engineering degree from a well-recognised university, the experience of being an overseas student has been fascinating." **_Lui Ching Dawn Lim, Malaysia_**

LSE
THE LONDON SCHOOL
OF ECONOMICS AND
POLITICAL SCIENCE ■

The London School of Economics & Political Science

Write to: Student Recruitment Office, London School of Economics, Houghton Street, London WC2A 2AE

Tel: 020 7955 6750

Fax: 00 7955 7421

Email: stu.rec@lse.ac.uk

Website: www.lse.ac.uk

Students: 7,137 in 1998/9 (3,253 undergraduate, 3,884 graduates and 4,542 international, from 130 countries), 56:44 male:female.

Accommodation: single sex, married, vacation, storage facilities. University residences £40 to £90 a week self-catered/catered; room in town from £60 a week.

Entrance requirements: for undergraduates, AAB-BCC at A level, International Baccalaureate 34 to 38; for postgraduates, second class honours degree from good university.

EFL: for undergraduate IELTS 7.0; for postgraduate IELTS 6.5, TOEFL 603.

Foundation: not applicable.

Fees: undergraduate courses £9,072 a year, postgraduate courses £9,360 a year.

The London School of Economics and Political Science (LSE) is unique in the UK in its concentration on teaching and research across the full range of the social, political and economic sciences. It was founded in 1895 by Beatrice and Sidney Webb, founding members of the Fabian Society and became part of the federal University of London (UL) in 1900. Today LSE is one of the largest institutions within UL. With over half of the school's students coming from overseas, LSE has a particularly large international student community. Alumni include MPs and members of the House of Lords, 26 current or former heads of government around the world and figures such as George Soros, Romano Prodi and Mick Jagger.

LSE is located in Holborn, central London, an area lying between the West End and the City. The British Library, the University of London's Senate House library and smaller specialist

LSE

libraries are within easy reach of the school. Students naturally benefit from the wider social and cultural opportunities and travel connections of London.

Academic strengths

The school teaches more than just economics and political science. Teaching is carried out through 18 academic departments and 26 research centres and institutes. While degrees are awarded through the University of London, the school has total autonomy over the content and structure of its degree courses, some of which involve intercollegiate collaboration within the federal university. In previous teaching quality assessments LSE was awarded an "excellent" in anthropology, economic history, information systems, international history, law, management, operational research and social policy. In the most recent research exercise, LSE achieved the rating of 5 or 5* in 13 subject areas including accounting, economics and international relations.

There is a range of facilities to aid students' study at LSE. The British Library of Political and Economic Science is the working library of the school and also serves as a national collection of material for research. It is one of the largest libraries in the world devoted exclusively to the economic and social sciences. The school is committed to ensuring that staff and students have access to necessary IT tools and support.

Student life

LSE has various support networks for its students. For either academic or personal advice and support, students consult personal tutors. Students can find three chaplains – Roman Catholic, Church of England and Free Church – and a Rabbi at the school. There is also an Islamic prayer room and student societies for all major religions. In 1998 the school made available some £1.2 million in entrance awards to self-financed undergraduate and postgraduate students of all nationalities. Additional scholarships are available for students from particular countries or taking particular courses. Both the school and the students union run hardship funds. As members of UL union, students have access to all the university's facilities including health and dental care, counselling services and the students' union itself, which has bars, cafes, a gym and a swimming pool. There is pre-sessional English language support, and ongoing academic support available.

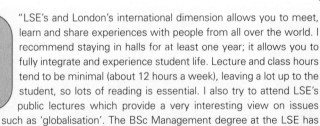

"LSE's and London's international dimension allows you to meet, learn and share experiences with people from all over the world. I recommend staying in halls for at least one year; it allows you to fully integrate and experience student life. Lecture and class hours tend to be minimal (about 12 hours a week), leaving a lot up to the student, so lots of reading is essential. I also try to attend LSE's public lectures which provide a very interesting view on issues such as 'globalisation'. The BSc Management degree at the LSE has provided me with significant business knowledge and access to management based careers where I can use my skills."

Gursheen Khandari

University of Luton

Write to: Tim Gutsell, International Office, University of Luton, Park Square, Luton LU1 3JU

Tel: 01582 489 346

Fax: 01582 486 260

Email: international-office@luton.ac.uk

Website: www.luton.ac.uk

Students: 15,000 in 1998/9 (225 postgraduate, 520 international, from 110 countries), 47:53 male:female.

Accommodation: single-sex, vacation, storage facilities. University residences from £55 a week self-catering. Room in town £40 a week.

Entrance requirements: 14 points minimum at A level or international equivalent.

EFL: IELTS 6, TOEFL 550.

Foundation: full range of foundation courses at undergraduate and postgraduate levels.

Fees: undergraduate courses £5,400 to £5,950 a year, postgraduate courses £4,950 to £6,200 a year.

Luton's situation means that London is easily accessible, by road, rail and air. There is an international airport just three miles from the university campus. The University of Luton has students across four faculties – the Luton Business School, Health Care and Social Studies, Humanities, and Science, Technology and Design. Facilities are modern, and the university has a compact, town centre location. Those wishing to visit the University of Luton can arrange to have a tour. Luton is an industrial town surrounded by countryside. It has several venues for the arts, including St George's Theatre, Luton Museum, the Art Gallery, a multiplex cinema, and the Stockwood Living Craft Museum. The Arndale Centre houses over 120 large department stores and smaller shops, and there is also a covered market just across the road from the university. The population of Luton is multinational; facilities include a mosque and worship facilities for many faiths. Halal food and other ethnic cuisines are widely available.

The Learning Resources Building

Academic strengths

The university has expanded in recent years, accompanied by investment in new resources for teaching, learning and other student support services. More than £40 million has been spent on the development programme, on new halls of residence, a design studio, a media studio, a computer centre, a learning resources centre and a refurbishment programme for the research centre. The degree scheme is modular, allowing students to create programmes of study to suit their professional and academic needs. Courses have a strong vocational emphasis. The learning resources centre has traditional library and audio-visual facilities, as well as modern electronic systems. Through a connection to SuperJANET (the United Kingdom's higher education and research network) users can reach the Internet and access information and communications world-wide. There is a studio at Park Square with broadcast-standard facilities for editing video material. There is a computerised caption generator and extensive digital effects. Foreign language programmes are received through a satellite dish. International students may take English language support modules as part of the full-time degree or diploma programme. Additionally, there are part-time evening English language courses available.

Student life

The students' union offers a range of clubs and societies to cater for most interests. There is a union bar and nightclub, and a subsidised minibus service. The annual May Ball is the biggest student ball in the country, catering for 6,000 students. There are a range of sports teams; in 1998 the University of Luton beat 80 per cent of other universities in the UK in team sports. There is an international student society and the town of Luton offers worship facilities for all faiths. A range of different ethnic cuisines is available locally. International students benefit from a dedicated induction programme. An airport pick-up service is available on request. There is a team of staff to support international students on all welfare and academic issues. The university is associated with a local medical practice; a free and confidential counselling service is also available. Those students with children can make use of nursery links in the town. The accommodation office organises the allocation of places in university halls of residence located within easy walking distance, and they help those looking for accommodation independently. There are several university managed properties.

"I am a first year BSc (Hons) Architecture student. My origins are Armenian – my grandparents emigrated to Bulgaria in the 1950s. I have spent most of my life in Sofia, Bulgaria. A friend in Montreal, Canada who teaches architecture recommended I try Luton as she had heard it was very good. The course is fascinating – it grabs you. The studio is spacious and you get the opportunity to meet and discuss issues with students from all three levels. The lecturers are excellent and very supportive. Socially, the culture here is to go out at 9pm and be back by midnight. I'm used to starting at midnight! Also I don't get a lot of spare time for socialising, as there are so many projects; but you accept this as being part of the course."

Susan Haroutunian, Bulgaria

the
MANCHESTER
METROPOLITAN
UNIVERSITY

manchester
manchester
manchester

Manchester Metropolitan University

Write to: Dr C D Rogers, Manchester Metropolitan University, All Saints, Manchester M15 6BH

Tel: 0161 247 1022

Fax: 0161 247 6310

Email: C.D.Rogers@mmu.ac.uk

Website: www.mmu.ac.uk

Students: 31,000 in 1997/8 (5,527 postgraduates, 2,195 international, from 93 countries), 43:57 male:female.

Accommodation: single-sex, married/family, vacation – extra charge, storage facilities. University residences from £42 to £52 a week self-catered, £62 to £65 a week catered. Room in town from £33 to £45 a week.

Entrance requirements: wide variation from course to course.

EFL: IELTS 6.0, traditional TOEFL 550, computer based TOEFL 213.

Foundation: Art and Design Foundation course leads to most degrees in art and design; Science and Engineering foundation stage is 'year 0' for large number of science and engineering degrees.

Fees: undergraduate classroom courses £6,560 a year, laboratory courses £7,100 a year. Postgraduate classroom courses £7,100 a year, laboratory courses £7,656 a year.

Manchester, with its 2.5 million inhabitants, is a cosmopolitan city with over 50,000 students studying at universities and colleges. Manchester is hosting the Commonwealth Games in 2002. A major construction initiative is providing the city with some of the best sporting facilities in the country. The compact city centre ensures easy access to facilities and amenities, and the city isn't far from the Peak District, Pennines, Yorkshire Dales, Lake District and North Wales.

Manchester is also known as being a city of entertainment. Its large student population has a wide choice of bars, clubs, comedy and music venues. With regard to musical talent, The Smiths, Happy Mondays, Stone Roses, Simply Red, M-People, Take That and the Bee Gees all started out in Manchester.

The city also houses many theatres, art galleries and Britain's first African and Caribbean Arts Centre, and over 20 cinemas. The university is spread out over seven campuses, five in the Manchester area and two in Cheshire.

Manchester Metropolitan University campus

UNIVERSITIES AND COLLEGES

Academic strengths

Manchester Metropolitan University offers 400 courses, many of which are practical in nature, equipping students with transferable skills valued by employers. The university also has links with industry, business, and professional bodies – many staff members are involved in applied research, and have business backgrounds. There is a range of courses that are popular with international students, including accounting, law, art and design, librarianship, business, and hotel and catering. Students also have the opportunity to study in the USA or Australia in year two.

The university works to improve its facilities for students. There has recently been extensive refurbishment and new building on the university's campuses. This includes split level library facilities, lecture theatres, seminar rooms, new laboratories, new design studios for the Art and Design faculty, and a purpose-built Faculty of Humanities and Social Science.

Seven site libraries and language labs hold over a million print and electronic materials. Students can reserve and renew books on-line, and search a number of bibliographic databases either from the drop-in centres or from home. The full text of many of the articles referenced are also on-line.

Student life

The students' union hosts a range of services for the student community. In addition to providing a busy entertainment schedule for students, including comedy nights, live music and club nights, the union also offers a welfare service, minibus service for women, and several bars and shops.

The union also organises over 80 clubs and societies. The Athletic Union, together with the University Sport and Recreational Unit co-ordinates over 45 sports clubs ranging from water polo to badminton. International students are welcomed to the university with airport and station pick-ups and an orientation week at the beginning of term. Pre-sessional English language courses are also offered to international students.

The university provides a meeting/prayer space for Jewish, Muslim and Christian students. The city of Manchester is a multicultural, multi-faith society and students of other religions will, more than likely, be able to contact members for worship.

"Leaving Kenya, my friends and family to study in Manchester was one of the hardest decisions I've had to make. I am a Business Studies student at Manchester Metropolitan University (MMU). I believe in taking every opportunity as it comes along, and my degree has offered me many. In my second year, I went to Flinders University, South Australia. I travelled around Adelaide and I also visited Melbourne and Sydney. I loved the people and the wide variety of culture in Australia, and have made a promise to myself to return. MMU also provided a student work placement. This involved a marketing role at Siemens, a large company based in Manchester. This placement has given me the advantage of having a whole year's valuable work experience. Living so far away from home has made me more independent and responsible and I have made many friends. I am glad I was strong enough to leave home and mum's cooking."

Natasha Montet, Kenya

THE UNIVERSITY
of MANCHESTER

manchester
manchester
manchester

The University of Manchester

Write to: Kate Cohoon, International Office, Beyer Building, The University of Manchester, Oxford Road, Manchester M13 9PL

Tel: 0161 275 2059

Fax: 0161 275 2058

Email: international.unit@man.ac.uk

Website: www.man.ac.uk

Students: 23,496 in 1998/99 (5,471 postgraduate, 2,570 international, from over 130 countries), 48:52 male:female.

Accommodation: single sex, married, vacation – sometimes extra charge. Storage facilities. University residences from £43 to £57 a week self-catered, from £75 a week catered.

Entrance requirements: vary according to subject, generally three high grades at A level.

EFL: Cambridge Certificate of Proficiency in English Grade C. GCSE English Language Grade C, IELTS average 7.0 (not less than 6.0 in any one component), TOEFL 550.

Foundation: none on campus. Two available at City College, Manchester for entry to science and engineering programmes or economics and social studies.

Fees: classroom courses £6,800 a year, laboratory courses £9,000 a year, clinical courses £16,500 a year.

The University of Manchester, founded in 1851, was one of the first 'redbrick', or civic, universities in England. Over the years several major scientific and technological advances have been made here including the world's first working prototypes of the computer in 1948 and Rutherford's work leading to the splitting of the atom. The university occupies a compact campus site, half a mile to the south of the centre of Manchester.

The city itself is relatively large and cosmopolitan (it has a population of over 500,000). Manchester is particularly renowned for its club and music scene. However, other tastes are catered for; it is home to two symphony

University of Manchester, Main building

UNIVERSITIES AND COLLEGES

orchestras – the Hallé and the BBC Philharmonic. Recently the city has undergone rejuvenation through public and private projects, such as the Bridgewater Concert Hall and the Metrolink tram system, and this cultural and economic revival has been recognised internationally by Manchester being given the opportunity to host the Commonwealth Games in 2002.

Academic strengths

The university is divided into eight academic areas: the faculties of art, business administration, economic and social studies, education, law, medicine, (including dentistry and nursing), science and engineering and the School of Biological Sciences. In the recent teaching quality assessments the university scored Excellent in several areas, including, law in 1993/4, business and management studies and computer science in 1994 and anthropology, music and geography in 1994/5.

Among the university's study facilities is the John Rylands University library. This is the third largest university library in the country and houses more than 3.5 million books. The library also distributes electronic information resources across the campus via the computer networks which are available 24 hours a day.

Student life

Manchester has a number of services in place for international students. Before the start of term students can be picked up at airports and railway stations. A four-day residential course for new students is then available to help students settle in and meet people. The International Student Welfare Officer and Welfare Advisor also organise a welcome desk for the first two weeks of the term and then later host a welcome reception event for all new international students. The society also runs a hospitality scheme, giving international students the opportunity to meet and briefly stay with local families.

Manchester University's students' union has welfare and advice services and organises a variety of social events through its societies, which number over 100. Societies include religious and national groups and students have access to two chapels – one Roman Catholic, the other covering all denominations. Two large indoor sports centres include gymnasiums, swimming pools, tennis courts and football pitches. The university also has a student health and counselling service.

"The University of Manchester is one of the best places to get a good education. I heard about my course from my brother who graduated with a BA (Econ) from here. He has gone on to become a very successful chartered accountant back home. My course is very demanding. It is difficult to stay on top of things, but everyone gets a lot of assistance from the academic personnel whose greatest concern is about the students' progress. Combining the above with the campus facilities, the people and the city itself, I would say that the University of Manchester was the best choice I could have made."

Apollo Athanasiades, Greece

MIDDLESEX
UNIVERSITY

Middlesex University

Write to: Admissions Enquiries, Middlesex University, White Hart Lane, London N17 8HR

Tel: 020 8362 5000

Fax: 020 8362 5649

Email: admissions@mdx.ac.uk

Website: www.mdx.ac.uk

Students: 22,000 full-time in 1998 (3,000 postgraduates, 3,400 international, from over 100 countries), 48:52 male:female.

Accommodation: single, single-sex, vacation. University residences from about £50 a week. Room in town from about £50 to £65 a week.

Entrance requirements: generally two or three GCSEs plus two or three A level passes, but a wide range of educational qualifications and experience is considered. International Baccalaureate pass.

EFL: Cambridge Advanced English, TOEFL 550, IELTS 6.0.

Foundation: international foundation course – see EFL chapter.

Fees: international foundation course £4,750 a year, art, design, performing arts £7,200 a year, other subjects £6,650 a year.

Building on its 19th century origins, Middlesex is now one of the largest universities in the UK offering lifelong learning to a diverse range of students from over a hundred countries around the world. As well as a broad range of undergraduate and postgraduate programmes, there are opportunities for summer, semester and year-long study.

Middlesex is located in London's pleasant northern suburbs, almost in the country yet only 35 minutes by underground from central London. Students are based at one of seven major campuses, depending on their study programme. Campuses range in architectural style from modern centres to period buildings. Each campus has its own learning resource centre, including

Middlesex University

modern libraries, IT equipment, language centres and media facilities all aiming to provide a conducive environment for effective study.

Academic strengths

The School of Art, Design and Performing Arts offers many programmes; pioneering courses in complementary medicine have been developed by the School of Nursing Studies; and the School of Social Science runs a criminology research centre. The Middlesex University Business School MBA carries AMBA accreditation and the School of Computing Studies has developed a portfolio of courses such as the new Masters in Ecommerce as well as innovative courses in computing/design. During five weeks in July and August, more than 1,000 students take credit-bearing courses in an extensive range of subjects offered by the Summer School and Middlesex operates work-based learning centres in Cyprus and Hong Kong. Degrees normally take three years but international students can add a one-year foundation course in intensive English study skills combined with courses in their chosen field. Although most international students come to Middlesex to obtain a degree, many also attend professional short courses or study for credit towards home degrees through study abroad arrangements offering a semester or year at Middlesex. Academic study can also be integrated with work experience through internships undertaken alongside taught courses, while sandwich years usually involve a full year's placement.

Student life

Each campus provides many ways to relax and enjoy the lighter side of university life; discos at Trent Park, tennis in Tottenham, a new sports centre at Hendon. A packed social calendar at every site, organised by the students' union, also offers many opportunities to mix. From arrival to degree ceremony, students are looked after by academic tutors and welfare and other services. The university guarantees all international students, including postgraduates, accommodation on campus for their first year; and students should have no difficulty finding university-recommended accommodation in the following years.

The orientation programme is planned to introduce students to London. There are outings and social events throughout the year. Middlesex has set up regional offices in five cities across the world (Hong Kong, Kuala Lumpur, New Delhi, Rio de Janeiro and Tel Aviv) to provide counselling and guidance for intending students.

"As an undergraduate, I studied degrees in communications and psychology at the University of Costa Rica. The university has an exchange programme with Middlesex and I won a bursary to study for an MA in Interactive Media from which I transferred to an MPhil. Studying and researching here has been a very intensive and interesting experience. The content and methods of teaching have been explorative and very well organised. On the MA we had guest lecturers from many different professional areas. This made the teaching really rich and gave me a panoramic view of the industry. For my MPhil I'm looking at ways of enhancing the role of the user in interactive narratives. When I return to Costa Rica, I'm hoping to set up a masters degree like the Middlesex one."

Mari Lopardo-Solano, Costa Rica

NAPIER UNIVERSITY
EDINBURGH

Napier University

Write to: The International Office, Old Craig, Craighouse Campus, Edinburgh EH10 5LG

Tel: 0131 455 6331

Fax: 0131 455 6334

Email: intoffice@napier.ac.uk

Website: www.napier.ac.uk

Students: 11,412 in 1998/9 (1,484 postgraduate, 8.5 per cent international, from 80 countries), 51:49 male:female.

Accommodation: mainly single-sex flats. University residences from £35 to £57 a week. Room in town from £45 to £55 a week.

Entrance requirements: generally two or three A levels in appropriate subjects. 24 points in International Baccalaureate.

EFL: IELTS 5.5, TOEFL 550 (computer-based test 215).

Fees: classroom courses £6,300 a year, laboratory courses £6,950 a year. Postgraduate: classroom courses £7,200 a year, laboratory courses £8,450 a year.

Napier University is named after the 16th-century philosopher and mathematician John Napier, one of Scotland's most illustrious sons and the man who developed the concept of logarithms. In the last three decades Napier has progressed from polytechnic to university status and, in The Times Good University Guide 1999, was rated as one of the top two new universities in the UK. The university is based on 11 sites in Edinburgh, Scotland's capital. Edinburgh is a compact city and students may move

Edinburgh Castle from the Grassmarket

around easily and cheaply. Architec-turally, the city centre is full of beautiful, historic buildings, ranging from the 16th-century Royal Mile to the 18th- and 19th-century New Town. The main campuses are at Craiglockhart, Merchiston, Sighthill, Craighouse and Canaan Lane. The Merchiston campus incorporates Napier Tower, the castle where John Napier was born in 1550.

Academic strengths

The university is divided into five faculties: Arts and Social Sciences; Engineering; Health Studies; Science; and the Napier Business School.

Napier University Business School is the largest in Scotland and the Engineering Faculty is the biggest in eastern Scotland. The university produces more graduates of mathematics than any other institution in Scotland and is situated in the European equivalent of the Silicon Valley. Napier's School of Communication Arts offers programmes including: communication; journalism; publishing; design; photog-raphy; film; and television. The university's careers advisory service provides a series of seminars and workshops to assist with careers prepa-ration and planning. The Financial Times league table of the top 100 universities in the UK has placed Napier amongst the top 10 in terms of students finding jobs once they graduate.

Student life

All of the university's sites in southwest Edinburgh have their own libraries. These are open seven days a week dur-ing term time and have extensive collec-tions of books, printed materials, audio-visual, CD-ROM and self-instruc-tional materials. Both individual and group study rooms are available, the latter accommodating between three and eight people and offering students the opportunity to work together on proj-ects. Computing facilities are available at each campus and students are given their own email address on enrolment. The university's computer services unit provides expertise and support to all the campuses, while help-desks are avail-able to answer questions and offer advice on computer usage. Media units, providing both audio and visual servic-es, are available at each of the main campuses. These offer a range of sup-port services, from graphics to photog-raphy, as well as facilities for in-house video production and editing. Achievements in sport include the foot-ball team winning the Scottish Universities League and the badminton club winning the Scottish Universities Badminton Championship.

"In 1998 Napier University was granted a joint scholarship with the British Trade and Cultural Office (BTCO) Taiwan, for students apply-ing for the MSc Information Technology (Multimedia Technology) degree. The scholarship covered full tuition fees for the master's programme and the cost of a pre-sessional English language course. I was the first successful applicant for the joint scholarship and joined the course for 1998/9. The scholarship really helped me fulfil my dream to study in the UK. I received a lot of support from BTCO and Napier University when I needed it, not just in terms of the tuition fees, but also from the people around me. I very much appreciate the scholarship and Edinburgh is a very good place to study".

Jack Chu, Taiwan

UNIVERSITY OF
NEWCASTLE

newcastle
newcastle
newcastle

University of Newcastle

Write to: Mr T T McCarthy, Director, International Office, 10 Kensington Terrace, Newcastle-upon-Tyne NE1 7RU

Tel: 0191 222 8152

Fax: 0191 222 5212

Email: international.office@ncl.ac.uk

Website: www.ncl.ac.uk

Students: 13,255 in 1997/8 (3,145 postgraduate, 1,183 international, from 122 countries), 60:40 male:female.

Accommodation: family, vacation. University residences from £38 to £62 a week self-catered, £60 to £80 a week catered. Room in town from £45 a week.

Entrance requirements: vary according to subject, minimum of EE at A level and three GCSEs. 24 points in International Baccalaureate.

EFL: for postgraduates IELTS 6.5, TOEFL 575 (for English Literary and Linguistic Studies and Law IELTS 7.0).

Foundation: for most science and engineering courses; bridging course in English language and British culture, history and society for arts and social sciences courses (successful completion guarantees admission to BA Combined Studies programme).

Fees: in 1999/2000 classroom courses £6,770 a year, laboratory courses £8,920 a year, clinical courses £16,520 a year.

Newcastle University

The University of Newcastle is a campus-based institution situated on a site of about 45 acres just north of the centre of Newcastle. These central facilities are supplemented by others further afield, including Close House, the university's country mansion in the Tyne Valley. This has extensive playing fields and a golf course, as well as an observatory and research facilities for the agricultural, biological and environmental sciences.

Newcastle is the largest city in northeast England. It became famous as a coal exporting port in the 19th century and some of the grandeur of this period remains in the city's buildings and six bridges spanning the Tyne. The locals are known for their friendliness and the city's nightlife frequently involves beer and dancing in pubs and clubs.

Newcastle is compact but has plenty of parks and green spaces. In the surrounding countryside tourists head to the Northumberland National Park, Kielder Water and castles such as Bamburgh and Warkworth. Another big attraction to the city is Newcastle United Football Club.

Academic strengths

With over 220 degree programmes to choose from, Newcastle has a diverse range of subjects on offer, from medicine and engineering to humanities, education and agriculture. In the teaching quality assessments of 1994 to 1996, Newcastle received Excellent ratings for architecture, English, geology, and social policy and administration and ratings for 22 out of 24 for modern languages and linguistics. The medical school recieved 24 out of 24.

The university's Robinson library, extended in 1996, has received a charter mark for excellence. Other university facilities include a total of over 700 computer terminals – including PCs and Apple Macs – a language centre, two university farms at Nafferton and Cockle Park, a marine laboratory, the Hatton Gallery and the Shefton Museum of Greek Art and Archaeology.

Student life

New international students can be met at the station or Newcastle airport and prior to the start of term they can attend a three-day orientation programme. During the academic session English classes are provided free of charge. Students are also encouraged to make use of the Open Access Centre, where they can learn a range of languages, including English, at their own pace. The cost of living in Newcastle is low in comparison to many other areas of the UK. Religious life is taken care of in the university chaplaincy, which local Christian and Jewish chaplains visit, and there is a mosque on campus. The chaplaincy also maintains contact with groups of other faiths in both the university and the city.

The students' union offers a number of clubs and societies which cater for sporting interests as well as religious and national societies. One of these is the International Students' Society which annually organises an international festival for members of the public as well as students. The union also runs social events which range from pub quizzes to discos and gigs by well-known bands.

"I am now in my fifth year at Newcastle, so I must like it! I'm doing the MEng in Civil and Environmental Engineering, but I started on the one-year foundation course to improve my English. I really enjoyed the First Year Conference (Freshers' Week), when everything was provided for meeting new people and exploring the university and city. I have found my course and the breadth of subjects it covers particularly interesting and rewarding. In general, the MEng was as I expected, but the tutors were definitely friendlier than I had imagined. The main benefit of coming to Newcastle to study was the language; I now have a near native knowledge of the language as well as a specialist vocabulary. The international flavour on campus has given me a different view of other cultures and the ability to adapt to new environments. Newcastle is an excellent place and I can highly recommend the nightlife, with its variety of pubs, clubs and relaxed atmosphere."

Milly Svenheim, Norway

University of North London

Write to: Mark Bickerton, International Office, University of North London, Holloway Road, London N7 8DB

Tel: 020 7753 5190

Fax: 020 7753 5015

Email: oncourse@unl.ac.uk

Website: www.unl.ac.uk/international

Students: 17,000 in 1998/9 (2,205 postgraduates, 700 international, from 114 countries), 47:53 male:female.

Accommodation: single-sex, vacation - extra charge in summer. University residences from £56 to £77 a week. Room in town £50 upwards a week.

Entrance requirements: generally 14 A level points, 24 in International Baccalaureate, at least 60 in European Baccalaureate.

EFL: for foundation IELTS 4.5, TOEFL 450, for undergraduate IELTS 5.5, TOEFL 550, for postgraduate IELTS 6.0, TOEFL 580.

Foundation: one-year courses (foundation, JYA), including English language, leading to degree courses in architecture, computing, law, science, social sciences, business, interior design or engineering.

Fees: foundation £4,800 a year, undergraduate £6,600 a year, MA/MSc £6,600 to £7,200 a year, MBA £9,000 a year.

The university is situated in Holloway Road in Islington, close to the centre of London, with the Faculty of Environmental and Social Studies nearby in Highbury Fields. Whether you are interested in music, film, dance, theatre, comedy or sport, London can provide suitable entertainment. The University of North London began as the Northern Polytechnic Institution in 1896 with a mission to 'promote the industrial skill, general knowledge, health and well-being of young men and women'. Today the focus remains on employability, with IT-based modules in all its undergraduate programmes and the opportunity for all students to learn a foreign language. The university has developed its own 'Capability Curriculum' – a method of teaching which takes into account the capabilities and attributes sought by employers.

University of North London

Academic strengths

Courses which are popular with international students include business, architecture, computing, tourism development, polymer technology and law. The university's art and design course achieved a rating of 22 out of 24 in the 1999 Teaching Quality Assessment (TQA) and electronic and electrical engineering and drama, dance and cinematics achieved 22 out of 24 in 1998.

There are a number of resources available to assist students in their study. The university's learning centre, opened in 1995, is housed in a mirrored glass building on the Holloway Road site. It holds extensive book and journal collections, computing and audio-visual facilities, areas for group work and individual quiet study spaces. Students also have access to CD-ROMs and the Internet. The university is continuing to develop its resources and a new building providing 4,000 square metres of space for learning facilities, such as web-linked computers, is due to be completed in 1999. It will be ready for opening in 2000. Students can also take advantage of the number of facilities geared towards specific courses which include Sun computing workstations, a teacher education gymnasium, meteorological equipment and a polymer laboratory.

Student life

Alongside the cultural, social and sporting activities available in the city, the University of North London has a number of its own facilities. The popular sports and recreation programme offers activities including aerobics, dance, badminton, volleyball, football and yoga. On-site the university has two gymnasia, a dance studio and a fitness suite and arrangements are made with local swimming pools and sports centres to provide canoeing, cricket, squash, sub-aqua, swimming and tennis. The new student centre brings together the students' union offices with facilities such as a shop, bars and an entertainment venue for music, comedy and dancing. Meeting spaces are available for the following denominations: Church of England; Roman Catholic; Muslim and the Free Church.

International students can benefit from additional facilities and services. An induction and familiarisation programme is held at the beginning of the first semester, in September; students receive general advice about living and studying in Britain and get an opportunity to meet international office and teaching staff as well as other new international students. The university also has an airport welcome service.

"I come from Montpellier and started a PhD in biology and molecular physiology in October 1995. I am working on a collaborative project with the Royal Veterinary College in Camden Town. I think it is quite nice to work in two different environments. I like it here because I've got my own lab and my own equipment. The technicians are around but I am learning how to sort my problems out by myself before asking for help. I get on very well with my supervisor; she's very helpful. We meet weekly but I can call or email her whenever I want. I think I want to stay in the research field when I finish my degree and I am thinking of doing a post-doctorate. I haven't decided whether to stay in England or not – probably I shall. I like London; it is very cosmopolitan."

Stephanie Bayol, France

UNIVERSITIES AND COLLEGES

UNIVERSITY of NORTHUMBRIA *at* NEWCASTLE

University of Northumbria at Newcastle

Write to: The International Office, Ellison Building, Ellison Place, Newcastle upon Tyne NE1 8ST

Tel: 0191 227 4271

Fax: 0191 261 1264

Email: er.intoff@unn.ac.uk

Website: www.unn.ac.uk

Students: 24,000 in 1998/9 (2,600 postgraduate, 2,200 from overseas, from about 100 countries), 45:55 male:female.

Accommodation: single-sex, married, vacation. University residences £45 a week. Room in town from £42 a week.

Entrance requirements: generally BCC at A level or equivalent (AAB for law; BBB English and film studies). Accept International and European Baccalaureates and many overseas qualifications.

EFL: Cambridge Advanced English, IELTS 5.5 to 7.5 depending on course, TOEFL 550. Credit transfer is possible.

Foundation: Diploma in Art and Design for students whose portfolio is not yet at year one level; also includes English language options. Also available in engineering, science and technology.

Fees: classroom courses from £6,180, laboratory courses from £6,375, MBA £12,000 a year.

Recently voted one of the world's most lively cities by US travel experts, Newcastle is easy to recommend. It's famous for its friendly people, good shopping and active club scene. For those who prefer the tranquillity of the countryside, the rural areas of Cumbria and Northumberland are nearby. Newcastle – the regional capital of the northeast of England – has been voted the best place to work in Britain due to its good transport system (the simple and efficient Metro) and its variety of cheap and interesting eateries. Its unofficial symbol is the beautiful Tyne Bridge which stretches majestically across the River Tyne.

Academic strengths

Founded in 1870 as the Rutherford College of Engineering, the university became Newcastle Polytechnic in 1969

The Angel of the North

before becoming a university in 1992. Its ethos has always been to maintain good standards of teaching. This is reflected in the Design Department's award-winning fashion design course, the reputation of which stems from the high standards of those who teach it. The Law School at the University is also well regarded, having been rated Excellent in a recent HEFCE survey, along with English, and business and management. In terms of research, the university specialises in photovoltaics (the science of converting solar light into energy) and it is highly regarded in the field of information and library management.

Northumbria prides itself on other academic areas including social sciences, business, management studies, engineering and special needs education. It also offers courses in environmental studies and management, a one-semester diploma in international business (starting in September or January), a Combined Honours Programme, and, for those interested in sport, bursaries for rugby players. Northumbria has an innovative Student Law Centre, which gives law students the opportunity to advise people on legal matters. Most courses last three years except for degrees such as modern languages, which involve an extra year abroad. The academic year at Newcastle is divided into two semesters.

Student life

The university's four campuses are located at varying distances from the city centre, and a free shuttle bus connects the two farthest campuses to the city. The Carlisle Campus won an award recently for being an outstanding example of architectural revival. All campuses have student residences, and priority for the rooms is given to international students and first-year undergraduates.

The students' union, the focal point of student life, organises an induction day for recently arrived international students, which is run by first- and second-year international students. It also helps run the 'Meet and Greet service' at the airport. The number of international students has grown steadily from 200 in 1991 to over 2,000 in 1999. Seminars on learning methods and short, intensive English language courses help integration and the university strives to maintain a good support network.

"From the age of 14 I knew that I wanted to study the law. It must be in my blood because back home in Nazareth (I'm Palestinian) all my relatives work for the family firm. I'm very young, so it's been quite hard for me to settle into student life at the university. Before I applied to Northumbria I came to visit the university for two months in order to see the city and the surrounding countryside and get the feel of it. I fell in love with the place! Now that I'm studying here I still like it, though I've found some of the rowdier students a bit hard to deal with. My university experience started off being quite difficult, but since I've got used to studying under a new system and in English, it's definitely got better. If you come here, be prepared to work hard – the teachers really can push you."

Sammer Abu-Ahmed, Palestine

Nottingham Trent University

Write to: Nottingham Trent University, International Office, Burton Street, Nottingham NG1 4BU

Tel: 0115 848 6515

Fax: 0115 848 6528

Email: int.office@ntu.ac.uk

Website: www.ntu.ac.uk

Students: around 23,000 in 1999 (3,484 postgraduates, 1,600 international, from over 80 countries),

The Nottingham Trent University Boots Library

49:51 male:female.

Accommodation: single-sex, vacation. University residences from £38 to £56 a week self-catered. Room in town from £35 to £50 a week.

Entrance requirements: normally two A levels plus three GCSE passes at grade C or equivalent, 24 points in International Baccalaureate.

EFL: Cambridge Certificate of Proficiency in English, GCSE English, IELTS 6.0, TOEFL 550.

Foundation: course available in art and design for international students. Courses also available at partner further education colleges.

Fees: classroom courses £6,510 a year, laboratory courses £7,270 a year, MBA £9,400 a year.

Nottingham is a vibrant city situated in the very heart of England, just two hours away from London. With over 50,000 students, the city has proved to be popular choice for prospective undergraduates. Nottingham Trent University has around 23,000 students, studying a variety of undergraduate, professional, postgraduate and unique courses, making it one of the largest universities in the UK. It consists of three campuses, one located in the centre of the city, one in a green-belt campus just outside the centre, and a third based in a rural market town near Southwell.

Academic strengths

The university offers a wide range of courses that are designed to be flexible and prepare students for the world of work.

They are grouped into nine faculties: Business School; Law School; Art and Design; Engineering and Computing; Economics and Social Sciences; Construction and the Environment; Science and Mathematics; and Humanities and Education. Subjects including chemistry, business and management studies, physics, and biological sciences received a rating of Excellent from the Higher Education Funding Council for England.

Students may benefit from the university's new £13 million electronic library and education resource centre which holds over 800 study spaces and more than 500,000 books. The university has many links with local and international businesses and institutions, and statistics show that, upon graduation, 96 per cent of students either enter into employment or continue with their education.

A Study Abroad Programme enables students already doing a degree in their home country to study for one semester at Nottingham Trent.

Student life

The university has committed some £30 million to new buildings and refurbishment in its aim to provide high-quality student residences. There are over 3,000 bed spaces available in university owned and managed residences and international students are given priority during their first year of study.

The university's sheer size means that it provides for a vast range of interests and activities. The students' union offers a variety of facilities, clubs and societies. The city students' union offers a bank, insurance and travel agents, a general shop and a specialist shop as well as a nightclub and bar. It also has its own radio station which offers many opportunities for students to get involved and receive both experience and training.

International students also benefit from a free, five-day orientation programme. Religious and cultural advisors are available to offer support and there are Muslim prayer room facilities. The university's Language Centre provides English language support throughout students' studies, and undergraduate students on registered courses are eligible for free English language classes.

"Everything is different in England: the culture, food and the language. The British people smile a lot, which makes you feel at ease, and they have always been nice to me. Teaching methods are also different; it is more in-depth and there's lots of access to information. I had heard about the reputation of Nottingham Law School, which is one of the best in the country. The course has more than met my expectations. The lecturers are very good, professional, encouraging and supportive. The international student support is brilliant. The orientation week is a real ice-breaker and I was able to help out with it this year. I have been on a trip to Edinburgh and there are events here every weekend. My aim is to do a BVC, and then a pupilage, either in the UK or in Ghana."

Irene Dodoo, Ghana

University of Oxford

Write to: Oxford Colleges Admissions Service, Undergraduates / Graduate Admissions Office, University of Oxford, University Offices, Wellington Square, Oxford OX1 2JD

Tel: 01865 270208 (undergraduates) 01865 270059 (graduates)

Fax: 01865 270 708

Email: Undergraduate.admissions @ox.ac.uk or Graduate.admissions@admin.ox.ac.uk

Website: www.ox.ac.uk

Students: 16,185 in 1998/9 (4,816 postgraduates, 2,431 international from over 130 countries), male:female 58:42.

Accommodation: varies from college to college. St. Hilda's College is all female. Other colleges are sympathetic to requests for single sex and married/family accommodation. Vacation. University residences from £60 a week self catered, £98 a week catered. Room in town from £55 a week.

Entrance requirements: Typically AAB at A level or 75 to 80 per cent in European baccalaureate (with scores of 8 to 9 in specified subjects). 36 points required in International baccalaureate with 6 to 7 in one or more specified subjects at higher level. For postgraduate entry an upper second class honours degree or equivalent is required.

EFL: IELTS 7.5 or TOEFL 600 for postgraduate courses.

Foundation: No foundation courses offered.

Fees: Classroom courses £6,684 a year; Laboratory courses £8,910 a year; Clinical courses £16,337 a year. In addition college fees must be paid, typically £3,235 a year for undergraduates and £1,650 a year for postgraduates.

Magdalen College, Oxford

Oxford is one of Britain's most famous educational institutions, and it has an enormous amount to offer to international students. A wealth of historical buildings, known as the 'dreaming spires' combine with many green spaces and a modern city centre. Famous alumni include Margaret Thatcher, Tony Blair and Bill Clinton, as well as countless well-known writers, philosophers and scientists. As an undergraduate, you apply to study at one of Oxford's 39 colleges rather than applying directly to the university itself, and as colleges can vary considerably in terms of atmosphere, facilities and academic strengths you need to do some careful research before you make your application (graduates apply first to the university and then to colleges). You could be studying at a college founded in 1249 or one founded in 1996. Undergraduates should note that although applications are through UCAS, the deadline is October 15th rather than December 15th for entry the following year. As a city, Oxford is multicultural, something to which its large numbers of international students undoubtedly contribute. It used to be a large industrial city with strong connections to the motor industry (Lord Nuffield established Morris Motors in nearby Cowley earlier this century). With the decline of the British motor industry, this is no longer so much the case, but it is certainly feels a more 'bustling' city than Cambridge which would probably claim to be more peaceful and secluded.

Academic strengths

Oxford's academic tradition speaks for itself. In the 1996 research assessment exercise no less than 25 of its faculties/departments received a 5* rating (with another 15 receiving a 5). Oxford also does extremely well in the teaching quality assessments, and you may well find yourself being taught by academics with a worldwide reputation in their field.

Student life

A visit to Fresher's Fair in your first week will reveal the remarkable number of student clubs and societies, many of which relate to specific countries and cultures. Many international students take up rowing, and are well represented in the Oxford team at the annual boat race against Cambridge. There is an orientation programme for international students, and the language centre provides free English language classes throughout the year. There are a number of scholarship schemes for international students and you can find details of these in the undergraduate and postgraduate prospectuses.

"I came from China to study at Magdalen College, Oxford. Maybe we Chinese are particularly fussy about food, but the first thing I really had to get used to was student food. Actually food in Britain is a lot better than it used to be, but eating out is expensive and so you really depend on the quality of food served in your college. I remember on Valentine's Day I received a romantic card from the President of my college. I was extremely worried about what to do, until I discovered that it was a practical joke played by an English friend of mine. The English sense of humour certainly takes a while to get used to! I found English people cold at first but the friends I made have become friends for life."

XiaoPei He, China

OXFORD
BROOKES
UNIVERSITY

Oxford Brookes University

Write to: The International Office, Oxford Brookes University, Gipsy Lane Campus, Headington, Oxford OX3 0BP

Tel: 01865 484 880

Fax: 01865 484 861

Email: international@brookes.ac.uk

Website: www.brookes.ac.uk/

Students: 11,516 full-time students in 1998/9 (17 per cent postgraduate, 2,132 international, from 100 countries), 41:59 male:female.

Accommodation: some single sex, vacation (except in summer). University residences from £50 to £55 a week self-catered, from £65 to £75 a week catered.

Entrance requirements: for undergraduates two A levels, International Baccalaureate or equivalent: 28+ points.

EFL: for undergraduates IELTS 6, TOEFL 550.

Foundation: international foundation diploma (study skills and English language tuition); foundation diploma in liberal arts (study skills, no language tuition); foundation programmes in building, and art and design. Most engineering degrees incorporate a foundation year into a four-year course.

Fees: from £6,900, £6,210 for foundation courses.

Oxford is a historic city with academic traditions extending back over eight centuries. Characterised by stunning historical architecture, and the River Isis, Oxford is a lively cosmopolitan centre with successful publishing, car-manufacturing, and new technology industries. In addition, it enjoys a good location, only an hour away from London and its international airports. Public transport in Oxford is reliable and cheap, although most people prefer to cycle.

Oxford Brookes University originates from the 19th century when it was a School of Art. Today, it has a large

Oxford city centre

international community of students and staff, with comprehensive provision for international students.

Academic strengths

Oxford Brookes' reputation has been upheld by high ratings in teaching quality assessments. Several subject areas have achieved Excellent ratings including anthropology, English, geography and law, and, in 1998, areas such as real estate, building and art history all scored 23 out of 24. In 1997 the School of Planning achieved the maximum rating of 24 out of 24. Every subject assessed achieved top marks in the student support and guidance category.

The university operates a modular degree programme, based on a system of credit accumulation and transfer, thereby providing opportunities for overseas exchanges and admission with credit. The range of courses offers students the flexibility and choice to devise programmes which suit their individual interests and strengths.

Up-to-date learning resources include three university libraries, each providing texts and reading rooms. Over 800 study areas are provided throughout the libraries, along with audio visual materials, the internet, electronic journals, library web pages and a web-based library catalogue. Networked computers can be found in open access rooms, departments, and halls of residence. Almost half the computer rooms are open 24 hours a day, 365 days a year.

Student life

Oxford Brookes' students' union has restaurants, bars, shops and a new venue, which is used for club nights, live music, comedy events and guest lectures. In addition, there are more than 65 student run societies covering a diverse range of interests and an advice centre and representation service. An interdenominational Christian chaplaincy, two Muslim prayer rooms, and a directory of the different faiths represented at the university along with contact numbers are offered to students.

The International Student Advisory Service offers international students advice on financial, personal and immigration matters through a team of student advisers who also provide newsletters and a number of social events. There is also an airport pick-up service, and a welcome programme when students arrive. Students can take English language modules to support their studies, which sometimes count towards their final degree mark.

"I completed my International Foundation Diploma (IFD) in July 1996, and I am now studying for a Masters of Business Administration (MBA) at Oxford Brookes University. I am the first Japanese student on the full-time MBA course. Before I came to Oxford in September 1995 I worked for the head office of Mitsubishi Motors Corporation in Japan, and was in charge of part of the recruitment and training of staff. The MBA course consists of people from 31 nationalities, so I not only gained academic knowledge but also a broader view through interactions with my classmates who have various cultural backgrounds, and different ways of thinking. The course is very difficult and involves a high degree of commitment and dedicated study; however, the MBA degree is of great value, and my two years at Oxford Brookes University have been worthwhile and rewarding for me."

Junko Noguchi, Japan

University of Plymouth

Write to: The International Office, Drake Circus, Plymouth, Devon PL4 8AA

Tel: 01752 233 345

Fax: 01752 232 014

Email: intoff@plymouth.ac.uk

Website: www.plym.ac.uk

Students: 23,680 in 1998/9 (2,496 postgraduate, 1,876 international, from over 100 countries), 47:53 male:female.

Accommodation: single-sex, vacation. University residence from £45 to £65 a week. Room in town from £35 to £45 a week, flat from £60 to £75 a week.

Entrance requirements: CCC at A level or equivalent (Bs and Cs for media, economics, social sciences, art, English, business and related subjects, biology, languages, geography, law). European or International Baccalaureate and other overseas qualifications accepted.

EFL: IELTS 6.0, TOEFL 600.

Fees: 1999 classroom courses £6,000 a year, laboratory courses £6,900 a year.

Foundation: Courses available.

The University of Plymouth is based on four main campuses in Devon and provides a pleasant location for learning and leisure: here students can both study in and enjoy an area of wonderful scenery. The largest campus is in Plymouth, a historic city set between the sea and Dartmoor, providing plenty of opportunity for outdoor and cultural activities. The Exeter campus is one of the bases for the Faculty of Arts and Education, the other being at Exmouth. Exeter is one of England's oldest and most graceful cities and has a lively cultural environment. The small town of Exmouth is the 'seaside' campus with bracing sea air, miles of beach and cliff walks. The Seale-Hayne estate covers nearly 200 hectares, of which 160

University of Plymouth - the Plymouth campus

are farmed, and it is close to the market town of Newton Abbot.

Academic strengths

Plymouth University was founded in 1970, but its roots go back nearly 200 years when it provided a range of education and training for all kinds of maritime activities. Since those days the university has grown into one of the UK's largest universities, offering flexible modular programmes within 28 subject-based departments and schools. The Faculty of Science on the Plymouth campus, built when the university was founded, is still one of its main strengths, along with technology, human sciences and the business school.

The university has six campuses in the South West of England, a network of regional partner colleges and is in the process of developing a technological infrastructure that links them all. There is an active research programme which supports teaching carried out there. The university received Excellent ratings in six of the areas most recently assessed.

The university has libraries, computing laboratories and media workshops on their sites to support student's work. These facilities are well staffed and advice is readily available. Most courses include the development of IT skills and an increasing number of tutors are using technology to deliver teaching materials. Students have their own email and access to the university's software libraries and the Internet.

Student life

With campuses on or near the coast, each with its own students' union, at Plymouth, Exeter, Exmouth and Newton Abbot, virtually every imaginable coastal and river sport is open to students, including a Diving and Sailing Centre at Plymouth with a sports diving course. Students can join winning teams for national student yachting, waterski and surfing events – or lounge on a beach on warm summer days.

In addition to water sports, there is a host of clubs and societies run by the university. Drama, arts, political and cultural groups and fantasy gaming, include those on offer. Students can also make music with the orchestra or sing with the choral society. The students' union is the base for entertainments and tries to provide something to suit everyone's taste.

The university arranges approved accommodation for all international students during their first year. There is an international office with a specific responsibility to look after international students and support them in any welfare issues.

"I am an Egyptian postgraduate student and I worked as an assistant lecturer at the Suez Canal University in Egypt. I completed my master's in Genetic Plant Studies and after that my government offered me a fellowship to study for a PhD in the UK. I am now studying at the Seale-Hayne Faculty of Agriculture, Food and Land Use which is located in an attractive setting with nice views of the Devon countryside all around the campus. Although the campus is small and peaceful, it has good resources including a large library and computing service which provides access to electronic mail, Internet and electronic information sources. The community on campus is very helpful and friendly. Teaching staff maintain a high research and consultancy profile and they have excellent contacts in the UK and overseas. All these factors have helped and encouraged me to overcome my homesickness, continue with my course of study and enjoy my life in the UK."

Manal Hassan Eid, Egypt

University of Portsmouth

Write to: Karen Arnold, International Office, University of Portsmouth, Town Mount, Hampshire Terrace, Portsmouth PO1 2QG.

Tel: 023 9284 5118

Fax: 023 9284 3538

Email: karen.arnold@port.ac.uk

Website: www.port.ac.uk/international

Students: 17,000 in 1998/9 (3,000 postgraduates, 2,000 international from 130 countries), 50:50 male:female.

Accommodation: vacation – extra charge. University residences from £50 to £80 a week self-catered. Room in town from £40 to £60 a week.

Entrance requirements: 12 to 22 points in two A levels. Minimum 24 points at International Baccalaureate.

EFL: IELTS 6, TOEFL 550.

Foundation: courses available in engineering, business, science, art, design and media.

Fees: classroom courses £6,300 a year (some business courses mark up fees by £200 to £400), laboratory courses £7,300.

Portsmouth University, an educational institution for 129 years, was made a university in 1992. It is based around three campuses – the main one situated in the city centre around Guildhall Square. The business school is based on the Milton campus three miles to the east and Langstone campus, home to sports fields and some accommodation, is a further mile away. The sites vary from modern tower blocks to lovely listed buildings and an ex-army barracks.

Some halls of residence overlook the sea and one appealing aspect of Portsmouth is that it is a southern, coastal town. This gives it one of the warmest climates in Britain with average temperatures of 20 degrees in summer months. It is well positioned for water

University of Portsmouth campus

UNIVERSITIES AND COLLEGES

sports and close to the continent. Portsmouth is good for cyclists as Portsea (the island that Portsmouth and Southsea are built on) is flat. "Bikeabout" is a cycle loan scheme that operates in the town. Trains and coaches both run from Portsmouth and London is one hour and 20 minutes away.

Academic strengths

The first degree from the University of Portsmouth was awarded in 1900 from the Faculty of Technology. Today the university is divided into five faculties that are all continually developing new courses and research.

The Faculty of Technology is divided into five main areas: electrical and electronic engineering; mechanical and manufacturing engineering; computer science; information systems; and mathematics. The Faculty of Science's teaching areas include biology, physics, earth science, geology and earth science. The Business School has become one of the largest in Britain with 180 academic research staff and 2,400 students on award-bearing courses. The school's four departments are: accounting and management science; business and management; economics and project; and quality management. The largest department in the university, with over 400 members of staff, is the Faculty of Humanities and Social Science. The School of Language and Area Studies has achieved high ratings in both research and teaching, with a top grade 5 in Russian. Finally, the Faculty of the Environment covers a broad mix of disciplines concerned with the operation, interpretation, design, construction and management of the environment.

Student life

There are over 200 clubs and societies at the university. Some of these, such as the Latin-American Society and the Malaysian Society, have a multicultural feel. There are university chaplains who have links with all faiths. International students can also benefit from free language classes, either pre-sessional or ongoing. Taking English courses can fulfil some of international students' academic requirements.

On arrival at Portsmouth, airport pick-ups can be arranged and a four-day, free induction period is laid on for international students. First year students are guaranteed accommodation and most halls of residence are within walking distance of teaching blocks. Competitive bursaries of £500 are available for international students. Study grants for Malaysian students are also available and for the 2000 entry, this is £1,200.

"I am Esra Kulan and I come from Istanbul, Turkey. I studied for the MA in Marketing at the University of Portsmouth. This was a one year, full-time course. During this time, I had a chance to meet students from different cultures, which was fantastically interesting. The tutors were also very helpful. For the rest of my life, I will never forget my time in Portsmouth and always remember it with a smile. I now have my own insurance agency business and I am honestly very happy there. I use the skills and the background gained from my marketing studies in my own business, which is very exciting."

Esra Kulan, Turkey

QUEEN MARY
AND WESTFIELD COLLEGE
UNIVERSITY OF LONDON

Queen Mary & Westfield College University of London

Write to: Cathy Shaw, International Office, Queen Mary and Westfield College, Mile End Road, London E1 4NS

Tel: 020 7882 5378

Fax: 020 7882 5556

Email: international-office@qmw.ac.uk

Website: www.qmw.ac.uk

Students: 8,181 (1,666 postgraduates; 20% international, from 130 countries), 56:44 male:female.

Accommodation: single sex, married/family, vacation. College residences from £53 to £67 a week. Room in town from £55 a week.

Entrance requirements: BCC at A levels (ABB for medicine); 26 in International Baccalaureate.

EFL: minimum IELTS 6.5.

Foundation: International Foundation Course and Science and Engineering Foundation programme (see below)

Fees: Arts, Social Studies and Law £7,300 a year; Engineering and Science £9,200 a year; Pre-clinical medicine and dentistry £9,600 (year one).

Queen Mary and Westfield is one of the only campus universities in London, and it therefore combines the attractions of living and working near other students with the various excitements of living in London. It is an amalgamation of four colleges: Queen Mary College, Westfield College, St Bartholomew's Hospital Medical School and the

The Queen's Building, Queen Mary and Westfield College

London Hospital Medical School (England's first medical school). It is also part of the federal University of London. The university's main campus is at Mile End, where most of the academic facilities are located, including the Harold Pinter Drama Studio. The university has three other sites for medical and dental students: Whitechapel, West Smithfield and Charterhouse Square (all located in the East End and the City). Famous alumni include Graham Chapman, Malcolm Bradbury, Sir Roy Strong and Dr Barnardo. Mile End is situated in London's East End, a short tube journey from the centre of London.

Academic strengths

Academically the college has particular strengths in English, maths, computer science and engineering. The Medical School and the Centre for Commercial Law Studies are particularly popular with overseas students. Over 80 per cent of QMW's departments scored 4 or 5 in the research assessment exercise of 1996, and English, geography and modern languages all scored well in the teaching quality assessments.

The International Foundation Course at Queen Mary and Westfield is a one-year course preparing students for degree studies in social sciences, humanities and law. There is also a science and engineering foundation programme which forms the first year of an integrated four year programme leading to a BSc.

Student life

QMW's students' union is located in Bancroft Road, behind the main campus facilities. It provides a bar, catering and the only shop on campus. The union also provides squash courts and a sports hall as well as entertainments every day. Annual events include the Valentine's Ball, Rag Week and the Summer Ball, and a large nightclub has just been opened. There are about 75 non-sporting clubs and societies. On campus facilities include the 500-seat refectory, the Gallery restaurant and the Café Bar. Welfare services include a bus service, a nightline and a college nursery, as well as the College Welfare Service and a Union Sabbatical Officer dedicated to student welfare. There is also a counselling service, a College Health Centre, a nursery and an ecumenical chaplaincy. Sports facilities include a gym, tennis courts, sports fields and a boat house. Students can also use the University of London pool. There are about 25 sports clubs ranging from Aikido to Volleyball.

International students are invited to a pre-sessional orientation course and receive free English language support and training throughout the academic year. Some scholarship funds are available through the different departments.

"I've joined the Aikido club and I go to lessons as often as I can whenever I have time off from my studies. I am studying English on the one-year foundation programme. I find it very intensive and challenging. I wanted to study in the UK, because I feel that Japan has more access to American culture, and I want to experience European culture. At QMW I find that the students are very friendly and there are a lot of students from Asia."

Takayoshi Takayama, Japan

Queen's University of Belfast

Write to: Mr S. M. Wisener, The Admissions Office, The Queen's University of Belfast, Belfast, Northern Ireland BT7 1NN

Tel: 02890 335 081

Fax: 02890 247 895

Email: admissions@qub.ac.uk

Website: www.qub.ac.uk

Students: 14,000 in 1998/99 (2,000 postgraduates, 1,750 international, from over 60 countries), 48:52 male:female.

Accommodation: single sex, vacation, storage facilities. University residences £36 to £45 self-catered, from £49 to £57 a week catered; room in town from £35 a week.

Entrance requirements: CCC to ABB (for Medicine). Other qualifications also considered.

EFL: TOEFL 550 minimum, IELTS 6.0-6.5.

Foundation: science, engineering and agriculture and food science have two levels of entry, level 0 (for students with qualifications which would normally require a foundation course) and level

1. *Those requiring a foundation or Foundation courses available through the Joint Training Centre, established with Shenzhen University in South China. Successful completion of these one-year courses can lead to admission to three-year Honours degree programmes in the School of Management and the Faculty of Engineering.*

Fees: undergraduate: classroom £5,935 a year, laboratory £7,705 per year, medicine and dentistry pre-clinical £9,300 per year, clinical £17,135 a year, postgraduate: £7,100 per year (excluding clinical) medical and dental £11,205 per year.

Queen's recently celebrated its 150th anniversary. Established in 1845 it became a full university in 1908. It has a long history but is modern in its outlook, with four major library complexes and computerised study facilities. While not a campus university, everything is compact and within easy walking distance, including the main accommodation complex. For two and a half weeks each November it organises the Belfast festival during which over 200 performances cater for all tastes. The

Queen's University Belfast

university is near the Ulster museum and the city art gallery. Former students include Seamus Heaney, recently awarded the Nobel Prize for literature as well as Mary McAleese, the current President of Ireland.

Academic strengths

A number of departments have been rated highly by recent research assessments. In TQAs they scored highly in Psychology (24/24, 1998), Dentistry (24/24, 1998) and Medicine (24/24, 1998). Electrical and electronic engineering was given a research rating of 5; mechanical, aeronautical and manufacturing engineering obtained a 5*, the highest award possible. Queen's also offers Irish studies, awarded a rating of 5.

The Northern Ireland Technology Centre offers industrial short courses to keep practising engineers abreast of new developments such as computer-aided design or robotics. The centre is next to the main engineering schools, and its state-of-the-art facilities are used to support undergraduate programmes and postgraduate curricula.

Queen's has established a new Multimedia Language Centre, with a CAN-8 VirtuLab system. Courses incorporate audio material, video images and text; they can be used to improve pronunciation, and to practise conversation, grammar and comprehension skills.

Students can use the self-access area on a 'drop-in' basis, with access to satellite TV and audio booths. There is a large library of audio tapes in over 30 languages.

Student life

Queen's is a mile from the city centre and at the heart of Belfast's social and cultural scene. The city also has good transport systems that can help you escape to the surrounding stunning scenery. Nearby, is one of the largest unspoilt lakes in Europe. In contrast you could visit the world's oldest whiskey distillery.

The students' union has over 100 clubs and societies which include Malaysian, Singaporean and Chinese societies. There are plenty of bars and live music venues, one of which has recently been refurbished. Queen's University has its own full-time two-screen cinema plus a dedicated Physical Education Centre, playing fields and an athletics arena. International students are offered a 'meeting and greeting' service at the airport and halls of residence. There is a three-day orientation programme in collaboration with the students' union and international friendship association. Each student has access to an International Student Adviser who acts as a personal adviser. Pre-sessional English courses are available as well as year-long English language courses.

"I completed a BA in Politics and Sociology at the University of San Diego and during those studies I spent a semester at Queen's University as a visiting student. My parents were originally concerned about me coming to Northern Ireland, but one of my teachers had spent time there and he soon put their minds at ease. The quality of teaching at Queen's impressed me so much that, when I decided to study law I applied to Queen's and was accepted. I like the modular degree structure at Queen's. The study facilities are first rate and the whole academic experience is at a high level. It is also economical to study here."

Jacob Maguire Emry, USA

Write to: International Office OC, PO Box 217, Reading RG6 6AH

Tel: 0118 987 5123

Fax: 0118 975 2252

Email: intoff@reading.ac.uk

Website: www.rdg.ac.uk

Students: 12,324 in 1999/00 (5,222 postgraduates, 2,550 international, from 136 countries), 50:50 male:female.

Accommodation: single room, married/family, vacation storage facilities. University residences from £43 to £64 a week self-catered, from £76 to £97 a week catered. Room in town from £56 a week.

Entrance requirements: range from CDD to BBB to ABC at A level according to course, 27 to 33 points in International Baccalaureate. Postgraduate admissions: applications are made direct to the university and are welcomed from highly qualified graduates from recognised institutions.

EFL: IELTS 6.5, TOEFL 575

(for linguistically demanding courses: IELTS 7.0, TOEFL 590).

Foundation: preparatory course on campus, includes English language and three subject options relevant to intended degree (success in exam guarantees place on degree course). Foundation students are full members of the university. Course also recognised by other universities.

Fees: classroom courses £6,462 a year, laboratory courses £8,370 a year.

The University of Reading is situated in the heart of the Thames Valley, 60km west of London. Though its main buildings are modern, the university was first set up as a university college in the 19th century. It was granted its Royal Charter in 1926. In 1954 the university's development was begun at Whiteknights, once the manorial estate of the Marquis of Blandford. Some of his beautiful eighteenth-century landscaping is still in evidence and parkland development continues today in the green open spaces surrounding the residential and academic areas. At

Whiteknights Campus

the centre of the campus is the library, with the academic buildings and the students' union grouped around it. Most of the halls of residence lie around the northern perimeter and in the nearby residential streets. The university also has two other sites: Bulmershe Court, housing the Faculty of Education and Community Studies, and London Road.

Academic strengths

The University of Reading is divided into five faculties: agriculture and food, education and communication studies, letters and social sciences, science, and urban and regional studies. Over 60 per cent of departments were rated 4 and above in the 1996 research assessment exercise and several received 5* or 5 ratings including agriculture, archaeology, business and management, classics, built environment, environmental sciences, French and Italian. The university also scored Excellent in the 1994/5 teaching quality assessments for geography, geology, and mechanical engineering, 24 out of 24 in the 1998 assessment for film and drama, and physics, and 22+ for five out of eight subjects assessed in the last three years. The university has a range of facilities to aid academic study: the library offers over one million books, periodicals and special collections; students have 24-hour use of PCs linked to the university network and the university runs over 800 hectares of farmland which are used for agricultural teaching and research.

Student life

The university has a long history of international activity; its international office is one of the longest established in the UK and the first Thai student graduated in 1901. All new international students can attend the university's week-long welcome programme and support continues for the duration of your course. The university's Centre for Applied Language Studies provides full-time pre-entry English courses running from April to September and other languages can be studied. In-session English language tuition is also provided free of charge for students paying overseas fees.

Other support services and facilities in place include a university chaplaincy catering for Protestant, Roman Catholic and Jewish students and for Islamic students there is a Muslim centre. Students holding an International Baccalaureate may be eligible to apply for one of the three scholarships that are available for undergraduates. More scholarships are available for postgraduate students.

Social life is taken care of on campus by more than 100 university clubs and societies. There are also extensive sports facilities on campus and on the river. In addition each hall of residence has its own social and sporting programmes.

"I belong to the State Civil Service and have been posted as private secretary to the Commerce and Industry Minister of West Bengal. My work is closely related to the MA course in Rural Social Development I'm studying here. Important features of it include the interchange of theory and practice and the interaction between students from different parts of the world. 'Students' in the Agricultural Extension and Rural Development Department refer, of course, to professionals from government and non-government organisations. So, working together, we find out about social development problems and policies in different parts of the world which give us all a new perspective. I find the course very valuable."

Prabir Bannerjee, India

RIPON & YORK
A COLLEGE OF THE UNIVERSITY OF LEEDS

College of Ripon & York St John

Write to: International Office, Lord Mayor's Walk, York YO31 7EX

Tel: 01904 716942

Fax: 01904 716928

Email: m.williams@ucrysj.ac.uk

Web: www.ucrysj.ac.uk

Students: over 4,000 in 1999 (500 postgraduate, 250 international, from over 15 countries), 33:67 male:female.

Accommodation: University residences from £50 a week self-catering, £68 a week catered.

Entrance requirements: normally two A levels plus 3 GCSE passes at grade C, or equivalent, pass in European Baccalaureate, 20 points in International Baccalaureate.

EFL: Cambridge Certificate of Proficiency in English, GCSE English, IELTS 6.0, TOEFL 550.

Foundation: in marketing and management, humanities and social science, creative and performing arts.

Entrance requirements: IELTS 4.0, TOEFL 450.

Fees: classroom courses £5,400 a year, laboratory and workshop courses £7,900 a year, foundation £4,200 a year.

The two main campuses of the college are located in two of northern England's most beautiful, unspoilt cathedral cities. York's 13th-century Minster, ringed by narrow streets, overlooks the surrounding medieval buildings and the city's Roman walls. Ripon, 25 miles (40 kilometres) north west of York, is built around an ancient market square and a 12th-century cathedral. Both cities are particularly attractive places in which to study.

York and Ripon colleges were founded in the mid-19th century as teacher training colleges for men and women respectively. The York campus occupies sites around the city centre and the international office is located in a medieval building beside the Minster. The swimming pool, squash courts,

Students at Ripon & York

chapel, library and student residences are built around the original college building. Ripon Campus is spacious and attractively landscaped, covering 50 acres (20.25 hectares), and including tennis courts, playing fields and the international office. It is surrounded by the beautiful scenery of the Yorkshire Dales National Park and many outdoor pursuits are available. London is just two hours away and Hull is close to York and Ripon.

Academic strengths

The college offers a range of modular degree programmes validated by the University of Leeds. There is a wide choice of subject combinations together with a range of specialist degrees. Many of the degrees have an international slant; they include American studies, cultural studies and English studies. The college places emphasis on vocational courses leading to specific careers, including: leisure and tourism management; management studies; film, television and theatre studies; communication arts with options in music; dance and drama; physical education; sport and exercise science; counselling; and occupational therapy. The college also has a strong tradition and reputation in teacher education. Other options include social sciences, psychology, theology and religious studies, art and design, geography and history. The International Short Course Centre offers a variety of EFL programmes, including a one-year foundation course in English with options in marketing and management, creative and performing arts, humanities and social science.

Student life

The college places great emphasis on international contact. It organised its first exchange programme with a college in New Hampshire, USA, 25 years ago. Students can study abroad in North America and Europe and every year students from North America, Europe and East and South-East Asia come to Ripon and York to study. All international students are warmly welcomed to the small, friendly campuses with their international tradition, and they are guaranteed accommodation on campus. In one residence on the Ripon campus, all rooms are linked to the university college's computer network. English language tuition and help in developing study skills are readily available.

York and Ripon are small but far from sleepy; they have pubs with jazz and folk music, theatre, art and cinemas, plus over 50 social and sports clubs supported by the students' union.

"I come from Juneau, Alaska, and I'm on a 'Year Abroad' exchange from York College of Pennsylvania, where I'm majoring in psychology, with minors in art and theology. I'm continuing with all these subjects here at York, England. It was the opportunity of a lifetime to be offered this exchange. When I arrived I was looked after by the International Society students, who were very kind and understood how I felt. I'm getting a different outlook on my subjects of study – there's more social psychology in my studies here and I'm learning to work more on my own. I've been on trips to Whitby and the Lake District, and I've been on visits to abbeys as part of the Historic Buildings course I'm taking. What I miss most about being away from home is the food."

Elsa Endorff, USA

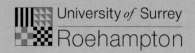

University of Surrey, Roehampton

Write to: David Street, International Unit, Roehampton Institute London, Roehampton Lane, London SW19 5PH

Tel: 020 8392 3151

Fax: 020 8392 3717

Email: d.Street@roehampton.ac.uk

Website: www.roehampton.ac.uk

Students: 7,000 in 1997/8 (1,000 postgraduate, 600 international, from 80 countries), 30:70 male:female.

Accommodation: single sex, vacation, storage facilities. Institute residences from £60 to £65 a week self-catered, from £78 a week catered. Room in town from £60 to £80 a week.

Entrance requirements: generally 10 to 14 points at A level. 24 points in International Baccalaureate. Some programmes require an audition, interview or portfolio.

EFL: IELTS 6.0, TOEFL 550.

Foundation: English for academic purposes, aims to raise students from entrance requirement – TOEFL 400 – to undergraduate entry level, lasts one or two semesters.

Fees: undergraduate courses £5,500 a year, postgraduate courses from £3,000 a year.

Roehampton Institute was formed in 1975 from four historic colleges – Digby Stuart, Froebel, Whitelands and Southlands – and it retains a collegiate structure but with additional shared resources. The colleges are a mixture of old and new and are housed in either purpose-built or historic buildings, all with their own gardens and grounds.

The institute is set in parkland in southwest London, close to Richmond Park and Wimbledon Common. A 10-minute train journey to Waterloo Station will take you within walking distance of the cultural venues and institutions of the South Bank Arts Centre, the Royal Festival Hall, the Globe Theatre, the National Theatre and the Museum of the Moving Image.

Froebel College

Academic strengths

Roehampton graduates receive their degrees from the University of Surrey.

Students can choose their study programme from a number of subject areas, including education, performing arts, commerce, humanities, life sciences and social sciences. In teaching quality assessments the institute was awarded 20 out of 24 for sociology in 1996 and 22 out 24 for linguistics in 1995. Roehampton also gained 4 out of 5 in both dance and theology, divinity and religious studies in the 1996 research assessment exercise.

The institute had recently invested £20 million in upgrading and developing its facilities, including the £4.5 million Learning Resources Centre. This centre and Whitelands College offer access to their computer suites up to 24 hours a day. Staff are invloved in external activities – the Head of the English Department is Ann Thompson, a Shakespeare scholar and Editor of the New Arden Shakespeare series and in the Faculty of Social and Life Sciences, Professor Martin Albrow is currently President of the Sociology and Social Policy section of the British Association for the Advancement of Science. The institute also receives guest lecturers and visits from business and industry professionals.

Student life

The staff of the International Unit are able to help students complete their application forms, assist in selecting their course and answer any questions they might have before leaving home. Then, on arrival, international students can use the 'meet and greet' service, which is available at nearby London airports. There is also a full orientation week to help students settle into life in London. For those needing assistance with their language, there is a free English language support unit and the institute runs pre-sessional courses in the summer.

The students' union is divided into three portfolios: entertainments, communications and equal opportunities /welfare. Each is responsible for different areas, for example, the organisation of weekly discos, or the production of the student magazine and there is an International Student Group, which organises weekly trips and excursions and social activities. The university has meeting spaces for Christian denominations and for Muslim students. Should students encounter exceptional financial difficulties, they can apply to the international unit for some support.

"I was born and raised in Seattle, Washington, and am currently in my fourth year of studying music performance at Biola University in Los Angeles, California. When Biola offered me the opportunity to study abroad at Roehampton Institute London, I jumped at the chance. Travelling to Britain has long been a dream of mine, and the prospect of living in London was incredible. Roehampton has perfect placement: minutes from the excitement of downtown, yet distant enough to enjoy park-like tranquility. The institute has a truly beautiful campus, even by a Washingtonian's standards! The architecture is varied, from the nobility of age-old brickwork to the contemporary style of wood and glass, set in grounds filled with lawns, trees and lakes. The faculty and staff are knowledgeable, friendly and accessible, and fitting in with the cosmopolitan student body is natural. I would heartily recommend Roehampton Institute London. The experience is unforgettable!"

Jack Wingard, USA

Rose Bruford College

Rose Bruford College

Write to: Sue McTavish (Registrar), The Admissions Office, Rose Bruford College, Lamorbey Park, Sidcup, Kent DA15 9D

Tel: 020 8300 3024

Fax: 020 8308 0542

Email: admiss@bruford.ac.uk

Website: www.bruford.ac.uk

Students: 630 in 1998/99 (74 international, from 23 countries), 40:60 male:female.

Accommodation: college residences from £60 per week self-catered; room in town from £55 to £65 a week.

Entrance requirements: two A levels or equivalent.

EFL: for BA degrees IELTS 6.5; for foundation course, IELTS 5.5.

Foundation: one year course to bring students to entry requirement standard for degree courses at Rose Bruford and other UK universities. International Summer School:

students study acting and technical subjects. English language classes are taught through role-play and improvisation.

Rose Bruford, a former teacher of speech and drama at the Royal Academy of Dramatic Art, founded the college in 1950 by setting up a course that combined both acting and teacher training. Recognised by the Department of Education and Science in 1951, it has remained in the public sector ever since. Today the college is very different: a university sector institution operating internationally to offer a range of degree courses in all areas of theatre and related arts. The college has two campuses: Lamorbey Park in the London Borough of Bexley, and another campus eight miles away in Greenwich. Both are about 20 minutes from central London. The city naturally has much to offer students interested in the theatre, from large scale West End shows to small, innovative productions in fringe venues.

Rose Bruford College

Academic strengths

The college is known for its pioneering work in the field of theatre training and offered the UK's first degree in acting in 1976. Courses range from summer schools, an international foundation course, BA (Hons) and MA degrees, through to MPhil and PhD. All degrees at Rose Bruford are validated by the University of Manchester and accredited, where appropriate, by the National Council for Drama Training. The college was awarded 20 out of 24 in the teaching quality assessment for drama in 1997. Full-time BA (Hons) degrees in all major aspects of the theatre are available, including acting, directing, actor-musicianship, music technology, sound and image design, stage management, lighting design, costume production, scenic arts, theatre design, European theatre arts and American Theatre Arts. The college also offers an MA degree in Theatre Practices. By distance learning the college offers BA (Hons) degrees in Opera Studies and Theatre Studies, and MA courses in Theatre and Performance Studies and Dramatic Writing. The college has links with institutions in Japan, China, the USA, Australia and Spain.

Performances take place in London's West End, as well as the college's own theatres and studios. These include a proscenium theatre, and a new, 330-seat, theatre-in-the-round. The college also has lighting studios, a MIDI laboratory, and recording and rehearsal studios. The college has a £12 million building programme underway which aims to provide students with the most comprehensive theatre training facilities in the UK.

Student life

Rose Bruford has facilities to take care of most aspects of student life. The students' union arranges various social events, including concerts, cabarets, outings and theatre visits. There are meetings and social evenings organised for international students who are also granted free membership of the London International Student House – a centre in London's West End offering facilities such as bars, restaurants, study rooms, a disco, nightclub and sports amenities. The college's student advisor helps students to find accommodation and advises on any problems that might arise. In addition, the college provides purpose-built residences to a limited number of students. A number of bursaries are also available to international students.

"I come from Singapore and I first heard about Rose Bruford College when I went to an exhibition of British universities. The reputation of theatre in Britain is very good and that is why I wanted to study here. On the course I am learning about all areas of theatre and gaining the technical knowledge I need with the help and support of good tutors. I enjoy being so involved in the shows we put on which give me the experience I need. When I first came to Britain I found it difficult to find my way, but I soon made friends who helped me discover London. Before I came to Britain I worked in theatre and television in Singapore as a production assistant. When I finish I want to stay in the UK and work in stage management on West End musicals."

Joy Lee, Singapore

Royal Holloway University of London

Write to: Educational and International Liaison Office, Royal Holloway, University of London, Egham, Surrey TW20 0EX

Tel: 01784 443957

Fax: 01784 471381

Email: liaison-office@rhbnc.ac.uk

Website: www.rhbnc.ac.uk

Students: 5,766 in 1998/9 (1,106 postgraduate, 24 per cent international, from 90 countries), 45:55 male:female.

Accommodation: single, married/family. College residences from £41 to £75 a week. Room in town from £60 a week.

Entrance requirements: BCC to ABB at A level. 28 to 35 points in International Baccalaureate.

EFL: IELTS 6.5 (some courses 6.0), TOEFL 570 to 550 (230 to 213 in computer-based tests). Postgraduate: IELTS 7.0 (some courses 6.5), TOEFL 600 to 570 (250 to 230 in computer-based test).

Fees: foundation £6,750 a year, classroom courses £7,890 a year, laboratory courses £9,473 a year. Postgraduate: £7,890 to £9,665 a year.

Founded in 1886, Royal Holloway will celebrate 100 years as a member college of the University of London in the year 2000. Although part of the University of London, Royal Holloway is situated in Egham in Surrey, 19 miles from the centre of the capital. The location of the college is quite rural and relatively peaceful compared with London. The college's campus covers over 120 acres with modern academic, residential and recreational facilities located alongside the Founder's Building. However, London does play a significant part in the lives of most students and travel to the centre is easy: four trains an hour take you to London Waterloo. It is also conveniently situated for Heathrow Airport, which is just eight miles away.

The Founder's Building

UNIVERSITIES AND COLLEGES

Academic strengths

The college comprises 21 departments covering: the humanities; performing arts; social sciences; and sciences. In addition to single honours degrees, a variety of joint honours and major-minor courses are offered. In the latest research assessment exercise Royal Holloway was ranked 13th overall in the UK, coming 3rd in the arts. The following subjects scored ratings of 5 and 5*: psychology; geography; French; classics; Italian; music; drama and theatre; media arts; and history. In teaching quality assessments the university gained 23 out of 24 for: physics; drama and theatre; and media arts. The main library stocks over half a million volumes and subscribes to 1,700 periodical titles. The majority of stock is housed in three separate buildings: the Bedford Library for history, social science and science texts; the Founder's library for modern and classical languages and literature; and the music library, which is alongside the Music Department. Students using the library can access a variety of equipment, from microfilm, audio and video cassettes to CD-ROM databases, the Internet and computer-based literature catalogues.

The college's proximity to London means that all of the capital's academic facilities and services, including national, university and specialist libraries are within easy reach.

Student life

There is an orientation programme at the beginning of each year for all international students. There is also in-sessional as well as pre-sessional language support for non-native English speakers. The students' union can be found in the centre of the campus. Facilities include three bars, a function space and a coffee bar. A number of clubs and societies are available for international students (mostly run by the students themselves and supported by the union). Most nights of the week there is some form of entertainment on campus including discos, cabaret, live bands, stand-up comedy and theme nights. London also offers a variety of alternative activities. Religious amenities include an interdenominational chaplaincy and a Muslim prayer room. The University of London Union (ULU) have hailed Royal Holloway as the best sporting college in London.

"I did my first degree in Moscow and chose Royal Holloway for my computer science PhD as it was recommended by my tutors and had a strong academic reputation. I have found the academic staff to be both supportive and approachable. Learning a foreign language (and even passing the exams) in your home country and using this language in everyday life are completely different things. A couple of years ago I could never have imagined that I would have friends from countries all over the world: Japan, Nigeria, Spain and, of course, Britain. The sort of experience I am getting here, in the heart of England, is unique. Our beautiful location has to be mentioned and the campus is close to both Heathrow and central London, 40 minutes by train and you can see Westminster Abbey, Trafalgar Square... everything you have read about in your English textbooks. Believe me you can only benefit from being an overseas student here!"

Yuri Kalnishkan, Russia

Write to: The International Office, University of Salford, Salford M5 4WT

Tel: 0161 295 5543

Fax: 0161 295 5256

Email: intoff@salford.ac.uk

Website: www.salford.ac.uk/homepage.html

Students: 17,750 in 1999 (2,049 postgraduate, 1,275 international), 56:44 male:female.

Accommodation: single, single-sex, married, vacation. University residence from £40 a week self-catering. £65 a week with all meals. Room in town from £35 to £43 a week.

Entrance requirements: generally high: a minimum CCC in A levels or equivalent for most subjects; European Baccalaureate: pass; International Baccalaureate: full Diploma (minimum 28 points).

EFL: Cambridge Certificate of Proficiency in English grade C; GCSE English grade C, IELTS 6.0; TOEFL 550 (new computer based systems 215).

Fees: Preliminary Year £6,375 a year (Science), £5,865 a year (Arts); Undergraduate classroom-based subjects £6,600, a year; Laboratory/Art & Design £8,500.

Manchester United Football Ground is just about one mile (1.6 kilometres) from Salford University and Old Trafford Cricket Ground is approximately two miles (three kilometres) away. Transport links to the university are excellent – the university has its own railway station and the International Airport is only six miles away. Manchester, just minutes away from the campus, was an important textile town during the period of Britain's industrial expansion and has many fine neogothic buildings and a network of canals from that era. It's an important, lively and attractive city with four universities, two football teams, its own orchestra and a reputation for musical innovation. Manchester is also an international city, with its own Chinatown, and is conveniently located for weekends in the Lake District, and day trips into the Pennines' hills and Welsh mountains.

University of Salford

Academic strengths

Salford's courses are designed with careers in mind. Work placements and partnerships with industry are built into many courses. The university has four faculties offering courses from foundation studies to HNDs and degrees. Postgraduate courses and research are provided by the Graduate School. There is a wide range of engineering courses available, including audio engineering, acoustics, and environmental engineering. Science programmes offered include information technology, computing, mathematics, and futuristic courses such as physics with optoelectronics or space technology. Accounting and business courses are particularly popular with international students. Health courses are also popular at the university and include podiatry, nursing, midwifery, radiography, occupational therapy, physiotherapy, sports rehabilitation, prosthetics, orthotics and social work.

Music is graded Excellent and biological sciences obtained a maximum 24 points for teaching quality. The research teams in all academic disciplines gained good ratings in the recent research exercise. The Faculty of Art and Design Technology is housed in a new hi-tech building which, appropriately, won the first Sterling Prize for Architectual Design. The International Institute runs courses to help those international students from pre-sessional English and study skills to English language modules in a study programme.

Student life

All first-year students are guaranteed accommodation, if they apply early enough. Also international students can usually remain in university residences or flats through their course. The residences are well planned, all within walking distance of the campus, and there are flats for postgraduate students and for married students with children.

The students' union runs about 80 clubs and societies covering most sports, party political groups, ethnic groups, departmental groups and religious groups. Discos, concerts, cabarets and balls are held at various times through the year. There are also regular film shows and other special events such as the popular International Students Evening. The university has a great variety of sports facilities including a new swimming pool.

The academic year is organised around two semesters, starting in September and February. Most degree courses last three years, but there are one-year foundation courses for some subjects.

"When I arrived in Salford, I thought I could speak and understand English. I'd been studying it since school and I'm reading for a degree in English at Fukuoka University in Japan. Salford has an exchange scheme with Fukuoka. I arranged to arrive early and spend the summer doing an intensive course in London before coming to Salford. I've been surprised at the difference in teaching. In Japan I hardly had to speak, but at Salford I have to speak a lot, and give opinions. I've realised how important it is to live in England among the people. I've discovered all sorts of new things – musicals in London, Chinese food in Chinatown, and I've joined an aerobics club. At the weekends I travel somewhere with a friend. So far we've been to Liverpool, Edinburgh and the Lake District."

Naoko Ogawa, Japan

School of Pharmacy
University of London

Write to: The Registry, The School of Pharmacy, University of London, 29–39 Brunswick Square, London WC1N 1AX

Tel: 020 7753 5831

Fax: 020 7753 5829

Email: registry@cua.ulsop.ac.uk

Website: www.ulsop.ac.uk

Students: 800 in 1999 (270 postgraduates, 130 international, from 30 countries), 40:60 male:female.

Entrance requirements: generally BBB at A level or equivalent, including chemistry and one other science. International Baccalaureate accepted.

EFL: IELTS 6.5 or equivalent.

Fees: all courses £9,540 (provisional) a year.

The School of Pharmacy, a specialist school of the University of London, is located in the beautiful and historic part of central London known as Bloomsbury, around the corner from the capital's hectic West End. The international officer, Edwin Cox, and his wife show their concern for the school's international students by making every effort to know each one by name and taking the time to get to know their parents. Edwin Cox's wife, Peggy Stone, is the school's registrar and welfare officer.

Academic strengths

The SOP was founded in 1842 as the training institute for the Royal Pharmaceutical Society, and it received its charter as a university in 1952. One of only 16 pharmacy schools in the UK today, it has a strong international reputation. In the research assessment exercise it was awarded an excellent

Practical work at the SOP

rating of 5. Students from the School of Pharmacy (known as 'The Square' to alumni, because of its location) can be found working all over the world. The SOP does not simply train students to become retail or hospital pharmacists. Its brief encompasses all topics in this field, such as toxicology, drug development and control, haematology and pollution.

The curriculum for undergraduate students of pharmacy has recently undergone a radical change. Students now work for the four-year Master of Pharmacy degree; the one-year MSc in Clinical Pharmacy; the two-year Diploma/ MSc in Pharmacy Practice; or the 18-months, part-time Certificate/ Diploma in Medicines in Healthcare. The new method of teaching emphasises working in small groups, laboratory work, and participation in projects rather than lectures. The new strategy has so far proved successful.

Because of its small size and its students' commonality of purpose, research students at the SOP can be seen taking time to help undergraduates. And because SOP is a small institution, everyone's social and academic problems can usually be sorted out within 48 hours.

Because entry into the SOP is highly competitive, entrance requirements are high. The school runs an MSc in Clinical Pharmacy, International Policy and Practice for registered pharmacists from different countries (1999/00 fee £9,240 plus a £500 bench fee).

Student life

Its international officer describes the School of Pharmacy as a campus without walls, as it has a clear academic base (the Brunswick Square building) yet its students live in the same residences as those from the other faculties of the University of London. This enables them to make friends with two separate groups of people: those with whom they study and those with whom they live. International Hall is one of about six halls within five or 10 minutes' walk of SOP. The school also has an arrangement with International Students' House nearby with its social and recreational programmes, and has its own students' union and sports ground (owned jointly with the Royal Free Hospital). And SOP students are members of the University of London, whose active collegiate union, ULU, is conveniently just round the corner.

"I had an English education in Singapore and received a government scholarship, enabling me to study in the UK. Chemistry was one of my favourite subjects, but as I didn't want to do it on its own I chose pharmacy, which has better job prospects. I wanted to come to the SOP because of its reputation. I also preferred the idea of studying in London to anywhere else in the UK. One of the best things about the undergraduate course is the emphasis on understanding and applying rather than memorising facts. I'm living in a university residence, where life is busy and exciting. Making friends has been easy, and with other Singaporeans I've helped set up a Singaporean Society. I haven't been homesick, partly because Peggy Stone in the Registry is always around to make sure all is well." (Sheila Rankin graduated with a first-class honours degree in 1999)

Sheila Rankin, Singapore

The University of Sheffield

Write to: The University of Sheffield, International Office, 2 Palmerston Road, Sheffield S10 2TE

Tel: 0114 276 8966

Fax: 0114 272 9145

Email: international@sheffield.ac.uk

Website: www.shef.ac.uk/~io

Students: 21,726 (15,283 post-graduate, 3,884 international, from over 106 countries), 48:52 male:female.

University of Sheffield

Accommodation: single-sex, married/family, vacation, storage facilities. University residences from £36 a week self-catered, from £73 a week catered. Room in town from £36.

Entrance Requirements: ABB to BBC at A level at postgraduate, upper second degree or equivalent at postgraduate.

EFL: Cambridge Certificate of Proficiency in English grades A,B,C; GCSE or O level English grade C; IELTS average of 6.0, no section less than 5; TOEFL at least 550; NEAB university entrance test, pass; Hong Kong Examination authority, use of English grade C or above.

Foundation: courses are available but are currently under review. Contact the international office for further details.

Fees: from £7,050 to £9,300 a year. Clinical £17,000 a year.

Sheffield, the fifth largest city in the UK, is surrounded by beautiful countryside and there are over 50 parks within its boundaries. The city has more woodland than in any other English city. The university's origins go back to the 19th century but the university as it is today was founded in 1905. The main campus is central but the university buildings spread into the surrounding countryside and most student accommodation is in the residential suburbs of Broomhill, not far from the centre. It is a lively city. Once famous for its steel production, it

UNIVERSITIES AND COLLEGES

has since become a city of sport, with ice hockey at the Sheffield Arena, and athletics and rugby at the Don Valley Stadium. Sheffield is also a city for shoppers – Meadowhall an out-of-town shopping and entertainment centre attracts millions every year.

Academic strengths

Sheffield has been associated with four Nobel prizes, the two most recent being in 1993 and 1996. Dr Richard Roberts, a graduate in the Department of Chemistry, won a share in the Nobel prize for medicine/physiology in 1993 and 1996; and in 1996 Professor Harry Kato, graduate of the same department, won a share in the Nobel prize for chemistry.

Subject areas rated Excellent in recent teaching quality assessments include: architecture; East Asian studies; English; geography; history; law; mechanical engineering; electronic and electrical engineering; engineering materials; linguistics; music; sociology; social policy and administration; town and regional planning. A number of other departments also scored very highly. Sheffield has a strong engineering faculty offering a range of different courses from aerospace engineering to control engineering (see Engineering chapter). 80 per cent of departments assessed in the 1996 research assessment exercise were awarded one of the top two grades (4 or 5). Some computer rooms can be accessed 23 hours a day. Famous alumni include Britain's first astronaut Helen Sharman, as well as the current UK Secretary of State for Education, David Blunkett.

Student life

The students' union funds over 120 societies reflecting the huge range of interests shared by students. They range from religious and cultural societies to folk music and juggling. There are over 60 clubs devoted to sport. The university helped host the World Student Games in 1991 and has an all-weather 500m jogging track, tennis courts and a floodlit artificial turf pitch. There is a 33m swimming pool and 26 hectares of playing fields. The union runs plenty of entertainment attracting big names to the Octagon Centre, a major venue for live music, as well as providing usual services such as a bank, a launderette and bars and food outlets. The International Office runs a 'meet and greet' scheme for students arriving at Manchester International Airport as well as a week-long orientation programme before the beginning of their first semester. Students also receive free English language support throughout their course.

"I chose Sheffield firstly because of its reputation as a research university and because of the Excellent rating the psychology department received. Secondly, the idea of a university in a city which is close to a national park appealed to me. The lecturers and tutors are professional and very friendly. There is hardly any barrier between a lecturer and a student. Lectures are accompanied by state-of-the-art multimedia presentations which make them more interesting."

Terence Quek, Singapore

School of Oriental & African Studies

Write to: Fiamma Shani, School of Oriental and African Studies (SOAS), University of London, Russell Square, London WC1H 0XG

Tel: 020 7898 4032

Fax: 020 7898 4039

Email: study@soas.ac.uk

Website: www.soas.ac.uk

Students: 2,591 in 1998 (1,131 postgraduate, 29 per cent international, from over 80 countries), 40:60 male:female.

Accommodation: single-sex, married, vacation. University residences from £75 a week self-catered; room in town: prices vary enormously.

Entrance requirements: generally BBB at A level, 30 to 32 points at international baccalaureate.

EFL: IELTS: 7.0 overall and minimum or 5.5 in each sub test; TOEFL: minimum of 640.

Foundation: several available, intermediate certificate course (ICC) one-year, full-time for prospective undergraduates offers help with English; includes modules in business, international relations, European culture. The Diploma in English for Academic Purposes helps students improve their language skills. Diploma for prospective postgraduates; includes independent study project. Both recognised by UK universities.

Fees: £7,950 a year.

Housed in attractive buildings on Russell Square, SOAS is one of the world's major centres for the study of Africa and Asia. It was founded in 1916 and is part of the University of London. There are five regional departments, (Africa, East Asia, Near and Middle East, South Asia and South East Asia), which teach the language and culture of these areas. There are also 11 subject or discipline departments (anthropology and sociology, art and archaeology, development studies, economics,

SOAS main entrance

geography, history, law, linguistics, music, political studies and the study of religion). In addition, the school provides a range of English and foundation preparatory courses for overseas students ranging from three weeks to one year.

Academic Strengths

SOAS has been awarded high research ratings in music, history, linguistics, anthropology, archaeology and religious studies and the excellence of its teaching is widely recognised. Students can choose from over 400 undergraduate degree combinations including law, economics, history, politics, geography, linguistics, art and archaeology, music and one of more than 40 non-European languages. Graduate students can take an intensive one-year master's degree or a three-year PhD programme. The school specialises in the social sciences, humanities and languages of Asia and Africa and its alumni are found in many institutions around the world.

SOAS has a library of almost a million volumes in 1,000 languages. It has language teaching facilities that include computerised language learning facilities and a language laboratory that uses a Sony digital system. The library also plays a national role, and is used by readers from industry and government.

In 1995 SOAS opened the Brunei gallery. It has been designed to provide two distinct areas, a teaching block and a gallery. There is space for a small permanent art collection as well as facilities for visiting exhibitions.

Student Life

SOAS is centrally located, very near to the British Museum, the West End and Covent Garden. Despite being right at the heart of London, the school itself is set in a leafy and peaceful location. SOAS has long had an international community and caters for students' many different religions. There are two single sex prayer rooms, a number of religious communities and five Anglican chaplaincies. The students' union runs its own student newspaper, and organises entertainment from all over the world through its twice-weekly discos. There are over 30 registered societies within the union, many of which represent a region or country.

SOAS can offer modern accommodation with en suite study bedrooms 15 minutes' walk from the main building. Students are also eligible to apply for University of London accommodation. International students take part in a welcome session when they arrive and can study English for up to four hours a week in the English language centre.

I have always been interested in development economics, and enrolled to do an MSc in Development at SOAS because of its reputation for expertise in matters to do with African and Asian countries. Although I was daunted before starting, it was in fact not as difficult as I feared, and the highlight was the Environmental Development course which had an extremely interesting set of guest lecturers. SOAS is very cosmopolitan – I made friends from all over Europe and Asia, not just from England. And of course living in London was a big highlight.

Yoko Hashimoto, Japan

london
london
london

South Bank University

Write to: Christiane Buxton, Head of International Office, International Office, 103 Borough Road, London SE1 OAA

Tel: 020 7815 6138/6137/6711

Fax: 020 7815 6199

Email: internat@sbu.ac.uk

Website: www.sbu.ac.uk/internat/

Students: 20,500 in 1998/9 (6,000 postgraduates, 2,500 international students, from 120 countries) 49:51 male:female.

Accommodation: vacation university accommodation from £62 to £75 a week self-catering. Room in town from £50 a week.

Entrance requirements: two to three A levels, depending on the type of degree. One A level for HND programmes. Equivalent qualifications and work experience are also considered.

EFL: IELTS 6.0 to 6.5, TOEFL 550 to 580.

Foundation: available leading to degree programme.

Fees: classroom courses £6,000, laboratory courses £6,400. Postgraduate classroom courses £6,800. MBA £7,650.

South Bank University was founded in 1892 as the Borough Polytechnic and was granted university status in 1992. It is a cosmopolitan institution, located in the centre of London. The courses tend to share a strong practical element. The many attractions of London are within the easy reach of the university. This includes theatres, cinemas, museums, parks and pubs, as well as all the famous London landmarks. South Bank is, for example, in walking distance of the famous South Bank Arts Complex, and Covent Garden can be reached within 10 minutes on the bus. The university is connected to the city by two tube lines, the Northern and the Bakerloo lines. The university has 20,500 students. First-year, full-time international students are guaranteed a place in one of the halls of residence, all of which are in walking distance of the university.

South Bank University

Accommodation is self-catering with shared kitchen facilities. In their newest hall of residence, McLaren House which was opened in September 1995, rooms are en suite with toilets and showers. Students can also pay to have a telephone in their room.

Academic strengths

The university offers a learning resource centre which provides access to information on the Internet, on-line databases and CD-ROMs. Students are provided with email accounts after enrolment. There are two main libraries with extensive collections of information sources including books, newspapers, journals, slides and audio-visual material. The language centre offers access to live satellite broadcasts and self-study materials such as books, tapes, and CD-ROMs. In total South Bank University has over half a million volumes and over 30,000 periodicals. There are extensive computer facilities in each university building.

In *The Times* 'Good University Guide 1998/99' South Bank's staff to student ratio was the 32nd best in the UK with 10.8 students to every member of staff. In the same guide, South Bank was ranked as being the 82nd best university in the country at research, while its teaching was assessed as being 79th best.

Student life

There is an active students' union that runs a variety of clubs and societies for people with sporting, cultural and social interests. Amongst the many sports clubs, there are football, basketball and badminton clubs. Cultural associations include African, Islamic and Chinese societies. There is also an active branch of Amnesty International and a film society. The sport facilities on the campus include a fitness suite and 21 acres of outdoor pitches in Dulwich. A regular student magazine is produced by the union. The chaplaincy includes both Anglican and Catholic chaplains who are open to meet students from other faiths and provide contact names and addresses of other religious organisations. The university also has a prayer room for Muslim students.

There is a meet and greet service for new international students arriving at the airport. There is also an introductory course for international students, free English language classes for two hours a week and an international student adviser. A scholarship scheme worth £2,000 in the form of tuition fee reduction for each year of study is available for new applicants. The international office may be contacted for further details.

"I took an MSc in International Business and Marketing at South Bank Business School and I am now working for the university's international office as their China representative. 'I want Chinese people to know the name South Bank, just like they might recognise the Oxbridge names. In China, people know about London but they don't realise what a good place this is to study. When I came to South Bank, I felt it was a very warm and friendly place. I am determined to put South Bank firmly on the map in the minds of Chinese students and to tell them about the very strong advantages they will have in studying here."

Min Liu, China

SOUTHAMPTON INSTITUTE

Southampton Institute

Write to: International Marketing Officer, Southampton Institute, East Park Terrace, Southampton SO14 0YN

Tel: 023 8031 9422

Fax: 023 8031 9412

Email: peggy.lardot@solent.ac.uk

Website: www.solent.ac.uk

Students: around 13,500 in 1999 (670 postgraduate, around 1,000 international, from nearly 50 countries), 60:40 male:female.

Accommodation: single, single-sex, vacation. Institute residences from £69 to £76 a week self-catering. Room in town from £45 to £50 a week.

Entrance requirements: two or three A levels in appropriate subjects or equivalent.

EFL: Cambridge Certificate: Advanced or Proficiency depending on course, IELTS 6.0 to 6.5, TOEFL 550 to 600.

Foundation: none.

Fees: £5,400 a year, plus £50 annual studio fees for some courses or £83 registration fee for BTEC courses.

Southampton is a large medieval city with a rich maritime history, but it has up-to-date shopping, sporting and cultural centres. It has a student population of over 20,000. The Southampton Institute's city campus is close to the centre of town, giving easy access to these facilities and numerous parks. The climate in Southampton, situated on England's south coast, is milder than most other parts of the British Isles.

Academic strengths

Southampton's college of higher education was founded in 1969 and

Southampton Institute's Mountbatten Library

merged with the Southampton College of Art in 1981. Southampton Institute was founded in 1984 with the incorporation of the College of Nautical Studies at Warsash. This heritage is reflected in the strengths of the institute's design and maritime courses. Southampton Institute's mission is to provide "courses for careers, research for results." Vocational, practical and innovative courses offered by the institute include a four-year sandwich BA (Hons) in Financial Services and a Yacht and Powercraft Design course. Many student projects are linked to local businesses. The institute offers degrees in fine art and graphic design, international design, and the more unusual degree in fine arts valuation and antiques (history and collecting), in which students are able to handle real art objects from the unique study collection. Many of the courses offered combine academic work with vocational skills. Southampton Business School (with over 4,400 students) offers more than 20 courses with a greater flexibility and choice of options for students. Degrees offered by Southampton Institute are validated by The Nottingham Trent University. The academic year has currently two 15-week (teaching) semesters, starting in September and February.

Student life

The institute has well-developed student support systems, including full-time counselling, study assistance, information services and careers services, backed up by modern IT systems and easy access to computers, software and networks. There are six new student residences providing 2,300 rooms (over 1,000 with en suite facilities), within easy walking distance of the main campus. Facilities on the campus include a bookshop, general shops, cashpoints, a sports hall and a library.There is also a fitness suite and swimming pool, and saunas and solariums are available to all. Southampton itself can offer all kinds of entertainments, including bowling, a multiscreen cinema. as well as many pubs, clubs, bars and restaurants.

An induction programme before enrolment, and social events throughout the year are organised for international students. The institute is committed to ensuring that international students settle in well, and provides support services to deal with any difficulties that may arise.

"Although I am from the USA, I was actually brought up in Germany. I chose Southampton Institute because it is one of the top five institutions in the UK for film studies. Southampton is also ideal for student life as nothing is futher than 15 minutes walk away. The only surprise to me has been the amount of course work we have to do. Staff at the International Affairs Office provide all-year-round support for international students, which is important because it's often hard to make friends with British students. I have been involved in the Institute's meet-and-greet service for the last couple of years. I think it's a very important first point of contact for all new arrivals."

Michael Deming, USA

University of Southampton

Write to: Jo Nesbitt or Sian Williams, Academic Registrar's, University of Southampton, Highfield, Southampton SO17 1BJ

Tel: 023 8059 2761

Fax: 023 8059 5789

Email: ednfairs@soton.ac.uk

Website: www.soton.ac.uk

Students: 16,883 in 1999/2000 (3,211 postgraduates, 1,787 international students, from over 100 countries).

Accommodation: Catered, self-catered, limited family facilities. Vacation facilities. University residences from £45 to £100 a week. Rooms in town from £40 a week.

Entrance requirements: vary according to subject, please refer to the prospectus for details.

EFL: TOEFL 600, IELTS 6.5 minimum. Lower qualifications for pre-sessional English courses.

Foundation: courses in engineering, art and design, science, social sciences and arts. Successful completion of foundation courses leads to degree course entry.

Fees: classroom courses £6,900 a year, laboratory courses £9,050 a year, clinical medicine £17,540 a year, (1999/2000 rates).

The University of Southampton has its roots in the Hartley Institute, founded in 1862. The university was granted its royal charter in 1952. Since then it has had some notable, international alumni including John Hyde, who played a part in designing the Intel Pentium, and Dr Jason Hu, the Taiwan foreign minister.

The main campus at Southampton is at Highfield, situated two miles from the city centre. The Avenue campus is home to the Faculty of Arts while the School of Ocean and Earth Science is based at the dockside Southampton Oceanography Centre. Art and design are taught in the nearby historic town of Winchester, at the Winchester School of Art.

Southampton has a population of 200,000, including 40,000 students. It is situated on the south coast – just a

University of Southampton campus

ferry ride away from France and the rest of Europe. The marina, Ocean Village, regularly plays host to international sailing events such as the Whitbread Round-the-World yacht race. The city also boasts two cinemas, two large theatres, several concert halls and art galleries.

Academic strengths

The University of Southampton has seven faculties that cover most academic disciplines. All departments that have been assessed scored over 18 out of 24 in teaching quality assessments. The electrical engineering and electronics, and computer science departments both obtained 24 out of 24.

The university prides itself on research and 32 departments assessed by the research assessment exercise obtained ratings of 4 and above. Southampton is also one of the top five universities in the UK in terms of research income. It is the only university in the country to have had six millennium products approved for display in the Millennium Dome.

There are seven libraries affiliated to the university, the largest of which is the Hartley Library housing over one million books on the main campus. Networked computer workstations can be found throughout the campus and may be accessed by all students.

Student life

The student scene is based around the Highfield campus although students are sufficiently near to the town to take advantage of facilities there. The students' union supports over one hundred clubs and societies. Many of these have an international dimension such as the Chinese, Singapore and Turkish societies. Furthermore, there are religious societies including the Buddhist society and the Islamic society. The Christian chaplaincy caters for all denominations and there is a Muslim prayer room on the campus.

The university has an international students' welfare adviser and offers many English language courses both before courses start and during term time. All international students are invited to attend a welcome conference.

A hardship fund exists to which all students, home or international, may apply if the need arises. This caters for students whose hardship has arisen since they began the course. A limited number of scholarships exist in a range of departments.

"From the age of eleven I heard about the UK from my English pen pal. I'm from a Singaporean, middle-income family and I regard the chance to study in England as a blessing. I chose the University of Southampton for a degree in computer engineering because it has a strong reputation throughout the world for electronics and computer science courses. As an undergraduate, I have been involved in sports and other club events. As a result, I have both British and overseas friends. Mental preparation is the key to success and I have had to be more independent. But if I have problems, there are plenty of people around to help me. For the first time in my life I have faced culture shock, getting used to British food, weather, accents and customs. But now I enjoy all these things. Studying in Southampton is the experience of a lifetime."

Steven Kok Liang Yeo, Singapore

UNIVERSITY OF ST ANDREWS

University of St Andrews

Write to: The International Office, University of St Andrews, Butts Wynd, St Andrews, Fife, Scotland KY16 9AJ

Tel: 01334 463323

Fax: 01334 462270

Email: elt@st-and.ac.uk

Website: www.st-and.ac.uk

Students: 5,878 in 1998/9 (900 postgraduates, 12 per cent international students, from 70 countries), 48:52 male:female.

Accommodation: married, family, vacation and storage facilities. University residence from £31 a week self-catered, from £61 to £82 a week full board. Room in town from £45 to £50 a week.

Entrance requirements: BBB to BBC at A level. 28 to 32 points at International Baccalaureate. For other entrance qualifications, contact Admissions (admissions@st-and.ac.uk).

EFL: TOEFL 580 minimum, IELTS 6.0 to 6.5.

Foundation: English language teaching, year-long access courses.

Fees: classroom courses £6,950 a year, laboratory courses £9,175 a year.

St Andrews is home to the oldest university in Scotland and the third oldest in the UK. The university is not campus-based and its buildings are spread throughout the town of St Andrews which lies on the Fife coast, north of Edinburgh. St Andrews enjoys excellent road connections with larger centres. Leuchars, the nearest railway station on the main east coast rail line from Aberdeen to London, is easily accessed by public transport.

St Andrews is a relatively small university with around 5,000 under-graduates and students are guaranteed university-owned accommodation in their first year. The university has a mix of modern and traditional housing, which ensures that there is accommodation to suit every character.

University of St Andrews campus

UNIVERSITIES AND COLLEGES

442

St Andrews is steeped in history and this antiquity is still visible in its monuments, beautiful old buildings and city walls. Nevertheless the city thrives today, having expanded threefold since the turn of the century. St Andrews is a safe place to study with crime rates below the UK average. It is also a tourist centre, famous both as "the Home of Golf" and for its long, sandy beaches.

Due to its large international student population, the university is cosmopolitan in its outlook. There are many pubs and cafes in St Andrews, many of which are frequented by students.

Academic strengths

St Andrews has the highest accumulated teaching quality assessment average in Scotland. In terms of research, the university has won the most consistently high set of research ratings in Scotland.

Students join one of three faculties: Arts, Science, and Divinity. Modules are studied which provide credits. In the first two years, different general subject areas are studied whereas the last two years are more specialised. Teaching primarily takes place through lectures that are supported, depending on the subject, by tutorials, seminars, laboratory work, fieldwork and individual study.

Students can take advantage of the 750,000 books provided by the modern, main library in the centre of town. There are also substantial departmental libraries. Computing laboratories are available 24-hours a day, 7-days a week and all university bedrooms can support networked computers. The university also boasts an observatory and a marine laboratory.

Student life

Students can participate in a host of activities offered by the university. There are over 100 societies and 50 sports clubs. The students' association is very active and there are undergraduate and postgraduate representatives on many university committees.

International students have their own overseas society that offers entertainment and activities for its members. At the beginning of each semester, the international office runs an orientation weekend for international students. They are also provided with an international student guide. The English Language Teaching provides free proof-reading support; and a low-cost, year-round English course for students.

"I chose computer science at St Andrews University both because of my instant love of the town and because of the excellent reputation which precedes St Andrews and its associated departments. The computer science department offered an exceptional range of topics to study throughout the four-year course. This, coupled with the opportunity to change direction at any point, meant that I had the freedom to let my studies develop and to decide on the direction in the computing industry that I wanted to take. Having graduated in 1998, I am working as a software engineer for Integrated Sales Systems UK Ltd, a cutting edge marketing software company. Thanks to my time at St Andrews, I have developed the technical and social skills necessary to make my career enjoyable and successful, and feel prepared for the challenges that the future holds."

Iain Ollerenshaw, UK

Staffordshire University

Write to: Ariel Edge, International Office, Staffordshire University, College Road, Stoke-on-Trent, ST4 2DE

Tel: 01782 292 718

Fax: 01782 292 796

Email: a.m.edge@staffs.ac.uk

Website: www.staffs.ac.uk/ welcome.html

Students: 14,623 in 1998/9 (621 postgraduates, 412 international from 76 countries). 53:47 male:female

Accommodation: single or twin rooms, vacation. University residences from £27 to £56 a week self-catering. Some en suite rooms.

Entrance requirements: two subjects at A level plus GCSE passes in three other separate subjects/three subjects at A level plus one GCSE in another separate subject, or international equivalent.
EFL: Cambridge proficiency Grade C IELTS 6, TOEFL 550.

Foundation: in design, fine art, applied science, computing, business, extended technology programme, extended engineering programme, and BTEC foundation art and design.

Fees: Fees 2000/2001 classroom courses £5,950 per year, studio and laboratory courses £6,500, MBA £7,800. Scholarships available.

Staffordshire is located in the heart of England between Birmingham and Manchester, in a region known as the Midlands. The area is famous for the death-defying adventure theme park Alton Towers, the beautiful countryside of the Staffordshire Moorlands and an internationally renowned ceramic industry. A network of roads and railways enables easy access to major cities in England such as Birmingham and Manchester. London is only 1 hour 45 minutes away on the train.

Staffordshire University began as an assortment of technical and art colleges in the early part of this century and has grown into a thriving institution. Based at two campuses the university offers a mix of city and country, with one campus located at a greenfield site at

Staffordshire University

Stafford and one in the centre of the busy city of Stoke on Trent. Students are attracted to the region and its university by the relatively low cost of living and competitive tuition fees.

Academic Strengths

The university has eight academic schools. The School of Art and Design is pioneering the use of computers in art and design practice. Students enjoy the use of well-equipped studios, work-spaces, and a gallery in New York. The School of Computing has ten courses within the undergraduate 'Computing Degree Scheme', offering a wide range of programmes from computer science to internet technology and computer graphics, imaging and visualisation. Staffordshire University has one of the largest higher education Computing Schools in the UK. The university operates a modular programme for its degree courses and has strong links with both local industry and international institutions. The well-stocked libraries contain over 300,000 books, and 2,000 up-to-date periodical titles along with 80 databases on CD ROM for reference catalogues. Students can research on-line and benefit from free induction and study skill sessions offered by the library. Computer facilities are available to all students and are accessible throughout the evenings and on Saturdays. They include a choice of Apple Macs and PCs, with access to the Internet.

Student Life

The students' union provides an assortment of bars, shops and catering outlets. Students can join a number of societies according to their religious, political, cultural, or recreational interests. The International Society welcomes students from all over the world, and arranges social events throughout the year. There are also specific national societies such as the Chinese or Malaysian society. The Film Theatre shows popular films on campus during term time.

Students can participate in a number of sports at the university. The sports hall provides facilities for most indoor sports and activities from badminton to yoga to indoor climbing.

International students are welcomed with an induction week at the beginning of term, with a packed programme of orientation and social activities. Coach transfers from Heathrow airport are arranged for specific days. Students are offered a wide choice in English language provision. There is a Foundation English course, an intensive Summer School, and a two-week pre-sessional course in addition to free modules that can be taken alongside a degree.

"It was through a friend of mine that I heard about Staffordshire University. The first time I came here from Taiwan it felt like a great place to study and I was very impressed with the staff and lecturers who are so friendly and helpful. I love my course, (an MSc degree in International Finance), and it has given me the chance to visit other countries and undertake research overseas. This year we went to the Czech Republic and had a great time experiencing a different environment to the UK. As part of my research I also got a chance to interview our vice chancellor about overseas students choosing to study in the UK. Apart from university life, there is lots to do in Stoke on Trent, and I have made many good friends in the church that I have joined."

Emily Liao Yuan Ying, Taiwan

University of Stirling

Write to: Student Recruitment and Admissions Service, University of Stirling, Stirling FK9 4LA

Tel: 01786 467 046

Fax: 01786 466 800

Email: international@stir.ac.uk

Website: www.stir.ac.uk

Students: 7,500 in 1999/00 (1200 postgraduates, 600–900 international, from over 70 countries), 49:51 male:female.

Accommodation: single, married, single-sex, vacation. University residences from £45 a week. Room in town from £45 to £50 a week.

Entrance requirements: Bs and Cs in Scottish Highers, A levels or equivalent required for most subjects (BBC for business, English, film and media, human resource management, marketing and Scottish studies).

EFL: Cambridge Advanced Certificate grade A, Cambridge Proficiency grade C, IELTS 6, TOEFL 550.

Fees: classroom courses £5,950 a year, laboratory courses £7,850 a year, taught MA, some MSc and MBA £8,900 a year.

Stirling's Bridge of Allan campus is built around a lake, Airthrey Loch, and is surrounded by the steep, wooded Ochil Hills. The stark, white university buildings rising through the treetops have a certain grandeur, although those who decry modern architecture compare them unfavourably with the beautiful green, landscaped grounds and the area's solid, typically Scottish stone houses. This region preserves sacred monuments of Scottish history, so it isn't surprising that Stirling is a popular

Stirling Campus

choice for history students. The Wallace Monument, commemorating one of Scotland's most famous fighters for independence, William Wallace, who won a victory there in the 13th century, looms over the campus. The university lies just outside the town of Stirling, whose castle was the home of Scottish kings. Close by is Bannockburn, site of the battle of 1314 where Robert the Bruce defeated an English army three times larger than his own.

Frequent buses connect the university with Stirling, whose railway service is prompt, clean and efficient, and serves Glasgow and Edinburgh, respectively. It also has direct services to London, Perth and Aberdeen. Not bad for a small town, considering that students are 10 per cent of the population.

Academic strengths

Stirling is one of Scotland's smaller universities and one of its most modern, having been founded as recently as 1967. It is also one of its most innovative – it was the first in the UK to introduce a semester system of two terms of fifteen weeks each, from September and February, with a short summer semester from late June to mid-August. It puts a higher value on teaching standards than on research. The country's teaching quality assessors recently awarded

Excellent ratings in economics, environmental science, religious studies and sociology. The university has four faculties: Arts, Human Sciences, Management and Natural Sciences, and offers many attractive and unusual courses. The Faculty of Management offers the widest range, including sports studies with management. Stirling is the Scottish centre for Japanese studies and has strong courses in film and media, an aquaculture course in its Environmental Science Department, and a degree in English as a foreign language. Flexibility is the keyword – there are many routes through the curriculum, and combined degrees in many subjects are offered by different faculties.

Student life

The campus is the focus of university life; there is enough accommodation for all first-year students, and amenities include cafes, shops and the McRobert Arts Centre, which provides a venue for film-showings, concerts and theatre. All students have an adviser to help plan coursework and achieve goals and deadlines. English language classes are available for international students (at a cost). The Student Information and Support Service also offers specialist assistance and advice.

"I came to Stirling at the beginning of the autumn semester, to read for an MPhil in Publishing Studies. I graduated in English from the University of Beijing four years ago, and then I joined a publishing company. I work with English clients like Longmans, the Oxford University Press, and BBC Books, so they sent me on this course to improve my knowledge of Western publishing. At the British Council in Beijing I found out that Stirling's Media Studies courses are famous internationally. It's hard work, but fruitful. I'm learning everything about publishing – editing, electronic publishing, printing, production, even marketing. Stirling is very peaceful. I live in a university flat, and it's comfortable, but there's no TV. I wish I'd known... I was looking forward to watching TV in English."

Sheng Chiang, China

 **University of Sunderland**

University of Sunderland

Write to: Centre for International Education, Technology Park, Chester Road, Sunderland SR2 7PS

Tel: 0191 515 2648

Fax: 0191 515 2960

Email: international@sunderland.ac.uk

Website: www.sunderland.ac.uk

Accommodation: single-sex, some married accommodation. University residences from £45 a week. Room in town from £30 to £35 a week.

Students: 15,700 in 1998 (1,500 postgraduate, 1,200 international, from 66 countries), 50:50 male:female.

Entrance requirements: many international qualifications are recognised as meeting the university's requirements and students from all countries are encouraged to apply.

EFL: IELTS 6, TOEFL 550.

Fees: classroom courses £6,300 a year undergraduates, £6,400 postgraduates; laboratory courses £7,300 a year undergraduates, £7,400 postgraduates, MBA £6,950, foundation programmes £6,300, PhD band 1 £6,400, PhD band 2 £7,400, study abroad £5,100. The university also has an extensive scholarship scheme and all international applicants are encouraged to apply.

Sunderland, Britain's newest city, is on the coast of north-eastern England. Some 300,000 people live and work here and it is a fast expanding city. The friendliness of the people mean that students soon feel at home, and they are able to take part in the life of a city that still has a strong sense of community.

St Peter's Campus, University of Sunderland

UNIVERSITIES AND COLLEGES

Sunderland is home to the spectacular new National Glass Centre built on the banks of the River Wear, next to St Peter's campus, with workshop and gallery facilities. Nearby is Sunderland Football Club's Stadium of Light which seats 42,000 and is one of the UK's largest football stadiums.

St Peter's and the main university campus at Chester Road are just minutes away from the city centre. Most students are able to live very close by, thanks to the compact nature of the city and the extent of the university accommodation. Student clubs and associations are always popular and the city has all the cultural, entertainment and shopping amenities that you expect of a major city.

Academic strengths

The university is organised into six "schools", each of which is responsible for a number of related disciplines and for the programmes within those disciplines: art, design and media; computing and engineering technology; education; sciences; social and international studies and business.

During the past year the university has been rated as Excellent in every one of the subjects in which they were assessed including Communication and Media Studies; Pharmacy and Pharmacology; Physiology and now Biological Sciences. Additionally, nearly all of Sunderland's teacher training courses have been given the highest possible ranking.

Student life

Sunderland is a city you can walk across in 15 minutes and it is, on average, safe and cheap to live in. There are few traffic jams. It has good clubs and the students' union owns a nightclub, Manor Quay. From Sunday to Thursday, Sunderland is a quiet town, but on Fridays and Saturdays it comes to life. The union operates late-night transport to collect women students from late venues and drive them home. There are two theatres and the union film club.

Advise the university of your arrival and they will direct you to Sunderland and meet you when you get there. You will be offered accommodation throughout your course, and have access to all student welfare services. Students are encouraged to meet people through induction weeks, social events and societies. At the weekends there is a choice of venues. Sunderland is a short train trip from the lively city of Newcastle; there are big, sandy beaches about five minutes away; and several national parks – Weardale, the North York Moors and the North Pennines. In addition, Sunderland, Middlesbrough and Newcastle all have their own well-supported football teams.

"When I decided my career was in science, I surfed the net to find out about studying in the UK. I came to Sunderland in 1996 to do a BSc (Hons) in Chemical and Pharmaceutical Science. The lecturers are helpful and you can go and talk to them whenever you need to. There is easy access to computers, and I can check things out on the Internet whenever I need to. Accommodation is comfortable, and although there are five Portuguese speakers in my hall I enjoy being able to get to know people from other countries."

Maria Cabaco, Portugal

The Surrey Institute of Art & Design University College

Write to: The Registry, The Surrey Institute of Art and Design, Falkner Road, Farnham Campus, Surrey GU9 7DS

Tel: 01252 722441

Fax: 01252 892616

Email: registry@surrart.ac.uk

Website: www.surrart.ac.uk

Students: 3,080 (including 2,525 undergraduates, 30 postgraduates and 130 international students from 66 countries). 57:43 male female ratio.

Accommodation: single sex, vacation summer extra charge. Institute residences from £33 to £55.80 a week self-catered. Room in town from £45 to £60 a week.

Entrance requirements: A levels in appropriate subjects or Foundation Diploma in Art and Design. International Baccalaureate accepted. IELTS 6 or TOEFL 550.

Fees: Undergraduate £7,804, Postgraduate £6,042 (£3,020 part-time)

Situated in picturesque Surrey, the Surrey Institute of Art and Design has two purpose-built campuses in Epsom and Farnham, small market towns half an hour from London by train. Both towns are pleasant, rather genteel market towns, set in attractive countryside but close enough to get to London easily for shopping or clubbing.

The Farnham campus is set in 16 acres of grounds beneath Farnham castle and has a spectacular new entrance building that doubles as a gallery. The Epsom campus is not far from the famous racecourse.

The Surrey Institute of Art & Design, University College

Academic strengths

The Institute is one of the largest independent colleges specialising in art, design and communication in Europe, with 20 programmes offering progression routes from a Foundation Diploma right through to undergraduate and post-graduate degrees as well as short courses. All courses have a professional practice element in each year of the programme giving students the chance to understand the business side of their subject and develop contacts. Many of the lecturers are also professional practitioners, and there is a strong emphasis on developing practical, employable skills.

Popular with overseas students is the one year Foundation Diploma in Art and Design, which can be taken at both the Epsom and Farnham campuses. For this you need one A level and three GCSE passes or international equivalent.

Epsom offers degrees in graphic design and fashion and fashion promotion, and illustration. Animation is a popular area, and the Farnham campus offers degrees in this as well as fine art, three dimensional design, film and video and photography. It also offers journalism, design management, packaging design, visual communications, interior design and textiles courses.

Student life

Much of the social life of students is based around the busy students' union (SU). It hosts a number of clubs and societies and organises bands, dances and films. As well as Epsom's famous racecourse, both towns have a number of pubs, bars, restaurants, theatres and sporting facilities. The towns are close to London so students can benefit from all the cultural and entertainment opportunities the capital has to offer.

There is an International Welfare Officer with specific responsibility to look after international students, and advice is also available for health matters and careers. International students have priority in booking rooms in the student village in Farnham. There is also a "meet and greet" programme and induction course when they first arrive. English language classes are available free of charge at three levels of tuition.

"After graduating from high school I did a foundation course in European Studies and it was then that I first became attracted to the world of fashion and communication. I heard about the degree in fashion promotion and illustration at the Surrey Institute of Art and Design from an English friend. A year later I found myself at Heathrow Airport ready to start a new life in a different country. Having spent almost three years here, it has been the best experience of my life so far. Apart from learning how to become more independent, I have also cultivated all the intellectual and practical skills I need in order to enter the fashion industry. I have found it very interesting to study a foreign fashion industry that is so different from that of my own culture. I recently did my work placement at a model agency and plan to work there as a booker once I have graduated."

Harris Spyropoulou, Greece

University of Sussex

Write to: Dr Philip Baker, International and Study Abroad Office, Arts B, University of Sussex, Falmer, Brighton BN1 9QN

Tel: 01273 678 422

Fax: 01273 678 640

Email: international.off@sussex.ac.uk

Website: www.sussex.ac.uk

Students: 9,176 in 1998/9 (2,205 postgraduate, 3,365 international, from 116 countries), 45:55 male:female.

Accommodation: single-sex (female), family, vacation. University residences from £50 a week self-catered. Room in town £45 a week (1999 figures).

Entrance requirements: vary according to subject, generally BBB-BCD. Overall pass in International Baccalaureate, including 14-17 in the 3 appropriate highers.

EFL: for undergraduate IELTS 6.5, TOEFL paper-based test 600 and TWE 4, computer-based test 250; for postgraduate IELTS 6.0-7.0, TOEFL 550 and TWE 4 or 600 and TWE 5, computer-based test 213-250.

Foundation: courses are currently available at local colleges in most subjects in the arts and sciences. Please contact the university for further details.

Fees: classroom courses £6,870 a year, laboratory courses £9,120 a year (1999/2000 figures).

The University of Sussex is a campus university and most of its residences, lecture theatres, seminar rooms, laboratories, restaurants, bars and sports facilities are situated within close proximity to each other in the university's parkland. Sussex is the only university in England with the whole of its academic campus situated in a designated area of outstanding natural beauty. The South Downs countryside, consisting of historic villages, hills and open farmland, is popular with day trippers, hikers, and mountain bikers.

Within a few minutes' train journey of the university is the seaside town of Brighton. Students form a large proportion of the town's population – over ten per cent – and many of the local bars and clubs have nights geared towards student entertainment. The atmosphere of the town is liberal and

University of Sussex campus

cosmopolitan. One major cultural attraction is the annual Brighton Festival. For three weeks in May international musicians, dancers and performers come to the town for England's biggest arts festival.

Academic strengths

The University of Sussex offers nearly 200 undergraduate degrees and over 100 taught postgraduate programmes. In the 1996 research assessment exercise, Sussex was awarded 5 or 5* in the following subjects: American studies, biological sciences, chemistry, computer science, English, history, history of art, pure mathematics, French, German, media studies and the science policy research unit. A total of 83% of academic staff at the university work in subject areas which have received a rating of 4 or 5. Nine of the ten subjects assessed under the current teaching quality assessment scheme (i.e. since 1995) have scored 20 or more points out of 24, with sociology achieving the maximum score of 24 in 1995. Under the previous scheme, those subjects which were awarded an Excellent were English (in 1994), and music and anthropology (in 1995).

The university library has a collection of over 750,000 books. It also has special collections which include the papers of Leonard and Virginia Woolf, Rudyard Kipling, and the archive of the *New Statesman* journal.

Student life

To ease international students into the start of their courses a 'Welcome and Information Programme' runs before the start of the autumn term. Pre-sessional English language courses are available and, during term-time, there are classes in English for academic purposes for those who should require them. Students can take the Cambridge exams in English at the university.

The International and Study Abroad Office organises day trips to places of interest, social events, and trips for international students. There is also the 'HOST' scheme, in which students can go and stay with a British family for a weekend and see more of Britain.

The students' union is the focus of many student activities at Sussex. Alongside its over 100 clubs and societies, it runs a newspaper, a radio station and an award-winning magazine. One of the clubs matches international students with home students to exchange conversational language skills. The university's sports facilities include 14 acres of playing fields, sports halls and squash courts.

"I studied Sociology at Universidad Complutense in Madrid, and I spent my last year as an ERASMUS student at the University of Sussex at Brighton, specialising in 'Development Studies'. I chose to stay for my MA in Migration Studies because of the excellent resources this university offers, and its brilliant teachers. At first it was a bit difficult to get used to such a different academic system, especially when participating in seminars with very few students and having to write essays in English, but everybody is very helpful. Brighton is also a great place to live. Its location by the sea and the young and cosmopolitan atmosphere of its inhabitants make it an ideal place to spend a year abroad. It is close to London and the sun shines more than elsewhere in the UK! Definitely, this is one of the best (if not 'the' best) places to choose!!! Enjoy it!"

Maira Vergara, Spain

UNIVERSITY OF TEESSIDE

middlesbrough
middlesbrough
middlesbrough

University of Teesside

Write to: Academic Registry, University of Teesside, Middlesbrough TS1 3BA

Tel: 01642 218 121

Fax: 01642 342 067

Email: h.cummins@tees.ac.uk

Website: www.tees.ac.uk

Students: 11,397 undergraduates (1,766 postgraduates, around 400 international students, from 45 countries).

Accommodation: Priority is given to international students, with 1000 places available in halls of residence and 400 in university-managed private housing in and around Middlesbrough. Prices from £39 to £47.50 a week self-catering, private rented accommodation from £29 to £33 a week.

Entrance requirements: HND: A level pass + 3 GCSE passes; Undergraduate degrees: 5 GCSE passes + 2 A levels; Postgraduates: first degree in relevant subject area.

Foundation: HND courses available.

Fees: £6,000 a year + supplements for health-related courses.

Located on a single campus in the centre of Middlesbrough, the University of Teesside offers more than 200 full-time courses from HND through to degree and postgraduate qualifications. Middlesbrough is in the Teesside region of North East England, which is undergoing somewhat of a renaissance at the moment with a number of new developments. For students one of the big benefits is that this is one of the cheapest places to live in the UK, as well as being near some beautiful coast and countryside. Other attractions include the multimillion pound Riverside Stadium - home to Middlesbrough Football Club, and the international standard water sports facility on the Tees Barrage.

Academic strengths

The university is divided into six schools: Business and Management, Computing and Mathematics, Health, Law, Arts and Humanities, International Studies, Science and Technology and Social Sciences. The university's principal

Learning Resource Centre

strengths are in computing, where it got an Excellent teaching quality rating, and in engineering, business and health-related subjects. It also offers courses in social sciences, law, art and design and humanities. Many programmes are offered in a flexible modular form and students may tailor some of their studies to meet their own needs or interests. Most undergraduate programmes are professionally orientated and many include an opportunity to undertake a work placement with a relevant business or commercial organisation.

The brand new Learning Resource Centre is a combined IT and library centre and has over 1,300 specially designed study places, 300 open access computer workstations with email and Internet software, language learning facilities and video viewing stations.

Student life

The university has spent over £30 million on new buildings and improvements to the facilities, and many are brand new or have recently been upgraded. These include new student accommodation and an Innovation and Virtual Reality Centre, which is home to the School of Science and Technology.

The students' union offers a varied programme of events. Features include theme nights such as "Fruity" and "Liquid Cool", live bands, DJs, comedy and big screen coverage of sporting events. Social events are focused around the union's three bars, "Union Central", "Central Cafe" and "The Zoo", a 1,000 capacity venue. The union building is fully accessible to students with disabilities, with lifts running to each floor. Students have access to a chaplaincy, a nursery, a health service, an advice centre and a counselling service. The university also has its own cinema.

North Yorkshire's coastline and moors provide opportunities for a wide range of outdoor activities. Sporting strengths at national level include rugby league, canoeing, martial arts, women's rugby, cycling, athletics and soccer. Trips are arranged internationally for skiing, squash, basketball, soccer and watersports. The fitness centre has a gym, sauna and climbing wall, and there are outdoor tennis courts. The Student Support Unit provides welfare and advice services to help international students adjust to the environment as well as practical assistance with accommodation, health care and immigration procedures. Subject to availability the university also provides English language courses. Students in financial difficulty can apply to the hardship fund run by the students' union.

"My government has sent me to Britain from Qatar to do an HND course in fabrication and welding engineering. They sent me because I can speak English and I have a Diploma in Sciences from the USA, and they operate a scheme with the University of Teesside. My wife is American and she'd wanted to see Britain, so we were glad to come. We found a nice house quickly and the people of Teesside are really friendly. We've brought our two older children over and they go to school in Middlesbrough, but we miss our youngest daughter who needs to stay at her school in Qatar. There are fantastic facilities at Teesside. The workshops have all the machinery you ever wanted to learn about and some you've never seen in your life. I'd like to transfer to a BSc degree course and later try for a master's degree if I can."

Ateeq Al-khulaifi, Qatar

Thames Valley University

Write to: Thames Valley University Learning Advice Centre, 18-22 Bond Street, Ealing, London, W5 5RF

Tel: 020 8579 5000

Fax: 020 8231 2900

Email: learning.advice@tvu.ac.uk

Web: www.tvu.ac.uk

Students: 25,112 in 1998 (4,760 postgraduates, 2 per cent of undergraduates and 5 per cent of postgraduates international), 36:64 male:female.

Accommodation: no university accommodation available. Room in town from £50 to £105 a week.

Entrance requirements: two A levels or international equivalent.

EFL: IELTS 5.5, TOEFL 550.

Fees: undergraduate £6,000 a year; postgraduate £3,090 to £9,270 a year.

In terms of student numbers, TVU is one of the UK's largest universities, yet its two campuses – one in the west London suburb of Ealing and one out to the west of London in the thriving town of Slough, near Windsor – are fairly compact. The university's large complement of more than 18,000 part-time and open or distance learning students account for this discrepancy. More than 85 per cent of TVU's students are over 21; more than 30 per cent are members of ethnic minorities; and some 20 per cent are from overseas. TVU goes back a long way, to a school founded in 1860 by a local philanthropist on the main site in St Mary's Road, Ealing. But since 1966, when it became a higher education institution, it has taught international students. Tutors who were there in the 1960s remember students and teachers from the USSR and China.

Students from overseas flying into Heathrow Airport don't have far to travel. The Ealing site is just a few underground stops away. Ealing is one of the more pleasant London suburbs, with accommodation at prices that are resonable for London. It's within easy reach of some of London's most spectacular sights: Hampton Court Palace, Eton School and Windsor Castle. In the other direction,

The Paul Hamlyn Learning Resource Centre

it's just half an hour by underground into central London.

Academic strengths

TVU has just revised its entire undergraduate curriculum to give students the greatest possible flexibility of choice. Subjects can be taken in major/minor combinations, business studies with information systems, for example, or as a specialisation: law is often studied by itself. A range of experts are available to help students design their courses according to their needs, and each student is allocated a personal tutor for advice and support. The idea is that students become independent learners, and the 700 computers, software, tapes, journals, books and other learning resources they may need are organised in new, extensively-equipped learning resource centres. Of TVU's four faculties, the Wolfson Institute of Health Sciences is the most heavily subscribed. Nursing and midwifery are taught at a number of hospitals across the region. There are also short courses in alternative therapies.

A large selection of business, management and accounting courses ranges from HNDs to the MBA. They have an international slant, and include hospitality, tourism and leisure management courses. Closely allied to these are degrees in computing, information systems and multimedia. Music, media and creative technologies are combined in the London College of Music and Media, offering degrees in everything from digital arts to popular music performance.

Student life

TVU has no student accommodation, but it is not difficult to find somewhere near the campuses. The university accommodation service helps students find family accommodation, lodgings, rooms, flats and houses reasonably near the campuses.

TVU's students' union supplements the theatre, cinema, club and music entertainment to be found in west London with its own entertainment programme; and with a Student Sports Card you can use the university and Borough of Ealing sports facilities at low prices.

London may be large, but TVU's international office and student support services are geared to ensure that international students have a source of help and information, starting with a one-month pre-sessional English course, which includes study skills.

"I come from Kuala Lumpur, the capital of Malaysia. I came to London in September 1997 to begin my career as a student on an undergraduate LLB Law degree with Thames Valley University (TVU). I chose to study law in the UK, because it is the head of all the Commonwealth countries which means I will eventually be able to practise in other Commonwealth nations. I am currently in my third year of a three-year course. In the past year I have learnt a lot about English culture and people and also visited many cities in the country. I have many friends studying law in other universities across London and, from talking to them, I learned that TVU's module, called 'legal skills', is not offered in most universities. In my opinion, it teaches the skills necessary for becoming a lawyer and I feel it could be beneficial to me in my plans of becoming a barrister."

Steven TK Lum, Malaysia

UEA Norwich

Write to: International Office,
University of East Anglia,
Norwich NR4 7TJ

Tel: 01603 592048

Fax: 01603 458596

Email: intl.office@uea.ac.uk

Website: www.uea.ac.uk/international

Students: 9,500 in 1998/9 (2,500 postgraduates, 1,500 international, from over 90 countries), 40:60 male:female.

Accommodation: married/family, vacation – extra charge, storage facilities. University residences from £37 to £55 a week self-catered. Room in town from £30 to £40 a week.

Entrance requirements: two or three A level passes or equivalent, European Baccalaureate Diploma pass.

EFL: TOEFL 500, computer-based TOEFL 215, IELTS 6, English language GCE/GCSE.

Foundation: one-year Business and English foundation to degree programme, IELTS level 5.5 required.

Fees: classroom courses £6,650 a year, laboratory courses £8,650, business courses £6,980 a year.

Set in 320 acres of parks and woodland, the University of East Anglia campus was originally designed so that no building was more than five minutes walk away from any other. There are plenty of places to eat and drink, including hot food at the self-service diner, an Italian-style restaurant, snack bars and cafés. Shopping facilities include a food outlet, newsagent, post office, two book-shops and a travel agent. There is also a 24-hour laundrette service and an indoor market on campus.

Norwich city centre is a 15-minute bus ride from the campus, and central London is only two hours away. There is also beautiful unspoilt coastline nearby.

Academic strengths

As well as the traditional humanities, science and social science courses

University of East Anglia, Norwich

458

UNIVERSITIES AND COLLEGES

available at UEA, there is a wide range of vocational courses available. The university operates a modular system, whereby students are given a broad introduction to a particular subject and then the opportunity to specialise further, or chose a series of modules to suit their interests. Some courses offer one-year industrial placements, and others study-abroad options.

The academic year is divided up into two semesters, and students are assessed at the end of each one. This continual assessment removes the pressure of final exams, whilst the modular programme breaks down the traditional boundaries between arts and science subjects. Students can take business, language and computer modules alongside their degrees.

The following subjects were rated Excellent in the most recent teaching quality assessments: applied social work, environmental science, development studies, and law. The following departments were awarded 5 ratings in the 1996 research assessment exercise: biological sciences, pure mathematics, social work, history, communication and media studies, and education, and environmental sciences. German, Scandinavian and Dutch languages were awarded top 5* ratings.

All students have access to computers. There are 2,000 terminals throughout the campus with a further 200 available in the Computer Centre, which has trained staff to deal with queries. 150 rooms in halls of residence are connected up to the campus network.

Student Life

The students' union organises most of the campus entertainment, from regular showings of films, to live concerts, dance nights and live comedy. The union also manages a live music venue in the city centre which was recently host to Ocean Colour Scene, Finlay Quaye, and Sleeper concerts.

There are over 100 student-run societies for students, ranging from bell-ringing to American football. The Norwich International Club meets weekly for people who wish to widen their knowledge and experience of other cultures.

There are religious facilities for students of all faiths – a multi-faith chaplaincy, Christian and Chinese fellowships and a mosque on campus all complement the places of worship in Norwich. Kosher and halal food is available locally, too.

International students are welcomed to the university by airport pick-ups, and an activities-packed induction programme. There is free English language support throughout the year.

"I wanted to get to know a different legal system before taking my final examinations in Germany, so I decided to spend a term at the University of East Anglia, Norwich. What has impressed me most is the friendly and personal atmosphere and the commitment and open-mindedness of the teachers who seem to have a personal interest in the students' progress. The advantages of a campus university are not to be disregarded: numerous bars, pubs and clubs as well as cultural events of all kinds offer sufficient (often too much!) distraction. Living in close quarters with British and international students of all subjects provides a unique opportunity for personal interchange, which is very enriching and helps you make life-long friends."

Nicolai von Cube, Germany

University of the West of England

BRISTOL

University of the West of England

Write to: Enquiry and Admissions Services, Frenchay Campus, Coldharbour Lane, Bristol BS16 1QY

Tel: 0117 965 6261

Fax: 0117 976 3804

Email: admissions@uwe.ac.uk

Website: www.uwe.ac.uk

Students: 23,644 in 1998 (3,158 postgraduate, 1,269 international, from over 40 countries), 50:50 male:female.

Accommodation: University residence from £43 a week, self-catering. Room in town from £42 to £55 a week.

Entrance requirements: minimum two A levels at grade E plus three GCSE subjects grade C, or equivalent. European or International Baccalaureates accepted.

EFL: Cambridge Certificate of Proficiency grade C. Undergraduate: IELTS 6.0, TOEFL 570. Postgraduate: IELTS 6.5, TOEFL 600.

Fees: classroom courses £6,150 a year, laboratory courses £6,500 a year.

Foundation: Programmes available in English language, art and design, built environment, engineering and science.

UWE, established as a university in 1992, is already in the first division of new universities according to recent league tables. It began life in 1885 as Bristol Merchant Venturers' School, established by the merchants of the time to further the artistic and scholastic life of the city.

Its blend of Victorian-to-modern architecture and its mix of classic and innovative programmes give the impression that it is a new university with a traditional slant. The university's programmes are grouped into 12 faculties

University of the West of England campus

and one associated faculty. Over 300 programmes of study are available at degree level and there is a range of taught professional and masters programmes.

Close links with industry and the professions ensure that programmes are relevant and innovative. Many degrees offer a period of industrial experience and a large number of students undertake their placements abroad. Research programmes exist in all faculties.

The university is the largest educational institution in the city and is similar in structure and status to an American state university. It is located on five campuses around Bristol, the natural capital of the south west.

Bristol is a city of fine architecture and culture set in the undulating valley of the River Avon. Excellent road and rail connections enable London, Oxford, the spectacular scenery of Wales, Devon and the Cotswolds to be reached in an hour and a half.

Academic strengths

UWE has scored highly in recent government assessments of teaching quality, reaching 20 or more out of a possible 24 in all the subjects which have so far been assessed. The university has Excellent ratings in business and law – subjects with a lasting appeal for international students. The university aims to develop skilled graduates with experience of their chosen fields of work. Placements in commercial companies are an important constituent of the business programmes. The law faculty has a replica law court in which students can stage trials.

Information technology and computer science programmes benefit from high research standards in the Faculty of Computer Studies and Mathematics. British culture and media studies also won a respectable research rating. The art, media and design faculty has programmes in fashion and textile design, ceramics and time-based media (television, video, multimedia, radio and sound).

Student life

UWE, though large, is friendly and not impersonal. Refectories, bars, shops and banking facilities are on or near all campuses along with a full range of student advisory services. There are fitness facilities and over 40 union sports clubs. Culturally there is the Centre for Performing Arts, promoting music and theatre and an active student union. There are prayer facilities for all religious groups.

"I worked on building sites for about five years back in Hong Kong to save the money to study here. I studied part-time for an HND in Building Studies so that I can do this BSc in Construction Management in one year instead of two or three, which I'd have to do in Hong Kong. I've been here for just a couple of weeks – and it's challenging. The culture is so different it's hard to see how to communicate with everyone, especially in class. It's easier in my residence. The library's too good - there's too much information! I feel free here – there's plenty of time to do research, and I like the seminars. It's a flexible system. What I love most in Britain is the space. What do I hate? Well, the food is... different. And I can't believe what they charge in Chinese restaurants."

David Tze Tung Ngi, Hong Kong

UWIC

UNIVERSITY OF WALES INSTITUTE CARDIFF

cardiff
cardiff
cardiff

University of Wales Institute Cardiff

Write to: The International Office, University of Wales Institute Cardiff, Western Avenue, Cardiff CF5 2SG.

Tel: 029 2041 6045

Fax: 029 2041 6928

Email: jphillips@uwic.ac.uk

Website: www.uwic.ac.uk

Students: 7,400 in 1997/8 (418 postgraduate, about 250 international, from over 10 countries), 50:50 male:female.

Accommodation: single-sex, vacation. University residences from £45 a week. Room in town from £40 a week.

Entrance requirements: two A level passes minimum Grade E, or equivalent. European or International Baccalaureate pass is accepted.

EFL: Cambridge Certificates: Advanced English grade A;

Proficiency in English grade C, IELTS 5.5, TOEFL 600.

Fees: foundation year £4,000, classroom courses £6,200 a year, laboratory courses and postgraduate courses £6,500 a year.

Cardiff, capital of Wales, is the location of UWIC, one of the constituent colleges of the federal University of Wales. Cardiff is the home of the respected Welsh National Opera, and Wales's national rugby team. An important port on the Bristol Channel, Cardiff is at the heart of Wales's industrial south but close to the beautiful Brecon Beacons, the green Vale of Glamorgan, miles of beaches and many historic castles.

Academic strengths

UWIC has four faculties. The Faculty of Art, Design and Engineering is on a modern campus in the cathedral town of Llandaff on the city's outskirts. Art,

Student Centre at the Llandaff Campus

design and engineering are major strengths – UWIC received an Excellent rating in the teacher quality assessment for ceramics and interior architecture, courses with a practical and technical focus, and a research rating for art and design. Fine art, which also received an Excellent rating, aesthetics, graphic design, and the history and theory of art and design have a more theoretical bias.

The art faculty is linked with engineering and offers courses in electronics design, design engineering, and industrial and product design and manufacture. The engineering workshops are equipped with everything from new computer rooms to miniaturised and factory-sized electronic manufacturing plants. Industrial experience is part of many UWIC courses, which carry transferable credit points. Commerce, in the Faculty of Business, Leisure and Food at the modern Colchester Avenue Campus, attracts many international students. You can take a two-year HND course in Business and Finance or Computing and go on to a BA degree in Business and Management or a BSc in Business Information Systems. Hotel, tourism, catering and institution management and food science and technology are taught in this faculty – at all levels, ranging from a diploma in Baking Technology to an HND or degree in Food Technology.

The professional emphasis of most courses is evident in the Faculty of Community Health Sciences, which offers courses in dental technology. Psychology and communication received an Excellent rating in the latest teaching quality assessment. Other courses include biomedical sciences, speech therapy, nutrition, podiatry and environmental risk management. The Faculty of Education and Sport is a leading centre for teacher education, sports science and human movement.

Student life

The sport faculty also has the college's best sports grounds and facilities on Cyncoed Campus. Off campus, the Welsh National Sports Centre is one of 15 leisure centres in the city, which also has eight golf courses. Town and gown share the Welsh obsession with rugby, so UWIC is certainly an option for sports-inclined students; the alumnus list includes a number of Olympic medallists and stars of past rugby internationals.

UWIC has some good, modern accommodation and guarantees a place to international students, who from induction to graduation can draw on a range of services – English language provision and study and welfare support to ensure that their studies are successful and enjoyable.

"I was born in Hong Kong, but my family went to live in Vancouver, Canada, about 10 years ago. I graduated in genetics from the University of British Columbia and after that I went to Hong Kong and worked for NatWest as a credit risk officer. I got a buzz off the Hong Kong Stock Exchange. At an education exhibition I discovered this one-year MBA at Cardiff and I was sold. It was a good move to come here, the facilities are good and so are the teaching staff, and the atmosphere is great. People really want to study – not just to get a degree."

Samuel Wong, Hong Kong

coventry
coventry
coventry

The University of Warwick

Write to: The International Office, The University of Warwick, Coventry CV4 7AL

Tel: 024 7652 3706

Fax: 024 7646 1606

Email: int.office@admin.warwick.ac.uk

Website: www.warwick.ac.uk

Students: 13,764 (5,769 postgraduate, 2,292 international, from 106 countries), 54:46 male:female.

Accommodation: single-sex, married/family, vacation, storage facilities. University residences from £40 a week self-catered, from £67 a week catered. Room in town from £40 a week.

Entrance requirements: three A levels average BBB or 32 points at International Baccalaureate.

Foundation: courses available in law, business studies, social sciences and science/engineering, taught in local colleges and supervised by Warwick.

Fees: classroom courses £7,100 a year, laboratory courses £9,140 a year.

Warwick University received its royal charter in 1965 when it admitted 450 students. It is spread across three neighbouring modern campuses about three miles from Coventry – a city whose cathedral is famed as a centre for international peace and reconciliation. The smaller Westwood and Gibbet Hill campuses are both 10 minutes' walk from the central campus. The university also has a site in Venice where history of art students spend time studying. The Warwick campus is very modern and provides accommodation for a large number of students. Because everything

Warwick campus

is on-site the campus is both lively and safe. Student-organised entertainment always has a large audience.

In 1984, the university established the science park to foster the growth of new technology. It is now home to over 65 technology-based companies and is strategically placed in one of the UK's major business regions. The surrounding countryside has plenty of historic attractions such as Warwick Castle and Shakespeare's birthplace in Stratford upon Avon.

Academic strengths

The university is divided into three faculties: Arts, Sciences and Social Sciences. Warwick is one of the country's leading research universities and was awarded consistently high scores in recent research and teaching quality assessment. Pure mathematics, computer science, and history were all awarded 5* for research, with 5s awarded to a long list including: biological sciences, statistics and operational research, economics and econometrics, social work, sociology, business and management studies, French, communication, cultural and media studies, and drama, dance and performing arts. There are two main libraries on campus which are open seven days a week during term time. There is an extensive network of PCs available for students to use. Some computer rooms are open 24 hours a day.

Student life

Warwick's students' union has five large bars, a nightclub, a radio station (where Radio 1 DJ Simon Mayo began his career), snack bars, a restaurant, shops and a bookshop as well as three high street banks. Also on campus is one of the largest arts centres in England. This houses a large concert hall, two theatres, a cinema, a music centre, two bookshops, a bar and restaurant.

Warwick has plenty of sporting facilities including a swimming pool. It is also one of the few universities in the UK to play frisbee and has a frisbee pitch. There are 60 acres of outdoor playing fields in total and the sports federation recognises over 70 sports clubs and societies.

International students are picked up from Gatwick and Heathrow airports and take part in an orientation programme for a week before term. There are pre-sessional English courses and support lessons through term time. The university organises a social programme and arranges weekend homestays with British families.

"I came to Warwick to complete my history degree and I liked it so much that I have decided to stay another year to complete a Diploma in International Studies. The tutors on my course were really helpful. I found the coursework to be very different but, in the end, I enjoyed it more than the American system as the work was spread out over a longer period. I lived on campus with British third years and I have made plenty of new friends. I also met students from all over the world and now have friends from Germany, Sweden and Finland. The international office was extremely helpful and gave us plenty of opportunities to meet people by organising social events and activities. They organised trips to Oxford, Warwick Castle and York and encouraged us to see Britain. I've really enjoyed my year here and I'm looking forward to starting my next course."

Kate Rounds, USA

University of Westminster

Write to: International Education Office, University of Westminster, 16 Little Titchfield Street, London W1P 7FH

Tel: 020 7911 5769

Fax: 020 7911 5132

Email: international-office @westminster.ac.uk

Website: www.westminster.ac.uk /international/

Students: 19,690 in 1997, (4,155 postgraduate, 2,500 international, from over 120 countries), 49:51 male:female.

Accommodation: single-sex, married, vacation. University residences from £60 to £100 a week self-catering. Room in London from £55 to £100 a week.

Entrance requirements: two or three A levels at grade C (BCCs for business studies, law and media) or international equivalent. Contact the International Education Office for detailed course requirements.

EFL: for undergraduate courses Cambridge Advanced English, IELTS 6.0, TOEFL 550; for postgraduate courses IELTS 6.5, TOEFL 600.

Fees: classroom courses £6,420 a year, laboratory courses £6,735 a year; postgraduate taught courses £5,200 to £8,000, MBA £8,500 a year, research degrees £7,000 to £9,000.

Entering the impressive marble entrance of the main university site (a listed building in central London) you will immediately be aware of a sense of history and grandeur. The university was founded as the Royal Polytechnic in 1838. Today, remnants of the time when it was a boys-only institution still adorn the walls. Yet the feel of the place is decidedly modern as men and women of all ages and origins rush from one lecture to another or linger on the stone steps on Upper Regent Street. This contrast reflects the institution's ethos: a sense of history combined with a modern outlook.

University of Westminster main entrance

Academic strengths

The university's reputation is one of innovation and of being at the cutting edge of the wide spectrum of subjects it provides. This can be seen in its newly introduced MA in International Business and Management by distance learning or in the opportunity for language students to interpret at live conferences. Historically, this is illustrated by the fact that the first-ever showing of moving images, by the Lumière brothers, took place at the Regent Street campus.

One of Westminster University's particular strengths is the highly-rated Design, Media and Communication Department, whose successful alumni include Michael Jackson, the former controller of BBC2. This exceptionally well-equipped department is located on another of the university's four campuses, at Harrow in north London. This was formerly an independent college and when the two merged in 1992, a £35 million programme was undertaken to completely modernise it.

Student life

The University of Westminster is known for its English language provision and it has one of the largest EFL schools in the world. PELAS (Preparation in English Language and Academic Skills) is designed to prepare international students to study in the UK. PELAS courses take place in June, July, August and September. Students who want to study English during their university course can take EAP (English for Academic Purposes) which lasts all year. This counts as a course module for most undergraduate degree programmes. Many of the staff in the International Education Office are from overseas or have studied abroad themselves. The office also runs a study abroad programme for those who wish to do part of their degree in the UK and part in their home country. Students on this programme follow university classes combined with English language classes, if required, for one or two semesters, and can then transfer the credits gained to a university in their home country.

The university has campuses in central and suburban London and gives priority in accommodation to international students. There is also an orientation programme to help them find out more about London and the university, and to meet other students. There is an International Student Advisor with responsibility for giving help and advice to international students and organising social events.

"Before I came here I was studying in Kuala Lumpur, working in a travel agency in order to gain experience in the tourism industry. I managed to get sponsorship from my government and I decided to come to Westminster because I'd heard it did a very useful degree in Business Studies with Tourism, and because they offered me a place on the spot. The international office has been really helpful and I use it a lot. Since I've been here, I've already set up a Malaysian Student Society and last year I set up the International Student Society, that aims to provide a meeting place for international students and society members are from all over the world. We feel it is important to mix not only with our own nationality, but with students from other countries, as well as British students."

Shazly Bashah, Malaysia

WIMBLEDON | SCHOOL OF ART

Wimbledon School of Art

Write to: The Academic Registrar, Wimbledon School of Art, Merton Hall Road, London SW19 3QA

Tel: 0208 408 5000

Fax: 0208 408 5050

Email: art@wimbledon.ac.uk

Website: www.wimbledon.ac.uk

Students: 800 in 1999 (110 postgraduates, 80 international, from 17 countries), 30:70 male:female.

Accommodation: institute and private residences from £60 to £65 a week self-catering. Some vacation storage facilities available.

Entrance requirements: all applications should be supported with slides or photos of your work. Interview not necessary for international students, but further photographs or slides of work may be requested.

EFL: proficiency in written and spoken English.

Foundation: courses available, along with pre-foundation classes in the summer vacation.

Fees: Foundation course £4,390 a year, other courses £7,267 a year.

Wimbledon School of Art was founded in 1890 and is based in the pleasant suburb of Wimbledon. It is situated only 20 minutes, by train, from the centre of London. Wimbledon has a large park, Wimbledon Common, and good transport connections to Waterloo international train station from where you can get Eurostar trains to Paris and Brussels. It has a number of distinguished alumni, including three Oscar winners, and winners of the

Wimbledon School of Art, Foundation Course

Turner Prize and the Olivier Award. Wimbledon's degrees are accredited by the University of Surrey.

The school's largest site is in Merton Hall Road. Foundation courses take place in an annexe about a mile away. There is also a sculpture facility in Cannizaro Park and additional studio spaces off the main sites.

Academic strengths

All the staff are practising artists, designers or practitioners involved in their professional fields. The school has four departments: Foundation Studies, Theatre, Fine Art, and History of Art and Contextual Studies. Art and Design won a 5 rating for research in 1996.

Foundation courses take place at the Palmerston Road site. This has good studio and technical facilities, including a large workshop with a welding bay, a vacuum form press, a ceramics studio, a black and white darkroom, video and editing facilities, a computer suite and a life drawing studio. The foundation course in Art and Design is a one-year, full-time course which offers an introduction to the specialist areas within art and design. The course enables students to progress onto suitable degree courses.

The Theatre Department offers 5 undergraduate courses and an MA in Theatre Design/Scenograpy. The department has purpose-built facilities including workshop space, a studio equipped with lighting and sound and a technical workshop for scenic construction.

Other postgraduate degrees on offer are in Fine Art: Drawing; Print; Sculpture; or Painting, and Theorisation of Contemporary Practice in Art and Performance. These are subject-specific degrees but they have shared elements of study that facilitates the exchange of ideas and practices across disciplines.

Student life

Students enjoy all the benefits of living in London, with easy access by tube and train to the city centre. From an artistic point of view, London has a lot to offer in terms of art galleries and exhibitions, and this is a major attraction of the school for international students. There is also a large learning resources centre, opened in 1999, which consists of a library, slide library and IT centre. This gives students access to over 28,000 books, slides, video and audio tapes, periodicals, the Internet, CD-ROMs and other computer facilities. All students can make use of the school's photography facilities, including a studio, cameras and a dark room. English language classes are provided for students where necessary.

"I'm studying an MA Drawing in Fine Art practice and am really enjoying it. Friends recommended I study at Wimbledon School of Art, so I applied. The course is quite different to what is on offer in Taiwan. Here I have more freedom to choose materials and I can try sculpture or painting as well as improving my drawing and sketching. There are more options available. The tutors are really helpful and very accessible. The best thing about the college is its 24-hour work space. This access is wonderful and I use it a lot. Fortunately I do not live very far away and I usually cycle to college."

Miin Heuey, Taiwan

THE UNIVERSITY *of York*

The University of York

Write to: Simon Willis, University of York, International Office, York YO10 5DD

Tel: 01904 433 534

Fax: 01904 433 538

Email: international@york.ac.uk

Website: www.york.ac.uk

Students: 8,240 in 1998/9 (1,800 postgraduate, 1100 international, from 71 countries), 49:51 male:female.

Accommodation: guaranteed for single overseas students. Some family and vacation accommodation available. University residences from £42 a week self-catered. Room in town from £45 a week.

Entrance requirements: three A level passes or international equivalent, see prospectus for grade requirements.

EFL: IELTS 6, TOEFL: paper-based 550, computer-based 213, Cambridge proficiency grade C.

Foundation: six-month English Language Foundation programme, one-year York International Foundation programme at local college for entrance to undergraduate courses at York or elsewhere.

Fees: classroom courses £6,810 a year, laboratory courses £9,090 a year.

York University is proud of its national and international reputation for teaching and research. The university is based on two sites, one a 200-acre campus at Heslington on the edge of the city, and the other in the city centre. The Heslington campus is quiet, and relatively traffic free. There is a regular and speedy bus service to the city centre from the campus. The Kings Manor, the city campus, houses the Department of History of Art, and parts of the English and History departments. This is a historic building that dates back to the medieval period.

York itself is a historic city that has been an important political, cultural, religious and trading centre since Roman times. This rich heritage is visible in the ancient walls encircling the city, the winding medieval lanes, Georgian-terraced townhouses, and York Minster – the largest medieval cathedral in Europe.

University of York campus

Academic Strengths

The university's 24 departments offer a wide range of courses across subjects in the arts, sciences and social sciences. As the university's strong performance in the teaching quality and research assessment exercise demonstrates, York has strengths in all these areas. Departments which have so far received Excellent ratings are: computer science, electronics, English, history, history of art, language and linguistics, mathematics, music, physics, social policy and sociology. Other departments not yet assessed for teaching, but which have performed strongly in the 1996 research assessments include biology, economics, politics and psychology.

International students are found in all subject areas at York. Particularly popular are undergraduate courses in computer science, economics, electronics, English, history, music, psychology and combined courses in the School of Politics, Economics and Philosophy.

The main library provides for all the information needs of undergraduate students. There are over 700 PCs around the campus. These are available 24 hours a day and give students access to word processing, spreadsheets and database programmes as well as email and the Internet.

English language support is available for students through the EFL unit.

Student life

International students are guaranteed accommodation throughout their time at York, and the university provides most other students with accommodation. This large resident population generates a varied and lively social life with over 60 clubs and societies.

International students form a sizeable proportion of the university community – about 12 per cent in 1998/9. For many, the focus is the Overseas Students' Association, which represents specific interests of the international population. As well as providing advice and guidance on a range of issues, the OSA also arranges a programme of social events throughout the year.

The International Office offers support for students on various issues and acts as a focal point for student enquiries. On arrival, students take part in an orientation programme, which complements freshers' activities on campus. All international students are assigned to a supervisor who is responsible for the their progress during their time at York. Supervisors form part of a welfare network which is designed to give students maximum support.

"I came to York in 1994 from Singapore to read an undergraduate degree in English language and linguistics. The main reasons I chose York were the glowing reports I had heard from friends and relatives who had studied here, and its excellent academic reputation. I have to say that I have not been at all disappointed – if anything all my expectations have been surpassed! At York I have been encouraged to flourish both academically and personally, with the staff providing guidance and assistance as and when I needed it. I even spent a year studying in America as part of my course – that was an amazing experience. I graduated in 1997 and decided I had to come back to study for a PhD, which I am doing at the moment. All in all, everyone I know who has come to York has found it to be an extremely rewarding and fulfilling experience."

Dinesh Vaswani, Singapore

If you want a valuable business degree, we're completely flexible

With the Heriot-Watt degree programme you can start earning a valuable business qualification right now - without putting your career on hold or saddling yourself with debt.

That's because we offer a choice of routes to a respected degree in either business administration, management or financial management and accounting.

Our distance learning programme provides the same syllabus and bachelor degrees as awarded at Heriot-Watt University, one of Europe's leading business schools. The difference is that you study at home and in your own time. You can take your exams at a centre near you, wherever you are in the world.

So if you have 3 Grade C 'A' level passes or equivalent you can start your course straight away.

Find out how flexible we can be. Call, fax or email us for an information pack quoting reference HBA0601.

FT Knowledge
12-14 Slaidburn Crescent
Southport PR9 9YF
United Kingdom

Tel: +44 (0)1704 508306
Fax: +44 (0)1704 506723
E-mail: hwattba@ftknowledge.com

Heriot-Watt University
Edinburgh

World Business Education

Department for Education and Employment
Student Support
Division 1
Mowden Hall
Staindrop Road
Darlington DL3 9BG
Tel: (01325) 392 822
Fax: (01325) 392 464
Website: dfee.gov.uk

Department for Education for Northern Ireland
Rathgael House
Bangor
Northern Ireland
Tel: (01247) 279 279
Fax: (01247) 279 100
Email: deni@nics.gov.uk
Website: www.deni.gov.uk

Higher Education Funding Council for England and Northern Ireland (HEFCE)
Northavon House
Coldharbour Lane
Bristol
BS16 1QD
Tel: (0117) 931 7317
Fax: (0117) 931 7203
Email: hefce@
hefce.ac.uk
Website: www.hefce.ac.uk

The Scottish Higher Education Funding Council (SHEFC)
Donaldson House
97 Haymarket Terrace
Edinburgh, EH12 5HD
Tel: (0131) 313 6500
Fax: (0131) 313 6501
Website: www.shefc.ac.uk

Higher Education Funding Council for Wales (HEFCW)
Linden Court
The Orchards
Ty Glas Avenue
Llanishen, Cardiff
CF4 5DZ
Tel: (01222) 761 861
Fax (01222) 763 163
Email: hefcw@wfc.ac.uk
Website: www.niss.ac.uk/
education/hefcw

The Northern Consortium
PO Box 88
Manchester M60 1QD
Tel: (0161) 200 4029
Email: pgorham@
fs2.ba.umist.ac.uk

THE BRITISH COUNCIL
The British Council has offices all over the world, and they are usually extremely helpful. Their offices are listed below. Please note that telephone and fax numbers are written as if dialled locally, and you will need to add a country code and delete the initial zero if dialled internationally. You can also try the British Council website: www.britcoun.org

Algeria
British Embassy
Résidence Cessiopée
Bâtiment B
7 Chemins des Glycines
Algiers
Tel: (213 2) 230 068
Fax:(213 2) 230 751

Argentina
Marcelo T de Alvear
590 (4th floor)
1058 Buenos Aires
Tel: (54 11) 4 311
9814/7519
Fax: (54 11) 4 311 7747
Email: britcoun@
britcoun.int.ar

Australia
Edgecliff Centre
203-235 New South
Head Road, (PO Box 88)
Edgecliff NSW 2027
Sydney
Tel: (61 2) 9 326 2022
Fax: (61 2) 9 327 4868
Email: Enquiries@
bc.org.au

Austria
Schenkenstraße 4
A-1010 Vienna
Tel: (431) 533 26 16
Fax:(431) 533 26 16 85
Email: bc.vienna@
bc-vienna.at

Azerbaijan
British Council
1 Vali Mammador Street
Bakü 370004
Tel: (994 12) 971 593/ 972
013
Fax: (994 12) 989 236
Email: dstaff@british
council.az

Bahrain
AMA Centre
146 Shaikh Salman
Highway
P.O.Box 452
Manama 356, Bahrain
Tel: (973) 261 555
Fax: (973) 241 272
Email: bc.manama@
bc-bahrain.bcouncil.org

Bangladesh
5 Fuller Road
PO Box 161
Dhaka 1000
Tel: (880 2) 868 905-7/ 868
8678
Fax: (880 2) 863 375/ 861
3255
Email: tcowin@
britishcouncil.net

Belgium and Luxembourg
Rue de la Charité 15 /
Liefdadigheidstraat 15
1210 Brussels
Belgium
Tel: (32 2) 227 08 40
Fax: (32 2) 227 08 49
Email: ken.churchill@
bc.brussels.sprint.com

Bolivia
La Paz Avenida Arce (eq.
Campos)
Casilla 15047
La Paz
Tel: (591) (2) 431 240
Fax: (591) (2) 431 377
Email: internet:info@
bcouncil.org.bo

Botswana
British High Commission
Building
Queens Road,
The Mall (PO Box 439)
Gaborone
Tel: (267) (3) 53602
Fax: (267) (3) 56643

Bosnia-Herzegovina
Obala Kulina Bana,
4, 2nd Floor
Sarajevo
Tel: (387 71) 207 836/200
895
Fax: (387 71) 200 890
Email: british.council@ ba.
britcoun.org

Brazil
SCS, Quadra 1,
Bloco H
Edificio Morro Vermelho,
8° Andar
70399-900 Brasília DF
Tel: (556 1) 323 7440
Email: brasilia@
britcoun.org.br

Brunei
No 45 Simpang 100
Jalan Tungku Link
Gadong BE3619
Bandar Seri Begawan 3192
Tel: (673 2) 453 220 / 216 /
218 / 219
Fax: (673 2) 453 221
Email: bcbrunei@ brunet.bn

Bulgaria
7 Tulovo Street
1504 Sofia
Tel: (359 2) 946 0098 /
946 0099 / 463 346 /
943 4425
Fax: (359 2) 946 0102 /
462 065
Email:
bc.sofia@bcsofia.ttm.bg

Burma
British Council
78 Kanna Road
PO Box 638
Yangon, Union of
Mayanmar
Tel: (95 1) 254 658 / 256
290 / 256 291
Fax: (95 1) 245 345
Email:admin@bc.burma.bc
ouncil.org

Cameroon
Avenue Charles de Gaulle
PO Box 818 Yaoundé
Tel: (237) 211 696 /
203 172
Fax: (237) 215 691

Canada
80 Elgin Street
Ottawa
Ontario K1P 5K7
Tel: (1 613) 237 1530
Fax: (1 613) 569 1478
Email: af572@
freenet.carleton.ca

Caribbean (Jamaica and Trinidad)
PCMB Building
64 Knutsford Boulevard
P O Box 235
Kingston 5,
Jamaica
Tel: 929 6915/7049
Fax: 929 7090
Email: bcjamaica@
bc-caribbean.org

Chile
Eliodoro Yáñes 832
Providencia
Santiago
Tel: (56 2) 236 1199 /
236 0193
Fax: (56 2) 235 7375 / 235
9690
Email:info@britcoun.cl

China
Beijing
Cultural and Education
Section
British Embassy
Landmark Building
8 North Dongsanhuan
Road
Chaoyang District
Beijing 100004
Tel: (86 10) 6590 6903
Fax: (86 10) 6590 0977
Email: bc.beijing@
bc-beijing.sprint.com

Shanghai
British Consulate
Dong Yi Plaza
88 Chang Shu Lu

Shanghai 200040
Tel: (86 21) 6249 3412/3 /4
Fax: (86 21) 6249 3410
Email:bc.shanghai@
bc-shanghai.sprint.com

Guangzhou
British Consulate-General
2nd Floor
GITIC Plaza Hotel
339 Huanshi Dong Lu
Guangzhou 510098
Tel: (86 20) 8335 1316 /
1354
Fax: (86 20) 8335 1321
Email: bc.guangzhou@
bc.guangzhou.sprint.com

Chengdu
Rm 1410, Shaocheng
Building
225 Shaocheng Rd
Chengdu 610015
Tel: (86 28) 624 7870
Fax: (86 28) 625 0424
Email: bccd@
public.cd.sc.cn

Columbia
Calle 87 No. 12-79
Apartado Aéreo 089231
Santafé de Bogota
Tel: (57 1) 618 0118 /
6103077
Fax: (57 1) 2187754 /
6167227
Email: brit.council@
bc-bogota.sprint.com

Croatia
Ilica 12/1, PO Box 55
10000 Zagreb
Tel: (385 1) 481 3700
Fax: (385 1) 421 725
@bc.tel.hr

Cyprus
PO Box 5654
3 Museum Street
CY-1387 Nicosia
Tel: (357 2) 442 152
Fax: (357 2) 677 257
Email: stamatis.dracos
@britcoun.org.cy

Czech Republic
Národní 10
12501 Prague 1
Tel: (420 2) 2199 1111
Fax: (420 2) 2491 3839
Email: bcprague
@britcoun.anet.cz

Denmark
Gammel Mønt 12,3
1117 Copenhagen K
Tel: (45) 33 369 400
Fax: (45) 33 369 406
Email: british.council@
britcoun.dk

**East Jerusalem
(West Bank and Gaza)**
Al-Nuzha Building
4 Abu Obeida Street
PO Box 19136
Jerusalem
Tel: (972 2) 628 2545 /
627 1131 / 626 4392
Fax: (972 2) 628 3021

Ecuador
Av. Amazonas 1646 y
La Niña
Casilla 17-07-8829, Quito
Tel: (593 2) 540 225 / 225
421 / 508 282 / 4

Fax: (593 2) 508 283
Email: erey@
bricoun.org.ec

Egypt
192 Sharia el Nil
Agouza, Cairo
Tel: (20 2) 303 1514
Fax: (20 2) 344 3076
Email: david.marler@
bc-cairo.sprint.com

Eritrea
Lorenzo Taza Street,
No. 23
PO Box 997, Asmara
Tel: (2911) 123415 /
120529
Fax: (2911) 127230
Email: britcoun@
eol.com.er

Estonia
Tallinn Resource
CentreVana Posti 7, Tallinn
EE0001
Tel: (372 6) 441 550 / 314
010 / 418 288
Fax: (372 6) 313 111
Email: british.council@
bctallinn.ee

Ethiopia
PO Box 1043
Adwa Avenue
Artistic Building
Addis Ababa
Tel: (251 1) 550 022
Fax: (251 1) 552 544
Email: britcoun@
telecom.net.et

Finland
Hakaniemenkatu 00530
Helsinki
Tel: (358 9) 701 8731
Fax: (358 9) 701 8725
Email: british.council@
cimo.fi

France
9/11 rue de Constantine
75007 Paris
Tel: (33 1) 4955 7300
Fax: (33 1) 4705 7702
Email: bc.paris@
bc-paris.sprint.com

Germany
Berlin
Hardenbergstraße 20
10623 Berlin
Tel: (49 30) 311 0990
Fax: (49 30) 311 099 20
Email: bc.berlin@
britcoun.de

Cologne
Hahnenstraße 6
50667 Cologne
Tel: (49 221) 206 440
Fax: (49 221) 206 4455
Email: bc.cologne@
britcoun.de

Hamburg
Rothenbaumchaussee 34
20148 Hamburg
Tel: (49 40) 446 057
Fax: (49 40) 447 114

Leipzig
Katharinen Strasse 1-3
(alte Waage)
04109 Liepzig
Tel: (49 341) 140 641-0
Fax: (49 341) 140 641-41

Munich

Rumfordstraße 7
80496 Munich
Tel: (49 89) 290 0860
Fax: (49 89) 290 08688
Email: bc-munich@
britcoun.de

Ghana
11 Liberia Road
P O Box 711 Accra
Tel: (233 21) 223415 /
663979 / 244744 / 235429
Fax: (233 21) 240330
Email:
bcaccra@bcgha.africaon
line.com.gh

Greece
17 Kolonaki Square
106 73 Athens
Tel: (30 1) 369 2333
/ 363 3211 - 5
Fax: (30 1) 363 4769
Email: british.council@
britcoun.gr

Hong Kong
3 Supreme Court Road
Admiralty, Hong Kong
Tel: (852) 2913 5100
Fax: (852) 2913 5102
Email: info@bc
hongkong.sprint.com

Hungary
Benczúr u. 26
H-1068 Budapest
Hungary
Tel: (36 1) 321 4039
Fax: (36 1) 342 5728 / 352
8779
Email: hungary@
britcoun.hu

India
New Delhi
17 Kasturba Gandhi Marg
New Delhi
Tel: (91 11) 371 1401 /
371 0111 / 371 0555
Fax:(91 11) 371 0717 /
371 9616
Email: colin.perchard@
bcdelhi.bcindia.sprintsmx.
vsnl.net.in

Bombay
Mittal Tower
C Wing Nariman Point
Bombay 400 021
Tel: (91 22) 282 3530
Fax: (91 22) 282 3560
Email: robert.frost@
bc-bombay.
bcindia.sprintsmx.ems.vsn
l.net.in

Calcutta
5 Shakespeare Sarani
Calcutta 700 071
Tel: (91 33) 282 5370
Fax: (91 33) 282 4804
Email: adrian.thomas@
bc-calcutta.bcindia.
sprintsmx.ems.vsnl.net.in

Madras
737 Anna Salai
Madras 600 002
Tel: (91 44) 852 5432
Fax: (91 44) 852 3234
Email: jaspar.utley@bc-
madras.bcindia.sprintsmx.
ems.vsnl.net.in

Indonesia
S. Widjojo Centre
Jalan Jenderal

Sudirman 71
Jakarta 12190
Tel: (62 21) 252 4115 /
4122 / 4126
Fax: (62 21) 252 4129
Email: bc.indonesia@
jakarta.wwbc.britcoun.gb.
sprint.com

Irish Republic
Newmount House
22/24 Lower Mount
Street, Dublin 2
Tel: (353 1) 676 4088 /
676 6943
Fax: (353 1) 676 6945
Email: bcdublin@iol.ie

Israel
140 Hayarkon Street
P.O. Box 3302
Tel Aviv 61032
Tel: (972 3) 522 2194 /
524 2558 / 524 1350
Fax: (972 3) 522 1229
Email: david.eliot@
britcoun.org.il

Italy
Via delle Quattro Fontane 20
00184 Rome
Tel: (39 06) 478 141
Fax: (39 06) 481 4296
Email: carol.mariotti@
britcoun.it

Japan
Tokyo 2 Kagurazaka 1 -
chome Shinjuku-ku
Tokyo 162-0825
Tel: (81 3) 3235 8031
Fax: (81 3) 3235 8040
Email: bc.tokyo@
bctokyo.sprint.com

Nagoya
Nagoya Daiya Building 11
5F, 3-15-1 Meieki 3
Nakamura - ku
Nagoya 450 0002
Tel: (81 52) 581 2016
Fax: (81 52) 581 2017
Email: bcnagoya@bc
tokyo.sprint.com

Sapporo
Sapporo International
Communication Plaza
Main Building 3F
North 1, West 3, Chuo-ku
Sapporo 060 0001
Tel: (81 11) 211 3672
Fax: (81 11) 219 1317
Email: bcsapporo@bc-
tokyo.sprint.com

Kyoto
77 Kitashirakawa
Nishimachi, Sakyo-ku
Kyoto 606-8267
Tel: (81 75) 791 7151
Fax: (81 75) 791 7154

Osaka
Seiko Osaka Building
19 Floor
3-5-1 Bakuromachi
Chuo-ku, Osaka 541 0059
Tel: (81 06) 6282 1984
Fax: (81 06) 6282 1985

Fukuoka
Zenrosai Molty Tenjin
Building 2F 1-1-7, Maizuru
Chuo-ku , Fukuoka 810
Tel: (81 92) 752 3750
Fax: (81 92) 752 3774 /
752 6622

Email: bc-fukuoka@bc
tokyo.sprint.com

Jordan
Rainbow Street
Jabal Amman
PO Box 634
Amman, 11118
Tel: (962 6) 463 6147
Fax: (962 6) 461 3389 / 465
6413
Email: bc.amman@bc
amman.sprint.com

Kazakhstan
Panfilova 158 - 1
(Corner Abaya)
Almaty
480091
Kazakhstan
Tel: (7 3272) 637743 /
633339
Fax: (7 3272) 633443
Email: bc@britcoun.almaty.kz

Kenya
ICEA Building
Kenyatta Avenue
PO Box 40751
Nairobi
Tel: (254 2) 334 811 /
334 855 / 6 / 7
Fax: (254 2) 339 854 / 334
875
Email: info@
britcoun.or.kr

Korea
The British Council
Joongwhoo Building
61-21 Taepyungro Ila
Choong-Ku
100-101 Seoul-Korea
Tel: (82) (2) 3702 0610
Fax: (82) (2) 3702 0660 / 61

Kuwait
2 Al Arabi Street
Block 2 PO Box 345,
13004 Safat
Mansouriya
Tel:(965) 253 3204 /
251 5512/ 253 3227/
252 0067/8
Fax: (965) 252 0069 /
255 1376
Email: britcoun@
kuwait.net

Latvia
5A Blaumana iela
Riga LV-1011
Tel: (371) 732 0468 / 1165 /
728 3875 / 8782 / 8723
Fax: (371) 783 0031
Email: bc.riga@british
council.sprint.com

Lebanon
Sidani Street
Fawzi Azar Building
Ras Beirut
Tel: (96 11) 740123 / 4 / 5
Fax: (96 11) 739 461
Email: ann.
malamahthomas@bc
beirut.sprint.com

Lithuania
Vilniaus 39/6
2600 Vilnius
Tel: (370 2) 616 607 / 222
615
Fax: (370 2) 221 602
Email: egle@
bc-vilnius.ot.lt

Lesotho
Hobson's Square (PO Box
429)
Maseru 100
Tel: (266) 312 609
Fax: (266) 310 363
Email: bclib@
lesoff.co.za

Macedonia
Bulevar Goce Delcev 6
P.O. Box 562
91000 Skopje
Tel: (389 91) 135 034 / 5
Fax: (389 91) 135 036
Email: britcoun@
nic.mpt.com.mk

Malawi
P O Box 30222
Lilongwe 3
Tel: (265) 783 244 / 419
Fax: (265) 782 945
Email: bc.lilongwe@
bc-lilongwe.sprint.com

Malaysia
Jalan Bukit Aman
50480 Kuala Lumpur
PO Box 10539
50916 Kuala Lumpur
Tel: (60 3) 298 7555
Fax: (60 3) 293 7214 / 293
0807
Email:
brcokl@britcoun.org.my

Malta
c/o British High
Commission
7 St Anne Street
Floriana VLT 15
Tel: (356) 226 227
Fax: (356) 226 207
Email: britcoun@
waldonet.net.mt

Mauritius
Royal Road
PO Box 111
Rose Hill
Tel: (230) 454 9550
Fax: (230) 454 9553
Email: bcouncil@
bow.intnet.mu

Mexico
Lopede Vega 316
Col. Chaputepec Morales,
11570 Mexico, DF
Tel: (52 5) 263 1900
Fax: (52 5) 263 1910
Email: bc.mexicocity@
bc-mexico.sprint.com

Morocco
36 Rue de Tanger
BP 427, Rabat
Tel: (212 7) 760 836
Fax: (212 7) 760 850
Email: britcoun.
morocco@bcmor.org.ma

Mozambique
Rua John Issa 226
PO Box 4178
Maputo
Tel: (258 1) 310 921 / 923 /
455 / 302 455
Fax: (258 1) 421 577
Email: root@
bcmaputo.uem.mz

Namibia
74 Bulow Strasse
PO Box 24224
Windhoek 9000

Tel: (264 61) 226776
Fax: (264 61) 227 530
Email: general.enquiries@
bc-namibia.bcouncil.org

Netherlands
Keizersgracht 2691016
1016 ED
Amsterdam
Tel: (31 20) 550 6060
Fax: (31 20) 620 7389

Nepal
Kantipath, PO Box 640
Kathmandu
Tel: (977 1) 221 305 / 223
796 / 222 698
Fax: (977 1) 224 076
Email: bcnepal@
bc-nepal.wlink.com.np

New Zealand
c/o British High Commission,
44 Hill Street
PO Box 1812, Wellington 1
Tel: (64 4) 495 0880
Fax: (64 4) 473 6261
Email: paul.smith@
bc-wellington.sprint.com

Nigeria
11 Kingsway Road
Ikoyi (PO Box 3702 Lagos)
Tel: (234 1) 269 2188 / 89 /
90 / 91 / 92
Fax: (234 1) 269 2193
Email: bc.lagos@
bc-lagos.bcouncil.org

Norway
Fridtjof Nansens Plass 5
0160, Oslo 1
Tel: (47 22) 396 190
Fax: (47 22) 424 039
Email: rosalind.olsen@
britcoun.no

Oman
Road One
Medinat Qaboos West
(PO Box 73, Postal Code
115, Medinat al Sultan
Qaboos)
Tel: (968) 600 548
Fax: (968) 699 163 / 698
018
Email: bc.muscat@
om.britishcouncil.org

Pakistan
Block 14, Civic Centre G 6
PO Box 1135,
Islamabad
Tel: (92 51) 111424 424 /
829 041
Fax: (92 51) 276 683
Email: bc-islamabad@
bc-islamabad.
sprint.com

Peru
Calle Alberto Lynch 110
San Isidro, Lima 27
Tel: (51 1) 221 7552
Fax: (51 1) 421 5215
Email: postmaster@
bc-lima.org.pe

Philippines
10th Floor, Taipan Place
Emerald Avenue
Ortigas Centre
Pasig City 1605,
Metro Manila, Philippines
Tel: (63 2) 914 1011/2/3/4
Fax: (63 2) 914 1020
Email: britcoun@
britcoun.org.ph

Poland
Al. Jerozolimskie 59
00-697, Warsaw
Tel: (48 22) 695 5900
Fax: (48 22) 621 9955
Email: bc.warsaw@
britcoun.org.pl

Portugal
Rua de Sao Marçal
1741294 Lisbon Codex
Tel: (35 11) 347 6141-7
Fax: (35 11) 347 6152

Qatar
93 Al Sadd Street
PO Box 2992
Doha, Qatar
Tel: (974) 426 193 / 4
Fax: (974) 423 315
Email: john.gildea@
bc-doha.sprint.com

Romania
Calea Dorobantilor 14
Bucharest 71132
Tel: (40 1) 211 6635 /
210 0314 / 210 5347
Fax: (40 1) 210 0310
Email: bc.romania@
bc-bucharest.
sprint.com

Russia
Moscow
Ulitsa Nikoloyamskaya 1
Moscow 109189
Tel: (095) 234 0201
Fax: (095) 975 2561/ 234
0207
Email: bc.moscow@
bc-moscow.sprint.com

St Petersburg
Naberezhnayareki Fontanki
46
St Petersburg 191025
Tel: (7 812) 325 6074
Fax: (7 812) 325 6073
Email: bc.stpeterbug@
britco.spb.su

Nizhny Novgorod
Dom Uchitelya
Bolshaya Pokrovskaya 2
Nizhny Novgorod 603005
Tel: (7 8312) 301 846
Fax: (7 8312) 337 673
Email: bc.nizhny@
bc.sci-nnov.ru

Ekaterinburg
Gogolya 15a
4th floor
Ekaterinburg 620075
Tel: (7 343) 59 29 02
Fax: (7 343) 59 29 04
Email: bic.ekat@
sovcust.sprint.com

Saudi Arabia
Tower B Second Floor
Al Mousa Centre
Olaya Street
PO Box 58012
Riyadh 11594
Tel: (966 1) 462 1818
Fax: (966 1) 462 0663
Email: enquiries@bc
riyadh.bcouncil.org

Senegal
34/36 Boulevard de la
Republique
(BP 6232), Dakar
Tel: (221) 822 2015
Fax: (221) 821 8136

Email: bcdakar@sonatel.
senet.net

Singapore
30 Napier Road
Singapore 258509
Tel: (65) 473 1111
Fax: (65) 472 1010
Email: reception@
britcoun.org.sg

Slovakia
Dolna 7, PO Box 12
974 00
Banska Bystrica
Tel: (421 88) 412 4216
Fax: (421 88) 412 4217
Email: bcbb@isternet.sk

Slovenia
Cankarjevonabrezje 27
27 Ljubljana 1000, Slovenia
Tel: (386 61) 125 9292 /
9032
Fax: (386 61) 126 4446
Email: info@
britishcouncil.si

South Africa
Johannesburg
PO Box 30637
76 Juta Street
Braamfontein
Johannesburg 2017
Tel: (27 11) 403 3316
Fax: (27 11) 339 7806
Email: enquiries.
johannesburg@
britcoun.org.za

Cape Town
3rd Floor, Associated
Magazine House
St John's Street
Cape Town 8001
PO Box 1469,
Cape Town 8000
Tel: (27 21) 462 3921
Fax: (27 21) 462 3960
Email: enquiries.
capetown@brit
coun.org.za

Durban
Ground floor
Marine Building
22 Gardiner Street
Durban 4000
Tel: (27 31) 305 7356/7 /8 /9
Fax: (27 31) 305 7335
Email: enquiries.
durban@britcoun.org.za

Spain
Paseo del General
Martinez, Campos 31
28010 Madrid
Tel: 337 3500
Fax: 337 3573
Email: general.enquiries@
bc-madrid.sprint.com

Sri Lanka
49 Alfred House Gardens
(PO Box 753)
Colombo 3
Tel: (941) 587 078 / 580
301 / 581 171 / 2
Fax: (941) 01587 079
Email: enquiries@
britcoun.lk

178 DS Senanayaka Vidiya
Kandy
Tel: (94 8) 222 410/234
284
Fax: (94 8) 222 410

Email: kandy@
britcoun.lk

Sudan
14 Abu Sin Street
(PO Box 1253)
Central Khartoum
Tel: (249 11) 780 817
Fax: (249 11) 774 935
Email: bc.khartoum@
bc-khartoum.sprint.com

Swaziland
The British Council
Ground and Third Floors
Lilunga House
Gilfillan Street, Mbabne
Swaziland
Tel: (268) (40) 43101 /
44605 / 42918
Fax: (268) (40) 42641

Sweden
c/o British Embassy
P O Box 27819
S-115 93 Stockholm
Tel: (46 8) 663 6004
Fax: (46 8) 663 7271
Email: british.council@
britcoun.se

Switzerland
Sennweg 2
PO Box 532
CH 3000, Berne 9
Tel: (41 31) 301 1473 / 1426
Fax: (41 31) 301 1459

Syria
Al Jala'a Abu Rumaneh
Maser Street
PO B 33105, Damascus
Tel: (963 11) 331 0631 / 2
Fax: (963 11) 331 0630
Email: david.baldwin@
bc-damascus.sprint.com

Taiwan
7F-1
99, Jen Ai Road,
Section 2 , Taipei 10625
Tel: (886 2) 396 2238
Fax: (886 2) 341 5749
Email: inquiries@
britcoun.org.tw

Tanzania
Samora Ave/Ohio St
PO Box 9100
Dar es Salaam
Tel: (255 51) 116 574 / 5 /
6 / 7 / 118 255
Fax: (255 51) 112 669
Email: bc.tanzania@
ics-dar.sprint.com

Thailand
254 Chulalongkorn Soi 64
Siam Square
Phyathai Road
Pathumwan
Bangkok 10330
Tel: (66 2) 252 6136 / 7 / 8
/ 611 6830 - 9
Fax: (66 2) 253 5312 / 253
5311
Email: bc.bangkok@
britcoun.or.th

Tunisia
c/o British Embassy
5 Place de la Victoire,
BP229 Tunis 1015 RP
Tel: (216 1) 259 053 / 351
754
Fax: (216 1) 353 411
Email:

general.enquiries@bc
tunis.sprint.com

Turkey
Esat Caddesi No. 41
Kucukesat
06660 Ankara
Tel: (90 312) 468 6192
Fax: (90 312) 427 6182
Email: bcankara@
britcoun.org.tr

Uganda
IPS Building
Parliament Avenue
(PO Box 7070), Kampala
Tel: (256 41) 234 725 /
730 / 737
Fax: (256 41) 254 853
Email: roger.wilkins@
bc-kampala.
swiftuganda.com

Ukraine
9/1 Besarabska Ploshcha,
Flat 9, 252004 Kyiv
Tel: 247 7235
Fax: 247 7280
Email:
michael.bird@bc.kiev.ua

United Arab Emirates
Villa no. 7, Al Nasr Street
Khalidiya, PO Box 46523
Dubai, Abu Dhabi
Tel: (971 2) 659 300
Fax: (971 2) 664 340
Email: information@
bc-abudhabi.
bcouncil.org

Tariq bin Zaid Street,
(near Rashid Hospital)
PO Box 1636, Dubai
Tel: (971 4) 370 109 / 371 540
Fax: (971 4) 370 703
Email: information@
bc-dubai.bcouncil.org

UNITED KINGDOM

London
10 Spring Gardens
London , SW1A 2BN
Tel: (020 7) 930 8466
Fax: (020 7) 839 6347
Email: enquiries@
britcoun.org

Manchester
Bridgewater House
58 Whitworth Street
Manchester M1 6BB
Tel: (0161) 957 7000
Fax: (0161) 957 7111
Email: alan.webster@
britcoun.org

Belfast
1 Chlorine Gardens
Belfast BT9 5DJ
Tel: (02890) 666 770
Fax: (02890) 665 242
Email: lynda.wilson@
britcoun.org

Edinburgh
3 Bruntsfield Crescent
Edinburgh EH10 4HD
Tel: (0131) 446 3000
Fax: (0131) 452 8487
Email: alison.kanbi@
britcoun.org

Cardiff
28 Park Place
Cardiff CF1 3QE
Tel: (01222) 397 346
Fax: (01222) 237 494

Email: lindahall@
britcoun.org

**United States of
America**
3100 Massachusetts
Avenue NW, Washington
DC 20008-3600
Tel: (1 202) 588 6500
Fax: (1 202) 588 7918
Email: enquiries@
bcwashingtondc.sprint.com

Uzbekistan
University of World
Languages Building
11 Kounoev Street
Tashkent
Tel: (998 71) 1206 752-3 /
998 712 / 567973
Fax: (998 71) 120 6371
Email: michael.moor@
bc-tashkent.sprint.com

Venezuela
Pisa 3, Torre Credit Card
Av. Principal El Bosque
Av. Sta Isabel/Sta Lucia
El bosque, Caracas
Tel: (582) 952 9965 / 9757
Fax: (582) 952 9691
bc-venezuela@
bc-caracas.sprint.com

Vietnam
Hanoi
18b Cao Ba Quat
Ba Dinh District, Hanoi
Tel: (844) 843 6780 / 1 / 2
Fax: (844) 843 4962
Email: bc.hanoi@
bc-hanoi.sprint.com

Ho Chi Minh City
25 Le Duan Street,
District 1, Ho Chi Minh City
Tel: (848) 823 862/823 863
Fax: (848) 823 2861/822
2105
Email: ukcouncil.hcmc@
bdvn.vnd.net

Yemen
Sana'a
As-Sabain Street No 7
PO Box 2157, Sana'a
Tel: (967 1) 244 121 / 2 /
244 153 / 4 / 5
Fax: (967 1) 244 120
Email:brendan.
mcharry@
bc-sanaa.sprint.com

Zambia
Heroes Place
Cairo Road
Lusaka
PO Box 34571
Tel: (260 1) 223 602 / 228
332 / 3 / 4
Fax: (260 1) 224 1222 /
226 756
Email:
bclusaka@zamnet.zm

Zimbabwe
23 Jason Moyo Avenue
P.O. Box 664
Harare
Tel: (263 9) 75815 / 6
Fax: (263 9) 75815
Email: general.enquiries@
bc-harare.sprint.com

Source: The British
Council

The University of Aberdeen
University Office
Regent Walk
Aberdeen AB24 3FX
Tel: 01224 272 090/272 091
Fax: 01224 272 576
Email:intoff@admin.abdn. ac.uk
Website: www.abdn.ac.uk/
Status: university

University of Abertay Dundee
Bell Street
Dundee DD1 1HG
Tel: 01382 308 919
Fax: 01382 308 081
Email: j.salters@tay.ac.uk
Website:www.abertay_ dundee.ac.uk
Status: university

The University of Wales, Aberystwyth
Old College
King Street
Aberystwyth
Ceredigion SY23 2AX
Tel: 01970 622 021
Fax: 01970 627 410
Email: undergraduate-admissions@ aber.ac.uk
Website: www.aber.ac.uk/
Status: university

Anglia Polytechnic University
East Road, Cambridge CB1 1PT
Tel: 01245 493 131
Fax: 01245 348 772
Email: international@ anglia.ac.uk
Website: www.anglia.ac.uk
Status: university

The Arts Institute at Bournemouth
Wallisdown
Poole
Dorset BH12 5HH
Tel: 01202 533011
Fax: 01202 537729
Email: general@arts-inst-bournemouth.ac.uk
Website: www.arts-inst-bournemouth.ac.uk

Askham Bryan College
Askham Bryan
York YO2 3PR
Tel: 01904 772 277
Fax: 01904 772 288
Status: college of higher education

Aston University
Aston Triangle
Birmingham B4 7ET
Tel: 0121 359 7046
Fax: 0121 359 1139
Email: international@ aston.ac.uk
Website : www.aston.ac.uk/
Status: university

St Austell College
Trevarthian Road
St Austell PL25 4BU
Tel: 01726 67911
Fax: 01726 68499
Email: info@stacoll.demon.co.uk
Website: www.st-austell.ac.uk

Babel Technical College
David Game House
69 Notting Hill Gate
London W11 3JS
Tel: 020 7221 1483
Fax: 020 7243 1730
Email: babel@babeltech.ac.uk

University of Wales, Bangor
Bangor
Gwynedd
LL57 2DG
Tel: 01248 382 017
Fax: 01248 370 451
Email: Ainsley@bangor. ac.uk
Website:www.bangor.ac.uk/
Status: university

Barking College
Dagenham Road
Dagenham RM7 OXU
Tel: 01708 766 841
Fax: 01708 731 067
Status: college of higher education

Barnsley College
HE Admissions Registry
Old Mill Lane Site
Church Street
Barnsley S70 2AX
Tel: 01226 730 191/216 229
Fax: 01226 216 613
Email: L.Kirk@barnsley.ac.uk
Website: www.barnsley.ac.uk/he
Status: college of higher education

Basford Hall College
Stockhill Lane
Nottingham
NG6 ONB
Tel: 0115 916 2001
Fax: 0115 916 6242
Email: bits@basford.demon.co.uk
Website: www.demon.co.uk./basford
Status: college of higher education

University of Bath
Bath BA2 7AY
Tel: 01225 826 832
Fax: 01225 826 366
Email: International-Office@bath.ac.uk
Contact: Admissions Office
Website: www.bath.ac.uk
Status: university

Bath Spa University College
Newton Park, Bath BA2 9BN
Tel: 01225 875 577
Fax: 01225 875 501
Email: international-office@bathspa.ac.uk
Contact: Doris Bechstein,
The International Office
Website:www.bathspa.ac.uk
Status: university

Bell College of Technology
Almada Street,
Hamilton
Lanarkshire ML3 OJB
Tel: 01698 283 100
Fax: 01698 282 131
Email: registry@bell.ac.uk
Contact: Registry Admissions
Status: college of higher education

Bell Language School
Hillscross
Red Cross Lane
Cambridge CB2 2QX
Tel: 01223 246644
Fax: 01223 414080
Email: registry@bell.ac.uk

The University of Birmingham
Edgbaston
Birmingham B15 2TT
Tel: 0121 414 3697
Fax: 0121 414 3850
Email: prospectus@bham.ac.uk
Contact: Director of Admissions
Website: www.birmingham.ac.uk
Status: university

Birmingham College of Food, Tourism and Creative Studies
Summer Row
Birmingham B3 1JB
Tel: 0121 604 1040
Fax: 0121 608 7100
Email: admissions@bcftcs.ac.uk
Contact: International
Admissions Officer
Website: www.bcftcs.ac.uk
Status: college of higher education

Bishop Burton College
Bishop Burton
Beverley
East Yorkshire HU17 8QG
Tel: 01964 553 000
Fax: 01964 553 101
Email: enquiries@bishopb-college.ac.uk
Website: www.bishops.college.ac.uk
Status: college of HE and FE

Bishop Grosseteste University College
Newport
Lincoln LN1 3DY
Tel: 01522 527 347
Fax: 01522 530 243
Email: registry@bgc.ac.uk
Contact: College Registry
Status: university

Blackburn College
Feilden Street, Blackburn
Lancashire BB2 1LH
Tel: 01254 551 440
Fax: 01254 682 700
Contact: Student Services
Status: college of higher education

Blake College
162 New Cavendish Street
London W1M 7FJ
Tel: 020 7636 0658
Fax: 020 7436 0049
Email: study@blake.ac.uk
Website: www.blake.ac.uk

Blackpool and the Fylde College
Ashfield Road
Bispham, Blackpool
Lancashire FY2 0HB
Tel: 01253 352 352
Fax: 01253 356 127
Email: visitors@blackpool.ac.uk
Contact: Admissions Office

Website: www.blackpool.ac.uk
Status: college of higher education

Bolton Institute of Higher Education
Deane Road
Bolton
BL3 5AB
Tel: 01204 528 851/900 600
Fax: 01204 399 074
Email: admiss@uel.ac.uk.
Contact: Senior Assistant Registrar
Website: www.bolton.ac.uk
Status: college of higher education

Bournemouth University
Poole House, PG134
Talbot Campus
Fern Barrow
Poole
BH12 5BB
Tel: 01202 595 651
Fax: 01202 595 287
Email: curran@bournemouth.ac.uk
Contact: Mr Chris Curran,
International Affairs
Website: www.bournemouth.ac.uk
Status: university

The University of Bradford
Richmond Road, Bradford
West Yorkshire
BD7 1DP
Tel: 01274 233 023
Fax: 01274 235 950
Email: international-office@ bradford. ac.uk
Website: www.brad.ac.uk
Status: university

Bradford and Ilkley Community College
Great Horton Road
Bradford
West Yorkshire
BD7 1AY
Tel: 01274 753 348
Fax: 01274 736 175
Email: international@bilk.ac.uk
Website: www.bilk.ac.uk
Status: college of higher education

Bretton Hall
West Bretton, Nr Wakefield
West Yorkshire
WF4 4LG
Tel: 01924 830 261
Fax: 01924 832 016
Website: www.bretton.ac.uk/
Status: college of higher education

University of Brighton
Mithras House
Lewes Road, Brighton
East Sussex
BN2 4AT
Tel: 01273 600 900
Fax: 01273 642 825
Email: admissions@bton.ac.uk.
Website: www.brighton.ac.uk/
Status: university

University of Bristol
Senate House, Tyndall Avenue,
Bristol
BS8 1TH
Tel: 0117 928 7678
Fax: 0117 925 1424
Email: admissions@bristol.ac.uk
Website: www.bris.ac.uk
Status: university

University of the West of England, Bristol
Frenchay Campus
Coldharbour Lane
Bristol
BS16 1QY

Tel: 0117 965 6261
Fax: 0117 976 3804
Email: admissions@uwe.ac.uk.
Website: www.uwe.ac.uk
Status: university

British College of Naturopathy and Osteopathy
Lief House
3 Sumpter Close
120/122 Finchley Road
London NW3 5HR
Tel: 0171 435 6464
Fax: 0171 431 3630
Status: college of higher education

The British Institute in Paris, University of London
Department d'Etudes
Francaises
Institut Britannique de Paris
11 rue de Constantine
75340 Paris Cedex 07, France
Tel: 1 44 11 73 83/4
Fax: 1 45 50 31 55
Email: campos@ext.jussieu.fr
Website: www.bip.lon.ac.uk
Status: university

Bromley College of Further and Higher Edication
Bromley College of Further and Higher Education
Rookery Lane
Bromley BR2 8HE
Tel: 020 8295 7031
Fax: 020 8295 7051
Email: phigham@bromley.ac.uk
Website: www.bromley.ac.uk

Brunel University
Registry,
Uxbridge
UB8 3PH
Tel: 01895 274 000
Fax: 01895 203 167
Email: courses@brunel.ac.uk
Website: www.brunel.ac.uk
Status: university

British School of Osteopathy
275 Borough High Street
London
SE1 1JE
Tel: 0171 407 0222
Fax: 0171 839 1098
Email: Admissions@bso.ac.uk
Website: www.bso.ac.uk
Status: college of higher education

The University of Buckingham
Buckingham MK18 1EG
Tel: 01280 814 080
Fax: 01280 824 081
Email: admissions@buck.ac.uk
Website: www.buck.ac.uk
Status: private university

Buckinghamshire Chilterns University College
Queen Alexandra Road
High Wycombe,
Bucks HP11 2JZ
Tel: 01494 522 141
Fax: 01494 524 392
Website: www.buckscol.ac.uk
Status: university

Butlers Wharf Chef School
The Cardamom Building
31 Shad Thames
London
SE1 2YR
Tel: 020 7357 8842
Fax: 020 7403 2368
Email: enquiries@chef-school.co.uk
Website: www.chef-school.co.uk

Cambridge University
Kellet Lodge, Tennis Court Road,
Cambridge CB2 1QJ
Tel: 01223 333 308
Fax: 01223 366 383
Email: ucam-undergraduate-admissions@lists.cam.ac.uk
Website: www.cam.ac.uk
Status: university

Canterbury Christ Church College of Higher Education
North Holmes Road
Canterbury
Kent CT1 1QU
Tel: 01227 767 700
Fax: 01227 470 442
Email: admissions@cant.ac.uk.
Website: www.cant.ac.uk
Status: college of higher education

Cardiff University
PO Box 921, Cardiff
Wales CF1 3XQ
Tel: 01222 874 432
Fax: 01222 874 622
Email: internat@cf.ac.uk
Website: www.cf.ac.uk
Status: university

University of Wales Institute, Cardiff
Western Avenue
Cardiff
Wales CF5 2SG
Tel: 01222 506 045
Fax: 01222 506 928
Email: jphillips@uwic.ac.uk
Website: www.uwic.ac.uk
Status: university

Carmarthenshire College
Graig Campus, Sand Road
Llanelli
Dyfed SA15 4DN
Tel: 01554 748 000
Fax: 01554 756 088
Email: eirian.davies@ccta.ac.uk
Contact: Admissions Unit
Website: www.ccta.ac.uk
Status: college of higher education

Cavendish College
35-37 Alfred Place
London WC1E 7DP
Tel: 020 7580 6043
Fax: 020 7255 1591
Email: learn@cavendish.ac.uk
Website: www.cavendish.ac.uk

University of Central England in Birmingham
Academic Registry
Perry Barr
Birmingham B42 2SU
Tel: 0121 331 6650
Fax: 0121 331 6706
Email: susan.lewis@uce.ac.uk
Website: www.uce.ac.uk
Status: university

University of Central Lancashire
Foster Building, Preston
Lancashire PR1 2HE
Tel: 01772 892 400
Fax: 01772 892 935
Email: c.enquiries@uclan.ac.uk
Website: www.uclan.ac.uk
Status: university

The Central School of Speech and Drama
Embassy Theatre
64 Eton Avenue
London NW3 3HY
Tel: 0171 722 8183

Fax: 0171 722 4132
Status: college of higher education

Cheltenham and Gloucester College of Higher Education
The Park, Cheltenham
Glos GL50 2QF
Tel: 01242 532 824/6
Fax: 01242 256 759
Email: admissions@chelt.ac.uk
Website: www.chelt.ac.uk
Status: college of higher education

Chichester College of Arts, Science and Technology
Westgate Fields, Chichester
West Sussex PO19 1SB
Tel: 01243 786321
Fax: 01243 539481
Email: info@chichester.ac.uk
Website: www.chichester.ac.uk

University College Chester
Co-ordinator, Parkgate Road, Chester
CH1 4BJ
Tel: 01244 375 444
Fax: 01244 373 379
Email: s.cranny@chester.ac.uk
Website: www.chester.ac.uk
Status: university

City Business College
178 Goswell Road
London EC1V 7DT
Tel: 020 7251 6473/0427
Fax: 020 7251 9410
Email: info@cbcenglish.bdx.co.uk

City of Bristol College
Brunel Centre, Ashley Down
Bristol BS7 9BU
Tel: 0117 904 5000
Fax: 0117 904 5050
Status: college of higher education

City College Manchester
Fielden Centre, 141 Barlow Moor Road,
West Didsbury
Manchester M20 2PQ
Tel: 0161 957 1609
Fax: 0161 957 8613
Email: igarcia@manchester-city-coll.ac.uk
Website: www.manchester-city-coll.ac.uk
Status: college of higher education

City & Guilds of London Art School
124 Kennington Park Road
London SE11 4DJ
Tel: 020 7735 2306
Fax: 020 7582 5361
Email: cgartsc@rmplc.co.uk
Website:
www.cityandguildsartschool.ac.uk

City of London College
The Registry
71 Whitechapel High Street
London E1 7PL
Tel: 020 7247 2166
Fax: 020 7247 1226
Email: Registrar@clc-london.ac.uk
Website: www.clc-london.ac.uk

City University
Northampton Square
London EC1V 0HB
Tel: 020 7477 8000
Fax: 020 7477 8559
Email: international@city.ac.uk
Website: www.city.ac.uk

Clevedon College of Art and Design
Green Lane, Linthorpe
Middlesbrough TS5 7RJ
Tel: 01642 829 973
Fax: 01642 823 467
Status: college of higher education

Colchester Institute
Sheepen Road, Colchester
Essex CO3 3LL
Tel: 01206 718 777
Fax: 01206 763 041
Status: college of higher education

Cordwainers College
182 Mare Street
London E8 3RE
Tel: 0181 985 0273
Fax: 0181 985 9340
Email: enquiries@cordwainers.ac.uk
Website: www.wwt.co.uk/cordw/co-home.html
Status: college of higher education

Cornwall College with Duchy College
Pool, Redruth
Cornwall TR15 3RD
Tel: 01209 712 911
Fax: 01209 718 802
Email: enquiries@cornwall.ac.uk
Status: college of higher education

Courtauld Institute of Art, University of London
Somerset House, Strand
London WC2R 0RN
Tel: 0171 873 2645
Fax: 0171 873 2410
Email: jacqueline.a.sullivan@courtauld.ac.uk
Status: university

Coventry University
Priory Street
Coventry CU1 5FB
Tel: 01203 838 674
Fax: 01203 632 710
Email: daya.evans@coventry.ac.uk
Website: www.coventry.ac.uk
Status: university

Cranfield University
Shrivenham
Swindon SN6 8LA
Tel: 01793 785 400
Fax: 01793 783 966
Email: laxon@rmcs.cranfield.ac.uk
Website: www.cranfield.ac.uk
Status: university

Crawley College
College Road
Crawley RH10 1NR
Tel: 01293 442 205
Fax: 01293 442 399
Email: crawcol@rmplc.co.uk
Status: college of higher education

Christie's Education
63 Old Brompton Road
London SW7 3JS
Tel: 020 7581 3933
Fax: 020 7589 0383
Email: vvonstruensse@christies.com
Website: www.christies.com

Croydon College
Fairfield, Croydon
CR9 1DX
Tel: 0181 760 5999
Fax: 0181 760 5880
Email: info@croydon.ac.uk
Website: www.croydon.ac.uk
Status: college of higher education

Cumbria College of Art and Design
Brampton Road, Carlisle
Cumbria CA3 9AY
Tel: 01228 400 300
Fax: 01228 514 491
Email: aileenmc@cumbriacad.ac.uk
Status: college of higher education

David Game College
David Game House

69 Notting Hill Gate
London W11 3JS
Tel: 020 7221 6665
Fax: 020 7243 1730
Email: info@davidgame-group.com
Website: www.davidgame-group.com

Dartington College of Arts
Totnes, Devon TQ9 6EJ
Tel: 01803 861 620
Fax: 01803 863 569
Email: registry@dartington.ac.uk
Website: www.dartington.ac.uk
Status: college of higher education

De Montfort University
The Gateway
Leicester LE1 9BH
Tel: 0116 255 1551
Fax: 0116 257 7515
Website: www.dmu.ac.uk
Status: university

University of Derby
Kedleston Road
Derby DE22 1GB
Tel: 01332 622 289
Fax: 01332 622 754
Email: m.a.crowther@derby.ac.uk
Website: www.derby.ac.uk
Status: university

Dewsbury College
Halifax Road
Dewsbury
West Yorkshire WF13 2AS
Tel: 01924 465 916
Fax: 01924 457 047
Email: dewsbury.ac.uk
Status: college of higher education

Doncaster College
Waterdale
Doncaster DN1 3EX
Tel: 01302 553 718
Fax: 01302 553 559
Website: www.don.ac.uk
Status: college of higher education

Dudley College of Technology
The Broadway
Dudley DY1 4AS
Tel: 01384 455 433
Fax: 01384 454 246
Email: mark.ellerby@dudleycol.ac.uk
Website: www.dudleycol.ac.uk
Status: college of higher education

University of Dundee
Dundee DD1 4HN
Tel: 01382 344 160
Fax: 01382 221 554
Email: srs@dundee.ac.uk
Website: www.dundee.ac.uk/
Status: university

The University of Durham
Old Shire Hall, Old Elvet
Durham DH1 3HP
Tel: 0191 374 4694
Fax: 0191 374 7216
Website: www.dur.ac.uk
Status: university

University of East Anglia
Norwich, Norfolk NR4 7TJ
Tel: 01603 592 048
Fax: 01603 458 596
Email: int.office@uea.ac.uk
Website: www.uea.ac.uk
Status: university

University of East London
Longbridge Road, Dagenham
Essex RM8 2AS
Tel: 0181 849 3443
Fax: 0181 839 3438
Website: www.uel.ac.uk
Status: university

**East Surrey College
(incorporating Reigate
School of Art and Design)**
127 Blackborough Road
Reigate, Surrey RH2 7DE
Tel: 01737 766 137
Fax: 01737 768 643
Website: www.esc.org.uk/
Status: college of higher education

Edge Hill University College
Ormskirk
Lancs L39 4QP
Tel: 01695 584 312
Fax: 01695 579 997
Email: ibisona@staff.ehche.ac.uk
Website: www.ehche.ac.uk/
Status: university

The University of Edinburgh
57 George Square
Edinburgh EH8 9JU
Tel: 0131 650 4360
Fax: 0131 668 4565
Email: slo@ed.ac.uk
Website: www.ed.ac.uk/
Status: university

EF International Language School
Kensington Cloisters
South Kensington Church Street
London W8 4LD
Tel: 020 7878 3530
Fax: 020 7795 6625
Email: ils.uk.agents@ef.com
Website: www.ef.com or www.english-town.com

The University of Essex
Wivenhoe Park, Colchester
Essex CO4 3SQ
Tel: 01206 873 666
Fax: 01206 873 423
Email: admit@essex.ac.uk
Website: www.essex.ac.uk
Status: university

European Business School, London
Regent's College
Regent's Park
London NW1 4NS
Tel: 0171 487 7507
Fax: 0171 487 7465
Email: exrel@regents.ac.uk
Website: www.regents.ac.uk/
Status: college of higher education

European School of Economics
8/9 Grosvenor Place
London SW1X 75H
Tel: 020 7245 6148
Fax: 020 7245 6164
Email: info@eselondon.ac.uk
Website: www.eselondon.ac.uk

European School of Osteopathy
Boxley House,
The Street
Boxley, Kent ME14 3DZ
Tel: 01622 671 558
Fax: 01622 662 165
Status: college of higher education

Exeter College
Brittany House
Exeter EX4 4EP
Tel: 01392 205 581
Fax: 01392 279 972
Status: college of higher education

**Executive Centre, International
House**
106 Piccadilly
London W1V 9FL
Tel: 0207 518 6936
Fax: 0207 518 6938
Website: www.international-house-london.ac.uk

University of Exeter
Northcote House
The Queen's Drive
Exeter EX4 4QJ
Tel: 01392 263 032
Fax: 01392 263 857
Email: J.C.Clissold@exeter.ac.uk
Website: www.ex.ac.uk/
Status: university

Faculty of Astrological Studies
FAS Registrar
BM 7470
London WC1N 3XX
Tel: 07000 790143
Fax: 01689 603537
Email: info@astrology.org.uk
Website: www.astrology.org.uk

Falmouth College of Arts
Woodlane, Falmouth
Cornwall TR11 4RH
Tel: 01326 211 077
Fax: 01326 212 261
Email: international@falmouth.ac.uk
Website: www.falmouth.ac.uk
Status: college of higher education

Franciscan Study Centre
Giles Lane
Canterbury
Kent CT2 7NA
Tel: 01227 769 349
Fax: 01227 786 648
Status: college of higher education

University of Glamorgan
Pontypridd
Mid Glamorgan CF37 1DL
Tel: 01443 482 684
Fax: 01443 482 014
Email: registry@glam.ac.uk
Website: www.glam.ac.uk/home.html
Status: university

**Glamorgan Centre for Art and
Design Technology**
Glyntaff Road, Pontypridd
South Wales CF37 4AT
Tel: 01443 662 800
Fax: 01443 663 313
Email: artcol@pontypridd.ac.uk
Status: college of higher education

University of Glasgow
Glasgow G12 8QQ
Tel: 0141 330 5185
Fax: 0141 330 4045
Email: sro@gla.ac.uk
Website: www.gla.ac.uk
Status: university

Glasgow Caledonian University
City Campus
70 Cowcaddens Road
Glasgow G4 0BA
Tel: 0141 331 3334
Fax: 0141 331 3449
Email: d.black@gcal.ac.uk
Website: www.gcal.ac.uk/
Status: university

**Gloucestershire College of Arts and
Technology**
Brunswick Road
Gloucester
Gloucestershire GL1 1HU
Tel: 01452 426 557
Fax: 01452 426 531
Status: college of higher education

**Goldsmiths College,
University of London**
New Cross
London SE14 6NW
Tel: 0171 919 7700
Fax: 0171 919 7704
Email: international-office@gold.ac.uk

Website: www.goldmiths.ac.uk
Status: university

University of Greenwich
Bank House
Wellington
Woolwich
London SE18 6PF
Tel: 0181 331 8590
Fax: 0181 331 8145
Email: courseinfo@gre.ac.uk
Website: www.gre.ac.uk
Status: university

**Greenwich School of
Management**
Meridian House
Royal Hill, Greenwich
London SE10 8RD
Tel: 0181 516 7800
Fax: 0181 516 7801
Email: enquiry@greenwich-college.ac.uk
Website: www.greenwich-college
Status: private college

**Guy's, King's and St Thomas's
Hospitals Medical and Dental
School**
Ceremonies Office
57 Waterloo Road
London SE1 8TY
Tel: 020 7836 5454
Fax: 020 7836 1799
Email: ucas.enquiries@kcl.ac.uk
Website: www.kcl.ac.uk

Gyosei International College
London Road
Reading, Berkshire
RG1 5AQ
Tel: 01189 209 357
Fax: 01189 310 137
Status: college of higher education

Halton College
Kingsway
Widness
Cheshire WA8 7QQ
Tel: 0151 423 1391
Fax: 0151 420 2408
Email: halton.college@cityscape.co.uk
Website: www.cityscape.co.uk/
users/aj75/index.html
Status: college of higher education

Hampstead School of Art
19-21 Kidderpore Avenue
London NW3 7ST
Tel: 020 7431 1292
Fax: 020 7431 1292

Handsworth College
The Council House
Soho Road
Birmingham, B21 9DP
Tel: 0121 551 6031
Fax: 0121 523 4447
Status: college of higher education

**Harper Adams
University College**
Newport
Shropshire TF10 8NB
Tel: 01952 815 000
Fax: 01952 814 783
Email: gpodmore@haac.ac.uk.
Website: www.haac.ac.uk/
Status: university

**Heatherley's School
of Fine Art**
80 Upcerne Road
Chelsea
London SW10 0SH
Tel: 020 7351 4190
Fax: 020 7351 6945
Email: info@heatherleys.org
Website: www.heatherleys.org

Hereford College of Technology
Folly Lane, Hereford
Herefordshire
HR1 1LS
Tel: 01432 352 235
Fax: 01432 353 449
Website: www.herefordshire.com/hct/
Status: college of higher education

**Herefordshire College of Art
and Design**
Folly Lane, Hereford
Herefordshire HR1 1LT
Tel: 01432 273 359
Fax: 01432 341 099
Status: college of higher education

Heriot-Watt University, Edinburgh
Riccarton
Edinburgh EH14 4AS
Tel: 0131 451 3877
Fax: 0131 449 5153
Email: International@hw.ac.uk
Website: www.hw.ac.uk/
Status: university

University of Hertfordshire
College Lane
Hatfield
Herts AL10 9AB
Tel: 01707 284 800
Fax: 01707 284 870
Email: international@herts.ac.uk
Website: www.herts.ac.uk
Status: university

Hertford Regional College
Ware Centre
Scotts Road
Ware
Hertfordshire SG12 9JF
Tel: 01920 465 441
Fax: 01920 462 772
Email: sfb1@sfb1.demon.co.uk
Website: www.hertreg.ac.uk/
Status: college of higher education

**Heythrop College, University of
London**
Kensington Square
London W8 5HQ
Tel: 0171 795 6600
Fax: 0171 795 4200
Email: a.clarkson@heythrop.ac.uk
Status: university

Holborn College
200 Greyhound Road
London W14 9RY
Tel: 0171 385 3377
Fax: 0171 381 3377
Email: hlt@holborncollege.ac.uk
Website: www.holborncollege.ac.uk
Status: college of higher education

Hove College
Medina House
Medina Villas
Hove
East Sussex BN3 2RP
Tel: 01273 772 577
Fax: 01273 208401
Email: courses@hovecollege.co.uk

The University of Huddersfield
Queensgate
Huddersfield
West Yorkshire HD1 3DH
Tel: 01484 422 288
Fax: 01484 516 151
Email: prospectus@hud.ac.uk
Website: www.hud.ac.uk/
Status: university

The University of Hull
Cottingham Road
Hull HU6 7RX
Tel: 01482 466 100

Fax: 01482 442 290
Email: admissions@admin.hull.ac.uk
Website: www.hull.ac.uk/
Status: university

**Imperial College of Science,
Technology and Medicine,
University of London**
Registry
London SW7 2AZ
Tel: 0171 594 8014
Fax: 0171 594 8004
Email: admissions@ic.ac.uk
Website: www.ic.ac.uk/
Status: university

**Institute of Education,
University of London**
20 Bedford Way
London WC1H 0AL
Tel: 0171 612 6102
Fax: 0171 612 6097
Email: overseas.liaison@ioe.ac.uk
Website: www.ioe.ac.uk
Status: university

Jetset Training
Kenilworth House
79-80 Margaret Street
London
W1N 7HB
Tel: 020 7436 3737
Fax: 020 7436 5737
Email: london@jetset-europe.plc.uk
Website:
www.jetsetworldwide.com/training.htm

Keele University
Office, Keele
Staffs ST5 5BG
Tel: 01782 621 111
Fax: 01782 632 343
Email: aaa20@admin.keele.ac.uk
Website: www.keele.ac.uk/depts/aa/
homepage.htm
Status: university

**The University of Kent at
Canterbury**
Canterbury
Kent CT2 7NZ
Tel: 01227 827 272
Fax: 01227 827 077
Email: admissions@ukc.ac.uk
Website: www.ukc.ac.uk/
Status: university

Kensington College of Business
52a Walham Grove
Fulham
London
SW6 1QR
Tel: 020 7381 6360
Fax: 020 7386 9650
Email: course@kensington-
coll.demon.co.uk
Website: www.mazware.com/kcb

**Kent Institute of
Art and Design**
Oakwood Park
Maidstone
Kent ME16 8AG
Tel: 01622 757 286
Fax: 01622 621 100
Email: intloff@kiad.ac.uk
Website: www.kiad.ac.uk
Status: college of higher education

Kidderminster College
Hoo Road,
Kidderminster
Worcs DY10 1LX
Tel: 01562 820 811
Fax: 01562 748 504
Email: staff@kcfe.prestel.ac.uk.
Status: college of higher education

King Alfred's Winchester
Saprkford Road
Winchester
Hampshire SO22 4NR
Tel: 01962 827 491
Fax: 01962 827 436
Email: international@wkac.ac.uk
Website: www.wkac.ac.uk
Status: college of higher education

**King's College London,
University of London**
Ceremonies Office
57 Waterloo Road
London SE1 8TY
Tel: 0171 836 5454
Fax: 0171 836 1799
Email: ucas.enquiries@kcl.ac.uk
Website: www.kcl.ac.uk/
Status: university

King Street College
4 Hammersmith Broadway
London W6 7AL
Tel: 020 8748 0971
Fax: 020 8741 1098
Emai: info@kingstreet.co.uk
Website: www.kingstreet.co.uk

Kingston University
Cooper House
40-46 Surbiton Road
Surrey KT1 2HX
Tel: 0181 547 8230
Fax: 0181 547 7080
Email: C.Gerrard@kingston.ac.uk
Website: www.kingston.ac.uk
Status: university

The University of Wales, Lampeter
College Street, Lampeter
Ceredigion SA48 7ED
Tel: 01570 423 530
Fax: 01570 423 423
Email: recruit@admin.lamp.ac.uk
Website: www.lamp.ac.uk
Status: university

Lancaster University
University House
Lancaster LA1 4YW
Tel: 01524 65 201
Fax: 01524 846 243
Email: ugadmissions@lancaster.ac.uk
Website: www.lancs.ac.uk/
Status: university

Lansdowne College
40/44 Bark Place
London W2 4AT
Tel: 0171 616 4410
Fax: 0171 616 4401
Status: college of higher education

Le Cordon Bleu,
14 Marylebone Lane
London W1M 6HH
Tel: 020 7935 3503
Fax: 020 7935 7621
Email: london@cordonbleu.net
Website: www.cordonbleu.net

University of Leeds
Leeds LS2 9JT
Tel: 0113 233 2332
Fax: 0113 233 2334
Email: prospectus@leeds.ac.uk
Website: www.leeds.ac.uk/
Status: university

Leeds, Trinity and All Saints College
Brownberrie Lane
Horsforth
Leeds LS18 5HD
Tel: 0113 283 7123
Fax: 0113 283 7200
Website: www.tasc.ac.uk/
Status: college of higher education

Leeds Metropolitan University
Calverley Street
Leeds LS1 3HE
Tel: 0113 283 6737
Fax: 0113 283 3129
Email: N.Slater@lmu.ac.uk
Website: www.lmu.ac.uk
Status: university

Leeds College of Art and Design
Jacob Kramer Building
Blenheim Walk
Leeds
LS2 9AQ
Tel: 0113 243 3848
Fax: 0113 244 5916
Status: college of higher education

Leeds College of Music
3 Quarry Hill
Leeds
W Yorkshire LS2 7PD
Tel: 0113 222 3400
Fax: 0113 243 8798
Status: college of higher education

University of Leicester
Leicester
LE1 7RH
Tel: 0116 252 5281
Fax: 0116 252 2447
Email: admissions@le.ac.uk
Website: www.le.ac.uk/
Status: university

Leicester South Fields College
Aylestone Road
Leicester LE2 7LW
Tel: 0116 224 2200
Fax: 0116 224 2190
Email: info@lsfe.ac.uk
Website: www.lsfe.ac.uk
Status: college of higher education

Leith's School of Food and Wine
21 St Alban's Grove
London W8 5BP
Tel: 020 7229 0177
Fax: 020 7937 5257
Email: info@leiths.com
Website: www.leiths.com

Leo Baeck College
80 East End Road
London
N3 2SY
Tel: 0181 349 4525
Fax: 0181 343 2558
Email: Leo-Baeck-College@mailbox.ulcc.ac.uk
Website: www.LB-College.demon.co.uk
Status: college of higher education

University of Lincolnshire and Humberside
Cottingham Road
Kingston upon Hull,
HU6 7RT
Tel: 01482 440 550
Fax: 01482 463 532
Email: tjohnson@humber.ac.uk
Website: www.ulh.ac.uk/
Status: university

The University of Liverpool
Schools, Colleges,
International Liaison and Admissions
Service (SCILAS)
Student Services Centre
Liverpool
L69 3GD
Tel: 0151 794 5927
Fax: 0151 708 2060
Email: scilas@liv.ac.uk
Website: www.liv.ac.uk/
Status: university

Liverpool Community College
Bankfield Centre
Bankfield Road
Liverpool L13 OBQ
Tel: 0151 252 3840
Fax: 0151 228 3231
Status: college of higher education

Liverpool Hope University College
Hope Park
Liverpool L16 9JD
Tel: 0151 291 3856
Fax: 0151 291 3116
Email: daviesj3@livhope.ac.uk
Website: www.livhope.ac.uk
Status: university

The Liverpool Institute for Performing Arts
Mount Street,
Liverpool L1 9HF
Tel: 0151 330 3232
Fax: 0151 330 3131
Email: admissions@lipa.ac.uk
Status: college of higher education

Liverpool John Moores University
4 Rodney Street
Liverpool L1 2TZ
Tel: 0151 231 3522/3169
Fax: 0151 707 0199
Email: international@livjm.ac.uk
Website: www.livjm.ac.uk
Status: university

London Centre for Fashion Studies
Bradley Close
White Lion Street
London N1 9PF
Tel: 020 7713 1991
Fax: 020 7713 1997
Email: learnf@shion.demon.co.uk
Website: www.fashionstudies.com

London Centre of International Relations (University of Kent)
Awdry House
11 Kingsway
London WC2B 6YF
Tel: 020 7565 6826
Fax: 020 7565 6827
Email: LCIR@ukc.ac.uk
Website: www.ukc.ac.uk

Llandrillo College, North Wales
Llandudno Road,
Colwyn Bay
North Wales LL28 4HZ
Tel: 01492 546 666
ext 338/9
Fax: 01492 543 052
Email: admissions@llandrillo.ac.uk
Status: college of higher education

London City College
51-55 Waterloo Road
London SE1 8TX
Tel: 020 7928 0029
Fax: 020 7401 2231
Email: lcclist@aol.com
Website: www.londoncitycollege.com

London College of English
178 Goswell Road
London
EC1L 7DT
Tel: 020 70610/251 6473
Fax: 020 7251 9410
Email: info@cbc.english.bdx.co.uk

London College of International Business Studies
14/15 Southampton Place
London WC1A 2AJ
Tel: 020 7242 1004
Fax: 020 7242 1005

London English Academy
85-87 The Broadway
Ealing
London W13 98P
Tel: 020 8579 9661
Fax: 020 8579 3919
Email: info@london-english-language-academy.co.uk
Website: www.london-english-lan-guage-academy.co.uk

London Esthetique
75-77 Margaret Street
London W1N 7HB
Tel: 020 7636 1893
Fax: 020 7323 1805
Website: www.london-est.com

London Hotel School
1 Bedford Avenue
London WC1B 3AS
Tel: 020 7665 0000
Fax: 020 7665 0001
Email:
Registrar@londonhotelschool.com
Website: www.londonhotelschool.com

London Institute of Technology and Research
213 Borough High Street
London SE1 1JA
Tel: 020 7787 4545
Fax: 020 7403 6726
Email: litrkazi@aol.com
Website: www.litr.co.uk

London Guildhall University
133 Whitechapel High Street
London E1 7QA
Tel: 0171 320 1616
Fax: 0171 320 1163
Email: enqs@lgu.ac.uk
Website: www.lgu.ac.uk
Status: university

The London Institute
65 Davies Street,
London W1Y 2DA
Tel: 0171 514 6000
Fax: 0171 514 6212
Email: bm@linst.ac.uk or ck@linst.ac.uk
Website: www.linst.ac.uk
Status: university

London Institute of Technology and English
11a Pratt Street
Camden Town
London NW1 0AE
Tel: 020 7284 2559/482 3444
Fax: 020 7323 4582
Email: oxhc@easynet.co.uk

London School of Economics and Political Science, University of London
Houghton Street
London WC2A 2AE
Tel: 0171 955 7440
Fax: 0171 955 7421
Email: stu-rec@lse.ac.uk
Website: www.lse.ac.uk
Status: university

London School of Jewish Studies
Schaller House
Albert Road, Hendon
London NW4 2SJ
Tel: 0181 203 6427
Fax: 0181 203 6420
Email: jewscoll@ulcc.clusi.ac.uk
Status: college of higher education

Loughborough University
Admissions Office
Ashby Road
Loughborough

Leics LE11 3TU
Tel: 01509 222 233
Fax: 01509 223 905
Email: c.e.prendargast@lboro.ac.uk
Website: www.lboro.ac.uk
Status: university

Lowestoft College
St Peters Street
Lowestoft
Suffolk NR32 2NB
Tel: 01502 583 521
Fax: 01502 500 031
Email: info@lowestoft.ac.uk
Website: www.lowestoft.ac.uk/
Status: college of higher education

Lucie Clayton College
4 Cornwall Gardens
London SW7 4AJ
Tel: 020 7581 0024
Fax: 020 7589 9693

University of Luton
Park Square
Luton
Beds LU1 3JU
Tel: 01582 489 346
Fax: 01582 489 260
Email: tim.gutsell@luton.ac.uk.
Website: www.luton.ac.uk/
Status: university

Manchester College of Arts and Technology
City Centre Campus
Lower Hardman Street
Manchester M3 3ER
Tel: 0161 953 5995
Fax: 0161 953 2259
Email: jim.whitham@mancat.ac.uk
Status: college of higher education

The University of Manchester
Beyer Building
Manchester M13 9PL
Tel: 0161 275 2059
Fax: 0161 275 2058
Email: international.unit@man.ac.uk
Website: www.man.ac.uk
Status: university

The University of Manchester Institute of Science and Technology (UMIST)
Admissions Officer
PO Box 88
Manchester M60 1QD
Tel: 0161 200 4033
Fax: 0161 200 8765
Email: ug.prospectus@umist.ac.uk
Website: www.umist.ac.uk/
Status: university

The Manchester Metropolitan University
Academic Division
All Saints
Manchester M15 6BH
Tel: 0161 247 1022
Fax: 0161 247 6310
Email: C.D.Rogers@mmu.ac.uk
Website: www.mmu.ac.uk
Status: university

Matthew Boulton College of Further and Higher Education
Sherlock Street
Birmingham, B5 7DB
Tel: 0121 446 4545
Fax: 0121 446 3105
Email: bmolneux@matthew-boulton. ac.uk
Status: college of higher education

Mid-Cheshire College
Hartford Campus
Chester Road, Northwich

Cheshire CW8 1LJ
Tel: 01606 74 444
Fax: 01606 75 101
Website: www.midchesh.u-net.com/
Status: college of higher education

Middlesex University
White Hart Lane
London N17 8HR
Tel: 0181 362 5000
Fax: 0181 362 5649
Email: admissions@mdx.ac.uk
Website: www.mdx.ac.uk
Status: university

Napier University
219 Colinton Road
Edinburgh EH14 1DJ
Tel: 0131 455 4330
Fax: 0131 455 4666
Email: info@napier.ac.uk
Website: www.napier.ac.uk
Status: university

University of Newcastle upon Tyne
10 Kensington Terrace
Newcastle upon Tyne
NE1 7RU
Tel: 0191 222 8152
Fax: 0191 222 5212
Email: international. office@ncl.ac.uk
Website: www.ncl.ac.uk
Status: university

Newcastle College
Rye Hill Campus
Scotswood Road
Newcastle upon Tyne
NE4 7SA
Tel: 0191 200 4110
Fax: 0191 272 4297
Email: sdoughty@ncl-coll.ac.uk
Website: www.ncl-coll.ac.uk/
Status: college of higher education

New College Durham
Framwellgate Moor
Durham DH1 5ES
Tel: 0191 375 4210
Fax: 0191 375 4222
Email: admissions@newdur.ac.uk
Website: www.newdur.ac.uk/
Status: college of higher education

Newham College of Further Education
School of Art Design & Fashion
East Ham Campus
High Street South
London E6 4ER
Tel: 0181 257 4377
Fax: 0181 257 4308
Website: www.newhamcfe.ac.uk/
Status: college of higher education

Newman College of Higher Education
Genners Lane
Bartley Green
Birmingham
B32 3NT
Tel: 0121 476 1181
Fax: 0121 476 1196
Email: registry@newman.ac.uk
Website: www.newman.ac.uk/
Status: college of higher education

University of Wales College, Newport
Caerleon Campus
PO Box 101
Newport NP6 1YH
Tel: 01633 432 432
Fax: 01633 432 850
Email: uic@newport.ac.uk
Website: www.newport.ac.uk/
Status: university

The Norwich School of Art and Design
St George Street
Norwich
NR3 1BB
Tel: 01603 610 561
Fax: 01603 615 728
Status: college of higher education

Northbrook College Sussex
Littlehampton Road,
Worthing
West Sussex BN12 6NU
Tel: 01903 606 060
Fax: 01903 606 007
Email: admissions@MBCOL.ac.uk
Website: www.NBCOL.ac.uk
Status: college of higher education

Nescot
Reigate Road, Ewell
Surrey KT17 3DS
Tel: 0181 394 3042/3300
Fax: 0181 394 3030
Email: rwood@nescot.ac.uk mkristensen@nescot.ac.uk
Website: www.nescot.ac.uk/
Status: college of higher education

The North East Wales Institute of Higher Education
Plas Coch
Mold Road
Wrexham LL11 2AW
Tel: 01978 290 666
Fax: 01978 290 008
Email: k.mitchell@newi.ac.uk
Website: www.newi.ac.uk/
Status: college of higher education

North East Worcestershire College
Peakman Street,
Redditch
Worcs B98 8DW
Tel: 01527 570 020
Fax: 01527 572 901
Status: college of higher education

Northern College
Aberdeen Campus
Hilton Place
Aberdeen AB24 4FA
Tel: 01224 283 500
Fax: 01224 283 900
Website: www.norcol.ac.uk/
Status: college of higher education

University of North London
166-220 Holloway Road
London N7 8DB
Tel: 0171 753 5190
Fax: 0171 753 5015
Email: international@unl.ac.uk
Website: www.unl.ac.uk
Status: university

North Tyneside College
Embleton Avenue, Wallsend
Tyne and Wear NE28 9NJ
Tel: 0191 229 5000
Fax: 0191 295 0301
Email: admissions@ntyneside.ac.uk
Website: www.ntyneside.ac.uk
Status: college of higher education

University of Northumbria at Newcastle
Ellison Building,
Ellison Place
Newcastle upon Tyne
NE1 8ST
Tel: 0191 227 4271
Fax: 0191 227 1264
Email: lyn.thompson@unn.ac.uk
Website: www.unn.ac.uk
Status: university

Northumberland College
College Road, Ashington
Northumberland
NE63 9RG
Tel: 01670 841200
Fax: 01670 841201
Website: www.northland.ac.uk/
Status: college of higher education

**North Warwickshire
and Hinckley College**
Hinckley Road, Nuneaton
Warwickshire CV11 6BH
Tel: 01203 243 000
Fax: 01203 329 056
Email: admissions@nwarks-
hinkley.ac.uk
Status: college of higher education

Norwich City College
Ipswich Road
Norwich
Norfolk NR2 2LJ
Tel: 01603 773 136
Fax: 01603 773 334
Email: registry@ccn.ac.uk
Website: www.ccn.ac.uk/
Status: college of higher education

The University of Nottingham
University Park
Nottingham
NG7 2RD
Tel: 0115 951 5247
Fax: 0115 951 5155
Email: international-office@notting-
ham.ac.uk
Website: www.nottingham.ac.uk
Status: university

The Nottingham Trent University
Burton Street
Nottingham NG1 4BU
Tel: 0115 948 6515
Fax: 0115 948 6528
Email: int.office@ntu.ac.uk
Website: www.ntu.ac.uk
Status: university

The Old Vicarage
Marden
Nr Tonbridge
Kent TN12 9AG
Tel: 01622 832200
Fax: 01622 832200

Oxford University
University Offices
Wellington Square
Oxford
OX1 2JD
Tel: 01865 270 208 (undergraduates)
01865 270 059 (graduates)
Fax: 01865 270 708
Email: undergraduate.admissions@
admin.ox.ac.uk or graduate.admis-
sions@admin.ox.ac.uk
Website: www.ox.ac.uk
Status: university

Oxford House College
28-30 Market Place
London W1N 7AL
Tel: 020 7580 9785
Fax: 020 7323 4582
Email: english@oxfordhouse.co.uk
Website: www.oxford-house-
college.ac.uk

**Oxford International College of
Beauty**
96a High Street
Witney
Oxford OX8 68L
Tel: 01993 775858
Fax: 01993 775858
Email: oicb@oxbox.com
Website: www.oxbox.com/oicb

Oxford Media and Business School
Rose Place
Oxford OX1 1SB
Tel: 01865 240963
Fax: 01865 242783
Email: courses@oxfordbusiness.co.uk
Website: www.oxfordbusiness.co.uk

Oxford Westminster College
Oxford OX2 9AT
Tel: 01865 247 644
Fax: 01865 251 847
Email: registry@ox-west.ac.uk
Website: www.ox-west.ac.uk
Status: university

Oxford Brookes University
Gipsy Lane Campus
Headington, Oxford
Oxon OX3 0BP
Tel: 01865 484 880
Fax: 01865 484 861
Website: www.brookes.ac.uk
Status: university

**Oxfordshire School of Art and
Design**
Broughton Road, Banbury
Oxon OX16 9QA
Tel: 01295 257 979
Fax: 01295 250 381
Email: enquiries@northox.ac.uk
Website: www.northox.ac.uk/Banbury/
default.htm
Status: college of higher education

University of Paisley
High Street
Paisley PA1 2BE
Tel: 0141 848 3000
Fax: 0141 848 3947
Email: international@paisley.ac.uk
Website: www.paisley.ac.uk
Status: university

University of Plymouth
Drake Circus, Plymouth
Devon PL4 8AA
Tel: 01752 233 340
Fax: 01752 232 014
Email: intoff@plymouth.ac.uk
Website: www.plym.ac.uk
Status: university

Plymouth College of Art and Design
Tavistock Place, Plymouth
Devon PL4 8AT
Tel: 01752 203 434
Fax: 01752 203 444
Email: enquiries@pcad.ply.ac.uk
Website: www.pcad.plymouth.ac.uk
Status: college of higher education

University of Portsmouth
University House
Winston Churchill Avenue
Portsmouth PO1 2UP
Tel: 01705 876 543
Fax: 01705 843 082
Email: admissions@port.ac.uk
Website: www.port.ac.uk/
Status: university

**Purley Secretarial and Language
College**
14 Brighton Road
Purley CR8 3AB
Tel: 020 8660 5060
Fax: 020 8668 4022
Email: purleycollege@compuserve.com

**Queen's Business and Secretarial
College**
24 Queensbury Place
London SW7 2DS
Tel: 0171 589 8583
Fax: 0171 823 9915
Status: private college

**Queen Mary and Westfield College,
University of London**
Mile End Road
London E1 4NS
Tel: 0171 775 3066
Fax: 0171 975 5556
Email: international-office@qmw.ac.uk
Website: www.qmw.ac.uk
Status: university

**The Queen's
University of Belfast**
Admissions Office
Belfast BT7 1NN
Tel: 01232 335 081
Fax: 01232 247 895
Email: admissions@qub.ac.uk
Website: www.qub.ac.uk
Status: university

**Ravensbourne College of Design
and Communication**
Walden Road
Chislehurst
Kent BR7 5SN
Tel: 0181 289 4900
Fax: 0181 325 8320
Email: info@rave.ac.uk
Website: www.rave.ac.uk/
Status: college of higher education

**Reading College and School of Arts
and Design**
Crescent Road
Reading
Berks RG1 5RQ
Tel: 0118 967 5555
Fax: 0118 967 5001
Status: college of higher education

The University of Reading
PO Box 217
Reading RG6 6AH
Tel: 0118 987 5123
Fax: 0118 931 4404
Email: intoff@reading.ac.uk
Website: www.rdg.ac.uk
Status: university

**Regents Business
School London**
Regent's College
Regent's Park
London NW1 4NS
Tel: 0171 487 7654
Fax: 0171 487 7425
Email: rbs@regents.ac.uk
Website: www.regents.ac.uk
Status: college of higher education

**University College of Ripon and
York St John**
Lord Mayor's Walk
York YO3 7EX
Tel: 01904 616 942
Fax: 01904 616 928
Email: m.williams@ucrysj.ac.uk
Website: www.ucrysj.ac.uk
Status: university

The Robert Gordon University
Schoolhill, Aberdeen
Scotland AB10 1FR
Tel: 01224 262 105
Fax: 01224 262 147
Email: j.youngson@rgu.ac.uk
Website: www.rgu.ac.uk/
Status: university

Roehampton Institute London
Downshire House
Roehampton Lane
London SW19 5PH
Tel: 0181 392 3151
Fax: 0181 392 3717
Email: D.Street@roehampton.ac.uk
Website: www.roehampton.ac.uk
Status: college of higher education

Rose Bruford College
Lamorbey Park
Burnt Oak Lane
Sidcup
Kent DA15 9DF
Tel: 0181 300 3024
Fax: 0181 308 0542
Email: admiss@bruford.ac.uk
Status: college of higher education

Royal Academy of Dancing
36 Battersea Square
London SW11 3RA
Tel: 020 7636 7076
Fax: 020 7924 3129

Royal Agricultural College
Cirencester
Gloucestershire GL7 6JS
Tel: 01285 652 531
Fax: 01285 650 219
Email: admissions@royagcol.ac.uk
Website: www.royagcol.ac.uk
Status: college of higher education

The Royal Ballet School
155 Talgarth Road
Barons Court
London W14 9DE
Tel: 020 8237 7128
Fax: 020 8237 7127
Website: www.royal-ballet-school.org.uk

Royal College of Music
Prince Consort Road
London SW7 2BS
Tel: 020 7589 3643
Fax: 020 7589 7740
Email: dharpham@rcm.ac.uk
Website: www.rcm.ac.uk

Royal Holloway, University of London
Liaison Office, Egham
Surrey TW20 0EX
Tel: 01784 443 399
Fax: 01784 471 381
Email: liaison-office@rhbnc.ac.uk
Website: www.rhbnc.ac.uk/
Status: university

Royal Veterinary College, University of London
Royal College Street
London NW1 0TU
Tel: 0171 468 5149
Fax: 0171 388 2342
Website: www.rvc.ac.uk/
Status: university

The Royal Veterinary College
Hawkshead House
Hawkshead Lane
North Mimms
Hatfield AL9 7TA
Tel: 020 7468 5000
Fax: 020 7388 2342
Website: www.rvc.ac.uk

Rycotewood College
Priest End, Thame
Oxfordshire OX9 2AF
Tel: 01844 212 501
Fax: 01844 218 809
Email: enquiries_rycote@oxfe.ac.uk
Website: www.oxfe.ac.uk/rycote
Status: college of higher education

University of St Andrews
Old Union Building
North Street, St Andrews
Fife KY16 9AJ
Tel: 01334 462 150
Fax: 01334 463 388
Email: admissions@st.andrews.ac.uk
Website: www.st-and.ac.uk/
Status: university

St George's Hospital Medical School, University of London
Cranmer Terrace
London SW17 ORE
Tel: 0181 725 5992
Fax: 0181 725 3426
Email: w.evans@sghms.ac.uk.
Website: www.sghms.ac.uk/
Status: university

St Helen's College
Brook Street,
St Helens WA10 1PZ
Tel: 01744 623 338
Fax: 01744 623 400
Website: www.sthelens.mernet.org.uk/
Status: college of higher education

St Loye's School of Occupational Therapy
Millbrook House, Millbrook Lane
Topsham Road
Exeter EX2 6ES
Tel: 01392 219 774
Fax: 01392 435 357
Email: A.Clark@exeter.ac.uk
Website: www.ex.uk/stloyes
Status: college of higher education

St Patrick's International College
24 Great Chapel Street
London W1V 3AF
Tel: 020 7734 2156
Fax: 020 7287 6282
Email: esther@elcgroup.net

The College of St Mark and St John
Derriford Road
Plymouth
Devon PL6 8BH
Tel: 01752 636 827
Fax: 01752 636 819
Email: kearnh@marjon.ac.uk
Website: http://194.80.168.100/
Status: college of higher education

University College of St Martin, Lancaster and Cumbria
Bowerham Road
Lancaster
Lancashire LA1 3JD
Tel: 01524 384 444
Fax: 01524 384 567
Email: admissions@ucsm.ac.uk
Website: www.ucsm.ac.uk/
Status: university

St Mary's University College
Waldegrave Road
Twickenham TW1 4SX
Tel: 0181 240 4000
Fax: 0181 240 4255
Website: www.smuc.ac.uk/
Status: university

The University of Salford
Maxwell Building
Salford
Greater Manchester
M5 4WT
Tel: 0161 295 5543
Fax: 0161 295 5256
Email: intoff@ext-rel.salford.ac.uk
Website: www.salford.ac.uk
Status: university

Salisbury College
Southampton Road
Salisbury
Wilts SP1 2LW
Tel: 01722 323 711
Fax: 01722 326 006
Status: college of higher education

Sandwell College
Wednesbury Campus

Woden Road South
Wednesbury
West Midlands WS10 0PE
Tel: 0121 556 6000
Fax: 0121 253 6104
Status: college of higher education

School of Oriental and African Studies (SOAS), University of London
Thornhaugh Street
Russell Square
London WC1H 0XG
Tel: 0171 691 3309
Fax: 0171 691 3362
Email: study@soas.ac.uk
Website: www.soas.ac.uk
Status: university

The School of Pharmacy, University of London
29-39 Brunswick Square
London WC1N 1AX
Tel: 0171 753 5831
Fax: 0171 753 5829
Email: registry@cua.ulsop.ac.uk
Contact: The Registry
Website: www.ulsop.ac.uk
Status: university

School of Slavonic and East European Studies, (SSEES) University of London
Senate House
Malet Street
London WC1E 7HU
Tel: 0171 862 8519
Fax: 0171 862 8641
Email: c.morley@ssees.ac.uk
Website: www.ssees.ac.uk/
Status: university

Scottish Agricultural College
Auchincruive
Ayr KA6 5HW
Tel: 01292 525 350
Fax: 01292 525 349
Email: etsu@au.sac.ac.uk
Website: www.sac.ac.uk/
Status: college of higher education

Sels College London
64-65 Longacre
Covent Garden
London WC2E 9JH
Tel: 020 7240 2581
Fax: 020 7323 4582
Email: english@sels.co.uk
Website: www.sels.co.uk

The University of Sheffield
6 Claremont Place
Sheffield S10 2TN
Tel: 0114 276 8966
Fax: 0114 272 9145.
Email: international@sheffield.ac.uk
Website: www.shef.ac.uk
Status: university

Sheffield Hallam University
City Campus, Pond Street
Sheffield S1 1WB
Tel: 0114 253 3490
Fax: 0114 253 4023
Email: c.arnold@shu.ac.uk
Website: www.shu.ac.uk/
Status: university

Shrewsbury College of Arts and Technology
London Road, Shrewsbury
Shropshire SY2 6PR
Tel: 01743 342 342
Fax: 01743 241 684
Email: mail@s-cat.ac.uk
Status: college of higher education

Solihull College
Blossomfield Road
Solihull B91 1SB
Tel: 0121 678 7001/2
Fax: 0121 678 7200
Email: enquiries@staff.solihull.ac.uk
Website: www.solihull.ac.uk/
Status: college of higher education

**Somerset College of Arts
and Technology**
Wellington Road, Taunton
Somerset TA1 5AX
Tel: 01823 366 366
Fax: 01823 355 418
Website: www.zynet.co.uk/scat1/
Status: college of higher education

Southampton Institute
East Park Terrace
Southampton
Hants SO14 0YN
Tel: 01703 319 807
Fax: 01703 319 412
Email: Marianne.Geach@ Solent.ac.uk
Website: www.solent.ac.uk
Status: college of higher education

University of Southampton
Highfield
Southampton SO17 1BJ
Tel: 01703 595 000
Fax: 01703 593 037
Email: prospenq@soton.ac.uk
Website: www.soton.ac.uk
Status: university

South Bank University
103 Borough Road
London SE1 0AA
Tel: 0171 815 8158
Fax: 0171 815 8273
Email: enrol@sbu.ac.uk
Website: www.sbu.ac.uk/
Status: university

Southport College
Mornington Road
Southport PR9 0TT
Tel: 01704 500 606
Fax: 01704 546 240
Status: college of higher education

Southwark College
Waterloo Centre,
The Cut
London SE1 8LE
Tel: 0171 815 1600
Fax: 0171 261 1301
Email: ucas@southwark.ac.uk
Website: www.southwark.ac.uk
Status: college of higher education

Sparsholt College Hampshire
Sparsholt
Winchester SO21 2NF
Tel: 01962 776 441
Fax: 01962 776 587
Email: enquiry@sparsholt.ac.uk
Website: www.sparsholt.ac.uk
Status: college of higher education

Spectrum Group
14 Burma Road
London N16 98J
Tel: 020 7275 7667
Fax: 020 7275 8922
Email: gill@spedas.demon.co.uk

Stafford College
Earl Street
Stafford ST16 2QR
Tel: 01785 223 800
Fax: 01785 259 953
Email: 104361.101@
compuserve.com
Status: college of higher education

Staffordshire University
College Road
Stoke on Trent ST4 2DE
Tel: 01782 292 718
Fax: 01782 292 796
Email: a.m.edge@staffs.ac.uk
Website: www.staffs.ac.uk
Status: university

The University of Stirling
Stirling FK9 4LA
Tel: 01786 467 046
Fax: 01786 466 800
Email: international@stir.ac.uk
Website: www.stir.ac.uk/
Status: university

**Stockport College of Further and
Higher Education**
Wellington Road South
Stockport SK1 3UQ
Tel: 0161 958 3416
Fax: 0161 958 3305
Website: www.stockport.ac.uk/
Status: college of higher education

The University of Strathclyde
Graham Hills Building
50 George Street
Glasgow G1 1QE
Tel: 0141 548 2814
Fax: 0141 552 7362
Email: j.foulds@mis.strath.ac.uk
Website: www.strath.ac.uk/Campus/
prospect/info/index3.htm
Status: university

University College Suffolk
Ipswich IP4 1LT
Tel: 01473 255 885
Fax: 01473 230 054
Website: www.suffolk.ac.uk/
Status: university

University of Sunderland
Technology Park
Chester Road
Sunderland SR2 7PS
Tel: 0191 515 2648
Fax: 0191 515 2960
Email: international@sunderland.ac.uk
Website: www.sunderland.ac.uk
Status: university

The University of Surrey
The Registry
Guildford
Surrey GU2 5XH
Tel: 01483 300 800
Fax: 01483 300 803
Website: www.surrey.ac.uk/
Status: university

University of Surrey, Roehampton
International Unit
Roehampton Lane
London SW19 5PH
Tel: 020 8392 3151
Fax: 020 8392 3717
Email: d.Street@roehampton.ac.uk
Website: www.roehampton.ac.uk

**Surrey Institute of Art
and Design**
Falkner Road
Farnham Campus
Surrey GU9 7DS
Tel: 01252 722 441
Fax: 01252 892 616
Email: registry@surrart.ac.uk
Website: www.surrart.ac.uk/
Status: college of higher education

University of Sussex
International and Study Abroad Office,
Arts B, Falmer
Brighton, Sussex BN1 9QN
Tel: 01273 678 422

Fax: 01273 678 640
Email: international.off@sussex.ac.uk
Website: www.sussex.ac.uk
Status: university

Sutton Coldfield College
Lichfield Road
Sutton Coldfield
West Midlands B74 2NW
Tel: 0121 355 5671
Fax: 0121 355 0799
Email: cnewman@sutcol.ac.uk
Website: www.sutcol.ac.uk/
Status: college of higher education

University of Wales, Swansea
The Registry
Singleton Park
Swansea SA2 8PP
Tel: 01792 295 111
Fax: 01792 295 110
Email: admissions@swan.ac.uk
Website: www.swan.ac.uk/
Status: university

**Swansea Institute of Higher
Education**
Mount Pleasant
Swansea SA1 6ED
Tel: 01792 481 094
Fax: 01792 481 085
Email: enquiry@sihe.ac.uk
Website: www.sihe.ac.uk/home.html
Status: college of higher education

Swindon College
Regent Circus
Swindon SN1 1PT
Tel: 01793 498 308
Fax: 01793 641 794
Status: college of higher education

**The Tate Gallery of
British Art**
Interpretation and Education
Tate Britain
Millbank
London SW1P 4RG
Tel: 020 7887 8922
Fax: 020 7887 8762
Email: gavin.street@tate.org.uk
Website: www.tate.org.uk

Tameside College
Ashton Campus
Beaufort Road
Ashton-under-Lyne
Lancs OL6 6NX
Tel: 0161 908 6600
Fax: 0161 343 2738
Email: info@tamesidecollege.ac.uk
Status: college of higher education

Tante Marie School of Cookery
Woodham House
Carlton Road, Woking
Surrey GU21 4HF
Tel: 01483 726957
Fax: 01483 724173
Email: info@tantemarie.co.uk
Website: www.tantemarie.co.uk

University of Teesside
Middlesbrough TS1 3BA
Tel: 01642 218 121
Fax: 01642 342 067
Email: h.Cummins@tees.ac.uk
Website: www@tees.ac.uk/
Status: university

Thames Valley University
18-22 Bond St, Ealing
London W5 5RF
Tel: 0181 579 5000
Fax: 0181 231 2900
Email: learning.advice@tvu.ac.uk
Website: www.tvu.ac.uk
Status: university

The Thomas Chippendale School of Furniture
Gifford
East Lothian EH41 4JA
Scotland
Tel: 01620 810680
Fax: 01620 810701
Email: info@chippendale.co.uk
Website: www.chippendale.co.uk

Trinity College Carmarthen
College Road
Carmarthenshire SA31 3EP
Tel: 01267 676 767
Fax: 01267 676 766
Status: college of higher education

University of Ulster
Cromore Road
Coleraine
County Londonderry
BT52 1SA
Tel: 01265 44 141
Fax: 01265 323 005
Email: sda.barnhill@ulster.ac.uk
Website: www.ulst.ac.uk/
Status: university

University College London, University of London
Gower Street
London WC1E 6BT
Tel: 0171 380 7365
Fax: 0171 380 7920
Email: degree-info@ucl.ac.uk
Website: www.ucl.ac.uk/
Status: university

University of Wales College of Medicine
Heath Park
Cardiff CF4 4XN
Tel: 01222 742 027
Fax: 01222 742 914
Website: www.uwcm.ac.uk/
Status: university

University College Warrington
Padgate Campus
Crab Lane
Warrington WA2 0DB
Tel: 01925 494 494
Fax: 01925 494 289
Email: registry.he@warr.ac.uk
Website: www.warr.ac.uk/unicoll/
Status: university

The University of Warwick
Coventry CV4 7AL
Tel: 01203 523 706
Fax: 01203 461 606
Email: intoff@admin.warwick.ac.uk
Website: www.warwick.ac.uk
Status: university

Warwickshire College, Royal Leamington Spa and Moreton Morrell
Warwick New Road
Leamington Spa
Warks CV32 5JE
Tel: 01926 318 000
Fax: 01926 318 111
Email: s.aslam@midwarks.demon.co.uk
Status: college of higher education

Welsh College of Music and Drama
Cathays Park
Cardiff CF1 3ER
Tel: 01222 342 854
Fax: 01222 237 639
Email: ROBERTSkT@wcmd.ac.uk
Website: www.wcmd.ac.uk/
Status: college of higher education

West Herts College, Watford
Hempstead Road, Watford
Herts WD1 3EZ
Tel: 01923 812 565
Fax: 01923 812 540
Status: college of higher education

University of West of England
Enquiry and Admissions Services
Frenchay Campus
Coldharbour Lane
Bristol BS16 1QY
Tel: 0117 965 6261
Fax: 0117 976 3804
Email: admissions@uwe.ac.uk
Website: www.uwe.ac.uk

Westhill College of Higher Education
Weoley Park Road
Selly Oak
Birmingham B29 6LL
Tel: 0121 415 2206
Fax: 0121 415 5399
Email: c.evans@westhill.ac.uk
Website: www.westhill.ac.uk/
Status: college of higher education

West London College
Parliament House
35 North Row
Mayfair
London W1R 2DB
Tel: 020 7491 1841
Fax: 020 7499 5853
Email: courses@w-l-c.co.uk
Website: www.w-l-c.co.uk

Weston College
Knightstone Road
Weston-super-Mare
BS23 2AL
Tel: 01934 411 411
Fax: 01934 411 410
Website: www.weston.ac.uk/
Status: college of higher education

University of Westminster
16 Little Titchfield Street
London W1P 7FH
Tel: 0171 911 5769
Fax: 0171 911 5132
Email: international-office@westminster
Website: www.westminster.ac.uk
Status: university

Westminster College
Battersea Park Road
London SW11 4JR
Tel: 0171 556 8068
Fax: 0171 498 4765
Email: tony_tucker@westminster-cfe.ac.uk
Website: www.westminster-cfe.ac.uk
Status: college of higher education

Westminster College of Computing
5 Sherwood Street
London W1V 7RA
Tel: 020 7287 6299
Fax: 020 7287 6297
Email: training@wcc.co.uk
Website: www.wcc.co.uk

West Thames College
London Road, Isleworth
Middlesex TW7 4HS
Tel: 0181 568 0244
Fax: 0181 569 7787
Email: admissions@west-thames.ac.uk
Website: www.west-thames.ac.uk/
Status: college of higher education

Wigan Leigh College
PO Box 53, Parsons Walk
Wigan
Lancashire WN1 1RS
Tel: 01942 761 601

Fax: 01942 501 533
Status: college of higher education

Wimbledon School of Art
Merton Hall Road
London SW19 3QA
Tel: 0181 408 5000
Fax: 0181 408 5050
Email: art@wimbledon.ac.uk
Website: www.wimbledon.ac.uk
Status: college of higher education

Wirral Metropolitan College
Borough Road
Birkenhead
Wirral
Merseyside L42 9QD
Tel: 0151 551 7472
Fax: 0151 551 7401
Email: h.e.enquiries@wmc.ac.uk
Website: http:/www.wmc.ac.uk
Status: college of higher education

University College Worcester
Henwick Grove
Worcester
WR2 6AJ
Tel: 01905 855 111
Fax: 01905 855 132
Website: www.worc.ac.uk/worcs.html
Status: university

Worcester College of Technology
Deansway
Worcester WR1 2JF
Tel: 01905 725 555
Fax: 01905 28 906
Status: college of higher education

Writtle College
Chelmsford
Essex
CM1 3RR
Tel: 01245 424 200
Fax: 01245 420 456
Email: postmaster@writtle.ac.uk
Website: www.writtle.ac.uk/
Status: college of higher education

Wye College, University of London
Wye
Ashford
Kent TN25 5AH
Tel: 01233 812 401
Fax: 01233 813 320
Email: registry@wye.ac.uk
Website: www.wye.ac.uk/
Status: university

The University of York
Heslington
York YO1 5DD
Tel: 01904 433 533
Fax: 01904 433 538
Email: admissions@york.ac.uk
Website: www.york.ac.uk
Status: university

York College of Further and Higher Education
Tadcaster Road
York YO2 1UA
Tel: 01904 770 200
Fax: 01904 770 499
Status: college of higher education

Yorkshire Coast College of Further and Higher Education
Lady Edith's Drive
Scarborough
North Yorkshire
YO12 5RN
Tel: 01723 372 105
Fax: 01723 501 918
Email: admissions@ycoastco.ac.uk
Website: www.ycoastco.ac.uk
Status: college of higher education

This chapter is a summary of the institutions offering undergraduate degrees in the main subject areas. A comprehensive listing can be found in the UCAS Directory available from UCAS (01242 223707).

Accountancy and Finance

Aberdeen, Abertay Dundee, Aberystwyth, APU, Aston, Bangor, Bell Col, Birmingham, Blackburn Col, Blackpool Col, Bolton Inst, Bournemouth, Bradford & Ilkley Col., Brighton, Bristol, UWE, Brunel, Buckingham, Buckinghamshire College, Buckland, Cardiff, Cardiff Inst, UCE, Central Lancashire, Chelt & Glos College, City, Coventry, Croydon Col, De Montfort, Derby, Dundee, Durham, UEA, East London, Edinburgh, Essex, Exeter Col, Exeter, Farnborough Col Of Tech, Glamorgan, Glasgow, Glasgow Caledonian, Greenwich, Heriot-Watt, Hertfordshire, Huddersfield, Hull, Keele, Kent at Canterbury, Kingston, Lancaster, Leeds, Leeds Metropolitan, Lincolnshire And Humberside, Liverpool, Liverpool John Moores, London Guildhall, LSE, Loughborough, Luton, Manchester, UMIST, Manchester Metropolitan, Mid-Cheshire Col, Middlesex, Napier, Nene, Newcastle, Newport Col, NE Wales Inst, North London, Northumbria, Norwich City Col, Nottingham, Nottingham Trent, Oxford Brookes, Paisley, Plymouth, Portsmouth, Queen's Belfast, Reading Col of Arts, Reading, Regents Business School, Robert Gordon, Royal Agricultural Col, Salford, Sheffield, Sheffield Hallam, Southampton, Southampton Inst, South Bank, Staffordshire, Stirling, Strathclyde, Uni Col Suffolk, Sunderland, Swansea, Swansea Inst, Teesside, Thames Valley, Ulster, Uni Col Warrington, Warwick, West Herts Col, Westminster, Wolverhampton.

Agriculture and Forestry

Aberdeen, Aberystwyth, APU, Askham Bryan, Bangor, Bath, Birmingham, Bolton Inst, Bournemouth, Brighton, Bristol, UWE, Buckinghamshire College, UCE, Central Lancashire, Chelt & Glos College, Chester, Cornwall College, Coventry, Cranfield, De Montfort, Derby, Dundee, UEA, East London, Edinburgh, Essex, Glamorgan, Glasgow, Greenwich, Harper Adams, Hertfordshire, Imperial, Kent at Canterbury, Leeds, Liverpool John Moores, Middlesex, Napier, Nene, Newcastle, New College Durham, Nescot, Northumbria, Nottingham, Nottingham Trent, Plymouth, Queen's Belfast, Reading, Roehampton Inst, Royal Agricultural Col, Scottish Agricultural Col, Sheffield Hallam, Southampton, Somerset Col of Art, South Bank, Sparsholt Hampshire, St Helens Col, Stirling, Strathclyde, Uni Col Suffolk, Sunderland, Sussex, Trinity Carmarthen, Warwickshire Col, Wolverhampton, Worcester, Writtle Col, Wye.

American Studies

Aberystwyth, Birmingham, Brunel, Canterbury Col, Central Lancashire, Chelt & Glos College, Chester, De Montfort, Derby, Dundee, UEA, Edinburgh, Essex, Exeter, Glamorgan, Hull, Keele, Kent at Canterbury, King Alfred's, King's, Lampeter, Lancaster, Leicester, Liverpool Hope, Liverpool John Moores, London Guildhall, Manchester, UMIST, Manchester Metropolitan, Middlesex, Nene, Nottingham, Plymouth, Queen's Belfast, Reading, Ripon & York St John, Sheffield, Staffordshire, Sunderland, Sussex, Swansea, Thames Valley, Ulster, Warwick, Wolverhampton.

Anatomy/Physiology/ Genetics

Aberdeen, Abertay Dundee, Aberystwyth, APU, Barnsley Col, Birmingham, Bradford, Bristol, UWE, Brunel, Brit Schl of Osteopathy, Cambridge, Cardiff, Central Lancashire, Dundee, UEA, East London, Edinburgh, Farnborough Col Of Tech, Glasgow, Greenwich, Hertfordshire, Huddersfield, Keele, King's, Kingston, Lancaster, Leeds, Leeds Metropolitan, Leicester, Lincolnshire And Humberside, Liverpool, Liverpool John Moores, Loughborough, Luton, Manchester, UMIST, Middlesex, Nene, Newcastle, Nescot, North London, Northumbria, Norwich City Col, Nottingham, Nottingham Trent, Oxford, Oxford Brookes, Plymouth, Queen Mary & Westfield, Queen's Belfast, Reading, Royal Holloway, Salford, Sheffield, Sheffield Hallam, Southampton, South Bank, St Andrews, St Mary's, Staffordshire, Strathclyde, Uni Col Suffolk, Sunderland, Sussex, Swansea, Teesside, UCL, Westminster, Wolverhampton, York.

Archaeology

Bangor, Birmingham, Bournemouth, Bradford, Bristol, Cambridge, Cardiff, Chester, Cumbria Col of Art, Durham, UEA, East London, Edinburgh, Exeter, Glasgow, Kent at Canterbury, King Alfred's, King's, Lampeter, Leicester, Liverpool, Luton, Manchester, Manchester Metropolitan, Nene, Newcastle, Newport Col, Nottingham, Oxford, Queen's Belfast, Reading, SOAS, Sheffield, Southampton, St Andrews, Trinity Carmarthen, UCL, Warwick, York.

Architecture

Bath, Brighton, UWE, Cambridge, Cardiff, UCE, Chelt & Glos College, De Montfort, Derby, Dundee, East London, Edinburgh, Glamorgan, Glasgow, Greenwich, Heriot-Watt, Huddersfield, Kent Inst of Art & Design, Kingston, Leeds, Leeds Metropolitan, Lincolnshire And Humberside, Liverpool, Liverpool John Moores, Luton, Manchester, Manchester Metropolitan, Middlesex, Newcastle, NE Wales Inst, North London, Northumbria, Nottingham, Nottingham Trent, Oxford Brookes, Paisley, Plymouth, Portsmouth, Queen's Belfast, Robert Gordon, Sheffield, Sheffield Hallam, South Bank, Strathclyde, Swansea Inst, Ulster, UCL, Westminster, Wolverhampton.

Art and Design

Abertay Dundee, Aberystwyth, APU, Barking Col, Barnsley Col, Basford Col, Bath Spa, Blackburn Col, Blackpool Col, Bolton Inst, Bournemouth, Art Inst Bournemouth, Bradford & Ilkley Col., Bretton Hall, Brighton, UWE, Brunel,

Buckinghamshire College, Canterbury Col, Cardiff Inst, Carmarthenshire Col, UCE, Central Lancashire, Ctrl Schl Speech & Drama, Chelt & Glos College, Chester, Chichester Inst, Bristol Col, City Col Manchester, Cleveland Col of Art, Colchester Inst, Cordwainers Col, Cornwall College, Coventry, Croydon Col, Cumbria Col of Art, Dartington Col of Arts, De Montfort, Derby, Dewsbury Col, Doncaster Col, Dudley Col of Tech, Dundee, UEA, East London, East Surrey Col, Edge Hill, Edinburgh, Exeter, Falmouth Col of Arts, Farnborough Col Of Tech, Glamorgan, Glamorgan Cntr For Art and Tech, Glasgow, Glasgow Caledonian, Gloucestershire Col of Arts, Goldsmiths, Greenwich, Halton Col, Handsworth Col, Herefordshire Col Of Tech, Herefordshire Col of Art, Heriot-Watt, Hertfordshire, Hertford Regional Col, Huddersfield, Keele, Kent Inst of Art & Design, Kidderminster Col, Kingston, Lancaster, Leeds, Leeds Metropolitan, Leeds Col of Art, Leicester, Leicester South Fields Col, Lincolnshire And Humberside, Liverpool Com Col, Liverpool Hope, Liverpool Inst for Perf Arts, Liverpool John Moores, Llandrillo Col, London Guildhall, London Institute, Loughborough, Lowestoft Col, Luton, Manchester Col of Arts And Tech, UMIST, Manchester Metropolitan, Mid-Cheshire Col, Middlesex, Napier, Nene, Newcastle, Newcastle Col, Newham Col, Newport Col, Norwich Schl of Art, Northbrook College, Nescot, NE Wales Inst, NE Worcestershire Col, North London, N Tyneside Col, Northumbria, N Warwickshire and Hinckley Col, Nottingham Trent, Oxford, Oxford Brookes, Oxfordshire Schl of Art, Plymouth, Plymouth Col of Art, Portsmouth, Ravensbourne Col of Design And Comm, Reading Col of Arts, Reading, Ripon & York St John, Robert Gordon, Roehampton Inst, Rose Bruford, Rycotewood Col, Salford, Salisbury Col, Scarborough, Sheffield Hallam, Sheffield Col, Shrewsbury Col of Arts & Tech, St Martin, Lancaster & Cumbr, Solihull Col, Southampton, Somerset Col of Art, Southampton Inst, South Devon Col, South Bank, Southport Col, Southwark Col, Stafford Col, St Helens Col, Col of St Mark & St John, Staffordshire, Stockport Col, Strathclyde, Uni Col Suffolk, Sunderland, Surrey Inst Of Art, Sutton Coldfield Col, Swansea Inst, Swindon Col, Tameside Col, Teesside, Thames Valley, Trinity Carmarthen, Ulster, UCL, Uni Col Warrington, Warwickshire Col, West Herts Col, Westhill Col, Weston Col, Westminster, West Thames Col, Wigan And Leigh Col, Wimbledon School Of Art, Wirral Met Col, Wolverhampton, Worcester, Worcester Col, Writtle Col, York Col, Yorkshire Coast Col.

Biochemistry/Biophysics/Biotechnology

Aberdeen, Aberystwyth, APU, Bangor, Barnsley Col, Bath, Birmingham, Bradford, Bristol, UWE, Brunel, Cambridge, Cardiff, Central Lancashire, Coventry, De Montfort, Dundee, Durham, UEA, East London, Edinburgh, Essex, Exeter, Glamorgan, Glasgow, Greenwich, Halton Col, Heriot-Watt, Hertfordshire, Huddersfield, Imperial, Keele, Kent at Canterbury, King's, Kingston, Lancaster, Leeds, Leicester, Liverpool, Liverpool John Moores, Luton, Manchester, UMIST, Manchester Metropolitan, Newcastle, Nescot, North London, Northumbria, Norwich City Col, Nottingham, Nottingham Trent, Oxford, Oxford Brookes, Paisley, Portsmouth, Queen Mary & Westfield, Queen's Belfast, Reading, Robert Gordon, Royal Holloway, Salford, Sheffield, Sheffield Hallam, Southampton, South Bank, St Andrews, Staffordshire, Stirling, Stockport Col , Strathclyde, Sunderland, Surrey, Sussex, Swansea, Teesside, Ulster, UCL, Warwick, Westminster, Wolverhampton, Wye, York.

Biology

Aberdeen, Abertay Dundee, Aberystwyth, APU, Aston, Bangor, Barnsley Col, Bath, Bath Spa, Bell Col, Birmingham,

Bolton Inst, Bradford, Bradford & Ilkley Col, Brighton, Bristol, UWE, Brunel, Cambridge, Canterbury Col, Cardiff, Cardiff Inst, Central Lancashire, Chester, Cornwall College, Coventry, De Montfort, Derby, Dundee, Durham, UEA, East London, Edge Hill, Edinburgh, Essex, Exeter, Glamorgan, Glasgow, Glasgow Caledonian, Greenwich, Halton Col, Heriot-Watt, Hertfordshire, Huddersfield, Hull, Imperial, Keele, Kent at Canterbury, King's, Kingston, Lancaster, Leeds, Leicester, Lincolnshire And Humberside, Liverpool, Liverpool Hope, Liverpool John Moores, Luton, Manchester, UMIST, Manchester Metropolitan, Middlesex, Napier, Nene, Newcastle, Newman Col, Nescot, NE Wales Inst, North London, Northumbria, Norwich City Col, Nottingham, Nottingham Trent, Oxford, Oxford Brookes, Paisley, Plymouth, Portsmouth, Queen Mary & Westfield, Queen's Belfast, Reading, Robert Gordon, Roehampton Inst, Royal Holloway, Scottish Agricultural Col, Salford, Scarborough, Sheffield, Sheffield Hallam, Southampton, South Bank, Sparsholt Hampshire, St Andrews, St Mary's, Staffordshire, Stirling, Stock-port Col, Strathclyde, Uni Col Suffolk, Sunderland, Sussex, Swansea, Trinity Carmarthen, Ulster, UCL, Warwick, Westminster, Wolverhampton, Worcester, Writtle Col, Wye, York.

Botany

Aberdeen, Aberystwyth, Askham Bryan, Bangor, Barnsley Col, Birmingham, Bristol, Cambridge, Dundee, Durham, UEA, East London, Edinburgh, Glasgow, Imperial, Leeds, Leicester, Liverpool, Luton, Manchester, Newcastle, Nottingham, Plymouth, Queen's Belfast, Reading, Royal Holloway, Sheffield, Southampton, St Andrews, Wolverhampton, Wye.

Building and Surveying

Abertay Dundee, APU, Bell Col, Blackburn Col, Blackpool Col, Bolton Inst, Bradford & Ilkley Col, Brighton, UWE, Brunel, Cardiff Inst, UCE, Central Lancashire, Colchester Inst, Coventry, Crawley Col, De Montfort, Derby, Doncaster Col, Dudley Col of Tech, Dundee, Edinburgh, Glamorgan, Glasgow Caledonian, Gloucestershire Col of Arts, Greenwich, Heriot-Watt, Hertfordshire, Huddersfield, Kingston, Leeds Metropolitan, Lincolnshire And Humberside, Liverpool, Liverpool John Moores, Loughborough, Luton, UMIST, Napier, Nene, Newport Col, Nescot, NE Wales Inst, Northumbria, Nottingham, Nottingham Trent, Oxford Brookes, Paisley, Plymouth, Portsmouth, Queen's Belfast, Reading Col of Arts, Reading, Robert Gordon, Salford, Sheffield Hallam, Sheffield Col, Somerset Col of Art, Southampton Inst, South Devon Col, South Bank, St Helens Col, Staffordshire, Stockport Col, Strathclyde, Uni Col Suffolk, Swansea Inst, Teesside, Ulster, UCL, Warwickshire Col, Westminster, Wigan And Leigh Col, Wirral Met Col, Wolverhampton.

Business and Management

Aberdeen, Abertay Dundee, Aberystwyth, APU, Askham Bryan, Aston, Bangor, Barnsley Col, Bath, Bath Spa, Bell Col, Birmingham, Birmingham Col Of Food Tourism, Blackburn Col, Blackpool Col, Bolton Inst, Bourne-mouth, Art Inst Bournemouth, Bradford, Bradford & Ilkley Col, Bretton Hall, Brighton, Bristol, UWE, Brunel, Buckingham, Buckinghamshire College, Buckland, Canterbury Col, Cardiff, Cardiff Inst, Carmarthenshire Col, UCE, Central Lancashire, Chelt & Glos College, Chester, Chichester Inst, City, Bristol Col, City Col Manchester, Colchester Inst, Cornwall College, Coventry, Cranfield, Crawley Col, Croydon Col, Cumbria Col of Art, Dartington Col of Arts, De Montfort, Derby, Dewsbury Col, Doncaster Col, Dudley Col of Tech, Dundee, Durham, UEA, East London, Edge Hill, Edinburgh, Essex, European Business Schl, Exeter Col, Exeter, Farnborough Col Of Tech, Galm-organ, Glasgow, Glasgow

Caledonian, Gloucestershire Col of Arts, Goldsmiths, Greenwich, Gyosei Int Col, Halton Col, Harper Adams, Herefordshire Col Of Tech, Heriot-Watt, Hertfordshire, Holborn Col, Huddersfield, Hull, Imperial, Keele, Kent at Canterbury, King Alfred's, King's, Kingston, Lampeter, Lancaster, Leeds, Leeds, Trinity And All Saints, Leeds Metropolitan, Leicester, Lincolnshire And Humberside, Liverpool, Liverpool Com Col, Liverpool Hope, Liverpool John Moores, Llandrillo Col, London Guildhall, London Institute, LSE, Loughborough, Luton, Manchester, UMIST, Manchester Metropolitan, Matthew Boulton Col, Mid-Cheshire Col, Middlesex, Napier, Nene, Newcastle, Newcastle Col, New College Durham, Newport Col, Northbrook College , Nescot, NE Wales Inst, NE Worcestershire Col, North London, N Tyneside Col, Northumbria, Norwich City Col, Nottingham, Nottingham Trent, Oxford, Oxford Brookes, Paisley, Plymouth, Portsmouth, Queen Margaret Col, Queen Mary & Westfield, Queen's Belfast, Reading Col of Arts, Reading, Regents Business School, Ripon & York St John, Robert Gordon, Roehampton Inst, Royal Agricultural Col, Royal Holloway, Scottish Agricultural Col, Salford, Sandwell Col, SOAS, Scarborough, Sheffield, Sheffield Hallam, Sheffield Col, Shrewsbury Col of Arts & Tech, St Martin, Lancaster & Cumbr, Solihull Col, Southampton, Somerset Col of Art, Southampton Inst, South Devon Col, South Bank, Southport Col, St Andrews, Southwark Col, St Helens Col, St Mary's, Staffordshire, Stirling, Stockport Col, Strathclyde, Uni Col Suffolk, Sunderland, Surrey, Sussex, Swansea, Swansea Inst, Swindon Col, Tameside Col, Teesside, Thames Valley, Ulster, UCL, Uni Col Warrington, Warwick, Warwickshire Col, West Herts Col, Westminster, Westminster Col, West Thames Col, Wigan And Leigh Col, Wirral Met Col, Wolverhampton, Worcester, Worcester Col, Writtle Col, Wye, York, York Col, Yorkshire Coast Col.

Chemistry

Aberdeen, Abertay Dundee, APU, Aston, Bangor, Barnsley Col, Bath, Bell Col, Birmingham, Bradford, Bradford & Ilkley Col, Brighton, Bristol, UWE, Cambridge, Cardiff, Central Lancashire, Coventry, De Montfort, Derby, Dundee, Durham, UEA, Edinburgh, Exeter, Glamorgan, Glasgow, Glasgow Caledonian, Greenwich, Halton Col, Heriot-Watt, Hertfordshire, Huddersfield, Hull, Imperial, Keele, Kent at Canterbury, King's, Kingston, Lancaster, Leeds, Leeds Metropolitan, Leicester, Liverpool, Liverpool John Moores, Loughborough, Manchester, UMIST, Manchester Metropolitan, Napier, Nene, Newcastle, North London, Northumbria, Nottingham, Nottingham Trent, Oxford, Oxford Brookes, Paisley, Plymouth, Queen Mary & Westfield, Queen's Belfast, Reading, Robert Gordon, Salford, Sheffield, Sheffield Hallam, Southampton, St Andrews, St Mary's, Staffordshire, Stirling, Stockport Col, Strathclyde, Sunderland, Surrey, Sussex, Swansea, Teesside, Ulster, UCL, Warwick, Wirral Met Col, Wolverhampton, York.

Cinematics - Film, TV, Photography

Aberdeen, Aberystwyth, APU, Bangor, Blackpool Col, Bolton Inst, Bournemouth, Art Inst Bournemouth, Bradford & Ilkley Col, Brighton, UWE, Brunel, Buckinghamshire College, Canterbury Col, Carmarthenshire Col, UCE, Central Lancashire, Chelt & Glos College, City Col Manchester, Cleveland Col of Art, Croydon Col, Cumbria Col of Art, De Montfort, Derby, UEA, Essex, Falmouth Col of Arts, Glamorgan, Glasgow, Greenwich, Heriot-Watt, Kent at Canterbury, Kent Inst of Art & Design, King Alfred's, Leeds Col of Art, Leicester South Fields Col, Lincolnshire And Humberside, Liverpool John Moores, London Guildhall,

London Institute , Manchester, Manchester Metropolitan, Mid-Cheshire Col, Middlesex, Napier, Newcastle, Newcastle Col, Newport Col, Northbrook College, Nescot, NE Wales Inst, North London, Northumbria, Northumberland Col, Nottingham Trent, Oxfordshire Schl of Art, Plymouth Col of Art, Reading Col of Arts, Reading, Roehampton Inst, Royal Holloway, Salisbury Col, Sandwell Col, Sheffield Hallam, Southampton, Southampton Inst, St Helens Col, Staffordshire, Stockport Col, Sunderland, Surrey Inst Of Art, Swansea Inst, Tameside Col, Thames Valley, Uni Col Warrington, Warwick, Warwickshire Col, West Herts Col, Westminster, Wolverhampton.

Computer Sciences and Engineering

Aberdeen, Abertay Dundee, Aberystwyth, APU, Aston, Bangor, Barnsley Col, Bath, Bell Col, Birmingham, Birmingham Col Of Food Tourism, Blackburn Col, Blackpool Col, Bolton Inst, Bournemouth, Bradford, Bradford & Ilkley Col, Brighton, Bristol, UWE, Brunel, Buckingham, Buckinghamshire College, Buckland, Cambridge, Canterbury Col, Cardiff, Cardiff Inst, Carmarthenshire Col, UCE, Central Lancashire, Chelt & Glos College, Chester, City, Bristol Col, City Col Manchester, Colchester Inst, Cornwall College, Coventry, Cranfield, Croydon Col, Cumbria Col of Art, De Montfort, Derby, Doncaster Col, Dudley Col of Tech, Dundee, Durham, UEA, East London, Edge Hill, Edinburgh, Essex, Exeter, Farnborough Col Of Tech, Glamorgan, Glasgow, Glasgow Caledonian, Goldsmiths, Greenwich, Halton Col, Herefordshire Col Of Tech, Heriot-Watt, Hertfordshire, Huddersfield, Hull, Imperial, Keele, Kent at Canterbury, King's, Kingston, Lampeter, Lancaster, Leeds, Leeds, Trinity And All Saints, Leeds Metropolitan, Leeds Col of Art, Leicester, Lincolnshire And Humberside, Liverpool, Liverpool Com Col, Liverpool Hope, Liverpool John Moores, Llandrillo Col, London Guildhall, Loughborough, Luton, Manchester, UMIST, Manchester Metropolitan, Mid-Cheshire Col, Middlesex, Napier, Nene, Newcastle, Newcastle Col, Newport Col, Northbrook College, Nescot, NE Wales Inst, NE Worcestershire Col, North London, N Tyneside Col, Northumbria, Norwich City Col, Nottingham, Nottingham Trent, Oxford, Oxford Brookes, Oxfordshire Schl of Art , Paisley, Plymouth, Portsmouth, Queen Mary & Westfield, Queen's Belfast, Ravensbourne Col of Design And Comm, Reading Col of Arts, Reading, Robert Gordon, Roehampton Inst, Royal Holloway, Salford, Sandwell Col, Sheffield, Sheffield Hallam, Sheffield Col, Shrewsbury Col of Arts & Tech, St Martin, Lancaster & Cumbr, Solihull Col, Southampton, Somerset Col of Art, Southampton Inst, South Devon Col, South Bank, Southport Col, St Andrews, St Helens Col, Col of St Mark & St John, Staffordshire, Stirling, Stockport Col, Strathclyde, Uni Col Suffolk, Sunderland, Surrey, Sussex, Swansea, Swansea Inst, Swindon Col, Tameside Col, Teesside, Thames Valley, Trinity Carmarthen, Ulster, UCL, Uni Col Warrington, Warwick, Warwickshire Col, West Herts Col, Westminster, Westminster Col, West Thames Col, Wigan And Leigh Col, Wirral Met Col, Wolverhampton, Worcester, Worcester Col, Writtle Col, York, Yorkshire Coast Col.

Dentistry

Birmingham, Bristol, Dundee, Glasgow, King's, Leeds, Liverpool, Manchester, Newcastle, Queen Mary & Westfield, Queen's Belfast, Sheffield, Col of Medicine Wales.

Drama, Dance and Performance Arts

Aberystwyth, APU, Bangor, Barnsley Col, Bath Spa, Birmingham, Bishop Grosseteste, Blackpool Col, Bolton

Inst, Bretton Hall, Brighton, Bristol, UWE, Brunel, Buckinghamshire College, Cambridge, Carmarthenshire Col, UCE, Central Lancashire, Ctrl Schl Speech & Drama, Chelt & Glos College, Chester, Chichester Inst, City Col Manchester, Clarendon College Notts, Cleveland Col of Art, Coventry, Croydon Col, Cumbria Col of Art, Dartington Col of Arts, De Montfort, Derby, Doncaster Col, Dudley Col of Tech, UEA, East London, Edge Hill, Exeter, Glamorgan, Glasgow, Gloucestershire Col of Arts, Goldsmiths, Greenwich, Heriot-Watt, Hertfordshire, Huddersfield, Hull, Kent at Canterbury, Kidderminster Col, King Alfred's, Lancaster, Leeds, Leicester South Fields Col, Lincolnshire And Humberside, Liverpool Com Col, Liverpool Hope, Liverpool Inst for Perf Arts, Liverpool John Moores, Llandrillo Col, London Institute, Loughborough, Luton, Manchester, Manchester Metropolitan, Middlesex, Nene, Newcastle Col, Newman Col, Northbrook College, Nescot, NE Worcestershire Col, North London, N Tyneside Col, Northumbria, Nottingham Trent, Plymouth, Queen Margaret Col, Queen Mary & Westfield, Queen's Belfast, Reading, Ripon & York St John, Roehampton Inst, Rose Bruford, Royal Holloway, Salford, Salisbury Col, Scarborough, Shrewsbury Col of Arts & Tech, St Martin, Lancaster & Cumbr, Somerset Col of Art, Southampton Inst, South Devon Col, South Bank, Southwark Col, St Helens Col, St Mary's, Staffordshire , Uni Col Suffolk, Surrey, Sussex, Swansea Inst, Tameside Col, Thames Valley, Trinity Carmarthen, Ulster, Uni Col Warrington, Warwick, Warwickshire Col, Welsh Col of Mus & Drama, Westhill Col, Wigan And Leigh Col, Wimbledon School Of Art, Wolverhampton, Worcester, Worcester Col.

Economics

Aberdeen, Abertay Dundee, Aberystwyth, APU, Aston, Bangor, Bath, Birmingham, Bolton Inst, Bournemouth, Bradford, Bristol, UWE, Brunel, Buckingham, Buckinghamshire College, Buckland, Cambridge, Cardiff, UCE, Central Lancashire, City, Coventry, De Montfort, Derby, Dundee, Durham, UEA, East London, Edinburgh, Essex, Exeter, Glamorgan, Glasgow, Glasgow Caledonian, Goldsmiths, Greenwich, Heriot-Watt, Hertfordshire, Huddersfield, Hull, Keele, Kent at Canterbury, Kingston, Lancaster, Leeds, Leeds Metropolitan, Leicester, Lincolnshire And Humberside, Liverpool, Liverpool John Moores, London Guildhall, LSE, Loughborough, Luton, Manchester, Manchester Metropolitan, Middlesex, Napier, Nene, Newcastle, North London, Northumbria, Nottingham, Nottingham Trent, Oxford, Oxford Brookes, Paisley, Plymouth, Portsmouth, Queen Mary & Westfield, Queen's Belfast, Reading, Royal Holloway, Salford, SOAS, SSEES, Sheffield, Southampton, Southampton Inst, South Bank, St Andrews, Staffordshire, Stirling, Strathclyde, Uni Col Suffolk, Sunderland, Surrey, Sussex, Swansea, Teesside, Thames Valley, Ulster, UCL, Warwick, Westminster, Wolverhampton, York.

Education Studies

Aberdeen, Abertay Dundee, Aberystwyth, Bangor, Barnsley Col, Bath, Bath Spa, Bell Col, Birmingham Col Of Food Tourism, Blackpool Col, Bradford & Ilkley Col, Bretton Hall, Bristol, UWE, Buckingham, Cambridge, Canterbury Col, Cardiff, Cardiff Inst, Central Lancashire, Ctrl Schl Speech & Drama, Chelt & Glos College, Chester, Chichester Inst, Bristol Col, De Montfort, Derby, Durham, East London, Edge Hill, Edinburgh, Essex, Exeter, Glamorgan, Greenwich, Herefordshire Col Of Tech, Heriot-Watt, Hertfordshire, Huddersfield, Keele, Kidderminster Col, King Alfred's, King's, Kingston, Lancaster, Leeds, Leeds Metropolitan, Liverpool, Liverpool Com Col, Liverpool John Moores, Llandrillo Col, Loughborough, Manchester, Manchester Metropolitan, Middlesex, Nene, Newcastle, Newman Col, Northbrook

College, NE Wales Inst, NE Worcestershire Col, Northern Col, North London, N Tyneside Col, Northumbria, Norwich City Col, Nottingham Trent, Oxford Westminster Col, Oxford Brookes, Plymouth, Ripon & York St John, Roehampton Inst, Scarborough, Sheffield Hallam, Sheffield Col, Shrewsbury Col of Arts & Tech, St Martin, Lancaster & Cumbr, Southampton, Somerset Col of Art, St Helens Col, Col of St Mark & St John, St Mary's, Stirling, Stockport Col, Strathclyde, Uni Col Suffolk, Sunderland, Swansea, Tameside Col, Trinity Carmarthen, Uni Col Warrington, Warwick, Warwickshire Col, West Herts Col, Westhill Col, Wolverhampton, Worcester, York, Yorkshire Coast Col.

Engineering - Aeronautical

Bath, Brighton, Bristol, UWE, Brunel, City, Cornwall College, Coventry, Cranfield, Crawley Col, Farnborough Col Of Tech, Glasgow, Hertfordshire, Imperial, Kingston, Lincolnshire And Humberside, Liverpool, Loughborough, Manchester, UMIST, Northbrook College, NE Wales Inst, Queen Mary & Westfield, Queen's Belfast, Salford, Sheffield, Southampton, Staffordshire, Stockport Col, Strathclyde.

Engineering - Chemical

Aston, Bath, Birmingham, Bradford, Brighton, Cambridge, Central Lancashire, Dudley Col of Tech, Edinburgh, Glamorgan, Halton Col, Heriot-Watt, Huddersfield, Imperial, Leeds, Loughborough, UMIST, Newcastle, Northumbria, Nottingham, Oxford, Paisley, Queen's Belfast, Sheffield, South Bank, Strathclyde, Surrey, Swansea, Teesside, UCL.

Engineering - Civil

Aberdeen, Abertay Dundee, APU, Aston, Bath, Bell Col, Birmingham, Bolton Inst, Bradford, Brighton, Bristol, UWE, Buckinghamshire College, Cardiff, City, Coventry, Cranfield, Derby, Doncaster Col, Dundee, Durham, East London, Edinburgh, Exeter, Glamorgan, Glasgow, Glasgow Caledonian, Gloucestershire Col of Arts, Greenwich, Heriot-Watt, Hertfordshire, Imperial, Kingston, Leeds, Leeds Metropolitan, Liverpool, Liverpool John Moores, Loughborough, Manchester, UMIST, Napier, Newcastle, Newport Col, Nescot, Northumbria, Nottingham, Nottingham Trent, Oxford, Oxford Brookes, Paisley, Plymouth, Portsmouth, Queen's Belfast, Salford, Sheffield, Sheffield Hallam, Southampton, Southampton Inst, South Bank, St Helens Col, Stockport Col, Strathclyde, Sunderland, Surrey, Swansea, Swansea Inst, Teesside, Ulster, UCL, Warwick, Westminster, Wigan And Leigh Col, Wolverhampton, Writtle Col.

Engineering - Electrical and Electronic

Aberdeen, Abertay Dundee, APU, Aston, Bangor, Barnsley Col, Bath, Bell Col, Birmingham, Blackburn Col, Blackpool Col, Bolton Inst, Bournemouth, Bradford, Brighton, Bristol, UWE, Brunel, Cardiff, Cardiff Inst, Carmarthenshire Col, UCE, Central Lancashire, City, Coventry, Cranfield, De Montfort, Derby, Doncaster Col, Dudley Col of Tech, Dundee, Durham, UEA, East London, Edinburgh, Essex, Exeter, Farnborough Col Of Tech, Glamorgan, Glasgow, Glasgow Caledonian, Greenwich, Halton Col, Herefordshire Col Of Tech, Heriot-Watt, Hertfordshire, Huddersfield, Hull, Imperial, Kent at Canterbury, King's, Kingston, Lancaster, Leeds, Leeds Metropolitan, Leicester, Lincolnshire And Humberside, Liverpool, Liverpool Com Col, Liverpool Inst for Perf Arts, Liverpool John Moores, Llandrillo Col, London Guildhall, Loughborough, Luton, Manchester, UMIST, Manchester Metropolitan, Middlesex, Napier, Newcastle, New College Durham, Newport Col, Northbrook College, Nescot, NE Wales Inst, North London, N Tyneside Col,

Northumbria, Norwich City Col, Nottingham, Nottingham Trent, Oxford, Oxford Brookes, Paisley, Plymouth, Portsmouth, Queen Mary & Westfield, Queen's Belfast, Ravensbourne Col of Design And Comm, Reading Col of Arts, Reading, Robert Gordon, Royal Holloway, Salford, Sandwell Col, Sheffield, Sheffield Hallam, Shrewsbury Col of Arts & Tech, Southampton, Southampton Inst, South Devon Col, South Bank, St Andrews, St Helens Col, Staffordshire, Stockport Col, Strathclyde, Uni Col Suffolk, Sunderland, Surrey, Sussex, Swansea, Swansea Inst, Teesside, Thames Valley, Ulster, UCL, Warwick, Warwickshire Col, Westminster, Wigan And Leigh Col, Wolverhampton, York, Yorkshire Coast Col.

Engineering – General

Aberdeen, Abertay Dundee, APU, Aston, Bangor, Barnsley Col, Birmingham, Blackburn Col, Blackpool Col, Bolton Inst, Bournemouth, Bradford, Bradford & Ilkley Col, Brighton, Bristol, UWE, Brunel, Buckinghamshire College, Cambridge, Cardiff, Cardiff Inst, UCE, Central Lancashire, City, Cornwall College, Coventry, Cranfield, De Montfort, Derby, Doncaster Col, Dundee, Durham, East London, Edinburgh, Exeter, Glamorgan, Glasgow, Glasgow Caledonian, Greenwich, Halton Col, Heriot-Watt, Hertfordshire, Huddersfield, Hull, Imperial, Kingston, Lancaster, Leeds, Leeds Metropolitan, Leicester, Lincolnshire And Humberside, Liverpool, Liverpool John Moores, Llandrillo Col, Loughborough, Luton, UMIST, Manchester Metropolitan, Mid-Cheshire Col, Middlesex, Napier, Nene, Newport Col, Northumbria, Norwich City Col, Nottingham, Nottingham Trent, Oxford, Oxford Brookes, Paisley, Plymouth, Portsmouth, Queen Mary & Westfield, Reading Col of Arts, Reading, Robert Gordon, Royal Agricultural Col, Salford, Sandwell Col, Sheffield Hallam, Solihull Col, Southampton, Somerset Col of Art, Southampton Inst, South Bank, Southport Col, St Helens Col, Staffordshire, Strathclyde, Sunderland, Surrey, Swansea, Swansea Inst, Teesside, Ulster, UCL, Uni Col Warrington, Warwick, Westminster, Wolverhampton, Worcester Col.

Engineering - Mechanical and Production

Aberdeen, Abertay Dundee, APU, Aston, Bangor, Barking Col, Barnsley Col, Bath, Bell Col, Birmingham, Blackburn Col, Blackpool Col, Bolton Inst, Bournemouth, Bradford, Brighton, Bristol, UWE, Brunel, Buckinghamshire College, Cardiff, Cardiff Inst, Carmarthenshire Col, UCE, Central Lancashire, City, Coventry, Cranfield, De Montfort, Derby, Doncaster Col, Dudley Col of Tech, Dundee, Durham, East London, Edinburgh, Exeter, Farnborough Col Of Tech, Glamorgan, Glasgow, Glasgow Caledonian, Gloucestershire Col of Arts, Greenwich, Halton Col, Harper Adams, Herefordshire Col Of Tech, Heriot-Watt, Hertfordshire, Huddersfield, Hull, Imperial, King's, Kingston, Lancaster, Leeds, Leeds Metropolitan, Leicester, Lincolnshire And Humberside, Liverpool, Liverpool Com Col, Liverpool John Moores, Llandrillo Col, Loughborough, Luton, Manchester, UMIST, Manchester Metropolitan, Middlesex, Napier, Nene, Newcastle, Newcastle Col, Newport Col, Northbrook College, NE Wales Inst, Northumbria, Nottingham, Nottingham Trent, Oxford, Oxford Brookes, Paisley, Plymouth, Portsmouth, Queen Mary & Westfield, Queen's Belfast, Reading Col of Arts, Reading, Robert Gordon, Rycotewood Col, Salford, Sheffield, Sheffield Hallam, Shrewsbury Col of Arts & Tech, Southampton, Somerset Col of Art, Southampton Inst, South Bank, St Helens Col, Staffordshire, Stockport Col , Strathclyde, Uni Col Suffolk, Sunderland, Surrey, Sussex, Swansea, Swansea Inst,

Teesside, Ulster, UCL, Warwick, Warwickshire Col, Westminster, Wigan And Leigh Col, Wolverhampton, Writtle Col, Yorkshire Coast Col.

English

Aberdeen, Aberystwyth, APU, Bangor, Bath Spa, Birmingham, Bishop Grosseteste, Blackburn Col, Bolton Inst, Bretton Hall, Bristol, UWE, Brunel, Buckingham, Buckinghamshire College, Cambridge, Canterbury Col, Cardiff, UCE, Central Lancashire, Chelt & Glos College, Chester, Chichester Inst, Colchester Inst, Coventry, Cumbria Col of Art, De Montfort, Doncaster Col, Dundee, Durham, UEA, East London, Edge Hill, Edinburgh, Essex, Exeter, Falmouth Col of Arts, Glamorgan, Glasgow, Goldsmiths, Greenwich, Hertfordshire, Huddersfield, Hull, Keele, Kent at Canterbury, King Alfred's, King's, Kingston, Lampeter, Lancaster, Leeds, Leeds, Trinity And All Saints, Leicester, Lincolnshire And Humberside, Liverpool, Liverpool Hope, Liverpool John Moores, London Guildhall, Loughborough, Luton, Manchester, Manchester Metropolitan, Middlesex, Nene, Newcastle, Newman Col, Newport Col, NE Wales Inst, North London, Northumbria, Norwich City Col, Nottingham, Nottingham Trent, Oxford, Oxford Brookes, Plymouth, Portsmouth, Queen Mary & Westfield, Queen's Belfast, Reading, Ripon & York St John , Roehampton Inst, Royal Holloway, Salford, SOAS, Scarborough, Sheffield, Sheffield Hallam, St Martin, Lancaster & Cumbr, Solihull Col, Southampton, South Bank, St Andrews, Col of St Mark & St John, St Mary's, Staffordshire, Stirling, Strathclyde, Sunderland, Surrey, Sussex, Swansea, Swansea Inst, Teesside, Trinity Carmarthen, Ulster, UCL, Warwick, Westhill Col, Westminster, Wolverhampton, Worcester, York.

Environmental Studies, Technology and Oceanography

Aberdeen, Abertay Dundee, Aberystwyth, APU, Askham Bryan, Aston, Bangor, Barnsley Col, Bath Spa, Bell Col, Birmingham, Blackpool Col, Bolton Inst, Bournemouth, Bradford, Brighton, UWE, Brunel, Buckinghamshire College, Cambridge, Canterbury Col, Cardiff Inst, UCE, Central Lancashire, Chelt & Glos College, Chester, Chichester Inst, Colchester Inst, Cornwall College, Coventry, Cranfield, De Montfort, Derby, Dundee, Durham, UEA, East London, Edge Hill, Edinburgh, Exeter, Farnborough Col Of Tech, Glamorgan, Glasgow Caledonian, Greenwich, Halton Col, Harper Adams, Heriot-Watt, Hertfordshire, Huddersfield, Hull, Imperial, Keele, Kent at Canterbury, King's, Kingston, Lampeter, Lancaster, Leeds, Leeds Metropolitan, Lincolnshire And Humberside, Liverpool, Liverpool Hope, Liverpool John Moores, LSE, Loughborough, Luton, Manchester, UMIST, Manchester Metropolitan, Middlesex, Napier, Nene, Newcastle, Newport Col, NE Wales Inst, North London, Northumbria, Norwich City Col, Nottingham, Nottingham Trent, Oxford Brookes, Paisley, Plymouth, Portsmouth, Queen Mary & Westfield, Reading, Ripon & York St John, Robert Gordon, Roehampton Inst, Royal Holloway, Scottish Agricultural Col, Salford, Scarborough, Sheffield, Sheffield Hallam, Sheffield Col, Southampton, Southampton Inst, South Bank, St Helens Col, Staffordshire, Stirling, Strathclyde, Uni Col Suffolk, Sunderland, Sussex, Swansea Inst, Teesside, Trinity Carmarthen, Ulster, Westminster, Wigan And Leigh Col, Wolverhampton, Worcester, Writtle Col, Wye, York.

European Studies and Languages

Aberdeen, Abertay Dundee, Aberystwyth, APU, Aston, Bangor, Bath, Bath Spa, Bell Col, Birmingham, Birmingham Col Of Food Tourism, Blackpool Col, Bolton Inst, Bournemouth, Bradford, UWE, Buckingham,

Buckhinghamshire College, Cambridge, Cardiff, Cardiff Inst, UCE, Central Lancashire, Chelt & Glos College, Coventry, De Montfort, Derby, Dundee, Durham, UEA, East London, Edge Hill, Edinburgh, Essex, European Business Schl, Exeter, Glamorgan, Glasgow, Glasgow Caledonian, Goldsmiths, Greenwich, Gyosei Int Col, Heriot-Watt, Hertfordshire, Huddersfield, Hull, Keele, Kent at Canterbury, King's, Kingston, Lampeter, Lancaster, Leeds, Leeds Metropolitan, Leicester, Lincolnshire And Humberside, Liverpool, Liverpool Hope, Liverpool John Moores, London Guildhall, Loughborough, Luton, Manchester, UMIST, Manchester Metropolitan, Mid-Cheshire Col, Middlesex, Napier, Nene, Newcastle, Newport Col, Northbrook College, North London, Northumbria, Nottingham, Nottingham Trent, Oxford, Oxford Brookes, Paisley, Plymouth, Portsmouth, Queen Mary & Westfield, Queen's Belfast, Reading, Ripon & York St John, Robert Gordon, Roehampton Inst, Royal Agricultural Col, Royal Holloway, Salford, SOAS, Sheffield, Sheffield Hallam, St Martin, Lancaster & Cumbr, Southampton, South Bank, St Andrews, Staffordshire, Stirling, Strathclyde, Uni Col Suffolk, Sunderland, Surrey, Sussex, Swansea, Swansea Inst, Teesside, Thames Valley, Ulster, UCL, Westminster, Wolverhampton, Worcester, York.

Food Science/Technology and Nutrition

APU, Askham Bryan, Bath Spa, Birmingham Col Of Food Tourism, Blackpool Col, Bournemouth, Cardiff Inst, Central Lancashire, Chester, Coventry, Cranfield, De Montfort, Dundee, Glamorgan, Glasgow, Glasgow Caledonian, Greenwich, Harper Adams, Huddersfield, Hull, King's, Kingston, Leeds, Leeds, Trinity And All Saints, Leeds Metropolitan, Lincolnshire And Humberside, Liverpool John Moores, Llandrillo Col, Luton, Manchester Metropolitan, Newcastle, North London, Northumbria, Nottingham, Nottingham Trent, Oxford Brookes, Plymouth, Queen Margaret Col, Queen's Belfast, Reading, Robert Gordon, Roehampton Inst, Scottish Agricultural Col, Salford, Sheffield Hallam, Southampton, South Bank, Staffordshire, Uni Col Suffolk, Surrey, Teesside, Ulster, Westminster, Wolverhampton, Wye.

Geography

Aberdeen, Aberystwyth, APU, Aston, Barnsley Col, Bath Spa, Birmingham, Bournemouth, Bradford, Brighton, Bristol, UWE, Brunel, Cambridge, Canterbury Col, Cardiff, UCE, Central Lancashire, Chelt & Glos College, Chester, Chichester Inst, Coventry, Cranfield, De Montfort, Derby, Dundee, Durham, East London, Edge Hill, Edinburgh, Exeter, Glamorgan, Glasgow, Greenwich, Hertfordshire, Huddersfield, Hull, Keele, King's, Kingston, Lampeter, Lancaster, Leeds, Leeds, Trinity And All Saints, Leeds Metropolitan, Leicester, Liverpool, Liverpool Hope, Liverpool John Moores, London Guildhall, LSE, Loughborough, Luton, Manchester, UMIST, Manchester Metropolitan, Middlesex, Nene, Newcastle, Newman Col, Newport Col, NE Wales Inst, North London, Northumbria, Nottingham, Nottingham Trent, Oxford, Oxford Brookes, Plymouth, Portsmouth, Queen Mary & Westfield, Queen's Belfast, Reading, Ripon & York St John, Roehampton Inst, Royal Holloway, Salford, SOAS, Scarborough, Sheffield, Sheffield Hallam, St Martin, Lancaster & Cumbr, Southampton, Southampton Inst, South Bank, St Andrews, Col of St Mark & St John, St Mary's, Staffordshire, Stirling, Strathclyde, Sunderland, Sussex, Swansea, Trinity Carmarthen, Ulster, UCL, Westminster, Wolverhampton, Worcester.

Geological Sciences

Aberdeen, Aberystwyth, Bangor, Bath Spa, Birmingham, Bournemouth, Brighton, Bristol, Cambridge, Cardiff, Chelt &

Glos College, Derby, Durham, UEA, Edge Hill, Edinburgh, Exeter, Glamorgan, Glasgow, Greenwich, Hertfordshire, Huddersfield, Imperial, Keele, Kingston, Lancaster, Leeds, Leicester, Liverpool, Liverpool John Moores, Luton, Manchester, Nene, Oxford, Oxford Brookes, Paisley, Plymouth, Portsmouth, Reading, Royal Holloway, Southampton, St Andrews, Staffordshire, Sunderland, UCL, Wolverhampton.

Health Care and Therapies

Aberdeen, Abertay Dundee, APU, Aston, Bangor, Barnsley Col, Birmingham, Birmingham Col Of Food Tourism, Blackpool Col, Bolton Inst, Bournemouth, Bradford, Bradford & Ilkley Col, Brighton, UWE, British Col of Naturopathy And Osteopathy, Brunel, Canterbury Col, Cardiff, Cardiff Inst, UCE, Central Lancashire, Chester, Chichester Inst, City, City Col Manchester, Coventry, Cranfield, De Montfort, Derby, Dudley Col of Tech, Durham, UEA, East London, Euro Schl Of Osteopathy, Glamorgan, Glasgow, Glasgow Caledonian, Greenwich, Heriot-Watt, Hertfordshire, Huddersfield, Hull, Imperial, Keele, King's, Kingston, Lancaster, Leeds, Leeds Metropolitan, Lincolnshire And Humberside, Liverpool, Liverpool Hope, Liverpool John Moores, Llandrillo Col, London Institute, Luton, Manchester, UMIST, Manchester Metropolitan, Matthew Boulton Col, Middlesex, Napier, Nene, Newcastle, New College Durham, Nescot, North London, Northumbria, Norwich City Col, Nottingham, Nottingham Trent, Oxford Brookes, Paisley, Plymouth, Portsmouth, Queen Margaret Col, Queen Mary & Westfield, Queen's Belfast, Reading, Ripon & York St John , Robert Gordon, Roehampton Inst, Salford, Sheffield, Sheffield Hallam, St Martin, Lancaster & Cumbr, Uni Col Suffolk, Southampton, Somerset Col of Art, South Bank, Southport Col, St George's Hosp Med Schl, St Loye's Schl Of Occup Ther, Col of St Mark & St John, St Mary's, Staffordshire, Stockport Col , Strathclyde, Uni Col Suffolk, Sunderland, Teesside, Trinity Carmarthen, Ulster, UCL, Col of Medicine, Wales, Warwickshire Col, Westminster, Wolverhampton, Worcester, York.

History

Aberdeen, Aberystwyth, APU, Bangor, Barnsley Col, Bath Spa, Birmingham, Bishop Grosseteste, Bolton Inst, Bradford, Brighton, Bristol, UWE, Brunel, Buckingham, Cambridge, Canterbury Col, Cardiff, Central Lancashire, Chelt & Glos College, Chester, Chichester Inst, Colchester Inst, Coventry, Cumbria Col of Art, De Montfort, Derby, Dundee, Durham, UEA, East London, Edge Hill, Edinburgh, Essex, Exeter, Glamorgan, Glasgow, Goldsmiths, Greenwich, Hertfordshire, Huddersfield, Hull, Keele, Kent at Canterbury, King Alfred's, King's, Kingston, Lampeter, Lancaster, Leeds, Leeds, Trinity And All Saints, Leeds Metropolitan, Leicester, Leo Baeck Col, Lincolnshire And Humberside, Liverpool, Liverpool Hope, Liverpool John Moores, London Guildhall, LSE, Luton, Manchester, Manchester Metropolitan, Middlesex, Nene, Newcastle, Newman Col, Newport Col, NE Wales Inst, North London, Northumbria, Norwich City Col, Nottingham, Nottingham Trent, Oxford, Oxford Brookes, Plymouth, Portsmouth, Queen Mary & Westfield, Queen's Belfast, Reading, Ripon & York St John, Roehampton Inst, Royal Holloway, Salford, SOAS, Scarborough, SSEES, Sheffield, Sheffield Hallam, St Martin, Lancaster & Cumbr, Southampton, Southampton Inst, South Bank, St Andrews, Col of St Mark & St John, St Mary's, Staffordshire, Stirling, Strathclyde, Uni Col Suffolk, Sunderland, Sussex, Swansea, Teesside, Thames Valley, Trinity Carmarthen, Ulster, UCL, Warwick, Westhill Col, Westminster, Wolverhampton, Worcester, Writtle Col, York.

History of Art

Aberdeen, Aberystwyth, APU, Birm-ingham, Bolton Inst,

Brighton, Bristol, Buckingham, Buckinghamshire College, Cambridge, UCE, Chester, Courtauld Inst of Art, Cumbria Col of Art, De Montfort, Derby, UEA, East London, Edinburgh, Essex, Falmouth Col of Arts, Glamorgan, Glasgow, Goldsmiths, Kent at Canterbury, Kingston, Lancaster, Leeds, Leicester, Liverpool, Liverpool John Moores, London Institute, Loughborough, Manchester, Manchester Metropolitan, Middlesex, Nene, Newcastle, Norwich Schl of Art, Northumbria, Nottingham, Oxford Brookes, Oxfordshire Schl of Art, Plymouth, Reading, SOAS, Scarborough, Sheffield Hallam, Southampton, St Andrews, Staffordshire, Sunderland, Sussex, Swansea Inst, Thames Valley, Trinity Carmarthen, UCL, Warwick, York.

Hotel, Institutional and Recreation Management

APU, Bangor, Barnsley Col, Bath, Bath Spa, Bell Col, Birmingham Col Of Food Tourism, Blackburn Col, Blackpool Col, Bolton Inst, Bournemouth, Bradford & Ilkley Col, Brighton, UWE, Brunel, Buckingham, Buckinghamshire College, Canterbury Col, Cardiff Inst, Central Lancashire, Chelt & Glos College, Chester, Chichester Inst, Bristol Col, City Col Manchester, Colchester Inst, Cornwall College, Coventry, Crawley Col, Croydon Col, De Montfort, Derby, Doncaster Col, Dundee, Edge Hill, Edinburgh, Farnborough Col Of Tech, Glamorgan, Glasgow Caledonian, Gloucestershire Col of Arts, Greenwich, Herefordshire Col Of Tech, Huddersfield, King Alfred's, Leeds Metropolitan, Leicester South Fields Col, Lincolnshire And Humberside, Liverpool Com Col, Liverpool John Moores, Llandrillo Col, London Institute, Loughborough, Luton, Manchester, Manchester Metropolitan, Mid-Cheshire Col, Middlesex, Napier, Nene, Newcastle Col, Nescot, NE Worcestershire Col, North London, Northumbria, Norwich City Col, Nottingham Trent, Oxford Brookes, Plymouth, Portsmouth, Queen Margaret Col, Reading Col of Arts, Ripon & York St John, Robert Gordon, Roehampton Inst, Scottish Agricultural Col, Salford, Scarborough, Sheffield Hallam, Shrewsbury Col of Arts & Tech, St Martin, Lancaster & Cumbr, Solihull Col, Southampton, Somerset Col of Art, Southampton Inst, South Devon Col, South Bank, Southwark Col, St Helens Col, Col of St Mark & St John, Staffordshire, Strathclyde, Uni Col Suffolk, Sunderland, Surrey, Swansea Inst, Teesside, Thames Valley, Ulster, Uni Col Warrington, Warwickshire Col, West Herts Col, Westminster, Westminster Col, West Thames Col, Wigan And Leigh Col, Wirral Met Col, Wolverhampton, Worcester, Worcester Col, Writtle Col, York Col, Yorkshire Coast Col.

Languages - African, Asian and Oriental

Birmingham, Bradford & Ilkley Col, Cardiff, Central Lancashire, De Montfort, Durham, Edinburgh, European Business Schl, Hertfordshire, Hull, Leeds, Liverpool John Moores, London Guildhall, Middlesex, Newcastle, North London, Nottingham, Oxford, Oxford Brookes, Reading, Royal Holloway, Salford, SOAS, Sheffield, Stirling, Sunderland, Sussex, Ulster, Westminster, Wolverhampton, York.

Languages – Celtic

Aberdeen, Aberystwyth, Bangor, Bath Spa, Bolton Inst, Cambridge, Cardiff, Edinburgh, Glamorgan, Glasgow, Lampeter, Liverpool, Luton, NE Wales Inst, North London, Queen's Belfast, St Mary's, Swansea, Trinity Carmarthen, Ulster, Westminster.

Languages - Classical and Ancient

Birmingham, Bolton Inst, Bristol, UWE, Cambridge, Durham, Edinburgh, Exeter, Glasgow, Keele, Kent at Canterbury,

King's, Lampeter, Leeds, Leo Baeck Col, Liverpool, Manchester, Newcastle, Nottingham, Oxford, Queen's Belfast, Reading, Royal Holloway, SOAS, St Andrews, St Mary's, Swansea, UCL, Warwick.

Languages - East European

Glasgow, King's, Nottingham, SSEES, Sheffield.

Languages - French

Aberdeen, Aberystwyth, APU, Aston, Bangor, Bath, Birmingham, Bolton Inst, Bradford, Brighton, Bristol, UWE, Brit Inst in Paris, Brunel, Buckingham, Buckinghamshire College, Canterbury Col, Cardiff, Cardiff Inst, UCE, Central Lancashire, Chelt & Glos College, Chester, Coventry, De Montfort, Derby, Dundee, Durham, UEA, East London, Edge Hill, Edinburgh, European Business Schl, Exeter, Glamorgan, Glasgow, Goldsmiths, Greenwich, Heriot-Watt, Hertfordshire, Huddersfield, Hull, Keele, Kent at Canterbury, King's, Kingston, Lampeter, Lancaster, Leeds, Leeds Trinity And All Saints, Leeds Metropolitan, Leicester, Liverpool, Liverpool Hope, Liverpool John Moores, London Guildhall, Loughborough, Luton, Manchester, UMIST, Manchester Metropolitan, Middlesex, Nene, Newcastle, North London, Northumbria, Nottingham, Nottingham Trent, Oxford Brookes, Plymouth, Portsmouth, Queen Mary & Westfield, Queen's Belfast, Reading, Ripon & York St John, Robert Gordon, Roehampton Inst, Royal Holloway, Salford, SSEES, Sheffield, Sheffield Hallam, Southampton, Southampton Inst, South Bank, St Andrews, Staffordshire, Stirling, Strathclyde, Sunderland, Surrey, Sussex, Swansea, Thames Valley, Ulster, UCL, Warwick, Westminster, Wolverhampton, York.

Languages - German

Aberdeen, Aberystwyth, APU, Aston, Bangor, Bath, Birmingham, Bolton Inst, Bradford, Bristol, UWE, Brunel, Buckinghamshire College, Cardiff, Cardiff Inst, UCE, Central Lancashire, Chester, Coventry, De Montfort, Derby, Dundee, Durham, UEA, East London, Edin-burgh, European Business Schl, Exeter, Glamorgan, Glasgow, Goldsmiths, Greenwich, Heriot-Watt, Hertfordshire, Huddersfield, Hull, Keele, Kent at Canterbury, King's, Kingston, Lampeter, Lancaster, Leeds, Leeds Metropolitan, Leicester, Liverpool, Liverpool John Moores, London Guildhall, Loughborough, Luton, Manchester, UMIST, Manchester Metropolitan, Middlesex, Nene, Newcastle, North London, Northumbria, Nottingham, Nottingham Trent, Oxford Brookes, Plymouth, Portsmouth, Queen Mary & Westfield, Queen's Belfast, Reading, Robert Gordon, Royal Holloway, Salford, SSEES, Sheffield, Sheffield Hallam, Southampton, Southampton Inst, South Bank, St Andrews, Staffordshire, Stirling, Strathclyde, Sunderland, Surrey, Sussex, Swansea, Thames Valley, Ulster, UCL, Warwick, Westminster, Wolverhampton, York.

Languages - Italian

Aberystwyth, APU, Aston, Bangor, Bath, Birmingham, Bradford, Bristol, Buckinghamshire College, Cardiff, Central Lancashire, Coventry, Durham, East London, Edinburgh, European Business Schl, Exeter, Glasgow, Greenwich, Hull, Kent at Canterbury, Lancaster, Leeds, Leicester, Liverpool, Liverpool John Moores, London, Manchester, Manchester Metropolitan, Middlesex, Nene, Nottingham, Nottingham Trent, Oxford Brookes, Plymouth, Portsmouth, Reading, Royal Holloway, Salford, Sheffield Hallam, St Andrews, Strathclyde, Sussex, Swansea, UCL, Warwick, Westminster, Wolverhampton.

Languages - Middle Eastern

Durham, Edinburgh, Exeter, Glasgow, Lampeter, Leeds, Manchester, Oxford, Salford, SOAS, St Andrews, UCL, Westhill Col, Westminster.

Languages - Russian

Bath, Birmingham, Bradford, Bristol, Chester, Coventry, Durham, Edinburgh, Essex, European Business Schl, Exeter, Glasgow, Heriot-Watt, Keele, King's, Leeds, Liverpool, LSE, Manchester, Nottingham, Portsmouth, Queen Mary & Westfield, SSEES, Sheffield, St Andrews, Strathclyde, Sunderland, Surrey, Sussex, Swansea, Westminster, Wolverhampton.

Languages – Scandinavian

UEA, Edinburgh, Hull, UCL.

Languages - Spanish/Latin American

Aberdeen, Aberystwyth, APU, Bangor, Birmingham, Bolton Inst, Bradford, Bristol, UWE, Buckingham, Buckinghamshire College, Cardiff, Cardiff Inst, UCE, Central Lancashire, Chester, Coventry, De Montfort, Derby, Dundee, Durham, East London, Edinburgh, Essex, European Business Schl, Exeter, Glasgow, Goldsmiths, Greenwich, Heriot-Watt, Hertfordshire, Huddersfield, Hull, Kent at Canterbury, King's, Kingston, Lancaster, Leeds, Leeds, Trinity And All Saints, Leeds Metropolitan, Leicester, Liverpool, Liverpool John Moores, London Guildhall, Loughborough, Luton, Manchester, UMIST, Manchester Metropolitan, Middlesex, Nene, Newcastle, North London, Northumbria, Nottingham, Nottingham Trent, Oxford Brookes, Plymouth, Portsmouth, Queen Mary & Westfield, Queen's Belfast, Roehampton Inst, Royal Holloway, Salford, Sheffield, Sheffield Hallam, Southampton, Southampton Inst, South Bank, St Andrews, Staffordshire, Stirling, Strathclyde, Sunderland, Sussex, Swansea, Thames Valley, Ulster, UCL, Warwick, Westminster, Wolverhampton.

Law

Aberdeen, Abertay Dundee, Aberystwyth, APU, Aston, Bangor, Bell Col, Birmingham, Blackburn Col, Blackpool Col, Bolton Inst, Bournemouth, Bradford, Bradford & Ilkley Col, Brighton, Bristol, UWE, Brunel, Buckingham, Buckinghamshire College, Buckland, Cambridge, Cardiff, UCE, Central Lancashire, City, Coventry, Croydon Col, De Montfort, Derby, Doncaster Col, Dundee, Durham, UEA, East London, Edge Hill, Edinburgh, Essex, Exeter, Glamorgan, Glasgow, Glasgow Caledonian, Greenwich, Herefordshire Col Of Tech, Heriot-Watt, Hertfordshire, Holborn Col, Huddersfield, Hull, Keele, Kent at Canterbury, King's, Kingston, Lancaster, Lansdowne Col, Leeds, Leeds Metropolitan, Leicester, Lincolnshire And Humberside, Liverpool, Liverpool John Moores, Llandrillo Col, London Guildhall, LSE, Luton, Manchester, Manchester Metropolitan, Middlesex, Napier, Nene, Newcastle, Newport Col, NE Wales Inst, NE Worcestershire Col, North London, Northumbria, Nottingham, Nottingham Trent, Oxford, Oxford Brookes, Paisley, Plymouth, Portsmouth, Queen Mary & Westfield, Queen's Belfast, Reading, Robert Gordon, SOAS, Sheffield, Sheffield Hallam, Southampton, Southampton Inst, South Bank, Staffordshire, Stirling, Strathclyde, Uni Col Suffolk, Sunderland, Surrey, Sussex, Swansea, Swansea Inst, Teesside, Thames Valley, Ulster, UCL, Warwick, Westminster, Wolverhampton.

Librarianship and Information Studies

Abertay Dundee, Aberystwyth, Bell Col, Brighton, UCE, East London, Lampeter, Leeds Metropolitan, Lincolnshire And Humberside, Liverpool John Moores, London Institute,

Loughborough, Manchester Metropolitan, Napier, NE Wales Inst, North London, Northumbria, Queen Margaret Col, Queen's Belfast, Robert Gordon, Sheffield, Southampton Inst, Staffordshire, Thames Valley, UCL, West Herts Col, Wolverhampton.

Linguistics and Literature

Aberdeen, APU, Bangor, Barnsley Col, Bolton Inst, Bradford, Brighton, UWE, Buckingham, Buckinghamshire College, Cardiff, Central Lancashire, Chichester Inst, Cumbria Col of Art, Derby, Durham, UEA, East London, Edge Hill, Edinburgh, Essex, Glamorgan, Glasgow, Hertfordshire, Kent at Canterbury, Lampeter, Lancaster, Leeds, Leeds Metropolitan, Luton, Manchester, UMIST, Middlesex, Nene, Newcastle, Northumbria, Nottingham Trent, Portsmouth, Queen Mary & Westfield, Reading, Ripon & York St John, Salford, SOAS, Sheffield, Col of St Mark & St John, Staffordshire, Stirling, Uni Col Suffolk, Sunderland, Sussex, Thames Valley, Ulster, UCL, Warwick, Westminster, Wolverhampton, York.

Marine Sciences and Technologies

Cornwall College, Glamorgan, Glasgow, Heriot-Watt, Liverpool, Liverpool John Moores, Newcastle, Plymouth, Southampton, Southampton Inst, Strathclyde, Sunderland, UCL.

Materials/Minerals Sciences and Technologies

Aberdeen, Bangor, Bath, Birmingham, Bolton Inst, Bradford, Bradford & Ilkley Col, Brunel, Buckinghamshire College, Camb-ridge, Canterbury Col, UCE, Central Lancashire, Cordwainers Col, Cornwall College, Coventry, De Montfort, Doncaster Col, Dundee, East London, Exeter, Farnborough Col Of Tech, Glamorgan, Glasgow Caledonian, Handsworth Col, Heriot-Watt, Huddersfield, Hull, Imperial, Leeds, Leeds Metropolitan, Leeds Col of Art, Leicester South Fields Col, Liverpool, Liverpool Corn Col, London Guildhall, London Institute, Loughborough, Manchester Col of Arts And Tech, Manchester, UMIST, Manchester Metropolitan, Napier, Nene, Newcastle, Northbrook College, NE Wales Inst, North London, Northumbria, N Warwickshire and Hinckley Col, Nottingham, Nottingham Trent, Oxford, Plymouth, Queen Mary & Westfield, Queen's Belfast, Sandwell Col, Sheffield, Sheffield Hallam, Shrewsbury Col of Arts & Tech, Solihull Col, Somerset Col of Art, St Andrews, Staffordshire, Strathclyde, Surrey, Surrey Inst Of Art, Sussex, Swansea, Swansea Inst, Swindon Col, Teesside, UCL, West Herts Col, Westminster, Wigan And Leigh Col, Wolverhampton.

Mathematics and Statistics

Aberdeen, Abertay Dundee, Aberystwyth, APU, Aston, Bangor, Barnsley Col, Bath, Bath Spa, Bell Col, Birmingham, Bolton Inst, Brighton, Bristol, UWE, Brunel, Cambridge, Canterbury Col, Cardiff, Central Lancashire, Chester, Chichester Inst, City, Coventry, De Montfort , Derby, Dundee, Durham, UEA, Edge Hill, Edinburgh, Essex, Exeter, Glamorgan, Glasgow, Glasgow Caledonian, Goldsmiths, Greenwich, Heriot-Watt, Hertfordshire, Huddersfield, Hull, Imperial, Keele, Kent at Canterbury, King's, Kingston, Lancaster, Leeds, Leeds, Trinity And All Saints, Leicester, Liverpool, Liverpool Hope, Liverpool John Moores, London Guildhall, LSE, Loughborough, Luton, Manchester, UMIST, Manchester Metropolitan, Middlesex, Napier, Nene, Newcastle, North London, Northumbria, Nottingham, Nottingham Trent, Oxford, Oxford Brookes, Paisley, Plymouth, Portsmouth, Queen Mary & Westfield, Queen's Belfast, Reading, Royal Holloway, Salford, Sheffield,

Sheffield Hallam, St Martin, Lancaster & Cumbr, Southampton, St Andrews, St Mary's, Staffordshire , Stirling, Strathclyde, Sunderland, Surrey, Sussex, Swansea, Teesside, Ulster, UCL, Warwick, Westhill Col, Westminster, Wolverhampton, York.

Media Studies - Communications, Journalism, Publishing

APU, Bangor, Barnsley Col, Bath Spa, Bell Col, Birmingham, Blackburn Col, Bournemouth, Bradford, Bretton Hall, Brighton, UWE, Brunel, Buckinghamshire College, Canterbury Col, Cardiff, UCE, Central Lancashire, Chelt & Glos College, Chichester Inst, City, Bristol Col, Cleveland Col of Art, Colchester Inst, Cornwall College, Coventry, Cumbria Col of Art, De Montfort, Doncaster Col, Dudley Col of Tech, UEA, East London, Edge Hill, Essex, Falmouth Col of Arts , Farnborough Col Of Tech, Glamorgan, Glasgow Caledonian, Goldsmiths, Greenwich, Hertfordshire, Huddersfield, King Alfred's, Lancaster, Leeds, Leeds, Trinity And All Saints, Leeds Metropolitan, Leicester, Lincolnshire And Humberside, Liverpool, Liverpool Com Col, Liverpool John Moores, Llandrillo Col, London Guildhall, London Institute, Loughborough, Luton, Manchester Metropolitan, Middlesex, Napier, Nene, Newport Col, Nescot, NE Wales Inst, NE Worcestershire Col, North London, Northumbria, Northumberland Col, N Warwickshire and Hinckley Col, Nottingham Trent, Oxford Westminster Col, Oxford Brookes, Oxfordshire Schl of Art, Paisley, Plymouth Col of Art, Portsmouth, Queen Margaret Col, Reading Col of Arts, Ripon & York St John, Robert Gordon, Roehampton Inst, Royal Holloway, Sheffield, Sheffield Hallam, Sheffield Col, Shrewsbury Col of Arts & Tech, Solihull Col, Somerset Col of Art, Southampton Inst, South Bank, St Helens Col, Col of St Mark & St John, St Mary's, Staffordshire, Stirling, Uni Col Suffolk, Sunderland, Surrey Inst Of Art, Sussex, Swansea Inst, Thames Valley, Trinity Carmarthen, Ulster, Uni Col Warrington, Warwick, Warwickshire Col, West Herts Col, Westminster, West Thames Col, Wigan And Leigh Col, Wirral Met Col, Wolverhampton, Worcester.

Medicine

Aberdeen, Birmingham, Bristol, Camb-ridge, Dundee, Edinburgh, Glasgow, Imperial, King's, Leeds, Leicester, Liverpool, Manchester, Newcastle, Nottingham, Oxford, Queen Mary & Westfield, Queen's Belfast, Royal Free Hosp Sch of Med, Sheffield, Southampton, St Andrews, St George's Hosp Med Schl, UCL, Col of Medicine, Wales.

Microbiology

Aberdeen, Aberystwyth, APU, Barnsley Col, Birmingham, Bradford, Bristol, UWE, Cardiff, Central Lancashire, Dundee, UEA, East London, Edinburgh, Glamorgan, Glasgow, Heriot-Watt, Hertfordshire, Huddersfield, Imperial, Kent at Canterbury, King's, Lancaster, Leeds, Leicester, Liverpool, Liverpool John Moores, Luton, Manchester, Napier, Newcastle, Nescot, North London, Nottingham, Nottingham Trent, Paisley, Plymouth, Portsmouth, Queen Mary & Westfield, Queen's Belfast, Reading, Sheffield, South Bank, Staffordshire, Strathclyde, Sunderland, Surrey, Teesside, UCL, Warwick, Westminster, Wolverhampton

Music

Aberdeen, APU, Bangor, Barnsley Col, Bath Spa, Birmingham, Blackpool Col, Bolton Inst, Bretton Hall, Brighton, Bristol, UWE, Brunel, Buckinghamshire College, Cambridge, Canterbury Col, Cardiff, Central Lancashire, Chichester Inst, City, Bristol Col, City Col Manchester, Colchester Inst, Coventry, Cumbria Col of Art, Dartington Col of Arts, De Montfort, Derby, Doncaster Col, Durham, UEA,

Edge Hill, Edinburgh, Exeter, Farnborough Col Of Tech, Glasgow, Glasgow Caledonian, Goldsmiths, Hertfordshire, Huddersfield, Hull, Imperial, Keele, King's, Kingston, Lancaster, Leeds, Leeds Metropolitan, Leeds Col of Mus, Lincolnshire And Humberside, Liverpool, Liverpool Com Col, Liverpool Hope, Liverpool Inst for Perf Arts, London Institute, Manchester, Manchester Metropolitan, Middlesex, Napier, Nene, Newcastle, Newcastle Col, Northbrook College , NE Wales Inst, Nottingham, Oxford, Oxford Brookes, Paisley, Plymouth, Queen's Belfast, Reading, Ripon & York St John , Roehampton Inst, Rose Bruford, Royal Holloway, Salford, SOAS, Scarborough, Sheffield, St Martin, Lancaster & Cumbr, Southampton, South Bank, St Helens Col, Staffordshire, Strathclyde, Sunderland, Surrey, Sussex, Thames Valley, Ulster, Uni Col Warrington, Warwickshire Col, Welsh Col of Mus & Drama, Westhill Col, Westminster, Wigan And Leigh Col, Wolverhampton, Worcester Col, York.

Nursing

Abertay Dundee, APU, Bangor, Birmingham, Bournemouth, Bradford, Brighton, UWE, Brunel, Buckinghamshire College, Canterbury Col, UCE, Central Lancashire, City, De Montfort, UEA, Edinburgh, Glamorgan, Glasgow, Glasgow Caledonian, Greenwich, Hertfordshire, Huddersfield, Hull, King's, Lancaster, Leeds, Leeds Metropolitan, Liverpool, Liverpool John Moores, Luton, Manchester, Middlesex, Nene, NE Wales Inst, North London, Northumbria, Nottingham, Oxford Brookes, Plymouth, Queen Margaret Col, Reading, Robert Gordon, Salford, Sheffield Hallam, St Martin, Lancaster & Cumbr, Southampton, South Bank, Stirling, Uni Col Suffolk, Sunderland, Surrey, Swansea, Teesside, Thames Valley, Ulster, Col of Medicine, Wales, Wolverhampton.

Pharmacy and Pharmacology

Aberdeen, APU, Aston, Barnsley Col, Bath, Bradford, Brighton, Bristol, UWE, Cambridge, Cardiff, Cardiff Inst, Central Lancashire, Coventry, De Montfort, Dundee, East London, Edinburgh, Glasgow, Greenwich, Hertfordshire, Huddersfield, King's, Kingston, Leeds, Liverpool, Liverpool John Moores, Luton, Manchester, Middlesex, Napier, Newcastle, Nescot, North London, Nottingham, Nottingham Trent, Oxford Brookes, Portsmouth, Queen's Belfast, Robert Gordon, Salford, Schl of Pharmacy, Sheffield, Southampton, St Andrews, Stockport Col, Strathclyde, Sunderland, UCL, Westminster, Wolverhampton.

Philosophy

Aberdeen, APU, Birmingham, Bolton Inst, Bradford, Bradford & Ilkley Col, Brighton, Bristol, Brunel, Cambridge, Cardiff, Central Lancashire, Chelt & Glos College, Chichester Inst, Dundee, Durham, UEA, Edinburgh, Essex, Glamorgan, Glasgow, Greenwich, Gyosei Int Col, Hertfordshire, Heythrop Col, Hull, Keele, Kent at Canterbury, King's, Kingston, Lampeter, Lancaster, Leeds, Leeds Metropolitan, Liverpool, Liverpool John Moores, London Guildhall, LSE, Manchester, Manchester Metropolitan, Middlesex, Nene, Newcastle, Newman Col, Newport Col, North London, Nottingham, Oxford, Queen's Belfast, Reading, Roehampton Inst, Sheffield, St Martin, Lancaster & Cumbr, Southampton, St Andrews, Col of St Mark & St John, Staffordshire, Stirling, Sunderland, Sussex, Swansea, Teesside, Ulster, UCL, Warwick, Wolverhampton, York.

Physical Science

Aberdeen, Aberystwyth, Bangor, Barnsley Col, Bath, Birmingham, Bradford & Ilkley Col, Brighton, Bristol, Cambridge, Cardiff, Central Lancashire, De Montfort, Dundee, Durham, UEA, Edinburgh, Essex, Exeter,

Glamorgan, Glasgow, Glasgow Caledonian, Heriot-Watt, Hertfordshire, Hull, Imperial, Keele, Kent at Canterbury, King's, Kingston, Lancaster, Leeds, Leicester, Liverpool, Liverpool John Moores, Loughborough, Manchester, UMIST, Napier, Newcastle, Northumbria, Nottingham, Nottingham Trent, Oxford, Paisley, Portsmouth, Queen Mary & Westfield, Queen's Belfast, Reading, Robert Gordon, Royal Holloway, Salford, Sheffield, Sheffield Hallam, Southampton, St Andrews, Staffordshire, Strathclyde, Surrey, Sussex, Swansea, UCL, Warwick, Westhill Col, York.

Planning (Town and Country)

Aberdeen, APU, Bangor, Bell Col, Birmingham, Bradford, UWE, Cambridge, Cardiff, Cardiff Inst, UCE, Chelt & Glos College, Coventry, De Montfort, Doncaster Col, Dundee, East London, Edge Hill, Glamorgan, Greenwich, Heriot-Watt, Kent at Canterbury, Leeds Metropolitan, Liverpool, Liverpool John Moores, Luton, Manchester, Middlesex, Napier, Newcastle, Northumbria, Nottingham Trent, Oxford Brookes, Paisley, Queen's Belfast, Reading, Salford, Sheffield, Sheffield Hallam, South Bank, Strathclyde, Ulster, UCL, Westminster, Wolverhampton.

Politics

Aberdeen, Aberystwyth, APU, Aston, Bangor, Barnsley Col, Bath, Birmingham, Bradford, Bradford & Ilkley Col, Brighton, Bristol, UWE, Brunel, Buckingham, Cambridge, Cardiff, UCE, Central Lancashire, Chelt & Glos College, Coventry, De Montfort, Derby, Dundee, Durham, UEA, East London, Edinburgh, Essex, Exeter, Glamorgan, Glasgow, Glasgow Caledonian, Goldsmiths, Greenwich, Hertfordshire, Huddersfield, Hull, Keele, Kent at Canterbury, Kingston, Lancaster, Leeds, Leeds Metropolitan, Leicester, Lincolnshire And Humberside, Liverpool, Liverpool John Moores, London Guildhall, LSE, Loughborough, Luton, Manchester, Manchester Metropolitan, Middlesex, Nene, Newcastle, North London, Northumbria, Nottingham, Nottingham Trent, Oxford, Oxford Brookes, Paisley, Plymouth, Portsmouth, Queen Mary & Westfield, Queen's Belfast, Reading, Robert Gordon, Royal Holloway, Salford, SOAS, SSEES, Sheffield, Sheffield Hallam, St Martin, Lancaster & Cumbr, Southampton, Southampton Inst, South Bank, St Andrews, Staffordshire, Stirling, Strathclyde, Sunderland, Sussex, Swansea, Teesside, Thames Valley, Ulster, Warwick, Westminster, Wolverhampton, York.

Psychology

Aberdeen, Abertay Dundee, APU, Aston, Bangor, Bath, Bath Spa, Birmingham, Bolton Inst, Bournemouth, Bradford, Bradford & Ilkley Col, Bristol, UWE, Brunel, Buckingham, Buckinghamshire College, Cambridge, Canterbury Col, Cardiff, Cardiff Inst, UCE, Central Lancashire, Chelt & Glos College, Chester, City, Coventry, De Montfort, Derby, Dundee, Durham, UEA, East London, Edge Hill, Edinburgh, Essex, Exeter, Glamorgan, Glasgow, Glasgow Caledonian , Goldsmiths, Greenwich, Halton Col, Hertfordshire, Huddersfield, Hull, Keele, Kent at Canterbury, King Alfred's, Kingston, Lancaster, Leeds, Leeds, Trinity And All Saints, Leeds Metropolitan, Leicester, Lincolnshire And Humberside, Liverpool, Liverpool Hope, Liverpool John Moores, London Guildhall, LSE, Loughborough, Luton, Manchester, Manchester Metropolitan, Middlesex, Napier, Nene, Newcastle, Newman Col, Newport Col, Northbrook College , NE Wales Inst, North London, Northumbria, Norwich City Col, Nottingham, Nottingham Trent, Oxford, Oxford Westminster Col, Oxford Brookes, Paisley, Plymouth, Portsmouth, Queen Margaret Col, Queen's Belfast, Reading, Ripon & York St John, Roehampton Inst, Royal Holloway, Sheffield, Sheffield Hallam, St Martin, Lancaster & Cumbr, Southampton, Southampton Inst, South Bank, St Andrews, Staffordshire, Stirling, Strathclyde, Uni Col Suffolk, Sunderland, Surrey, Sussex, Swansea, Teesside, Thames Valley, Ulster, UCL, Warwick, Westhill Col, Westminster, Wolverhampton, Worcester, York.

Sociology and Anthropology

Aberdeen, Abertay Dundee, Aberystwyth, APU, Aston, Bangor, Barnsley Col, Bath, Bath Spa, Bell Col, Birmingham, Blackburn Col, Blackpool Col, Bolton Inst, Bradford, Bradford & Ilkley Col, Bretton Hall, Brighton, Bristol, UWE, Brunel, Buckinghamshire College, Cambridge, Canterbury Col, Cardiff, UCE, Central Lancashire, Chelt & Glos College, Chester, Chichester Inst, City, Colchester Inst, Coventry, De Montfort, Derby, Doncaster Col, Durham, UEA, East London, Edge Hill, Edinburgh, Essex, Exeter, Glamorgan, Glasgow, Glasgow Caledonian, Goldsmiths, Greenwich, Gyosei Int Col, Hertfordshire, Heythrop Col, Huddersfield, Hull, Keele, Kent at Canterbury, King Alfred's, King's, Kingston, Lampeter, Lancaster, Leeds, Leeds, Trinity And All Saints, Leeds Metropolitan, Leicester, Lincolnshire And Humberside, Liverpool, Liverpool Hope, Liverpool John Moores, London Guildhall, LSE, Loughborough, Luton, Manchester, Manchester Metropolitan, Middlesex, Napier, Nene, Newcastle, Northbrook College, NE Wales Inst, North London, Northumbria, Norwich City Col, Nottingham, Nottingham Trent, Oxford, Oxford Brookes, Paisley, Plymouth, Portsmouth, Queen Margaret Col, Queen's Belfast, Reading Col of Arts, Reading, Ripon & York St John, Roehampton Inst, Royal Holloway, Salford, SOAS, Scarborough, Sheffield, Sheffield Hallam, St Martin, Lancaster & Cumbr, Solihull Col, Southampton, Southampton Inst, South Bank, St Andrews, Southwark Col, Col of St Mark & St John, St Mary's, Staffordshire, Stirling, Strathclyde, Uni Col Suffolk, Sunderland, Surrey, Sussex, Swansea, Swansea Inst, Teesside, Thames Valley, Ulster, UCL, Uni Col Warrington, Warwick, West Herts Col, Westhill Col, Westminster, Wolverhampton, Worcester, Worcester Col, York.

Social Policy, Social Work and Administration

Abertay Dundee, APU, Aston, Bangor, Barnsley Col, Bath, Bath Spa, Birmingham, Blackburn Col, Blackpool Col, Bolton Inst, Bournemouth, Bradford, Bradford & Ilkley Col, Brighton, Bristol, UWE, Brunel, Buckinghamshire College, Canterbury Col, Cardiff, Cardiff Inst, Carmarthenshire Col, UCE, Central Lancashire, Chelt & Glos College, Chester, Chichester Inst, Bristol Col, Colchester Inst, Cornwall College, Coventry, De Montfort, Derby, Dewsbury Col, Doncaster Col, Dudley Col of Tech, Dundee, Durham, East London, Edge Hill, Edinburgh, Essex, Glamorgan, Glasgow, Glasgow Caledonian, Gloucestershire Col of Arts, Goldsmiths, Greenwich, Herefordshire Col Of Tech, Hertfordshire, Huddersfield, Hull, Keele, Kent at Canterbury, King Alfred's, Kingston, Lampeter, Lancaster, Leeds, Leeds Metropolitan, Lincolnshire And Humberside, Liverpool, Liverpool Com Col, Liverpool John Moores, Llandrillo Col, London Guildhall, LSE, Loughborough, Luton, Manchester, Manchester Metropolitan, Middlesex, Napier, Nene, Newcastle, Newcastle Col, Newport Col, NE Wales Inst, NE Worcestershire Col, Northern Col, North London, N Tyneside Col, Northumbria, Nottingham, Nottingham Trent, Oxford Brookes, Paisley, Plymouth, Portsmouth, Queen Margaret Col, Queen's Belfast, Reading, Robert Gordon, Roehampton Inst, Royal Holloway, Salford, Sheffield, Sheffield Hallam, Sheffield Col, Shrewsbury Col of Arts & Tech, St Martin, Lancaster & Cumbr, Southampton, Somerset Col of Art, Southampton Inst, South Devon Col, South Bank, Southport Col, St Helens Col, Col of St Mark & St John, Staffordshire, Stirling, Stockport Col, Strathclyde,

Bank, St Andrews, Staffordshire, Stirling, Strathclyde, Uni Col Suffolk, Sunderland, Surrey, Sussex, Swansea, Teesside, Thames Valley, Ulster, UCL, Warwick, Westhill Col, Westminster, Wolverhampton, Worcester, York.

Uni Col Suffolk, Sunderland, Sussex, Swansea, Swansea Inst, Teesside, Thames Valley, Ulster, Uni Col Warrington, Warwick, Warwickshire Col, West Herts Col, Westhill Col, Wigan And Leigh Col, Wolverhampton, Worcester, Worcester Col, York, Yorkshire Coast Col.

Sport Science/Studies

Aberdeen, Abertay Dundee, APU, Bangor, Barnsley Col, Bath, Bell Col, Birmingham, Blackburn Col, Blackpool Col, Bolton Inst, Brighton, UWE, Brunel, Buckhinghamshire College, Canterbury Col, Cardiff Inst, Carmarthenshire Col, Central Lancashire, Chelt & Glos College, Chester, Chichester Inst, Coventry, De Montfort, Doncaster Col, Durham, East London, Edge Hill, Edinburgh, Essex, Exeter, Glamorgan, Glasgow, Greenwich, Halton Col, Hertfordshire, Huddersfield, Hull, King Alfred's, Kingston, Leeds, Leeds, Trinity And All Saints, Leeds Metropolitan, Liverpool Hope, Liverpool John Moores, Llandrillo Col, Loughborough, Luton, Manchester Metropolitan, Mid-Cheshire Col, Middlesex, Nene, Newcastle Col, Newport Col, Nescot, NE Wales Inst, North London, Northumbria, Nottingham Trent, Oxford Brookes, Portsmouth, Ripon & York St John, Roehampton Inst, Salford, Sheffield Hallam, Sheffield Col, Shrewsbury Col of Arts & Tech, St Martin, Lancaster & Cumbr, Solihull Col, Southampton, Somerset Col of Art, South Bank, Southwark Col, St Helens Col, Col of St Mark & St John, St Mary's, Staffordshire, Stirling, Stockport Col, Strathclyde, Sunderland, Swansea, Teesside, Trinity Carmarthen, Ulster, Uni Col Warrington, Warwickshire Col, Westhill Col, Westminster, Wigan And Leigh Col, Wolverhampton, Worcester, Yorkshire Coast Col.

Teacher Training

APU, Bangor, Bath, Bath Spa, Bishop Grosseteste, Bradford & Ilkley Col, Bretton Hall, Brighton, UWE, Brunel, Cambridge, Canterbury Col, Cardiff Inst, UCE, Chelt & Glos College, Chester, Chichester Inst, De Montfort, Derby, Durham, Edge Hill, Edinburgh, Exeter, Glasgow, Goldsmiths, Greenwich, Hertfordshire, Huddersfield, Hull, Keele, King Alfred's, Kingston, Leeds, Trinity And All Saints , Leeds Metropolitan, Liverpool Hope, Liverpool John Moores, Loughborough, Manchester Metropolitan, Middlesex, Nene, Newman Col, Newport Col, NE Wales Inst, Northern Col, North London, Northumbria, Nottingham Trent, Oxford Westminster Col, Oxford Brookes, Paisley, Plymouth, Reading, Ripon & York St John, Roehampton Inst, Scarborough, Sheffield Hallam, St Martin, Lancaster & Cumbr, Southampton, Col of St Mark & St John, St Mary's, Stirling, Strathclyde, Sunderland, Surrey, Swansea Inst, Trinity Carmarthen, Warwick, Wolverhampton, Worcester.

Theology

Aberdeen, Bangor, Bath Spa, Birmingham, Bristol, UWE, Cambridge, Canterbury Col, Cardiff, Chelt & Glos College, Chester, Chichester Inst, Derby, Durham, Edinburgh, Exeter, Franciscan Study Cntr, Glasgow, Greenwich, Hertfordshire, Heythrop Col, Hull, Kent at Canterbury, King Alfred's, King's, Lampeter, Lancaster, Leeds, Leeds, Trinity And All Saints, Liverpool Hope, Manchester, Manchester Metropolitan, Middlesex, Newcastle, Newman Col, Nottingham, Oxford, Oxford Westminster Col, Oxford Brookes, Queen's Belfast, Ripon & York St John, Roehampton Inst, SOAS, Scarborough, SSEES, Sheffield, St Martin, Lancaster & Cumbr, St Andrews, Col of St Mark & St John, St Mary's, Stirling, Uni Col Suffolk, Sunderland, Trinity Carmarthen, Westhill Col, Wolverhampton.

Tourism

Abertay Dundee, Aberystwyth, APU, Bangor, Barnsley Col, Bell Col, Birmingham Col Of Food Tourism, Blackburn Col, Blackpool Col, Bolton Inst, Bournemouth, Bradford & Ilkley

Col, Brighton, UWE, Buckingham, Buckhinghamshire College, Canterbury Col, Cardiff Inst, Central Lancashire, Chelt & Glos College, Chester, City Col Manchester, Colchester Inst, Cornwall College, Coventry, Croydon Col, Cumbria Col of Art, Derby, Dudley Col of Tech, Farnborough Col Of Tech, Glamorgan, Glasgow Caledonian, Gloucestershire Col of Arts, Greenwich, Herefordshire Col Of Tech, Hertfordshire, Huddersfield, King Alfred's, Leeds Metropolitan, Lincolnshire And Humberside, Liverpool John Moores, Llandrillo Col, London Institute, Luton, Manchester Metropolitan, Mid-Cheshire Col, Napier, Newcastle Col, Northbrook College, NE Worcestershire Col, North London, Northumbria, Norwich City Col, Oxford Brookes, Paisley, Plymouth, Portsmouth, Queen Margaret Col, Robert Gordon, Scottish Agricultural Col, Salford, Scarborough, Sheffield Hallam, Sheffield Col, Shrewsbury Col of Arts & Tech, St Martin, Lancaster & Cumbr, Solihull Col, Southampton Inst, South Devon Col, South Bank, Southport Col, Southwark Col, St Helens Col, Col of St Mark & St John, Staffordshire, Stockport Col, Uni Col Suffolk, Sunderland, Swansea Inst, Teesside, Thames Valley, Trinity Carmarthen, Ulster, Uni Col Warrington, West Herts Col, Westminster, Westminster Col, West Thames Col, Wirral Met Col, Wolverhampton, Worcester, Worcester Col, York Col, Yorkshire Coast Col.

Veterinary Science

Bristol, UWE, Cambridge, Edinburgh, Glasgow, Liverpool, Middlesex, Royal Vet Col.

Zoology

Aberdeen, Aberystwyth, Bangor, Barnsley Col, Birmingham, Bristol, Cambridge, Cardiff, Dundee, Durham, UEA, East London, Edinburgh, Glasgow, Imperial, Leeds, Leicester, Liverpool, Liverpool John Moores, Manchester, Newcastle, Nottingham, Queen Mary & Westfield, Queen's Belfast, Reading, Roehampton Inst, Royal Holloway, Sheffield, Southampton, Swansea, UCL.

Combined Programmes

Aberdeen, Abertay Dundee, Aberystwyth, APU, Bangor, Barnsley Col, Bath, Bath Spa, Birmingham, Bolton Inst, Bradford, Bradford & Ilkley Col, Brighton, UWE, Brunel, Buckingham, Cambridge, Canterbury Col, Cardiff, Central Lancashire, Chelt & Glos College, Cornwall College, Coventry, Cranfield, De Montfort, Derby, Doncaster Col, Dundee, Durham, UEA, East London, Edge Hill, Edinburgh, Essex, Exeter, Glamorgan, Glasgow, Glasgow Caledonian, Greenwich, Halton Col, Heriot-Watt, Hertfordshire, Huddersfield, Hull, Keele, Kent at Canterbury, King's, Kingston, Lampeter, Lancaster, Leeds, Leeds, Trinity And All Saints, Leeds Metropolitan, Leicester, Lincolnshire And Humberside, Liverpool, Liverpool John Moores, London Guildhall, LSE, London Schl of Jewish Studies, Luton, Manchester, Manchester Metropolitan, Middlesex, Napier, Nene, Newcastle, Newport Col, NE Wales Inst, North London, Northumbria, Norwich City Col, Nottingham Trent, Oxford, Oxford Brookes, Paisley, Plymouth, Portsmouth, Queen Margaret Col, Queen Mary & Westfield, Reading, Roehampton Inst, Royal Holloway, Scottish Agricultural Col, Salford, Sheffield, Sheffield Hallam, Shrewsbury Col of Arts & Tech, St Martin, Lancaster & Cumbr, Southampton, Somerset Col of Art, South Devon Col, Southport Col, St Andrews, Staffordshire, Stirling, Stockport Col, Strathclyde, Uni Col Suffolk, Sunderland, Sussex, Swansea, Swansea Inst, Teesside, Trinity Carmarthen, Ulster, UCL, Uni Col Warrington, Warwick, Westhill Col, Westminster, Wirral Met Col, Wolverhampton, York.

Index

501